PHP & MYSQL

server-side web development

JON DUCKETT

Design by:
EMME STONE

Additional material by:
CHRIS ULLMAN

WILEY

TABLE OF CONTENTS

Code download: http://phpandmysql.com

DOWNLOAD THE CODE FOR THIS BOOK FROM

http://phpandmysql.com

CREDITS

AUTHOR
Jon Duckett

ADDITIONAL MATERIAL
Chris Ullman

CREATIVE DIRECTION
Emme Stone

TECHNICAL REVIEW
Roman Schevchenko
Art Bergquist
Jack Shepler
Phil DeGeorge

REVIEW TEAM
Bob Erickson
Chris Dawson
Scott Weaver
Trevor Reynolds

THANKS TO...
Jim Minatel
Alcwyn Parker
Daniel Morgan
Richard Eskins

INTRODUCTION

This book will teach you how to build websites using a programming language called PHP and how to store the data that the website uses in a database such as MySQL.

PHP is a programming language that was designed to run on a web server so that when someone requests a web page, the server can generate an HTML page to send back to that specific user. This means that pages can be tailored to individual people. This is a requirement for any site that allows users to perform tasks such as:

- **Register or log in** because each user's name, email and password is different from the next
- **Make a purchase** because each customer's order, payment and delivery details are unique
- **Search the website** because the search results are tailored to each user

PHP was designed to work with databases like MySQL which can store data such as the content of the pages the site displays, the products a site sells, or details about members of the site. Using PHP, you will learn how to create web pages that allow members to update the data stored in the database. For example:

- **Content management systems** allow the owners of the site to update the site's content using a form and those updates are shown to visitors without any new code being written
- **Online shops** allow owners to list the products for sale and customers to make purchases
- **Social networks** allow visitors to register and log in, create user profiles, upload their own content, and see pages that are tailored to them or their interests

Because the information shown on these sites is stored in a database, they are known as **database-driven websites**.

Here is a guide to the types of pages that are in this book. Different designs for the pages convey different types of information.

INFORMATION PAGES

These appear on a white background and introduce topics, explaining context and how they are used.

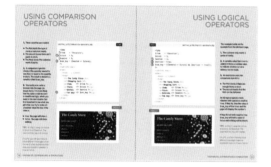

CODE PAGES

These appear on a beige background and show you how to apply individual sections of code.

DIAGRAM PAGES

These appear on a dark background and explain concepts using diagrams and infographics.

EXAMPLE PAGES

These appear in earlier chapters to bring together the topics you have learnt and how to apply them.

SUMMARY PAGES

These appear at the end of each chapter and remind you of the key topics covered.

STATIC VS DYNAMIC WEBSITES

When a site is built using only HTML and CSS, every visitor sees the same content because they are all sent the same HTML and CSS files.

1. When your browser asks for a page of a site built using HTML and CSS files, the request is sent to a **web server** that hosts the site.

2. The web server finds the HTML file the browser requested and sends it back to the browser. It may also send CSS to style the page, media (such as images), JavaScript, and other files the page uses.

Because all visitors are sent the same HTML files, they will all see the same content. Therefore, this type of site is known as a **static website**.

People who update static websites need to know HTML and CSS. If the owners want to update the text on a page, the HTML code must be manually updated and uploaded to the web server.

WEB BROWSER

WEB SERVER

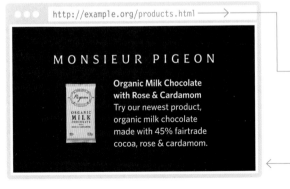

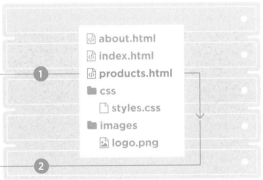

This book assumes you have knowledge of HTML and CSS. If you are new to them, try our book on the topic http://htmlandcssbook.com.

When websites are built using PHP, each visitor can see different content because the PHP page creates the HTML file that is sent to them.

Websites like eBay, Facebook and news sites often display new information each time you visit them. If you view the source of the pages in a browser, you will see HTML code, but a programmer will not have manually updated the code between your visits.

This type of site is known as a **dynamic website** because the HTML page that is sent back to the visitor is created using instructions written in a language like PHP.

1. When a browser asks for a page of a site built using PHP, the request is sent to the web server.
2. The web server finds the PHP file.
3. Any PHP code in the file is run through a piece of software called a **PHP interpreter**, and an HTML page is created for that one visitor.
4. The web server sends the HTML page it created for that visitor to their browser. (It does not keep a copy of the file; next time the PHP file is requested, it creates a new HTML page for that visitor).

WEB BROWSER   WEB SERVER

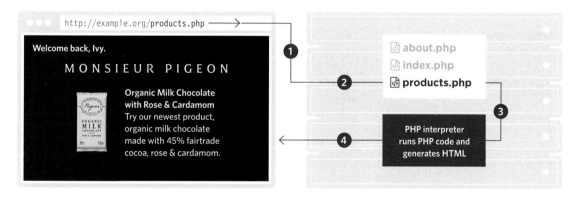

PHP code is not sent back to the web browser; it is used to create an HTML page that is then sent back to the browser. Because the PHP code runs on the web server, it is called **server-side programming**.

PHP can be used to create HTML pages that are tailored or **personalized** to each individual visitor. This may include showing the visitor's name, topics they are interested in, or posts from their friends.

PHP: THE LANGUAGE AND THE INTERPRETER

The PHP interpreter is a piece of software that runs on the web server. You can tell it what to do using code written in a language called PHP.

Software helps people use a computer to perform specific tasks without in-depth knowledge of how the computer achieves that task. For example:

- Email programs let you send and receive emails without needing to understand how computers store or transmit emails.

- Photoshop lets you edit pictures without you learning how computers manipulate images.

Each time you use a piece of software, it is capable of performing the same tasks, but it can perform those tasks with different data:

- An email program can be used to create, send, receive and store emails, but the content and recipient of each email can be different.

- Photoshop can perform tasks such as adding a filter to, resizing or cropping an image. It can achieve the same tasks with any image.

Both of these pieces of software have a graphical user interface that you interact with to achieve these tasks.

The PHP interpreter is also a piece of software. It runs as part of a web server. But, instead of using a graphical user interface, you tell the PHP interpreter what you want it to do using code written in a programming language called PHP.

When you create a web page using PHP, that page will always perform the same tasks, but it can perform those tasks using different data each time the page is requested. For example, a site written using PHP could have:

- One login page that every member uses to sign in, even though the email address and password that each member uses to log in are different.

- One user account page that every member can use to see the details of their account. Even if hundreds of different people use the page at the same time, they will only see their own details.

This is possible because the rules or instructions required to perform these tasks are the same for every user, but the data that every user supplies or sees can be different.

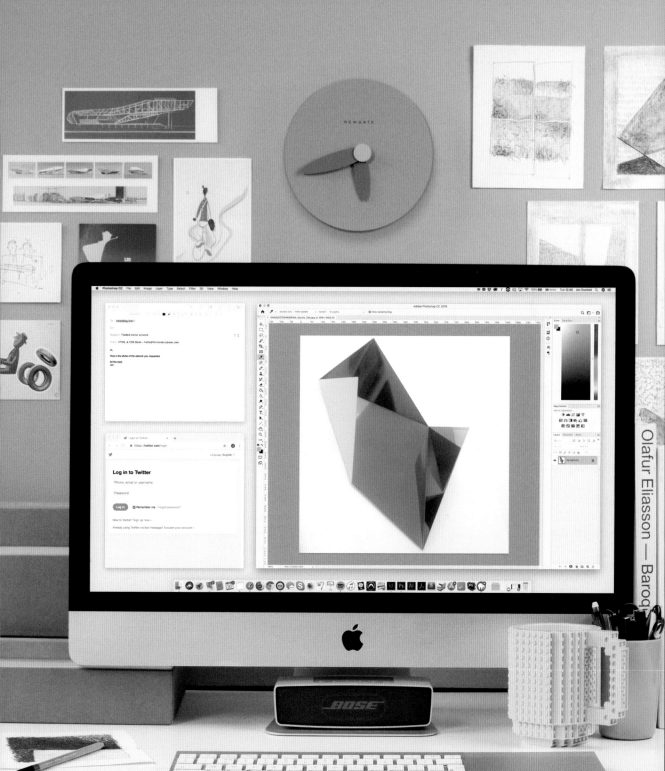

PERFORMING A TASK USING DIFFERENT DATA

Programming languages let you create rules that tell a computer how to perform a task. The data the program uses can be different each time the task is performed.

When you use any programming language, you have to give the computer precise instructions, telling it exactly what you want it to do. These instructions are very different than the type you might give when asking a person to perform a task.

Imagine you wanted to buy five candy bars and you needed to work out the total cost of the bars. To work out the total cost, you multiply the price of a single bar by the number of bars you want to buy. You could express this rule in the following way:

total = price x quantity

When it comes to working out the cost of the candy:

- If a candy bar costs $1, and you buy 5 of them, the total is $5.
- If the price of a single bar was $1.50, the rule is the same, but the total would be $7.50.
- If you wanted to buy 10 bars at $2 each, the rule is the same, but the total would be $20.

The values that are used instead of the words *total*, *price*, and *quantity* can change, but the rule used to calculate the total cost of the candy stays the same.

When you use PHP to create a web page, you first need to work out what:

- Task you want to achieve
- Data can change each time that task is performed

You then give the PHP interpreter detailed instructions on how to achieve the task and use names to represent the values that can change. If you told the PHP interpreter:

price = 3
quantity = 5

Then use the rule:

total = price x quantity

The word *total* would represent a value of 15. The next time you run the page, you could give the price or quantity different values, and it could work out the new total using the same rule.

Programmers call words that represent values **variables** because the value they represent can change (or vary) each time the program runs.

total = price x quantity

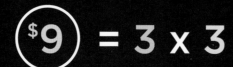

WHAT IS A PHP PAGE?

A PHP page often contains a mix of HTML and PHP code.
It can be used to send an HTML page back to the browser.

Below, on the left, you can see a PHP page that contains a mix of HTML and PHP code.

- HTML code is in blue
- PHP code is in purple

When the PHP interpreter opens the file it:

- Copies any HTML code straight into a temporary HTML file that it creates for that visitor.
- Follows any instructions written in PHP code (which often generate content for the HTML page).

The PHP code shown here determines the current year and writes it out inside the opening <p> and closing </p> tags.

PHP code can perform basic tasks such as arithmetic or getting the current date, and more complex tasks like using the information sent via an HTML form to update the data stored in a database.

When the PHP interpreter has finished processing the PHP file, it sends the temporary HTML page it created for that visitor back to their browser, then deletes the temporary HTML page.

Below, you can see the HTML page that would be sent back to the browser once the PHP interpreter had followed the PHP code.

The PHP interpreter has determined the current year and displayed it in the HTML page it created.

PHP
```
<!DOCTYPE html>
<html>
  <body>
    <h1>Current Year</h1>
    <p>It is: <?php echo date('Y'); ?></p>
  </body>
</html>
```

HTML
```
<!DOCTYPE html>
<html>
  <body>
    <h1>Current Year</h1>
    <p>It is 2021 </p>
  </body>
</html>
```

The PHP interpreter gets the current year
and writes it out inside the paragraph tags.

Each page typically performs the same task every time it is requested, but it can work with different information for each visitor to the site.

A PHP website is made up of a set of PHP pages and each page performs a specific task. For example, a site that allows members to log in might have a:

- Login page - to let members log into the site
- Profile page - to show members' profiles

Each time one of these pages is requested it needs to be able to work with different data that is specific to the current member. Therefore, the page needs to:

- Contain instructions on how to complete the task that the page is supposed to achieve.
- Give a name to each piece of data that might change every time the page is requested.

In PHP, variables use a name to represent a value that can change each time the page is requested. The PHP code can tell the PHP interpreter:

- What variable name to use for a piece of data that can change *every* time the page is requested.
- What value to use *this* time the page is requested.

Once the HTML page has been sent back to the user, the PHP interpreter forgets any values stored in variables, so it can perform the same task for the next person that requests the page (with different values).

To store data for longer, you put it in a database like MySQL, which you meet on the next page.

```
PHP
<!DOCTYPE html>
<html>
  <body>
    <h1>My Profile</h1>
    <p>Name: <?php echo $username; ?></p>
  </body>
</html>
```

```
HTML
<!DOCTYPE html>
<html>
  <body>
    <h1>My Profile</h1>
    <p>Name: Ivy Stone</p>
  </body>
</html>
```

The PHP interpreter gets the value stored in the $username variable and writes it out inside the paragraph tags.

WHAT IS MYSQL?

MySQL is a type of database. Databases store data in a structured manner so you can easily access and update the information they hold.

Spreadsheet programs like Excel store information in a grid made up of columns and rows. They can then use the data stored in the spreadsheet to perform calculations, or manipulate it using formulas.

MySQL is a piece of software that stores information in a similar way; in **tables** which are also made up of columns and rows. You can use PHP to access and update the information that the database stores.

One database can have multiple tables. Each table usually holds one type of data the site needs to store. Below are two examples of database tables that hold:
- Members (or users) of a site
- Articles that a site displays

Within each table, **column names** describe the type of information each column of the table holds:

- The member table stores each member's forename, surname, email address, password, date they joined, and profile picture.

- The article table stores each article's title, summary, content, date it was created, and some extra values discussed on the right-hand page.

Each **row** holds the data to describe one of the things that the table represents. In the:
- member table, each row represents one member
- article table, each row holds one article

TABLE NAME   COLUMN NAME   COLUMN

member

id	forename	surname	email	password	joined	picture
1	Ivy	Stone	ivy@eg.link	$2y$10$MAdTTCAOMiOw	2021-01-01 20:28:47	ivy.jpg
2	Luke	Wood	luke@eg.link	$2y$10$NN5HEAD3atar	2021-01-02 09:17:21	NULL
3	Emiko	Ito	emi@eg.link	$2y$10$/RpRmiUMStji	2021-01-02 10:42:36	emi.jpg

article

id	title	summary	content	created	category_id	member_id	image_id	published	
1	Systemic	Brochure	<p>This	2021-01-01	1	2	1	1	
2	Polite	Poster	<p>These	2021-01-02	1	1	2	1	ROW
3	Swimming	Architect	<p>This	2021-01-02	4	1	3	1	

Using PHP, you can:

- **Get data from the database** and show this information in a web page.

- **Add new rows of data**. To create a new article, you would add a row to the `article` table and provide the data that should be stored in each column.

- **Delete rows of data**. To delete an article, you would remove the entire row that represents the article.

- **Change data in an existing row**. To update a member's email address, you would find the row in the `member` table that represents them, then update the value in the `email` column of that row.

Note how both tables start with a column called `id`. Each row of a table has a unique value in this column (here, the values in these columns start at 1 and increases by 1 for each row). The values in the `id` column let you tell the database which row of data you want to work with. For example, you could get the member whose `id` is 2 or the article whose `id` is 1.

MySQL is called a **relational database** because it can explain the relationships between the types of data stored in the different tables.

In the tables below, for example, the articles are written by different members of the site. In the `article` table, the value in the `member_id` column tells you which user wrote the article because it holds a number that matches one of the values in the `id` column of the `member` table.

The first article was written by the member whose `id` column has a value of 2 (Luke Wood). The second and third articles are written by the user whose `id` column has a value of 1 (Ivy Stone).

These relationships:
- Structure the data, ensuring each table only holds one particular type of data (member or article).
- Save the database having to store the same data in multiple tables (saving space in the database).
- Make it easier to keep data up to date. If a member changes their name, it only needs to be updated in the `member` table (not in each article they wrote).

member

id	forename	surname	email	password	joined	picture
1	Ivy	Stone	ivy@eg.link	$2y$10$MAdTTCAOMiOw	2021-01-01 20:28:47	ivy.jpg
2	Luke	Wood	luke@eg.link	$2y$10$NN5HEAD3atar	2021-01-02 09:17:21	NULL
3	Emiko	Ito	emi@eg.link	$2y$10$/RpRmiUMStji	2021-01-02 10:42:36	emi.jpg

article

id	title	summary	content	created	category_id	member_id	image_id	published
1	Systemic	Brochure	<p>This	2021-01-01	1	2	1	1
2	Polite	Poster	<p>These	2021-01-02	1	1	2	1
3	Swimming	Architect	<p>This	2021-01-02	4	1	3	1

HISTORY OF PHP

As with most software, there have been many versions of PHP & MySQL. Newer versions have added features and run faster than older versions.

PHP was created by Rasmus Lerdorf in 1994. He then released the code to the public in 1995, encouraging users to improve on it. At that time, the letters stood for Personal Home Page. Now the acronym stands for PHP: Hypertext Processor.

PHP is now used on 80% of websites that use a programming language on the server.

Sites like Facebook, Etsy, Flickr and Wikipedia were all first developed in PHP (although some also use other technologies these days).

Popular open source software such as WordPress (which powers over 35% of the world's websites), Drupal, Joomla and Magento are all written in PHP. Learning PHP helps you work with them.

With each new version of PHP, extra features are added. This book will introduce features up to and including PHP 8, which was released in November 2020.

PHP 1	1995
	1996
	1997
PHP 2	1998
PHP 3	
	1999
PHP 4	2000
	2001
	2002
	2003
	2004
PHP 5	
	2005
PHP 5.1	2006
PHP 5.2	2007
	2008
	2009
PHP 5.3	2010
	2011
PHP 5.4	2012
	2013
PHP 5.5	2014
PHP 5.6	2015
PHP 7	2016

1995	———————— MYSQL 1 ————————
1996	··
1997	———————— MYSQL 3.2 ————————
1998	··
1999	———————— PHPMYADMIN ————————
2000	··
2001	··
2002	··
2003	············· MYSQL 4 ·············
2004	··
2005	··
2006	············· MYSQL 5 ·············
2007	··
2008	———————— SUN BUYS MYSQL ————————
2009	············· MYSQL 5.1 ·············
2010	— MARIADB ——— ORACLE BUYS SUN —
2011	············· MYSQL 5.5 ·············
2012	··
2013	············· MYSQL 5.6 ·············
2014	··
2015	··
2016	———————— MYSQL 5.7 ————————
2017	··
2018	············· MYSQL 8 ·············
2019	··

MySQL was first released in 1995. The letters SQL (pronounced either *ess-queue-el* or *sequel*) stand for Structured Query Language. SQL is a language that is used to get information into and out of relational databases.

MySQL was developed by a Swedish company called MySQL AB. They made MySQL available for free. Michael Widenius, one of the creators of MySQL, named MySQL after his daughter, My.

MySQL AB was sold to Sun Microsystems in January 2008, and then Oracle bought Sun in 2010.

When MySQL's developers learned that Oracle were going to buy Sun (and therefore own MySQL), they were concerned that it may not remain free, so they created an open source version of the database called MariaDB (named after the same founder's younger daughter, Maria).

Sites like Facebook, YouTube, Twitter, Neftlix, Spotify and Wordpress all use MySQL or MariaDB.

phpMyAdmin is a tool that can be used to administer MySQL and MariaDB databases. It was released in 1998 as a free tool to help manage MySQL databases (and it also works with MariaDB).

The code in this book works with either MySQL version 5.5 or MariaDB 5.5 and higher, and phpMyAdmin is used to work with them.

The latest version of MySQL (at the time of writing) is version 8. (MySQL 6 was never released, and version 7 is not shown because it was designed to run on clusters of servers, not on your personal

WHAT THIS BOOK COVERS

This book is divided into four sections.
Here is an overview of the topics you will learn in each section.

A: BASIC PROGRAMMING INSTRUCTIONS

The first section shows you how to use PHP code to write instructions that the PHP interpreter can follow. You will learn about:

- Basic programming instructions
- Running different code in different situations (e.g., running one set of code if a user is logged in, and another set of code if they are not)
- How functions can group together all of the code required to perform an individual task
- How classes and objects help organize code used to represent things in the world around us

B: DYNAMIC WEB PAGES

The second section of this book introduces a set of tools that PHP provides which enable you to build dynamic web pages. You will learn how to:

- Collect data sent from a web browser
- Check that users have supplied the data a page needs, and that it is in the right format
- Work with any data that has been sent
- Process files that users have uploaded
- Represent dates and times in PHP
- Temporarily store data in cookies and sessions
- Troubleshoot problems with your code

C: DATABASE DRIVEN WEBSITES

The third section shows you how to get data from a database and show it in your web pages, as well as how to update the data that is stored in the database. You will learn how:

- Databases store data
- A language called SQL is used to retrieve or update the data held in a database
- Data from the database is displayed in a PHP page
- HTML forms can be used to allow visitors to update the data that is stored in the database

D: EXTENDING THE SAMPLE APPLICATION

The fourth section shows you practical techniques for building websites and web applications in PHP. The sample application is a basic content management system with social features. You will learn how to:

- Improve the structure of your code
- Incorporate code that other programmers share
- Send emails using PHP
- Allow members to register and log in to a site
- Create pages tailored to individual members
- Use search engine friendly URLs
- Add social features such as likes and comments

A

BASIC PROGRAMMING INSTRUCTIONS

In the first section of this book, you will learn the basics of writing code in PHP.

Programming involves creating a series of instructions that a computer can follow in order to perform a specific task. You can compare these instructions to a recipe that contains steps you follow in order to create a dish. Each individual instruction in PHP is called a **statement**.

Because PHP was designed to build websites that can dynamically create HTML pages for each visitor, the statements you learn in this first section of the book focus on how PHP is used to create HTML pages.

A complete website is often made up of thousands of lines of code so it is important that you organize your code carefully. This section introduces two concepts that group together sets of related statements:

- **Functions** group together the statements that are required to perform an individual task.
- **Objects** group together a set of statements that represent concepts; for example, articles shown on a site, products a site sells, or members that have registered with a site.

The topics in this section form the foundations for everything else you learn in this book.

Before you delve into the first chapter, there are a few fundamentals to learn that will help you on your way.

HOW TO INSTALL THE SOFTWARE & CODE SAMPLES

To build sites using PHP and a database like MySQL on your desktop or laptop computer, you will need to install some software. Once it the required software has been installed, you will need to download the sample code files for the book from our website:
`http://phpandmysql.com/code/`

HOW PHP FILES CONTAIN A MIX OF HTML AND PHP CODE

Because PHP is used to create HTML pages, a PHP page often contains a mixture of HTML and PHP code, so you need to learn how the PHP interpreter tells the difference between these two types of code.

HOW PHP IS USED TO CREATE HTML

One of the most common instructions you will tell the PHP interpreter to perform is to add content to the HTML page that it sends back to the visitor. This instruction is used in every example in this section.

HOW TO ADD COMMENTS TO YOUR PHP CODE

Comments are not run by the PHP interpreter itself however they will help you (and others) understand what the code is supposed to do, and therefore it is important to learn how to add them. Comments are used throughout the code in this book to help explain what the code examples are doing.

INSTALLING SOFTWARE AND FILES

The tools below install all of the software you need to create database-driven websites on your desktop or laptop computer.

To work with this book, you need to install:

- A **web server** that runs a PHP interpreter. This book uses **Apache** (as it is the most widely used).
- **MySQL** or **MariaDB** which is database software.
- **phpMyAdmin** to manage the database.

Instead of downloading and installing each of these programs individually, the tools described below download and install all of them for you.

We also recommend using a code editor like those described here: `http://notes.re/php/editors`

INSTALLING ON A MAC

We recommend that Mac users install the required software using a tool called MAMP. A link to download it and instructions on using it are available here: `http://notes.re/php/mamp`

When you install MAMP on a Mac (using default settings), it creates the folder: `/Applications/MAMP`

There is another folder inside this called `htdocs`. Any web pages you write using PHP must be placed inside this folder. It is known as the **document root**.

INSTALLING ON A PC / LINUX

We recommend that PC and Linux users install the required software using a tool called XAMPP. A link to download it and instructions on using it are available here: `http://notes.re/php/xampp`

When you install XAMPP on a PC (using default settings), it creates the folder: `c:\xampp\`

There is another folder inside this called `htdocs`. Any web pages you write using PHP must be placed in this folder. It is known as the **document root**.

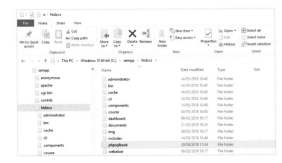

DOWNLOADING THE SAMPLE CODE

Download the sample code for the book using the download button here:
`http://phpandmysql.com/code`

The sample code is stored in a folder called `phpbook`. The `phpbook` folder contains sub-folders for each section of the book as well as each individual chapter. Place the `phpbook` folder inside the `htdocs` folder.

To open PHP files in your browser, you **must** type a URL into the address bar. (If you open a file using the `File` menu's `Open` command, double-click on it, or drag it onto the browser, the PHP code will not run.)

Try opening the URL shown below and you should see the test page shown underneath it. When opening files on your computer, instead of using a domain name, enter `localhost`. This is followed by the path from the `htdocs` folder to the file you want to open.

The path shown below tells the server to look in the `phpbook/section_a/intro` folder and find the file called `test.php`.

```
            HOSTNAME                    RELATIVE PATH

http://localhost/phpbook/section_a/intro/test.php

                                                  FILENAME
```

Welcome to PHP & MySQL

Your web server is working

PHP Version 5.6.10

TROUBLESHOOTING

If you do not see the page on the left, check out:
`http://notes.re/php/mamp` for MAMP
`http://notes.re/php/xampp` for XAMPP

MAMP sometimes requires a **port number**. It uses port 8888, so enter: `http://localhost:8888/` Port numbers help different programs installed on a computer share the same connection to the Internet. This is similar to how offices may have one telephone number, followed by an extension number to reach individual people's telephones.

HOW PHP PAGES MIX HTML & PHP CODE

Many PHP pages mix HTML and PHP code. The PHP code is written between PHP tags. The opening and closing PHP tags, plus any PHP code they contain, are known as a **PHP block**.

OPENING TAG

<?php

The opening tag indicates that the PHP interpreter must start processing the code before sending any content back to the browser.

CLOSING TAG

?>

The closing tag indicates that the PHP interpreter can stop processing the code until it comes across another opening **<?php** tag.

PHP is a type of programming language known as a **scripting language**. Scripting languages are designed to run in a particular environment; PHP was created to work with a PHP interpreter on a web server. An individual PHP page is often called a **script**.

You should treat all PHP code as if it is case-sensitive.

Although there are some parts of the language that are not case-sensitive, treating them as if they all are case-sensitive reduces errors.

A PHP page is a text file (just like an HTML file is). Its file extension is .php, which tells the web server to send the file to the PHP interpreter so that it can follow the instructions written in PHP.

Below, you can see a PHP page that contains:

- **PHP code between PHP tags shown on purple.**
  The PHP interpreter processes any code written inside the PHP tags.

- **HTML code outside the PHP tags shown on white.**
  This is automatically added to the HTML file that is sent to the browser (because the PHP interpreter does not need to do anything with it).

Each individual instruction inside the PHP tags is called a **statement**. Most statements start on a new line and end with a semicolon. You can omit the semicolon after a statement:

- On the last line of a PHP block
- If the PHP block only contains one statement

Including a semicolon at the end of each statement helps to avoid errors.

This page calculates the cost of 5 bags of candy at $3 each, and stores the price in a variable called **$total**. It then writes out that value in the HTML page. You will learn how the PHP code does this in Chapter 1.

```php
<?php
  $price    = 3;
  $quantity = 5;
  $total    = $price * $quantity;
?>
```

····· **OPENING PHP TAG** ·····
····· **STATEMENT**
····· **STATEMENT**   ····· **PHP BLOCK**
····· **STATEMENT**
····· **CLOSING PHP TAG** ·····

```html
<!DOCTYPE html>
<html>
  <head>
    <title>Cost of Candy</title>
  </head>
  <body>
    <p>Total: $<?php echo $total; ?></p>
  </body>
</html>
```

····· **PHP BLOCK**

HOW PHP SENDS TEXT AND HTML TO THE BROWSER

The echo command tells the PHP interpreter to add text or markup to the HTML page it is creating for the browser.

Any text and/or HTML that appears in quotes after an echo command gets sent to the browser so that it can be displayed in the page. You can use single or double quotes after the echo command, but the opening quote and closing quote must **match**.

The first quote mark tells the PHP interpreter where the text it should add to the page starts; the second tells it where it ends. The text is known as a **string literal**. The semicolon at the end of the line tells the PHP interpreter that it is the end of the statement.

```
echo '<b>Hello!</b>';
```

WRITE TO BROWSER   TEXT & MARKUP TO DISPLAY

To display a quote mark *in* the text you are sending to the browser, add a backslash immediately before the quote mark. The backslash tells the PHP interpreter not to treat the quote mark that comes after it as code. Programmers call this **escaping** the quote mark.

Below, the echo command uses double quotes to write out an HTML link. The URL in the href attribute must be in quotes, so those quotes are escaped. The code below writes out the following HTML link:
`<a href="http://notes.re/php">PHP</a>`

```
echo "<a href=\"http://notes.re/php\">PHP</a>";
```

OPENING QUOTE
FOR ECHO COMMAND   ESCAPED QUOTES
HOLD ATTRIBUTE   CLOSING QUOTE
FOR ECHO COMMAND

You can also display double quotes by placing any text and HTML you want to output in single quotes.

This works because the PHP interpreter looks for a matching single quote to indicate the end of the text.

```
echo '<a href="http://notes.re/php">PHP</a>';
```

OPENING QUOTE
FOR ECHO COMMAND   HTML ATTRIBUTE
IN DOUBLE QUOTES   CLOSING QUOTE
FOR ECHO COMMAND

WRITING CONTENT TO THE PAGE

`section_a/intro/echo.php`

```php
<!DOCTYPE html>
<html>
  <head>
    <title>echo Command</title>
    <link rel="stylesheet" href="css/styles.css">
  </head>
  <body>
    <h1>The Candy Store</h1>
①  <h2><?php echo 'Ivy\'s'; ?> page</h2>
②  <?php echo '<p class="offer">Offer: 20% off</p>' ?>
  </body>
</html>
```

RESULT

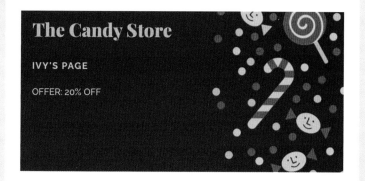

In the code box on the left:

- The filepath in the top-right corner corresponds to the file in the code download.
- The numbers correspond to the steps that describe the code below.

1. The echo command uses single quotes to write out the name of the visitor followed by 's. The backslash character is used to escape the ' between their name and the letter s.

2. The echo command adds a paragraph to the page. The <p> element has a class attribute.

Because the text and markup written to the page are placed in single quotes, the HTML attribute can use double quotes.

Although you can use single or double quotes after the echo command, it is better to choose one and stick with it. This book mostly uses single quotes so that the content can contain HTML attributes as shown here.

NOTE: If you use double quotes after an echo command, the PHP interpreter checks if the text contains variable names (which you meet on p32-36). If it does, it will write out the value that the variable holds. It does not do this with single quotes. See p52 for an example of this.

TRY: In Step 1, change the name Ivy to your name and save the file. When you refresh the page, the greeting will use your name.

COMMENTS

It is good practice to add comments that describe your PHP code. It reminds you what your code does when you come back to it after a break and it also helps others to understand your code.

Single-line comments start with either:
- Two forward slashes // or
- A single pound (or hash) symbol #

These characters tell the PHP interpreter to ignore any more PHP code on that line, until it comes across a closing ?> PHP tag.

```
echo "Welcome";   // Display greeting
echo "Welcome";   #  Display greeting
```

SINGLE-LINE COMMENT

Multi-line comments are comments that span more than one line in the PHP file. They let you add more detailed descriptions and/or notes to your code.

A forward slash and asterisk /* tells the PHP interpreter to ignore everything until it comes across an asterisk followed by a forward slash */.

```
echo "Welcome";
/*
After welcome message:
- Add profile image next to member's name
- Make both a link to the member's profile page
*/
```

MULTI-LINE COMMENT

ADDING COMMENTS TO YOUR CODE

```php
<?php
    /*
①  This page displays the member's name
    and details of a current offer
    */
?>
<!DOCTYPE html>
<html>
  <head>
    <title>Adding Comments to Your Code</title>
    <link rel="stylesheet" href="css/styles.css">
  </head>
  <body>
    <h1>The Candy Store</h1>
②  <h2><?php echo 'Welcome Ivy'; // Show name ?></h2>
    <?php echo '<p class="offer">Offer: 20% off</p>' ?>
  </body>
</html>
```

RESULT

The Candy Store

WELCOME IVY

OFFER: 20% OFF

This example is very similar to the previous one but it adds comments to the code.

1. The page starts with a multi-line comment that describes what the code does.

2. After the welcome message, a single-line comment indicates what is being shown.

The comments are not added to the HTML that is sent to the browser; they are only visible in the PHP code.

TRY: In Step 1, add another line of text into the comment.

TRY: In Step 2, change the double forward slash characters to a # (the pound/hash symbol).

NOTE: This book uses a lot of comments to help describe what individual lines of code do in the examples. Experienced programmers rarely use as many comments on a line-by-line basis as shown in this book.

IN THIS SECTION
BASIC PROGRAMMING INSTRUCTIONS

1 VARIABLES, EXPRESSIONS & OPERATORS

Each time a PHP page performs the task it was designed to achieve, it can use different values, so it is important to learn how to represent that data in code using **variables**. You will also learn how **expressions** and **operators** are used to work with these values.

2 CONTROL STRUCTURES

A PHP page will not always run the same lines of code in the same order. **Control structures** allow you to write rules that the PHP interpreter uses to determine which code it should run next.

3 FUNCTIONS

All of the individual statements that are required to perform a task can be grouped together using a **function**. This not only helps organize your code but also saves you repeating the same instructions if the page needs to perform a task multiple times.

4 CLASSES & OBJECTS

Code is used to represent concepts such as the site's members, the products being sold, and the articles being displayed. Programmers use **classes** and **objects** to group together the code that represents each of these different concepts.

1

VARIABLES, EXPRESSIONS & OPERATORS

This chapter shows how variables store data that can change each time a PHP page is requested, and how expressions and operators work with values in variables.

Variables use a name to represent a value that can change each time a PHP page is requested:

- The **name** describes the type of data that the variable holds
- The **value** is the value the variable should hold this time the page is requested

Once the page has finished running and HTML has been sent back to the browser, the PHP interpreter forgets the variable (so the next time the page runs, it can hold a different value).

PHP distinguishes between different types of values you can store in a variable (such as text and numbers); these are known as **data types**:

- A piece of text is called a **string**
- A whole number is called an **integer**
- A fractional number is represented using a **float**
- A value of true or false is called a **boolean**
- A series of related names and values can be stored in an **array**

Once you have learned about variables, you will see how **expressions** can use multiple values to create a single value. For example, text in two variables can be joined together to form one sentence, or a number stored in one variable can be multiplied by a number in another.

Expressions rely upon **operators** to create a single value. For example, the + operator is used to add two values together, and the - operator is used to subtract one value from another.

VARIABLES

Variables store data that can change (or vary) each time a PHP page is requested. They use a **name** to represent a **value** that can change.

To create a variable and store a value in it, you need:

- A variable **name** which must start with a dollar sign, followed by one or more words that describe the type of information the variable can hold

- An **equals sign** which is known as the **assignment operator** because it assigns a value to the variable name

- The **value** you want the variable to hold

If the variable holds text, the text is written between quotation marks. You can use single or double quotes, but they must match. (For example, do not start with a single quote and end with a double quote.)

If the variable stores a number or boolean value (true or false), you do not place it in quotes.

When a variable is created, programmers call this **declaring** a variable. When it is given a value, they say that a value is being **assigned** to the variable.

```
     NAME        VALUE

  $name   = 'Ivy';
  $price  = 5;

  ASSIGNMENT OPERATOR
```

Once a variable has been declared and a value has been assigned to it, the variable name can be used in the PHP code wherever you want to use the value that the variable currently holds.

When the PHP interpreter comes across a variable name, it replaces the name with the value it holds. Below, the echo command is used to display the value stored in the $name variable shown above.

```
  echo $name;

  DISPLAY   VALUE IN VARIABLE
```

CREATING AND ACCESSING VARIABLES

section_a/c01/variables.php

```php
<?php
$name  = 'Ivy';
$price = 5;
?>
<!DOCTYPE html>
<html>
  <head>
    <title>Variables</title>
    <link rel="stylesheet" href="css/styles.css">
  </head>
  <body>
    <h1>The Candy Store</h1>
    <h2>Welcome <?php echo $name; ?></h2>
    <p>The cost of your candy is
       $<?php echo $price; ?> per pack.</p>
  </body>
</html>
```

① `$name  = 'Ivy';`
② `$price = 5;`
③ `<h2>Welcome <?php echo $name; ?></h2>`
④ `$<?php echo $price; ?> per pack.</p>`

In this example, two variables are created and assigned values at the top of the page:

1. `$name` holds the name of the current visitor to the site. This is text so it is written in quotes.

2. `$price` holds the price of a single pack of candy. It is a number so the value is not placed in quotes.

Next, you can see the HTML that gets sent back to the visitor's browser. In the HTML:

3. The visitor's name is written into the page using the `echo` command.

4. The cost of the candy is written into the page.

TRY: In Step 1, change the value of the `$name` variable to hold your name. Save the file and then refresh the page in your browser. You will see your name shown.

TRY: In Step 2, change the price to 2. Save the file and then refresh the page. You will see the new price shown.

`RESULT`

The Candy Store

WELCOME IVY

The cost of your candy is $5 per pack.

In this chapter, values are assigned to variables in the PHP code. In later chapters, the values assigned to variables will come from HTML forms that visitors submit, from data in URLs, and from databases.

HOW TO NAME VARIABLES

A variable's name should describe the data that it stores.
Use the following rules to create a variable name.

1

Begin with a dollar sign ($).

- ✓ `$greeting`
- ✗ `greeting`

2

Follow it with a letter or an underscore (not a number).

- ✓ `$greeting`
- ✗ `$2_greeting`

3

Then use any combination of letters A-z (uppercase and lowercase), numbers, and underscores. (No dashes or periods are allowed.)

- ✓ `$greeting_2`
- ✗ `$greeting-2`
- ✗ `$greeting.2`

Note: $this has special meaning. Do not use it as a variable name.

- ✗ `$this`

Using variable names that describe the data your variable stores makes your code easier to understand and follow.

If you use more than one word to describe the data a variable holds, it is common to separate each word with an underscore.

Names are case-sensitive, so $Score and $score would be two different names. However, you should generally avoid creating two variables that use the same word and different combinations of uppercase/lowercase letters as they are likely to confuse other people reading your code.

Technically, you can use characters from different character sets (such as Chinese or Cyrillic characters) but it is often considered good practice to just use letters A-z, numbers, and underscores (as there are some complicated issues in supporting other characters).

SCALAR (BASIC) DATA TYPES

PHP distinguishes between three **scalar data types** that hold text, numbers, and booleans.

STRING DATA TYPE

Programmers call a piece of text a **string**. The `string` data type can consist of letters, numbers and other characters, but they are used to represent text.

```
$name = 'Ivy';
```

Strings are always enclosed in either single or double quotes. The opening quote must match the closing quote.

⊘ `$name = 'Ivy';`
⊘ `$name = "Ivy";`
⊗ `$name = "Ivy';`
⊗ `$name = 'Ivy";`

NUMERIC DATA TYPES

Numeric data types let you perform mathematical operations with the values that they hold, such as addition or multiplication.

```
$price = 5;
```

Numbers are not written in quotes. If you place numbers in quotes, they can be treated as strings rather than numbers.

PHP has two numeric data types:

`int` represents integers, which are whole numbers (e.g., 275)

`float` holds floating point numbers, which represent fractions (e.g., 2.75)

BOOLEAN DATA TYPE

The `boolean` data type can only have one of two values: `true` or `false`. These values are commonly in most programming languages.

```
$logged_in = true;
```

`true` and `false` should be written in lowercase, and are not placed in quotes. At first, boolean values might seem abstract, but many things can be represented using true or false, such as:

- Is a visitor logged in?
- Have they agreed to terms and conditions?
- Does a product qualify for free shipping?

NULL DATA TYPE

PHP also has a data type called `null`. It can only have the value `null`. It indicates that a value has not been specified for a variable.

TYPE JUGGLING

On p60-61 you see how the PHP interpreter can convert a value from one data type to another (e.g., a string to a number).

UPDATING A VALUE IN A VARIABLE

You can change or overwrite the value stored in a variable by assigning it a new value. This is done in the same way you assign a value to the variable when creating it.

1. The $name variable is **initialized**. This means it is declared and assigned an initial value, which will be used if the variable is not updated later in the page.

The initial value is Guest; it is written in quotes as it is text.

2. The $name variable is then assigned a new value of Ivy.

3. The $price variable holds the price of a single pack of candy.

Next, you can see the HTML that will be sent back to the visitor's browser. In the HTML:

4. The name is written into the page using the echo command. It shows the updated value that was assigned to the $name variable in Step 2.

5. The cost of the candy is written into the page.

```
section_a/c01/updating-variables.php                    PHP

<?php
$name  = 'Guest';          (1)
$name  = 'Ivy';            (2)
$price = 5;                (3)
?>
<!DOCTYPE html>
<html>
  <head>
    <title>Updating Variables</title>
    <link rel="stylesheet" href="css/styles.css">
  </head>
  <body>
    <h1>The Candy Store</h1>
    <h2>Welcome <?php echo $name; ?></h2>        (4)
    <p>The cost of your candy is
      $<?php echo $price; ?> per pack.</p>       (5)
  </body>
</html>
```

RESULT

The Candy Store

WELCOME IVY

The cost of your candy is $5 per pack.

TRY: In Step 2, change the value of the $name variable to hold your name. Save the file and then refresh the page in your browser. You will see your name shown.

TRY: Add a new line after Step 2 and set the $name variable to hold another name. Save the file and refresh the page. You will see the new name shown.

ARRAYS

A variable can also hold an **array** which stores a series of related values. Arrays are known as a **compound data type** because they can store more than one value.

An array is like a container that holds a set of related variables. Each item in the array is called an **element**. In the same way that a variable uses a name to represent a value, each element in an array has a:

- **Key** which acts just like a variable name
- **Value** which is the data that the name represents

PHP has two types of array:

- In **associative arrays**, the key for each element is a name that describes the data it represents

- In **indexed arrays**, the key for each element is a number known as an **index number**

ASSOCIATIVE ARRAY
The array below is designed to hold data that represents a member of a website. Each time the array is used, the names used in the keys (that describe the data stored in each element of the array) will remain the same.

INDEXED ARRAY
The array below is designed to hold a shopping list. Lists like this can hold a different number of elements each time they are used. The key does not use a name to describe each item in the list; it uses an index number (which is an integer and starts at 0).

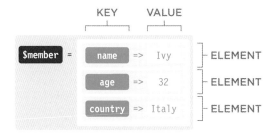

In these two examples, each value stored in the array is a scalar data type (an individual piece of data).

On p44, you can see examples of arrays where one element of the array holds another array.

NOTE: Index numbers start at 0, not 1. The first element in the list has an index number of 0. The second element is identified by the index number 1, and so on. The index number is often used to describe the order of the items in the list.

ASSOCIATIVE ARRAYS

To create an associative array, give each element (or item) in the array a **key** that describes the data it holds.

To store an associative array in a variable, use:

- A variable name that describes the set of values the array will hold
- The assignment operator
- Square brackets to create the array

Inside the brackets or parentheses, use:

- The key name in quotes
- The double arrow operator =>
- The value for this element (strings go in quotes; numbers and booleans do not)
- A comma after each element

```
    VARIABLE      CREATE ARRAY
       |              |
$member = [
        'name'    => 'Ivy',
        'age'     => 32,
        'country' => 'Italy',
];         |        |        |
         KEY    OPERATOR   VALUE
```

An associative array can also be created using the syntax shown below, with the word `array` followed by parentheses (instead of square brackets).

```
$member = array(
   'name'    => 'Ivy',
   'age'     => 32,
   'country' => 'Italy',
);
```

To access an element in an associative array, use:

- The name of the variable holding the array
- Followed by square brackets and quote marks
- The key for the element you want to retrieve

```
        VARIABLE   KEY
           |        |
        $member['name'];
```

CREATING & ACCESSING ASSOCIATIVE ARRAYS

`section_a/c01/associative-arrays.php`

```php
<?php
$nutrition = [
    'fat'   => 16,
    'sugar' => 51,
    'salt'  => 6.3,
];
?>
<!DOCTYPE html>
<html>
  <head> ... </head>
  <body>
    <h1>The Candy Store</h1>
    <h2>Nutrition (per 100g)</h2>
    <p>Fat:   <?php echo $nutrition['fat']; ?>%</p>
    <p>Sugar: <?php echo $nutrition['sugar']; ?>%</p>
    <p>Salt:  <?php echo $nutrition['salt']; ?>%</p>
  </body>
</html>
```

RESULT

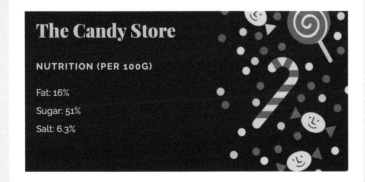

1. In this example, an associaive array is created and stored in a variable called `$nutrition`.

The array is created inside square brackets. It has three elements (each element has a key/value pair). The `=>` operator assigns the values to each of the keys.

2. To display data stored in the array, use:

- The **echo** command to indicate that the following value should be written out to the web page
- Followed by the name of the variable that holds the array
- Followed by square brackets and quotes holding the name of the key you want to access

For example, to write the sugar content into the page use:
`echo $nutrition['sugar'];`

TRY: In Step 1, change the values of the array. Give the key:
- fat a value of 42
- sugar a value of 60
- salt a value of 3.5
Save and refresh the page to see the updated values.

TRY: In Step 1, add another element to the array. Use the key `protein` and assign it a value of `2.6`. Then, in Step 2, show the protein value in the page.

INDEXED ARRAYS

When an array is created, if a key is not provided for each element, the PHP interpreter will assign it a number called an **index number**. Index numbers start at zero (0), not one (1).

To store an indexed array in a variable, use:

- A variable name that describes the set of values that the array will hold
- The assignment operator
- Square brackets to create the array

Inside the square brackets or parentheses, use:

- The list of values the array should hold (strings go in quotes, numbers and booleans do not)
- A comma after each value

Each element will be assigned an index number.

```
          ASSIGNMENT
VARIABLE  OPERATOR              VALUES

$shopping_list = ['bread', 'cheese', 'milk',];
```

Above, bread would be assigned the index number 0, cheese 1, and milk 2. Index numbers are often used to indicate the order of the items listed in the array.

An indexed array can also be created using the syntax shown below, with the word **array** followed by parentheses (instead of square brackets).

```
$shopping_list = array('bread',
                       'cheese',
                       'milk');
```

Each value that is being added to the array can be on the same line or on a new line (as shown above).

To access the items in an indexed array, use:

- The name of the variable holding the array
- Followed by square brackets (no quote marks)
- The index number of the item you want to access (in the square brackets)

The code below gets the third item in the array, so in this example it would get the value milk.

```
 VARIABLE      INDEX NUMBER

$shopping_list[2];
```

CREATING & ACCESSING INDEXED ARRAYS

section_a/c01/indexed-arrays.php

PHP

```php
<?php
$best_sellers = ['Chocolate', 'Mints', 'Fudge',
    'Bubble gum', 'Toffee', 'Jelly beans',];
?>
<!DOCTYPE html>
<html>
  <head> ... </head>
  <body>
    <h1>The Candy Store</h1>
    <h2>Best Sellers</h2>
    <ul>
      <li><?php echo $best_sellers[0]; ?></li>
      <li><?php echo $best_sellers[1]; ?></li>
      <li><?php echo $best_sellers[2]; ?></li>
    </ul>
  </body>
</html>
```

RESULT

1. This example starts by creating a variable called `$best_sellers`. Its value is an array holding a list of the best-selling items on the website.

This array is created using square brackets, and the items are added to the array inside those brackets. Because the items in the array are text, they are placed in quotes. (Numbers and booleans would not go in quotes.) Each item is followed by a comma.

2. The three best-selling items are written to the page:

- The `echo` command indicates that the following value should be written out
- Followed by the name of the variable that holds the array
- Then square brackets holding the index number of the item you want to retrieve. Remember that index numbers start at 0, not 1.

TRY: In Step 1, add Licorice to the array after Fudge. In Step 2, add the 4th and 5th items from the array.

UPDATING ARRAYS

Once an array has been created, you can add new items to it or update the value for any of the elements that are in it.

To update a value stored in an associative array, use:

- The name of the variable holding the array
- Followed by square brackets
- Then the key name in quotes
- An assignment operator
- The new value it should hold

```
$member['name'] = 'Tom';
```
VARIABLE   KEY   NEW VALUE

To add a new item to an associative array, do exactly the same as above, but use a new key name (not one that has already been used in the array).

The quotes go around the key name when it is a string because quotes indicate a string data type.

WHICH TYPE OF ARRAY TO USE

Associative arrays are best when you:

- Know exactly what information the array will hold. This is necessary in order to provide a key name for each of the elements.
- Need to get single pieces of data using a key name.

To update a value stored in an indexed array, use:

- The name of the variable holding the array
- Followed by square brackets
- The index number (not in quotes)
- An assignment operator
- The new value it should hold

```
$shopping_list[2] = 'butter';
```
VARIABLE   INDEX   NEW VALUE
             NUMBER

You will see how to add items to indexed arrays on p220. The process is different because you can specify the position of the new item in the array.

Quotes are not placed around index numbers because number data types are not quoted.

Indexed arrays are helpful when you:

- Do not know how many pieces of data are going to be stored in the array. (The index numbers increase as more items are added to the list.)
- Want to store a series of values in a specific order.

CHANGING VALUES STORED IN ARRAYS

section_a/c01/updating-arrays.php

```php
<?php
$nutrition = [
    'fat'   => 38,
    'sugar' => 51,
    'salt'  => 0.25,
];
$nutrition['fat']   = 36;
$nutrition['fiber'] = 2.1;
?>
<!DOCTYPE html>
<html>
  <head> ... </head>
  <body>
    <h1>The Candy Store</h1>
    <h2>Nutrition (per 100g)</h2>
    <p>Fat:   <?php echo $nutrition['fat']; ?>%</p>
    <p>Sugar: <?php echo $nutrition['sugar']; ?>%</p>
    <p>Salt:  <?php echo $nutrition['salt']; ?>%</p>
    <p>Fiber: <?php echo $nutrition['fiber']; ?>%</p>
  </body>
</html>
```

1. This example starts by storing an array in a variable called `$nutrition`.

The keys and values that make up each element in the array do not need to be on a new line (as shown here) but it makes them easier to read if they are.

2. The value that is stored for the fat content is updated from 38 to 36.

3. A new element is added to the array. The key is `fiber` and its value is `2.1`.

4. The values in the array are written out to the page.

TRY: After Step 3, add another key for `protein` and assign it a value of `7.3`.

RESULT

The Candy Store

NUTRITION (PER 100G)

Fat: 36%

Sugar: 51%

Salt: 0.25%

Fiber: 2.1%

STORING ARRAYS IN AN ARRAY

The value of any element in an array can be another array. When every element of an array holds another array, it is called a **multidimensional array** and it can be used to represent data that you may see in tables.

There are times when you need to store a related set of values in an element of an array (for example, when representing data that you may traditionally have seen in tables). Consider the table on the right with three members, their ages, and their countries.

NAME	AGE	COUNTRY
Ivy	32	UK
Emi	24	Japan
Luke	47	USA

Each row of this table (each member) can be represented using an element of an indexed array. Each element can then hold an associative array storing the name, age, and country of each member.

The index numbers for the indexed array are automatically assigned by the PHP interpreter. The comma after each of the associative arrays indicates the end of the value for that element.

```
$members = [
    ['name' => 'Ivy',  'age' => 32, 'country' => 'UK',],
    ['name' => 'Emi',  'age' => 24, 'country' => 'Japan',],
    ['name' => 'Luke', 'age' => 47, 'country' => 'USA',],
];
```

To get the array that holds data about Emi, use the:

- Name of the variable that holds the indexed array
- Index number of the element you want to access in square brackets (remembering that indexed arrays start at 0, and that numbers are not placed in quotes).

```
$members[1];
```

To get the age of Luke, use the:

- Name of the variable that holds the indexed array
- Index number of the element that holds the array of data about Luke, in square brackets
- Key of the element you want to access in the array about Luke in a second set of square brackets (because the key is a string, put it in quotes)

```
$members[2]['age'];
```

MULTIDIMENSIONAL ARRAYS

PHP   section_a/c01/multidimensional-arrays.php

```php
<?php
$offers = [
    ['name' => 'Toffee', 'price' => 5, 'stock' => 120,],
    ['name' => 'Mints',  'price' => 3, 'stock' => 66,],
    ['name' => 'Fudge',  'price' => 4, 'stock' => 97,],
];
?>
<!DOCTYPE html>
<html>
  <head> ... </head>
  <body>
    <h1>The Candy Store</h1>
    <h2>Offers</h2>
    <p><?php echo $offers[0]['name']; ?> -
      $<?php echo $offers[0]['price']; ?> </p>
    <p><?php echo $offers[1]['name']; ?> -
      $<?php echo $offers[1]['price']; ?> </p>
    <p><?php echo $offers[2]['name']; ?> -
      $<?php echo $offers[2]['price']; ?> </p>
  </body>
</html>
```

RESULT

The Candy Store

OFFERS

Toffee - $5

Mints - $3

Fudge - $4

1. This example starts by storing an indexed array in a variable called $offers.

Each element in the array stores an associative array holding the name, price, and stock level of an item that is on offer.

2. The name of the first product is written out. (The index number for the first product is 0.)

3. The price of the first product is written out.

4. The name and price of the second product are written out.

5. The name and price of the third product are written out.

TRY: In Step 1, add another product with a name of Chocolate to the array. Set the price to 2 and assign it a stock level of 83. Then, after Step 5, write out the name and price of the new product you just added.

In the next chapter, you will see how a loop can be used to write out the name and price of each product in the $offers array, no matter how many products the array contains.

SHORTHAND FOR ECHO

When a PHP block is only used to write a value to the browser, you can use shorthand instead of `<?php echo ?>`.

Instead of writing `<?php echo $name; ?>` you can use the shorthand `<?= $name ?>` this is the only time you do not need to use the full opening `<?php` delimiter.

You do *not* need:
- The letters **php** in the opening tag
- The **echo** command
- A semicolon before the closing tag

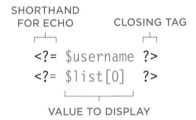

SHORTHAND FOR ECHO   CLOSING TAG

```
<?= $username ?>
<?= $list[0]  ?>
```

VALUE TO DISPLAY

In many of the examples in the early chapters of this book, you will see that each PHP file has two parts:

- First, the PHP code stores values in variables or arrays. (It may also perform tasks with the data they hold.)

- Then, the HTML code that is sent back to the browser. This second part of the page will show values that were stored in variables using the shorthand syntax shown above.

If you start each page by creating the values that the page will need to display, and storing them in variables, it will help create a clear separation between the PHP code that runs on the server, and the HTML code that the visitor will end up seeing.

The second part of the file, where the HTML page is created, should use the minimum amount of PHP code possible. In the early examples, the PHP code in this part of the page will only write out values stored in variables into the HTML.

USING THE SHORTHAND FOR ECHO

```php
<?php
$name      = 'Ivy';
$favorites = ['Chocolate', 'Toffee', 'Fudge',];
?>
<!DOCTYPE html>
<html>
  <head>
    <title>Echo Shorthand</title>
    <link rel="stylesheet" href="css/styles.css">
  </head>
  <body>
    <h1>The Candy Store</h1>
    <h2>Welcome <?= $name ?></h2>
    <p>Your favorite type of candy is:
       <?= $favorites[0] ?>.</p>
  </body>
</html>
```

(1) `$name      = 'Ivy';`
(2) `$favorites = ['Chocolate', 'Toffee', 'Fudge',];`
(3) `<h2>Welcome <?= $name ?></h2>`
(4) `<?= $favorites[0] ?>.</p>`

RESULT

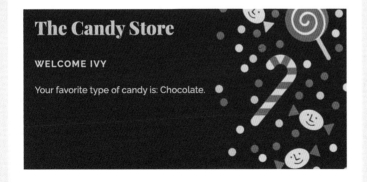

In this example, you can see that two different variables have been created and assigned values at the top of the page before the HTML starts:

1. $name holds the name of a member of the site. This is text so it is stored in quotes.

2. $favorites holds an array of the member's favorite types of candy.

3. The name is written into the page using the shorthand for the echo command.

4. The member's favorite type of candy is written out to the page using the shorthand for the echo command.

TRY: In Step 1, change the value stored in the $name variable to your name. In Step 2, add your favorite type of candy to the start of the array. Save the file, and refresh the page in your browser. You will see the content change.

EXPRESSIONS & OPERATORS

Two (or more) values are often used to create one new value.
Expressions consist of one or more constructs that **evaluate** to (result in) a single value. Expressions use **operators** to create a single value.

Basic math (addition, subtraction, multiplication, and division) uses two values to create one new value. The following expression multiplies the number 3 by the number 5 to create a value of 15:

```
3 * 5
```

Programmers say that expressions **evaluate** to a single value. Below, the new value that is created is stored in a variable called $total:

```
$total = 3 * 5;
```

The + - * / = symbols are all called **operators**.

You can join two or more strings together to create one longer piece of text using a string operator called the **concatenation operator**. The following expression joins the values 'Hi ' and 'Ivy' to create one string.

```
$greeting = 'Hi ' . 'Ivy';
```

The joining of these two strings evaluates into one single value of Hi Ivy, which is stored in the variable called $greeting.

In the rest of this chapter, you will meet the operators introduced on the right.

ARITHMETIC OPERATORS
p50-51

Arithmetic operators allow you to work with numbers, performing tasks such as addition, subtraction, multiplication, and division.

For example, if someone was purchasing 3 packets of candy and each packet cost $5, you could use a multiplication operator to work out the total cost of those three packets of candy.

STRING OPERATORS
p52-53

String operators allow you to work with text. There are two string operators that are used to combine different pieces of text into one single string.

For example, if you have a member's first name stored in one variable and their last name stored in a second variable, you could join the two variables together to create their full name.

COMPARISON OPERATORS
p54-55 and p58

As their name suggests, comparison operators *compare* two values and return a boolean value of either `true` or `false`.

For example, if you take the numbers 3 and 5, you could compare them to see if:

- 3 is greater than 5 (`false`)
- 3 is equal to 5 (`false`)
- 3 is less than 5 (`true`)

You can also compare strings to see if one value is greater or less than another:

- `'Apple'` is greater than `'Banana'` (`false`)
- `'A'` is equal to `'B'` (`false`)
- `'A'` is less than `'B'` (`true`)

LOGICAL OPERATORS
p56-57 and p59

Three logical operators `and`, `or`, and `not` work with two values of either `true` or `false`. To understand how they work, consider the following two questions; both can be answered with `true` or `false`:

Is the temperature hot? Is the weather sunny?

- The and operator checks if the temperature is hot **and** the weather is sunny.
- The or operator checks if the temperature is hot **or** the weather is sunny.
- The not operator can check if the answer to just one of these questions at a time is *not* true. For example, is the weather *not* sunny?

Each of these results in a value of `true` or `false`.

ARITHMETIC OPERATORS

PHP allows you to use the following mathematical operators.
They can be used with numbers or variables that store numbers.

NAME	OPERATOR	PURPOSE	EXAMPLE	RESULT
Addition	+	Add one value to another	10 + 5	15
Subtraction	-	Subtract one value from another	10 - 5	5
Multiplication	*	Multiply two values (NOTE: This is an asterisk and not the letter x)	10 * 5	50
Division	/	Divide two values	10 / 5	2
Modulus	%	Divide two values and return the remainder	10 % 3	1
Exponentiation	**	Raise a value to the power of another	10 ** 5	100000
Increment	++	Add one to the number and return the new value	$i = 10; $i++;	11
Decrement	--	Subtract one and return the new value	$i = 10; $i--;	9

ORDER OF EXECUTION

You can perform multiple arithmetic operations in a single expression but it is important to understand the order in which the result will be calculated: multiplication and division are performed *before* addition and subtraction.

This can affect the number you might expect to see. For example, the numbers here are calculated left to right. The result is 16:
$total = 2 + 4 + 10;
In the following, however, the result is 42 (not 60):
$total = 2 + 4 * 10;

Parentheses allow you to indicate which calculation you want performed first, so the following results in a total of 60:
$total = (2 + 4) * 10;
The parentheses indicate that 2 is added to 4 *before* being multiplied by 10.

USING ARITHMETIC OPERATORS

section_a/c01/arithmetic-operators.php

```php
<?php
$items    = 3;
$cost     = 5;
$subtotal = $cost * $items;
$tax      = ($subtotal / 100) * 20;
$total    = $subtotal + $tax;
?>
<!DOCTYPE html>
  <html>
  <head> ... </head>
  <body>
    <h1>The Candy Store</h1>
    <h2>Shopping Cart</h2>
    <p>Items: <?= $items ?></p>
    <p>Cost per pack: $<?= $cost ?></p>
    <p>Subtotal: $<?= $subtotal ?></p>
    <p>Tax: $<?= $tax ?></p>
    <p>Total: $<?= $total ?></p>
  </body>
</html>
```

① $items = 3;
② $cost = 5;
③ $subtotal = $cost * $items;
④ $tax = ($subtotal / 100) * 20;
⑤ $total = $subtotal + $tax;
⑥ (the `<p>` lines)

RESULT

The Candy Store

SHOPPING CART

Items: 3

Cost per pack: $5

Subtotal: $15

Tax: $3

Total: $18

This example shows how mathematical operators are used with numbers to calculate the cost of an order. First, two variables are created to store the:

1. Total number of items ordered ($items)
2. Cost of each packet of candy ($cost)

Next, calculations are performed and the results are stored in variables before the HTML is created. This helps separate the PHP code from the HTML content.

3. The cost of the order is calculated by multiplying the number of items by the cost of one packet of candy.

4. Tax needs to be added at a rate of 20%. To do this, the subtotal is divided by 100. (This is done in parentheses to ensure it is calculated first.) Next, the result is multiplied by 20.

5. Finally, the tax is added to the subtotal to find the total cost.

6. The results that were stored in variables are then written out in the HTML page.

TRY: Change the cost of items in Step 1 and the quantity in Step 2.

STRING OPERATORS

You may need to join two or more strings to create a single value. The process of joining two or more strings is called **concatenation**.

CONCATENATION OPERATOR

The concatenation operator is a period symbol. It joins the value in one string to the value in another. In the example below, the variable called $name would hold the string 'Ivy Stone':

```
$forename = 'Ivy';
$surname  = 'Stone';
$name     = $forename . ' ' . $surname;
```

Note that a space is added between the $forename and $surname variables; if the space was not there, the $name variable would hold the value IvyStone.

You can concatenate as many strings as you want in one statement providing the concatenation operator is used between every string.

You can join strings that are stored in variables without a concatenation operator. If a value is assigned with double quotes (rather than single quotes), the PHP interpreter replaces the variable names in double quotes with the values they contain. Below, $name would hold the value Ivy Stone.
```
$name = "$forename $surname";
```

CONCATENATING ASSIGNMENT OPERATOR

If you want to append some text to an existing variable, you can use the concatenating assignment operator. You can think of it as shorthand for creating an updated string:

```
$greeting = 'Hello ';
$greeting .= 'Ivy';
```

Here, the string 'Hello ' is stored in a variable called $greeting. On the next line, the concatenating assignment operator adds the string 'Ivy' to the end of the value held by the variable called $greeting.

Now, the $greeting variable holds the value 'Hello Ivy'. As you can see, it uses one less line of code than the example on the left hand side.

JOINING TOGETHER STRINGS

section_a/c01/string-operator.php

```php
<?php
$prefix  = 'Thank you';
$name    = 'Ivy';
$message = $prefix . ', ' . $name;
?>
<!DOCTYPE html>
<html>
  <head>
    <title>String Operator</title>
    <link rel="stylesheet" href="css/styles.css">
  </head>
  <body>
    <h1>The Candy Store</h1>
    <h2><?= $name ?>'s Order</h2>
    <p><?= $message ?></p>
  </body>
</html>
```

RESULT

This example will display a personalized message.

1. First, a variable called `$prefix` is created to store the start of the message for the visitor. It holds the words `Thank you`.

2. A second variable is created to store the visitor's name. The variable is called `$name`, and the visitor is called Ivy.

3. The personal message is created by concatenating (or joining) three values together and storing the new value in a variable called `$message`:

- First, the value stored in `$prefix` is added to `$message`
- Next, a comma and a space is added
- Finally, the value stored in `$name` is added

TRY: In Step 2, change the value stored in `$name` to your name.

TRY: In Step 3, assign the value of the `$message` variable using double quotes (and no concatenation operator):
`$message = "$prefix $name";`

COMPARISON OPERATORS

Comparison operators let you compare two or more values.
They result in a boolean value of either `true` or `false`.

IS EQUAL TO

This operator compares two values to see if they are the same.

`'Hello' == 'Hello'` results in `true`
because they *are* the same string.
`'Hello' == 'Goodbye'` results in `false`
because they are *not* the same string.

The operators above allow the PHP interpreter to determine whether or not the two values are equivalent. The operators below are more strict because they check both the value *and* the data type.

IS NOT EQUAL TO

These operators compare two values to see if they are *not* the same.

`'Hello' != 'Hello'` results in `false`
because they *are* the same string.
`'Hello' != 'Goodbye'` results in `true`
because they are *not* the same string.

The operators above would treat 3 (an integer) as equivalent to 3.0 (a float). The operators below would not. (p60-61 shows how 0 can be treated as a boolean value of `false` and 1 treated as `true`.)

IS IDENTICAL TO

This operator compares two values to check that both the value and data type are the same.

`'3' === 3` results in `false`
because they are *not* the same data type.
`'3' === '3'` results in `true`
because they *are* the same data type and value.

IS NOT IDENTICAL TO

This operator compares two values to check that both the value and the data type are *not* the same.

`3.0 !== 3` results in `true`
because they are *not* the same data type.
`3.0 !== 3.0` results in `false`
because they *are* the same data type and value.

If you use `echo` to write out the value of a boolean to the page, `true` will show 1 and `false` will not display anything.

LESS THAN and GREATER THAN

< checks if the value on the left is less than the value on the right.

4 < 3 results in `false`   3 < 4 results in `true`

> checks if the value on the left is greater than the value on the right.

z > a results in `true`   a > z results in `false`

LESS THAN OR EQUAL TO and GREATER THAN OR EQUAL TO

<= checks if the value on the left is less than or equal to the value on the right.

4 <= 3 results in `false`   3 <= 4 results in `true`

>= checks if the value on the left is greater than or equal to the value on the right.

z >= a results in `true`   z >= z results in `true`

SPACESHIP OPERATOR

The spaceship operator compares the values to the left and right of it and results in:

0 if both values are equal
1 if the value on the left is greater
−1 if the value on the right is greater

This operator was introduced in PHP 7 (and does not work with earlier versions of PHP).

1 <=> 1 results in: 0
2 <=> 1 results in: 1
2 <=> 3 results in: −1

LOGICAL OPERATORS

Comparison operators result in a single value that is `true` or `false`. Logical operators can be used with multiple comparison operators to compare the results of multiple expressions.

In this one line of code, there are three expressions, each of which will resolve to a single value of either `true` or `false`.

Expression 1 (on the left) and expression 2 (on the right) both use comparison operators, and both expressions result in a value of `false`.

Expression 3 uses a logical operator (rather than a comparison operator).

The logical and (`&&`) operator checks to see whether *both* of the expressions (either side of it) return `true`. In this case, they do not, so the entire expression will evaluate to a value of `false`.

Expressions 1 and 2 are evaluated before 3.

Each expression has been put in its own set of parentheses. This helps show that the code in each set of parentheses should evaluate into a single value. It works without parentheses, but that makes it harder to read.

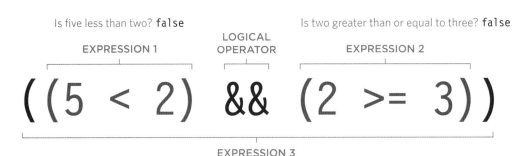

Is five less than two? `false`

EXPRESSION 1

LOGICAL OPERATOR

Is two greater than or equal to three? `false`

EXPRESSION 2

$$((5 < 2) \;\&\&\; (2 >= 3))$$

EXPRESSION 3

Do expression 1 and expression 2 both evaluate to `true`? `false`

&&

LOGICAL AND

This operator tests more than one condition.

```
((2 < 5) && (3 >= 2))
```
This results in a value of true

If both expressions evaluate to true, the expression returns true. If one of these results in false, the expression results in false.

```
true  && true   results in true
true  && false  results in false
false && true   results in false
false && false  results in false
```

You can use the word **and** instead of two ampersands.

||

LOGICAL OR

This operator tests at least one condition.

```
((2 < 5) || (2 < 1))
```
This results in a value of true

If either expression evaluates to true, the expression returns true. If both expressions result in false, the expression results in false.

```
true  || true   results in true
true  || false  results in true
false || true   results in true
false || false  results in false
```

You can use the word **or** instead of two pipestem characters.

!

LOGICAL NOT

This operator takes a single boolean value and negates it.

```
!(2 < 1)
```
This results in a value of true

The ! negates an expression. If it is false (without the ! before it), it results in true. If the statement is true, it results in false.

```
!true   results in false
!false  results in true
```

You *cannot* use the word **not** instead of the exclamation mark.

SHORT CIRCUIT EVALUATION

Logical expressions are evaluated left-to-right. Once the first expression has been evaluated and the PHP interpreter knows the logical operator, it might not need to evaluate the second condition, as you can see in the examples on the right.

```
((5 < 2) && (2 >= 2))
         ↑
```
A false value was found.

There is no point continuing to test the second condition because they cannot both result in a value of true.

```
((2 < 5) || (2 >= 2))
         ↑
```
A true value was found.

There is no point continuing to test the second condition because at least one of the values is true.

USING COMPARISON OPERATORS

1. Three variables are created:

- The first holds the type of candy a customer wants.
- The second shows there are 5 packs in stock.
- The third shows the customer wants 8 packs.

2. A comparison operator checks if the quantity wanted is less than or equal to the quantity in stock. The result is stored in a variable called $can_buy.

3. You hardly ever write a boolean into the page (as shown here). It is more likely that the value would be used in conditional logic, which you meet in the next chapter. But it is important to see what you get when you try to write out a boolean value like this; if the value is:

- `true`, the page will show 1
- `false`, the page will show nothing

TRY: In Step 1, swap the values in $stock and $wanted. The value in $can_buy will change.

On p75, you will learn how to show different messages when the result of an expression that uses a comparison operator is true or false.

`section_a/c01/comparison-operators.php` **PHP**

```php
<?php
$item   = 'Chocolate';
$stock  = 5;
$wanted = 8;
$can_buy = ($wanted <= $stock);
?>
<!DOCTYPE html>
<html>
  <head> ... </head>
  <body>
    <h1>The Candy Store</h1>
    <h2>Shopping Cart</h2>
    <p>Item:    <?= $item ?></p>
    <p>Stock:   <?= $stock ?></p>
    <p>Wanted:  <?= $wanted ?></p>
    <p>Can buy: <?= $can_buy ?></p>
  </body>
</html>
```

RESULT

The Candy Store

SHOPPING CART

Item: Chocolate

Stock: 5

Wanted: 8

Can buy:

USING LOGICAL OPERATORS

section_a/c01/logical-operators.php

PHP

```php
<?php
$item    = 'Chocolate';
$stock   = 5;
$wanted  = 3;
$deliver = true;
$can_buy = (($wanted <= $stock) && ($deliver == true));
?>
<!DOCTYPE html>
<html>
  <head> ... </head>
  <body>
    <h1>The Candy Store</h1>
    <h2>Shopping Cart</h2>
    <p>Item:    <?= $item ?></p>
    <p>Stock:   <?= $stock ?></p>
    <p>Ordered: <?= $wanted ?></p>
    <p>Can buy: <?= $can_buy ?></p>
  </body>
</html>
```

(1) $wanted = 3;
(2) $deliver = true;
(3) $can_buy = ...

RESULT

This example builds on the example from the left-hand page.

1. The customer only wants 3 packs of candy.

2. A variable called `$deliver` is added; it stores a boolean value to indicate whether or not a delivery can be made.

3. An expression uses two comparison operators:

- The first checks if there are enough items in stock
- The second checks that the item can be delivered

An `&&` logical operator tests whether both operators result in `true`. If they do, then the value of `$can_buy` will be `true`, and the page will display the number 1.

If they do not both result in `true`, `$can_buy` will hold a value of `false` and nothing will be shown.

TRY: In Step 1, swap the values in `$stock` and `$wanted`. The value in `$can_buy` will change.

On p75, you learn how to show different messages when an expression returns `true` or `false`.

TYPE JUGGLING: CONVERTING DATA TYPES

The PHP interpreter can convert a value from one data type to another. This is known as **type juggling** and can lead to unexpected results.

PHP is known as a **loosely typed** language because, when you create a variable, you do not need to specify the data type of the value it will hold. Below, the $title variable holds a string, then an integer:

```
$title = 'Ten';   // String
$title = 10;       // Integer
```

PHP's approach can be compared with **strictly typed** programming languages (such as C++ or C#), which require programmers to specify the data type that each variable will hold when it is declared.

When the PHP interpreter comes across a value that does not use the data type it expects to receive, it can try to convert the value to the expected data type. This a process called **type juggling**.

Type juggling can cause confusion because the PHP interpreter can generate surprising results or errors. For example, the addition operator below adds two values together. The number 1 is an integer, but 2 is a string because it is in quote marks.

```
$total =  1 + '2';
```

In this case, the PHP interpreter will automatically try to convert the string to a number so that it can perform the arithmetic. As a result, the $total variable will hold the number 3.

On the right-hand page, you can see rules that specify how a value is converted from one data type to another. There are examples to demonstrate type juggling at: http://notes.re/php/type-juggling.

When the data type for a value is changed to a different data type, programmers say that the value's data type is **cast** from one type to another. Type juggling is known referred to as **implicit casting** because the PHP interpreter performs the casting.

When a programmer explicitly changes the data type of a value using code, it is known as **explicit casting** because the PHP interpreter has been explicitly told to change the data type.

NUMBERS

When the PHP interpreter expects two numbers, it can perform a mathematical operation on them.

Below, you can see what happens when:
- A string is added to a number
- A boolean is added to a number

NUMBER + STRING	TREATED AS	RESULT	DESCRIPTION
1 + '1'	1 + 1	2 (int)	String holds a valid integer. It is treated as an integer.
1 + '1.2'	1 + 1.2	2.2 (float)	String holds a float. It is treated as a float.
1 + '1.2e+3'	1 + 1200	1201 (float)	String holds a float using an e (exponent of 10). Treated as a float.
1 + '5star'	1 + 5	6 (int)	String holds an integer followed by other characters. The number is treated as an integer. Later characters are ignored.
1 + '3.5star'	1 + 3.5	4.5 (float)	String holds a float followed by other characters. The number is treated as a float. Later characters are ignored.
1 + 'star9'	1 + 0	1 (int)	String starts with anything other than an integer or a float. It is treated as the number 0.

NUMBER + BOOLEAN	TREATED AS	RESULT	DESCRIPTION
1 + true	1 + 1	2 (int)	Boolean true is treated as the integer 1.
1 + false	1 + 0	1 (int)	Boolean false is treated as the integer 0.

STRINGS

When the PHP interpreter tries to concatenate two strings, it will follow these rules.

Below, you can see what happens when PHP:
- Concatenates a string with a number
- Concatenates a string with a boolean

STRING . NUMBER	TREATED AS	RESULT	DESCRIPTION
'Hi ' . 1	'Hi ' . '1'	Hi 1 (string)	Integer is treated as a string.
'Hi ' . 1.23	'Hi ' . '1.23'	Hi 1.23 (string)	Float is treated as a string.

STRING . BOOLEAN	TREATED AS	RESULT	DESCRIPTION
'Hi ' . true	'Hi ' . '1'	Hi 1 (string)	Boolean true is treated as an integer of 1.
'Hi ' . false	'Hi ' . ''	Hi (string)	Boolean false is treated as a blank string.

BOOLEANS

When the PHP interpreter expects a boolean value, all of the values shown in the table on the right will be treated as false.

Any other value is treated as true (any text, a number other than 0, or the boolean value true).

VALUE	DATA TYPE	TREATED AS
false	Boolean	false
0	Integer	false
0.0	Float	false
'0'	String with a value of 0	false
''	Empty string	false
array[]	Empty array	false
null	Null	false

The Candy Store

MULTI-BUY OFFER

Hello, Ivy.

Buy 5 packs of Chocolate for $20
(usual price $25)

Save $5

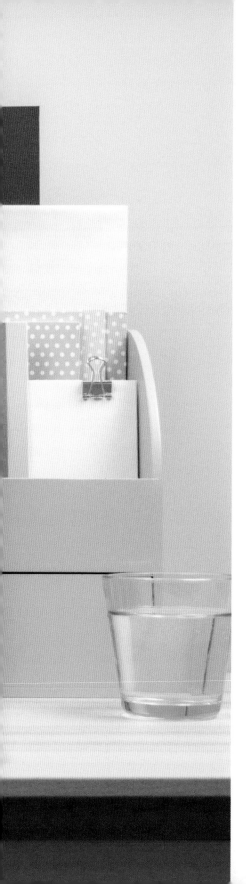

A BASIC
PHP PAGE

This example brings together several of the techniques you have seen in this chapter.

The PHP file creates an HTML page that tells visitors about a discount that is available when they purchase multiple packs of candy.

You will see how to:

- Store information in variables and arrays.

- Use the concatenation operator to join text in variables to create a personalized greeting for a visitor.

- Use arithmetic operators to perform calculations that determine the prices that are shown on the page.

- Write new values that have been created by the PHP interpreter into the HTML content of the page.

Additionally, if the values that are stored in the variables are updated then the page will automatically reflect the new products and prices.

PROCESSING AND DISPLAYING DATA

When you start writing PHP files, they often contain a mixture of HTML and PHP code. It is good practice to separate this code as much as possible:

- Start by using PHP to create the values that will be displayed in the HTML page, and store those values in variables. (On the right, this is above the dotted horizontal line.)

- Then, the lower part of the page can focus on the HTML content. PHP code should only be used in this part of the page to display the values that have been stored in the variables. (On the right, this is below the dotted horizontal line.)

Looking at the PHP code at the start of the page:

1. This example starts by declaring a variable to hold the visitor's username. It is called $username because a variable name should always start with a dollar symbol, followed by a name that describes the type of data it holds.

2. A variable called $greeting is declared to hold a greeting for the visitor. This uses the string operator to join the string Hello, and the name of the visitor.

3. A variable called $offer is created to hold the details of an item that is on special offer. Its value is an array with four elements:

- The item on offer
- The quantity they must purchase
- The normal price per pack (without discount)
- The discounted price per pack

The first element, which describes the item on offer, uses a string data type. The other values are integers.

4. A variable called $usual_price is created. Its value is the cost of the items without discount. This is calculated by multiplying two of the values stored in the array: the quantity and the price.

5. A variable called $offer_price is created. Its value is the cost of the items with the discount applied. This is calculated by multiplying the quantity and the discounted price that were stored in the array.

6. A variable called $saving is created to hold the total saving for the customer. This is calculated by subtracting the value stored in the $offer_price variable (created in Step 5) from the value stored in $usual_price (created in Step 4).

The second half of the page (below the dotted horizontal line) will create the HTML that is sent back to the browser. It starts with the HTML DOCTYPE declaration. PHP is only used to write out values that were stored in variables in the previous steps:

7. The greeting, which is the word Hello followed by the visitor's name, is written out to the page using the shorthand for the echo command.

8. The total saving, which is stored in the $saving variable (created in Step 6) is shown in a yellow circle. CSS is used to place this circle in the top right corner of the browser window.

9. A paragraph explains the details of the offer. It shows the quantity of candy the visitor has to buy, and the name of the candy.

10. This is followed by the discounted price stored in $offer_price and the usual price in $usual_price.

```php
<?php
$username = 'Ivy';                                      // Variable to hold username

$greeting = 'Hello, ' . $username . '.';                // Greeting is 'Hello, ' + username

$offer = [                                              // Create array to hold offer
    'item'     => 'Chocolate',                          // Item on offer
    'qty'      => 5,                                     // Quantity to buy
    'price'    => 5,                                     // Usual price per pack
    'discount' => 4,                                     // Offer price per pack
];

$usual_price = $offer['qty'] * $offer['price'];         // Usual total price
$offer_price = $offer['qty'] * $offer['discount'];      // Offer total price
$saving      = $usual_price - $offer_price;             // Total saving
?>
<!DOCTYPE html>
<html>
  <head>
    <title>The Candy Store</title>
    <link rel="stylesheet" href="css/styles.css">
  </head>
  <body>
    <h1>The Candy Store</h1>

    <h2>Multi-buy Offer</h2>

    <p><?= $greeting ?></p>

    <p class="sticker">Save $<?= $saving ?></p>

    <p>Buy <?= $offer['qty'] ?> packs of <?= $offer['item'] ?>
       for $<?= $offer_price ?><br>(usual price $<?= $usual_price ?>)</p>
  </body>
</html>
```

① ② ③ ④ ⑤ ⑥ ⑦ ⑧ ⑨ ⑩

TRY: In Step 1, change the username to your name.

In Step 2, update the greeting shown to the visitor to say Hi (instead of Hello).

In Step 3, update the number of packs of candy in the $offer array's qty key to 3.

In Step 3, update the price of the candy to 6.

SUMMARY
VARIABLES, EXPRESSIONS & OPERATORS

> Variables store data that varies each time a script runs.

> Scalar data types hold text, whole numbers, floating point numbers, and boolean values of `true` or `false`.

> An array is a compound data type, used to store a set of related values.

> Each item in an array is called an element. Elements in an associative array have a key and a value. Elements in an indexed array have an index number and a value.

> String operators join (concatenate) text in strings.

> Mathematical operators perform math using numbers.

> Comparison operators compare two values to see if one is equal, greater, or less than the other.

> Logical operators can combine the outcomes of multiple expressions using `and`, `or`, and `not`.

2
CONTROL STRUCTURES

This chapter shows you how to tell the PHP interpreter whether to run a block of code or not; when to repeat a set of statements; and when to include code from another file.

There are three ways to control when the PHP interpreter will run statements in a PHP file:

- **Sequence**: The PHP interpreter runs the statements in the order in which they are written. Line 1, line 2, line 3, and so on until it reaches the last line. All of the examples you have seen so far in the book run the code in sequence.

- **Selection**: The PHP interpreter uses a condition to check whether or not some code will run. For example, the condition could be, "Is the user logged in?" If the answer is "no" it could show a link to the login page. If the answer is "yes" it could show a link to the user's profile page. Programmers call these instructions **conditional statements** because they select which set of statements to run based upon a condition.

- **Repetition / iteration**: The PHP interpreter can repeat the same set of code multiple times. For example, if an array held a shopping list, the same instructions could run for each item in the list (whether it contains 1 or 100 items). **Loops** are used to repeat sets of statements.

When you change the order in which statements are run, you are changing the **control flow**.

In this chapter, you will also learn how to use **include files** to hold code that is used by multiple pages. This method allows you to include one file in several pages rather than repeating the same code over and over again in each file.

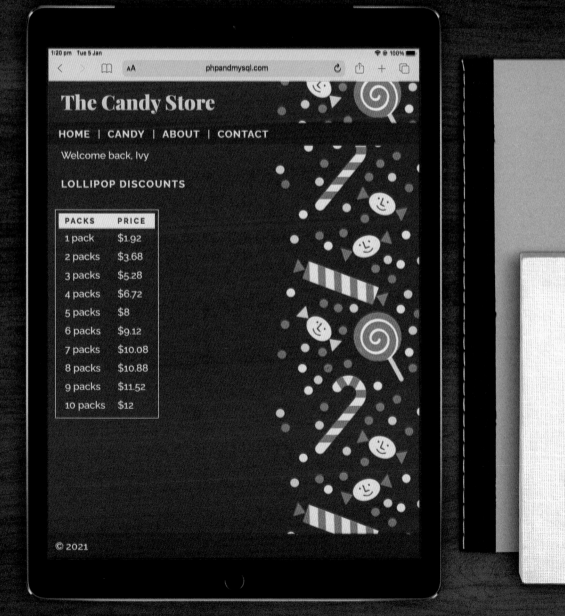

The Candy Store

HOME | CANDY | ABOUT | CONTACT

Welcome back, Ivy

LOLLIPOP DISCOUNTS

PACKS	PRICE
1 pack	$1.92
2 packs	$3.68
3 packs	$5.28
4 packs	$6.72
5 packs	$8
6 packs	$9.12
7 packs	$10.08
8 packs	$10.88
9 packs	$11.52
10 packs	$12

© 2021

CONDITIONAL STATEMENTS

Conditional statements test a **condition** to determine whether or not to run a block of code. They are similar to saying: "If this situation is true, perform task 1 (and optionally, if not, perform task 2)."

Some tasks are only performed if a **condition** is met. Consider a website where users can log in. If the user

- *is* logged in, a link to their profile page is shown.
- is *not* logged in, a link to the login page is shown.

Here, the condition would be: *"Is the user logged in?"* and it is used to determine which link to show.

Conditions are expressions that always result in a value of `true` or `false`. They often use comparison operators (see p54-55) to compare two values.

If a variable called `$logged_in` stores a value of `true` when a user is logged in and `false` when they are not logged in, the following will act as a condition:

`($logged_in === true)`

If the condition results in a value of:

- `true` it could then run statements that show a link to the user's profile page.
- `false` it could then run statements that show a link to the login page.

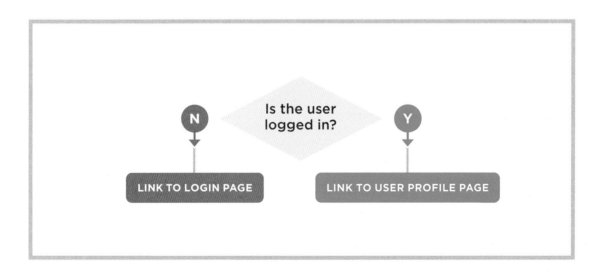

IF

p74

An if statement only runs a set of statements if a condition is met. The statements to use if the condition *is* met are surrounded by curly braces. If the condition is not met, the statements in the curly braces are skipped, and the PHP interpreter moves to the next line of code after it.

```
if ($logged_in === true) {
    // Statements to run if condition met
}
```

IF... ELSE

p75-77

An if... else statement checks a condition. If it returns true, the first set of statements is run. Otherwise, the second set of statements is run. You will also meet the ternary operator which provides a shorthand for an if... else statement.

```
if ($logged_in === true) {
    // Statements to run if condition is met
} else {
    // Statements to run if condition not met
}
```

IF... ELSEIF...

p78

In an if... elseif statement, if the first condition is not met, you can add a second condition. The statements that follow the second condition only run if the second condition is met.

You can provide a default set of statements to run if neither condition is met using the else option.

```
if ($logged_in === true) {
    // Statements to run if condition 1 met
} elseif ($time > 12) {
    // Statements to run if condition 2 met
} else {
    // Statements to run otherwise
}
```

SWITCH

p79

A switch statement doesn't rely on a condition; you specify a variable and then provide options that could match the value in the variable.

If none of the options match, a default set of statements can be run instead.

If there is no default *and* no match, the PHP interpreter goes to the next line after the switch statement.

```
switch ($option) {
    case 'option_1':
        // Statements to run go here
        break;
    case 'option_2':
        // Statements to run go here
        break;
    default:
        // Statements to run go here
}
```

MATCH

p80

PHP 8 added the match expression (a variation on the switch statement). If an exact match for a variable is found (it is the same value *and* data type as the variable) then an expression is run and the value that expression creates is returned. You can specify multiple options on one line, as well as provide a default in case no values match. However, if there is no match *and* no default, it will cause an error.

```
$result = match($option) {
    'option_1'              => // Expression,
    'option_2', 'option_3' => // Expression,
    'default'               => // Expression,
};
```

CURLY BRACES
FORM CODE BLOCKS

PHP uses curly braces to surround a related set of statements.
The braces and the statements inside them form a **code block**.

START CODE BLOCK

```
{

    // Curly braces indicate
    // the start and end of
    // a code block.

}
```

END CODE BLOCK

Curly braces let the PHP interpreter know where a
code block starts and ends:

- A left curly brace signals the start of a code block.
- A right curly brace signals the end of a code block.

There is no limit to how many statements can appear
inside the curly braces of a code block.

Code blocks allow the PHP interpreter to run, skip, or
repeat the statements that they contain.

There should not be a semi-colon after the closing
curly brace } at the end of a code block because
code blocks just indicate where a set of related
statements start and finish; the code block itself is
not an instruction that the PHP interpreter runs.

STRUCTURE OF CONDITIONAL STATEMENTS

A **condition** always results in, or **evaluates into**, a boolean value of either **true** or **false**. The result determines which code block is run.

The condition below checks if the value in the `$logged_in` variable is **true**:

- If it is, the condition results in a value of **true**.
- If it is not, the condition results in a value of **false**.

CONDITION TO TEST

```php
if ($logged_in === true) {
    $link = '<a href="member.php">My Profile</a>';
```
CODE TO EXECUTE IF VALUE IS TRUE
```php
} else {
    $link = '<a href="login.php">Login</a>';
```
CODE TO EXECUTE IF VALUE IS FALSE
```php
}
```

When the result of the condition is **true**, the first code block is run. The PHP interpreter then ignores the **else** keyword and skips the second code block. Next, it moves to the first line of code after the conditional statement.

When the result of the condition is **false**, the PHP interpreter skips the first code block and moves to the **else** keyword. It then runs the statements in the code block that follow it. Next, it moves to the first line of code after the conditional statement.

USING IF... STATEMENTS

This example displays a custom greeting if a visitor is logged in. It starts by creating two variables and storing values in them:

1. $name holds the visitor's name.

2. The $greeting variable is **initialized**; which means it is given an initial value that will be used if it is not updated in Steps 3 and 4. The greeting says Hello.

3. An if statement uses a condition to check if the $name variable is *not* an empty string.

If the variable is *not* empty then the subsequent code block is run.

4. The value in the $greeting variable is updated to say Welcome back, followed by the visitor's name.

5. The value stored in $greeting is written out to the page.

TRY: In Step 1, change the value of the $name greeting to store an empty string. Refresh the page, and the greeting will say Hello.

NOTE: A condition can just contain a variable name, e.g.:
```
if ($name) {
  $greeting = 'Hi, ' + $name;
}
```

section_a/c02/if-statement.php   `PHP`

```php
<?php
$name     = 'Ivy';
$greeting = 'Hello';

if ($name !== '') {
    $greeting = 'Welcome back, ' . $name;
}
?>
<!DOCTYPE html>
<html>
  <head> ... </head>
    <body>
      <h1>The Candy Store</h1>
      <h2><?= $greeting ?></h2>
    </body>
</html>
```

`RESULT`

The Candy Store

WELCOME BACK, IVY

This condition would check if the value stored in the $name variable would be treated as true after type juggling has occurred.

As you saw on p60-61, a string that holds any text, or a number other than 0, would be treated as a value of true.

USING IF... ELSE STATEMENTS

PHP   section_a/c02/if-else-statement.php

```php
<?php
$stock = 5;

if ($stock > 0) {
    $message = 'In stock';
} else {
    $message = 'Sold out';
}
?>
<!DOCTYPE html>
<html>
  <head> ... </head>
  <body>
    <h1>The Candy Store</h1>
    <h2>Chocolate</h2>
    <p><?= $message ?></p>
  </body>
</html>
```

① `$stock = 5;`
② `if ($stock > 0) {`
③ `    $message = 'In stock';`
④ `} else {`
⑤ `    $message = 'Sold out';`
⑥ `    <p><?= $message ?></p>`

RESULT

This example checks the stock level of an item and displays the corresponding message.

1. A variable called $stock holds the number of items in stock.

2. An if statement uses a condition to check if the quantity held in $stock is greater than 0.

3. If the condition results in true, a variable called $message is given a value of In stock. The PHP interpreter then skips the else keyword and the subsequent code block.

4. If the condition in Step 2 returns false, the else keyword tells the PHP interpreter to run the code block that follows it.

5. A variable called $message is given a value of Sold out.

6. The value stored in the $message variable is written out to the page.

TRY: In Step 1, change the value stored in $stock to 0.

In Step 5, change the message to More stock coming soon.

TERNARY OPERATORS

Ternary operators check a condition, then provide one value to use if the condition results in `true` and another value to use if it results in `false`. They are often used as a shorthand version of an `if... else` statement.

On the right, the condition of the `if... else` statement checks if a user's age is less than 16. If the condition results in:

- `true` then `$child` is assigned a value of `true`.
- `false` then `$child` is assigned a value of `false`.

Below, you can see how a ternary operator does this in just one line of code.

```
if ($age < 16) {
    $child = true;
} else {
    $child = false;
}
```

QUESTION MARK
COLON
CONDITION TRUE FALSE

```
$child = $age < 16 ? true : false;
```

RESULT STORED IN VARIABLE

TERNARY OPERATOR

A question mark separates the condition that is being tested from the values that will be used.

A colon separates the value that is returned if the condition results in `true` from the value that is returned if the condition results in `false`.

Here, the result returned by the ternary operator is being stored in a variable called `$child`.

Parentheses are sometimes placed around the condition (see right-hand page) to show that it will result in a single value, however they are not required.

USING TERNARY OPERATORS

PHP

section_a/c02/ternary-operator.php

```php
<?php
$stock = 5;

$message = ($stock > 0) ? 'In stock' : 'Sold out';
?>
<!DOCTYPE html>
<html>
  <head> ... </head>
  <body>
    <h1>The Candy Store</h1>
    <h2>Chocolate</h2>
    <p><?= $message ?></p>
  </body>
</html>
```

① ② ③

RESULT

This example replicates the previous example but uses a ternary operator (instead of an if... else statement).

1. A variable called $stock holds the number of items in stock.

2. A ternary operator is used to assign a value to the variable called $message. The condition checks if the value in $stock is greater than 0. If this condition evaluates to:

- true then In stock is stored in $message.
- false then Sold out is stored in $message.

3. The value stored in the $message variable is written into the page.

TRY: In Step 1, change the value stored in $stock to 0.

In Step 2, change the message to More stock coming soon.

USING IF... ELSEIF... STATEMENTS

This example builds on the previous examples.

1. A variable called $ordered indicates the number of items that the shop has ordered to replenish their stock.

2. An if statement uses a condition to check if the value in $stock is greater than 0. If it is, then a variable called $message will hold In stock, and the PHP interpreter moves to the end of the if... elseif statement.

3. If the first condition is not met, an elseif... statement uses a second condition to check if the value in $ordered is greater than 0. If it is, the variable called $message will hold Coming soon, and the PHP interpreter moves to the end of the if... elseif statement.

4. If neither condition resulted in a value of true, the PHP interpreter runs the else clause and the block of code that follows it, which stores the message Sold out in the $message variable.

5. The value stored in $message is written into the page.

section_a/c02/if-else-if-statement.php   `PHP`

```php
<?php
$stock   = 5;
$ordered = 3;

if ($stock > 0) {
    $message = 'In stock';
} elseif ($ordered > 0) {
    $message = 'Coming soon';
} else {
    $message = 'Sold out';
}
?>
<!DOCTYPE html>
<html>
  <head> ... </head>
  <body>
    <h1>The Candy Store</h1>
    <h2>Chocolate</h2>
    <p><?= $message ?></p>
  </body>
</html>
```

`RESULT`

TRY: In Step 1, change the value in the $stock variable to 0.

When you refresh the page, the message should say Coming soon.

USING SWITCH STATEMENTS

section_a/c02/switch-statement.php

```php
<?php
$day = 'Monday';

switch ($day) {
    case 'Monday':
        $offer = '20% off chocolates';
        break;
    case 'Tuesday':
        $offer = '20% off mints';
        break;
    default:
        $offer = 'Buy three packs, get one free';
}
?>
<!DOCTYPE html>
<html>
  <head> ... </head>
  <body>
    <h1>The Candy Store</h1>
    <h2>Offers on <?= $day; ?></h2>
    <p><?= $offer ?></p>
  </body>
</html>
```

RESULT

The Candy Store

OFFERS ON MONDAY

20% off chocolates

1. A variable called $day is set to hold a day of the week.

2. The switch statement starts with the command switch and a variable name in parentheses. The variable holds what is known as the **switch value**.

This is followed by a pair of curly braces containing options that may match the switch value.

3. There are two options. Both:
- Start with the word case
- Followed by a value
- Then a colon

4. If the switch value matches an option, the statements that follow it are run. (They set values for a variable called $offer.)

5. break tells the PHP interpreter to go to the end of the switch statement.

6. The last option is default. It is followed by the statements to run if none of the previous options match. (There is no break after the default option.)

7. The value in $offer is shown.

TRY: In Step 1, change the value to Wednesday. After Step 5, add an option to the switch statement for Wednesday.

USING MATCH EXPRESSIONS

NOTE: This example only works with PHP 8+.

1. A variable called $day is set to hold a day of the week.

2. A match expression is used to assign a value to the $offer variable. It starts with the word match, followed by parentheses that contain the name of a variable, then an opening curly brace.

3. The curly braces contain arms which start with values that are checked to see if they match the value stored in the $day variable.

If a match is found, the expression on the right of the double arrow operator runs.

Each arm can only run one expression and ends with a comma. Also, note that the match expression uses a strict type comparison; it will not perform type juggling.

4. The last arm uses the value default, followed by an expression to run if there is no match. (If there is no match *and* no default arm, an error is raised.)

5. The value in $offer is shown.

```
section_a/c02/match.php                                  PHP

    <?php
①  $day = 'Monday';

②  $offer = match($day) {
③      'Monday'              => '20% off chocolates',
        'Saturday', 'Sunday' => '20% off mints',
④      default              => '10% off your entire order',
    }
    ?>
    <!DOCTYPE html>
    <html>
      <head> ... </head>
      <body>
        <h1>The Candy Store</h1>
        <h2>Offers on <?= $day ?></h2>
⑤      <p><?= $offer ?></p>
      </body>
    </html>
```

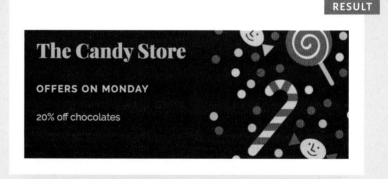

RESULT

The Candy Store

OFFERS ON MONDAY

20% off chocolates

TRY: In Step 1, change the value to Tuesday. In Step 3, add an offer to the match expression for Tuesday.

TRY: In Step 1, change the value to Wednesday. Then remove the default option. You should see an error.

LOOPS

Loops allow you to write a set of instructions once and then repeat them either a fixed number of times or until a condition has been met.

If you want a person to do the same task ten times, rather than writing the same instructions ten times, you can write the instructions once and tell them to repeat the task ten times. In PHP, loops allow you to:

- Write the statements to perform a task once in a pair of curly braces that create a code block.
- Use a condition to determine whether or not to run those statements (like the if statement on p74). If the condition returns true, the code block runs; if the condition returns false, it does not.
- Once the statements have run, the condition is tested again. If it returns true, the statements are repeated, and then the condition is tested again.

When the condition returns false, the interpreter moves to the line of code *after* the loop.

To perform a task ten times, you could use a variable to act as a counter, give it a value of 1, then:

1. Check if the value in the counter is less than 10.
2. If it is, the statements in the code block are run.
3. The value stored in the counter is increased by 1.
4. The PHP interpreter goes back to Step 1.

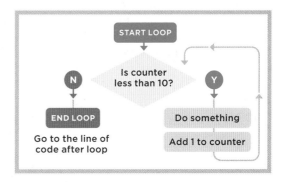

WHILE   p82-83
A while loop repeats the statements in the loop for as long as a condition results in a value of true.

DO WHILE LOOPS   p84-85
A do... while loop is like a while loop, except the condition is checked *after* the statement group has run, which means that the statements will run at least once, even if the condition evaluates to false.

FOR LOOPS   p86-89
A for loop lets you repeat the code block a specified number of times. The condition is followed by instructions that create the counter, and update the counter each time the loop is processed.

FOREACH LOOPS   p90-93
A foreach loop goes through each of the elements in an array and repeats the same series of statements for each of them. (It can also work with properties of objects, which you meet in Chapter 4.)

WHILE LOOPS

A `while` loop checks a condition; if it returns `true`, a code block runs. The condition is then checked again; if it returns `true`, the code block runs again. The loop repeats until the condition returns `false`.

TYPE OF LOOP
All loops start with a keyword which tells the PHP interpreter what kind of loop you are using. A **while loop** starts with the keyword `while`.

CONDITION
The condition checks values in the code. (The one below checks if the value in the `$counter` variable is less than 10.) If the condition evaluates to `true`, the statements in curly braces run.

STATEMENTS TO RUN
The statements that perform the task that is to be repeated are placed inside the curly braces. Loops repeat the code in these curly braces until the condition returns `false`.

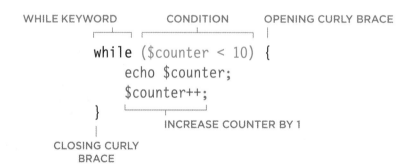

The example above says: While the value in the `$counter` variable is less than 10, repeat the instructions in the curly braces.

The code in the curly braces:
1. Writes out the value stored in the `$counter` variable
2. Adds 1 to the value in `$counter` using the ++ operator.

If `$counter` held the value 1 when this code started, it would display 123456789 (as it writes the content of the `$counter` until it reaches 10).

USING WHILE LOOPS

section_a/c02/while-loop.php

```php
<?php
$counter = 1;
$packs   = 5;
$price   = 1.99;
?>
...
<h2>Prices for Multiple Packs</h2>
<p>
  <?php
  while ($counter <= $packs) {
      echo $counter;
      echo ' packs cost $';
      echo $price * $counter;
      echo '<br>';
      $counter++;
  }
  ?>
</p>
```

RESULT

This example shows how much multiple packs of candy cost.

1. A variable called $counter is set to hold the value 1.

2. $packs holds the number of packs to show the prices for.

3. $price is the cost per pack.

4. The while loop starts with a condition. It checks if the value of $counter is less than or equal to the value stored in $packs. If it is, the statements in the curly braces are run.

5. The number in the counter is written out.

6. The text packs cost $ is shown (p100 shows how to use the singular pack for 1 pack).

7. The value in $price is multiplied by the value in $counter and is written out.

8. A line break is added.

9. The number in $counter is increased by 1 using the increment operator (see p50).

After Step 9, the PHP interpreter checks the condition in Step 4 again. It repeats the process until this condition returns false.

TRY: In Step 2, increase the number of packs to 10.

TRY: In Step 4, change the operator to < rather than <=.

DO WHILE LOOPS

A do `while` loop runs a set of statements in curly braces *before* it checks the condition, so the code block always gets executed at least once.

TYPE OF LOOP

A **do while loop** starts with the keyword do. The keyword `while` appears after the closing curly brace that holds the statements to run.

STATEMENTS TO RUN

The statements that need to be repeated are placed in the curly braces. These are run at least once because the condition comes after the curly braces.

CONDITION

The condition checks the current values in the code. If it evaluates to `true`, the PHP interpreter goes back to the start of the loop and repeats the statements.

```
DO KEYWORD   OPENING CURLY BRACE
      |     |
    do {
        echo $counter;
        $counter++;
    } while ($counter < 10);
    |   |         |
CLOSING  WHILE      CONDITION
CURLY BRACE  KEYWORD
```

The statements in this loop write out the value in the $counter variable and then add 1 to that number using the ++ operator.

The statements run before the condition, so it will always write out the value in $counter and add 1 to it at least once.

If $counter held a value of 3, then this code would write 3456789. If $counter held a value of 1, it would write 123456789.

USING DO WHILE LOOPS

section_a/c02/do-while-loop.php

```php
<?php
$packs = 5;
$price = 1.99;
?>
...
<h2>Prices for Multiple Packs</h2>
<p>
  <?php
  do {
      echo $packs;
      echo ' packs cost $';
      echo $price * $packs;
      echo '<br>';
      $packs--;
  } while ($packs > 0);
  ?>
</p>
```

1
2
3
4
5
6

RESULT

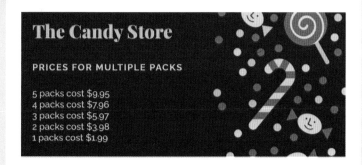

The Candy Store

PRICES FOR MULTIPLE PACKS

5 packs cost $9.95
4 packs cost $7.96
3 packs cost $5.97
2 packs cost $3.98
1 packs cost $1.99

TRY: In Step 1, change the value in $packs to 10 and change the value stored in $price to 2.99.

NOTE: There is no semicolon after the closing curly brace (before the while keyword) but there is one after the condition.

In this example, the code in the curly braces is run before the condition is checked, so the code block runs once even if the condition returns false.

1. Two variables are set up. The number of packs of candy is stored in $packs. The price per pack is stored in $price.

2. The do while loop starts with the keyword do and an opening curly brace. The code block comes before the condition, so it runs once whether or not the condition is met.

3. The number of packs (stored in $packs) is written out, followed by the words packs cost $. (p100 shows how to use the singular pack for 1 pack.)

4. The cost is written out by multiplying $packs by $price. This is followed by a line break.

5. The number stored in $packs is reduced by one using the -- decrement operator.

6. The code block ends with a closing curly brace. This is followed by the while keyword, then the condition. The condition checks if the number stored in $packs is greater than 0.

FOR LOOPS

A for loop repeats a set of statements a specified number of times.
To do this, it creates a counter and updates it each time the loop runs.

TYPE OF LOOP
A **for loop** begins with the keyword for.

CONDITION
In a for loop, the condition sits alongside the code to create and update the counter. This is shown in detail on the right-hand page.

STATEMENTS TO RUN
The statements that perform the task that must be repeated are placed inside the curly braces. They run a fixed number of times.

```
                    CONDITION & EXPRESSIONS
          FOR           (right-hand page shows
          KEYWORD          how these work)              OPENING CURLY BRACE

          for ($i = 0; $i < 10; $i++) {
                echo $i;
          }           CODE TO EXECUTE DURING LOOP

          CLOSING
          CURLY BRACE
```

The variable name $i or $index is often used for a counter.

The statement in the curly braces writes out the value stored in $i.

In this case, it would write out:
0123456789

FOR LOOPS USE THREE EXPRESSIONS

The for loop needs two extra expressions in addition to the condition.
One creates a counter and the other updates it.

EXPRESSION 1:
INITIALIZATION
This expression only runs once; the first time the loop is run. It creates the variable for the counter and sets its value to 0.

EXPRESSION 2:
CONDITION
The second expression is the condition. The statements in the for loop will repeat until the condition returns false.

EXPRESSION 3:
UPDATE
Once the statements in the curly braces have run, the third expression adds 1 to the number stored in the counter.

INITIALIZATION   CONDITION   UPDATE

$$(\$i = 0; \quad \$i < 10; \quad \$i++)$$

In the example above, the variable called $i is used as a counter. It is assigned an initial value of 0.

The condition checks if the value held in $i is less than 10. As long as it is, the statements in the code block are run.

Instead of using the number 10, this could be a variable that holds a value, e.g., $i < $max;

Each time the loop has run, the counter is updated using the ++ increment operator to add 1 to the value stored in $i.

USING FOR LOOPS

This example uses a for loop to repeat a task ten times.

1. A variable called $price stores the cost of a single pack of candy.

2. The for keyword indicates the type of loop, followed by the three expressions in parentheses:

- Expression one: $i = 1;
  This initializes the counter with a value of 1.

- Expression two: $i <= 10;
  This is the condition. It says that the code should repeat while the value in the counter is less than or equal to 10.

- Expression three: $i++
  This increases the number in the counter by 1 each time the loop runs.

3. The curly braces hold the statements used each time the loop runs. As before, it writes out the number of packs (the value stored in the counter), and the price (the value in the counter multiplied by the value in $price).

After the statements in the curly braces have run, the third expression (in Step 2) updates the counter by increasing the number stored in $i by 1.

`section_a/c02/for-loop.php` **PHP**

```php
<?php
$price = 1.99;
?>
...
<h2>Prices for Multiple Packs</h2>
<p>
  <?php
  for ($i = 1; $i <= 10; $i++) {
      echo $i;
      echo ' packs cost $';
      echo $price * $i;
      echo '<br>';
  }
  ?>
</p>
```

RESULT

The Candy Store

PRICES FOR MULTIPLE PACKS

1 packs cost $1.99
2 packs cost $3.98
3 packs cost $5.97
4 packs cost $7.96
5 packs cost $9.95
6 packs cost $11.94
7 packs cost $13.93
8 packs cost $15.92
9 packs cost $17.91
10 packs cost $19.9

TRY: In Step 1, increase the price from 1.99 to 2.99.

TRY: In Step 2, make the loop repeat 20 times.

section_a/c02/for-loop-higher-counter.php

```php
<?php
$price = 1.99;
?>

...

<h2>Prices for Large Orders</h2>
<p>
    <?php
    for ($i = 10; $i <= 100; $i = $i + 10) {
        echo $i;
        echo ' packs cost $';
        echo $price * $i;
        echo '<br>';
    }
    ?>
</p>
```

① ② ③

RESULT

The Candy Store

PRICES FOR LARGE ORDERS

10 packs cost $19.9
20 packs cost $39.8
30 packs cost $59.7
40 packs cost $79.6
50 packs cost $99.5
60 packs cost $119.4
70 packs cost $139.3
80 packs cost $159.2
90 packs cost $179.1
100 packs cost $199

On p216, you can learn how to format numbers so that they show two decimal places, to reflect how prices are commonly written.

This example shows discounts for buying multiple packs of candy.

1. A variable stores the price of a single pack of candy.

2. The for keyword indicates the type of loop, followed by the three expressions in parentheses:

- Expression one: $i = 10;
  This initializes the counter with a value of 10.

- Expression two: $i <= 100;
  This is the condition. It indicates that the code should repeat while the value in the counter is less than or equal to 100.

Expression three: $i = $i + 10
This increases the value in the counter by 10 each time the loop is run.

3. The curly braces hold the statements that are executed each time the loop runs. These are the same as the ones in the previous example.

TRY: In Step 2, update the condition to show prices for up to 200 packs of candy.

FOREACH LOOPS

A `foreach` loop is designed to work with compound data types like arrays. It works through each element in the array, one by one, and runs the same code block for each element.

Compound data types, like arrays, hold a series of related elements. Each element is made up of a key/value pair. In an associative array, the key is a string. In an indexed array, the key is an index number.

A `foreach` loop works through each element in an array, one by one. It runs the statements in the code block, then moves onto the next element.

Each time the code block runs, you can access the key and value of the current element in the array and use it inside the code block. To do this, in the parentheses after the `foreach` keyword, you specify:

- The name of the variable holding the array
- A variable name to represent the current key
- A variable name to represent the current value

TYPE OF LOOP
A **foreach loop** starts with the keyword `foreach`.

VARIABLE NAMES
The parentheses contain three variable names (shown in detail on the right-hand page).

STATEMENTS TO RUN
The statements that perform the task that is to be repeated are inside the curly braces.

NAME OF VARIABLE HOLDING ARRAY   VARIABLE NAME FOR KEY

KEYWORD   VARIABLE NAME FOR VALUE

```php
foreach ($array as $key => $value) {
    echo $key;
    echo ' - $';
    echo $value;
}
```

There are three statements inside the curly braces. They write out:
- The key
- A dash and a dollar symbol
- The value of the element

If you only want to use the values of the array, you can omit the key:
```php
foreach ($array as $value) {
    // Statements go here
}
```

Once the same statements have been repeated for each element in the array, the PHP interpreter moves on to the next line of code after the loop.

Below, $products stores an array of product names and prices.

A foreach loop is able to show a name and price for each item.

The loop works no matter how many items the array holds.

```
$products = ['toffee' => 2.99, 'mints' => 1.99, 'fudge' => 3.40,];
```

VARIABLE   KEY   VALUE   KEY   VALUE   KEY   VALUE

In the example below, the loop starts with the foreach keyword.

Then, in the parentheses:

- $products is the name of the variable holding the array.
- It is followed by the keyword as.

- $item is the variable name that will hold the **key** of the current element in the array.
- It is followed by a double arrow operator.
- $price is the variable name that will hold the **value** of the current element in the array.

In the code block, the variable names $item and $price will be used to represent the key and value of the current element in the array. First, the product name (stored in $item) is written out, followed by a dollar and a dash, then the price (stored in $price).

AS KEYWORD   DOUBLE ARROW OPERATOR

VARIABLE HOLDING ARRAY | VARIABLE NAME FOR KEY | VARIABLE NAME FOR VALUE

```
foreach ($products as $item => $price) {
    echo $item;
    echo ' - $';
    echo $price;
}
```

Loops are often used in the part of the page that generates HTML (see next page).

When they are, the first and last line of the loop above can be placed in their own code blocks.

The data in the keys and values of the array can then be written out using the shorthand for echo.

```
<?php foreach ($products as $item => $price) { ?>
  <li>
    <b><?= $item ?></b> - $<?= $price ?>
  </li>
<?php } ?>
```

LOOPING THROUGH KEYS AND VALUES

This example displays a table that shows the names and prices of products stored in an array.

1. A variable called $products stores an associative array that holds a list of products, along with their prices.

2. In the HTML part of the page, a heading and the start of the HTML table are written out.

3. A foreach loop is created. In the parentheses that follow the foreach keyword, you see:

- $products - the name of the variable holding the array
- The keyword as
- $item - a variable name used to represent the key of the current element in the array
- The double arrow operator
- $price - a variable name used to represent the value of the current element in the array

This is followed by an opening curly brace to start a code block.

4. A table row is written out for each element in the array showing its name and price.

5. The code block is closed.

TRY: In Step 1, add two more items to the array.

`section_a/c02/foreach-loop.php`   `PHP`

```php
<?php
$products = [
    'Toffee' => 2.99,
    'Mints'  => 1.99,
    'Fudge'  => 3.49,
];
?>
...
<h2>Price List</h2>
<table>
  <tr>
    <th>Item</th>
    <th>Price</th>
  </tr>
  <?php foreach ($products as $item => $price) { ?>
    <tr>
      <td><?= $item ?></td>
      <td>$<?= $price ?></td>
    </tr>
  <?php } ?>
</table> ...
```

`RESULT`

section_a/c02/foreach-loop-just-accessing-values.php

```php
<?php
$best_sellers = ['Toffee', 'Mints', 'Fudge',];
?>
...
<h2>Best Sellers</h2>
<?php foreach ($best_sellers as $product) { ?>
    <p><?= $product ?></p>
<?php } ?>
```

RESULT

In an indexed array, the index numbers often represent the order of items in the array. A foreach loop can be used to write out the values in that order.

1. The $best_sellers variable holds an indexed array representing the best selling products.

2. A foreach loop is used to display the best sellers. After the foreach keyword, in the parentheses, you see:

- $best_sellers – the name of the variable holding the array
- The keyword as
- $product – a variable name that will be used to represent the value of the current element in the array
- There is no variable for the key name (the index number)

This is followed by an opening curly brace to start a code block.

3. The value of the current element is shown in <p> tags.

4. The code block is closed.

TRY: In Step 1, add two more items to the array. Then, in Steps 2 and 3, change the variable name from $product to $candy.

USING INCLUDE FILES TO REPEAT CODE

Most websites need to repeat identical code on multiple pages.
For example, the header and footer are often the same on every page.
Include files save you repeating the same lines of code in multiple files.

Rather than duplicate the code for the header of a site in every page, you can:

- Put the code for the header in a separate PHP file which is known as an include file.
- Use PHP's `include` statement to add that code to every page that uses the header.

When the PHP interpreter comes across an `include` statement, it gets the contents of the include file and runs that code as if it were placed where the `include` statement is used.

Below-left, a file called `candy.php` includes two files:

- `header.php` contains the header for the site.
- `footer.php` contains the footer for the site.

Between the two `include` statements is the main content of the page. Using include files:

- Saves duplicating or repeating the same code.
- Makes the code easier to maintain because, when an include file is changed, it updates every page that uses it.

candy.php

```php
<?php include 'includes/header.php'; ?>

<h1>The Candy Store</h1>
<h2>Welcome</h2>
<p>A wide selection of delicious candy
   handmade in our kitchen...</p>

<?php include 'includes/footer.php'; ?>
```

includes/header.php

```php
<h1>The Candy Store</h1>
<nav>
  <a href="index.php">Home</a> |
  <a href="candy.php">Candy</a> |
  <a href="about.php">About</a> |
  <a href="contact.php">Contact</a>
</nav>
```

includes/footer.php

```php
<footer>
  &copy; <?php echo date('Y')?>
</footer>
```

INCLUDING AND REQUIRING FILES

Four keywords can be used to include code from an include file.
Each one behaves slightly differently, but uses the same syntax.

The `include` keyword tells the PHP interpreter to get another file from the server and treat it as if the contents of that file had been written where the `include` statement is written.

It is followed by the path to the file written in quotes. (You sometimes see the filename and quotes in parentheses, but they are not needed.) The include file should use the `.php` file extension.

INCLUDE STATEMENT

```
<?php include 'includes/filename.php'; ?>
```

RELATIVE PATH TO FILE

include / require

The `include` and `require` keywords both add the code from the file whose path follows the keyword.

The difference between them is how the PHP interpreter behaves if the included file cannot be found or read:

- `include`: the interpreter generates an error, but keeps trying to process the rest of the page.

- `require`: the interpreter generates an error, then stops trying to process the rest of the page.

include_once / require_once

The `include_once` and `require_once` keywords perform exactly the same job as `include` and `require`, but they ensure that the PHP interpreter only includes the code once in any given page.

Once a file has been included in the page using the `include_once` and `require_once` keywords, if the page then uses the same keywords to include the same file, it will not be included a second time.

The PHP interpreter uses extra resources to check if the file has already been included, so these options should only be used when there is a risk of duplication.

CREATING INCLUDE FILES

This page shows two include files:

- `header.php` contains the opening HTML markup, the name of the site, and the navigation that appears at the top of every page of the site.

- `footer.php` contains a copyright notice with the current year and the closing HTML for each page.

Both files use the `.php` file extension. This ensures that the PHP code is run through the PHP interpreter.

Include files are often stored in a folder called `includes` (as shown with these two files).

As this example shows, if you had to update the navigation, you would only need to update `header.php`, and it would automatically update every page that included this file.

NOTE: The links in `header.php` are used to demonstrate how to create a navigation bar; the code download does not have corresponding pages for each link.

```
section_a/c02/includes/header.php                            PHP

<!DOCTYPE html>
<html>
  <head>
    <title>The Candy Store</title>
    <link rel="stylesheet" href="css/styles.css" />
  </head>
  <body>
    <h1>The Candy Store</h1>
    <nav>
      <a href="index.php">Home</a> |
      <a href="candy.php">Candy</a> |
      <a href="about.php">About</a> |
      <a href="contact.php">Contact</a>
    </nav>
```

```
section_a/c02/includes/footer.php                            PHP

    <footer>&copy; <?php echo date('Y')?></footer>
  </body>
</html>
```

If the last line of an include file is a PHP statement, it often misses the closing ?> PHP tag because spaces after a closing tag can result in unwanted whitespace in the browser. It can also cause HTTP headers (see p180-82) to be sent to the browser too early.

You may also see a blank line at the end of the include file. This is sometimes added to help tools that are used to analyze changes between different versions of a file (which are often used by development teams and in code repositories such as GitHub).

USING INCLUDE FILES

section_a/c02/include-and-require-files.php

```php
<?php
$stock = 25;

if ($stock >= 10) {
    $message = 'Good availability';
}
if ($stock > 0 && $stock < 10) {
    $message = 'Low stock';
}
if ($stock == 0) {
    $message = 'Out of stock';
}
?>

<?php require_once 'includes/header.php'; ?>

<h2>Chocolate</h2>
<p><?= $message ?></p>

<?php include 'includes/footer.php'; ?>
```

(1) (2) (3) (4)

RESULT

This page uses the include files from the left-hand page.

1. The page starts by creating a message about stock levels and storing it in a variable called $message. If the stock level is:

- Greater than or equal to 10, the message is Good availability.
- Between 1 and 9, the message is Low stock.
- 0, it says Out of stock.

2. The HTML part of the page starts by including the header file (which contains the code that is used at the top of every page).

The require_once statement indicates that the file should only be included once. It is placed where the header should be displayed, and the PHP interpreter treats it as if this code were copied and pasted there.

3. This is followed by the content of the page, which shows the stock level message.

4. The include statement tells the PHP interpreter to add the code from the footer.php file.

TRY: Add a new link to the navigation in header.php.

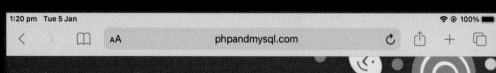

The Candy Store

HOME | CANDY | ABOUT | CONTACT

Welcome back, Ivy

LOLLIPOP DISCOUNTS

PACKS	PRICE
1 pack	$1.92
2 packs	$3.68
3 packs	$5.28
4 packs	$6.72
5 packs	$8
6 packs	$9.12
7 packs	$10.08
8 packs	$10.88
9 packs	$11.52
10 packs	$12

© 2021

EXAMPLE

This example shows a greeting, followed by any discounts that are applicable when a customer purchases multiple packs of candy. It uses a variety of the techniques that were introduced throughout this chapter.

- A variable stores the visitor's name.

- A conditional operator creates a greeting for the visitor.

- A `for` loop is used to create an indexed array that holds discounted prices that are on offer when customers buy multiple packs of candy.

- The header and footer of the page live in include files.

- A `foreach` loop is used to display the discounted prices from the array. For one pack there is a 4% discount, for two packs the discount is 8%, for three packs the discount is 12% and so on...

- A ternary operator ensures that the page displays the word `pack` when showing the price of a single pack of candy, or the word `packs` when showing the price of multiple packs.

EXAMPLE

The file starts by creating values that will be shown in the page and storing them in variables.

1. A variable called $name holds the user's name.

2. The $greeting variable is initialized; it stores the message Hello which can be shown to anyone.

3. The condition of an if statement checks if the $name variable has a value.

4. If it does, the value in $greeting is updated to hold a personal message using the visitor's name.

5. The name of a product is stored in $product.

6. The cost for one pack of it is stored in $cost.

7. A for loop creates an array to hold the prices of multiple packs of candy. The counter represents the number of packs of candy. In the parentheses the:

- Counter is set to 1 (representing 1 pack of candy)
- Condition checks if the counter is less than or equal to 10 (representing 10 packs of candy)
- The counter increments each time the loop runs

Inside the loop:

8. The $subtotal variable holds the price of an individual pack of candy multiplied by the counter (which represents the current number of packs).

9. The $discount variable holds the discount when buying this number of packs. It is calculated by dividing the cost by 100, then multiplying that figure by the number in the counter multiplied by 4.

10. The $totals variable holds an array; the key is the current value in the counter (representing the number of packs) and the value is the price for this number of packs of candy minus the discount.

11. The for loop is closed.

In the part of the page that generates the HTML that is sent back to the browser:

12. The header for the page is included using the require keyword because it is needed in order for the rest of the page to display correctly (the header file was shown on p96).

13. The greeting is written into the page.

14. The name of the product is written into the page.

15. An HTML table is created, and column headings are added to the first row of the table.

16. A foreach loop is used to display the data that was stored in the array that was created in Steps 7-11. A new row of data is added to the table for each element in that array. In the parentheses, the:

- Array to use is stored in a variable called $totals
- Key is stored in a variable called $quantity
- Value is stored in a variable called $price

17. The key for this element of the array is written out (this is the number of packs of candy).

18. The text pack is written out. The condition of a ternary operator then checks if the value in $quantity is 1. If it is, nothing is added. If it is any value other than 1, an s is added (so it reads packs rather than the singular pack).

19. The price for this quantity of candy (with the discount) is written out.

20. The foreach loop is closed.

21. The footer for the page is included using the include keyword (the footer was shown on p96).

TRY: In Step 6, change the value in $cost to 10. In Step 7, update the loop to run 20 times, showing the prices for up to 20 packs of candy.

PHP section_a/c02/example.php

```
   <?php
①  $name = 'Ivy';                                        // Store the user's name

②  $greeting = 'Hello';                                  // Create initial value for greeting
③  if ($name) {                                          // If $name has a value
④      $greeting = 'Welcome back, ' . $name;             // Create personalized greeting
   }

⑤  $product = 'Lollipop';                                // Product name
⑥  $cost    = 2;                                        // Cost of single pack

⑦  for ($i = 1; $i <= 10; $i++) {
⑧      $subtotal   = $cost * $i;                         // Total for this quantity
⑨      $discount   = ($subtotal / 100) * ($i * 4);       // Discount for this quantity
⑩      $totals[$i] = $subtotal - $discount;              // Add discounted price to indexed array
⑪  }
   ?>

⑫  <?php require 'includes/header.php'; ?>

⑬    <p><?= $greeting ?></p>
⑭    <h2><?= $product ?> Discounts</h2>
   ┌ <table>
   │   <tr>
⑮ ┤     <th>Packs</th>
   │     <th>Price</th>
   └   </tr>
⑯      <?php foreach ($totals as $quantity => $price) { ?>
       <tr>
         <td>
⑰          <?= $quantity ?>
⑱          pack<?= ($quantity === 1) ? '' : 's'; ?>
         </td>
         <td>
⑲          $<?= $price ?>
         </td>
       </tr>
⑳      <?php } ?>
     </table>

㉑  <?php include 'includes/footer.php' ?>
```

SUMMARY
CONTROL STRUCTURES

> Curly braces can be used around a group of related statements to form a code block.

> Conditional statements use a condition to determine whether or not to run the statements in a code block.

> Conditions result in a value of `true` or `false`.

> There are five types of conditional statements: `if`, `if... else`, `if... elseif`, `switch`, and `match`.

> Loops allow you to repeat the same code block multiple times while a condition remains true.

> There are four types of loops: `while`, `do... while`, `for`, and `foreach`.

> Include files store code that will be used in multiple pages to save having to duplicate it.

3

FUNCTIONS

A single web page often performs many tasks.
Functions organize your code by grouping together
the statements required to perform an individual task.

A PHP page can contain hundreds of lines of code and perform several distinct tasks.
Therefore, it is important that the code is carefully organized so that you (and others) can
easily understand what it is doing.

In the last chapter, you saw that code blocks help organize your code by placing a set of
related statements in a pair of curly braces. Those curly braces tell the PHP interpreter where
the set of related statements start and end. This means that a code block can be skipped over
(using conditional statements) or repeated (using loops).

A function groups together all the statements required to perform an individual task inside a
code block. It also gives the code block a **function name** that describes the task it performs
(which helps you find the code that performs an individual task). The opening curly brace tells
the PHP interpreter where the statements to perform the task start, and the corresponding
closing curly brace shows it where they end.

When the PHP interpreter comes across a function, it does not run the code immediately.
It waits until another statement in the PHP page **calls** the function using its name to say that
the task needs to be performed; only then will it run the statements in the code block. You can
also tell the PHP interpreter to use the function multiple times, to save repeating the same
lines of code when you need to perform the task more than once.

The Candy Store

STOCK CONTROL

PRODUCT	STOCK	RE-ORDER	TOTAL VALUE	TAX DUE
Toffee	12	No	$36	$7.2
Mints	26	No	$52	$10.4
Fudge	8	Yes	$32	$6.4

USING FUNCTIONS

Each task that a PHP page performs may require many PHP statements. The statements required to perform an individual task can be stored inside a function, and then called upon when needed.

DEFINING AND CALLING A FUNCTION
See p108-111

A function is created by being given a name that describes the task it performs. This is followed by the statements required to perform the task in a code block. Programmers call this the **function definition**.

When the page needs to perform the task, the function's name is used to tell the PHP interpreter to run the statements in that code block. Programmers refer to this as **calling** the function.

GETTING DATA OUT OF FUNCTIONS
See p112-113

When a function has performed its task, it usually **returns** a value to indicate the result of the task it performed. For example:

- If a function is used to log a user into the site, the function could return `true` when a user successfully logs in and `false` when they do not.

- If a function is used to calculate the total cost of an order, it will return that total.

DEFINING FUNCTIONS THAT NEED DATA
See p114-116

Functions often need information in order to perform their task.

If the task is to log a user into the site, the function may need two pieces of data; the user's email address and their password.

Parameters are like variable names that represent each piece of data the function needs to perform its task. The actual values used when the function is called are known as **arguments**.

The functions you meet in this chapter perform very simple tasks in order to explain how to create a function and why they are used. In later chapters, functions are used to perform more complicated tasks.

HOW VARIABLES WORK WITH FUNCTIONS
See p118-121

The code inside a function cannot access variables that were declared outside the function; therefore any data the function needs must be passed into the function using a parameter.

Similarly, variables declared in a function cannot be accessed by the code outside of the function. This is why a function is often designed to return a value to the the code that called it (after the function has run).

SPECIFYING DATA TYPES
See p124-127

Type declarations tell the PHP interpreter the data type you expect to be:

- Passed into a function (as an argument)
- Returned from a function

Using type declarations helps ensure that the function receives data it can use to perform its task. They also help track down problems in the code when it does not work as expected.

OPTIONAL AND DEFAULT VALUES
See p130-131

When you create a function, you can specify that one or more of the parameters (pieces of information it needs to perform its task) are optional and do not need to be specified.

When you indicate that an parameter is optional, you must provide a default value for the parameter. This is a value that the script should use when the function is called without a value for that parameter.

DEFINING AND CALLING A FUNCTION

A **function definition** stores the statements that perform a task in curly braces to form a code block, and gives them a name to describe the task. The function is then **called** when the task needs to be performed.

To define (or create) a function, use:

- The `function` keyword (this indicates that you are defining a new function)
- A name that describes the task this function performs followed by a pair of parentheses
- Curly braces to hold the code to perform the task

There is no semicolon after the closing curly brace.

The function below contains two statements:

- The first stores the current year in a variable called `$year` (you see how this works in Chapter 8).
- The second writes a copyright notice to the page using the value stored in the `$year` variable.

When you define a function, the code is not run. It is just stored in the function definition for later use.

```
                      KEYWORD                    NAME

                    function write_copyright_notice()
OPENING CURLY BRACE — {
                          $year = date('Y');
                          echo '&copy; ' . $year;
CLOSING CURLY BRACE — }
```

When you need to perform a task defined in a function, specify the function name followed by parentheses. This tells the PHP interpreter that you want to run the statements in the function.

You can call the same function as many times as you want within the same PHP file. Once a function has performed its task, the PHP interpreter moves on to the line of code after the one that called the function.

```
                    NAME

          write_copyright_notice();
```

BASIC FUNCTIONS

PHP

```php
<?php
function write_logo()
{
    echo '<img src="img/logo.png" alt="Logo">';
}

function write_copyright_notice()
{
    $year = date('Y');
    echo '&copy; ' . $year;
}
?> ...
  <header>
    <h1><?php write_logo(); ?> The Candy Store</h1>
  </header>
  <article>
    <h2>Welcome to the Candy Store</h2>
  </article>
  <footer>
    <?php write_logo(); ?>
    <?php write_copyright_notice(); ?>
  </footer>
```

(1) function write_logo()
(2) echo '<img src="img/logo.png" alt="Logo">';
(3) function write_copyright_notice()
(4) $year = date('Y');
(5) echo '© ' . $year;
(6) <h1><?php write_logo(); ?> The Candy Store</h1>
(7) <?php write_logo(); ?>
(8) <?php write_copyright_notice(); ?>

RESULT

This page uses two functions. The first function displays a logo. The second function creates a copyright notice.

1. The `write_logo()` function is defined.

2. In the curly braces, a single statement displays a logo.

3. A function called `write_copyright_notice()` is defined. The curly braces hold two statements.

4. The current year is stored in a variable called `$year` (you learn how this works in Chapter 8).

5. The copyright symbol © is written to the page, followed by the year.

6. The first function is called to add a logo to the top of the page.

7. The same function is called to add a logo to the footer.

8. The second function is called to add the copyright notice in the footer for the page.

TRY: After Step 5, inside the function, write out the company name (The Candy Store) after the copyright notice.

CODE DOES NOT ALWAYS RUN IN SEQUENCE

A function definition stores the statements needed to perform a task. Those statements are only run (or executed) when the function is called. This means code is not always run in the same order in which it is written.

When people first look at PHP code, it is common to think that the statements will run in the order in which they are written. In practice, the PHP interpreter can execute the statements in a very different order.

You often see functions defined near the top of a PHP page. (If the page also declares variables at the top of the page, those variables usually come before the function definitions.)

The functions are then called later in the code where the task needs to be performed.

As you can see on these two pages, although functions may be written near the top of a page, a function definition only *stores* the statements in a code block (and gives the function a name to identify what it does). The PHP interpreter does not run (or execute) that code until the function is called. This can mean that the statements run in a very different order than they appear in the code.

```php
    <?php
①  function write_logo()
    {
②      echo '<img src="img/logo.png" alt="Logo" />';
    }

③  function write_copyright_notice()
    {
④      $year = date('Y');            // Get and store year
⑤      echo '&copy; ' . $year;   // Write copyright notice
    }
    ?>
    <!DOCTYPE html>
    <html>
      <header>
⑥      <h1><?php write_logo(); ?> The Candy Store</h1>
      </header>
      <article>
        <p>Welcome to The Candy Store</p>
      </article>
      <footer>
⑦      <?php write_logo(); ?>
⑧      <?php write_copyright_notice(); ?>
      <footer>
    </html>
```

The left-hand page shows the example on the page before it.
Below, you can see the order in which the statements are run.
The first line that the PHP interpreter actually runs is at Step 6.

STEP	WHAT THE INTERPRETER DOES
6	The first line to be executed is Step 6. It calls the `write_logo()` function.
1, 2	The PHP interpreter goes to Step 1 where the function was defined, then runs Step 2.
6	When the function has run, the interpreter returns to the line of code that called the function.
7	It now moves onto the next line of PHP code. Step 7 calls the `write_logo()` function again.
1, 2	The PHP interpreter goes to Step 1 where the function was defined, then runs Step 2.
7	When the function has run, the interpreter returns to the line of code that called the function.
8	It now moves onto the next line of PHP code. Step 8 calls the `write_copyright_notice()` function.
3, 4, 5	It moves to Step 3 where that function was declared, then runs Steps 4-5.
8	Once the function has finished it returns to the line that called it.

You may see a function being called *before* it is defined but it is better to define functions before calling them.

If several pages need to use the same functions, the function definitions can be stored in an include file.

GETTING DATA OUT OF FUNCTIONS

Functions are often used to create new values. These values can be sent back to the statement that called the function using the return keyword.

Functions rarely write data straight to the page (like the previous example does). More often, a function creates a new value and returns it to the statement that called it. To return a value, use the return keyword, followed by the value you want to return.

The function below is similar to the ones on the previous four pages, but it creates a copyright notice and stores it in a variable called $message. It then returns the value stored in the $message variable (rather than writing the HTML directly into the page).

```php
function create_copyright_notice()
{
    $year    = date('Y');
    $message = '&copy; ' . $year;
    return $message;
}
```

KEYWORD   VALUE TO RETURN

When a function returns a value, and you want to display that data in the page, use the echo command (or the shorthand for echo), then call the function.

It is considered better practice to return a value from a function and then write that into the page, rather than use an echo command inside the function.

```php
<?= create_copyright_notice() ?>
```

You can also store the value that has been returned from a function in a variable.

To do this, use a variable name, followed by the assignment operator, then call the function.

```php
$copyright_notice = create_copyright_notice();
```

FUNCTIONS THAT RETURN A VALUE

section_a/c03/functions-with-return-values.php

```php
<?php
function create_logo()
{
    return '<img src="img/logo.png" alt="Logo" />';
}

function create_copyright_notice()
{
    $year    = date('Y');
    $message = '&copy; ' . $year;
    return $message;
}
?> ...
  <header>
    <h1><?= create_logo() ?>The Candy Store</h1>
  </header>
  <article>
    <h2>Welcome to The Candy Store</h2>
  </article>
  <footer>
    <?= create_logo() ?>
    <?= create_copyright_notice() ?>
  </footer>
```

RESULT

In this example, the functions are adapted to return values.

1. `create_logo()` is defined.

2. The `return` keyword is used, followed by the HTML needed to create the image.

3. `create_copyright_notice()` is defined. In the curly braces, there are three statements that:

4. Get the current year and store it in a variable called `$year`.

5. Create a variable called `$message`, and store the copyright symbol © followed by the current year in it.

6. Return the value stored in the `$message` variable.

7. The first function is called, and the value that is returned is written into the page using the shorthand for `echo`.

8. The first function is called again to repeat the logo.

9. The second function is called, and the value that is returned is written into the page using the shorthand for `echo`.

TRY: In Step 5, add the company name to the `$message` variable.

DEFINING FUNCTIONS THAT NEED INFORMATION

Parameters are like variable names that represent values a function needs to perform its task. The values that the parameter represents can change each time the function is called.

When defining a function, if it needs data to perform its task:

- List the pieces of information it requires
- Give each one a variable name (starting with $) that describes the type of data it represents
- Put these names inside the parentheses that come after the function name
- Separate each name with a comma
- These are known as the **parameters** of the function

Parameters act like variables, but they can only be used by the statements in the curly braces of the function definition. Code outside the function definition cannot access them.

The `calculate_cost()` function below works out the total when users purchase one or more of the same item. To perform this task, it needs two parameters:

- `$price` represents the price of one item
- `$quantity` represents the quantity of that item

Inside this function, `$price` and `$quantity` act like variables. They represent the values that are passed into the function when it is called.

The code inside the function definition calculates the total cost by multiplying the price by the quantity. This value is then sent back to the code that called the function using the `return` keyword.

PARAMETERS

```
function calculate_cost($price, $quantity)
{
    return $price * $quantity;
}
```

PARAMETER NAMES ARE USED LIKE
VARIABLES WITHIN THE FUNCTION

When the PHP interpreter reaches the closing curly brace, it forgets all values stored in the function. This is important because a page can call a function several times, using different values each time.

NOTE: In PHP 8, the function definition can add a comma after the last parameter name (not just between parameters) making the code more uniform. This would cause an error in earlier versions of PHP.

CALLING FUNCTIONS THAT NEED INFORMATION

When calling a function that has parameters, the value for each parameter is specified in parentheses after the function name. The values used when calling a function are known as **arguments**.

ARGUMENTS AS VALUES

Below, when the `calculate_cost()` function is called, it is given the values that it should use. The values are supplied in the same order that the parameters were specified in the function definition.

The number 3 is used for the price of the item and the number 5 is used for the quantity purchased, so `calculate_cost()` will return the number 15 and this value is stored in a variable called `$total`.

```
$total = calculate_cost(3, 5);
```

ARGUMENTS AS VARIABLES

This time, when `calculate_cost()` is called, it uses variable names rather than values:

- `$cost` represents the price of the item
- `$units` represents the quantity purchased

If variable names are used as arguments, the variable names do not need to match the parameter names.

When the function below is called, the PHP interpreter will send the values stored in the `$cost` and `$units` variables to the function.

Inside the function, those values are represented by the parameter names `$price` and `$quantity` (the names were specified in parentheses on the first line of the function definition).

```
$cost  = 4;
$units = 6;
$total = calculate_cost($cost, $units);
```

PARAMETERS VS ARGUMENTS

People often use the terms parameter and argument interchangeably, but there is a subtle difference. On the left-hand page, when the function is defined, you can see the names `$price` and `$quantity`. Inside the curly braces of the function, those words act like variables. These names are the **parameters**.

On this page, when the function is called, the code either specifies numbers that will be used to perform the calculation or variables that hold numbers. These values that are passed into the code (the information it needs to calculate the cost of this particular type of candy) are called **arguments**.

A FUNCTION USING PARAMETERS

1. `calculate_total()` is defined at the top of the page. It works out the total when someone buys one or more of the same item, then adds a 20% sales tax. It needs two pieces of data, and therefore has two parameters:

- `$price` will represent an individual item's price
- `$quantity` represents the number of units of the item being purchased

2. In the function definition, a variable called `$cost` stores the cost of the required number of units. This is calculated by multiplying the value stored in `$price` by the value in `$quantity`.

3. Next the sales tax due for those items is stored in a variable called `$tax`. It is calculated by multiplying the value in `$cost` (created in Step 2) by 0.2.

4. To get the total, the values in `$cost` and `$tax` are added.

5. The total is returned from the function to the code that called it.

6. The function is called three times. Each time, it uses different prices and quantities, and the value returned from the function is written into the page.

`section_a/c03/function-with-parameters.php` **PHP**

```php
<?php
function calculate_total($price, $quantity)
{
    $cost  = $price * $quantity;
    $tax   = $cost * (20 / 100);
    $total = $cost + $tax;
    return $total;
}
?> ...
<h1>The Candy Store</h1>
<p>Mints:  $<?= calculate_total(2, 5) ?></p>
<p>Toffee: $<?= calculate_total(3, 5) ?></p>
<p>Fudge:  $<?= calculate_total(5, 4) ?></p>
```

RESULT

The Candy Store

Mints: $12

Toffee: $18

Fudge: $24

TRY: In Step 6, call the function again to show the price of 4 packs of bubble gum at $1.50 each.

NAMING FUNCTIONS

The name of a function should clearly describe the task it performs. It is often made up of a word to describe what the function does and the type of information it works with or returns.

Rules for function names are the same as variables. They should start with a letter, followed by any combination of letters, numbers, or underscores. You cannot have two functions with the same name in the same PHP page.

In this book, all function names are in lowercase. If the function name requires more than one word, an underscore separates them. (You will see functions use different naming rules; the important point is to use a consistent naming strategy across a project.)

To help create a name that describes the task performed by the function, you would:

- State what the function does (e.g., calculate, get, or update)

- Followed by the type of information it either returns or processes (e.g., date, total, or message)

Below are two examples of descriptive function names you have already seen in this chapter:

- `calculate_total()` *calculates* the *total* cost of items for sale

- `create_copyright_notice()` *creates* a *copyright notice*

WHAT IT DOES

`calculate_total()`

DATA IT RETURNS

WHAT IT DOES

`create_copyright_notice()`

DATA IT RETURNS

SCOPE

When a function is called, the code runs in its own **scope**; it cannot access or update values stored in variables outside of the function.

The code in a function runs independently from the rest of the page.

- Any information a function needs to do its job must be passed to it using parameters. The parameters act like variables inside the function.

- When the function is called, statements in the function can create variables and give them values.

- The function can then return a value to the code that called the function.

- When the function has run, any parameters and variables created in the function are destroyed.

Because the code in the function is run separately from the rest of the page:

- The function cannot access or update variables outside of the function (which is why the information is passed in as parameters).

- The subsequent code cannot access the variables created inside of the function because they are destroyed as soon as the function has done its job.

Programmers say that each time a function is called, the PHP interpreter runs the code for that function in **local scope**. The code outside the function in the main part of the page is in **global scope**.

Where a variable is declared, in local or global scope, determines whether or not other code can access it.

In the diagram below, there are two variables that are both called $tax; each one runs in a different scope:

A: The first variable called $tax is created in global scope. (It is outside the function.)

B: The second variable called $tax is created inside the function definition, in local scope.

```php
<?php
$tax = 20;
function calculate_total($price, $quantity)
{
    $cost  = $price * $quantity;
    $tax   = $cost  * (20 / 100);
    $total = $cost  + $tax;
    return $total;
}
?>
```

SCOPE:　●　GLOBAL　　LOCAL

Ideally, two variables would not share a name in the same script, but this shows how the variables are treated entirely independent of each other.

DEMONSTRATING SCOPE

section_a/c03/global-and-local-scope.php

```php
<?php
$tax = '20';

function calculate_total($price, $quantity)
{
    $cost  = $price * $quantity;
    $tax   = $cost  * (20 / 100);
    $total = $cost  + $tax;
    return $total;
}
?> ...
<h1>The Candy Store</h1>
<p>Mints:  $<?= calculate_total(2, 5) ?></p>
<p>Toffee: $<?= calculate_total(3, 5) ?></p>
<p>Fudge:  $<?= calculate_total(5, 4) ?></p>
<p>Prices include tax at: <?= $tax ?>%</p>
```

(1) (2) (3) (4) (5) (6) (7) (8)

RESULT

1. A variable called $tax is declared in global scope so it can be used by any of the code outside the function.

2. The `calculate_total()` function is defined. It needs the price and quantity of an item. The variables created inside this function are in local scope.

3. The cost is calculated by multiplying the item's price by the required quantity. The result is stored in the $cost variable.

4. The tax due is calculated by multiplying the $cost by the tax rate (which is 20 divided by 100). The result is stored in a variable called $tax. **Note:** This does not overwrite the value stored in the $tax variable created in Step 1.

5. To get the total, the value in $cost is added to the value that was stored in $tax in Step 4.

6. The total is returned. When the function has run, the PHP interpreter will delete all of the parameters and the variables created in the function.

7. The function is called three times with new values each time.

8. The value stored in $tax (in global scope in Step 1) is shown.

TRY: In Step 1, change the tax rate to 25. It will change the tax rate displayed at the bottom of the page, but not the totals written out in Step 7.

The totals in Step 7 remain the same because a tax rate of 20% is used in Step 4 in the function. This shows how the two variables called $tax work independently.

GLOBAL AND STATIC VARIABLES

In limited cases, the code in a function can be allowed to access or update a global variable and told to remember a value that was stored in a variable in the function after that function has finished running.

ACCESSING OR UPDATING GLOBAL VARIABLES INSIDE A FUNCTION

The code inside a function can access or update a value stored in variable that was declared in global scope if the PHP interpreter is told it may access it.

At the start of the function's code block (before the variable is used), add the `global` keyword followed by the name of the variable. This allows the code in the function to access or update its value.

It is considered best practice to pass values into a function using parameters, but the ability to do this is mentioned here because you might see code that accesses a global variable using this technique.

```
global $cost;
```
KEYWORD VARIABLE

KEEPING A VALUE IN A FUNCTION AFTER IT HAS RUN

When a function has finished running, it usually deletes any local variables that were created inside the function.

The PHP interpreter can be told remember a value stored in a variable that was created in a function if that variable is created as a **static variable**.

To create a static variable, use:

- The `static` keyword
- Followed by a variable name
- Then an initial value it should hold the first time the function is called

When the function finishes running, this variable and the value it stores will not be deleted (but they are only available to the code inside the function).

```
static $quantity = 10;
```
KEYWORD VARIABLE INITIAL VALUE

ACCESSING VARIABLES OUTSIDE A FUNCTION

section_a/c03/global-and-static-variables.php

```php
<?php
$tax_rate = 0.2;

function calculate_running_total($price, $quantity)
{
    global $tax_rate;
    static $running_total = 0;
    $total = $price * $quantity;
    $tax   = $total * $tax_rate;
    $running_total = $running_total + $total + $tax;
    return $running_total;
}
?> ...
<h1>The Candy Store</h1>
<table>
  <tr><th>Item</th><th>Price</th><th>Qty</th>
    <th>Running total</th></tr>
  <tr><td>Mints:</td><td>$2</td><td>5</td>
    <td>$<?= calculate_running_total(2, 5); ?></td></tr>
  <tr><td>Toffee:</td><td>$3</td><td>5</td>
    <td>$<?= calculate_running_total(3, 5); ?></td></tr>
  <tr><td>Fudge:</td><td>$5</td><td>4</td>
    <td>$<?= calculate_running_total(5, 4); ?></td></tr>
</table>
```

Line markers: ① $tax_rate = 0.2; ② function calculate_running_total; ③ global $tax_rate; ④ static $running_total = 0; ⑤ $total = $price * $quantity; ⑥ $tax = $total * $tax_rate; ⑦ $running_total; ⑧ return $running_total; ⑨ the three calculate_running_total calls

RESULT

1. A variable called $tax_rate is created in global scope.

2. calculate_running_total() creates a running total.

3. The global keyword lets the function access/update the value in the global $tax_rate variable.

4. The static keyword says that the $running_total variable (and its value) must not be deleted when the function has finished running. (It gets an initial value of 0 when it is created.)

5. $total holds the price of a product multiplied by the quantity the customer wants.

6. $tax holds the amount of tax due on those items using the value in the global $tax_rate variable created in Step 1.

7. $running_total holds the:

- Value in $running_total
- Plus the value in $total
- Plus the value in $tax

8. The value in $running_total is returned but it is not deleted because it is a static variable.

9. The function is called three times. Each time, the total for this item is added to the previous total.

FUNCTIONS AND COMPOUND DATA TYPES

Compound data types (like arrays) can store multiple values. Functions can accept a compound data type as an argument, and return a compound data type from the function.

USING A COMPOUND DATA TYPE AS AN ARGUMENT

When defining a function, the parameters can be written so that they can accept either a scalar or a compound data type:

- Scalar data types hold one piece of data: a string, number or boolean.

- Compound data types can hold multiple pieces of data. You met arrays in Chapter 1 and you will learn about another compound data type called objects in Chapter 4.

On the right-hand page, you can see an example where an array holding three different exchange rates is passed into the function as a single parameter.

USING A COMPOUND DATA TYPE AS A RETURN VALUE

A function should only perform a single task (not multiple tasks) but an individual task can generate more than one value that needs to be returned.

If you want to return more than one value from a function, you must create an array or an object in the function and then return it. This is because a function can only return one scalar or compound value.

As soon as the PHP interpreter has run a statement beginning with the keyword `return`, it stops running the code in the function and goes back to the line of code that called the function (even if there are more statements in the function definition that have not been run).

On the right-hand page, the `calculate_prices()` function calculates three prices for an item in three currencies and returns the prices as an array.

ACCEPT AND RETURN MULTIPLE VALUES

section_a/c03/functions-with-multiple-values.php

```php
<?php
$us_price = 4;
$rates = [
    'uk' => 0.81,
    'eu' => 0.93,
    'jp' => 113.21,
];

function calculate_prices($usd, $exchange_rates)
{
    $prices =  [
        'pound' => $usd * $exchange_rates['uk'],
        'euro'  => $usd * $exchange_rates['eu'],
        'yen'   => $usd * $exchange_rates['jp'],
    ];
    return $prices;
}
$global_prices = calculate_prices($us_price, $rates);
?> ...
<h2>Chocolates</h2>
<p>US $<?= $us_price ?></p>
<p>(UK &pound; <?= $global_prices['pound'] ?> |
    EU &euro; <?= $global_prices['euro'] ?> |
    JP &yen; <?= $global_prices['yen'] ?>)</p>
```

1. The $us_price variable holds the US dollar price of an item.

2. The $rates variable stores an associative array of three exchange rates.

3. The calculate_prices() function calculates prices of an item in three currencies, then returns those prices as an array. It has two parameters: the price in US dollars, and the array holding the exchange rates.

4. An array is created and stored in a variable called $prices. The first element holds the UK price, which is calculated by multiplying the US price by the exchange rate for the UK. Then the EU and Japanese prices are added to the array.

5. The function returns the array containing the three new prices.

6. The function is called, and the array it returns is stored in a variable called $global_prices.

7. The US price is written out using the variable from Step 1.

8. Other prices from the array created in Step 6 are displayed.

TRY: Add an exchange rate for Australian dollars at 1.32.

RESULT

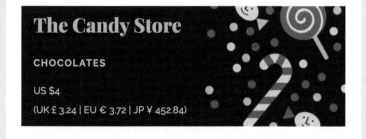

The Candy Store

CHOCOLATES

US $4

(UK £ 3.24 | EU € 3.72 | JP ¥ 452.84)

ARGUMENT AND RETURN TYPE DECLARATIONS

When defining a function, you can specify what data type each argument is supposed to be and what data type the function should return.

Some tasks require data in a specific data type. For example, functions that perform arithmetic require numbers as arguments, and functions that process text need strings.

A function definition can specify the data types that each parameter expects, and the data type that the function should return. This helps programmers because the first line of the function definition clearly shows them what data type each argument should be, and what data type the function should return.

Below, on the first line of the function definition:

- Inside the parentheses, an **argument type** is specified before each parameter name to indicate the data type the argument should use.
- After the parentheses, there is a colon followed by a **return type** to indicate the data type the function will return.

Here, both arguments should be an integer, and the value that is returned should also be an integer.

```
              ARGUMENT TYPE      ARGUMENT TYPE     RETURN TYPE

  function calculate_total(int $price, int $quantity): int
  {
      return $price * $quantity;        PARAMETERS     COLON
  }
```

The table on the right shows data types used in argument and return type declarations. PHP 8 added:

- **union types** to specify that an argument or return type can be one of a set of types. Each type is separated by a pipestem symbol |. For example, int|float indicates an integer or a float.
- **mixed** which indicates an argument or return type can be any of the data types (it is called a **pseudo-type** because variables cannot have this type).

DATA TYPE	DESCRIPTION
string	String
int	Integer (whole number)
float	Floating point number (decimal)
bool	Boolean (**true** or **false** / 0 or 1)
array	Array
className	Class of object (see Chapter 4)
mixed	A mix of the above data types (PHP8)

USING TYPE DECLARATIONS

section_a/c03/type-declarations.php

```php
<?php
$price    = 4;
$quantity = 3;

function calculate_total(int $price, int $quantity): int
{
    return $price * $quantity;
}

$total = calculate_total($price, $quantity);
?>
<h1>The Candy Store</h1>
<h2>Chocolates</h2>
<p>Total $<?= $total ?></p>
```

RESULT

The Candy Store

CHOCOLATES

Total $12

1. In this example, the first line of the function definition specifies:

- Argument type declarations for the $price and $quantity parameters, to show that their values should be integers.

- A return type declaration to show that the function should return an integer.

The type declarations do not affect the operation of this example; they only indicate what data types the arguments and return types should be. The next page shows how to enforce that these values use the correct data types.

TRY: Change the value stored in the $price variable to be a string instead of an integer, e.g.:

```php
$price = '1';
```

When you refresh the page you should see the same result because you need to turn on strict types (see next page).

NOTE: If an argument or return type can be null (rather than a value) you can use a question mark before the data type.

For example, ?int indicates the value will be an integer or null. In PHP 8, this could also use a union type int|null.

TRY: If you are running PHP 8, use union types to indicate that the values can be integers or floating point numbers.

ENABLING STRICT TYPES

When a function definition has argument and/or return type declarations, you can tell the PHP interpreter to generate an error if a function is called using the wrong data type, or if it returns the wrong data type.

When the arguments of a function are the wrong scalar data type, the PHP interpreter can try to convert them to the data type it expects to receive.

For example, to help it try to process data, the PHP interpreter can convert:

- The string '1' to the integer 1
- A boolean value of **true** into an integer of 1
- A boolean value of **false** into an integer of 0
- An integer of 1 into a boolean value of **true**
- An integer of 0 into a boolean value of **false**

These are examples of type juggling, which was introduced on p60-61.

You can tell the PHP interpreter to enable **strict types** so that it raises an error if a function:

- Is called using an argument that is the wrong data type (when an argument type declaration was used)
- Returns a value that is the wrong data type (when a return type declaration was provided)

The errors it raises can help track down the source of problems in the PHP code, but the PHP interpreter needs to be told to check the types in the page that **calls** the function using the declare construct below.

This **must** be the first statement in the page, and only turns on strict types for functions called in *that* page.

STRICT TYPES   ON

```
declare(strict_types = 1);
```

You learn about error handling and troubleshooting in Chapter 10, but you may have noticed that there are several files called .htaccess in the download code. These file control settings of the web server, such as whether or not to report errors in the HTML page that the web server sends back to the browser. If you cannot see these files, it is because operating systems treat them as hidden files (see p196).

Sometimes function definitions are placed in an include file so that they can be called by several pages of a site (as you will see in Chapter 6). Strict types do not need to be enabled in a file that just contains function definitions, but they must be enabled on pages that **call** the functions if you want the PHP interpreter to raise an error when the wrong data type is used.

USING STRICT TYPES

PHP

```php
<?php
(1) declare(strict_types = 1);

(2) $price    = 4;
    $quantity = 3;

(3) function calculate_total(int $price, int $quantity): int
    {
(4)     return $price * $quantity;
    }

(5) $total = calculate_total($price, $quantity);
?>
<h1>The Candy Store</h1>
<h2>Chocolates</h2>
(6) <p>Total $<?= $total ?></p>
```

RESULT

This example is almost the same as the one on the previous page, but strict types are enabled in the first statement to show an error if the arguments or return value are the wrong data type.

1. The `declare` construct enables strict types for the page.

2. Two variables are declared to hold a price and a quantity.

3. The `calculate_total()` function is defined. The:

- Argument type declarations indicate that both parameters expect integers.

- Return type declaration specifies that the function returns an integer.

4. The function multiplies the price by the quantity and returns this value.

5. The function is called, using the variables created in Step 2, and the result that is returned is stored in a variable called `$total`.

6. The total is written out.

TRY: In Step 2, set the value for the `$price` variable to a string: `$price = '4';`
When you refresh the page, you should see an error message.

TRY: If you are running PHP 8, in Step 2 use 4.5 for the price, and in Step 3 use union types to specify that arguments and return values can be an `int` or `float`.

MULTIPLE RETURN STATEMENTS

Functions can return different values depending on the result of a conditional statement inside the function.

A function can use conditional statements to determine what value should be returned. The function below returns different messages depending on the value passed in as an argument.

As soon as a function has processed one **return** statement, the PHP interpreter goes back to the line of code that called the function. None of the subsequent statements in that function are executed.

The function below has three **return** statements.

1. A condition checks if the value in the $stock parameter is 10 or more. If so, the first **return** statement is processed, and no subsequent statements in the function are run.

2. If the value is greater than 0 and less than 10, the second **return** statement is processed, and no subsequent code in the function is run.

3. If the function is still running, $stock must hold a value of 0 so the final **return** statement is processed.

```php
function get_stock_message($stock)
{
    if ($stock >= 10) {
        return 'Good availability';
    }
    if ($stock > 0 && $stock < 10) {
        return 'Low stock';
    }
    return 'Out of stock';
}
```

USING SEVERAL RETURNS IN A FUNCTION

PHP section_a/c03/multiple-return-statements.php

```php
<?php
$stock = 25;

function get_stock_message($stock)
{
    if ($stock >= 10) {
        return 'Good availability';
    }
    if ($stock > 0 && $stock < 10) {
        return 'Low stock';
    }
    return 'Out of stock';
}
?>
<h1>The Candy Store</h1>
<h2>Chocolates</h2>
<p><?= get_stock_message($stock) ?></p>
```

RESULT

1. The `$stock` variable holds the stock level.

2. The `get_stock_message()` function checks the stock level and returns one of three messages.

3. A conditional statement checks if the stock is greater than or equal to 10. If so, the first `return` statement is processed. It returns the message `Good availability` and no more of the code in the function is run.

4. If the stock was not 10 or more, the function would still be running and the next condition would check if the stock is greater than 0 and less than 10. If so, the second `return` statement is processed. It returns the message `Low stock`, and no more of the code in the function is run.

5. If the function is still running, there cannot be any stock, so the final `return` statement returns a message saying `Out of stock`.

6. The function is called, and the value that is returned is written out to the page.

TRY: In Step 1, change the stock level to 8. You should see the message `Low stock`.

OPTIONAL PARAMETERS AND DEFAULT VALUES

You can make a parameter of a function optional.
To do this, give it a default value to use when a value is not supplied.
Optional parameters usually appear after parameters that are required.

Some tasks can have optional information. This data is not *needed* for the function to do its job, but a value *can* be provided when the function is called.

To make a parameter optional, you give it a **default value**, which is used when the function is called without providing a value for that parameter.

The default value is provided after the parameter name in the function definition. The syntax is the same as if you were assigning a value to a variable.

The function below is called using two arguments, so the final parameter would use the default value of 0.

Optional parameters are placed *after* the required parameters because, until PHP 8, when calling a function, the arguments had to be in the order that the parameters were listed in the function definition.

You will learn about PHP 8's named parameters next, but it is likely that developers will continue to place the optional parameters after the required ones.

```
function calculate_cost($cost, $quantity, $discount = 0)
{                                          └──────┬──────┘
    $cost = $cost * $quantity;                 OPTIONAL
    return $cost - $discount;
}

$cost = calculate_cost(5, 3);
```

When documenting how a function works, any optional parameters are placed in square brackets. When calling the function, **do not** use the square brackets; they only indicate it is optional.

NOTE: The comma before optional parameters is in the square brackets because putting a comma after the last argument when calling a function caused an error up until PHP 8 (which allows trailing commas).

```
calculate_cost($cost, $quantity[, $discount])
                                └──────┬──────┘
```

OPTIONAL PARAMETER SHOWN IN SQUARE BRACKETS

USING DEFAULT VALUES FOR PARAMETERS

PHP
`section_a/c03/default-values-for-parameters.php`

```php
<?php
function calculate_cost($cost, $quantity, $discount = 0)
{
    $cost = $cost * $quantity;
    return $cost - $discount;
}
?>
<h1>The Candy Store</h1>
<h2>Chocolates</h2>
<p>Dark chocolate $<?= calculate_cost(5, 10, 5) ?></p>
<p>Milk chocolate $<?= calculate_cost(3, 4) ?></p>
<p>White chocolate $<?= calculate_cost(4, 15, 20) ?></p>
```

RESULT

The Candy Store

CHOCOLATES

Dark chocolate $45

Milk chocolate $12

White chocolate $40

1. The `calculate_cost()` function calculates the cost of one or more items based on three pieces of information, the:

- Cost
- Quantity
- Discount

When calling the function, the last argument is optional because the parameter is given a default value of 0. The function is then called three times.

2. The first time it is called, it is given a cost of 5, a quantity of 10 and a discount of 5, so the function will subtract 5 from the total of 50 and return 45.

3. The second time it is called, a cost of 3 and a quantity of 4 are given, but the discount is not supplied so the default value of 0 is applied. As a result, the function returns a cost of 12.

4. The third time it is called, it is given a cost of 4, a quantity of 15, and a discount of 20. As with Step 2, it will subtract a discount (this time, it is 20) from the cost (which is 60) to return a value of 40.

TRY: In Step 1, change the default discount to 2. In Step 2, change the discount to 7.

NAMED ARGUMENTS

When calling a function in PHP 8, you can put parameter names before the arguments. This means that arguments do not need to be given in the same order that the parameter names appear in the function definition.

Some functions have many parameters. In PHP 8, when you call a function, you can add parameter names before the arguments. These are called **named arguments** (or named parameters). They:

- Clearly indicate what each argument does
- Let you skip optional arguments without giving a default value or using empty quotes (see below)

The function definition does not change, just the way the arguments are provided when it is called. The example on the right-hand page has four parameters:

- $cost (required) is the cost of an item
- $quantity (required) is the number of that item
- $discount (optional) is the amount to discount
- $tax (optional) is the percentage of tax due

When calling a function without named arguments, the arguments *must* appear in the same order as the parameters in the function definition:

To use the default for $discount and then specify a value for $tax, you must specify the default value *or* use empty quotes as the argument because the $discount parameter comes before $tax.

```
calculate_cost(5, 10, 0, 5);   or   calculate_cost(5, 10, '', 5);
```

When using named arguments, the name is separated from the argument by a colon and the arguments can be in any order.

If an argument is supposed to use its default value (specified in the function definition) you do not need to provide a value for it or use blank quotes:

```
calculate_cost(quantity: 10, cost: 5, tax: 5);
```

Arguments without parameter names can appear before named arguments if they appear in the same order as the parameters in the function definition.

Below, the first two values will be used for cost and quantity; next the tax is provided; and note that the value for the discount is not specified.

```
calculate_cost(5, 10, tax: 5);
```

USING NAMED
ARGUMENTS

```php
<?php
function calculate_cost($cost, $quantity, $discount = 0, $tax = 20,)
{
    $cost = $cost * $quantity;
    $tax  = $cost * ($tax / 100);
    return ($cost + $tax) - $discount;
}
?>
<h1>The Candy Store</h1>
<h2>Chocolates</h2>
<p>Dark chocolate $<?= calculate_cost(quantity: 10, cost: 5, tax: 5, discount: 2); ?></p>
<p>Milk chocolate $<?= calculate_cost(quantity: 10, cost: 5, tax: 5); ?></p>
<p>White chocolate $<?= calculate_cost(5, 10, tax: 5); ?></p>
```

(1) (2) (3) (4)

1. The `calculate_cost()` function calculates the cost of one or more items based on four pieces of information; the:

- Cost (required)
- Quantity (required)
- Discount (optional – default 0)
- Tax (optional – default 20%)

Because this example uses PHP 8, a **trailing comma** can be added after the last parameter in the function definition (not just between parameters). This improves the uniformity in the code (because a comma can appear after every parameter).

After the function has been defined, it is called three times.

RESULT

The Candy Store

CHOCOLATES

Dark chocolate $50.5

Milk chocolate $52.5

White chocolate $52.5

2. The function is called with four named arguments. Because they are named, the arguments can appear in any order.

3. Named arguments are used for cost, quantity and tax. The default discount will be used.

4. The first two values do not use named arguments so they are used for the first two parameters ($cost and $quantity). No value is given for $discount so the final argument must be named in order for it to be used for the $tax parameter.

HOW TO APPROACH WRITING A FUNCTION

Following these four steps will help you write functions.

1: DESCRIBE THE TASK BRIEFLY
Use a combination of what it does (e.g. get, calculate, update, or save) followed by the type of data it works with. This will become the function name.
The function name never changes.

2: WHAT DATA IS NEEDED TO PERFORM THE TASK?
Each piece of data becomes a parameter.
The values passed to the parameter (the arguments) can change each time the function is called.

3: WHAT INSTRUCTIONS MUST IT FOLLOW TO PERFORM THE TASK?
The instructions will be represented using statements inside the curly braces.
The instructions that are followed will be the same each time the function is called.

4: WHAT IS THE RESULT YOU EXPECT?
This will be the value that is returned from the function. It is considered good practice for a function to return a value. If you are performing a task that does not calculate a new value or retrieve some information, then the function will often return true or false to indicate whether or not it has worked.
The value that is returned can change every time the function is given new values to work with.

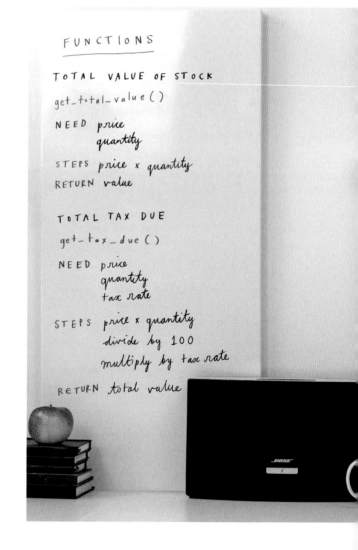

FUNCTIONS

TOTAL VALUE OF STOCK

get_total_value ( )

NEED price
        quantity

STEPS price x quantity
RETURN value

TOTAL TAX DUE

get_tax_due ( )

NEED price
        quantity
        tax rate

STEPS price x quantity
        divide by 100
        multiply by tax rate

RETURN total value

WHY USE FUNCTIONS?

There are benefits to writing the code that performs a task in a function.

REUSABILITY

As you have seen several times in this chapter, if a page needs to perform the same task multiple times (such as calculating the cost of items), then you only need to write the code to perform this task once. When the page needs to perform the task, it calls the function and gives it the values needed to do its job.

MAINTAINABILITY

If you find that the instructions needed to perform a task change, then you only need to change the code in the function definition (you do not need to make changes every time the task is performed). Once the function definition has been updated, any time that function is called, it will use the updated code.

ORGANIZATION

By placing the code that performs each task into a function, it becomes easier to find all of the statements required to perform that task.

TESTABILITY

By breaking up your code into the individual tasks it performs, you can test each individual task on its own, making it easier to isolate problems.

DOCUMENTING FUNCTIONS

Programmers often need to use functions that they did not write;
for example, when working on a large site in a team of programmers.
Documentation helps programmers learn how to use those functions.

To use a function in your PHP page, you do not need to understand *how* the statements that appear in the curly braces achieve the task, you only need to know:

- What the function is supposed to do
- The name of the function
- The parameters that it requires
- What it should return

On the right-hand page, you can see a page of the PHP.net website. It is the official home of PHP and hosts the documentation for the PHP language. It will be a very useful resource for you while you are learning the language.

The page on the right shows a function that determines how many characters are in a string. This page is a typical example of how functions are documented. You will usually see:

1. The function name and description

2. Syntax to call the function and use its parameters (argument and return types may be shown)

3. A description of its parameters

4. What value(s) the function will return

5. An example of how you might use the function

It is important to distinguish between two types of function:

- **User-defined functions** are functions that are defined in a PHP file by a programmer who is using the PHP language. (All of the functions in this chapter have been user-defined functions.)

- **Built-in functions** are defined by the people who create the PHP language, and their definitions are implemented in the PHP interpreter. This means that anyone can call those functions without including the function definition in a page.

Built-in functions perform tasks that programmers commonly need to achieve when writing PHP code. Therefore, they save developers from having to write their own code to perform these tasks, reinventing the wheel every time. You will learn more about the built-in functions in Chapter 5.

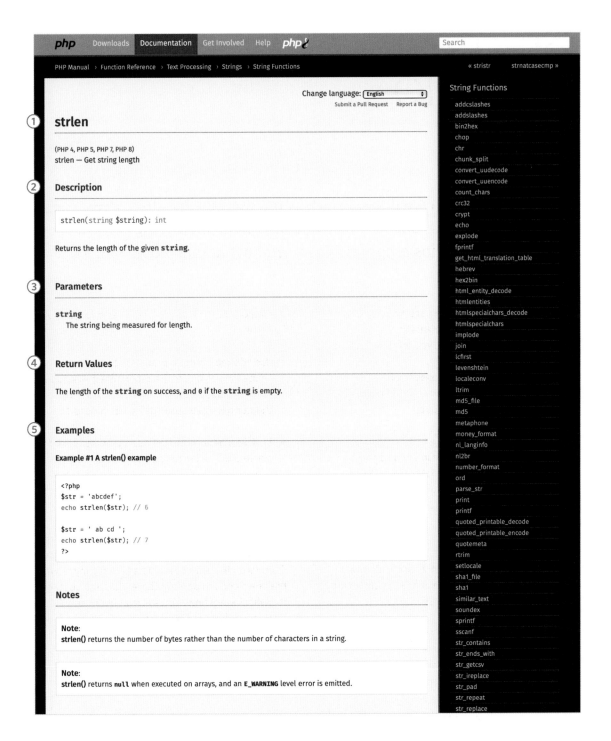

« stristr   strnatcasecmp »

Change language: [English ▼]

Submit a Pull Request   Report a Bug

① strlen

(PHP 4, PHP 5, PHP 7, PHP 8)
strlen — Get string length

② Description

```
strlen(string $string): int
```

Returns the length of the given **string**.

③ Parameters

string
   The string being measured for length.

④ Return Values

The length of the **string** on success, and 0 if the **string** is empty.

⑤ Examples

Example #1 A strlen() example

```php
<?php
$str = 'abcdef';
echo strlen($str); // 6

$str = ' ab cd ';
echo strlen($str); // 7
?>
```

Notes

> **Note:**
> strlen() returns the number of bytes rather than the number of characters in a string.

> **Note:**
> strlen() returns **null** when executed on arrays, and an **E_WARNING** level error is emitted.

String Functions

addcslashes
addslashes
bin2hex
chop
chr
chunk_split
convert_uudecode
convert_uuencode
count_chars
crc32
crypt
echo
explode
fprintf
get_html_translation_table
hebrev
hex2bin
html_entity_decode
htmlentities
htmlspecialchars_decode
htmlspecialchars
implode
join
lcfirst
levenshtein
localeconv
ltrim
md5_file
md5
metaphone
money_format
nl_langinfo
nl2br
number_format
ord
parse_str
print
printf
quoted_printable_decode
quoted_printable_encode
quotemeta
rtrim
setlocale
sha1_file
sha1
similar_text
soundex
sprintf
sscanf
str_contains
str_ends_with
str_getcsv
str_ireplace
str_pad
str_repeat
str_replace

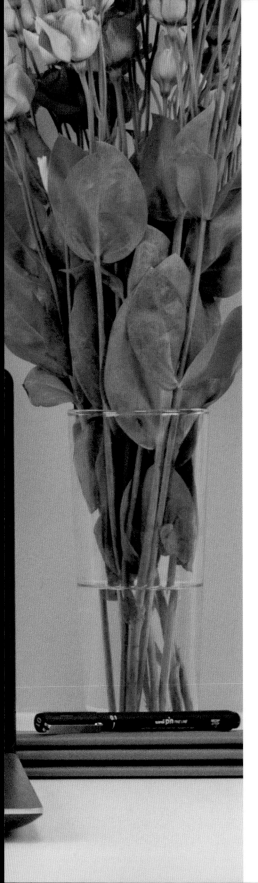

EXAMPLE

This example shows a page for monitoring stock levels in a candy shop.

An associative array is created to hold the names of the products that the store sells and the stock levels for each one. These values are shown in the first two columns of the table.

Then, three functions are created to generate the values that are shown in the next three columns:

- The first function looks at the stock levels and creates a message indicating whether or not more stock should be ordered.

- The second works out the total value of stock for each item that is sold.

- The third calculates how much tax will be due when all of the remaining stock has been sold.

```php
<?php
declare(strict_types = 1);
$candy = [
    'Toffee' => ['price' => 3.00, 'stock' => 12],
    'Mints'  => ['price' => 2.00, 'stock' => 26],
    'Fudge'  => ['price' => 4.00, 'stock' => 8],
];
$tax = 20;

function get_reorder_message(int $stock): string
{
    return ($stock < 10) ? 'Yes' : 'No';
}

function get_total_value(float $price, int $quantity): float
{
    return $price * $quantity;
}

function get_tax_due(float $price, int $quantity, int $tax = 0): float
{
    return ($price * $quantity) * ($tax / 100);
}
?>
```

1. Strict types are turned on.

2. A multidimensional array is created (see p44-45) and is stored in a variable called $candy. The:

- Keys are the names of the types of candy sold
- Values are arrays that hold the price and available stock level of that product

3. A global variable is declared to hold the tax rate.

4. A function called get_reorder_message() is defined. It has one parameter, the current stock level for a product (an int). It returns a message (a string) saying whether or not the item should be reordered.

5. A ternary operator is used to return a message. The condition checks if the stock level is less than 10:

- If it is, the function returns Yes.
- Otherwise, the function returns No.

6. A function called get_total_value() is defined. It has two parameters; the:

- Price of the product (float)
- Quantity of this product available (int)

It returns a float indicating the total value of the stock for this product (here, an int is also a valid number).

7. The function returns the price of the product multiplied by the quantity of stock available.

8. A function called get_tax_due() is defined. It has three parameters; the:

- Price of the product (float)
- Quantity of this product available (int)
- Tax rate as a percent with a default of 0% (int)

It returns a float, indicating the total amount of tax that will be due when these products are sold.

```php
<!DOCTYPE html>
<html>
  <head> ... </head>
  <body>
    <h1>The Candy Store</h1>
    <h2>Stock Control</h2>
    <table>
      <tr>
        <th>Candy</th><th>Stock</th><th>Re-order</th><th>Total value</th><th>Tax due</th>
      </tr>
      <?php foreach ($candy as $product_name => $data) { ?>
        <tr>
          <td><?= $product_name ?></td>
          <td><?= $data['stock'] ?></td>
          <td><?= get_reorder_message($data['stock']) ?></td>
          <td>$<?= get_total_value($data['price'], $data['stock']) ?></td>
          <td>$<?= get_tax_due($data['price'], $data['stock'], $tax) ?></td>
        </tr>
      <?php } ?>
    </table>
  </body>
</html>
```

(10) ... `<?php foreach ($candy as $product_name => $data) { ?>`
(11) ... `<tr>`
(12) ... `<td><?= $data['stock'] ?></td>`
(13) ... `<td><?= get_reorder_message($data['stock']) ?></td>`
(14) ... `<td>$<?= get_total_value($data['price'], $data['stock']) ?></td>`
(15) ... `<td>$<?= get_tax_due($data['price'], $data['stock'], $tax) ?></td>`
(16) ... `<?php } ?>`

9. The total tax due is returned. To calculate this, the total value of the stock (price of one item multiplied by the available quantity) is multiplied by the tax percentage (the tax rate divided by 100).

10. A foreach loop works through the products in the array stored in $candy. In the parentheses:

- $candy is the variable storing the array from Step 2
- $product_name is the name of the variable that will hold the key for the current element of the array (the name of the product: toffee, mints, or fudge)
- $data is the variable that will represent the value for the current element. This is the array that stores the price and stock level of that product.

11. A table row is created, and the name of the product that the loop is currently processing is written out in a <td> element.

12. $data holds an array containing the price and stock level of that product; the stock level is written out in the next table cell.

13. The get_reorder_message() function is called. The stock level is passed in as an argument. The value returned is shown in the table.

14. The get_total_value() function is called. The first parameter is the price of the product. The second parameter is the quantity available. The value returned will be written into the table.

15. The get_tax_due() function is called. The first parameter is the price of the product. The second parameter is the quantity available. The third parameter is the tax rate stored in Step 3. The value returned will be written into the table.

16. The closing curly brace ends the code block, and the loop repeats for each element of the array.

SUMMARY
FUNCTIONS

> Function definitions give a function a name and use a code block to store the statements to perform a task.

> Calling a function tells the PHP interpreter to run those statements to perform the task.

> The return keyword sends data back from a function.

> Parameters represent the data a function needs to perform its task. Parameter names act like variables in the function.

> When a function has run, the parameters and any variables declared in the function are deleted.

> When a function is called, the values used for the parameters are known as arguments.

> Type declarations specify the data type for arguments.

> Return types specify the data type a function returns.

> If a parameter is optional, it is given a default value.

4

OBJECTS & CLASSES

Objects group together a set of variables and functions that represent things you come across in day-to-day life, such as news articles, products for sale, or users of a website.

- In Chapter 2, you saw how variables can store individual pieces of information. When a variable is used in an object, it is called a **property** of the object.

- In Chapter 3, you saw how functions can represent a task that your code needs to perform. When a function is used in an object, it is called a **method** of the object.

Websites often need to represent multiples of the same types of things. A news site will publish many news articles, a shop will sell many products, and a site that allows users to register will have many members. Each one of these things can be represented in code using an **object**.

PHP uses something called a **class** as a template for creating objects that represent a type of thing. For example, it may use one class to create objects that represent products and another class to create objects that represent members. Each object that is created using a class is automatically given the properties and methods that are defined in that class.

Objects and classes help organize your code and make it easier to understand. It is also important to learn how objects work because the PHP interpreter has several built-in objects, which you will start to learn about in Section B of this book.

The first few pages of this chapter introduce the concepts behind objects and how they are used. Following that, you will learn the code required to create and use objects and classes.

WEBSITES AS MODELS

Models are representations of things from the world around us. Programmers create models using data; then they use code to perform tasks that manipulate the data stored in those models.

Websites use data to create models that represent things from day-to-day life. Programmers often refer to these *things* as different **types of objects**. E.g.:

- People (such as customers or members of a site)
- Products or services visitors might buy (such as books, cars, bank accounts, or TV subscriptions)
- Documents that were traditionally printed (such as news articles, calendars, or tickets)

For example, a bank might need certain pieces of data to represent each customer:

- Forename
- Surname
- Email
- Password

It would need the same pieces of data about each person, but the names, email addresses and passwords for each customer would be different.

It would also need to know the same pieces of data about every bank account, but the values used to represent each account would be different. E.g.:

- Account number
- Account type
- Balance

The bank can perform tasks using this data. E.g., tasks performed with a bank account might include:

- Checking the balance
- Making a deposit
- Withdrawing money

Tasks like these get or update data held in variables. E.g., if you withdraw money or make a deposit, it will change the amount stored for that account's balance. Similarly, tasks related to a customer could include:

- Authenticating a user (confirming they are who they claim to be) by checking that the email and password they give matches data stored for them
- Getting their full name (by combining the forename and surname)

An **object** groups together all the:

- Variables that store data needed to create a model of a concept, such as a customer or account
- Functions that represent tasks that type of object can perform

If you remove the photo on the right, you could still tell a lot by looking at the information in the boxes; the types of objects, the data needed to represent each one, and the tasks that the objects can perform.

OBJECT TYPE: CUSTOMER

DATA	VALUE
forename	Ivy
surname	Stone
email	ivy@eg.link
password	$2y$10$MAdTTCA0Mi0whewg...

TASK	PURPOSE
get full name	Retrieve full name
authenticate	Check email and password match

OBJECT TYPE: ACCOUNT

DATA	VALUE
number	20489446
type	Checking
balance	1000.00

TASK	PURPOSE
deposit	Deposit money
withdraw	Withdraw money
get balance	Retrieve balance

The information boxes show two types of objects: **customer** and **account**. For each type of object, the website must do two things:

1. Store the pieces of data used to represent it
The individual pieces of data it stores are the same for each customer or account, but the values that represent that customer or account are different.

2. Perform the same tasks with that type of object
You can perform the same tasks with each customer. You can perform the same tasks with each account.

These tasks can access or change the data that is stored for each customer or account. For example, when a deposit is made on an account, it will update the value that represents the balance of the account.

PROPERTIES & METHODS

In an object, variables are called **properties** and functions are called **methods**. Properties store the data needed to create a model of a concept. Methods represent the tasks that type of object can perform.

VARIABLES:
THE PROPERTIES OF AN OBJECT

In Chapter 1, you saw that variables can store data that changes each time a page is requested. When variables are used inside an object, they are called the properties of the object.

When creating an object, a programmer must decide what data they need to know about that type of object in order for the website to do its job.

For example, if objects are used to represent customers, each customer object will have:

- The *same* properties to hold their forename, surname, email address, and password; but
- *Different* values to represent each customer

If you use an object to represent an account, each account object would also have:

- The *same* properties to hold the account number, account type, and balance; but
- *Different* values to represent each account

The properties of the object are a set of variables that describe the individual *characteristics* that all of those objects have in common. The values that are stored for each property are what make one object different from the next.

FUNCTIONS:
THE METHODS OF AN OBJECT

In Chapter 3, you saw that PHP can group together all of the statements required to perform a task in a function. When functions are used inside an object, they are called the methods of the object.

When creating an object, a programmer decides what tasks users of their website can perform with each type of object. These tasks often:

- Ask questions that tell you something about that object using data stored in its properties
- Change the values stored in one or more of that object's properties

The tasks you can perform with an account (make a deposit, withdraw money, or check the balance) are applicable to every account, so all objects that represent an account have the same methods.

Similarly, you would need to perform the same tasks for every customer (authenticate them, get their full name), so every object that represents a customer would have the same methods.

On the right, you can see a similar diagram to the one on the previous page, but this time it shows the property and method names for two customer objects and two account objects.

OBJECT TYPE: CUSTOMER	
DATA	**VALUE**
forename	Ivy
surname	Stone
email	ivy@eg.link
password	$2y$10$MAdTTCA0Mi0whewg...

TASK	**PURPOSE**
getFullName()	Return values of **forename** and **surname** properties
authenticate()	Check **email** and **password** match

OBJECT TYPE: CUSTOMER	
DATA	**VALUE**
forename	Emiko
surname	Ito
email	emi@eg.link
password	$2y$10$NN5HEAD3atarECjRiir...

TASK	**PURPOSE**
getFullName()	Return values of **forename** and **surname** properties
authenticate()	Check **email** and **password** match

OBJECT TYPE: ACCOUNT	
DATA	**VALUE**
number	20489446
type	Checking
balance	1000.00

TASK	**PURPOSE**
deposit()	Increase value of **balance** property
withdraw()	Decrease value of **balance** property
getBalance()	Return value of **balance** property

OBJECT TYPE: ACCOUNT	
DATA	**VALUE**
number	10937528
type	Savings
balance	2346.00

TASK	**PURPOSE**
deposit()	Increase value of **balance** property
withdraw()	Decrease value of **balance** property
getBalance()	Return value of **balance** property

OBJECT DATA TYPE

An object is an example of a compound data type because it can store multiple values.

As you have seen, PHP has different data types:

- Scalar data types hold individual values: strings, integers, floats, booleans
- Compound data types hold multiple values: arrays and objects

Below, you can see two diagrams of objects that represent a customer and their account.

A variable that holds an object can be named like any other variable (in lowercase, with an underscore to separate each word when the name uses multiple words). For example:

- A variable called $customer could store an object that represents a customer.
- A variable called $account could store an object that represents an account.

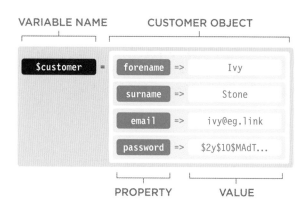

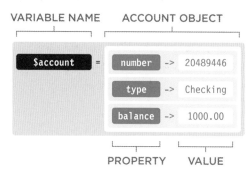

People often say that an object is stored *in* a variable but, as you learn on p530-31, the variable actually stores something called a **reference** to where the object was created in the PHP interpreter's memory.

When a page has finished running, and the PHP interpreter has sent an HTML page back to the browser, it forgets the object (removing it from its memory, like it forgets the values stored in variables).

CLASSES ARE TEMPLATES FOR CREATING OBJECTS

To create objects, you use a template called a **class**. A class definition specifies the property names and methods that a type of object has.

A class definition sets out:

- Property names that describe the data that you need to store for a type of object
- Methods that define tasks that can be performed with that kind of object

Each time you create an object using a class:

- You supply the values for the properties (those values make one object different from the next)
- The object automatically gets all of the methods that were defined in the class

Each individual object created using the class is referred to as an **instance** of that class.

For example, if you create an object to represent a bank account (as illustrated in this chapter), you would provide the values for the following properties:

- `$number`
- `$type`
- `$balance`

And it would automatically get these methods:

- `deposit()`
- `withdraw()`
- `getBalance()`

Some programmers use the terms class and object interchangeably but, strictly speaking, a class is a template that is used to create an object.

HOW TO CREATE AND USE OBJECTS

Below, you can see the steps that you need to learn to create and use classes and objects.

DEFINING A CLASS AS A TEMPLATE FOR AN OBJECT
See p154

A class is a template that is used to create one type of object. The class defines the:

- Properties that store the data used to represent that type of object
- Methods that contain the statements to achieve the tasks that kind of object can perform

A new class is created for each type of object that the website needs to deal with.

CREATING AN OBJECT AND STORING IT IN A VARIABLE
See p155

An object is created by:

- Specifying the name of the class that should be used as a template for it
- Supplying values for its properties

The object will automatically get the methods defined in the class.

When an object is created, it is usually stored in a variable so that it can be used by the rest of the code in the page.

SETTING AND ACCESSING PROPERTY VALUES
See p156-157

Once an object has been created, it is possible to:

- Set values for its properties
- Access values stored in its properties and use them in the rest of the code in the page

Every instance of an object will store different values in its properties because it represents a different instance of that kind of object (such as a different customer or a different account).

DEFINING AND CALLING METHODS OF AN OBJECT
See p158-159

A method defines the statements needed to achieve a task that a type of object is capable of performing. They are written just like function definitions, but live inside the class. They also usually return a value, like functions do.

When a method of an object is called, it will often need to access or update values stored in that object's properties.

PHP has a special variable called $this which allows methods to work with values stored in the properties of *this* object.

ASSIGNING PROPERTY VALUES WHEN CREATING OBJECTS
See p160-163

Rather than creating an object and then setting the values for each of its properties individually, you can create an object and assign values to the properties in a single line of code. To do this, something called a **constructor** function is added to the class.

In PHP 8, a constructor function can also define an object's properties (so you don't need to define them before setting their values in a constructor function).

CONTROLLING WHAT CODE CAN ACCESS PROPERTIES
See p164-165

Sometimes, you will not want to allow PHP pages to access or update the properties of an object directly. Instead, you can create methods to get or update values stored in those properties.

For example, you may hide the balance property of an account object, then use the methods getBalance(), deposit(), and withdraw() to work with the value that is stored in the balance property.

CLASSES: TEMPLATES FOR OBJECTS

When a **class definition** is created, the properties and methods that an object will have are stored inside curly braces.

A class definition uses:

- The `class` keyword.
- A name that describes the type of object it creates. The name should use UpperCamelCase where the first letter of each word starts with an uppercase letter (do not use underscores).
- A pair of curly braces to create a code block. The braces show where the class starts/ends. Each brace starts on a new line.
- **NOTE:** There is no semicolon after the closing curly brace that ends the class definition.

Inside the curly braces of the class, the properties for this type of object are listed using:

- A visibility keyword (see p164). The ones below use the keyword `public`.
- The data type that the property will hold. (This was added in PHP 7.4 and is optional.)
- The name of the property starting with a $ symbol.

The methods use the same syntax as function definitions, but are preceded by a visibility keyword (see p164); the methods below use `public`.

```
class Account
{
    public int    $number;
    public string $type;
    public float  $balance;

    public function deposit(float $amount): float
    {
        // Code to deposit money here
    }
    public function withdraw(float $amount): float
    {
        // Code to withdraw money here
    }
}
```

PROPERTIES

METHODS

CREATING AN OBJECT USING A CLASS

To create an object, use the **new** keyword followed by the class name and a pair of parentheses.

To create the object, use:

- The **new** keyword.
- The name of the class that will be a template for the object.
- Parentheses. These can contain parameter names (like a function has parameters in parentheses). They pass data to the object when it is created.

As you saw on p150, a reference to an object is often stored in a variable so that it can be used by the rest of the code in a PHP page. To do this:

- Create a variable to hold the object; its name should describe the type of object that it holds.
- Add the assignment operator =
- Create the object (as described on the left).

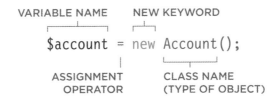

In the example above, the `$account` variable would store a reference to an object created using the `Account` class that is shown on the left-hand page.

It would have three properties: `$number`, `$type`, and `$balance`. None of these would have values yet. You will see how to assign their values on the next page.

The object would also automatically have the two methods that were in the class definition.

To create a second object that represents another account, you would do the same as shown above, but with a different variable name (otherwise the second object would overwrite the first one).

The class definition must be in any page that creates an object using the class. If a class definition is used by more than one page, it is put in a separate file which can then be included in both pages. That file is given the same name as the class (e.g., `Account.php`).

ACCESS AND UPDATE PROPERTIES

You access and update properties of an object like you do variables. If an object is stored in a variable, specify the variable name first, then use the object operator to specify the property you want to work with.

ACCESSING PROPERTIES

To access a value stored in a property, use the:

- Name of the variable holding the object
- Object operator -> with no space either side of it
- Name of the property (note that the property name does not start with the $ symbol here)

The object operator indicates that the property on the right of the operator belongs to the object stored in the variable on the left of the operator.

The code below shows how to display the value of the account balance on the page.

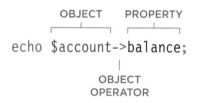

If the data type of a property was set in the class and you try to access the property before it has been assigned a value, the PHP interpreter will create an error that can stop the page running.

SETTING AND UPDATING PROPERTIES

To update the value stored in a property, use the:

- Name of the variable holding the object
- Object operator -> with no space either side of it
- Name of the property you want to update
- Assignment operator =
- New value (if the value is a string, it goes in quotes; numbers and booleans are not put in quotes)

If you try to set the value of a property that was not in the class definition, the property will be added to this one object. (It would not be added to any other objects created using the class.)

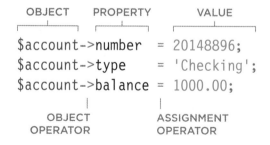

As you will see on p161, it is possible to specify default values for properties in the __construct() method. This will ensure that each property has a value when the object is created using the class.

USING OBJECTS AND PROPERTIES

`section_a/c04/objects-and-properties.php`

```php
<?php
class Customer
{
    public string $forename;
    public string $surname;
    public string $email;
    public string $password;
}

class Account
{
    public int    $number;
    public string $type;
    public float  $balance;
}

    $customer = new Customer();
    $account  = new Account();
    $customer->email  = 'ivy@eg.link';
    $account->balance = 1000.00;
?>
<?php include 'includes/header.php'; ?>
<p>Email: <?= $customer->email ?></p>
<p>Balance: $<?= $account->balance ?></p>
<?php include 'includes/footer.php'; ?>
```

1. The Customer class and its properties are defined.

2. The Account class and its properties are defined.

3. An instance of the Customer class is created and that object is stored in a variable called $customer.

4. An instance of the Account class is created and that object is stored in a variable called $account.

5. The email property of the Customer object is given a value.

6. The balance property of the Account object is given a value.

7. An include file adds a header to the page.

8. The two properties that have just been set are displayed.

9. An include file adds the HTML tags needed to close the page.

TRY: After Step 5, set the customer's forename and surname in the Customer object.

Then, in Step 8, display their name before the email address.

RESULT

NEO ⬤ BANK

Email: ivy@eg.link

Balance: $1000

DEFINING AND CALLING METHODS

A method is a function that is written inside a class definition. To call a method, use the name of the variable holding the object, the object operator, then the method name.

DEFINING A METHOD

To add a method to a class, use a visibility keyword (see p164 - the one below uses `public`), followed by a function definition. If a method needs to access or update a property of the object, use:

- A special variable called `$this` (known as a **pseudo-variable**) to indicate that you want to access a property of *this* object
- The object operator ->
- The name of the property you want to access

The `deposit()` method below has a parameter called `$amount`. When the method is called, the value used for `$amount` is added to the value in the `balance` property, and the new value in `balance` is returned.

```
class Account
{
  public int    $number;
  public string $type;
  public float  $balance;

  public function deposit($amount)
  {
    $this->balance += $amount;
    return $this->balance;
  }
}
```

$this PSEUDO-VARIABLE

CALLING A METHOD

To call a method, use the:

- Name of the variable holding the object
- Object operator ->
- Method name
- Arguments for the method's parameters

The example below deposits $50 into the account. The `deposit()` method (shown in the left-hand column) adds this amount to the value in the `balance` property; it then returns the new balance.

The `echo` command is used to write the new balance out to the page.

OBJECT METHOD NAME

```
echo $account->deposit(50.00);
```

OBJECT OPERATOR   ARGUMENT

USING METHODS OF OBJECTS

PHP   section_a/c04/objects-and-methods.php

```php
<?php
class Account
{
    public int    $number;
    public string $type;
    public float  $balance;

    public function deposit(float $amount): float
    {
        $this->balance += $amount;
        return $this->balance;
    }
    public function withdraw(float $amount): float
    {
        $this->balance -= $amount;
        return $this->balance;
    }
}

$account = new Account();
$account->balance = 100.00;
?>
<?php include 'includes/header.php'; ?>
<p>$<?= $account->deposit(50.00) ?></p>
<?php include 'includes/footer.php'; ?>
```

1. Define the Account class and its properties (as on p157).

2. Add the deposit() method. The $amount parameter is the amount to add to the balance.

3. The amount passed into the function is added to the value stored in the balance property:

- $this->balance gets the balance property of *this* object.
- += adds the value in $amount to the balance.

4. The new value stored in the balance property is returned.

5. withdraw() does the same as deposit(), but subtracts an amount from the balance.

6. An object is created using the Account class and stored in a variable called $account.

7. The balance property of the object is set to 100.00.

8. The deposit() method is called adding $50.00 to the account. It returns the updated balance, and that value is written to the page with the shorthand for echo.

TRY: After Step 8, use withdraw() to withdraw $75.

RESULT

NEO BANK

$150

CONSTRUCTOR METHOD

The `__construct()` method is known as a **constructor**.
It automatically runs when a class is used to create an object.

If you add a method called `__construct()` to a class definition (its name must start with **two** underscores), the statements inside that method are automatically run when the class is used to create an object.

A `__construct()` method can be used to allow you to create an object and add values to its properties in one line of code, rather than create the object and then set each property individually using a separate statement (as you saw on p156-157).

Below, an object is created using the `Account` class and stored in a variable called `$account`. When the object is created, the PHP interpreter looks in the class for a method called `__construct()`.

The arguments in the parentheses after the class name are passed to the `__construct()` method (as shown on the right-hand page). Inside the `__construct()` method, those values are used to set the properties of the object.

```
        VARIABLE        CLASS NAME     VALUES USED TO CREATE OBJECT

        $account  =  new Account(20148896, 'Checking', 1000.00);

                                   ACCOUNT NUMBER  ACCOUNT TYPE  BALANCE
```

NOTE: Do not start the name of your own functions with two underscores; this naming convention is only to be used for what PHP calls **magic methods**.

Magic methods are called automatically by the PHP interpreter; you do not need to call these methods in your own code.

Below, the __construct() method of the Account class has three parameters: $type, $number, and $balance, which correspond to its properties.

The three statements in the __construct() method take the values in the parameters and use those values to set the properties of the object.

As you saw on p158, the $this pseudo-variable lets you to access or update properties of *this* object.

If an object was created using the code on the left-hand page, the __construct() method shown below would automatically run and give the:

- $number parameter the value 20148896
- $type parameter the value 'Checking'
- $balance parameter the value 100.00

In the example on the next page, you will see how to specify default values for any of these properties.

```
class Account
{
    public int    $number;
    public string $type;
    public float  $balance;

    public function __construct($number, $type, $balance)
    {
        $this->number  = $number;
        $this->type    = $type;
        $this->balance = $balance;
    }

    function deposit($amount) {...}
    function withdraw($amount) {...}
    function getBalance() {...}
}
```

PHP 8 adds a simpler way to write class definitions by allowing you to declare the properties for a class inside the parentheses of the __construct() method.

When an object is created using the class, the arguments provided to the constructor are automatically assigned as values for these properties. This is called **constructor property promotion**.

If a property is optional, a default value can be given (see the $balance property on the right) and this value will be used if an argument is not specified.

```
class Account
{
    public function __construct(
        public int    $number,
        public string $type,
        public float  $balance = 0.00,
    ) {}

    function deposit($amount) {...}
    function withdraw($amount) {...}
    function getBalance() {...}
}
```

USING CONSTRUCTORS WITH A CLASS

1. The PHP page starts by enabling strict types because type declarations have been added to the methods (see p126-27).

2. The class name and its properties are defined.

3. The `__construct()` method from the previous page is added to set the values of the properties. Argument type declarations are added to the parameters. If a balance is not given when creating the object, a default value of `0.00` is used.

4. The `deposit()` and `withdraw()` methods update the value stored in the `balance` property. They are given argument and return type declarations of `float`. (When the data type is `float` an `int` can be used without causing an error.)

section_a/c04/constructor-methods.php `PHP`

```php
<?php
declare(strict_types = 1);
class Account
{
    public int    $number;
    public string $type;
    public float  $balance;

    public function __construct(int $number, string $type, float $balance = 0.00)
    {
        $this->number  = $number;
        $this->type    = $type;
        $this->balance = $balance;
    }

    public function deposit(float $amount): float
    {
        $this->balance += $amount;
        return $this->balance;
    }

    public function withdraw(float $amount): float
    {
        $this->balance -= $amount;
        return $this->balance;
    }
}
```

```php
⑤  $checking = new Account(43161176, 'Checking', 32.00);
    $savings  = new Account(20148896, 'Savings', 756.00);
    ?>

    <?php include 'includes/header.php'; ?>
    <h2>Account Balances</h2>
    <table>
⑥    <tr>
       <th>Date</th>
       <th><?= $checking->type ?></th>
       <th><?= $savings->type  ?></th>
     </tr>
     <tr>
       <td>23 June</td>
⑦    <td>$<?= $checking->balance ?></td>
       <td>$<?= $savings->balance  ?></td>
     </tr>
     <tr>
       <td>24 June</td>
⑧    <td>$<?= $checking->deposit(12.00)  ?></td>
       <td>$<?= $savings->withdraw(100.00) ?></td>
     </tr>
     <tr>
       <td>25 June</td>
⑨    <td>$<?= $checking->withdraw(5.00) ?></td>
       <td>$<?= $savings->deposit(300.00) ?></td>
     </tr>
    </table>
    <?php include 'includes/footer.php'; ?>
```

RESULT

5. Two objects are created to represent a checking account and a savings account.

The constructor assigns the values in the parentheses to the properties of each of the objects.

6. An HTML table is drawn into the page. The first row shows headings using the type property of the two objects. To access a property, use the:

- Name of the variable that holds the object
- Object operator
- Property name

7. The next table row shows the balance property of the objects.

8. In the third row of the table, the balance of each account is updated by calling the deposit() or withdraw() methods.

These methods return the new value of the balance property, and this is written out to the page. To call a method, use the:

- Name of the variable holding the object
- Object operator
- Method name with its arguments in parentheses

9. In the fourth row of the table, the previous step is repeated using different values.

TRY: In Step 6, create an object to represent a high-interest account.

In Steps 7-9, add rows to show its balance being updated.

VISIBILITY OF PROPERTIES AND METHODS

You can prevent code outside of an object from getting or setting the values stored in the properties inside it. You can also prevent the code outside of an object from calling its methods.

The properties and methods of a class are called **members** of a class. You can specify whether the code outside of an object created using this class can:

- Access or update the value stored in a property
- Call a method

This is done by setting the **visibility** when a property is declared or a method is defined.

So far in this chapter, all property and method names have been preceded by the word `public`, which means any other code can work with the properties and methods of the object.

There are times when you only want to allow the code inside the object to access or update properties or call the methods of that object. To do this, you change the word `public` to `protected`.

For example, the `Account` class has a property called `balance`. If it is declared using the `public` visibility keyword, any code that creates an object using this class can get or update the value in that property.

To prevent any other code updating the value stored in the `balance` property, its visibility can be set to `protected`. If you try to access a `protected` property using code that is outside the class, the PHP interpreter generates an error.

If code outside of the object needs to get the value stored in a `protected` property, you add a method to the class that returns its value. This method would be known as a **getter** (because it gets a value).

In the example on the right, a new method called `getBalance()` is added to the `Account` class; its job is to return the value stored in the `$balance` property.

To update the value stored in a `protected` property, you add a method to the class that updates its value. This is known as a **setter** (because it sets a value).

The `deposit()` and `withdraw()` methods in the `Account` class are already used to update the value stored in the `$balance` property.

These changes ensure that the balance is only updated by the `deposit()` or `withdraw()` methods. It could not be updated by any other code.

If you do not specify the visibility of a property or method in the class definition, it defaults to being `public`, but explicitly stating whether the property or method is `public` or `protected` is considered good practice and makes your code easier to understand.

There is also another setting for visibility called `private`, used in more advanced object-oriented code. It is beyond the scope of a beginner's book. These settings are also called **access modifiers**.

USING GETTERS AND SETTERS

section_a/c04/getters-and-setters.php

```php
<?php
declare(strict_types = 1);

class Account {
    public     int    $number;
    public     string $type;
    protected  float  $balance;

    public function __construct() {...}
    public function deposit() {...}
    public function withdraw() {...}

    public function getBalance(): float
    {
        return $this->balance;
    }
}

$account = new Account(20148896, 'Savings', 80.00);
?>

<?php include 'includes/header.php'; ?>
<h2><?= $account->type ?> Account</h2>
<p>Previous balance: $<?= $account->getBalance() ?></p>
<p>New balance: $<?= $account->deposit(35.00) ?></p>
<?php include 'includes/footer.php'; ?>
```

(1) (2) (3) (4) (5) (6) (7)

RESULT

SAVINGS ACCOUNT

Previous balance: $80

New balance: $115

1. The `balance` property was previously `public` and is now changed to `protected` so that it is not visible outside the class.

2. The existing `deposit()` and `withdraw()` methods act as setters to update the balance (the code for them is the same as the previous example).

3. A getter called `getBalance()` is added to the class to get the value of the protected `balance` property if it needs to be displayed.

4. An object is created using the Account class. It is stored in the $account variable.

5. The type of account is shown. Because this property is `public`, it can be accessed directly.

6. The `getBalance()` method is called to display the value in the $balance property.

7. The `deposit()` method is called. It adds $35 to the $balance property. This method also returns the new balance so it can be written out to the page.

TRY: After Step 6, use the `withdraw()` method to take $50 out of the account.

STORING AN ARRAY IN A PROPERTY OF AN OBJECT

A property of an object can store an array. Individual elements of the array can then be accessed using array syntax.

The properties of the objects you have seen so far all stored scalar data types (strings, numbers, and booleans). The property of an object can also store a compound data type such as an array. Below, an Account object is stored in a variable called $account, and its number property is set.

The value assigned to the number property is an associative array holding two separate values:

- An account number
- A routing number (known as a sort code or a BSB in some countries)

```
        OBJECT    PROPERTY              VALUE IS AN ARRAY
$account->number = ['account_number' => 12345678,
                    'routing_number' => 987654321,];
```

To access a value that has been stored as an array in the number property of an object, use the:

- Name of the variable holding the object
- Object operator
- Name of the property holding the array
- Key of the item in the array you want to access

Below, the account number and routing number that have been stored as an associative array in the number property of the Account object are retrieved using their key names and written out to the page using the echo command. (If the array was an indexed array, the key would be the index number of the element you wanted to access.)

```
        OBJECT    PROPERTY        KEY
echo $account->number['account_number'];
echo $account->number['routing_number'];
```

USING AN ARRAY IN A PROPERTY OF AN OBJECT

section_a/c04/array-in-object.php

```php
<?php
declare(strict_types = 1);

class Account {...}
// As on p165, but number property is an array not int

//Create an array to store in the property
$numbers = ['account_number' => 12345678,
            'routing_number' => 987654321,];

//Create an instance of the class and set properties
$account = new Account($numbers, 'Savings', 10.00);
?>
<?php include 'includes/header.php'; ?>
<h2><?= $account->type ?> account</h2>
Account <?= $account->number['account_number'] ?><br>
Routing <?= $account->number['routing_number'] ?>
<?php include 'includes/footer.php'; ?>
```

(1) `class Account {...}`

(2) `$numbers = ['account_number' => 12345678, 'routing_number' => 987654321,];`

(3) `$account = new Account($numbers, 'Savings', 10.00);`

(4) `<h2><?= $account->type ?> account</h2>`

(5) `Account <?= $account->number['account_number'] ?><br>`

(6) `Routing <?= $account->number['routing_number'] ?>`

RESULT

In this example, an object is created to represent an account. The account and routing numbers will both be stored in the $number property.

1. The Account class is the same as it was in the previous example on p165, but the argument type declaration for the $number parameter in the __construct() method indicates that the value will be an array.

2. A variable called $number is declared. It holds an associative array with two keys:
- account_number
routing_number

3. An object is created using the Account class. The first argument is the $numbers variable created in Step 2. This assigns the array to the $number property of the object.

4. The type of account is written out to the page.

5. The account number is shown.

6. The routing number is shown.

TRY: In Step 2, change the account number and routing number.

STORING AN OBJECT IN A PROPERTY OF AN OBJECT

A property of an object can store another object. You can then access or update individual properties of both objects and call their methods.

On the previous page, you saw that a property of an object can store an array. You can also store another object in the property of an object.

Below, the value assigned to the $number property is a new object created with the AccountNumber class (shown on the right-hand page).

The AccountNumber class is a template for an object that represents account numbers. It has two properties:

- $accountNumber holds the account number
- $routingNumber holds the routing number (known as a sort code or a BSB in some countries)

To access a property or method from the object stored in the $number property of the object, use the:

- Name of the variable holding the Account object
- Object operator
- Name of the property storing account numbers
- Object operator (to access *that* object)
- Property or method you want to use

Below, the $account variable holds the object that represents the bank account.

Its $number property stores a second object created using the AccountNumber class.

Its properties, $accountNumber and $routingNumber, are written out using the echo command.

<pre>
                    OBJECT IN A
          OBJECT   PROPERTY   PROPERTY
          ┌───┴──┐ ┌───┴──┐   ┌────┴────┐
echo $account->number->accountNumber;
echo $account->number->routingNumber;
</pre>

USING AN OBJECT AS A PROPERTY OF AN OBJECT

section_a/c04/object-in-object.php

```php
<?php
declare(strict_types = 1);
class Account {...}
// As p165, but the data type of the number property
// is the class name AccountNumber

class AccountNumber
{
    public int $accountNumber;
    public int $routingNumber;

    public function __construct(int $accountNumber,
                               int $routingNumber)
    {
        $this->accountNumber = $accountNumber;
        $this->routingNumber = $routingNumber;
    }
}

$numbers = new AccountNumber(12345678, 987654321);
$account = new Account($numbers, 'Savings', 10.00);
?>
<?php include 'includes/header.php';?>
<h2><?= $account->type ?> Account</h2>
Account <?= $account->number->accountNumber ?><br>
Routing <?= $account->number->routingNumber ?>
<?php include 'includes/footer.php'; ?>
```

RESULT

SAVINGS ACCOUNT

Account 12345678
Routing 987654321

1. The Account class is the same as the example on p165, except the argument type declaration for the $number parameter in the __construct() method shows the value for that parameter should be an object created using the AccountNumber class.

2. A class definition is added for the AccountNumber class. It has two public properties:

- $accountNumber
- $routingNumber

3. A constructor method is used to assign values to these properties when an object is created using this class.

4. An object is created using the AccountNumber class. It is stored in a variable called $numbers.

5. An object is created to represent an account using the Account class. The first argument is the variable holding the object that represents the account numbers.

6. The type of account is written out into the heading of the page.

7. The account number is shown.

8. The routing number is shown.

BENEFITS OF USING OBJECTS

The use of objects helps organize your code, saves repeating the same code in different pages, makes it easier to maintain, and easier to share.

BETTER ORGANIZATION

If a PHP page has hundreds of lines of code, one after the other, it can be hard to work out what each line of code is doing.

Grouping together the variables and functions used to represent a concept, such as a customer or their account, in a class helps keep all of the related code in one place.

When objects are created using a class, programmers can look at the class definition to see what:

- Data is available in its properties
- Tasks can be performed using its methods

As you will see in the final example for this chapter, shown on the next page, class definitions are often stored in separate files (which are called **class files**). This makes it easy to find the code for a class.

BETTER RE-USABILITY

There may be several pages of a site that need to represent the same things; for example, several pages may represent a customer or member of a site.

Rather than each page repeating the variable declarations (to store data that represents the customer) and the function definitions (to represent the tasks that they can perform), a class definition can be used as a template to create an object that represents them.

Any page that needs to represent a customer can include the class file in the page and create an object using that class definition as a template.

Programmers sometimes refer to the **Don't Repeat Yourself** or **DRY Principle**. According to this principle, if you find yourself repeating code, you should check whether or not a function or method of an object could be used to perform the task instead.

Programmers also refer to the **single responsibility principle**, which indicates that every function or method should have a single responsibility (rather than perform multiple tasks). This helps maximize re-use of the code and makes it easier to understand.

EASIER TO MAINTAIN

Careful organization of code, and maximizing the re-use of code, helps make that code easier to maintain. For example:

- If you need to store some extra information about the customers of a site, you can add a property to the class definition that represents the customers, and that information will be available on every object that represents a customer.

- If you need to change how a program performs a specific task (such as how interest is calculated for an account), you only need to update the code in one class, and it will update every object that is created using that class.

EASIER TO SHARE CODE

If you think about how a class is written, as long as you know its name, and the properties and methods it has, you do not need to know how it achieves all of the tasks that it performs. You only need to know:

- How to create an object using that class
- What data you can get from its properties
- What tasks you can perform with its methods

This helps programmers who are working together in a team because different programmers can be responsible for different class definitions.

In the next section of the book, you will see that the PHP interpreter has many built-in functions and classes that help you create web pages. You do not need to know how they achieve their tasks, you just need to know how to use them.

EXAMPLE

This example will display user information and bank balances for a customer with multiple bank accounts.

Two class definitions are used:

- A `Customer` class is used to create an object that represents a customer of the bank
- An `Account` class is used to create objects that represent the different accounts each customer has

The classes will be put in two separate files called `Customer.php` and `Account.php`, and those files will be stored in a folder called `classes`.

Any page that uses the classes to create an object will include the class definitions, just like the header and footer of the pages have been included in each page.

In the page shown on the left:

- A `Customer` object will be created using the `Customer` class

- A new property will be added to the `Customer` class called `$accounts`

- The `$accounts` property will hold an array

- That array will store two `Account` objects that represent the two types of account the customer has (created using the new `Account` class)

This shows how you can create a hierarchy of objects, where one object contains another.

The page displays the customer's name and uses a `foreach` loop to work through each of the accounts the customer has. Inside the loop, the account number, type, and balance of each account will be shown.

A conditional statement checks whether the user is overdrawn and, if so, displays the balance in orange rather than white.

EXAMPLE

section_a/c04/classes/Account.php `PHP`

```php
<?php
① class Account {...} // See p165
```

section_a/c04/classes/Customer.php `PHP`

```php
<?php
class Customer
{
    public  string $forename;
    public  string $surname;
    public  string $email;
    private string $password;
②  public  array  $accounts;

    function __construct(string $forename, string $surname, string $email,
③                         string $password, array $accounts)
    {
        $this->forename = $forename;
        $this->surname  = $surname;
        $this->email    = $email;
        $this->password = $password;
④      $this->accounts = $accounts;
    }
    function getFullName()
    {
⑤      return $this->forename . ' ' . $this->surname;
    }
}
```

The two class definitions are created in Account.php and Customer.php and stored in a folder called classes. The classes can be included in any page that needs to create that type of object using a PHP include statement (see Step 5).

1. The Account class was created on p162-167.

2. The Customer class builds on the one on p157. The new $accounts property holds an array of objects; each object represents one of the customer's accounts.

3 + 4. The $accounts property is added to the constructor method.

5. A new method returns the customer's full name.

6. The page to show the user's accounts includes the Account and Customer class definitions needed to create those objects.

7. An indexed array is created and stored in a variable called $accounts. It holds two objects created using the Account class. Each object represents one of the customer's bank accounts.

```php
<?php
include 'classes/Account.php';
include 'classes/Customer.php';

$accounts = [new Account(20489446, 'Checking', -20),
             new Account(20148896, 'Savings', 380),];

$customer = new Customer('Ivy', 'Stone', 'ivy@eg.link', 'Jup!t3r2684', $accounts);
?>
<?php include 'includes/header.php'; ?>
<h2>Name: <b><?= $customer->getFullName() ?></b></h2>

<table>
  <tr>
    <th>Account Number</th>
    <th>Account Type</th>
    <th>Balance</th>
  </tr>

  <?php foreach ($customer->accounts as $account) { ?>
    <tr>
      <td><?= $account->number ?></td>
      <td><?= $account->type ?></td>
      <?php if ($account->getBalance() >= 0) { ?>
        <td class="credit">
      <?php } else { ?>
        <td class="overdrawn">
      <?php } ?>
      $ <?= $account->getBalance() ?></td>
    </tr>
  <?php } ?>

</table>
<?php include 'includes/footer.php'; ?>
```

8. A new `Customer` object is created to represent the customer and is stored in a variable called `$customer`. The final argument is the array of accounts created in Step 7.

9. The `Customer` object's new `getFullName()` method returns the customer's full name, which is shown in the heading.

10. A `foreach` loop goes through the array stored in the `$accounts` property of the `Customer` object. In the loop, each account is held in a variable called `$account`.

11. The account number and type are written to the page.

12. An `if` statement checks if the balance is 0 or more.

13. If it is, a `<td>` element is created with the class `credit`.

14. If not, it sits in a `<td>` element with a class called `overdrawn`.

15. The balance is written out.

TRY: In Step 7, add a third account to the array.

SUMMARY
OBJECTS & CLASSES

> Objects group together variables and functions that represent something from the world around us.

> In an object, the variables are called properties and the functions are called methods.

> A class is used as a template to create objects.

> Class definitions set out the properties and methods that each object created using that class will have.

> The `__construct()` method runs when an object is created. It can be used to put values into properties.

> `$this` accesses a property or method of *this* object.

> Properties can be declared as `public` (they can be accessed by code outside the object) or `protected` (they can only be used by code inside the object).

> Classes and objects help organize, re-use, maintain, and share code more effectively.

B

DYNAMIC WEB PAGES

This section shows you how to use PHP to create dynamic web pages. These are pages where the content that users see can change without a programmer manually altering the file.

Section A introduced the syntax of the PHP language. It showed how:

- Variables and arrays store data
- Operators create a single value from multiple pieces of information
- Conditions and loops determine when code is run
- Functions and classes group together related statements

In this section, you learn how to apply these basic concepts to create dynamic web pages. At a basic level, a computer is a machine that is programmed to:

- Accept data known as **input**
- **Process** that data and perform tasks with it
- Then create **output** that users can see or hear
- They can also optionally **store** data for later use

The PHP pages you will learn to write in this section are like basic programs; they can accept input from a web browser, process that data, then use it to output an HTML page that is tailored to an individual visitor. You will learn how to:

- Use a set of functions and classes that are part of PHP
- Collect and process data that has been sent from browsers
- Work with images and other files that users can upload
- Store data about website visitors using cookies and sessions
- Deal with errors and troubleshoot your code

To read this section, you need to understand how the PHP interpreter handles requests and how it responds to them.

To handle page requests, servers follow rules set out in protocols and encoding schemes:

HTTP REQUESTS & RESPONSES

HyperText Transfer Protocol (HTTP) is a set of rules that control how browsers and servers communicate. This is why website URLs start with either `http://` or `https://`. HTTP specifies what data:

- Browsers send to a server when they request a file
- Servers send to the browser when they respond with the requested file

ENCODING SCHEMES

Computers represent text, images and audio using binary data, which is made up of a series of 0s and 1s.

Encoding schemes are rules that computers use to translate the things you see and hear into the 0s and 1s that the computer processes. If you do not know how to tell PHP which encoding scheme to use, it may not process or display data correctly.

The PHP interpreter comes with several tools that help you build dynamic web pages:

ARRAYS, FUNCTIONS, CLASSES

The PHP interpreter comes with sets of:

- **Superglobal arrays**: these are arrays that it creates each time a file is requested.
- **Built-in functions**: that perform tasks programmers often need to achieve.
- **Built-in classes**: to create objects that represent things programmers often need to deal with.

ERROR MESSAGES

The PHP interpreter creates **error messages** when it encounters a problem; learning how to read these messages will help you fix problems in your code.

SETTINGS

Like many pieces of software, the PHP interpreter and the web server both have settings you can control. You will see how to change the settings for both of these pieces of software using text files.

HTTP REQUESTS AND RESPONSES

HyperText Transfer Protocol (HTTP) is a set of rules that specify how browsers should **request** pages and how servers should format their **response**. It helps to understand what data is sent with each step.

When a web browser **requests** a PHP page, the browser's address bar shows a URL which specifies how the browser can find that page. Each URL has:

- A **protocol** (for web pages it is HTTP or HTTPS)
- A **host** (the server to send the request to)
- A **path** that identifies the requested file
- An optional **query string** with extra data the page might need

PROTOCOL   HOST   PATH   QUERY STRING

`http://eg.link/year.php?year=2021`

NAME VALUE

When a query string is added to the end of a URL, each piece of data it sends is like a variable; it has a:

- **Name** that describes the data that is being sent. The name is the same each time the URL is used.
- **Value** for this piece of data. The value can change each time the page is requested.

When a browser requests a web page, it also sends **HTTP request headers** to the server. They are not shown in the main browser window (like the URL), but they can be viewed in the developer tools that come with most browsers (see screen shot below).

The headers hold data the server may find helpful, and they are also similar to a variable; they have a:

- **Name** that describes what data is being sent. The name is the same each time a URL is used.
- **Value** for the piece of data.

The headers in the screenshot below show:

- The language the visitor speaks (US English). On multi-language sites, this could be used to select the correct language for a visitor.
- That the user's request came from another web page, along with the URL of that page.
- The browser is Chrome on a Mac, running OSX. This could be used to determine whether to send a visitor to a desktop/mobile version of the site.

LANGUAGE →
PAGE REQUEST IS FROM →
BROWSER →

```
×   Headers   Preview   Response   Initiator   Timing
▼ Request Headers      View source
    Accept-Language: en-GB,en-US;q=0.9,en;q=0.8
    Referer: http://localhost:8888/phpbook/section_b/intro/index.php
    User-Agent: Mozilla/5.0 (Macintosh; Intel Mac OS X 10_15_7) AppleWebKit/537.36
    (KHTML, like Gecko) Chrome/93.0.4577.63 Safari/537.36
```

When the web server receives a request for a PHP page, it **responds** to that request by:

- Finding the PHP file requested in the URL
- Getting the PHP interpreter to process any PHP code that the PHP file contains
- Sending an HTML page back to the browser that requested the page

When the server sends the HTML page back to the browser, it also sends **HTTP response headers** to the browser, which hold data that the browser might need to know about the file that it is returning. Like the request headers, each response header has a name and a value (like a variable), which can be viewed in the browser's developer tools. In the screenshot below, the server is sending HTTP response headers that tell the browser the:

- File's media type and the encoding scheme used (to help ensure that it displays the file correctly)
- Date and time the file was sent
- Type of web server used to send the file

The response headers can be updated using:

- The PHP interpreter's settings (see p196-99)
- A built-in function called `header()` (see p226-27)

When a browser receives the HTML file, it is shown in the same way it would display any HTML page.

The server also sends back two pieces of data to indicate whether the request was successful or not:

- A three-digit **status code** for software to interpret
- A **reason phrase** that people can read

For successful requests, the status code is 200 and the reason phrase is OK. If a server cannot find a file, the status code is 404 and the reason phrase is Not found. When browsing the web, you may have seen a screen like this, indicating that a page was not found.

Not Found

The requested URL /code/section_b/c5/test.php was not found on this server.

The table below shows the most common status codes and reason phrases. Codes such as 301 (moved permanently) and 404 (not found) help search engines index sites when they find links to pages that have been deleted or moved to a new URL.

STATUS CODE	REASON PHRASE
200	OK
301	Moved permanently
307	Temporary redirect
403	Forbidden
404	Not found
500	Internal server error

```
×   Headers   Preview   Response   Timing

▼ Response Headers      view source

TYPE & ENCODING →    Content-Type: text/html; charset=UTF-8
      DATE SENT →    Date: Fri, 15 Jan 2021 15:47:46 GMT
         SERVER →    Server: Apache/2.4.46 (Unix) OpenSSL/1.0.2u PHP/8.0.0
```

HOW DATA IS SENT USING HTTP GET AND POST

HTTP specifies two ways that browsers can send data to the server: HTTP GET puts the data in the query string at the end of the URL. HTTP POST adds the data to the HTTP headers.

When sending data to a web page via **HTTP GET**, the browser puts the data in a query string and adds it to the end of the URL for the page. A question mark separates the URL for the page from the query string.

A query string can hold several name/value pairs. An equals sign separates each name from its value. To send more than one name/value pair, separate each one with an ampersand.

QUERY STRING

http://eg.link/hotel.php?location=Paris&year=2021

NAME   VALUE   NAME   VALUE

When sending data via **HTTP POST**, the browser adds extra name/value pairs to the HTTP request headers. The browser can send multiple name/value pairs to the server with each request.

The headers are not shown in the main browser window, but you can see them in the developer tools that come with most browsers. Below, you can see three headers and their corresponding values.

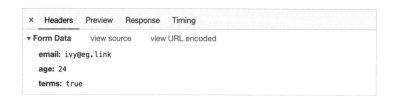

HOW DATA IS SENT FROM LINKS AND FORMS

HTML uses links and forms to send additional data to the server at the same time as requesting a page.

A link can use a query string to send extra data to the server. The data in the query string usually tells the server to get specific information and display that data in the page that it returns.

Typically, HTTP GET is used when a browser wants to get information from the server, and that information would be the same for every visitor to the site. For example, when they:

- Click links to display specific information
- Enter a search term into a form

Programmers sometimes refer to this type of request as a **safe interaction** because the user is not held accountable for the task they perform (for example., they are not agreeing to terms and conditions or purchasing a product).

Forms have inputs that allow users to enter text or numbers, select one of a list of options, or check a box. The form data can be added to the query string or sent in the HTTP headers.

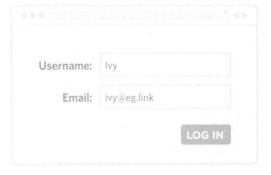

Typically, HTTP POST is used when a user is sending (or posting) information to the server that either identifies them or is used to update the data stored about them on the server. For example, when they:

- Sign into their personal account
- Purchase a product
- Subscribe to a service
- Agree to terms and conditions

In these situations, the user can be held accountable for their actions because they have to fill in the form, then submit it.

SECURING DATA SENT TO OR FROM A SERVER

When sensitive data is sent between a browser and a server, it should be encrypted. **Encryption** encodes data so that it cannot be read. **Decryption** turns the data back into a format that can be read.

When data is sent across the Internet, it can travel across different networks, passing through many routers and servers to reach its destination. During this journey, unauthorized parties could access the data and try to read it.

Any website that collects information about its members, or displays their personal data to them in a page, has a responsibility to ensure that data is transferred securely between the browser and server.

To send data securely between a browser and server, websites use **HyperText Transfer Protocol Secure (HTTPS)**. HTTPS adds extra rules to HTTP that govern how data should be sent securely between browsers and servers.

To send data securely across the Internet, it must be encrypted. This involves altering the data so that, even if it were intercepted during its journey, people would not be able to read it.

Messages are encrypted by replacing the original characters with a different set of characters. This is done using a set of rules known as a **cipher**.

The recipient of the message then needs to decrypt the message in order to make it readable again. To decrypt the message, the recipient needs to know how the message was encrypted.

The data needed to decrypt the message is known as a **key** because it "unlocks" the message.

1. When the user submits a form, the browser encrypts the data.

2. During transit, the encrypted data cannot be read.

3. The server uses a key to decrypt the data.

NKFAyGCNYKdbNCDTA+XIwR698oP
pAdN1ghyUmRPtkE8y2evzf8LEMe
rOQ89N6XJN2AFt919bAr+qk/qSv
C6b/dRAbb6NqIYXqc6sOIZta/VZ
lUwJTUJHOIo6Qj68+paMgZX/6wX
XOf2VWLxxBM7XwU7ufVZ53VLQA+
mz/wA4jbAFevz8y2f8dbNCBW2wA

To encrypt and decrypt the data sent between browsers and servers using HTTPS, a **certificate** must be installed on the web server. It tells the browser how to encrypt information it sends that server.

In order to obtain a certificate to install on a web server, you must follow these three steps:

1. Create a **certificate signing request** (CSR). These are generated by the web server the site lives on. They look like a series of random characters.

2. Purchase a certificate from a company called a **certificate authority** (CA). They ask for a certificate signing request, and information about the website and its owner. CAs charge per year for the certificate. A list of popular certificate authorities is shown here: `http://notes.re/certificate-authorities/`

3. Install the certificate (which is a text file) on the server the site runs on.

NOTE: Certificates are not always issued immediately, so they must be obtained before a site is due to go live.

When developing a site locally using MAMP or XAMPP, you can configure the web server to run using HTTPS without purchasing a certificate. You can see instructions on how to do this here: `http://notes.re/local-certificates/` To get a CSR and install a certificate on a hosting company's servers, check their support files.

Once a certificate has been installed on the web server, if a browser requests a URL for the site using `https://` rather than `http://` then the:

- Browser encrypts the request and HTTP request headers
- Server encrypts the page it returns and the HTTP response headers

When `https://` is being used, browsers usually display a padlock icon in the address bar.

Historically, HTTPS used two different protocols (set of rules) to add encryption to the requests and responses sent using HTTP:

- Secure Sockets Layer (**SSL**)
- Transport Layer Security (**TLS**)

You often hear people use the terms SSL and TLS interchangeably, but technically they are different.

You can think of TLS as being like a more recent version of SSL. TLS is the protocol that you should be using on your site.

ENCODING SCHEMES

Computers represent text, images and audio using **binary data**, which is made up of a series of 0s and 1s. **Encoding schemes** translate the things you see or hear into the 0s and 1s that the computer processes.

Understanding the role of encoding schemes is important because, if a computer uses the wrong encoding scheme to translate between the binary data and the text, images and audio that you see and hear, the data will not display/play correctly.

All of the data a computer processes and stores is represented using **bits** (**binary digits**). A bit is a 0 or a 1. So, everything in your computer (the letters you type, images you see, audio you hear) is represented in 0s and 1s. Below, you can see the binary equivalent of each letter in the word HELLO:

H	E	L	L	O
01001000	01000101	00101100	00101100	01001111

As this shows, even simple data requires a lot of bits. A series of 8 bits is called a **byte**.

Encoding schemes are rules that a computer uses to translate between text, images and audio and the binary data (combinations of 0s and 1s) the computer processes and stores.

- When you type text, upload images or record audio, an encoding scheme is used to translate that content into 0s and 1s.
- When the computer shows you text and images or plays an audio file, it uses an encoding scheme to translate the 0s and 1s into things you can see or hear.

Image encoding schemes specify how to represent images using bits. Computer images are made up of squares called pixels. Below, you can see how a basic black and white heart icon can be represented using 0s and 1s. Every white square is represented by a 0 and every black square is a represented by a 1.

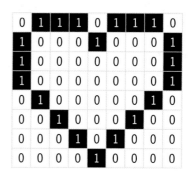

To recreate color images, the computer must know what color each pixel is, which requires more data. Different image formats (such as GIF, JPEG, PNG, and WebP) use different encoding schemes to represent the color of each pixel using 0s and 1s.

To manipulate the image, a computer can change the data it stores for each pixel. For example, a filter could be used to darken or lighten each pixel of the image, or an image could be cropped by removing pixels from the edges.

Character encoding schemes specify how to represent text using bits, and some character encoding schemes support more characters than others. The more characters an encoding scheme supports; the more bytes of data it needs in order to handle those characters.

When you create a website, in order to support an international audience, you should use a character encoding scheme that includes the characters used by the languages of those who visit your site.

ASCII

ASCII is an early character encoding scheme that uses 7 bits of data to represent each character. One drawback with ASCII is that there are only 128 possible combinations of 0 and 1 using 7 binary digits, so there are not enough combinations to support all of the characters used in every language. In fact, ASCII only supports 95 text characters.

ISO 8859-1

ISO 8859-1 uses 8 bits (1 byte) of data to represent each character. The extra bit of data means that there are enough combinations of 0 and 1 to represent the same characters as ASCII as well as the accented characters used in Western European languages. But it does not support languages that use different character sets, such as Chinese, Japanese or Russian.

UTF-8

UTF-8 represents all of the characters from every language, so it is the best character encoding scheme to use when creating websites.

To support these languages, UTF-8 needs up to four bytes of data to represent each character (four sets of 8 combinations of 0 and 1). Characters represented using more than one byte of data are known as **multi-byte characters**. For example, below you can see the binary equivalents for three different currency symbols:

SYMBOL	BINARY	BYTES
$	00100100	1
£	11000010 10100011	2
€	11100010 10000010 10101100	3

It is important to understand how character encoding schemes work because they:

- Need to be specified in several places
- Affect which characters you can use
- Determine which built-in functions can be used

BUILT-IN FUNCTIONS

Some of the PHP interpreter's built-in functions have a parameter that is used to specify the character encoding scheme that is being used.

There are also some built-in functions that work with a specific character encoding scheme. For example, PHP has a function that counts the number of characters in a string. This function was added to PHP when the default character encoding scheme was ISO 8859-1, and the function worked by counting the number of bytes a string uses (because each character used 1 byte of data). When PHP started to support UTF-8, this function gave inaccurate results because each character could use more than one byte. Therefore, a new built-in function was added that could count multi-byte characters.

PHP SETTINGS

When the PHP interpreter creates a page to send back to the browser, it tells the browser the character encoding scheme it used so that it can display the data correctly. The PHP interpreter has settings that specify the encoding scheme used to create the HTML pages it is sending back and, if the encoding scheme is not set correctly, the browser may show a ◆ symbol for characters it does not understand (or it might not show them at all).

CODE EDITORS

Because the PHP files themselves are text, code editors usually allow you to specify the character encoding scheme it should use to save the PHP files. The following link shows you how to set the character encoding scheme in some popular code editors: `http://notes.re/editors/set-encoding` If you see an option that says UTF-8 without BOM, you should select that option.

In Section C, you will also see that databases need to know the encoding scheme that a website uses.

THE PHP INTERPRETER'S BUILT-IN TOOLKIT

Throughout this section of the book, you will meet tools that are built into the PHP interpreter to help you create dynamic web pages.

You have seen that the PHP interpreter is a piece of software that runs on a web server.

When you open software on a desktop or laptop computer (such as a word processor or image editing software), there is a graphical user interface (GUI). The toolbars and menu options in the GUI are used to perform tasks that the software was designed to accomplish, and the results are shown on screen.

The PHP interpreter does not have a GUI. Instead, the PHP interpreter has a set of built-in arrays, functions, and classes that the PHP code in your PHP files can use to perform tasks that it commonly needs to when processing data and creating HTML pages to send back to the browser.

The PHP interpreter also uses text files to allow the control of options and preferences, and record any errors that may occur.

SUPERGLOBAL ARRAYS
p190-191

Every time a browser requests a PHP page, the PHP interpreter creates a set of arrays called **superglobal arrays** that hold data that can be accessed and used by the PHP code in that page.

The superglobal arrays are all associative arrays, so you need to know:

- What the arrays are called
- The keys in each of the arrays
- What each of those keys stores

Once the PHP interpreter has created the HTML page and sent it back to the browser, the data in these arrays is forgotten because the data only applies to that individual request for the page.

The next time the file runs, it will be able to access a set of superglobal arrays with data related to *that* specific request.

BUILT-IN FUNCTIONS
p192-193 and Chapter 5

The **built-in functions** can be compared to the commands found in the menus of software that has a GUI. For example, one function searches a string for characters and replaces them with other characters, like the search and replace function of a word processor. Instead of using a menu item in the GUI, you call the function in your PHP code.

In Chapter 3, you saw how to create a function definition and call the function. You call built-in functions in the same way but you do not include a function definition in the page because it is built into the PHP interpreter.

In order to use the built-in functions, you need to know the:

- Function name
- Parameter(s) it requires
- Value that it will return (or what it displays on the page)

BUILT-IN CLASSES
p318-27

The **built-in classes** are used to create objects that represent things programmers often need to deal with. For example, the `DateTime` class is used to create objects that represent dates and times. The class has properties and methods that let you work with the dates and times that an object created with it represents.

In Chapter 4, you saw how to write class definitions and use them to create objects. You do not include a class definition in a page when creating an object using a built-in class, because it is built into the PHP interpreter.

To use the built-in classes, you need to know how to create an object using that class, and what:

- Properties it has
- Methods it has
- Parameters each method has
- Value each method returns

ERROR MESSAGES
p194-195 and Chapter 10

If the PHP interpreter comes across errors in the code it is trying to run, it will generate an error message.

When a site is being developed, error messages should be displayed in the page that the PHP interpreter sends back to the browser. This enables the developers to immediately see any errors that occur when they try to run the page.

When a site goes live, the errors should be hidden from visitors. Because developers cannot see the errors as they occur in real time (they cannot look over the shoulders of every user), the error messages are saved to a text file called a **log file** that is stored on the server. The developers then check the log files to see if any errors were encountered that were missed when the site was being developed.

SETTINGS
p196-199

Desktop software often has menu options that bring up windows that allow users to control preferences or options for how the software operates. For example, the settings of a word processor might let the user select the paper size or default language that a document is in.

Because the PHP interpreter and web server do not have a GUI, they use text files to control a range of settings. For example, there are settings that control whether the PHP interpreter should show the error messages on the screen or save them to a log file, and where the error log file should live on the server.

These text files can be edited using the same code editor that you use to create the PHP pages.

SUPERGLOBAL ARRAYS

The $_SERVER superglobal array is an example of one of the superglobal arrays that the PHP interpreter creates each time a page is requested. Each superglobal array has data that the page's PHP code can use.

All of the superglobal arrays are associative arrays. You need to know the name of the array, the keys each array has, and the data that they hold.

Below, you can see what the $_SERVER superglobal array stores. It holds data about the:

- Browser (which is sent in the HTTP headers)
- Type of HTTP request (GET or POST)
- URL that was requested
- Location of the file on the server

The data that the superglobal arrays store is retrieved in the same way any associative array is accessed. To store the IP address of the user's browser in a variable called $ip you would use the following:

SUPERGLOBAL ARRAY

$ip = $_SERVER['REMOTE_ADDR'];

KEY

KEY	PURPOSE
$_SERVER['REMOTE_ADDR']	Browser's IP address
$_SERVER['HTTP_USER_AGENT']	Type of browser used to request the page
$_SERVER['HTTP_REFERER']	If the visitor came to this page via a link, a browser can send the URL of the page that linked to this one. Not all browsers send this data.
$_SERVER['REQUEST_METHOD']	The type of HTTP request: GET or POST
$_SERVER['HTTPS']	Only added to array if page accessed using HTTPS; if so, its value is true
$_SERVER['HTTP_HOST']	The host name (could be a domain name, IP address, or localhost)
$_SERVER['REQUEST_URI']	The URI (*after* the host name) used to request this page
$_SERVER['QUERY_STRING']	Any data in the query string
$_SERVER['SCRIPT_NAME']	Path from the document root folder to the file currently being executed
$_SERVER['SCRIPT_FILENAME']	Path from the filesystem root to the file currently being executed
$_SERVER['DOCUMENT_ROOT']	Path from the filesystem root to document root of the file being executed

The difference between a document root and filesystem root is described here: http://notes.re/php/filepaths

DATA IN THE $_SERVER SUPERGLOBAL ARRAY

Each element of the $_SERVER superglobal array stores a different piece of information about the request or the file that has been requested.

Below, individual values stored in the $_SERVER superglobal array are written out by selecting the data in the different keys of the array.

PHP

section_b/intro/server-superglobal.php

```
<table>
  <tr><th colspan="2" class="title">Data About Browser Sent in HTTP Headers  </th></tr>
  <tr><th>Browser's IP address      </th><td><?= $_SERVER['REMOTE_ADDR'] ?>      </td></tr>
  <tr><th>Type of browser           </th><td><?= $_SERVER['HTTP_USER_AGENT'] ?></td></tr>
  <tr><th colspan="2" class="title">HTTP Request                              </th></tr>
  <tr><th>Host name                 </th><td><?= $_SERVER['HTTP_HOST'] ?>       </td></tr>
  <tr><th>URI after host name       </th><td><?= $_SERVER['REQUEST_URI'] ?>     </td></tr>
  <tr><th>Query string              </th><td><?= $_SERVER['QUERY_STRING'] ?>    </td></tr>
  <tr><th>HTTP request method       </th><td><?= $_SERVER['REQUEST_METHOD'] ?> </td></tr>
  <tr><th colspan="2" class="title">Location of the File Being Executed        </th></tr>
  <tr><th>Document root             </th><td><?= $_SERVER['DOCUMENT_ROOT'] ?>   </td></tr>
  <tr><th>Path from document root   </th><td><?= $_SERVER['SCRIPT_NAME'] ?>     </td></tr>
  <tr><th>Absolute path             </th><td><?= $_SERVER['SCRIPT_FILENAME'] ?></td></tr>
</table>
```

RESULT

DATA ABOUT BROWSER SENT IN HTTP HEADERS	
BROWSER'S IP ADDRESS	::1
TYPE OF BROWSER	Mozilla/5.0 (Macintosh; Intel Mac OS X 10_15_7) AppleWebKit/605.1.15 (KHTML, like Gecko) Version/14.0.2 Safari/605.1.15
HTTP REQUEST	
HOST NAME	localhost:8888
URI AFTER HOST NAME	/phpbook/section_b/intro/server-superglobal.php
QUERY STRING	
HTTP REQUEST METHOD	GET
LOCATION OF THE FILE BEING EXECUTED	
DOCUMENT ROOT	/Users/Jon/Sites/localhost
PATH FROM DOCUMENT ROOT	/phpbook/section_b/intro/server-superglobal.php
ABSOLUTE PATH	/Users/Jon/Sites/localhost/phpbook/section_b/intro/server-superglobal.php

BUILT-IN FUNCTIONS SHOWING VARIABLE DATA

The `var_dump()` function is an example of one of PHP's built-in functions. It is used when developing sites to check what value(s) a variable is holding and what data type they are.

To use (or call) a built-in function, you only need to know its name, its parameters, and what values it will return or display in the page.

`var_dump()` has one parameter: a variable name. It does not return a value; it shows the values stored in the variable in the HTML page that is created.

```
var_dump($variable);
```

If the variable holds a scalar value (a string, number, or integer), it shows the data type and the value.

If the value is a string, the number of characters in the string is shown in parentheses after the data type.

```
DATA TYPE   LENGTH   VALUE
string(3) "Ivy"
```

If the variable holds an array, it shows the word `array` and the number of elements in the array in parentheses.

Then, in a pair of curly braces, it shows the key, the data type of the value, and the value of each element.

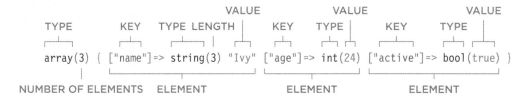

If the variable holds an object, it shows the word `object`, the class name, and the number of properties.

For each property, it shows the name, data type of the value, and the value. (Methods are not shown.)

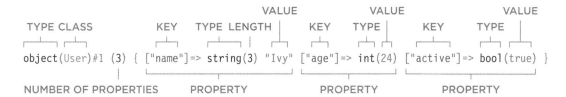

SHOWING THE CONTENTS OF A VARIABLE

section_b/intro/var-dump.php

```php
<?php
$username    = 'Ivy';

$user_array  = [
    'name'    => 'Ivy',
    'age'     => 24,
    'active'  => true,
];

class User
{
    public $name;
    public $age;
    public $active;
    public function __construct($name, $age, $active) {
        $this->name   = $name;
        $this->age    = $age;
        $this->active = $active;
    }
}

$user_object = new User('Ivy', 24, true);
?>
...
<p>Scalar: <?php var_dump($username); ?></p>
<p>Array:  <?php var_dump($user_array); ?></p>
<p>Object: <?php var_dump($user_object); ?></p>
```

This example creates variables to store a scalar value, an array and an object, then uses var_dump() to show what each variable holds.

1. A variable called $username stores the name of a member of a website as a string.

2. An array is stored in a variable called $user_array. The array stores the member's name, age, and if they are active.

3. A class called User is created to act as a template for objects that represent the members of a site. It has three properties: the user's name, age, and if they are active or not.

4. An object is created using the User class and is stored in a variable called $user_object.

5. The values stored in the variables are displayed using the var_dump() function.

NOTE: If you add HTML <pre> tags around each PHP block, this will spread the data that is displayed over separate lines making it easier to read.

```
<pre>
<?php var_dump($username) ?>
</pre>
```

RESULT

```
Scalar: string(3) "Ivy"

Array: array(3) { ["name"]=> string(3) "Ivy" ["age"]=> int(24) ["active"]=> bool(true) }

Object: object(User)#1 (3) { ["name"]=> string(3) "Ivy" ["age"]=> int(24) ["active"]=> bool(true) }
```

ERROR MESSAGES

When there is a problem with the PHP code, the PHP interpreter generates error messages which help you fix any mistakes.

If the PHP interpreter comes across a problem with the code it is running, it generates an error message. There are two ways to view the messages; they can be:

- Shown in the HTML that is sent to the browser
- Saved to a text file known as an **error log**

Each error message contains four pieces of data that help you locate the problem so you can fix it:

- The **error level** (or severity of the error; the levels are described in the table below)
- A description of the error
- The file that contained the error
- The line number where the error was found

When developing a site, error messages should be shown in the HTML pages that the PHP interpreter sends back to the browser so that the developer can see them immediately. When a site is live, they should be saved to an error log (a text file on the server); they should not be shown to visitors. You will learn how to change this setting on p352-53.

The code for this section of the book displays errors in the HTML page. If you try the exercises that follow many of the examples in this section, do not be disheartened if you see error messages. The messages help you find out where there are problems with your code and how to fix them. You learn more about handling errors in Chapter 10.

ERROR LEVEL	ERROR DESCRIPTION		PHP FILE	LINE NUMBER

```
Error: description goes here in test.php on line 21
```

LEVEL	DESCRIPTION
PARSE	Errors in the syntax of the PHP code prevent the PHP interpreter from trying to run the page at all
FATAL	An error in the PHP code that stops any further code (after the error) from running
WARNING	Something that will *probably* cause a problem, but the intepreter tries to run the rest of the page
NOTICE	Something that *could* indicate an problem, but the intepreter tries to run the rest of the page
DEPRECATED	PHP code that is likely to be removed from future versions of PHP
STRICT	PHP code that could be written in a better way and will be more future-proof

EXAMPLES OF ERROR MESSAGES

Error messages can look cryptic at first, but the information they contain helps you find out what is wrong with your code.

```php
PHP                                    section_b/intro/error1.php

   <?php
①  echo $name;
②  echo ' welcome to our site.';
   ?>
```

```
RESULT

   Warning: Undefined variable $name in
   /Users/Jon/Sites/localhost/phpbook/section_b/intro/error1.php on line 2
   welcome to our site.
```

1. The page tries to write out a variable that has not been created. A warning says there is an Undefined variable $name in error1.php on line 2. Because the error level is a warning, the interpreter continues to run.

(Up to PHP 7.4, this error created a notice, not a warning.)

2. The page writes out the text welcome to our site (which you can see on the last line of the result box).

```php
PHP                                    section_b/intro/error2.php

   <?php
③ ⎡ echo 'Hello ';
   ⎣ username = 'Ivy';
   ?>
```

```
RESULT

   Parse error: syntax error, unexpected token "=" in
   /Users/Jon/Sites/localhost/phpbook/section_b/intro/error2.php on line 3
```

3. The echo statement *would* write out the word Hello but the next line creates a parse error which prevents the PHP interpreter from running any of the code in the page.

The error is caused by a missing $ symbol at the start of the $username variable.

You will learn more about troubleshooting and error messages in Chapter 10.

SETTINGS & OPTIONS FOR THE PHP INTERPRETER

The settings and preferences for software on a desktop computer are often controlled via a menu in the user interface. The settings of the PHP interpreter and Apache web server are controlled using text files.

The Apache web server and PHP interpreter have settings that control things such as the default character encoding used, whether to show users error messages if there is a problem, and how much memory an individual web page is allowed to consume. The files that are used to control these settings can be edited in your code editor.

php.ini

A text file called `php.ini` controls the default settings for the PHP interpreter. The settings in this file can be changed, but must not be removed. Once changes have been made, the web server must be restarted for the changes to take effect.

To find where your `php.ini` file is located, PHP has a built-in function called `phpinfo()`. It displays the PHP interpreter's settings in an HTML table (see right-hand page). The path to the `php.ini` file is in the first table next to the title **Loaded configuration file**.

Some hosting companies do not give you access to the `php.ini` file because it usually controls how all the PHP files on that web server run (and would therefore affect other sites on the same server). If you do not have access to `php.ini`, you can use `.htaccess` to control many of the same settings.

If one file needs different settings to the other PHP files on the web server, a built-in PHP function called `ini_set()` can be used override some of the settings in the `php.ini` file.

httpd.conf

A text file called `httpd.conf` controls default settings for the Apache web server. Several settings overlap with those in `php.ini`, and Apache must be restarted for the changes to take effect. Hosts do not always give customers access to `httpd.conf` as it usually controls the settings for the whole web server.

.htaccess

Apache lets users add files called `.htaccess` to any folder in the document root of a site. The rules in an `.htaccess` file only apply to the files in the same directory as the `.htaccess` file and any of its child folders and they will override the settings in `httpd.conf` and `php.ini`.

Changes to `.htaccess` files take effect as soon as the file is saved. But you should only use `.htaccess` if you cannot use `httpd.conf` or `php.ini` to perform the task as it is slower than changing default settings.

Most hosting companies let you to create `.htaccess` files, but they may restrict the settings you can use (such as the maximum size of uploaded files).

Operating systems treat `.htaccess` files as hidden files so you may need to tell your file explorer or FTP program to show them. To learn how to view hidden files, go to: `http://notes.re/hidden_files`

The code for this book uses multiple `.htaccess` files so that different chapters can have different settings.

VIEWING SETTINGS FOR THE PHP INTERPRETER

Like most software, the PHP interpreter has settings (or preferences) that control how it works. The built-in `phpinfo()` function displays tables that show the settings you can configure and their current values.

section_b/intro/phpinfo.php

```php
<?php phpinfo(); ?>
```

RESULT

The `phpinfo()` function creates a long set of tables that show the settings for the PHP interpreter and their default values. These settings affect every PHP file that the PHP interpreter runs.

The text files described on the left-hand page can be used to change these settings.

The table below describes some of the settings that you will need to know how to control in this section. They can be found under the heading *Core* unless noted.

SETTING	DESCRIPTION
default_charset	Default character encoding. (This should be set to UTF-8.)
display_errors	Turn on/off errors on in HTML page. On for development. Off when site goes live.
log_errors	Turn on/off saving of errors to a log file. On when the site goes live.
error_log	Path to the log file that errors can be written to when the site goes live.
error_reporting	What errors should be recorded. (E_ALL is the setting to show all errors.)
upload_max_filesize	Maximum size of a single file a browser can upload to the server.
max_execution_time	Maximum number of seconds a script can run before the PHP interpreter stops it.
date.timezone	Default timezone used by the server. Shown under the heading Date.

CHANGING INTERPRETER SETTINGS: php.ini

php.ini is a file that allows you to edit the PHP interpreter's settings. You must only edit the values it uses; do not delete any of the settings.

The php.ini file is a long file as it contains all of the settings for the PHP interpreter. It also has a lot of comments to explain the settings. Anything after a semi-colon is a comment.

Settings are controlled using **directives** which are like variables. Only edit the values of the directives (do not delete any). To find a setting you want to control, open up the file and search for that setting.

For a full list of directives see:
http://php.net/manual/en/ini.list.php

Each directive starts on a new line and is made up of:

- An option to change
- An assignment operator
- The value it should have

When the value is a:

- String: place it in quotes
- Number: do not use quotes
- Boolean: do not use quotes

```
date.timezone   = "Europe/Rome"
display_errors  = On
```

OPTION   VALUE

php.ini (not included in code download)   `PHP`

```
; A selection of the values that can be changed in the php.ini file with comments
default_charset      = "UTF-8"          ; Default character set used
display_errors       = On               ; Whether or not to show errors on screen
log_errors           = On               ; Write errors to a log file
error_reporting      = E_ALL            ; Show all errors
upload_max_filesize  = 32M              ; Max size of a file that can be uploaded
post_max_size        = 32M              ; Max amount of data sent via HTTP POST
max_execution_time   = 30               ; Max execution time of each script, in seconds
memory_limit         = 128M             ; Max amount of memory a script may consume
date.timezone        = "Europe/Rome"    ; Default timezone
```

CHANGING SERVER SETTINGS: .htaccess

.htaccess files can be added to any directory on an Apache web server. It will override the settings of the PHP interpreter for files in that folder. It also affects child folders and the files they contain.

An .htaccess file only needs to contain the settings that you want to override in php.ini. The settings use the same names and values as those in php.ini except they are preceded by:

- php_flag if the directive's value is a boolean (representing a setting that can be on or off)
- php_value if there are more than two options (e.g. numbers, locations or encoding schemes)

Comments start with a # symbol and must appear on a new line (not the same line as the directive).

The .htaccess file below is included with the code download for this book. It will ensure errors are shown in the HTML pages in many of the examples.

If you do not see it (or it looks grayed out), this is because operating systems treat it as a hidden file.

To learn how to show hidden files see:
http://notes.re/hidden_files

The .htaccess file can also control options of the Apache web server that the php.ini file cannot.

```
php_value date.timezone    "Europe/London"
php_flag  display_errors   On
```

    TYPE   OPTION   VALUE

PHP   section_b/intro/.htaccess

```
# sample .htaccess file used in code examples (options described in php.ini example)
php_value  default_charset       "UTF-8"
php_flag   display_errors        On
php_flag   log_errors            Off
php_value  error_reporting       -1
php_value  upload_max_filesize   32M
php_value  post_max_size         32M
php_value  max_execution_time    30
php_value  memory_limit          128M
php_value  date.timezone         "Europe/London"
```

IN THIS SECTION

DYNAMIC WEB PAGES

5 BUILT-IN FUNCTIONS

Each of PHP's built-in functions performs a specific task programmers often need to achieve when working with data. The built-in functions are introduced first because they are used in each chapter of the rest of the book.

6 GETTING DATA FROM BROWSERS

This chapter shows how the PHP interpreter can access data sent from a browser, check that the data the page needs has been provided, and check that it is in the right format. You also learn how to make sure that data supplied by visitors is safe to display in a page.

7 IMAGES & FILES

If you allow users to submit images or other files to a website, you need to know how the PHP interpreter handles those files. This chapter also shows you how to perform tasks such as resizing images and creating smaller versions of images known as thumbnails.

8 DATES & TIMES

Dates and times are written in many different ways, so you need to know how PHP can help you format dates and times consistently. You will also learn how to perform common tasks such as representing an interval of time and handling recurring events.

9 COOKIES & SESSIONS

This chapter shows how text files called cookies can be saved in a user's browser in order to store information about that visitor. It also shows how sessions can be used to store information on the web server for a short period of time (such as a single visit to a site).

10 ERROR HANDLING

Everyone makes mistakes when writing code, which result in the PHP interpreter creating error messages. This chapter shows you how to read these error messages, as well as techniques that help you find and resolve errors in your code.

5

BUILT-IN FUNCTIONS

This chapter introduces a set of functions that are built into the PHP interpreter. Each function performs a specific task.

The function definitions for built-in functions are built into the PHP interpreter, which means they do not need to be included in a PHP page before they are called. They were designed to perform tasks that web developers often need to achieve when creating dynamic web pages and save them from having to write their own functions to perform those tasks.

To call a built-in function, you need to know its name, what parameters it has, and what data it will return. Therefore, this chapter contains several tables that show the function names and parameters, followed by descriptions of the functions, and what values they return.

The first set of functions are grouped in terms of the data types they are used to work with: strings, numbers, and arrays. Later in the chapter, you will also see:

- How to create constants (which are like variables whose values cannot change once set)
- A function that is used to control the HTTP headers that are sent back to the browser when the PHP interpreter returns a page that has been requested
- A set of functions that allow you to get information about files on the server

The functions you meet in this chapter will be used throughout the rest of this book.

UPPER & LOWERCASE, CHECKING LENGTH

These functions transform text into upper or lowercase characters and count the number of characters or words in the string.

The following functions are designed to work with text (the string data type). They take a string as an argument, update it, and return the amended string.

For example, the `strtolower()` function takes a string and converts all the text to lowercase. It then returns the updated value.

CHANGING THE CASE OF CHARACTERS

FUNCTION	DESCRIPTION
strtolower(*$string*)	Returns a string with all characters in lowercase.
strtoupper(*$string*)	Returns a string with all characters in uppercase.
ucwords(*$string*)	Returns a string with the first letter of every word in uppercase.

COUNTING CHARACTERS AND WORDS

FUNCTION	DESCRIPTION
strlen(*$string*)	Returns the number of characters in the string. Spaces and punctuation count as characters. (See also mb_strlen() on p210-211 for multibyte characters.)
str_word_count(*$string*)	Returns the number of words in the string.

CONVERTING CASE & COUNTING CHARACTERS

PHP   section_b/c05/case-and-character-count.php

```php
<?php
① $text = 'Home sweet home';
?>
<?php include 'includes/header.php'; ?>
<p>
    <b>Lowercase:</b>
② <?= strtolower($text) ?><br>
    <b>Uppercase:</b>
③ <?= strtoupper($text) ?><br>
    <b>Uppercase first letter:</b>
④ <?= ucwords($text) ?><br>
    <b>Character count:</b>
⑤ <?= strlen($text) ?><br>
    <b>Word count:</b>
⑥ <?= str_word_count($text) ?>
</p>
<?php include 'includes/footer.php'; ?>
```

RESULT

```
Lowercase: home sweet home
Uppercase: HOME SWEET HOME
Uppercase first letter Home Sweet Home
Character count: 15
Word count: 3
```

1. A string saying Home sweet home is stored in a variable called $text. This will be used as an argument when each of the functions is called.

2. The strtolower() function is called. The function converts the text to lowercase and returns that value. The value that the function returns is written out to the page using the shorthand for the echo command.

3. The strtoupper() function returns the string in uppercase.

4. The ucwords() function returns the string with the first letter of each word in uppercase.

5. The strlen() function counts how many characters are in the string and returns that number.

6. The str_word_count() counts the number of words in the string and returns that number.

TRY: In Step 1, change the string to read PHP and MySQL, then save the file and refresh the page.

FINDING CHARACTERS IN A STRING

These functions look for one or more characters in a string. If they find a match, they return the position of that character. If no match is found, they return `false`.

Each character in a string has a **position**; a number that starts at 0. So the first character is at position 0, the second is at position 1, and so on.

```
H  o  m  e     s  w  e  e  t     h  o  m  e
0  1  2  3  4  5  6  7  8  9  10 11 12 13 14
```

When you look for a set of characters inside a string, those characters are called a **substring**.

Some of the functions are **case-sensitive**; so a match is only found if the string and substring have the same combination of upper and lowercase characters.

FUNCTION	DESCRIPTION
strpos(*$string*, *$substring[, $offset]*)	Returns position of first match for substring (case-sensitive). If `offset` is used, it only looks *after* this character position.
stripos(*$string*, *$substring[, $offset]*)	Case-insensitive version of `strpos()`.
strrpos(*$string*, *$substring[, $offset]*)	Returns position of last match for substring (case-sensitive).
strripos(*$string*, *$substring[, $offset]*)	Case-insensitive version of `strrpos()`.
strstr(*$string*, *$substring*)	Returns text from first occurrence of a substring (including the substring) to the end of the string (case-sensitive).
stristr(*$string*, *$substring*)	Case-insensitive version of `strstr()`.
substr(*$string*, *$offset[, $characters]*)	Returns characters from the position specified in `$offset` to the end of the string. If the `$characters` parameter is used, it specifies the number of characters to return after `$offset`. For more options, see: http://notes.re/php/substr
* str_contains(*$string*, *$substring*)	Checks if a substring is found in a string, returns `true`/`false`.
* str_starts_with(*$string*, *$substring*)	Checks if string starts with substring, returns `true`/`false`.
* str_ends_with(*$string*, *$substring*)	Checks if string ends with substring, returns `true`/`false`.

The last three functions, marked with an asterisk were added in PHP 8; they are all case-sensitive.

NOTE: Optional parameters are shown in square brackets. Functions for multibyte characters are shown on p 210.

CHECKING FOR CHARACTERS IN A STRING

`section_b/c05/finding-characters.php`

```php
<?php
$text = 'Home sweet home';
?> ...
<b>First match (case-sensitive):</b>
<?= strpos($text, 'ho') ?><br>
<b>First match (not case-sensitive):</b>
<?= stripos($text, 'me', 5) ?><br>
<b>Last match (case-sensitive):</b>
<?= strrpos($text, 'Ho') ?><br>
<b>Last match (not case-sensitive):</b>
<?= strripos($text, 'Ho') ?><br>
<b>Text after first match (case-sensitive):</b>
<?= strstr($text, 'ho') ?><br>
<b>Text after first match (not case-sensitive):</b>
<?= stristr($text, 'ho') ?><br>
<b>Text between two positions:</b>
<?= substr($text, 5, 5) ?><br>
```

(1) (2) (3) (4) (5) (6) (7) (8)

RESULT

```
First match (case-sensitive): 11
First match (not case-sensitive): 13
Last match (case-sensitive): 0
Last match (not case-sensitive): 11
Text after first match (case-sensitive): home
Text after first match (not case-sensitive): Home sweet home
Text between two positions: sweet
```

1. The string Home sweet home is stored in `$text`.

2. The `strpos()` function is called to look for the first time the substring ho appears in the string. It returns 11.

3. The `stripos()` function is called to find the first time the substring me appears after position 5. It returns 13.

4. The `strrpos()` function is called to find the last time the substring Ho is found. It returns 0 because it is case-sensitive.

5. The `strripos()` function is called to find the last time the substring Ho is found. It returns 11 as it is not case-sensitive.

6. The `strstr()` function is called to get the text from the first occurrence of the substring ho. It returns home.

7. The `stristr()` function is called to get the text from the first occurrence of ho. It returns Home sweet home because it is not case-sensitive.

8. The `substr()` function is called and returns five characters, starting with the character in the fifth position.

TRY: In Step 1, change the string to say Home and family.

Then, in Step 8, use `substr()` to return the word and.

REMOVING AND REPLACING CHARACTERS

These functions can remove specified characters (including whitespace), replace characters (like a find and replace tool), and repeat a string a specified number of times.

The **trim** functions remove characters from a string. They can check for specific characters at the start and/or end of the string and delete them if they are present.

If you do not specify characters to remove, trim functions remove any whitespace found at the start and/or end of the string including spaces, tabs, carriage returns, and line feeds (soft returns).

The **replace** functions look for characters in a string. If a match is found, it replaces those characters with new characters. The **repeat** function repeats a string a fixed number of times.

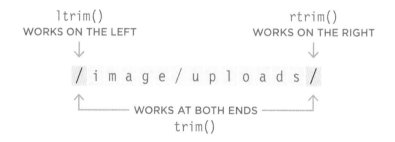

```
ltrim()                          rtrim()
WORKS ON THE LEFT            WORKS ON THE RIGHT
       ↓                            ↓
   / i m a g e / u p l o a d s /
       ↑                            ↑
       └───── WORKS AT BOTH ENDS ───┘
                  trim()
```

FUNCTION	DESCRIPTION
ltrim(*$string[, $delete]*)	Remove whitespace from the left-hand side of the string. If specified, $delete provides a set of characters that should be removed if they are found at the start of the string. It is case-sensitive.
rtrim(*$string[, $delete]*)	Removes whitespace from the right-hand side of the string.
trim(*$string[, $delete]*)	Removes whitespace from the left and right-hand sides of the string.
str_replace(*$old, $new, $string*)	Replaces the substring $old with the one in $new (case-sensitive).
str_ireplace(*$old, $new, $string*)	Replaces the substring $old with the one in $new (case-insensitive).
str_repeat(*$string, $repeats*)	Repeats the string a specified number of times.

REPLACING CHARACTERS IN A STRING

section_b/c05/removing-and-replacing-characters.php

```php
<?php
$text = '/images/uploads/';
?> ...
<b>Remove '/' from both ends:</b><br>
<?= trim($text, '/') ?><br>
<b>Remove '/' from the left of the string:</b><br>
<?= ltrim($text, '/') ?><br>
<b>Remove 's/' from the right of the string:</b><br>
<?= rtrim($text, 's/') ?><br>
<b>Replace 'images' with 'img':</b><br>
<?= str_replace('images', 'img', $text) ?><br>
<b>As above but case-insensitive:</b><br>
<?= str_ireplace('IMAGES', 'img', $text) ?><br>
<b>Repeat the string:</b><br>
<?= str_repeat($text, 2) ?></p>
```

(1) (2) (3) (4) (5) (6) (7)

RESULT

```
Remove '/' from both ends:
images/uploads
Remove '/' from the left of the string:
images/uploads/
Remove 's/' from the right of the string:
/images/upload
Replace 'images' with 'img':
/img/uploads/
As above but case-insensitive:
/img/uploads/
Repeat the string:
/images/uploads//images/uploads/
```

1. The path `'/images/uploads/'` is a string that is stored in a variable called `$text`.

2. The `trim()` function returns the string with / removed from the left and right of the text.

3. The `ltrim()` function returns the string with / removed from the left-hand side.

4. The `rtrim()` function returns the string with s/ removed from the right-hand side.

5. The `str_replace()` function returns the string with the letters images replaced with the letters img. It is case-sensitive.

6. The `str_ireplace()` function returns the string with the letters IMAGES replaced with the letters img. The substring search is case-insensitive, so it would find both IMAGES and images and replace them with img.

7. The `str_repeat()` function returns the string with all the characters repeated twice.

TRY: In Step 1, add a space before and after the file path, then refresh the page. The forward slashes / will not be removed in Steps 2, 3 or 4 because there is a space before or after them.

MULTIBYTE STRING FUNCTIONS

Some of the string functions you have seen so far return the wrong result if they are used with multibyte characters. The multibyte string functions below support all of the characters in UTF-8.

When text is encoded using UTF-8, some characters use more than one byte of data. E.g., the £ symbol uses two bytes and € uses three.

If you use multibyte characters as arguments for some of the string functions, they can produce an incorrect result (examples of inaccurate results are shown on the right-hand page).

The multibyte string functions shown below have the same names as functions you have met so far in this chapter but are preceded by the characters mb_.

Some string functions have no multibyte equivalent, e.g., trim() and str_replace(). They work with UTF-8 as long as it has been set as the default character encoding in php.ini or .htaccess files.

FUNCTION	DESCRIPTION
mb_strtoupper($string)	Returns string with all characters in uppercase.
mb_strtolower($string)	Returns string with all characters in lowercase.
mb_strlen($string)	Returns the number of characters in the string.
mb_strpos($string, $substring[, $offset])	Returns the position of the first place the substring is found (case-sensitive). If an $offset is specified, it only looks after this character position.
mb_stripos($string, $substring[, $offset])	Case-insensitive version of mb_strpos().
mb_strrpos($string, $substring[, $offset])	Returns position of last match for substring (case-sensitive).
mb_strripos($string, $substring[, $offset])	Case-insensitive version of mb_strrpos().
mb_strstr($string, $substring)	Returns text from the first occurrence of a substring (including the substring) to the end of the string (case-sensitive).
mb_stristr($string, $substring)	Case-insensitive version of mb_strstr().
mb_substr($string, $start[, $characters])	Returns characters from position specified in $start to the end of the string. If $characters is specified, it returns this number of characters after $start.

USING MULTIBYTE STRING FUNCTIONS

section_b/c05/multibyte-string-functions.php

```php
<?php
$text = 'Total: £444';
?> ...
<b>Character count using <code>strlen()</code>:</b>
<?= strlen($text) ?><br>
<b>Character count using <code>mb_strlen()</code>:</b>
<?= mb_strlen($text) ?><br>
<b>First match of 444 <code>strpos()</code>:</b>
<?= strpos($text, '444') ?><br>
<b>First match of 444 <code>mb_strpos()</code>:</b>
<?= mb_strpos($text, '444') ?><br>
```

RESULT

```
Character count using strlen(): 12
Character count using mb_strlen(): 11
First match of 444 strpos(): 9
First match of 444 mb_strpos(): 8
```

This example uses string functions with the £ symbol, which UTF-8 needs two bytes of data to encode.

1. A string is created using the £ symbol and stored in $text. It is 11 characters long.

2. The strlen() function works by counting the number of bytes taken to represent a string, not the number of characters in the string. This is why it says there are 12 characters in the string (not 11).

3. The function mb_strlen() takes into account the encoding that the PHP interpreter is using and displays the correct number of characters in the string as 11.

4. The strpos() function finds the first position of 444. The position is calculated using the number of bytes before the substring is found (not the number of characters). It returns 9, rather than 8.

5. mb_strpos() finds the first position of 444, correctly returning the number 8.

TRY: In Step 1, change the £ symbol in the string to the € symbol.

REGULAR EXPRESSIONS

Credit card numbers, zip codes and phone numbers use specific patterns of characters. Regular expressions describe a pattern of characters and PHP has built-in functions to check if those patterns are found in a string.

Regular expressions sit between two forward slashes. The pattern in the expression below describes:

[A-z] The letters A-z (upper/lowercase)
{3,9} occurring between 3 and 9 times

`/[A-z]{3,9}/`

The syntax for regular expressions can be quite complex, and there are entire books about how to write them, but these pages show you the basics.

If this expression was used to check the string Thomas was 1st! the PHP interpreter would find the **first** time that there is a sequence of 3-9 characters that use the uppercase or lowercase letters A-z. These characters are highlighted below:

T h o m a s   w a s   1 s t !

The table below demonstrates how to match specific characters, a range of characters, and characters at the start or end of a string.

EXPRESSION	DESCRIPTION	EXAMPLE
/1st/	Matches the characters 1st	Thomas was **1st**!
/[abcde]/	If characters are in square brackets, it matches any one of the letters; this matches any letter a, b, c, d or e	Thom**a**s was 1st!
/[K-Z]/	A hyphen in square brackets creates a range of characters to match. This matches any uppercase character between K and Z	**T**homas was 1st!
/[a-e]/	This matches any lowercase character between a and e	Thom**a**s was 1st!
/[0-9]/	This matches any number between 0 and 9	Thomas was **1**st!
/[A-z0-9]/	This matches any upper or lowercase letter A-z or number 0-9	**T**homas was 1st!
/^[A-Z]/	A caret ^ at the start of a pattern indicates that the string must start with these characters; this matches if the first character is A-Z	**T**homas was 1st!
/1st\!$/	A dollar $ at the end of a pattern indicates the string must end with the specified characters; this matches if the last characters are 1st!	Thomas was **1st!**
/\s/	Matches a space	Thomas**was** 1st!

The following characters have special meaning in regular expressions: \ / . | $ ( ) ^ ? { } + *

To create a pattern that matches any of these characters, place a **backslash** before the character.

EXPRESSION	DESCRIPTION	EXAMPLE
/[\!\?\(\)]/	Matches an exclamation mark, question mark or parentheses	Thomas was 1st**!**

You can add a **quantifier** to specify the number of times a pattern should appear in the string.

The examples below find characters that occur a specified number of times.

EXPRESSION	DESCRIPTION	EXAMPLE
/[a-z]+/	The plus sign + indicates one or more of the specified characters	**T**homas was 1st!
/[a-z]{3}/	A number in curly braces {} indicates exact number of times the pattern must be found	T**hom**as was 1st!
/[A-z]{3,5}/	Two numbers separated by a comma in curly braces {} indicate the minimum and maximum number of times the pattern must be found	T**homa**s was 1st!
/[a-z]{3,}/	A number, then a comma (without a second number) in curly braces is the minimum number of times the pattern can be found	T**homas** was 1st!

To look for a sequence of patterns, use one pattern followed by another.

Below, a match for the first pattern must be followed by a match for the second pattern.

EXPRESSION	DESCRIPTION	EXAMPLE
/[0-9][a-z]/	Matches a number 0-9 followed by a lowercase letter a-z	Thomas was **1s**t!

Placing parentheses around part of an expression creates a **group**. You can add a quantifier after the group to indicate how many times it should appear.

If you want to find one of a set of options, you can specify the options inside a group, and separate each option with a pipestem character.

EXPRESSION	DESCRIPTION	EXAMPLE
/[0-9]([a-z]{2})/	[0-9] matches any number 0-9; it is followed by ([a-z]{2}) which matches two lowercase letters	Thomas was **1st**!
/[1-31](st|nd|rd|th)/	[1-31] matches any number 1-31 followed by (st|nd|rd|th) which matches st, nd, rd or th	Thomas was **1st**!

REGULAR EXPRESSION FUNCTIONS

These functions check if a string contains a pattern of characters that are described by a regular expression. If they find a match, each one will perform a different task.

The functions below all use regular expressions to look for a specified pattern of characters in a string.

They perform tasks such as:

- Checking if the pattern is found
- Counting how many times a pattern is found
- Looking for the pattern of characters and replacing them with a new set of characters (like a find and replace feature in a word processor)

In each case, the function has parameters for the:

- Regular expression that describes the pattern of characters it is looking for (this goes in quotes because it is a string)
- String that it is looking for that pattern in

The function that will replace a matching set of characters with a new set of characters also needs to know what to replace those characters with.

FUNCTION	DESCRIPTION
preg_match($regex, $string)	Looks for a matching pattern in a string. It returns 1 if a match was found, 0 if no match was found, false if an error occurred.
preg_match_all($regex, $string)	Looks for a matching pattern in a string. It returns the number of matches found (0 if none found), or false if an error occurred.
preg_split($regex, $string)	Looks for a matching pattern in a string. It splits the string each time a match is found, then returns each of those parts in an indexed array.
preg_replace($regex, $replace, $string)	Replaces specified characters with an alternative string. It is similar to a find and replace tool in a word processor. It returns the string with characters replaced or null if an error occurred. To delete characters, replace them with a blank string.

NOTE: These function names start with the prefix preg (which stands for **P**erl **reg**ular expressions) because the regular expressions PHP uses follow those in another programming language called Perl.

USING REGULAR EXPRESSIONS

```php
<?php
$text = 'Using PHP\'s regular expression functions';
$path = 'code/section_b/c05/';

$match = preg_match('/PHP/', $text);
$path = preg_split('/\//', $path);
$text = preg_replace('/PHP/', '<em>PHP</em>', $text);
?> ...
<b>Was a match found?</b><br>
<?= ($match === 1) ? 'Yes' : 'No' ?><br><br>

<b>Parts of a path:</b><br>
<?php foreach($path as $part) { ?>
  <?= $part ?><br>
<?php } ?>

<b>Updated text:</b><br>
<?= $text ?>
```

Circled numbers mark lines: ① $text = 'Using PHP\'s regular expression functions'; ② $path = 'code/section_b/c05/'; ③ $match = preg_match('/PHP/', $text); ④ $path = preg_split('/\//', $path); ⑤ $text = preg_replace('/PHP/', '<em>PHP</em>', $text); ⑥ <?= ($match === 1) ? 'Yes' : 'No' ?>

 ⑦ foreach loop block ⑧ <?= $text ?>

RESULT

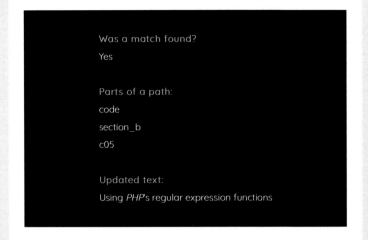

```
Was a match found?
Yes

Parts of a path:
code
section_b
c05

Updated text:
Using PHP's regular expression functions
```

1. Text is stored in a variable called $text.

2. A filepath is stored in a variable called $path.

3. The preg_match() function checks if the string PHP is found in the text that was stored in the variable called $text in Step 1. If it is found, $match stores 1.

4. The preg_split() function splits up the path that was stored in the $path variable in Step 2 each time there is a forward slash, and puts each part into a new element of an array.

5. The preg_replace() function looks for the letters PHP in the text that was stored in $text in Step 1. If it is found, then it is replaced with the same letters inside an HTML <em> element.

6. A ternary operator is used to check if the $match variable holds a value of 1. If it does then the word Yes is written out to the page. If it does not then the word No is shown instead.

7. A loop displays each element in the $path array on a new line.

8. The updated text stored in $text is displayed, with the characters PHP in <em> tags.

WORKING WITH NUMBERS

In addition to the mathematical operators you met in Chapter 1, there are functions for common tasks that programmers perform with numbers.

FUNCTION	DESCRIPTION
round(*$number*, *$places*, *$round*)	Rounds floating point numbers up or down: *$number* is the number to round up or down. *$places* is the number of decimal places to round the number to. *$round* specifies how to round numbers up or down, the options are: <table><tr><td>OPTION</td><td>PURPOSE</td></tr><tr><td>PHP_ROUND_HALF_UP</td><td>Rounds halves up (e.g., 3.5 becomes 4).</td></tr><tr><td>PHP_ROUND_HALF_DOWN</td><td>Rounds halves down (e.g., 3.5 becomes 3).</td></tr><tr><td>PHP_ROUND_HALF_EVEN</td><td>Rounds halves to the nearest even number.</td></tr><tr><td>PHP_ROUND_HALF_ODD</td><td>Rounds halves to the nearest odd number.</td></tr></table>
ceil(*$number*)	Rounds a number up to the nearest integer (whole number).
floor(*$number*)	Rounds a number down to the nearest integer (whole number).
mt_rand(*$min*, *$max*)	Creates a random number between *$min* and *$max*.
rand(*$min*, *$max*)	Since PHP 7.1 rand() has been the same as mt_rand(). Before this, rand() used an algorithm that was less random and slower.
pow(*$base*, *$exponent*)	Returns the base to the exponent power (e.g., 3^4 would return 81).
sqrt(*$number*)	Returns the square root of a number.
is_numeric(*$number*)	Checks if a value is a number (either an integer or a float). Returns true if it is a number, false if not.

number_format(
   $number
   [, *$decimals*]
   [, *$decimal_point*]
   [, *$thousand_separator*])
	Specifies how a number should be formatted. If just $number is given, it formats it without decimals and a comma is used to separate thousands.
	 $decimals shows the given number of decimal places with a dot to separate decimals and a comma to separate thousands.
	 $decimal_point and $thousand_separator let you specify the characters used to separate decimals and thousands.
	 To use decimal_point or thousand_separator you must use both.

NUMERIC FUNCTIONS

1. Numbers are rounded in various ways.

2. A random number between 0 and 10 is generated.

3. 4 to the power of 5 is shown.

4. The square root of 16 is shown.

5. Checks if a value is a number (an `int` or `float`). Returns `true` if it is (shows 1 in the page); `false` if not (shows nothing).

6. The number is formatted to 2 decimal places. A space separates thousands and a comma separates decimals.

TRY: In Step 2, create a random number between 50 and 100.

PHP

section_b/c05/numeric-functions.php

```php
<b>Round:</b>                        <?= round(9876.54321) ?><br>
<b>Round to 2 decimal places:</b> <?= round(9876.54321, 2) ?><br>
<b>Round half up:</b>                <?= round(1.5, 0, PHP_ROUND_HALF_UP) ?><br>
<b>Round half down:</b>              <?= round(1.5, 0, PHP_ROUND_HALF_DOWN) ?><br>
<b>Round up:</b>                     <?= ceil(1.23) ?><br>
<b>Round down:</b>                   <?= floor(1.23) ?><br>
<b>Random number:</b>                <?= mt_rand(0, 10) ?><br>
<b>Exponential:</b>                  <?= pow(4, 5) ?><br>
<b>Square root:</b>                  <?= sqrt(16) ?><br>
<b>Is a number:</b>                  <?= is_numeric(123) ?><br>
<b>Format number:</b>                <?= number_format(12345.6789, 2, ',', ' ') ?><br>
```

RESULT

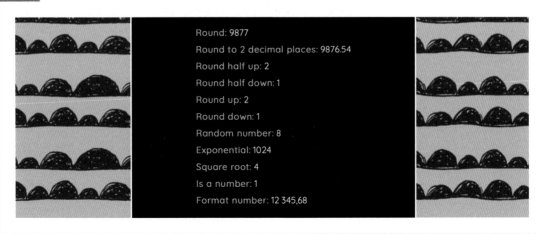

Round: 9877
Round to 2 decimal places: 9876.54
Round half up: 2
Round half down: 1
Round up: 2
Round down: 1
Random number: 8
Exponential: 1024
Square root: 4
Is a number: 1
Format number: 12 345,68

WORKING WITH ARRAYS

These functions can search the contents of an array, count the number of items they hold, and select random keys from them. They can also convert arrays into a string or a string into an array.

As you have seen, arrays hold a set of key/value pairs in a single variable.

In an indexed array, the key is an index number. It indicates the position of the item in the array.

An associative array acts more like a collection of related variables. Each key is a string.

GETTING INFORMATION ABOUT AN ARRAY

FUNCTION	DESCRIPTION
array_key_exists($key, $array)	Checks for a key in the array. Returns true if it exists, otherwise returns false.
array_search($value, $array[, $strict])	Searches the values stored in the array, and returns the key for the first match. If $strict has a value of true, it indicates that the match must be the same data type.
in_array($value, $array)	Checks if a value is in an array. Returns true if it is, false if not.
count($array)	Returns the number of items in the array.
array_rand($array[, $number])	Selects a random item from the array and returns its key. If a number is specified as the second parameter, it returns an array containing that number of random keys.

TURNING ARRAYS INTO STRINGS AND BACK AGAIN

FUNCTION	DESCRIPTION
implode([$separator,]$array)	Turns the values of an array into a string (keys are not included). If you specify a separator, it is inserted between each value.
explode($separator, $string[, $limit])	Turns a string into an indexed array. The separator is the character that separates each of the items in the string. An optional limit can be used to set the maximum number of items to add to the array.

ARRAY FUNCTIONS

section_b/c05/array-functions.php

```php
<?php
// Create array of greetings then get random value
$greetings    = ['Hi ', 'Howdy ', 'Hello ', 'Hola ',
                 'Welcome ', 'Ciao ',];
$greeting_key = array_rand($greetings);
$greeting     = $greetings[$greeting_key];
// Array of best sellers, count items, list top items
$bestsellers       = ['notebook', 'pencil', 'ink',];
$bestseller_count  = count($bestsellers);
$bestseller_text   = implode(', ', $bestsellers);
// Array holding customer details
$customer     = ['forename' => 'Ivy',
                 'surname'  => 'Stone',
                 'email'    => 'ivy@eg.link',];
// If you have a customer forename, add it to greeting
if (array_key_exists('forename', $customer)) {
    $greeting .= $customer['forename'];
}
?> ...
<h1>Best Sellers</h1>
<p><?= $greeting ?></p>
<p>Our top <?= $bestseller_count ?> items today are:
   <b><?= $bestseller_text ?></b></p>
```

Circled numbers in left margin: (1) lines for $greetings array, (2) $greeting_key, (3) $greeting, (4) $bestsellers, (5) $bestseller_count, (6) $bestseller_text, (7) $customer array, (8) if block, (9) greeting output, (10) top items output

RESULT

Best Sellers

Welcome Ivy

Our top 3 items today are: notebook, pencil, ink

1. An array called `$greetings` is created to hold several greetings.

2. A random key is selected from the array and stored in a variable called `$greeting_key`.

3. The random key is used to select the greeting from the array and store it in `$greeting`.

4. An array of best selling items is stored in `$bestsellers`.

5. The `count()` function is used to count the number of elements in the array; this is stored in `$bestseller_count`.

6. The array is converted to a string using `implode()`, with a comma to separate each item. It is stored in `$bestseller_text`.

7. An associative array is created holding details about a customer.

8. `array_key_exists()` checks if there is a value for the customer's forename. If there is, it is added to `$greeting`.

9. The greeting is written out.

10. The number of best sellers and their names are shown.

TRY: In Step 4, add another item to the array of best sellers.

ADDING AND REMOVING ELEMENTS IN AN ARRAY

These functions add elements to, and remove them from, an array. You can specify whether the new elements should be added at the start or end of the array.

To add an element to an array, you specify the value to add.

To remove an element from an array, you only specify its key.

The diagram shows positions of items that are added or removed.

FUNCTION	DESCRIPTION
array_unshift($array, $items)	Adds one or more items to the start of an indexed array. Returns number of items in the array. (For associative arrays, see p42.)
array_push($array, $items)	Adds one or more items to the end of an indexed array. Returns number of items in array. (For associative arrays, see p42.)
array_shift($array)	Removes the first item from the array. Returns value of the removed item.
array_pop($array)	Removes the last item from the array. Returns value of the removed item.
array_unique($array)	Removes duplicate entries from an array. Returns the new array.
array_merge($array1, $array2)	Joins two or more arrays and returns the new array. If both are indexed arrays, the index numbers of the new array start at 0. You can also join two arrays using the + operator: $array1 + $array2

ORIGINAL	UNSHIFT	PUSH	SHIFT	POP	UNIQUE
0 => paper	0 => glue	0 => paper	0 => paper	0 => paper	0 => paper
1 => pencil	1 => paper	1 => pencil	0 => pencil	1 => pencil	1 => pencil
2 => eraser	2 => pencil	2 => eraser	1 => eraser	2 => eraser	2 => pencil
	3 => eraser	3 => glue			

ARRAY UPDATING FUNCTIONS

     section_b/c05/array-updating-functions.php

```php
<?php
// Array of items being ordered
$order = ['notebook', 'pencil', 'eraser',];
array_unshift($order, 'scissors'); // Add to start
array_pop($order);                 // Remove last
$items = implode(', ', $order);    // Convert to string

// Array of classes
$classes = ['Patchwork' => 'April 12th',
            'Knitting'  => 'May 4th',
            'Lettering' => 'May 18th',];
array_shift($classes);                      // Remove 1st
$new     = ['Origami'   => 'June 5th',
            'Quilting' => 'June 23rd',]; // New items
$classes = array_merge($classes, $new);  // Add to end
?>
<h1>Order</h1>
<?= $items ?>
<h1>Classes</h1>
<?php foreach($classes as $description => $date) { ?>
  <b><?= $description ?></b> <?= $date ?><br>
<?php } ?>
```

(1) (2) (3) (4) (5) (6) (7) (8) (9) (10)

RESULT

1. An indexed array is created and stored in `$order`.

2. The `array_unshift()` function adds an element to the start of the array. The first parameter is the array; the second is the item to add (this only works with indexed arrays).

3. The `array_pop()` function removes the last item.

4. The array is converted into a string using `implode()` and stored in `$items`. Each element is separated by a comma and space.

5. An associative array is created and stored in `$classes`.

6. `array_shift()` removes the first item from the array.

7. Another associative array is created to hold new elements.

8. `array_merge()` is used to take the `$classes` array and add the new items created in Step 7.

9. `$items` is written out.

10. A `foreach` loop writes out the keys and values of the associative array.

TRY: In Step 4, separate the items in the string with a semi-colon.

SORTING ARRAYS (CHANGING ORDER)

The sorting functions change the order of the items listed in an array. Ascending lists order items from lowest value to highest (e.g., A-Z or 0-9). Descending lists order items from highest value to lowest (e.g., Z-A or 9-0).

SORT BY VALUE AND CHANGE KEYS

When you sort the array using the functions below, the keys become index numbers starting at 0 (whether it is an indexed or associative array). The r in rsort() stands for reverse.

FUNCTION	DESCRIPTION
sort($array)	Ascending according to value
rsort($array)	Descending according to value

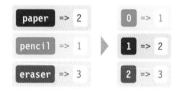

SORT BY VALUE AND MAINTAIN KEYS

When you sort the array using the functions below, the keys move with their values.

FUNCTION	DESCRIPTION
asort($array)	Ascending according to value
arsort($array)	Descending according to value

SORT BY KEY AND MAINTAIN VALUES

When you sort the array using the functions below, the values move with their keys.

FUNCTION	DESCRIPTION
ksort($array)	Ascending according to key
krsort($array)	Descending according to key

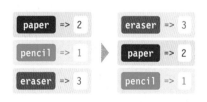

ARRAY SORTING FUNCTIONS

section_b/c05/array-sorting-functions.php

```php
<?php
// Array holding order
$order = ['notebook', 'pencil', 'scissors',
          'eraser', 'ink', 'washi tape',];
sort($order);                           // Sort ascending
$items = implode(', ', $order);         // Convert to text

// Create array holding classes
$classes = ['Patchwork' => 'April 12th',
            'Knitting'  => 'May 4th',
            'Origami'   => 'June 8th',];
ksort($classes);                        // Sort by key
?>

<h1>Order</h1>
<?= $items ?>
<h1>Classes</h1>
<?php foreach($classes as $description => $date) { ?>
  <b><?= $description ?></b> <?= $date ?><br>
<?php } ?>
```

Circled markers: ① ② ③ ④ ⑤ ⑥ ⑦

RESULT

Order

eraser, ink, notebook, pencil, scissors, washi tape

Classes

Knitting May 4th

Origami June 8th

Patchwork April 12th

1. An indexed array is created and stored in a variable called $order.

2. The values in the array are sorted in ascending alphabetical order using sort(). This gives each item in the array a new index number starting at 0.

3. The array is converted into a string using implode(). Each element is separated by a comma followed by a space. The resulting string is stored in a variable called $items.

4. An associative array is created and stored in $classes.

5. The keys in the array are sorted in alphabetical order using the ksort() function (their values move with them).

6. The string stored in $items is written out.

7. A foreach loop is used to write the keys and values of the $classes array to the page.

TRY: In Step 5, reverse the order of the array holding the classes.

CONSTANTS

A constant is a name/value pair and acts like a variable.
But, once its value has been assigned, it cannot be updated.

A constant is a name/value pair, like a variable, but:

- It is created using the `define()` function
- Its value cannot be updated once it has been set
- It can be accessed anywhere in the PHP page (including inside functions)

Its name should describe the type of data it holds and it should begin with a letter or underscore (not a dollar symbol). Its value can be a scalar data type or an array.

The `define()` function's parameters are:

- The constant name, which is usually in uppercase.

- Its value; strings should be placed in quotes, numbers and booleans should not.

- An optional boolean to say whether or not the name is case-sensitive (`true` if it is, `false` if not). If the third parameter is not supplied, the name will be case-sensitive.

```
define('SITE_NAME', 'Mountain Art Supplies');
```
NAME — VALUE

Constants are often used to store information that a site needs in order to work, but whose values only change when a site is installed (either the first time, when it moves to a new server, or when the same code is used to power a different website).

A constant can also be created using the keyword `const`, followed by the constant name, the assignment operator, and the value it should hold. This approach can be used to define a constant inside of a class (whereas the `define()` function cannot).

```
const SITE_NAME = 'Mountain Art Supplies';
```
NAME — VALUE

USING CONSTANTS

PHP section_b/c05/includes/settings.php

```php
<?php
① define('SITE_NAME', 'Mountain Art Supplies');
② const ADMIN_EMAIL = 'admin@eg.link';
```

PHP section_b/c05/includes/constants.php

```php
<?php
③ include 'includes/settings.php';
   include 'includes/header.php';
   ?>

④ <h1>Welcome to <?= SITE_NAME ?></h1>
⑤ <p>To contact us, email <?= ADMIN_EMAIL ?></p>

   <?php include 'includes/footer.php'; ?>
```

RESULT

MOUNTAIN ART SUPPLIES

Welcome to Mountain Art Supplies

To contact us, email admin@eg.link

In this example, an include file called `settings.php` will create two constants that hold information about the site.

1. The `define()` function is used to create a constant called `SITE_NAME`. Its value is the name of the site.

2. The `const` keyword is used to create a constant called `ADMIN_EMAIL`. Its value is the email address of the site owner.

The second file in this example is a page called `constants.php`, which uses the values in these two constants.

3. The `settings.php` file is included so that the page can access the constants.

4. The shorthand for the `echo` command is used to write out the contents of the constant that holds the site name.

5. The site owner's email address is displayed.

ADDING OR UPDATING HTTP HEADERS

The `header()` function updates the HTTP headers the PHP interpreter sends to the browser. It can also add new headers. Its one argument is the name of the header to set, followed by a colon, and its value.

Sometimes, users request one page, but you need to send them to another one. For example, if it:
- Is no longer available
- Has moved to a new URL
- Is missing data it needs

In this case, `header()` has one argument that is made up of three parts:
- The header name `Location`
- A colon
- The new URL

When the browser receives the `Location` header, it requests the new URL. This should be followed by the `exit` command to prevent the interpreter running more of the PHP code (see right).

```
header('Location: http://www.example.com/');
```
HEADER   NEW URL

Most PHP files create HTML to send to the browser, but PHP can be used to create other types of file such as JSON, XML or CSS.

To do this, `header()` needs:
- The header `Content-type`
- A colon
- The media type of the content

This creates an HTTP header that tells the browser the file's media type. For more on media types see:
`http://notes.re/media-types`

```
header('Content-type: application/json');
```
HEADER   MEDIA TYPE

Browsers can cache (store) pages users have viewed. If the user requests the page again, it can show the page that it has stored, rather than requesting the file again (this makes the page appear to load faster).

To tell the browser how long it can cache a page for, use:
- The header `Cache-Control`
- A colon
- `max-age=` followed by the number of milliseconds the page can be cached for

ISPs and networks use **proxies** to cache web pages. If pages hold personal data, follow the milliseconds with a comma, space, and the word `private`, to prevent a proxy caching it. If there is no personal data, set it to `public`.

```
header('Cache-Control: max-age=3600, public');
```
HEADER   VALID FOR   TIME (MS)   PROXY

REDIRECTING USERS USING HTTP HEADERS

section_b/c05/redirect.php

PHP

```php
<?php
$logged_in = true;

if ($logged_in == false) {
    header('Location: login.php');
    exit;
}
?>
<?php include 'includes/header.php'; ?>
<h1>Members Area</h1>
<p>Welcome to the members area</p>
<?php include 'includes/footer.php'; ?>
```

① ② ③ ④

PHP

section_b/c05/login.php

```php
<h1>Login</h1>
<b>You need to log in to view this page.</b>
<p>(You create a full login system in Chapter 16.)</p>
```

RESULT

This example shows how to redirect users to another page using the `header()` function. You cannot have sent any markup or text to the browser before using the `header()` function, not even a space or a carriage return.

1. A variable called `$logged_in` stores a boolean value indicating whether the user is logged in.

2. In an `if` statement, a condition checks if the value in `$logged_in` is `false`.

3. If it is `false`, the user is redirected to the `login.php` page using the `header()` function.

(You learn how to create a members area with a functioning login page in Chapter 16.)

4. After redirecting a visitor using the `header()` function, the `exit` command is used to prevent any more of the PHP code in the file being executed.

If the value in `$logged_in` is `true`, the previous code block will have been skipped and the rest of the page is shown.

TRY: In Step 1, change the value of the `$logged_in` variable to `false`. You will then be redirected to the login page.

DATA ABOUT FILES AND DELETING FILES

The file functions take a file path as a parameter then either return information about the file and its filepath, or delete the file.

The table below shows file functions. Some of these functions return different parts of a filepath; those parts are described in the diagram on the right.

PHP also has built-in constants that hold paths:
__FILE__ holds the current file's path.
__DIR__ holds the current file's directory.

FUNCTION	DESCRIPTION
file_exists($path)	Checks if a file exists. Returns true if it exists, false if not.
filesize($path)	Returns the size of the file in bytes.
mime_content_type($path)	Returns the media type of the file. (See http://notes.re/media-types)
unlink($path)	Tries to delete a file. Returns true if it worked, false if it did not.
pathinfo($path[, $part])	Returns parts of the filepath. You can specify the part of the path to retrieve. If you do not, it returns an array with the following four keys.

PART	DESCRIPTION
PATHINFO_DIRNAME	Path to directory the file is in.
PATHINFO_BASENAME	Basename of the file.
PATHINFO_FILENAME	Filename (no extension).
PATHINFO_EXTENSION	File extension.

FUNCTION	DESCRIPTION
basename($path)	Returns the basename of a file from a path.
dirname($path[, $levels])	Returns the path to the directory the specified file is in. If $levels is specified, this is the number of parent directories to go up.
realpath($path)	Returns the absolute path to the file.

The difference between absolute and relative paths is described here: http://notes.re/paths

GETTING FILE INFORMATION

section_b/c05/files.php

```php
<?php
$path = 'img/logo.png';
?>
<?php include 'includes/header.php'; ?>
<?php if (file_exists($path)) { ?>
  <b>Name:</b>        <?= pathinfo($path, PATHINFO_BASENAME) ?><br>
  <b>Size:</b>        <?= filesize($path) ?> bytes<br>
  <b>Mime type:</b> <?= mime_content_type($path) ?><br>
  <b>Folder:</b>      <?= pathinfo($path, PATHINFO_DIRNAME) ?><br>
<?php } else { ?>
  <p>There is no such file.</p>
<?php } ?>
<?php include 'includes/footer.php'; ?>
```

(1) (2) (3) (4) (5) (6) (7)

RESULT

```
Name: logo.png
Size: 12995 bytes
Mime type: image/png
Folder: img
```

1. $path stores a path to a file.

2. An if statement uses file_exists() to check if the file exists. If it does, it writes out information about the file.

3. pathinfo() shows the name of the file including its extension (known as the basename).

4. filesize() shows the size of the file in bytes.

5. mime_content_type() shows the media type of the file.

6. pathinfo() shows the folder the file is in.

7. If the file does not exist, the user is told there is no such file.

TRY: In Step 1, change $path to img/pattern.png. You will see the new name and size (the mime type and folder remain the same).

TRY: In Step 1, change $path to img/nologo.png. Because this file does not exist, you should see the error message in Step 7.

SUMMARY

BUILT-IN FUNCTIONS

> PHP's built-in functions achieve tasks that many programmers need to perform when creating sites.

> You call built-in functions just like any function, but you do not add a function definition in the page.

> String functions find, count and replace characters or change their case.

> Number functions round numbers, pick random numbers and perform mathematical functions.

> Array functions add and remove elements, sort the contents of an array, check for keys or values, and turn arrays into strings and back again.

> Constants are like variables, but the value cannot be updated once it has been set.

> The header() function updates the HTTP headers that are sent to the browser (and can redirect users to another page).

6

GETTING DATA FROM BROWSERS

In this chapter, you will learn how to access the data browsers send to the PHP interpreter, make sure that it is ready to use, and safe to display in dynamic web pages.

In the introduction to this section, you saw that HTML pages have two mechanisms for sending data to the server: adding information to links or providing forms to fill in. You also saw how this data is sent via HTTP GET (in a query string) or HTTP POST (in the HTTP headers that are sent with each page request).

In this chapter, you will learn how to access that data so it can be used in the page. This involves four key steps:

- **Collecting** each piece of data from the query string or HTTP headers.

- **Validating** each piece of data to check that a value has been given and that it is in the right format (e.g., if a page needs a number, you check that a number was provided, not text).

- **Deciding** whether or not the page can process the data that the visitor supplied. If not, the visitor may need to be shown error messages.

- **Escaping** or **sanitizing** the data to ensure it is safe to use in the page because certain characters can prevent a page displaying correctly or even cause harm to the site.

There is no one standard way to perform each of these four steps; different developers use different approaches. This chapter introduces a selection of the many different ways to collect data and make sure it is safe to use.

FOUR STEPS TO COLLECT AND USE DATA

There are four steps to collect data from visitors and make sure that the data is safe to use.

1. COLLECT DATA

First, you collect the data that browsers send to the server. You can do this using:

- Two superglobal arrays that the PHP interpreter creates each time a PHP file is requested.

- Two built-in functions called **filter functions**.

As you will see, a page will not always receive the values that it needs in order to perform its task, and this can cause an error.

If a piece of data is optional, you can specify a default value that the page should use if it is not supplied.

If it is not optional, and data is missing, you might need to tell the visitor that they have not provided enough information (see next step).

2. VALIDATE DATA

Once a PHP page has collected data from a browser, it will often **validate** each individual piece of data that it received to ensure that it will not cause errors when the page runs. This involves checking:

- If the page has the data it needs to perform its task. This is known as **required data**.

- If the data is in the **correct format**. For example, if your page needs a number to perform a calculation, you can check that you have received a number. Or, if you expect to receive an email address, you can check that the text is in the correct format to be a valid email address.

PHP provides two ways to validate data; you can:

- Write your own user-defined functions.

- Use a set of built-in filters with the filter functions. Each filter validates different types of data.

There are different ways to achieve each of these steps and you will meet several of them in this chapter.

3. DECIDE ACTION

Once a page has collected and validated all of the individual values it needs, it can determine whether or not it has all of the data it needs to run:

- If all of the data is valid, it can be processed.

- If any of the data is invalid or missing, it should not be used. Instead, the page can show the user an error message.

The process of displaying errors when data is invalid is slightly different for forms than for query strings.

- If form data is invalid, you can show the form again with messages next to any form controls that supplied invalid data. The messages should tell the user how to provide the data in the correct format.

- If a query string has incorrect data, you should not expect visitors to edit the query string. Instead, you should provide a message that explains how the user can request the data they wanted.

4. ESCAPE OR SANITIZE DATA

Whenever you display data that a visitor has supplied in a page, it needs to be **escaped** to make sure it is safe to display. This involves replacing a set of characters that browsers treat as code (such as the < and > symbols) with things called **entities**. The entities tell the browser to display those characters (rather than running them as HTML code).

If you do not perform this step before showing the data in a page, a hacker could try to get the page to run a malicious JavaScript file.

If the user provides data that is then used in a URL, you also need to escape any characters that have special meaning (such as forward slashes and question marks). If you don't escape these characters, the web server may not be able to process the URL.

GETTING DATA SENT VIA HTTP GET

When data is added to a query string at the end of a URL, the PHP interpreter adds that data to a superglobal array called $_GET so that the PHP code in the page can access it.

Below, you can see an HTML link. In its `href` attribute, you can see the URL of the page that it is linking to.

At the end of the URL, there is a query string that holds two name/value pairs which are sent to the server when the visitor clicks on the link.

URL   QUERY STRING

```
<a href="http://eg.link/hotel.php?location=Tokyo&year=2021">Tokyo</a>
```
NAME   VALUE   NAME   VALUE

When the PHP interpreter receives this request, it adds the data from the query string to a superglobal array called $_GET. Like all of the superglobal arrays that the PHP interpreter generates, $_GET is an associative array. It is given an element for each name/value pair that is in the query string. The:

- **key** is the name being sent
- **value** is the value sent with the name

The code in the PHP file can access the values in the $_GET superglobal array in the same way that it would access values from any associative array:

```
$location = $_GET['location'];
```
VARIABLE   KEY

Often, a single PHP file is used to display several pages of a website, and data in the query string is used to determine what data is shown in the page.

On the right-hand page, an array has three elements. Each element holds the city and address of a store. A value in the query string selects which store's data should be shown, so this one PHP file creates three pages of the site; each one is for a different store. The data in the array is also used to create the links that request these three pages.

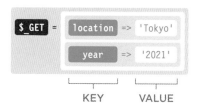

KEY   VALUE

USING A QUERY STRING TO SELECT CONTENT

section_b/c06/get-1.php?city=London

PHP

```php
<?php
$cities  = [
    'London' => '48 Store Street, WC1E 7BS',
    'Sydney' => '151 Oxford Street, 2021',
    'NYC'    => '1242 7th Street, 10492',
];
$city    = $_GET['city'];
$address = $cities[$city];
?>
...
<?php foreach ($cities as $key => $value) { ?>
  <a href="get-1.php?city=<?= $key ?>"><?= $key ?></a>
<?php } ?>

<h1><?= $city ?></h1>
<p><?= $address ?></p>
```

(1) · (2) · (3) · (4) · (5) · (6)

RESULT

London Sydney NYC

LONDON

48 Store Street, WC1E 7BS

TRY: In the browser's address bar, remove the query string from the URL and reload the page. It will display two errors.

This is because the city name was not in the query string and therefore was not added to the $_GET superglobal array.

This example collects a city name from the query string and shows the address of a store in that city.

1. The `$cities` variable holds an associative array. Each key is the name of a different city; each value is the address for a branch of the store in that city.

2. The name of the city is collected from the `$_GET` superglobal array and stored in a variable called `$city`. (Note that this is case-sensitive.)

3. The name of the city is used to select the address of the branch in that city from the array created in step 1, and store it in a variable called `$address`.

4. A `foreach` loop works through each element in the `$cities` array.

5. Inside the loop, a link is created for each city. The name of the city is written out in the query string, and again as link text. This shows how PHP can create links, and how those links can point to a single file that can display different data.

6. The values that were stored in the `$city` and `$address` variables in Steps 2 and 3 are displayed in the page.

HANDLING MISSING DATA IN SUPERGLOBAL ARRAYS

If you try to access a key that has not been added to a superglobal array, the PHP interpreter raises an error. To prevent such errors, you can check if the key is in the superglobal array before accessing it.

When someone shares a link to a page, they can accidentally miss part or all of its query string.

At the end of the previous example you saw that, if the query string is missing data, it cannot be added to the $_GET superglobal array. If a PHP file tries to access that data, the PHP interpreter raises an error saying Undefined array key or Undefined index because it is trying to access a key (or index) that has not been added to the $_GET superglobal array.

To prevent this error, pages should check if a value has been added to the $_GET superglobal array before trying to access it.

PHP has a built-in function called isset() which accepts a variable name, a key of an array, or a property of an object as an argument. It returns true if that variable, key, or property exists, and its value is not null. Otherwise it returns false. Importantly, it will not cause an error if the specified variable, key, or parameter does not exist.

Below, a variable called $city is declared. A ternary operator (the shorthand for an if... else statement, see p76-77) checks if the $_GET superglobal has a key called city and its value is not null. If it does, it will be stored in the $city variable. Otherwise, $city will hold a blank string.

```
$city = isset($_GET['city']) ? $_GET['city'] : '';
```

VARIABLE   DOES KEY EXIST?   YES: STORE ITS VALUE   NO: STORE BLANK STRING

PHP 7 introduced the null-coalescing operator ?? which acts as a shorthand for using isset() in the condition of a ternary operator.

If a value on the left of the null-coalescing operator does not exist, you supply an alternative value that should be used to the right of it.

```
$city = $_GET['city'] ?? '';
```

VARIABLE   TRY TO STORE THIS VALUE   IF IT DOES NOT EXIST: STORE BLANK STRING

USING A QUERY STRING TO SELECT CONTENT

section_b/c06/get-2.php

```php
<?php
$cities  = [
    'London' => '48 Store Street, WC1E 7BS',
    'Sydney' => '151 Oxford Street, 2021',
    'NYC'    => '1242 7th Street, 10492',
];
$city = $_GET['city'] ?? '';
if ($city) {
    $address = $cities[$city];
} else {
    $address = 'Please select a city';
}
?>
...
<?php foreach ($cities as $key => $value) { ?>
  <a href="get-2.php?city=<?= $key ?>"><?= $key ?></a>
<?php } ?>

<h1><?= $city ?></h1>
<p><?= $address ?></p>
```

① `$city = $_GET['city'] ?? '';`
② `if ($city) {`
③ `    $address = $cities[$city];`
④ `} else {`
⑤ `    $address = 'Please select a city';`

RESULT

London Sydney NYC

Please select a city

This example builds on the previous one. The differences are highlighted.

1. The value stored in the $city variable is assigned using the null-coalescing operator. If the $_GET superglobal array:

- Has a key called city and its value is not null, its value will be stored in the $city variable.

- Does not have a key called city, or its value is null, an empty string is stored in the $city variable.

2. The $city variable is used in the condition of an if statement. If the value is a string that is not empty, the PHP interpreter treats that value as true and runs the subsequent code block.

3. The $address variable stores the address of the branch in the city that was named in the query string.

4. Otherwise, if the value in the $city variable is a blank string, the second code block runs.

5. The $address variable stores a message telling the visitor to select a city.

TRY: In the query string, use Tokyo as the city. The page will show an error because it cannot find that key in the $cities array.

Add a new element to the array in Step 1 with the key Tokyo and add an address for it, then try using it in the query string again.

VALIDATING DATA

Before a PHP page uses the data it has collected, the data should be validated to ensure that it will not cause errors when the page runs.

Validating the data that a page receives involves checking that the PHP file has:

- The data needed to perform a task, which is known as **required data**.

- The data in the **right format**. E.g., if a page needs a number to perform a calculation, you can check that it received a number (rather than a string).

In the file on the previous page, the query string needed a:

- Name and value to specify the store to display
- Value that matched a key in the array of cities

If the value supplied in the query string is not in the array of cities, the PHP interpreter raises an error. Therefore, before trying to display the city in the page, the code can check if the value in the query string is present in the array of cities.

You will learn several ways to validate different types of data throughout the rest of this chapter. The example on the right-hand page uses PHP's built-in `array_key_exists()` function (see p218) to check if the value in the query string matches a key in the array of cities. The function returns `true` if the key is found, `false` if it is not; and the value the function returns is stored in a variable called `$valid`.

Once the data has been validated, the page then needs to determine whether or not it should run the rest of the code.

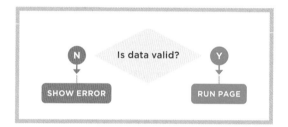

The example used so far in the chapter is extended on the right-hand page. The `$valid` variable is used in the condition of an `if` statement to determine whether or not the page can process the data:

- If the data is valid, the page can get the location of the store from the array and hold it in a variable called `$address` ready to show later in the page.

- If the data is not valid, the `$address` variable stores a message telling the visitor to select a city. This provides helpful feedback to the visitor telling them how to use the page and get the information that they are looking for.

Later in the chapter, you learn how to deal with pages that need to collect multiple values from the browser, and how to check if all the values are valid or not.

VALIDATING QUERY STRING DATA

section_b/c06/get-3.php

```php
<?php
$cities  = [
    'London' => '48 Store Street, WC1E 7BS',
    'Sydney' => '151 Oxford Street, 2021',
    'NYC'    => '1242 7th Street, 10492',
];
$city  = $_GET['city'] ?? '';
$valid = array_key_exists($city, $cities);

if ($valid) {
    $address = $cities[$city];
} else {
    $address = 'Please select a city';
}
?>
...
<?php foreach ($cities as $key => $value) { ?>
  <a href="get-3.php?city=<?= $key ?>"><?= $key ?></a>
<?php } ?>

<h1><?= $city ?></h1>
<p><?= $address ?></p>
```

(1) `$city = $_GET['city'] ?? '';`
(2) `$valid = array_key_exists($city, $cities);`
(3) `if ($valid) {`
(4) `    $address = $cities[$city];`
(5) `} else {`
(6) `    $address = 'Please select a city';`

RESULT

London Sydney NYC

Please select a city

This example builds on the previous ones and uses validation to check if the query string holds a valid location.

1. If the query string contains a city, it will be stored in a variable called `$city`. If not, `$city` will hold a blank string.

2. The `array_key_exists()` function checks if the value in `$city` is a key in the `$cities` array. If it is, the `$valid` variable will hold a value of `true`. If not, `$valid` will hold a value of `false`.

3. The `$valid` variable is used in the condition of an `if` statement. If the value it stores is `true`, the first code block will run.

4. The address for that city is collected from the `$cities` array and stored in the `$address` variable.

5. If the value in `$valid` is `false`, the second code block runs.

6. The `$address` variable holds a message telling the visitor to select a city.

TRY: In the browser's address bar, try entering the city name Shanghai in the query string: `get-3.php?city=Shanghai`

SHOWING AN ERROR PAGE IF DATA IS MISSING

If a page needs to get data from the query string, but that data is missing or is not valid, the PHP interpreter can tell the browser to request a different file containing an error message.

Validating data in the query string is important because, when people link to your site, it is easy for them to accidentally miss data from the query string.

You should not expect visitors to be able to edit the data in the query string so, if the data is not valid, you can help them by:

- Showing them a message in the page. This could tell them that the page they requested could not be found, or it could tell them to select from a list of options (like the example on the previous page).

- Sending them to a different page that contains an error message.

Note how the condition in the code below checks if the data is invalid by checking if the value stored in $valid is *not* true.

On p226, you saw that PHP's built-in header() function can be used to set the Location header that the PHP interpreter sends to the browser. This tells the browser to request a different page.

When a page cannot be displayed because the data was not valid, it is good practice to update the response code that the PHP interpreter sends back to the browser (see p181). This helps prevent search engines from adding incorrect URLs to their search results. PHP's built-in http_response_code() function is used to set the HTTP response code. Its one argument is the response code that should be used. Sending back a response code of 404 indicates that the requested page could not be found.

Once the response code and header have been set, the exit command stops any further code on the page from running (as this could cause an error).

```
IF NOT VALID ──→ if (!$valid) {
SET RESPONSE CODE ──────→ http_response_code(404);
REDIRECT TO ERROR PAGE ──────→ header('Location: page-not-found.php');
STOP CODE RUNNING ──────→ exit;
}
```

SENDING VISITORS TO AN ERROR PAGE

section_b/c06/get-4.php

```php
<?php
$cities  = [
    'London' => '48 Store Street, WC1E 7BS',
    'Sydney' => '151 Oxford Street, 2021',
    'NYC'    => '1242 7th Street, 10492',
];
$city   = $_GET['city'] ?? '';
$valid = array_key_exists($city, $cities);

if (!$valid) {
    http_response_code(404);
    header('Location: page-not-found.php');
    exit;
}
$address = $cities[$city];
?>
...
<?php foreach ($cities as $key => $value) { ?>
  <a href="get-4.php?city=<?= $key ?>"><?= $key ?></a>
<?php } ?>

<h1><?= $city ?></h1>
<p><?= $address ?></p>
```

(1) `$valid = array_key_exists($city, $cities);`
(2) `if (!$valid) {`
(3) `    http_response_code(404);`
(4) `    header('Location: page-not-found.php');`
(5) `    exit;`

RESULT

PAGE NOT FOUND

Sorry, we could not find the page you were looking for.

NOTE: The result box is showing the file called page-not-found.php because there is no city in the query string.

This example sends visitors to an error page if the data in the query string is not a valid city.

1. PHP's `array_key_exists()` function checks if the name of the city collected from the query string is one of the keys in the array of cities. The function returns `true` if it exists, and `false` if it does not. This value is stored in a variable called `$valid`.

2. The condition of an `if` statement checks if the value stored in `$valid` is *not* `true`. (The `!` operator indicates that it should *not* be `true`.) If it is `false`, the following code block runs.

3. PHP's `http_response_code()` function tells the PHP interpreter to send the response code 404 back to the browser, indicating that the page could not be found.

4. PHP's `header()` function tells the PHP interpreter to add a `Location` header to instruct the browser to request a file called `page-not-found.php` instead.

5. PHP's `exit` command tells the PHP interpreter not to run any more code in the file.

When the value in `$valid` is `true`, Steps 3-5 are ignored and the page is displayed.

ESCAPING OUTPUT

When values that have been submitted to the server are shown in a page, they must be **escaped** to ensure hackers cannot use them to run malicious scripts.

Escaping data involves removing (and optionally replacing) any characters that should not appear in a value. For example, HTML has five **reserved characters** that browsers treat as code:

< and > are used in tags
" and ' hold attribute values
& is used to create entities

In order to display these five characters on a page, they must be replaced with either an **entity name** or an **entity number** that represents them. Browsers then display the corresponding characters rather than treating them as code.

| < | > | & | " | ' |
| < | > | & | " | ' |

When a page receives values from a visitor and then needs to display those values in a page, it should check for these five reserved characters and replace them with their entities. This can be done using PHP's built-in htmlspecialchars() function (see p246).

If you do not replace HTML's reserved characters with entities, hackers could submit values that load a JavaScript file containing malicious code. This is called a **cross-site scripting** (**XSS**) attack.

For example, if a visitor provided the following username, then the page tried to display the username, it could cause the script to run.

Luke<script src="http://eg.link/bad.js"></script>

When the reserved characters are replaced with entities, the visitors would see the text above (and the script would not run). In the HTML source code for the page, the username would look like this:

Luke<script src="http://eg.link/bad.js"></script>

Data supplied by users should only appear in HTML markup that is visible on the web page (or in the <title> or <meta> elements). Do **not** show data supplied by a user in:

- Comments in your code
- CSS rules (as they can include a script in a page)
- <script> elements
- Tag names
- Attribute names
- As a value of HTML event attributes such as onclick and onload
- As a value of an HTML attribute that loads files (such as the src attribute)

As you see on p280, values that are used in a URL or query string must also be escaped.

RISK OF NOT ESCAPING OUTPUT

section_b/c06/xss-1.php

```
<a class="badlink" href="xss-1.php?msg=<script
src=js/bad.js></script>">LINK TO DEMONSTRATE XSS</a>

<?php
$message = $_GET['msg'] ?? 'Click link at top of page';
?>
...
<h1>XSS Example</h1>
<p><?= $message ?></p>
```

RESULT

NOTE: As you will see on the next page, escaping text in the query string means that the script tags are displayed in the page, and the browser does not treat them as code.

This example shows what happens if data is not escaped.

1. For the purposes of this example, a link to this same page is shown. The link has a query string containing `<script>` tags. (In a real XSS attack, the link to this page could appear on another website, in an email, or another kind of message.)

2. The PHP page checks the `$_GET` superglobal array to see if the query string contains a name called `msg`.

- If it is does, the corresponding value is stored in a variable called `$message`.

- If it does not, `$message` stores an instruction telling users to click on the link.

3. The value in `$message` is shown in the page.

When you click on the link at the top of the page, the script will be run because the value in the query string has not been escaped.

ESCAPING RESERVED HTML CHARACTERS

PHP's built-in `htmlspecialchars()` function replaces HTML's reserved characters with their corresponding entities so that those characters are displayed and cannot be run as code.

The `htmlspecialchars()` function has four parameters; the first is required, the rest are optional.

- `$text` is the text you want escaped.
- `$flag` is an option to control which characters are encoded (see table below for common options).
- `$encoding` is the encoding scheme used in the string (if not specified, the default is UTF-8).
- `$double_encode` Because HTML entities start with an ampersand, if a string contains an entity, the ampersand is encoded and the page displays the entity (rather than the reserved character). Using a value of `false` for this parameter tells the PHP interpreter not to encode entities in the string.

If the string that is being escaped is made up of characters that are all valid for the encoding scheme that is used, the function returns the string with the reserved characters replaced by entities.

If the string contains characters that are invalid, it returns an empty string (unless the `ENT_SUBSTITUTE` flag is used, as described in the table below).

Because `htmlspecialchars()` is quite a long function name, and has four parameters, some programmers create user-defined functions with a shorter name to escape values and return the encoded version (as shown on the right-hand page).

```
htmlspecialchars($text[, $flag][, $encoding][, $double_encode]);
```

FLAG	DESCRIPTION
ENT_COMPAT	Convert double quotes, leave single quotes alone (this is the default if no flag is supplied)
ENT_QUOTES	Convert double and single quotes
ENT_NOQUOTES	Do not convert double or single quotes
ENT_SUBSTITUTE	To prevent the function returning an empty string, replace invalid characters with the replacement character: ◆ (in UTF-8 this is U+FFFD, in any other encoding it is &#xFFFD)
ENT_HTML401	Treat code as HTML 4.01
ENT_HTML5	Treat code as HTML 5
ENT_XHTML	Treat code as XHTML

To specify multiple flags, separate each one with a pipestem symbol, e.g., ENT_QUOTES|ENT_HTML5.

ESCAPING CONTENT PROVIDED BY USERS

PHP

section_b/c06/xss-2.php

```php
<a class="badlink" href="xss-2.php?msg=<script
src=js/bad.js></script>">ESCAPING MARKUP</a>

<?php
$message = $_GET['msg'] ?? 'Click the link above';
?> ...
<h1>XSS Example</h1>
```
① `<p><?= htmlspecialchars($message) ?></p>`

PHP

section_b/c06/xss-3.php

```php
<a class="badlink" href="xss-3.php?msg=<script
src=js/bad.js></script>">ESCAPING MARKUP</a>

<?php
function html_escape(string $string): string
{
    return htmlspecialchars($string,
        ENT_QUOTES|ENT_HTML5, 'UTF-8', true);
}
$message = $_GET['msg'] ?? 'Click the link above';
?> ...
<h1>XSS Example</h1>
```
② (bracket spanning function definition)
③ `<p><?= html_escape($message) ?></p>`

RESULT

XSS EXAMPLE

<script src=js/bad.js></script>

1. The first example only has one change from the previous example; when the value in $message is written out, it uses PHP's htmlspecialchars() function to replace HTML's reserved characters with their corresponding entities. Therefore, when the link is clicked on, the HTML for the <script> tags will be shown on the screen, rather than being run by the browser.

2. A second version of the same example adds a user-defined function called html_escape(). It accepts a string as an argument, and returns that string with all of the reserved characters replaced by entities. When it calls htmlspecialchars(), it provides values for all four parameters.

3. The html_escape() function is called to write out the message from the query string.

The result of both examples looks exactly the same.

NOTE: In the code download for this chapter, the html_escape() function definition is also in an include file functions.php.

TRY: In Step 2, replace the function definition with an include statement that includes the functions.php file.

HOW FORM DATA IS SENT TO THE SERVER

Forms allow visitors to enter text and select options. For each form control, the browser can send a name and value to the server along with a page request.

The HTML `<form>` tag requires two attributes:

- The value of the `action` attribute is the PHP file that the form data should be sent to.

- The value of the `method` attribute indicates how to send the form data to the server.

The `method` attribute should have one of two values:

- GET sends the form data using HTTP GET in a query string added to the end of the URL.

- POST sends the data using HTTP POST in the HTTP headers sent from the browser to the server.

PAGE TO SEND DATA TO   HTTP METHOD TO SEND DATA

```
<form action="join.php" method="POST">
    <p>Email: <input type="email" name="email"></p>
    <p>Age:   <input type="number" name="age"></p>
    <p><input type="checkbox" name="terms" value="true">
        I agree to the terms and conditions.</p>
    <input type="submit" value="Save">
</form>
```

When the visitor submits the form, the browser requests the page specified in the `action` attribute.

The value of the `action` attribute can be a relative path from the page that creates the form to the page that processes the form, or it can be a full URL.

Often, the form will be submitted to the same PHP page that was used to display the form.

The form above is sent via HTTP POST, so the browser will add the names and values of the form controls to the HTTP headers. The headers are sent with the request for `join.php`. For each header:

- The **name** is the value of the `name` attribute of that form control.
- The **value** is the text the user entered or the value of the item they selected.

The HTML form controls below fall into one of two categories: text inputs which allow visitors to enter text, and options which allow visitors to select an option.

If a visitor fills in a text input, the name that is sent to the server is the value of the `name` attribute, and the value is the text they entered. If the user does not enter any text for that form control, the name is still sent to the server and the value is a blank string.

If an option is selected, the name is the value of the `name` attribute and the value is the data in the `value` attribute for the option they selected. If the user did not select an option, the browser does not send any data for that form control to the server.

TEXT INPUT	EXAMPLE	PURPOSE
Text input	`<input type="text" name="username">`	Enter single line of text
Number input	`<input type="number" name="age">`	Enter number
Email input	`<input type="email" name="email">`	Enter email
Password	`<input type="password" name="password">`	Enter password
Text area	`<textarea name="bio"></textarea>`	Enter longer text

OPTION	EXAMPLE	PURPOSE
Radio buttons	`<input type="radio" name="rating" value="good">` `<input type="radio" name="rating" value="bad">`	Select one of multiple options

Select boxes	`<select name="preferences">`
	  `<option value="email">Email</option>`
	  `<option value="phone">Phone</option>`
	`</select>`
		Select one of multiple options

Checkboxes	`<input type="checkbox" name="terms" value="true">`	Select a single option

To demonstrate server-side validation, this book only validates data on the server. Live sites should use JavaScript and number and email inputs to validate data in the browser before it is sent to the server, and then validate the data again on the server (because it is possible to bypass validation in the browser).

NOTE: When the PHP interpreter adds data from the browser to a superglobal array, it is always a string data type, even if the value is a number or a boolean.

You will meet the file upload control used to send files to the server in the next chapter.

GETTING FORM DATA

When the PHP interpreter receives data sent via HTTP POST, it is added to the $_POST superglobal array.

When the visitor submits a form via HTTP POST, the PHP interpreter receives the request for the page and adds the form data (sent in the HTTP headers) to the $_POST superglobal array. The:

- **key** is the name of the form control
- **value** is the value the user entered or selected

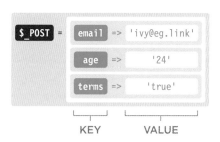

KEY   VALUE

If the form was sent using HTTP GET, the PHP interpreter gets the form data from the query string and adds it to the $_GET superglobal array.

The code in the PHP file can access the values in the $_POST superglobal array in the same way that it would access values from any associative array. If the form control is a text input, there will always be a value for it (unless it has been disabled):

$email = $_POST['email'];

VARIABLE   KEY

If the form control is an option, the name and value is only added to the HTTP headers if the visitor selects an option. Therefore, the null-coalescing operator is used to collect options from the $_POST superglobal array (in the same way it was used to collect values from the query string).

$age = $_POST['age'] ?? false;

VARIABLE   KEY   DEFAULT VALUE

The example on the right shows what the superglobal arrays hold when pages use forms. The var_dump() function (see p192) is used to show the contents of the superglobal array so that you can see which elements are added to the array, and also so that you can see that all data is these superglobal arrays is a string data type - even if it is a number or boolean.

It is important to try this example out for yourself and see how the data in the superglobal array changes when the:

- Page first loads, before the form is sent
- Form is submitted, without filling in any data
- Form fields are completed

HOW FORM DATA IS RECEIVED

PHP   section_b/c06/collecting-form-data.php

```php
<form action="collecting-form-data.php" method="POST">
  <p>Name:     <input type="text" name="name"></p>
  <p>Age:      <input type="text" name="age"></p>
  <p>Email:    <input type="text" name="email"></p>
  <p>Password: <input type="password" name="pwd"></p>
  <p>Bio:      <textarea name="bio"></textarea></p>
  <p>Contact preference:
    <select name="preferences">
      <option value="email">Email</option>
      <option value="phone">Phone</option>
    </select></p>
  <p>Rating:
   1 <input type="radio" name="rating" value="1"> 
   2 <input type="radio" name="rating" value="2"> 
   3 <input type="radio" name="rating" value="3"></p>
  <p><input type="checkbox" name="terms" value="true">
    I agree to the terms and conditions.</p>
  <p><input type="submit" value="Save"></p>
</form>
<pre><?php var_dump($_POST); ?></pre>
```

(1) (2) (3)

1. Five text controls ask for the user's name, age, email, password, and bio.

2. Three form controls present options to the visitor.

3. The contents of the $_POST superglobal array is written out using the var_dump() function.

When the page loads, the form has not been submitted, so the $_POST superglobal will be empty.

If the form is submitted without entering any data, the $_POST superglobal array contains an element for each of the text inputs; its value is a blank string. The select box is sent to the server with the default value shown when the page loaded. But the names and values of the radio buttons and checkbox are not sent to the server.

If all of the form controls are filled in, the $_POST superglobal array will hold an element for each form control. Each value sent to the server is a string.

TRY: Change the value in the method attribute of the `<form>` tag to GET, and the data will be sent via HTTP GET. Then, in Step 3, display the contents of the $_GET superglobal array.

RESULT

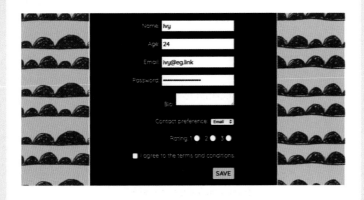

HOW TO CHECK A FORM HAS BEEN SUBMITTED

A form must be submitted before you can collect and process its data. There are different techniques to check if the form has been submitted depending on whether the form was sent via HTTP POST or HTTP GET.

HTTP POST

The $_SERVER superglobal array (see p190) has a key called REQUEST_METHOD, which stores the HTTP method used to request the page. When a form is submitted using HTTP POST, it has a value of POST.

To check if a form has been submitted using HTTP POST, the condition of an if statement checks if the REQUEST_METHOD key has a value of POST. The code to process the form goes in the following code block.

```php
if ($_SERVER['REQUEST_METHOD'] == 'POST') {
    // Code to collect and process form data goes here
}
```

HTTP GET

When a user clicks on a link or enters a URL into the browser's address bar, the request is always sent via HTTP GET. Therefore, you cannot use the $_SERVER superglobal to check when a form has been sent via HTTP GET. Instead, you can either add a:

- Hidden input to the form, or
- Name and value to the submit button

When the form is submitted, the name and value of the hidden input or submit button will be added to the $_GET superglobal array.

The condition of an if statement can then check whether the $_GET superglobal has the value that is sent when the form is submitted. If it has, the code to collect and process the data can run.

```php
$submitted = $_GET['submitted'] ?? '';
if ($submitted === 'true') {
    // Code to collect and process form data goes here
}
```

CHECKING A FORM HAS BEEN SUBMITTED

PHP section_b/c06/check-for-http-post.php

```php
<?php
if ($_SERVER['REQUEST_METHOD'] == 'POST') {
    $term = $_POST['term'];
    echo 'You searched for ' . htmlspecialchars($term);
} else { ?>
    <form action="check-for-http-post.php" method="POST">
      Search for: <input type="text" name="term">
      <input type="submit" value="search">
    </form>
<?php } ?>
```

(1) (2) (3)

PHP section_b/c06/check-for-http-get.php

```php
<?php
$submitted = $_GET['sent'] ?? '';
if ($submitted === 'search') {
    $term = $_GET['term'] ?? '';
    echo 'You searched for ' . htmlspecialchars($term);
} else { ?>
    <form action="check-for-http-get.php" method="GET">
      Search for: <input type="search" name="term">
      <input type="submit" name="sent" value="search">
    </form>
<?php } ?>
```

(4) (5) (6)

RESULT

1. The condition of an `if` statement checks the `$_SERVER` superglobal array to see if the key called `REQUEST_METHOD` has a value of `POST`.

2. If it does, the search form has been sent via HTTP POST, and a message will be used to display the search term.

3. Otherwise, it is skipped and the form is displayed.

In this example, the submit button's name is `sent` and its value is `search`. If the form was submitted, they are added to the `$_GET` superglobal array.

4. The null-coalescing operator checks if the `$_GET` superglobal array has a value for the key `sent`. If it does, a variable called `$submitted` stores its value; if it does not, it stores a blank string.

5. The condition of an `if` statement checks if the value in `$submitted` is `search`. If it is, the form was sent via HTTP GET and the search term is displayed.

6. Otherwise, the form is shown.

TRY: Use a hidden form input to indicate the form was submitted.

VALIDATING NUMBERS

When form data is collected it should be validated to ensure that all of the required values have been provided and the data is in the correct format. This prevents bad data causing errors when the page runs.

To check if a value is a number, use PHP's built-in `is_numeric()` function (p216). Or, if you need to check that a number is within a specified range of allowed numbers, you can create a user-defined function to perform the task. Below, you can see a function that uses comparison operators to check if a number is within the minimum and maximum range of allowed values. The function has three parameters:

- `$number` is the value that it needs to check
- `$min` is the minimum permitted number
- `$max` is the maximum permitted number

In the function, the condition contains two expressions that check if the number is:

- Greater than or equal to the minimum number
- Less than or equal to the maximum number

If both expressions evaluate to `true`, the function returns `true`. If either of the expressions result in `false`, the function returns `false`.

Once a page has collected a number, it can check if the value is valid by calling this function.

```
function is_number($number, int $min = 0, int $max = 100): bool
{
    return ($number >= $min and $number <= $max);
}
```
                    IS IT >= MINIMUM?   IS IT <= MAXIMUM?

If the form data is not valid, the user is often shown the form again so that they can try again. In such cases, the number that they provided can be shown in the form control by writing it out in the `value` attribute of the `<input>` tag. The `htmlspecialchars()` function is used when displaying the value to prevent an XSS attack.

Because the value the user entered is only collected if the form has been submitted, the `$age` variable must be decalared at the top of the page and given an initial value of a blank string. If the variable were not declared at the top of the page, then trying to show it in the `value` attribute of the form control would result in an `Undefined variable` error in the text input.

```
<input type="text" name="age" value="<?= htmlspecialchars($age) ?>">
```

CHECKING IF A NUMBER IS VALID

section_b/c06/validate-number-range.php

```php
<?php
declare(strict_types = 1);
$age     = '';
$message = '';

function is_number($number, int $min = 0, int $max = 100): bool
{
    return ($number >= $min and $number <= $max);
}

if ($_SERVER['REQUEST_METHOD'] == 'POST') {
    $age   = $_POST['age'];
    $valid = is_number($age, 16, 65);
    if ($valid) {
        $message = 'Age is valid';
    } else {
        $message = 'You must be 16-65';
    }
}
?> ...
<?= $message ?>
<form action="validate-number-range.php" method="POST">
  Age: <input type="text" name="age" size="4"
        value="<?= htmlspecialchars($age) ?>">
  <input type="submit" value="Save">
</form>
```

RESULT

You must be 16-65

Age: 15   SAVE

1. Two variables, $age and $message, are initialized with values that are blank strings.

2. The is_number() function (see left-hand page) is defined.

3. The page checks if the form has been submitted. If it has...

4. The age is collected from the $_POST superglobal array. The data comes from a text input, so a value will always be sent for it when this form is submitted.

5. The is_number() function is called. The value the user submitted is the first argument, and the numbers 16 and 65 are the minimum and maximum valid numbers. The boolean value it returns is stored in $valid.

6. The condition of an if statement checks if the value in $valid is true. If it is, the $message variable holds a message saying the age is valid.

7. Otherwise, $message stores an error message.

8. The message is shown.

9. The number the user entered (or the initial value from Step 1) is shown in the number input using htmlspecialchars().

VALIDATING TEXT LENGTH

Sites often limit the number of characters that can appear in things like usernames, posts, article titles, and profiles. A single function can be used to check the length of any string the site receives.

To test if the text supplied by users is between a minimum and maximum number of characters:

- PHP's built-in `mb_strlen()` function (see p210) is used to count how many characters are in the string. This number is stored in a variable.

- Then a condition uses two expressions to check if the number of characters is within the permitted range (in the same way that they were used on the previous page to check that a number was within a permitted range).

If the number of characters is valid, the function returns `true`; if not, it returns `false`.

When code to validate data is placed in a function, it can be used to validate multiple form controls. This saves repeating code to perform the same task.

The function below (and the previous example) use parameters so that, each time they are called, they can have different minimum and maximum values.

When multiple pages perform the same validation tasks, you should place the function definitions in an include file. Then you can include that file rather than duplicating the same function definitions in each page. The download code for this chapter has an include file called `validate.php` which contains three function definitions from this chapter.

```php
function is_text($text, int $min = 0, int $max = 100): bool
{
    $length = mb_strlen($text);
    return ($length >= $min and $length <= $max);
}
```
IS IT >= MINIMUM?   IS IT <= MAXIMUM?

CHECKING TEXT LENGTH

section_b/c06/validate-text-length.php

```php
<?php
declare(strict_types = 1);
$username = '';
$message  = '';

function is_text($text, int $min = 0, int $max = 1000): bool
{
    $length = mb_strlen($text);
    return ($length >= $min and $length <= $max);
}
if ($_SERVER['REQUEST_METHOD'] == 'POST') {
    $username = $_POST['username'];
    $valid    = is_text($username, 3, 18);
    if ($valid) {
        $message = 'Username is valid';
    } else {
        $message = 'Username must be 3-18 characters';
    }
}
?> ...
<?= $message ?>
<form action="validate-text-length.php" method="POST">
  Username: <input type="text" name="username"
    value="<?= htmlspecialchars($username) ?>">
  <input type="submit" value="Save">
</form>
```

RESULT

Username: Ivy   SAVE

1. The $username and $message variables are initialized.

2. The user-defined function called is_text() (shown on the left-hand page) is defined.

3. The page checks if the form has been submitted. If it has...

4. The text is collected from the $_POST superglobal array.

5. The is_text() function is called to check if the text the user entered is between 3 and 18 characters long. The value it returns is stored in $valid.

6. The condition of an if statement checks if the value in $valid is true. If it is, $message holds a message saying the username is valid.

7. Otherwise, $message stores a message telling the user that the username must be between 3-18 characters long.

8. The value in the $message variable is displayed.

9. The value in $username is shown in the text input. This is either the value the user sent, or the blank string used to initialize the variable in Step 1.

VALIDATING DATA USING REGULAR EXPRESSIONS

A regular expression can be used to check if the value that a visitor provided matches a specified pattern of characters.

As you saw on p214-17, regular expressions can describe a permitted pattern of characters, such as those used in credit card numbers, ZIP/postal codes and phone numbers. The function below uses regular expressions to check the strength of users' passwords.

It accepts a password as a parameter and then checks if it is 8 or more characters. It then uses regular expressions to check if it contains:

- Uppercase characters
- Lowercase characters
- Numbers

Each check is separated using the and operator. If all conditions evaluate to true, the function returns true; otherwise it returns false. (A single regular expression could be used to perform all the checks in one go, but the regular expression would be harder to read.)

The function contains a condition with four expressions:

First, mb_strlen() checks if the value contains 8 or more characters.

Next, PHP's preg_match() function is used three times to check if the pattern of characters described in a regular expression is found in the password.

If all of the expressions result in true, the following code block returns the value true (because it met the requirements). Otherwise, if the function is still running, it returns false.

```
function is_password(string $password): bool
{
    if (
        mb_strlen($password) >= 8
        and preg_match('/[A-Z]/', $password)
        and preg_match('/[a-z]/', $password)
        and preg_match('/[0-9]/', $password)
    ) {
        return true;      // Passed all tests
    }
    return false;         // Invalid
}
```

NOTE: Although browsers will hide a password when it is typed in, the data it is still sent as plain text in the HTTP headers. Therefore, all personal data should be sent via HTTPS (see p184-85).

CHECKING PASSWORD STRENGTH

     section_b/c06/validate-password.php

```php
<?php
declare(strict_types = 1);
$password = '';
$message  = '';
function is_password(string $password): bool
{
    if (
        mb_strlen($password) >= 8
        and preg_match('/[A-Z]/', $password)
        and preg_match('/[a-z]/', $password)
        and preg_match('/[0-9]/', $password)
    ) {
        return true;   // Passed all tests
    }
    return false;      // Invalid
}
if ($_SERVER['REQUEST_METHOD'] == 'POST') {
    $password = $_POST['password'];
    $valid    = is_password($password);
    $message  = $valid ? 'Password is valid' :
        'Password not strong enough';
}
?> ...
<?= $message ?>
<form action="validate-password.php" method="POST">
  Password: <input type="password" name="password">
  <input type="submit" value="Save">
</form>
```

RESULT

Password: ●●●●●●●●●●●●●●   SAVE

1. The `$password` and `$message` variables are initialized.

2. The `is_password()` function is defined with one parameter: the password to check.

3. An `if` statement uses four expressions; each one results in `true` or `false`. They are separated by the and operator, so the subsequent code block only runs if they *all* result in `true`.

4. The code block returns `true`, and the function stops running.

5. Otherwise, if any condition failed, the function returns `false`.

6. If the form was submitted, the following code block runs.

7. The password is collected from the `$_POST` superglobal.

8. `is_password()` is called to check the user's password. The result is stored in a variable called `$valid`.

9. A ternary operator checks if the `$valid` variable holds `true`. If so, `$message` holds a success message; otherwise, it holds an error message.

10. The value in the `$message` variable is displayed.

SELECT BOXES AND RADIO BUTTONS

Select boxes and radio buttons let users select one from a list of options. Browsers only send the name and value to the server if an option was selected. The value is validated by seeing if it matches one of the options.

When a form uses a select box or radio buttons, you can create an indexed array holding all the options the user can choose from, and store it in a variable. The array below stores star ratings from 1-5.

Then, the array can be used to:

- Create the options in select boxes or radio buttons
- Check that the user picked one of these options

```php
$star_ratings = [1, 2, 3, 4, 5,];
```

To check that the user selected a valid option, PHP's built-in in_array() function is used.

If the submitted value is found in the array of options, in_array() returns true. If not, it returns false.

```php
$valid = in_array($stars, $star_ratings);
```
SUBMITTED VALUE   VALID OPTIONS

To create the form controls, you can loop through the options and add an element for each one. If the form is shown to the user again, the selected option can be highlighted using a ternary operator.

The condition of a ternary operator checks if the value in the $stars variable matches the current value in the loop. If so, the checked attribute is added. If not, a blank string is written out instead.

```php
<?php foreach ($option as $star_ratings) { ?>
  <?= $option ?>
  <input type="radio" name="stars" value="<?= $option ?>"
    <?= ($stars == $option) ? 'checked' : '' ?>>
<?php } ?>
```

NOTE: This example relies on the $stars variable having been initialized (see Step 1 on the right-hand page).

VALIDATING OPTIONS

PHP   section_b/c06/validate-options.php

```php
<?php
$stars   = '';
$message = '';
$star_ratings = [1, 2, 3, 4, 5,];

if ($_SERVER['REQUEST_METHOD'] == 'POST') {
    $stars   = $_POST['stars'] ?? '';
    $valid   = in_array($stars, $star_ratings);
    $message = $valid ? 'Thank you' : 'Select an option';
}
?> ...
<?= $message ?>
<form action="validate-options.php" method="POST">
  Star rating:
  <?php foreach ($star_ratings as $option) { ?>
    <?= $option ?> <input type="radio" name="stars"
         value="<?= $option ?>"
         <?= ($stars == $option) ? 'checked' : '' ?>>
  <?php } ?>
  <input type="submit" value="Save">
</form>
```

(1) $stars / $message
(2) $star_ratings
(3) if
(4) $stars
(5) $valid
(6) $message
(7) <?= $message ?>
(8) foreach
(9) option
(10) ternary

RESULT

1. The $stars and $message variables are initialized.

2. The $star_ratings variable holds an indexed array of values that will be used to create a set of radio buttons.

3. An if statement checks if the form has been submitted.

4. If so, the selected option is collected from the $_POST superglobal array.

5. PHP's in_array() function checks if the value that the user selected is one of the permitted options.

6. A ternary operator is used to create a message that indicates whether or not the data was valid.

7. The value in $message is shown.

8. A foreach loop creates the options in the HTML form. It works through the values in the $star_ratings array. For each:

9. The option is shown, followed by a radio button with the option added in the value attribute.

10. A ternary operator checks if an option has been selected. If so, the checked attribute is added.

HOW TO TELL IF A CHECKBOX IS CHECKED

A checkbox is either checked or not, but the name and value of the checkbox is only sent to the server when the checkbox is checked.

Determining whether or not a checkbox was selected, involves two steps:

- First, use PHP's isset() function to check if there is a value for the checkbox in the superglobal array.
- If there is, then check if the value provided was the value that you expected to be sent.

Both of these two checks can be performed in the condition of a ternary operator. If both checks result in values of true, you know that the user checked the box and you can assign a boolean value of true.

Below, if both checks result in true, $terms will store the value true, otherwise it will store false.

```
$terms = (isset($_POST['terms']) and $_POST['terms'] == true) ? true : false;
```

IF VALUE WAS ADDED TO
SUPERGLOBAL ARRAY

AND THE VALUE
PROVIDED IS CORRECT

If the form is shown to the user again, to check a box that they had selected, you just need to check if the value for that checkbox is true.

If it is, then the checked attribute is added to the control. If it is not, then a blank string is written out instead.

```
<input type="checkbox" name="terms" value="true"
    <?= $terms ? 'checked' : '' ?>>
```

IF CHECKBOX
WAS SELECTED

ADD CHECKED
ATTRIBUTE

OTHERWISE ADD
A BLANK STRING

VALIDATING CHECKBOXES

PHP

```php
<?php
$terms   = '';
$message = '';

if ($_SERVER['REQUEST_METHOD'] == 'POST') {
    $terms   = (isset($_POST['terms']) and $_POST['terms'] == true) ? true : false;
    $message = $terms ? 'Thank you' : 'You must agree to the terms and conditions';
}
?> ...
<?= $message ?>
<form action="validate-checkbox.php" method="POST">
  I agree to the terms and conditions: <input type="checkbox" name="terms" value="true"
    <?= $terms ? 'checked' : '' ?>>
  <input type="submit" value="Save">
</form>
```

RESULT

You must agree to the terms and conditions

I agree to the terms and conditions: ☐ SAVE

1. The $terms and $message variables are initialized.

2. If the form has been submitted...

3. Two expressions are used in the condition of a ternary operator to determine if the checkbox was checked. First, PHP's isset() function checks if the checkbox was sent. If it was, the second expression checks if its value is true. If both expressions evaluate to true, the $terms variable is assigned a value of true; if not, it is assigned a value of false.

4. If $terms stores a value of true, $message stores the words Thank you; if not, it holds a message telling the user to agree to the terms and conditions.

5. The message is displayed in the page.

6. A ternary operator is used to check if the $terms variable holds a value of true (indicating that it was checked). If so, the checked attribute is added to the checkbox. If not, a blank string is written out instead.

CHECKING IF MULTIPLE VALUES ARE VALID

Pages often need to check if several pieces of data are valid before working with that data. For example, most forms ask visitors to provide more than one piece of information.

Take a look at the form below. It asks visitors to provide the following data (using three data types):

- Name (a string between 2 and 10 characters long)
- Age (an integer between 16 and 65)
- Agreement to the terms and conditions (a boolean value of true or false)

When the user submits the form, if any of the data is invalid, the page should:

- Not process the data
- Create error messages telling the visitor how to correct each of the issues
- Display any values that the user entered

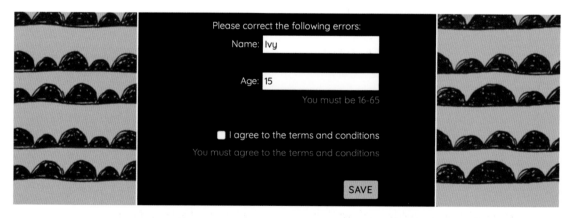

In addition to showing the form, this page can display error messages and any values the user entered. To do this, it starts by declaring two arrays:

- One with an element to hold each of the values that the user will supply.

- One with an element to hold each of the error messages that might be displayed in the page.

Both of these arrays must be initialized with a name for each element and a value that can be shown when the page first loads (before the form has been submitted). If this were not done, and the PHP interpreter tried to access an element of an array that did not have a value, it would raise an error.

The array that holds error messages stores a blank string for each potential form error because there are no errors when the page first loads.

1. If the form has been submitted, the data that the user supplied is collected.

These values overwrite the initial values stored in the array that was created to hold the user's data.

ARRAY TO HOLD
USER DATA
                             GET VALUES

```php
$user['name']  = $_POST['name'];
$user['age']   = $_POST['age'];
$user['terms'] = (isset($_POST['terms']) and $_POST['terms'] == true) ? true : false;
```

2. Next, each piece of data is validated. If it is not valid, an error message will be stored in the corresponding element of the $errors array.
The data is validated using the validation functions you have seen in the chapter, which return true if the value the user supplied is valid and false if it is not.

This means that the validation functions can be called in the condition of a ternary operator. If the data is:

- Valid: the element stores a blank string.
- Invalid: an error message is stored telling the user why the data is not valid.

ARRAY TO HOLD   VALIDATE   BLANK   ERROR
ERROR MESSAGES   FORM VALUES   STRING   MESSAGE

```php
$errors['name']  = is_text($user['name'], 2, 20)   ? '' : 'Name must be 2-20 characters';
$errors['age']   = is_number($user['age'], 16, 65) ? '' : 'You must be 16-65';
$errors['terms'] = $user['terms']                  ? '' : 'You must agree to the terms';
```

3. To check if there were errors, PHP's built-in implode() function is used to join all the values in the $errors array into one string.

The result is stored in a variable called $invalid. If $invalid holds a blank string, the data was valid. If not, there was at least one error.

```php
$invalid = implode($errors);
```

VARIABLE TO HOLD   ARRAY HOLDING
ALL ERRORS   ERRORS

4. An if statement is used to check if $invalid contains any text. If it does, it will be treated as true and the error messages are displayed with the form.

If there were no errors, $invalid will hold a blank string (which is treated as false), and the page can process the data that it received.

```php
if ($invalid) {
    // Show error messages and do not process the data
} else {
    // Data is valid, the page can process the data
}
```

VALIDATING FORMS

This example shows how to validate multiple form controls. The result was shown on the previous page.

1. `validate.php` is included in the page. It contains the definitions for three of this chapter's validation functions. Placing them in an include file allows any page to include this file and then use its functions.

2. The `$user` variable holds an array with an element for each form control; they are assigned an initial value to use in the form when the page first loads.

3. The `$errors` variable stores an array that has an element for each piece of data that is being validated.

4. `$message` is assigned a blank string. Once the data is validated, it will hold a success or error message.

5. An `if` statement checks if the form was submitted.

6. If so, the three pieces of data from the form are collected, and the data the user supplied overwrites the initial values that were stored in the `$user` array.

7. The name the user supplied is validated using the `is_text()` function. It returns `true` if the data is valid; `false` if not. If it is valid, the corresponding element in the `$errors` array (see Step 3) holds a blank string. If not, it holds a message telling the user how to fix it.

8. The user's age is validated using `is_number()`. It returns `true` if the data is valid; `false` if not. If it is valid, the corresponding element of the `$errors` array holds a blank string. If not, it holds an error message.

9. If the user checked the `terms` checkbox, the corresponding element of the `$errors` array holds a blank string. If not, it holds an error message saying they need to accept the terms and conditions.

10. All of the values in the `$errors` array are joined into a single string using PHP's `implode()` function. The result is stored in a variable called `$invalid`.

11. The condition of an `if` statement checks if the value in `$invalid` is `true`. If it contains any text it will be treated as `true`. A blank string is treated as `false`.

12. If the data is invalid, the `$message` variable stores a message telling the user to correct the form errors.

13. Otherwise, `$message` stores a message to say the data was valid. If the data is valid, the page can then process it.

(Often, when a page has received valid data, the form will not need to be displayed again.)

14. The value stored in `$message` is displayed.

15. If the user has submitted the form, the value they entered for their name is written out in the `value` attribute of the form control. (This text is escaped using PHP's `htmlspecialchars()` function.)

If the form was not submitted, it will display the blank string that was stored in the corresponding key of the `$user` array when it was initialized in Step 2.

16. The value of the element in the `$errors` array that corresponds to this form control is shown.

17. If the user supplied their age, it is shown in the `value` attribute of the form control. This is followed by the corresponding value in the `$errors` array.

18. If the visitor checked the terms and conditions checkbox, the `checked` attribute is added to it. It is followed by the relevant value in the `$errors` array.

```php
<?php
declare(strict_types = 1);                                 // Enable strict types
require 'includes/validate.php';                           // Validation functions

$user = [
    'name'  => '',
    'age'   => '',
    'terms' => '',
];                                                         // Initialize $user array
$errors = [
    'name'  => '',
    'age'   => '',
    'terms' => '',
];                                                         // Initialize errors array
$message = '';                                             // Initialize message

if ($_SERVER['REQUEST_METHOD'] == 'POST') {                // If form submitted
    $user['name']  = $_POST['name'];                       // Get name
    $user['age']   = $_POST['age'];                        // Get age then check T&Cs
    $user['terms'] = (isset($_POST['terms']) and $_POST['terms'] == true) ? true : false;

    $errors['name']  = is_text($user['name'], 2, 20)   ? '' : 'Must be 2-20 characters';
    $errors['age']   = is_number($user['age'], 16, 65) ? '' : 'You must be 16-65';
    $errors['terms'] = $user['terms']                  ? '' : 'You must agree to the
        terms and conditions';                             // Validate data

    $invalid = implode($errors);                           // Join error messages
    if ($invalid) {                                        // If there are errors
        $message = 'Please correct the following errors:'; // Do not process
    } else {                                               // Otherwise
        $message = 'Your data was valid';                  // Can process data
    }
}
?> ...
<?= $message ?>
<form action="validate-form.php" method="POST">
  Name: <input type="text" name="name" value="<?= htmlspecialchars($user['name']) ?>">
  <span class="error"><?= $errors['name'] ?></span><br>
  Age:  <input type="text" name="age" value="<?= htmlspecialchars($user['age']) ?>">
  <span class="error"><?= $errors['age'] ?></span><br>
  <input type="checkbox" name="terms" value="true" <?= $user['terms'] ? 'checked' : '' ?>>
    I agree to the terms and conditions
  <span class="error"><?= $errors['terms'] ?></span><br>
  <input type="submit" value="Save">
</form>
```

① ② ③ ④ ⑤ ⑥ ⑦ ⑧ ⑨ ⑩ ⑪ ⑫ ⑬ ⑭ ⑮ ⑯ ⑰ ⑱

COLLECTING DATA USING FILTER FUNCTIONS

PHP also has two built-in functions that collect data sent from the browser and store it in variables. They are called filter functions because they can apply a filter to the data that the browser sent.

`filter_input()` gets a single value that has been sent to the server. It requires two arguments. The first argument is the **input source** (which is not written in quotes). Use:

- `INPUT_GET` to get data sent via HTTP GET
- `INPUT_POST` to get data sent via HTTP POST
- `INPUT_SERVER` to get the same data that was made available in the `$_SERVER` superglobal array.

The second argument is the name of a name/value pair that was sent to the server, which should be in quotes. Used like this, `filter_input()` returns:

- The value if it was sent to the server
- `null` if the data was not sent to the server

Once you have learned how to use this function, you will learn how to apply a filter as a third parameter.

```
$data = filter_input(INPUT_SOURCE, 'name');
```
INPUT SOURCE   NAME

`filter_input_array()` collects all of the values that were sent to the server via HTTP GET or POST and stores each one as an element of an array.

Because it gets all of the values, it only requires one argument; the input source. The values for the input source are the same as they are for `filter_input()`.

```
$data = filter_input_array(INPUT_SOURCE);
```
INPUT SOURCE

When the data is received, it is stored as a string data type. Some of the filters you can apply using these filter functions will convert the data type.

The next few pages use PHP's `var_dump()` function to display values collected using these functions as it's important to see the data types of each value.

USING FILTER FUNCTIONS TO COLLECT DATA

PHP   section_b/c06/filter_input.php

```php
① <?php $location = filter_input(INPUT_GET, 'city'); ?> ...
② <a href="filter_input.php?city=London">London</a> |
   <a href="filter_input.php?city=Sydney">Sydney</a>
③ <pre><?php var_dump($location); ?></pre>
```

RESULT

```
London | Sydney

string(6) "London"
```

PHP   section_b/c06/filter_input_array.php

```php
④ <?php $form = filter_input_array(INPUT_POST); ?> ...
  <form action="filter_input_array.php" method="POST">
    Email: <input type="text" name="email" value=""><br>
    I agree to terms and conditions:
⑤   <input type="checkbox" name="terms" value="true"><br>
    <input type="submit" value="Save">
  </form>
⑥ <pre><?php var_dump($form); ?></pre>
```

RESULT

```
Email: [            ]
I agree to terms and conditions: ☐
                          SAVE

array(2) {
   ["email"]=>
   string(11) "ivy@eg.link"
   ["terms"]=>
```

When these two examples first load, the value shown will be NULL as the query string is empty.

1. The filter_input() function collects a single value sent via HTTP GET in the query string. The name for the name/value pair is city. The value that is collected is stored in a variable called $location.

2. Two links use query strings to send a name called city; their values are different city names.

3. var_dump() is used to display the value stored in $location and its data type (a string).

4. The filter_input_array() function is used to get all values from the form when it is submitted using HTTP POST. The array that the function creates is stored in a variable called $form.

5. The form sends a text input and a checkbox via HTTP POST.

6. var_dump() displays the names and values stored in $form along with the data type of each value.

TRY: Submit the form without filling it in. The array will hold a blank string for the text input and nothing for the checkbox.

VALIDATION FILTERS

When filter functions get data sent from a browser, it is stored as a string. Below you can see three validation filters that check if a value is a boolean, an integer or a float. Each filter has a filter ID used to identify it.

If a page expects to receive a value that is a boolean, an integer or a float, the filter functions can use the three filters below to check if the value provided is the correct data type.

When these filters check if a value is a boolean, an integer or a float, the filter functions convert the value from the string data type to the data type specified in the filter. You will see how to use the filters on p273.

FILTER ID	DESCRIPTION
FILTER_VALIDATE_BOOLEAN	Checks if a value is true. 1, on, and yes all count as true. It is not case-sensitive. If it is true, the function returns a boolean value of true. If not, it returns false.
FILTER_VALIDATE_INT	Checks if a number is an integer (0 is not counted as a valid integer). If valid, it returns the number as an int data type. If not, it returns false.
FILTER_VALIDATE_FLOAT	Checks if a number is a floating point number (decimal). Integers pass the filter (0 does not as it is not counted as a valid integer). If valid, it returns the value as a float data type. If not, it returns false.

Each filter also has two types of settings that can be used to control how the filter behaves:

- **Flags** are settings that you can turn on / off.
- **Options** are settings where you must set a value.

For example, the integer and float filters have options that allow you to specify the minimum and maximum number that the user is allowed to provide. So, if a visitor was asked to provide their age and they needed to be between 16 and 65, the filter could check if the number provided was within this range. If the number was not provided, or if the number was too low or too high, it would be invalid.

All of the validation filters also have an option that allows you to specify a default value that should be used if data that has been received is invalid.

The flags are options that can only be turned on. For example, the integer filter has a flag you can turn on in order to allow visitors to provide numbers using hexadecimal notation in addition to the standard digits 0-9. (Hexadecimal notation uses the digits 0-9 and letters A-F to represent numbers 10-15; you may have seen it used to specify colors in HTML and CSS.)

A full list of the validation filters, along with their flags and options is shown on p278-79.

Below, you can see the validation filters that are used to collect text. Regular expressions can also be used to write custom filters.

Data often follows rules regarding:

- The number of characters it may contain
- Permitted characters it may use
- The order those characters may appear in

For example, there are rules that control how characters are used in email addresses, URLs, domain names, and IP addresses. The four filters below check if a value follows these rules.

FILTER ID	DESCRIPTION
FILTER_VALIDATE_EMAIL	Checks if the structure of a string matches that of an email address.
FILTER_VALIDATE_URL	Checks if the structure of a string matches that of a URL.
FILTER_VALIDATE_DOMAIN	Checks if the structure of a string matches that of a valid domain name.
FILTER_VALIDATE_IP	Checks if the structure of a string matches that of a valid IP address.

Regular expressions can be used to write other filters that check if a value contains a pattern of characters.

The regular expression is specified as an option for the FILTER_VALIDATE_REGEXP filter.

FILTER ID	DESCRIPTION
FILTER_VALIDATE_REGEXP	Checks if a string contains a pattern of characters described using a regular expression (see p212-15).

USING FILTERS TO VALIDATE SINGLE VALUES

When the filter functions are used to check data, they must be told the ID of the filter to use, and any flags or options the filter should follow.

When `filter_input()` is used to collect an individual piece of data, the third parameter is the ID of the filter to use, and the fourth (optional) parameter holds the settings the filter can use.

The function returns:
- The value it received if it passes the filter
- `false` if it does not pass the filter
- `null` if the name was not sent to the server

```
$data = filter_input(INPUT_SOURCE, 'name', FILTER_ID[, $settings]);
                     └─────┬─────┘  └─┬─┘   └──┬──┘   └────┬────┘
                     INPUT SOURCE    NAME     ID      FLAGS/OPTIONS
```

When a filter uses flags and options, they are stored in an associative array, with two keys:

- `flags` holds settings that can be turned on
- `options` holds settings that require a value

Below, an array of flags and options is stored in a variable called `$settings`.

The value for the `flags` key is the name of the flag that should be turned on (this is not written in quotes). To use multiple flags, separate each flag name with the pipestem character |.

The value for the `options` key is another associative array; each element's key is the name of the option that is being set and the value is the value to use.

```
                                    FLAGS
                          ┌──────────┴──────────┐
$settings['flags'] = FLAG_NAME1 | FLAG_NAME2;
$settings['options']['option1'] = value1;
$settings['options']['option2'] = value2;
                     └───┬───┘    └──┬──┘
                       OPTION       VALUE
```

When one element of an array stores another array, the syntax above can be easier to read. This approach was demonstrated as a way to update arrays on p42.

NOTE: When `filter_input()` collects data that is not valid, it returns `false`, which means that the value the user supplied cannot be shown in a form.

COLLECTING VALUES USING FILTERS

PHP

```php
<?php
$settings['flags']                      = FILTER_FLAG_ALLOW_HEX;    // Allow hex flag
$settings['options']['min_range'] = 0;                              // Min number option
$settings['options']['max_range'] = 255;                            // Max number option

$number = filter_input(INPUT_POST, 'number', FILTER_VALIDATE_INT, $settings);
?> ...
<form action="validate-input.php" method="POST">
  Number: <input type="text" name="number" value="<?= htmlspecialchars($number) ?>">
  <input type="submit" value="Save">
</form>
<?php var_dump($number); ?>
```

RESULT

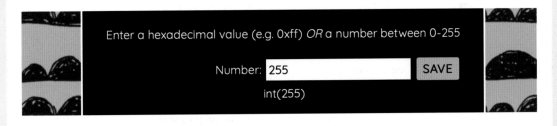

Enter a hexadecimal value (e.g. 0xff) *OR* a number between 0-255

Number: 255   SAVE

int(255)

1. The $settings variable holds an array of flags and options used to validate a number. The flag allows the number to be given in hexadecimal notation. The options state that the minimum number allowed is 0 and the maximum number allowed is 255.

2. The filter_input() function gets the value sent via HTTP POST from a form control whose name is number. The third parameter is the filter ID. The fourth parameter is the name of the variable that holds the array of options and flags to use with the filter.

3. The value stored in $number is shown in the form control. If the value in $number is null (because the form was not submitted) or false (because the data was not valid), you will not see it shown in the form control. This is because PHP does not display anything for false or null values.

4. var_dump() is used to show the value stored in $number (because false or null are not shown in a browser). It also shows the data type because all valid numbers are converted from strings to integers.

FILTERS TO VALIDATE MULTIPLE INPUTS

To collect and validate a set of values at the same time, you can use
`filter_input_array()`, and specify a filter to use for each piece
of data that is collected.

When a page expects to receive multiple values, create an associative array with an element for each value the page expects to receive. The keys for each element of the array are the names of the form controls or the names in the query string.

The value for each element is either:
- The name of the filter to use when the data is collected (if it has no flags or options)
- An array holding the name of the filter *and* any flags or options it should use

```
$filters['name1'] = FILTER_ID;
$filters['name2']['filter'] = FILTER_ID;
$filters['name2']['options']['option1'] = value1;
$filters['name2']['options']['option2'] = value2;
```

The `filter_input_array()` function is then called with two parameters, the:
- Input source (`INPUT_GET` or `INPUT_POST`)
- Array of filters that should be used with the values the page expects to receive for each input

It returns a new associative array. The key for each element is the name of the input; the value is:
- The value provided if it is valid
- `false` if the value was provided, but not valid
- `null` if the name was not provided

```
$data = filter_input_array(INPUT_SOURCE, $filters);
```
INPUT SOURCE   FILTERS ARRAY

If the page receives extra data that was not specified in the array of filters, that data is **not** added to the array that `filter_input_array()` returns.

If a piece of data is missing, it is given a value of `null`. To stop missing values from being added to the array, specify `false` as the third argument.

VALIDATING MULTIPLE INPUTS WITH FILTERS

PHP

```php
<?php
$form['email'] = '';                                                  // Initialize email
$form['age']   = '';                                                  // Initialize age
if ($_SERVER['REQUEST_METHOD'] == 'POST') {                           // If submitted
    $filters['email']                       = FILTER_VALIDATE_EMAIL;  // Email filter
    $filters['age']['filter']               = FILTER_VALIDATE_INT;    // Integer filter
    $filters['age']['options']['min_range'] = 16;                     // Min value 16
    $form = filter_input_array(INPUT_POST, $filters);                 // Validate data
}
?> ...
<form action="validate-multiple-inputs.php" method="POST">
    Email: <input type="text" name="email" value="<?= htmlspecialchars($form['email']) ?>">
    Age: <input type="text" name="age" value="<?= htmlspecialchars($form['age']) ?>"><br>
    I agree to the terms and conditions: <input type="checkbox" name="terms" value="1"><br>
    <input type="submit" value="Save">
</form>
<pre><?php var_dump($form); ?></pre>
```

Labels: ① ② ③ ④

RESULT

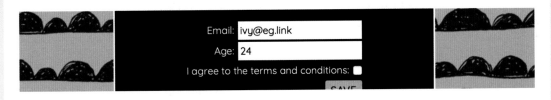

1. The `$form` array is initialized with values for the email and age inputs.

2. If the form has been submitted, `$filters` stores an array. The key for each element is the name of a form control. The values are the filters/options to use:

- `email` must follow the format of an email address
- `age` must be an integer that is 16 or more

3. `filter_input_array()` collects and validates the data and overwrites the values stored in `$form`.

4. The `var_dump()` function displays the data.

NOTE: When the form is sent, even if the terms checkbox is checked, it is not added to the `$form` array as it was not named in the `$filters` array. Also, invalid data is not displayed in the form control.

FILTER FUNCTIONS TO WORK WITH VARIABLES

PHP has two built-in filter functions to filter values stored in variables. `filter_var()` applies a filter to a single value stored in a variable. `filter_var_array()` applies filters to a set of values stored in an array.

The `filter_var()` function requires the:

- Name of the variable whose value will be checked
- Filter ID

Values for options or flags are set in the same way they are for `filter_input()`. The values it returns are also the same: if it is valid, it returns the value; if invalid, it returns `false`; if missing, it returns `null`.

$$\underbrace{\text{filter\_var(\$variable,}}_{\text{VARIABLE HOLDING DATA}} \underbrace{\text{FILTER\_ID}}_{\text{FILTER}}\underbrace{\text{[, \$settings]);}}_{\text{FLAGS/OPTIONS}}$$

The `filter_var_array()` function also has two parameters, the:

- Name of the variable holding an array whose data will be checked
- Array of filters and their options/flags

The values for the options or flags are set in the same way that they are for the `filter_input_array()` and the values that are returned are also the same.

If only one filter is named, the same filter is applied to all of the values in the array.

$$\underbrace{\text{filter\_var\_array(\$array,}}_{\text{VARIABLE HOLDING ARRAY}} \underbrace{\text{\$filters);}}_{\text{FILTERS TO USE}}$$

When `filter_input()` or `filter_input_array()` are used to validate data, they return `false` for any invalid pieces of data (replacing the value the user submitted).

This means that if the form contains invalid data, the user would not be able to see any invalid values that they had entered into the form.

To show incorrect values, collect the data and store it in a variable or array. Then, when it is validated using `filter_var()` or `filter_var_array()`, the result can be stored in a new variable. If the data is:

- valid: the page uses the data in the new variable
- invalid: the form displays the data as it was originally collected before it was validated

VALIDATING DATA IN VARIABLES

`PHP`

```php
<?php
$form['email'] = '';                                                    // Initialize
$form['age']   = '';
$form['terms'] = 0;
$data          = [];
if ($_SERVER['REQUEST_METHOD'] == 'POST') {                             // If submitted
    $filters['email']                        = FILTER_VALIDATE_EMAIL;   // Email filter
    $filters['age']['filter']                = FILTER_VALIDATE_INT;     // Integer filter
    $filters['age']['options']['min_range'] = 16;                       // Min age
    $filters['terms']                        = FILTER_VALIDATE_BOOLEAN; // Boolean filter
    $form = filter_input_array(INPUT_POST);                            // Get all values
    $data = filter_var_array($form, $filters);                         // Apply filters
}
?> ...
<form action="validate-variables.php" method="POST">
    Email: <input type="text" name="email" value="<?= htmlspecialchars($form['email']) ?>">
    Age: <input type="text" name="age" value="<?= htmlspecialchars($form['age']) ?>"><br>
    I agree to the terms and conditions: <input type="checkbox" name="terms" value="1"><br>
    <input type="submit" value="Save">
</form>
<pre><?php var_dump($data); ?></pre>
```

This example looks the same as the previous one.

1. The $form and $data arrays are initialized with values to show if the form has not been submitted.

2. If the form has been sent, the $filters array will store the filters and options to validate the data.

3. filter_input_array() collects the data from the form, overwriting the values stored in $form in Step 1.

4. filter_var_array() validates the form data (using the filters specified in the $filters array). It stores the array of results in a variable called $data.

5. The text inputs display the values that the user supplied (which were stored in the $form array before the data was validated).

6. The var_dump() function shows the data that has been validated and stored in the $data array (or null if the form was not sent).

TRY: Remove the age input controls, then resubmit the form. The var_dump() function will still show a value for the age control in Step 6 because it was listed in the array of filters, but not supplied when filter_var_array() was called.

VALIDATION FILTERS, FLAGS AND OPTIONS

The tables below show the filters, flags, and options for working with booleans and numbers. The tables on the right show the filters, flags, and options for working with strings.

All of the validation filters also have an option called default.

This option lets you provide a default value if the data is invalid.

FILTER_VALIDATE_BOOLEAN

Checks if a value is true (1, on, or yes are treated as true). Returns boolean value of true if the value is true, false if it is not true, null if the name was not present. Not case-sensitive.

FLAG	DESCRIPTION
FILTER_NULL_ON_FAILURE	Returns null (not false) if invalid

FILTER_VALIDATE_INT

Checks if a number is an integer (0 is not counted as a valid integer). If valid, returns the number as an int data type.

FLAG	DESCRIPTION
FILTER_FLAG_ALLOW_HEX	Allow hexadecimal numbers
FILTER_FLAG_ALLOW_OCTAL	Allow octal numbers
OPTION	DESCRIPTION
min_range	Minimum allowed number
max_range	Maximum allowed number

FILTER_VALIDATE_FLOAT

Checks if a number is a floating point number (decimal). Integers are valid (but 0 is not counted as a valid integer). If valid, returns the value as a float data type.

FLAG	DESCRIPTION
FILTER_FLAG_ALLOW_THOUSAND	Allows float to have thousand separator Returns null (not false) if invalid

FILTER_VALIDATE_REGEXP

Checks if a string contains a pattern of characters described in a regular expression (which were introduced on p214-17).

OPTION	DESCRIPTION
regexp	The regular expression to use

FILTER_VALIDATE_EMAIL

Checks if the structure of a string matches that of an email address.

FLAG	DESCRIPTION
FILTER_FLAG_EMAIL_UNICODE	Allows unicode characters in name part of address (part before @ symbol)

FILTER_VALIDATE_URL

Checks if the structure of a string matches that of a valid URL.

FLAG	DESCRIPTION
FILTER_FLAG_SCHEME_REQUIRED	Must contain a scheme e.g., `http://` or `ftp://`
FILTER_FLAG_HOST_REQUIRED	Must contain a hostname
FILTER_FLAG_PATH_REQUIRED	Must contain a path to file or directory
FILTER_FLAG_QUERY_REQUIRED	Must contain a query string

FILTER_VALIDATE_DOMAIN

Checks if the structure of a string matches that of a domain name.

FLAG	DESCRIPTION
FILTER_FLAG_HOSTNAME	Validates a hostname

FILTER_VALIDATE_IP

Checks if the structure of a string matches that of a valid IP address.

FLAG	DESCRIPTION
FILTER_FLAG_IPV4	Checks if it is a valid IPV4 IP address
FILTER_FLAG_IPV6	Checks if it is a valid IPV6 IP address
FILTER_FLAG_NO_RES_RANGE	Doesn't allow IPs from reserved range (addresses used on local networks and not sent across the Internet)
FILTER_FLAG_NO_PRIV_RANGE	Doesn't allow IPs from private range (a subset of reserved IP addresses)

SANITIZATION FILTERS

Sanitizing data involves removing characters that are not allowed to be in a value (and optionally replacing them). All four of PHP's filter functions can use a set of built-in filters to sanitize data.

In addition to the validation filters, PHP's built-in filter functions can also use a set of built-in **sanitization filters** that remove (and sometimes replace) any characters that should not appear in a value.

The first filter in the table below performs the same task as the `htmlspecialchars()` function (p246); it replaces the five reserved characters that HTML treats as code with entities.

The second filter encodes a URL, replacing the characters that are not allowed to appear in a URL with encoded versions of those characters.

The remaining filters remove characters that are not allowed to appear in text, numbers, email addresses, and URLs (but they do not replace those characters).

You should escape or sanitize data when it is being used (rather than when it is collected) because it will change the data. For example, imagine a visitor supplied the text `Fish & Chips`.

To display this text in a page, the ampersand must be escaped: `Fish &amp; Chips`. But, if the text was escaped when it was collected, a search feature might not be able to find the text `Fish & Chips` because the ampersand has already been escaped.

Also, characters are escaped in different ways depending on how the data is used; this is known as the **context** of how the data is used. To display the same text in a query string, the space is replaced with `%20` and the ampersand with `%26`, so it becomes:
`http://eg.link/search.php?Fish%20%26%20Chips`

FILTER ID	DESCRIPTION
`FILTER_SANITIZE_FULL_SPECIAL_CHARS`	Equivalent to `htmlspecialchars()` with ENT_QUOTES on
`FILTER_SANITIZE_ENCODED`	Converts URL to a URL-encoded version of the same URL
`FILTER_SANITIZE_STRING`	Removes tags from a string
`FILTER_SANITIZE_NUMBER_INT`	Removes characters other than 0-9 and + or -
`FILTER_SANITIZE_NUMBER_FLOAT`	Removes characters other than 0-9 and + or -. Has flags to allow a thousand and decimal separators and e or E for scientific notation
`FILTER_SANITIZE_EMAIL`	Removes characters not allowed in email addresses. Permits A-z 0-9 ! # $ % & ' * + - = ? ^ _ ` {	} ~ @ . [ ]
`FILTER_SANITIZE_URL`	Removes characters not allowed in URLs. Permits A-z 0-9 $ - _ . + ! * ' ( ) , { }	\ \ ^ ~ [ ] ` <> # % " ; / ? : @ & =

APPLYING SANITIZATION FILTERS TO VARIABLES

section_b/c06/sanitization-filters.php

```php
<?php
$user['name']  = 'Ivy<script src="js/bad.js"></script>';   // User's name
$user['age']   = 23.75;                                     // User's age
$user['email'] = '£ivy@eg.link/';                           // User's email

$sanitize_user['name']  = FILTER_SANITIZE_FULL_SPECIAL_CHARS; // HTML Escape filter
$sanitize_user['age']   = FILTER_SANITIZE_NUMBER_INT;         // Integer filter
$sanitize_user['email'] = FILTER_SANITIZE_EMAIL;             // Email filter

$user = filter_var_array($user, $sanitize_user);            // Sanitize output
?> ...
<p>Name:  <?= $user['name'] ?></p>
<p>Age:   <?= $user['age'] ?></p>
<p>Email: <?= $user['email'] ?></p>
<pre><?php var_dump($user); ?></pre>
```

1. The $user variable holds an array of data about a user.

2. The $sanitize_user variable holds an array with three keys whose names match the keys in the $user array. The values are the names of the sanitization filter to use with that value.

RESULT

Name: Ivy<script src="js/bad.js"></script>

Age: 2375

Email: ivy@eg.link

3. The filter_var_array() function is called to apply the sanitization filters to the values that are stored in the $user array. The name is escaped, and unwanted characters are removed from the age and email.

4. The sanitized data is shown.

5. PHP's var_dump() function shows the sanitized $user array (not shown in the result above).

TRY: In Step 2, remove the age element from the $user array. Because it is named in the array of filters, it will be given a value of null in the $user array.

NOTE: The decimal separator has been removed from the age, making it 2375. You must be careful that sanitization does not change the values you receive. To permit decimals or thousand separators, or scientific notation, add flags for the number filter: http://notes.re/php/sanitize

VALIDATING FORMS USING FILTERS

This example uses validation filters to validate data from multiple form controls, and uses sanitization filters to ensure that any data supplied by users is safe to display in the page. The result of this example looks the same as the one on p264.

1. The $user and $error arrays and the $message variable are initialized. This allows them to be used in the form at the bottom of the page when it first loads (before it is submitted).

2. An if statement checks if the form was submitted.

3. The $validation_filters variable holds an array of filters that will be used to validate the form data.

4. filter_input_array() collects the values from the form and applies the validation filters to the values that are collected. The results overwrite the values that were stored in $user in Step 1. If a value is:

- Valid, it is stored in the array
- Invalid, false is stored
- Missing, it will be given a value of null

5. Each value in the $errors array is set using a ternary operator. The condition checks if each piece of data is valid. If the value is counted as:

- true, it will hold a blank string
- false or null, the value will be an error message telling the user how to correct that piece of data

6. PHP's implode() function is used to join all of the values in the $errors array into a single string and store them in a variable called $invalid.

7. The condition of an if statement checks if the $invalid variable contains text, which is treated as true (a blank string is treated as false).

8. If the data is invalid, the $message variable holds a message telling the visitor to correct the form errors.

9. Otherwise, the $message variable tells the user that the data was valid. At this point, the page could process the data it received (and there would be no need to show the form again).

10. The name and age that were stored in the $user array are sanitized to make sure that they are safe to display in the page. This is done using PHP's filter_var() function:

- The name is sanitized to replace any HTML reserved characters with entities.
- The number is sanitized so that it only contains characters that are allowed in an integer.

11. The value in the $message variable is shown.

12. The form is displayed. If the user has supplied data that is:

- Valid, those values are shown in the form controls
- Invalid, the form controls will be blank

If the user has not submitted the form, the form controls use the initial values that were assigned to each element of the $user array in Step 1.

If any data is invalid, an error message is shown after the corresponding form control.

```php
<?php
$user    = ['name' => '', 'age' => '', 'terms' => '', ];          // Initialize
$errors  = ['name' => '', 'age' => '', 'terms' => false, ];
$message = '';

if ($_SERVER['REQUEST_METHOD'] == 'POST') {                        // If form submitted
    // Validation filters
    $validation_filters['name']['filter']               = FILTER_VALIDATE_REGEXP;
    $validation_filters['name']['options']['regexp']    = '/^[A-z]{2,10}$/';
    $validation_filters['age']['filter']                = FILTER_VALIDATE_INT;
    $validation_filters['age']['options']['min_range']  = 16;
    $validation_filters['age']['options']['max_range']  = 65;
    $validation_filters['terms']                        = FILTER_VALIDATE_BOOLEAN;

    $user = filter_input_array(INPUT_POST, $validation_filters); // Validate data

    // Create error messages
    $errors['name']  = $user['name']  ? '' : 'Name must be 2-10 letters using A-z';
    $errors['age']   = $user['age']   ? '' : 'You must be 16-65';
    $errors['terms'] = $user['terms'] ? '' : 'You must agree to the terms & conditions';
    $invalid = implode($errors);                                  // Join error messages

    if ($invalid) {                                               // If there are errors
        $message = 'Please correct the following errors:';        // Do not process
    } else {                                                      // Otherwise
        $message = 'Thank you, your data was valid.';             // Can process data
    }

    // Sanitize data
    $user['name'] = filter_var($user['name'], FILTER_SANITIZE_FULL_SPECIAL_CHARS);
    $user['age']  = filter_var($user['age'],  FILTER_SANITIZE_NUMBER_INT);
}
?> ...
<?= $message ?>
<form action="validate-form-using-filters.php" method="POST">
  Name: <input type="text" name="name" value="<?= $user['name'] ?>">
  <span class="error"><?= $errors['name'] ?></span><br>
  Age: <input type="text" name="age" value="<?= $user['age'] ?>">
  <span class="error"><?= $errors['age'] ?></span><br>
  <input type="checkbox" name="terms" value="true"
      <?= $user['terms'] ? 'checked' : '' ?>> I agree to the terms and conditions
  <span class="error"><?= $errors['terms'] ?></span><br>
  <input type="submit" value="Save">
</form>
```

SUMMARY
GETTING DATA FROM BROWSERS

> Data sent via query strings and forms is added to the $_GET and $_POST superglobal arrays, which store all the data they receive as strings.

> If a value may be missing from a superglobal array, use the isset() function to check if it is present or supply a default with the null-coalescing operator.

> Data can also be collected using the filter_input() or filter_input_array() functions.

> Before processing data, validate it. Check required data was supplied and that it is in the right format.

> Before showing user data, sanitize it to prevent XSS attacks. Replace reserved characters with entities.

> Validation filters are used in filter functions to validate values and convert them into the correct data type.

> Sanitization filters are used in filter functions to replace or remove unwanted characters.

7

IMAGES & FILES

This chapter shows you how to let visitors upload images to the server and how to safely display them in your PHP pages. These techniques also work for other types of file.

First, you learn how users upload images and how the server receives them. You see how the:

- HTML file upload control is used in an HTML form so that users can upload files.
- PHP interpreter adds data about the file to a superglobal array called $_FILES.
- File is placed in a temporary folder on the server.
- File must be moved to a folder where the uploaded files will be stored.

Next, you will learn how to validate the files that have been uploaded and check that:

- The filename only contains permitted characters.
- There is not already a file with that name.
- It is a permitted media type and file extension.
- The size of the file is not too large.

Finally, you will learn how to manipulate the images to create:

- Thumbnails of the image.
- Cropped versions of the image.

Throughout the chapter, you will meet more built-in functions that help with these tasks. While the chapter demonstrates these techniques using images, they can also be used to let visitors upload audio, video, PDF, and other types of files.

UPLOADING FILES FROM A BROWSER

HTML forms can contain a file upload control, which visitors can use to upload files to the server.

When creating an HTML form that allows visitors to upload files, the opening `<form>` tag must have the following three attributes:

- `method` with a value of POST to specify that the form should be sent via HTTP POST (because files should not be sent using HTTP GET)

- `enctype` with a value of `multipart/form-data` to specify the encoding type that the browser should use to send the data)

- `action` whose value is the PHP file that the form data should be sent to

The file upload control is created using the HTML `<input>` element. Its `type` attribute must have a value of `file`. In the browser, this creates a button which opens a new window that allows the user to select the file they want to upload:

```
<input type="file" name="image">
```

Like the other form controls, the file input control sends a name/value pair to the server:

- The name is the value of the `name` attribute for that file control (above it is called `image`)

- The value is the file that the user is sending

To help restrict the type of file a user can upload, the file input control has an `accept` attribute. Its value should be a comma-separated list of media types that the site accepts. (Media types are often referred to as MIME types; you can find out about them here: `http://notes.re/media-types`)

```
<input type="file" name="image"
       accept="image/jpeg, image/png">
```

If the `accept` attribute is used, when the visitor clicks on the button to upload a file, modern browsers will disable files that are not in the list of accepted types so that they cannot be selected.

This is helpful for usability, but you cannot rely upon the `accept` attribute to restrict the type of files visitors upload because they can override the setting and older browsers do not support it. (Chrome 10, Internet Explorer 10, Firefox 10, and Safari 6 were the first versions of the major browsers to support this feature.) Therefore you should also try to validate the media type on the server using PHP (see p295).

To permit all of the subtypes of a media type, you can add an asterisk character instead of a subtype. The following allows all formats of image (including BMP, GIF, JPEG, PNG, TIFF, and WebP):

```
<input type="file" accept="image/*">
```

1. The form below allows visitors to upload images. It is used in all of the examples in this chapter. The opening `<form>` tag needs a:

- `method` attribute with a value of `POST`
- `enctype` attribute set to `multipart/form-data`
- `action` attribute specifying the file to send the form data to (this value changes in each example)

2. To create a file upload control, the `<input>` element carries a `type` attribute whose value is `file`.

Because the examples in this chapter demonstrate how to allow visitors to upload an image, the value of the `name` attribute is `image`.

3. The submit button is used to submit the form.

```
① <form method="post" action="filename.php" enctype="multipart/form-data">
      <label for="image"><b>Upload file:</b></label>
② <input type="file" name="image" accept="image/*" id="image"><br>
③ <input type="submit" value="Upload">
   </form>
```

The first result box below shows the form that the file upload control creates. When an image is selected, the text next to the button is replaced by the filename.

In the second result box, you see the window that opens when the user clicks on *Choose File*. A text file and zip file are disabled because they are not images.

The visual appearance of the window that pops up to select files varies between browsers and operating systems (you cannot control its appearance using CSS).

RECEIVING FILES ON THE SERVER

When a file is uploaded via a web page, the web server saves it in a temporary folder, and the PHP interpreter stores details about the file in a superglobal array called $_FILES.

A form can have multiple file upload controls, so the PHP interpreter will create an element in the $_FILES superglobal array for each file upload control that the form sends.

The name of the element matches the name of the file upload control and its value is an array of data about the file that was uploaded via that form control.

The table below shows the information that the $_FILES superglobal array stores for each file that has been uploaded.

The images in this chapter are uploaded using a file upload control whose name is image, so the $_FILES array will have an element called image, and its value will be an array holding information about that image.

KEY	VALUE	HOW TO ACCESS VALUE
name	File name	$_FILES['image']['name']
tmp_name	Temporary location of the file (set by the PHP interpreter)	$_FILES['image']['tmp_name']
size	Size in bytes	$_FILES['image']['size']
type	Media type (according to the browser)	$_FILES['image']['type']
error	0 if file uploaded successfully, an error code if there was a problem	$_FILES['image']['error']

Once a file has been uploaded, the PHP code should check that the PHP interpreter did not find any errors with the upload.

If the **error** key in the array that was created for this file has a value of 0 then it means that the PHP interpreter did not encounter any errors.

```
if ($_FILES['image']['errors'] === 0) {
    // Process image
} else {
    // Show error message
}
```

CHECKING A FILE HAS BEEN UPLOADED

1. The $message variable is initialized with a blank string. It stores a message if the form is submitted.

2. If the form has been submitted using HTTP POST...

3. An if statement checks that there are no errors.

4. If there are no errors, the name and size of the file are stored in $message.

5. Otherwise, $message stores an error message.

6. The value in the $message variable is shown.

section_b/c07/upload-file.php

PHP

```php
<?php
$message = '';                                              // Initialize
if ($_SERVER['REQUEST_METHOD'] == 'POST') {                 // If form sent
    if ($_FILES['image']['error'] === 0) {                  // If no errors
        $message  = '<b>File:</b> ' . $_FILES['image']['name'] . '<br>';   // File name
        $message .= '<b>Size:</b> ' . $_FILES['image']['size'] . ' bytes'; // File size
    } else {                                                // Otherwise
        $message  = 'The file could not be uploaded.';      // Error message
    }
}
?> ...
<?= $message ?>
<form method="POST" action="upload-file.php" enctype="multipart/form-data">
  <label for="image"><b>Upload file:</b></label>
  <input type="file" name="image" accept="image/*" id="image"><br>
  <input type="submit" value="Upload">
</form>
```

Circled numbers: ① $message = ''; ② if ($_SERVER...; ③ if ($_FILES['image']['error']...; ④ $message = 'File:'... / $message .= 'Size:'...; ⑤ $message = 'The file could not be uploaded.'; ⑥ <?= $message ?>

RESULT

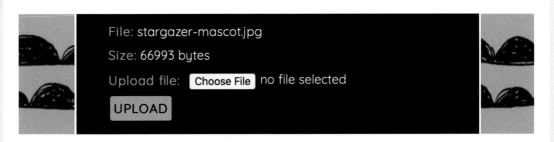

File: stargazer-mascot.jpg
Size: 66993 bytes
Upload file: Choose File no file selected
UPLOAD

MOVING A FILE TO ITS DESTINATION

PHP's `move_uploaded_file()` function moves a file from its temporary location to where it should be stored on the server.

When a file is uploaded to the server, it is given a temporary filename and placed in a temporary folder. (The temporary filename is created by the PHP interpreter.)

The PHP interpreter will delete the temporary file from this folder when the script finishes running. Therefore, to store an uploaded file on the server, you must call the `move_uploaded_file()` function to move it to another folder. It has two parameters:

- The temporary location of the file
- The destination where the file should be saved

It returns `true` if it was able to move the file to the new location and `false` if not.

The destination (the location where the file should be saved) is made up of the:

- Path to the folder that will store the uploaded file (this folder must have been created before you try to move a file into it).
- Filename (its original filename or a new name).

If you want to use the original name of the file that was uploaded, you can access it via the array that the PHP interpreter created for that file. Its key is `name`.

Below, the destination filepath is stored in a variable called `$destination`. It is created by specifying the `uploads` folder, followed by the original name of the file used when uploading the image.

NEW FOLDER   FILENAME

```
$destination = '../uploads/' . $_FILES['image']['name'];
move_uploaded_file($_FILES['image']['tmp_name'], $destination);
```

TEMPORARY LOCATION   DESTINATION FILEPATH

FILE PERMISSIONS
The permissions for the destination directory should:
- Permit the web server to read/write files - this allows it to save and display images
- Disable execute permissions - this prevents malicious scripts from being executed

CHECK A FILE WAS UPLOADED
PHP's `move_uploaded_file()` function checks that a file was uploaded via HTTP POST before moving it. If you need to use a file *before* you move it, use PHP's `is_uploaded_file()` to perform this check for you. (This helps prevent someone accessing other files.)

MOVING AN UPLOADED FILE

section_b/c07/move-file.php

```php
<?php
$message = '';                              // Initialize
$moved   = false;                           // Initialize

if ($_SERVER['REQUEST_METHOD'] == 'POST') { // If sent +
    if ($_FILES['image']['error'] === 0) {  // No errors
        // Store temporary path and new destination
        $temp = $_FILES['image']['tmp_name'];
        $path = 'uploads/' . $_FILES['image']['name'];
        // Move the file and store result in $moved
        $moved = move_uploaded_file($temp, $path);
    }

    if ($moved === true) { // If move worked, show image
        $message = '<img src="' . $path . '">';
    } else {               // Else store error message
        $message = 'The file could not be saved.';
    }
}
?> ...
<?= $message ?>
```

RESULT

1. A variable called $moved is initialized with a value of false. This will change to true if the image is successfully moved.

2. If the form was submitted and there were no errors...

3. $temp holds the location where the PHP inpterpreter temporarily stored the file.

4. $path stores the path where the file will be saved. (The file will keep the same filename that it had when it was uploaded.)

5. move_uploaded_file() tries to move the file from its temporary location (in $temp) to the new location (in $path). The function returns true if it worked or false if it failed. This value replaces the value stored in the $moved variable in Step 1.

6. A conditional statement tests if $moved has a value of true, indicating that the move worked.

7. If so, $message stores an HTML <img> tag that shows the uploaded image.

8. Otherwise, $message stores an error message.

9. The value stored in $message is displayed to the user.

CLEANING A FILENAME AND DUPLICATE FILES

Before moving a file from its temporary location, you should:
a) Remove characters in the filename that could cause problems
b) Ensure that it will not overwrite another file with the same name

Characters such as ampersands, colons, periods and spaces should be removed from filenames as they can cause problems. To do this, you can replace characters other than A-Z, a-z, and 0-9, with a dash.

1. Use PHP's `pathinfo()` function (see p228), to get the file's basename and extension.

2. Use PHP's `preg_replace()` function (see p214) to replace any characters in the basename other than A-Z, a-z, and 0-9, with a dash.

3. Create the destination filepath by joining the upload directory, basename, a period, and the file extension. This value should be saved in a variable.

```
①  $basename  = pathinfo($filename, PATHINFO_FILENAME);
    $extension = pathinfo($filename, PATHINFO_EXTENSION);
②  $basename  = preg_replace('/[^A-z0-9]/', '-', $basename);
③  $filepath  = 'uploads/' . $basename . '.' . $extension;
```

If `move_uploaded_file()` is called and a file with the same name exists, the old file is replaced by the new one. To prevent this, each file needs a unique name:

4. Set a counter to 1 and store it in a variable called i.

5. In the condition of a `while` loop, use PHP's `file_exists()` function (see p228) to check if a file with the same name already exists.

6. If it does, add 1 to the value stored in the counter.

7. Update the filename, adding the value in the counter after the basename, before the extension. E.g., if `upload.jpg` exists, call the file `upload1.jpg`.

The loop's condition then runs again to check if the new filename exists. The loop repeats Steps 5-7 until it has a unique filename.

```
④  $i = 1;
⑤  while (file_exists('uploads/' . $filename)) {
⑥      $i = $i + 1;
⑦      $filename = $basename . $i . '.' . $extension;
    }
```

VALIDATING FILE SIZE AND FILE TYPE

To ensure a site can work with an uploaded file, before moving it, check:
a) The file is not too large (large files take longer to download/process)
b) The site can work with the media type and file extension

You can set a maximum file upload size in php.ini or .htaccess (see p196-9), or you can create validation code to restrict sizes in pages that accept uploads.

To see if a file is larger than the maximum upload size set in php.ini or .htaccess look in the $_FILES array. If it is, the error key for that file will have a value of 1.

You can also check the size of a file in the $_FILES array; the size key for the file holds the size in bytes. The two ternary operators below are used to perform both of these checks. The condition of the:

- First ternary operator checks if the error code is 1
- Second, checks if the size is larger than 5mb

```
$error = ($_FILES['image']['error'] === 1)      ? 'Too large' : '';
$error = ($_FILES['image']['size'] <= 5242880) ? '' : 'Too large';
```

Validating a file's media type and file extension helps ensure that a site can safely handle a file. Below:

1. $allowed_types is an array of allowed media types.

2. PHP's mime_content_type() function tries to detect the file's media type and stores it in $type.

3. PHP's in_array() function checks if this file's media type is in the array of allowed media types.

4. $allowed_exts stores an array of allowed extensions.

5. The filename is converted to lowercase and is stored in $filename.

6. The file extension is collected and stored in $ext.

7. PHP's in_array() function checks if this file extension is in the array of allowed extensions.

```
① $allowed_types = ['image/jpeg', 'image/png', 'image/gif',];
② $type  = mime_content_type($_FILES['image']['tmp_name']);
③ $error = in_array($type, $allowed_types) ? '' : 'Wrong file type ';
④ $allowed_exts = ['jpeg', 'jpg', 'png', 'gif',];
⑤ $filename = strtolower($_FILES['image']['name']);
⑥ $ext      = pathinfo($filename, PATHINFO_EXTENSION));
⑦ $error   .= in_array($ext, $allowed_exts) ? '' : 'Wrong extension ';
```

VALIDATING FILE UPLOADS

This example brings together the code to upload, validate, and save a file.

1. Six variables are created to hold the:

- Result of whether or not the file was uploaded
- Success / failure message the user sees
- Errors if there are problems with the image
- Path to the folder storing the uploaded files
- Maximum file size in bytes
- Allowed media types
- Allowed file extensions

2. A function called `create_filename()` is defined. It uses the code from p294 to clean the filename and ensure the filename is unique, then return the new filename. Its two parameters are the:

- Name of the file
- Relative path to the folder where it will be stored

3. An `if` statement checks if the form was posted.

4. A ternary operator is used to check if there was an error uploading this image because it was larger than the size limit set in `php.ini` or `.htaccess`. If so, an error message is stored in `$error`.

5. Another `if` statement checks if the file was uploaded without any errors.

6. The size of the file is validated. If it is less than or equal to the maximum size stored in `$max_size` in Step 1, `$error` stores a blank string; if it is larger than the maximum permitted size, `$error` holds the message `'too big '`.

7. PHP's built-in `mime_content_type()` function gets the media type of the file and stores it in `$type`.

8. PHP's `in_array()` function checks if the media type stored in `$type` is in the `$allowed_types` array. If it is, a blank string is added to the `$error` variable. If it is not, an error message is added to `$error`.

9. PHP's `pathinfo()` function gets the file extension of the uploaded image. This function is called inside PHP's `strtolower()` function to ensure that the extension is in lowercase. It is then stored in `$ext`.

10. PHP's `in_array()` function is used to check if the file extension is permitted. If it is, a blank string is added to the `$error` variable. If it is not, a message is added to indicate that it is the wrong extension.

11. The condition of an `if` statement checks if `$error` holds a value that is *not* treated as `true`. A blank string is treated as `false` (there are no errors).

12. If there are no errors, the `create_filename()` function (from Step 2) is called to ensure that the filename is clean and unique.

13. `$destination` holds the path to save the new file.

14. PHP's `move_uploaded_file()` function is called to move the file from its temporary location to the the `uploads` folder. It returns `true` if it works; `false` if not. The result is stored in a variable called `$moved`.

15. If the `$moved` variable has a value of `true`, the image was uploaded, passed the checks, and has been saved, so the `$message` variable stores an HTML `<img>` tag that will display the image.

16. If not, an error message is stored in `$message`.

17. The value stored in the `$message` variable is displayed before the upload form.

```php
<?php
$moved          = false;                                      // Initialize
$message        = '';                                         // Initialize
$error          = '';                                         // Initialize
$upload_path    = 'uploads/';                                 // Upload path
$max_size       = 5242880;                                    // Max file size (in bytes)
$allowed_types  = ['image/jpeg', 'image/png', 'image/gif',];  // Allowed file types
$allowed_exts   = ['jpeg', 'jpg', 'png', 'gif',];             // Allowed file extensions

function create_filename($filename, $upload_path)             // Function to make filename
{
    $basename   = pathinfo($filename, PATHINFO_FILENAME);     // Get basename
    $extension  = pathinfo($filename, PATHINFO_EXTENSION);    // Get extension
    $basename   = preg_replace('/[^A-z0-9]/', '-', $basename); // Clean basename
    $i          = 0;                                          // Counter
    while (file_exists($upload_path . $filename)) {           // If file exists
        $i        = $i + 1;                                   // Update counter
        $filename = $basename . $i . '.' . $extension;        // New filepath
    }
    return $filename;                                         // Return filename
}
if ($_SERVER['REQUEST_METHOD'] == 'POST') {                   // If form submitted
    $error = ($_FILES['image']['error'] === 1) ? 'too big ' : '';  // Check size error

    if ($_FILES['image']['error'] == 0) {                              // If no upload errors
        $error .= ($_FILES['image']['size'] <= $max_size) ? '' : 'too big ';  // Check size
        // Check the media type is in the $allowed_types array
        $type   = mime_content_type($_FILES['image']['tmp_name']);
        $error .= in_array($type, $allowed_types) ? '' : 'wrong type ';
        // Check the file extension is in the $allowed_exts array
        $ext    = strtolower(pathinfo($_FILES['image']['name'], PATHINFO_EXTENSION));
        $error .= in_array($ext, $allowed_exts) ? '' : 'wrong file extension ';
        // If there are no errors, create the new filepath and try to move the file
        if (!$error) {
            $filename    = create_filename($_FILES['image']['name'], $upload_path);
            $destination = $upload_path . $filename;
            $moved       = move_uploaded_file($_FILES['image']['tmp_name'], $destination);
        }
    }

    if ($moved === true) {                                       // If it moved
        $message = 'Uploaded:<br><img src="' . $destination . '">';  // Show image
    } else {                                                     // Otherwise
        $message = '<b>Could not upload file:</b> ' . $error;    // Show errors
    }
}
?> ... <?= $message ?> <!-- Show form -->
```

RESIZING IMAGES

When users upload images, sites will often resize them so that they are all a similar size; this makes the page look neater and load faster. To resize an image, you need its **ratio**: its width divided by its height.

Uploaded images are often resized for two reasons:

- When a set of images are similar sizes, they look neater than when they are very different sizes.
- When an uploaded file is larger than the size it is shown at, this slows down the loading of the page.

When resizing images, you should keep the same ratio (the width divided by the height), otherwise the resized images look distorted (see right-hand page). If you want all images to be *exactly* the same size, you can crop the image (select part of it) then resize that selection, retaining its ratio (see p300-301).

LANDSCAPE

With landscape images, the width is greater than the height, so the ratio is greater than 1.

In the example below, if the width is 2000 and the height is 1600, the ratio will be:
2000 ÷ 1600 = 1.25

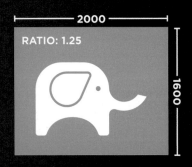

RATIO: 1.25

2000 · 1600

SQUARE

With square images, the height and the width are the same, so the ratio is exactly 1.

In the example below, if the width is 2000 and the height is 2000, the ratio will be:
2000 ÷ 2000 = 1

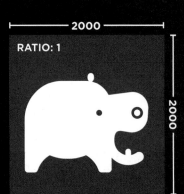

RATIO: 1

2000 · 2000

PORTRAIT

With portrait images, the width is always less than the height, so the ratio is less than 1.

In the example below, if the width is 1600 and the height is 2000, the ratio will be:
1600 ÷ 2000 = 0.8

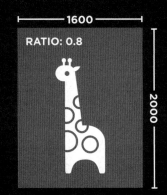

RATIO: 0.8

1600 · 2000

Below, you can see how to work out the new width and height an image will be when resizing it. By retaining the same ratio as the original image, the resized image will not look distorted.

To make a set of resized images look more consistent, they are resized to fit inside a square **containing box** (or **bounding box**) which sets the maximum width and height the image can be.

When the image is resized, the longer side of the image (the width *or* height) will fill the container, and the shorter side will be calculated using the image's ratio.

The width and height of the container must be defined. This is the maximum width and height the resized image can be.

In this example, the maximum width and height are set to 1000.

LANDSCAPE

├── 1000 ──┤
1000

PORTRAIT

├── 1000 ──┤
1000

1

Get the width and height of the original image that was uploaded.

Use them to calculate the image's ratio (width ÷ height).

├────── 2000 ──────┤
RATIO: 1.25
1600

├───── 1600 ─────┤
RATIO: 0.8
2000

2

If the width is greater than the height, the image is landscape. Otherwise it is portrait.

Set the longer side of the image to the size of the container.

├── 1000 ──┤
1600

├───── 1600 ─────┤
1000

3

Calculate the length of the shorter side of the resized image.
Landscape: *Divide* the container height by the ratio.
Portrait: *Multiply* the container width by the ratio.

├── 1000 ──┤
800

A **landscape** image will not fill the full height of the container.

├── 800 ──┤
1000

A **portrait** image will not fill the full width of the container.

CROPPING IMAGES

Cropping images allows you to create a set of images that are all exactly the same size, and allows the new images to fill the containing box. When images are cropped, part of the original image is removed.

To crop an image, you need to select the part of the original image that you want to keep.

To make a set of images a consistent shape, the cropped section of each image should have the same ratio.

Once you have selected an area to crop, you can then resize it to make sure that all of the images are the same size.

To select the area of the image you want for the crop, you need four pieces of data:

- **Selection width:** The width of the area in the image you want keep from the x-offset

- **Selection height:** The height of the area in the image you want to keep from the y-offset

- **X-offset:** The distance from the left-hand side of the image to where the selection should start

- **Y-offset:** The distance from the top of the image to where the selection should start

There are JavaScript tools that allow users to crop images in the browser before the image is uploaded. For some of the available options, see:
`http://notes.re/php/images/crop-javascript`

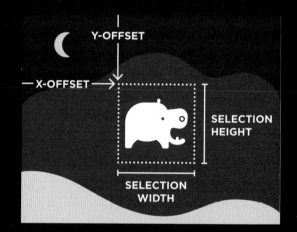

To ensure that the uploaded images are all the same size, you need to specify the width and height that you want them to be. Those values will be used to calculate the new image's ratio (width ÷ height).

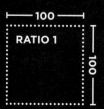

1

Get the width and height of the uploaded image and calculate the uploaded image's ratio (width ÷ height).

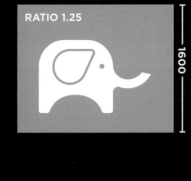

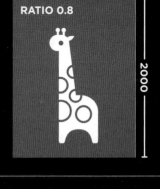

2

Select the relevant part of the image to keep.

This selection should have the same ratio as the new image.

The calculations for selections and offset are shown below.

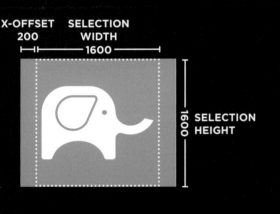

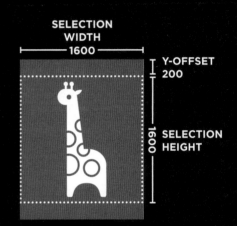

If new image ratio is less than uploaded image ratio:

- **Selection width** = original height x new ratio
- **Selection height** = original height
- **X-offset** = (original width - selection width) / 2
- **Y-offset** = 0

Otherwise use the following calculations:

- **Selection width** = original width
- **Selection height** = original width x new ratio
- **X-offset** = 0
- **Y-offset** = (original height - selection height) / 2

3

The cropped area is resized so it is the size of the new image (as defined on the left-hand page).

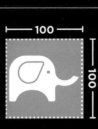

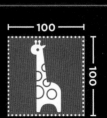

EDITING IMAGES USING EXTENSIONS

Extensions add functionality to the PHP interpreter, allowing it to perform extra tasks. GD and Imagick are two popular extensions that allow the PHP interpreter to resize and crop images.

When extensions are installed on a web server, they usually give you extra functions or classes that your PHP pages can use (in the same way that your code uses PHP's built-in functions and classes).

The GD and Imagick extensions perform tasks similar to the basic features of Photoshop but, instead of manipulating images using a graphical user interface, they let you edit the image using PHP code.

The rest of this chapter explains how to resize images using GD, then how to resize and crop images using Imagick. (An example of cropping images using GD is available online: `http://notes.re/php/gd-crop`)

GD is more complicated to use than Imagick but it has been installed by default with the PHP interpreter since PHP 4.3, whereas Imagick must be installed on the web server before it can be used.

USING GD

If you use MAMP on a Mac, GD should be enabled by default.

If you use XAMPP on a PC, you probably need to enable the GD extension before you can use it, see: `http://notes.re/php/enable-gd`

In order to resize and crop an image using GD, you must call five of GD's functions (shown below). GD has set functions to open different media types (GIF, JPEG, PNG, WEBP etc.), and corresponding functions to save them (the italic *mediatype* below is replaced by the type of file - see right-hand page).

FUNCTION	DESCRIPTION
`getimagesize()`	Get the dimensions and media type of an image
`imagecreatefrommediatype()`	Open the image (replace *mediatype* with the image's media type)
`imagecreatetruecolor()`	Create a new blank image using the dimensions of the resized or cropped image
`imagecopyresampled()`	Take the selected part of the original image, resize it and paste it into the new image created in the previous step
`imagemediatype()`	Save the image (replace *mediatype* with the image's media type)

DETERMINING THE MEDIA TYPE

To select the correct function to open or save an image, you need to know the media type of the image.

GD's `getimagesize()` function requires a path to an image as an argument. It returns an array containing data about the image including its media type. The table on the right shows the data held in that array (the keys are a mix of numbers and words).

KEY	DESCRIPTION
0	Width of the image (in pixels)
1	Height of the image (in pixels)
2	Constant describing the image type
3	String with dimensions for use in an `<img>` tag: `height="yyy" width="xxx"`
mime	Media type of the image
channels	3 if image is RGB, 4 if it is CMYK
bits	Number of bits used for each color

OPENING & SAVING IMAGES

The media type of the image can be used in a `switch` statement (as shown on the next page) so that the right function is called to open or save the image.

The table on the right shows some of the functions GD offers to open and save image formats.

FORMAT	OPEN	SAVE
GIF	`imagecreatefromgif()`	`imagegif()`
JPEG	`imagecreatefromjpeg()`	`imagejpeg()`
PNG	`imagecreatefrompng()`	`imagepng()`
WEBP	`imagecreatefromwebp()`	`imagewebp()`

RESIZING AND CROPPING IMAGES

The `imagecopyrempled()` function copies part (or all) of an image into a new blank image.

To do this, the function has 10 parameters, but it can be easier to think of them as 5 pairs of parameters:

- `$new, $orig`
  New and original images (stored in variables before the function is called – see p304)
- `$new_x, $new_y`
  X-offset and Y-offset where it should position the copied area in the new image
- `$orig_x, $orig_y`
  X-offset and Y-offset where it should take the selection from the original image
- `$new_width, $new_height`
  Selection width and height in the new image
- `$orig_width, $orig_height`
  Selection width and height from the original image

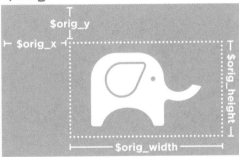

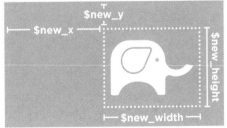

```
imagecopyresampled($new, $orig, $new_x, $new_y, $orig_x, $orig_y,
                   $new_width, $new_height, $orig_width, $orig_height);
```

RESIZING IMAGES USING GD

The function on the right-hand page uses GD to create a thumbnail. The thumbnail will keep the same aspect ratio as the original. The new size is based on a maximum width and height given as arguments.

The complete example in the code download follows the example on p297. The only differences are that it creates a path for the resized thumbnail image, then calls this function to create a thumbnail once the uploaded image has been moved (Steps 14-15).

1. `resize_image_gd()` has four parameters, the:

- Path to the uploaded image
- Path to save the resized image
- Maximum width of the new image
- Maximum height of the new image

2. GD's `getimagesize()` function returns an array holding data about the image, including its dimensions and media type (see previous page).

3. The image's width, height, and media type are taken from the array and stored in variables.

4. The `$new_width` and `$new_height` variables are initialized with the maximum width and height that the thumbnail can be.

5. `$orig_ratio` stores the uploaded image's ratio.

6. If the width is greater than the height of the image, then the image is a landscape image.

7. For a landscape image, the width of the resized image will be the maximum width. This value was set when the variable was initialized in Step 4. But the new height of the image must be calculated; to do this, divide the width of the image by its ratio.

8. Otherwise, the image is portrait or square. Its height remains the maximum height set in Step 4. The new width is calculated by multiplying the image's new height by its ratio.

9. A `switch` statement is used to select the correct function to open the image. (As shown on the previous page, GD uses separate functions to open images that are different media types.) The image's media type (stored in `$media_type` in Step 3) is used as the condition of the `switch` statement. The opened image is stored in `$orig`.

10. GD's `imagecreatetruecolor()` function creates a blank image, which is stored in `$new`. The two arguments provided are the width and height that the new image should be.

11. GD's `imagecopyresampled()` function copies the original image, resizes it, and pastes it into the new image created in Step 10. It needs to be given values for all 10 of the parameters that were described on the previous page.

12. Another `switch` statement is used to select the correct function to save the resized image. This time, a shorthand form of the `switch` statement is used (so the example fits on the page). The functions that save images return `true` if the image is saved, and `false` if not; this value is stored in `$result`.

13. The value stored in `$result` is returned.

14. Once the image has been uploaded and moved, the path where the new thumbnail image will be saved is created by joining the path to the uploads folder, the text `thumb_`, and the filename.

15. `resize_image_gd()` is called.

```php
<?php
function resize_image_gd($orig_path, $new_path, $max_width, $max_height)
{
    $image_data   = getimagesize($orig_path);              // Get image data
    $orig_width   = $image_data[0];                        // Image width
    $orig_height  = $image_data[1];                        // Image height
    $media_type   = $image_data['mime'];                   // Media type
    $new_width    = $max_width;                            // Maximum new width
    $new_height   = $max_height;                           // Maximum new height
    $orig_ratio   = $orig_width / $orig_height;            // Original image ratio

    // Calculate new size
    if ($orig_width > $orig_height) {                      // If landscape
        $new_height = $new_width / $orig_ratio;            // Set height using ratio
    } else {                                              // Otherwise
        $new_width  = $new_height * $orig_ratio;           // Set width using ratio
    }

    switch($media_type) {                                 // Check the media type
        case 'image/gif' :                                // If it is a GIF
            $orig = imagecreatefromgif($orig_path);       // This function opens image
            break;                                        // End switch statement
        case 'image/jpeg' :                               // If it is a JPG
            $orig = imagecreatefromjpeg($orig_path);      // This function opens image
            break;                                        // End switch statement
        case 'image/png' :                                // If it is a PNG
            $orig = imagecreatefrompng($orig_path);       // This function opens image
            break;                                        // End switch statement
    }

    $new = imagecreatetruecolor($new_width, $new_height); // Create a blank image

    imagecopyresampled($new, $orig, 0, 0, 0, 0, $new_width, $new_height,
        $orig_width, $orig_height);                       // Copy orig to new image

    // Save image - The thumbs folder must have been created + have the right permissions
    switch($media_type) {
        case 'image/gif' : $result = imagegif($new, $new_path);  break;
        case 'image/jpeg': $result = imagejpeg($new, $new_path); break;
        case 'image/png' : $result = imagepng($new, $new_path);  break;
    }
    return $result;
} ... // Code to upload and validate the image is the same as on p296-7
$moved     = move_uploaded_file($_FILES['image']['tmp_name'], $destination); // Move file
$thumbpath = $upload_path . 'thumb_' . $filename;                 // Create thumbnail path
$resized   = resize_image_gd($destination, $thumbpath, 200, 200); // Create thumbnail
```

RESIZING AND CROPPING WITH IMAGICK

The Imagick PHP extension lets you to control a piece of open source image editing software called ImageMagick using PHP code. The Imagick extension:

- Requires much less code than GD
- Calculates ratios and dimensions to resize images (you do not need to calculate them in your code)
- Uses the same methods for all image formats
- Supports more image formats than GD

But it does require both the Imagick extension and the ImageMagick software to be installed on the web server; they are not installed by default. So you must:

- Enable Imagick for MAMP on a Mac
- Install Imagick + ImageMagick for XAMPP on PCs
  See: `http://notes.re/php/install-imagick`
- Check if your hosting provider supports it

To use Imagick, you create an object that represents the image using the `Imagick` class, and pass the constructor the path to the image it will represent.

| VARIBLE TO STORE OBJECT | CLASS NAME | PATH TO IMAGE |

```
$image = new Imagick($filepath);
```

The `Imagick` object it creates has a set of methods that manipulate and save the image.

METHOD	DESCRIPTION
`thumbnailImage()`	Resize image
`cropThumbnailImage()`	Crop and resize image
`writeImage()`	Save image

On a PC, the path Imagick uses to save a file *must* be an absolute (not relative) path, and absolute paths are different on a PC compared with Mac and Unix.

- On a PC, they start with a drive letter e.g., `C:/`
- On a Mac and Unix, they start with a backslash \

The directory separator is also different: on a PC it is a forward slash, on a Mac and Unix it is a backslash. To create the correct path to the upload directory (and store it in a variable), the code below is used.

The statement below uses:

- PHP's `dirname()` function to return the path to the directory holding the file specified as an argument.

- The `__FILE__` constant, which holds the path to the file that is currently running.

- The `DIRECTORY_SEPARATOR` constant, which stores the correct directory separator for the operating system being used to run the PHP file.

CURRENT FILE   DIRECTORY SEPARATOR

```
$upload_path = dirname(__FILE__) . DIRECTORY_SEPARATOR . 'uploads' . DIRECTORY_SEPARATOR;
```

PATH TO PARENT DIRECTORY

The two examples below show two user-defined functions that use Imagick to resize and crop images.

The statements that call these functions appear just after the code that moves the uploaded file to its destination, just like the previous example on p305.

The code to upload, validate, and move the image is the same as the code on p296-7.

1. The create_thumbnail() function creates a thumbnail of an image using Imagick. Its two parameters are the:

- Path to the image that was just uploaded
- Path for the new thumbnail Imagick will create

2. A new object is created using the Imagick class. It needs the path to the image that was uploaded.

3. The Imagick object's thumbnailImage() method resizes the image. To do this, it uses three arguments:

- The new width of the image
- The new height of the image
- A boolean value of true to tell Imagick that the width and height are *maximum* values and that the thumbnail should be the same ratio as the original

4. Imagick's writeImage() method saves the image to the location stored in the $destination parameter.

5. The function returns true to show that it worked.

6. Once the file has moved, the $thumbpath variable stores a path where the new thumbnail will be saved.

7. create_thumbnail() is called, and it is given the path of the uploaded image and the thumbnail path.

```
PHP                                                    section_b/c07/resize-im.php

① function create_thumbnail($temporary, $destination)
   {
②     $image = new Imagick($temporary);              // Object to represent image
③     $image->thumbnailImage(200, 200, true);        // Create thumbnail
④     $image->writeImage($destination);              // Save file
⑤     return true;                                   // Return true to show success
   } ... // Once file has been validated and moved, create the thumbnail path, then thumbnail
   $moved      = move_uploaded_file($_FILES['image']['tmp_name'], $destination); // Move
⑥ $thumbpath = $upload_path . 'thumb_' . $filename;       // Path to thumbnail
⑦ $thumb     = create_thumbnail($destination, $thumbpath);  // Create thumbnail
```

8. create_cropped_thumbnail() creates a square crop of the uploaded image. This ensures that all of the thumbnails are the same size.

9. The only difference from the example above is that it uses the cropThumbnailImage() method of the Imagick object to create the cropped thumbnail.

```
PHP                                                    section_b/c07/crop-im.php

⑧ function create_cropped_thumbnail($temporary, $destination)
   {
       $image = new Imagick($temporary);              // Object to represent image
⑨     $image->cropThumbnailImage(200, 200, true);    // Create thumbnail
       $image->writeImage($destination);             // Save file
       return true;                                  // Return true to show success
   }
```

SUMMARY
IMAGES & FILES

> HTML forms use a file upload control to upload files.

> When a file is uploaded, the $_FILES superglobal array stores data about it.

> When files are uploaded, they are placed in a temporary location. They must then be moved to a different folder in order to save them.

> Before trying to work with files, check that they were uploaded via HTTP, and that there were no errors.

> Ensure that the filename only uses allowed characters.

> Validate the size and media type of uploaded files before saving them.

> When resizing an image, retain the same ratio; otherwise, it will look stretched and distorted.

> GD and Imagick are extensions that allow you to resize and crop images on the server using PHP.

8
DATES & TIMES

Dates and times can be written in many different ways. PHP provides built-in functions and classes that help to process and display dates and times in various formats.

In this chapter, you will learn the different ways in which the PHP interpreter can accept dates and times as input, and how it can format them as output when they are displayed to visitors. PHP can work with dates and times using:

- Components such as years, months, days, hours, minutes, and seconds
- Formats such as '1st June 2001', '1/6/2001' or 'next Tuesday'
- Unix timestamps which count the number of seconds since January 1st 1970 (this may seem an odd way to represent dates/times, but many programming languages use them)

Once you have understood how PHP processes date and time formats, you will meet a set of built-in functions that generate Unix timestamps, and convert them back into a human-readable format.

You will then learn how dates and times can be represented using objects that are created using four built-in classes:

- DateTime creates objects that represent a specific date and time
- DateInterval creates objects that represent an interval of time (e.g., an hour or a week)
- DatePeriod creates objects that represent recurring events that happen at regular intervals (e.g., every day, month, or year)
- DateTimeZone creates objects that represent a time zone

DATE FORMATS

Dates can be displayed in many different ways. PHP uses a set of **format characters** to describe how a date is written.

Dates can consist of the following components:

- Day of week
- Day of month
- Month
- Year

PHP uses format characters to represent each of these components. For example, **m-d-Y** represents the date format 04-06-2022. Format characters tell the PHP interpreter how dates will be:

- Processed when they are received
- Formatted when they are displayed

You can add spaces, forward slashes, dashes, and periods between the format characters to visually separate each component.

Below, you see how the format characters describe different ways of writing the same date:

FORMAT CHARACTERS	DATE FORMAT
l m j Y	Saturday April 6 2022
D jS F Y	Sat 6th April 2022
n/j/Y	4/6/2022
m/d/y	04/06/22
m-d-Y	04-06-2022

DAY OF WEEK

CHARACTER	DESCRIPTION	EXAMPLE
D	First three letters	Sat
l	Full name	Saturday

DAY OF MONTH

CHARACTER	DESCRIPTION	EXAMPLE
d	Digits with leading zero	09
j	Digits no leading zero	9
S	Suffix	th

MONTH

CHARACTER	DESCRIPTION	EXAMPLE
m	Digits with leading zero	04
n	Digits no leading zero	4
M	First three letters	Apr
F	Full name	April

YEAR

CHARACTER	DESCRIPTION	EXAMPLE
Y	Four digits	2022
y	Two digits	22

TIME FORMATS

These format characters can be used to represent different ways of displaying time.

HOUR

CHARACTER	DESCRIPTION	EXAMPLE
h	12-hour with leading zero	08
g	12-hour no leading zero	8
H	24-hour with leading zero	08
G	24-hour no leading zero	8

MINUTE

CHARACTER	DESCRIPTION	EXAMPLE
i	Digits with leading zero	09

SECOND

CHARACTER	DESCRIPTION	EXAMPLE
s	Digits with leading zero	04

AM/PM

CHARACTER	DESCRIPTION	EXAMPLE
a	Lowercase	am
A	Uppercase	AM

Times can consist of the following components:

- Hours
- Minutes
- Seconds
- am/pm (if 24-hour time is not used)

Each one can be represented using format characters. For example, **g:i a** represents a time in the format 8:09 am. These format characters are used to tell the PHP interpreter how times will be:

- Processed when they are received
- Formatted when they are displayed

You can add spaces, colons, periods, and parentheses between the format characters to visually separate each component.

Below, you see how the format characters can describe different ways of writing the same time:

FORMAT CHARACTERS	DATE FORMAT
g:i a	8:09 am
h:i(A)	08:09(AM)
G:i	08:09

SPECIFYING DATES & TIMES USING STRINGS

Some functions and methods allow you to specify a date and time using a string. The string must be in an accepted format as described below.

The PHP interpreter can accept dates using the following string formats. If forward slashes are used, the PHP interpreter expects the month before the day of the month. If dashes or dots are used, it expects the day of the month before the month.

DATE FORMAT	EXAMPLE
d F Y	04 September 2022
jS F Y	4th September 2022
F j Y	September 4 2022
M d Y	Sep 04 2022
m/d/Y	09/04/2022
Y/m/d	2022/09/04
d-m-Y	04-09-2022
n-j-Y	9-4-2022
d.m.y	04.09.22

You can use the relative times on the right. E.g.:
+ 1 day
+ 3 years 2 days 1 month
- 4 hours 20 mins
next Tuesday
first Sat of Jan
First/Last only work for days of the month.
If no time is specified, it will be set to midnight.

The PHP interpreter can accept times using the following string formats. You can also:
- Use uppercase or lowercase for am and pm.
- Use a letter **t** to separate a date from a time.
- Add a timezone after it.

12-HOUR TIME FORMAT	EXAMPLE
ga	4am
g:i a	4:08 am
g:i:s a	4:08:37 am
g.i.s a	4.08.37 am

24-HOUR TIME FORMAT	EXAMPLE
H:i	04:08
H:i:s	04:08:37
His	040837
H.i.s	04.08.37

TYPE	RELATIVE TIME
Add/subtract	+ -
Quantity	0 - 9
Units of time (can be plural)	day, fortnight, month, year, hour, min, minute, sec, second
Day names	Monday - Sunday and Mon - Sun
Relative terms	next, last, previous, this
Ordinal terms	first - twelfth

UNIX TIMESTAMPS

Unix timestamps represent dates and times using the number of seconds that have elapsed since midnight on January 1, 1970.

DATE	TIME	UNIX TIMESTAMP
31 DEC 1969	+ 23:59:00	= -60
1 JAN 1970	+ 00:02:00	= 120
11 APR 1975	+ 11:00:00	= 166878000
30 AUG 2000	+ 14:00:00	= 967644000
31 DEC 2020	+ 15:00:00	= 1609426800

The PHP interpreter lets you specify and retrieve dates and times using Unix timestamps.

On the left, you can see some specific examples of dates and times, followed by their corresponding Unix timestamp.

Dates before January 1, 1970 are written using negative numbers.

As you will see, PHP's built-in functions and classes help you work with Unix timestamps. They use the format characters you just met to describe how the functions and classes should transform a Unix timestamp into something that is human-readable.

The maximum date of a Unix timestamp is 19 January 2038.

Unix is an operating system that was developed in the 1970s.

BUILT-IN DATE AND TIME FUNCTIONS

PHP has built-in functions that can create Unix timestamps to represent dates and times. It also has built-in functions to convert these Unix timestamps into a format that is easy to read.

The three functions below are all used to create a Unix timestamp.

If they are not able to create a timestamp, they return `false`.

If you do not specify a time for `strtotime()` or `mktime()`, the time is set to midnight.

FUNCTION	DESCRIPTION
`time()`	Returns the current date and time as a Unix timestamp.
`strtotime($string)`	Converts a string to a Unix timestamp (accepts formats shown on p314).

	EXAMPLE
	`strtotime('December 1 2020');`
	`strtotime('1/12/2020');`

FUNCTION	DESCRIPTION
`mktime(H, i, s, n, j, Y)`	Converts date/time components (in arguments) into a Unix timestamp.

	EXAMPLE	REPRESENTS
	`mktime(17, 01, 05, 2, 1, 2001);`	February 1 2001 17:01:05
	`mktime(01, 30, 45, 4, 29, 2020);`	April 29 2020 01:30:45

`date()` converts Unix timestamps into a human-readable format.

The format is specified using the format characters on p312-3.

If no timestamp is provided, the current date and time is shown.

FUNCTION	DESCRIPTION
`date($format[, $timestamp])`	Returns a Unix timestamp formatted in a human-readable way: The first parameter specifies how the date should be formatted. The second parameter is the Unix timestamp to format.

	EXAMPLE	OUTPUT
	`date('Y');`	Current year
	`date('d-m-y h:i a', 1609459199);`	31-12-20 11:59 pm
	`date('D j M Y H:i:a', 1609459199);`	Thu 31 Dec 2020 23:59:59

DATE FUNCTIONS

section_b/c08/date-functions.php

```php
<?php
$start      = strtotime('January 1 2021');
$end        = mktime(0, 0, 0, 2, 1, 2021);
$start_date = date('l, d M Y', $start);
$end_date   = date('l, d M Y', $end);
?>
<?php include 'includes/header.php'; ?>

<p><b>Sale starts:</b> <?= $start_date ?></p>
<p><b>Sale ends:</b> <?= $end_date ?></p>

<?php include 'includes/footer.php'; ?>
```

PHP

section_b/c08/includes/footer.php

```php
<footer>&copy; <?php echo date('Y')?></footer> ...
```

RESULT

1. The `strtotime()` function creates a Unix timestamp to represent a date in the past. It is stored in a variable called `$start`.

2. The `mktime()` function creates a Unix timestamp to represent a date one month later. It is stored in `$end`.

3. The `date()` function converts these Unix timestamps into a readable format using the:
- Day name
- Day (with leading zero)
- Month (first three letters)
- Year (four digits)

They are stored in the variables `$start_date` and `$end_date`.

4. The human-readable version of each date is shown.

5. The include file for the footer adds a copyright notice. The year is written out using the `date()` function. As no timestamp is given, it uses the current date.

TRY: In Step 2, change the date and time to next week at midday. In Step 3, change the date format to Mon 1st February 2021.

NOTE: If the time is out by a few hours, check the default timezone setting in the `php.ini` file (see p198).

OBJECTS TO REPRESENT DATES & TIMES

PHP's built-in `DateTime` class creates an object that represents a date and time. Its methods can return the date and time the object represents either in a human-readable format or as a Unix timestamp.

To create a `DateTime` object, use:

- A variable to hold the object
- The assignment operator
- The `new` keyword
- The class name `DateTime`
- A pair of parentheses

In the parentheses, add the date/time the object should represent.

You can use any of the date and time formats that were shown on p314. The value should be placed in quotes.

If you do not specify a date and time, the object will use the current date and time.

If you specify a date but no time, the object will use midnight on the specified day.

```
$date = new DateTime('2001-02-01 15:01:05');
```

VARIABLE   CLASS NAME   DATE AND TIME

You can also use the function `date_create_from_format()` to create a `DateTime` object.

The first argument is the format that the date and time will be supplied in.

The second argument is the date and time in the specified format. Both arguments go in quotes.

```
$date = date_create_from_format('j-M-Y', '15-Jan-2020');
```

VARIABLE   FUNCTION   FORMAT   DATE/TIME

The methods of the `DateTime` object below return the date and time that the object represents.

To get the date/time in a human-readable format, use the `format()` method.

To get the date/time as a Unix timestamp, use the `getTimestamp()` method.

METHOD	DESCRIPTION
`format($format[, $DateTimeZone])`	Gets the date and time in the specified format. The optional second parameter sets a time zone (see p326).
`getTimestamp()`	Returns the Unix timestamp for the date and time the object represents.

DateTime OBJECT

`section_b/c08/datetime-object.php`

```php
<?php
$start = new DateTime('2021-01-01 00:00');
$end   = date_create_from_format('Y-m-d H:i',
    '2021-02-01 00:00');
?>
<?php include 'includes/header.php'; ?>

<p><b>Sale starts:</b>
    <?= $start->format('l, jS M Y H:i') ?></p>
<p><b>Sale ends:</b>
    <?= $end->format('l, jS M Y') ?> <b>at</b>
    <?= $end->format('H:i') ?></p>

<?php include 'includes/footer.php'; ?>
```

① `$start = new DateTime('2021-01-01 00:00');`
② `$end   = date_create_from_format('Y-m-d H:i',`
③ `<?= $start->format('l, jS M Y H:i') ?></p>`
④ `<?= $end->format('l, jS M Y') ?> <b>at</b>`
⑤ `<?= $end->format('H:i') ?></p>`

RESULT

Sale starts: Friday, 1st Jan 2021 00:00

Sale ends: Monday, 1st Feb 2021 at 00:00

© 2021

1. This example starts by creating an object using the `DateTime` class. It is stored in a variable called `$start`.

2. A second `DateTime` object is created using the function `date_create_from_format()`. The first parameter specifies the format the date will be provided in. The second parameter sets the date and time. This object is stored in a variable called `$end`.

3. The start date and time are written into the page using the `format()` method of the `DateTime` object. The argument specifies the format that the date and time should be written out in.

4. The end date (not time) is written into the page using the `format()` method of the `DateTime` object. Its parameter specifies the format that the date should be written out in.

5. The end time is written out separately and also uses the `format()` method. This shows how you can just write out the date *or* time the object holds.

TRY: In Step 1, set the date to hold yesterday's date. In Step 2, change the date to 7 days after the offer starts.

UPDATING DATE & TIME IN DateTime OBJECTS

Once an object has been created with the DateTime class, you can use the methods below to set or update the date/time that it represents.

The methods that set a date/time overwrite any date/time the object currently represents.

The add() and sub() methods use a DateInterval object which will be introduced on p322.

METHOD	DESCRIPTION
setDate(*$year*, *$month*, *$day*)	Sets a date for the object
setTime(*$hour*, *$minute* [, *$seconds*][, *$microseconds*])	Sets a time for the object
setTimestamp(*$timestamp*)	Sets the date/time using a Unix timestamp
modify(*$DateFormat*)	Updates the date/time using a string
add(*$DateInterval*)	Adds an interval of time using a DateInterval object (see p322)
sub(*$DateInterval*)	Subtracts an interval of time using a DateInterval object (see p322)

When the PHP interpreter creates a variable, it can hold a scalar value or array in the variable. When the PHP interpreter creates an object, it stores the object in an independent location in its memory. Then, if that object is stored in a variable, the variable stores the location of where the object was created in the PHP interpreter's memory (rather than storing the object itself).

This means that, if you create an object and store it in a variable, then declare a second variable and assign the same object as the value of that variable, both variables would hold the location of the same object.

Therefore, if you update the object in one variable, it will also be updated in the other:

```php
$start = new DateTime('2020/12/1');
$end   = $start;
// Both variables point to same object
$end->modify('+1 day');
```

To get around this, you can use a keyword called clone to create a copy of the object:

```php
$start = new DateTime('2020/12/1');
$end   = clone $start;
// Only object in $end is modified
$end->modify('+1 day');
```

HOW TO SET DATE & TIME
IN A DateTime OBJECT

PHP section_b/c08/datetime-object-set-date-and-time.php

```php
<?php
$start = new DateTime();
$start->setDate(2021, 12, 01);
$start->setTime(17, 30);
$end = clone $start;
$end->modify('+2 hours 15 min');
?>
<?php include 'includes/header.php'; ?>

<p><b>Event starts:</b>
    <?= $start->format('g:i a - D, M j Y') ?></p>

<p><b>Event ends:</b>
    <?= $end->format('g:i a - D, M j Y') ?></p>

<?php include 'includes/footer.php'; ?>
```

(1) `$start = new DateTime();`
(2) `$start->setDate(2021, 12, 01);`
(3) `$start->setTime(17, 30);`
(4) `$end = clone $start;`
(5) `$end->modify('+2 hours 15 min');`
(6) `<?= $start->format('g:i a - D, M j Y') ?></p>`
(6) `<?= $end->format('g:i a - D, M j Y') ?></p>`

RESULT

1. A new object is created using the `DateTime` class. The object is stored in a variable called `$start`; it holds the current date and time.

2. The date is set using the `setDate()` method of the `DateTime` object.

3. The time is updated using the `setTime()` method of the `DateTime` object.

4. The object that is stored in `$start` is cloned using the `clone` keyword and the clone is stored in a variable called `$end`.

5. The `modify()` method of the `DateTime` object is used to update the object stored in `$end` so that it represents a date and time that is 2 hours 15 minutes after the date and time that was represented by the object stored in `$start`.

6. The dates and times that both objects represent are written out using the `format()` method.

TRY: In Step 5, modify the end of the event to be two days after the start date.

REPRESENT AN INTERVAL USING DateInterval

The DateInterval class is used to create an object that represents an interval of time measured in years, months, weeks, days, hours, minutes, and seconds.

The DateTime object's add() and sub() methods use a DateInterval object to specify an interval of time to add to or remove from the current date/time. You specify the duration of the interval using the format shown in the table on the right.

The letter P precedes each interval. The letter T precedes a period of time.

INTERVAL	REPRESENTED
1 year	P1Y
2 months	P2M
3 days	P3D
1 year, 2 months, 3 days	P1Y2M3D
1 hour	PT1H
30 mins	PT30M
15 seconds	PT15S
1 hour, 30 minutes, 15 seconds	PT1H30M15S
1 year, 1 day, 1 hour, and 30 minutes	P1Y1DT1H30M

```
$interval = new DateInterval('P1M');
```
VARIABLE   CLASS NAME   INTERVAL

The DateTime object's diff() method (short for difference) compares two DateTime objects and returns a DateInterval object that represents the interval between them.

To display the interval stored in a DateInterval object, use its format() method. Its argument is a string that uses the format characters on the right where you want the interval to appear.

INTERVAL	DESCRIPTION
%y	Years
%m	Months
%d	Days
%h	Hours
%i	Minutes
%s	Seconds
%f	Microseconds

STRING TO DISPLAY

```
$interval->format('%h hours %i minutes');
```
INTERVAL   INTERVAL

DateInterval OBJECT

PHP

```php
<?php
$today     = new DateTime();
$event     = new DateTime('2025-12-31 20:30');
$countdown = $today->diff($event);

$earlybird = new DateTime();
$interval  = new DateInterval('P1M');
$earlybird->add($interval);
?>
<?php include 'includes/header.php'; ?>

<p><b>Countdown to event:</b><br>
    <?= $countdown->format('%y years %m months %d days') ?>
</p>
<p><b>50% off tickets bought by:</b><br>
    <?= $earlybird->format('D d M Y, g:i a') ?>
</p>

<?php include 'includes/footer.php'; ?>
```

(1) (2) (3) (4) (5) (6) (7) (8)

RESULT

1. The current date and time are represented using a `DateTime` object, and stored in `$today`.

2. An event date is represented using a `DateTime` object stored in a variable called `$event`.

3. The `DateTime` object's `diff()` method gets the interval of time between now and the event date. The `DateInterval` object that is returned is stored in `$countdown`.

4. The current date and time are stored in `$earlybird`.

5. An interval of one month is represented by a `DateInterval` object stored in `$interval`.

6. The `DateTime` object's `add()` method adds the interval in the `DateInterval` object to the current date in `$earlybird`.

7. The interval stored in `$countdown` is written out. Note how the % symbol is put before the format characters that represent the intervals.

8. The date stored in `$earlybird` is written out.

TRY: In Step 2, change the event date to 3 months in the future. In Step 5, make the interval 12 hours.

RECURRING EVENTS USING DatePeriod

The DatePeriod class can create an object that stores a set of DateTime objects that occur at regular intervals between a start and end date. You can then loop through each of the DateTime objects it creates.

To create a DatePeriod object, you need three things:

- A start date (DateTime object)
- The frequency of the event (a DateInterval object)
- An end date for the period

The end date for the date period can be either:

- A DateTime object; or
- An integer that says how many times the event should occur (after the start date)

When a DatePeriod object is created, it holds a series of DateTime objects; each one represents a point in time between the start and end date at the interval specified in the DateInterval object.

```
$period = new DatePeriod($start, $interval, $end);
```
VARIABLE — CLASS NAME — START DATE/TIME — INTERVAL — END DATE/TIME

You can access each DateTime object in a DatePeriod object using a foreach loop.

As with all loops, use a variable name to hold each DateTime object as it loops through them.

In the code block, you can use the methods of the DateTime object to work with that date/time.

DatePeriod OBJECT HOLDS DateTime OBJECTS — VARIABLE NAME TO REPRESENT EACH DateTime OBJECT

```
foreach($period as $occurrence) {
    echo $occurrence->format('Y jS F');
}
```

DatePeriod OBJECT

section_b/c08/dateperiod-object.php

```php
<?php
$start    = new DateTime('2025-1-1');
$end      = new DateTime('2026-1-1');
$interval = new DateInterval('P1M');
$period   = new DatePeriod($start, $interval, $end);
?>
<?php include 'includes/header.php'; ?>

<p>
  <?php foreach ($period as $event) { ?>
    <b><?= $event->format('l') ?></b>,
    <?= $event->format('M j Y') ?></b><br>
  <?php } ?>
</p>

<?php include 'includes/footer.php'; ?>
```

(1) (2) (3) (4) (5) (6)

RESULT

Wednesday Jan 1 2025
Saturday Feb 1 2025
Saturday Mar 1 2025
Tuesday Apr 1 2025
Thursday May 1 2025
Sunday Jun 1 2025
Tuesday Jul 1 2025
Friday Aug 1 2025
Monday Sep 1 2025
Wednesday Oct 1 2025
Saturday Nov 1 2025
Monday Dec 1 2025

1. The `$start` variable holds a `DateTime` object representing 1st January 2025.

2. The `$end` variable holds a `DateTime` object representing 1st January 2026.

3. The `$interval` variable holds a `DateInterval` object representing one month.

4. The `$period` variable will hold the `DatePeriod` object. It requires three parameters (the values were defined in Steps 1-3):

- A start date
- An interval
- An end date

It will hold twelve `DateTime` objects (one for each month of the year 2025).

5. A `foreach` loop goes through each of the `DateTime` objects. Inside the loop, `$event` represents each `DateTime` object. For each one:

6. The `format()` method is used to write out the name of the day and then the month, day and year.

TRY: In Step 3, change the interval to three months (P3M).

MANAGING TIME ZONES USING DateTimeZone

When creating a DateTime object, you can specify a time zone. This is represented using an object created using the DateTimeZone class.

The DateTimeZone class creates an object that represents a time zone. It will store information about that time zone.

In the parentheses, specify the time zone using an IANA time zone (for a full list, see http://notes.re/timezones).

You can use this object when creating a DateTime object to specify its time zone, which also controls daylight savings.

VARIABLE   CLASS NAME   TIME ZONE

```
$tz_LDN = new DateTimeZone('Europe/London');
$LDN = new DateTime('now', $tz_LDN);
```

DateTimeZone
OBJECT

METHOD	DESCRIPTION	
getName()	Returns the name of this time zone	
getLocation()	Returns an indexed array holding the following information:	
	KEY	VALUE
	country_code	Short code for country
	latitude	Latitude of this location
	longitude	Longitude of this location
	comments	Any comments about this location
getOffset()	Returns the offset from UTC for this timezone in seconds (UTC is the same time as GMT but it is a standard, and is not tied to a country/territory)	
getTransitions()	Returns an array indicating when daylight savings time takes effect in the given time zone	

DateTimezone OBJECT

section_b/c08/datetimezone-object.php

```php
<?php
$tz_LDN    = new DateTimeZone('Europe/London');
$tz_TYO    = new DateTimeZone('Asia/Tokyo');
$location = $tz_LDN->getLocation();

$LDN       = new DateTime('now', $tz_LDN);
$TYO       = new DateTime('now', $tz_TYO);
$SYD       = new DateTime('now',
                 new DateTimeZone('Australia/Sydney'));
?> ...
<p><b>LDN: <?= $LDN->format('g:i a') ?></b>
   (<?= ($LDN->getOffset() / (60 * 60)) ?>)<br>
   <b>TYO: <?= $TYO->format('g:i a') ?></b>
   (<?= ($TYO->getOffset() / (60 * 60)) ?>)<br>
   <b>SYD: <?= $SYD->format('g:i a') ?></b>
   (<?= ($SYD->getOffset() / (60 * 60)) ?>)<br></p>

<h1>Head Office</h1>
<p><?= $tz_LDN->getName() ?><br>
   <b>Longitude:</b> <?= $location['longitude'] ?><br>
   <b>Latitude:</b>  <?= $location['latitude'] ?></p>
```

①②③④⑤⑥⑦

1. Two `DateTimeZone` objects are created to represent the time zones for London and Tokyo.

2. `getLocation()` returns location data for the London timezone as an array. The array is stored in `$location`.

3. Two `DateTime` objects are created using the `DateTimeZone` objects from Step 1. They represent the current time in two time zones.

4. A third `DateTime` object is created to show how the `DateTimeZone` object can be created at the same time as the `DateTime` object.

5. For each of `DateTime` object:
- `format()` shows the current time in that location.
- `getOffset()` shows the time difference between those locations and UTC. It returns the time difference in seconds, so this is divided by 60 * 60 to show the offset in hours.

6. The first time zone's name is retrieved using `getName()`.

7. The longitude and latitude of the time zone are written out.

TRY: Create an object for an LA office and display the time there.

```
LDN: 11:11 am (0)
TYO: 8:11 pm (9)
SYD: 10:11 pm (11)

Head Office

Europe/London
Longitude: -0.12528
Latitude: 51.50833
```

SUMMARY
DATES & TIMES

> Format characters let you specify the way that a date or time should be formatted.

> A Unix timestamp represents a date and time using seconds elapsed since January 1, 1970.

> The `time()`, `strtotime()`, and `mktime()` functions create Unix timestamps. The `date()` function converts a Unix timestamp to a human-readable format.

> The `DateTime` class creates objects that represent dates and times. It has methods to modify dates and times and show them in human-readable formats.

> The `DateInterval` class creates objects that represent an interval of time, such as a month or year.

> The `DatePeriod` class creates a set of `DateTime` objects that represent recurring events.

> The `DateTimeZone` class creates objects to represent time zones and hold information about them.

9

COOKIES & SESSIONS

To create web pages that contain personal data such as a username, profile picture, or list of recently viewed pages, the site would need to know who is requesting each page.

The HTTP protocol provides rules that specify how a browser should request a web page and how the server should respond, but it treats each request and response separately. HTTP does not provide a mechanism for a website to tell which visitor is requesting a page.

If a site needs to tell who is requesting a web page or show any personalized information, it can keep track of each visitor and store information about their preferences using a mix of cookies and sessions.

- **Cookies** are text files that are stored in the user's browser. A site can tell the browser what data to store in a cookie, and the browser will then send that data back to the website with every subsequent page it requests from that site.

- **Sessions** allow a site to temporarily store data about a user on the server. When a visitor requests another page from the site, the PHP interpreter can access the data from that individual user's session.

Cookies and sessions store small amounts of data temporarily, but they are not guaranteed to store data for a long period of time because users can delete cookies (or access the site from a different browser that does not have the cookie), and sessions are only designed to last for the duration of one visit to the site (they do not store data between visits).

When data about users must be stored for longer periods, it is saved in a database. You will learn how to do this in Chapter 13. This requires knowledge of how cookies and sessions work.

WHAT ARE COOKIES?

A website can tell a browser to store data about the user in a text file called a **cookie**. Then, each time the browser requests another page from that site, the browser sends the data in the cookie back to the server.

WHAT IS A COOKIE
A website can tell a browser to create a cookie, which is a text file that is stored in the browser.

Each cookie has a name, which should describe the type of information the cookie holds. The cookie name will be the same for each visitor.

The value stored in each user's cookie can change. So a cookie is like a variable that is stored in a text file in the user's browser.

CREATING COOKIES
When a browser requests a web page, the website can send an extra HTTP header back to the browser with the page.

That HTTP header tells the browser the name of the cookie to create and the value that should be stored in the cookie.

The value stored in the cookie is text, and it should not be longer than 4,096 characters. A site can also create more than one cookie.

GETTING COOKIE DATA
If the browser requests another page from the site that created the cookie, it will send the name of the cookie and the value it stores to the server along with the page request.

The PHP interpreter then adds the cookie data to a superglobal array called $_COOKIE so that the PHP code in that page can use it. The name of the cookie is the key, and its value is the value the cookie stored.

WHO CAN ACCESS A COOKIE
Browsers only send data in a cookie to a server when it is requesting a page from the same domain that created it. For example, if google.com creates a cookie, it is only sent when the browser requests pages from google.com. It would never be sent to facebook.com.

JavaScript can also access cookie data if it was sent from the same domain that created the cookie.

COOKIES ARE TIED TO ONE BROWSER
Because it is the browser that creates and stores the cookies:

- If more than one browser is installed on a device, the cookie is only sent from the browser it was stored in (not any other browsers installed on that device).

- If a user gets a new device, that device will not have the cookie to send to the server.

HOW LONG COOKIES LAST
The server can specify a date and time when a cookie expires. This is the date and time when the browser should stop sending the data in the cookie to the server. If an expiry date is not supplied, the browser stops sending the cookie to the server when the user closes their browser.

Users can also refuse or delete cookies, so a site should be able to operate without them.

FIRST PAGE REQUEST

- Browser requests a page using an HTTP request

REQUEST: page.php

- Server sends back the requested page
- Adds an HTTP header telling the browser the name of a cookie to create and its value

RESPONSE: page.php

HEADER: counter = 1

- Browser displays the page
- Creates a cookie using data in the HTTP header

COOKIE: counter = 1

A cookie should not be used to store sensitive data (e.g., email addresses or credit card numbers) because the contents of the cookie can be viewed in the developer tools of a browser and is sent between a browser and a server as plain text.

SUBSEQUENT PAGE REQUESTS

- Browser requests a page using an HTTP request
- Sends HTTP header with name and value of cookie

REQUEST: page.php

HEADER: counter = 1

- Server adds cookie data to $_COOKIE
- Creates page using data in $_COOKIE
- Sends back the requested page
- Can update value stored in cookie

RESPONSE: page.php

HEADER: counter = 2

- Browser shows page created using its cookie data
- Updates the cookie using data in the HTTP header

COOKIE: counter = 2

To prevent someone from reading the HTTP headers when they are sent between the browser and server, run your site using HTTPS rather than HTTP (see p184). This encrypts the information in the headers.

HOW TO CREATE AND ACCESS COOKIES

PHP's built-in `setcookie()` function is used to create a cookie. To access cookies you can use the `$_COOKIE` super global array, or the `filter_input()` and `filter_input_array()` functions.

PHP's `setcookie()` function creates an HTTP header that is sent with the web page and tells the browser to create a cookie. The function allows you to set a name and a value for the cookie.

As this function creates an HTTP header, it must be used **before** content is sent to the browser (as shown with `header()` on p226). Even a space before the opening `<?php` tag is treated as content.

If you do not set an expiry date for a cookie, the browser stops sending the cookie data to the server when the user closes their browser. You learn how to set an expiry date for a cookie on p336.

```
setcookie($name, $value);
```

Once the browser has stored the cookie, if that browser requests another page from the site, the cookie name and value are sent to the server with the request. When the PHP interpreter receives the request, it adds the cookie data to a superglobal array called `$_COOKIE`.

A new element is added to the array for each cookie. The:

- **Key** is the name of the cookie
- **Value** is the value the cookie holds (it is stored as a string)

This data is often collected and stored in a variable.

If the code tries to access a key that does not exist in `$_COOKIE` an error is generated. To prevent this, the null-coalescing operator can be used to check if the key is in the array. If it is, the value from the cookie is stored in the variable. If not, the variable stores the value `null`.

```
$preference = $_COOKIE['name'] ?? null;
```

PHP's `filter_input()` and `filter_input_array()` functions (p268) can also collect cookie data. The input type should be set to `INPUT_COOKIE`.

The second parameter is the name of the cookie. The third and fourth parameters are optional; they specify the ID of the filter to use and any options for the filter.

If a cookie has not been sent, the function does not raise an error. Also, if integer, float or boolean filters are used, they convert the value to that data type.

```
$preference = filter_input(INPUT_COOKIE, $name[, $filter[, $options]]);
```

SETTING AND ACCESSING COOKIES

section_b/c09/cookies.php

```php
<?php
$counter = $_COOKIE['counter'] ?? 0;   // Get data
$counter = $counter + 1;                // +1 to counter
setcookie('counter', $counter);         // Update cookie

$message = 'Page views: ' . $counter; // Message
?>
<?php include 'includes/header.php'; ?>

<h1>Welcome</h1>
<p><?= $message ?></p>
<p><a href="sessions.php">Refresh this page</a> to see
the page views increase.</p>

<?php include 'includes/footer.php'; ?>
```

(1) (2) (3) (4) (5)

RESULT

This example uses a cookie to count the number of pages a visitor has viewed.

1. The `$counter` variable stores the number of pages the visitor has viewed. If the browser sends data from a cookie called `counter` to the server, `$counter` will store that value. If not, the null-coalescing operator is used to store a value of 0 instead.

2. 1 is added to the value in `$counter`, as the visitor has just viewed a page.

3. The `setcookie()` function is used to tell the browser to create or update a cookie called `counter`, and store the value from `$counter` in that cookie.

4. The `$message` variable stores a message saying the number of pages the visitor has viewed.

5. The message is displayed.

TRY: Once you have viewed the page once, refresh the page and watch the counter go up.

TRY: Store your name in a cookie called `name`, then show it after the page views.

SECURING COOKIES

`setcookie()` has parameters that control how browsers use cookies. You should also validate data received from cookies and use `htmlspecialchars()` if their contents are shown in a page.

To update a value stored in a cookie, call `setcookie()` again with a new value for the cookie. To stop the browser sending a cookie, call `setcookie()` again. Set the value to a blank string and the expiry to a time in the past. If you update the value or expiry time of a cookie, the last four arguments **must** use the same values that were used when the cookie was created.

Because it is possible to send HTTP headers that mimic cookies with a page request:

- The server should validate cookie data before using it (using techniques from Chapter 6).
- If a cookie value is shown in a page, it should use `htmlspecialchars()` to prevent an XSS attack.

`setcookie($name[, $value, $expire, $path, $domain, $secure, $httponly])`

PARAMETER	DESCRIPTION
$name	The name of the cookie.
$value	The value the cookie should hold (this gets treated as a string - cookies do not store data types).
$expire	The date and time the browser should stop sending the cookie to the server (as a Unix timestamp).

To set the timestamp, use PHP's `time()` function and add the period you want the cookie to last for.

PERIOD	NOW		SECS		MINS		HRS		DAYS
1 day	time()	+	60	*	60	*	24		
30 days	time()	+	60	*	60	*	24	*	30

$path	If a cookie is only needed for part of the site, specify the directories it should be used for. By default, the path is the root folder '/' which means all directories. Setting this to /members means it is only sent to pages in the members folder of the site.
$domain	If the cookie is only needed on a subdomain, set the URL for the subdomain. By default, it is sent to all subdomains of a site. If it is set to the subdomain members.example.org, the cookie is only sent to files in the subdomain members.example.org.
$secure	If this is given a value of true, the cookie will be created in the browser, but the browser only sends it back to the server if the page is requested using a secure HTTPS connection (see p184).
$httponly	If given a value of true, the cookie is only sent to the server (it cannot be accessed by JavaScript).

CONTROLLING COOKIE SETTINGS

section_b/c09/cookie-preferences.php

```php
<?php
$color   = $_COOKIE['color'] ?? null;        // Get data
$options = ['light', 'dark',];               // Options

if ($_SERVER['REQUEST_METHOD'] == 'POST') {  // If posted
    $color = $_POST['color'];                // Get color
    setcookie('color', $color, time() + 60 * 60,
        '/', '', false, true);               // Set cookie
}

// If color is valid option, use it - otherwise use dark.
$scheme = (in_array($color, $options)) ? $color : 'dark';
?>
<?php include 'includes/header-style-switcher.php'; ?>
    <form method="POST" action="cookie-preferences.php">
      Select color scheme:
      <select name="color">
        <option value="dark">Dark</option>
        <option value="light">Light</option>
      </select><br>
      <input type="submit" value="Save">
    </form>
<?php include 'includes/footer.php'; ?>
```

PHP
section_b/c09/includes/header-style-switcher.php

```php
<body class="<?= htmlspecialchars($scheme) ?>">
```

RESULT

Select color scheme: Dark

SAVE

1. The variable $color stores the value sent for a cookie called color (or null if it was not sent).

2. An array holds the permitted options for the color scheme.

3. An if statement checks if the form has been submitted.

4. If it has, the value for the select box called color is stored in the $color variable. This overwrites the value in Step 1.

5. The setcookie() function is called to set a cookie called color. Its value is the option that the user selected from the select box. It also:

- Expires in one hour
- Is sent to all pages of the site
- Gets sent via HTTP or HTTPS
- Is hidden from JavaScript

6. The condition of a ternary operator checks if the value in $color is in the $options array. If it is, the value is saved to the variable called $scheme. If not, $scheme stores the value dark.

7. A new header is included. It writes the value in the $color variable into the class attribute of the <body> tag to ensure the CSS rules for the page use the correct color scheme.

WHAT ARE SESSIONS?

Sessions store information about a user and their preferences on the server. They are called sessions because they only store the data for the duration of a single visit to the site.

WHAT IS A SESSION?

When a session starts, the PHP interpreter creates three things:

- A **session ID**, a string used to identify an individual visitor.
- A **session file**, which is a text file that is stored on the server. It is used to hold data about that user. Its filename will contain the session ID.
- A **session cookie**, which is stored in the browser. Its name is PHPSESSID and its value is that user's session ID.

GETTING SESSION DATA

If a browser has a session cookie, it is sent to the server every time the user requests another page from that site. The session ID is used to identify the user, so that the server can:

- Find the session file whose filename contains the session ID sent in the cookie.
- Take data from the session file and put it into the $_SESSION superglobal array so the page can access it.

SAVING SESSION DATA

Once a session has been created, new data can be saved to that users' session by adding it to the $_SESSION superglobal array.

When a page has finished running, the PHP interpreter takes all of the data from the $_SESSION superglobal array and saves it in that user's session file. Saving data to the session file updates its last modified time, and the PHP interpreter can check this time to tell if a session was used recently.

HOW LONG SESSIONS LAST

To work, a session needs both the session cookie in the browser and the session file on the server.

- Session cookies expire when users close the browser.
- Session files can be deleted by the server if they are not modified within a time period (the default is 24 minutes).

HOW SESSIONS ARE STARTED

When a site uses sessions, every page should call PHP's built-in `session_start()` function. When this function is called, if the browser requesting the page did not send a session cookie or if a matching session file cannot be found, the PHP interpreter automatically starts a new session for that user.

OTHER WAYS TO USE SESSIONS

Instead of using session cookies, it is possible to add a session ID to URLs, but this is less secure. It is also possible to store session data in a database, but that topic is beyond the scope of this book. (It is usually only used on sites that have very high volumes of traffic and require several servers to handle the load.)

FIRST PAGE REQUEST

- Browser requests a page using an HTTP request

REQUEST: `page.php`

On the server, the PHP page calls `session_start()`. The browser did not send a session cookie, so it:

- Generates a **session ID** for that user
- Creates a **session file** to hold that user's data (the filename includes the session ID)

The page adds data to the $_SESSION superglobal; when it has finished running, values from this array are added to the session file it created for this user.

- The server sends back the requested page
- Sends an HTTP that will create a **session cookie** holding the session ID

RESPONSE: `page.php`

HEADER: `PHPSESSID = 1234567`

- Browser displays the page
- Creates session cookie holding the session ID

COOKIE: `PHPSESSID = 1234567`

SUBSEQUENT PAGE REQUESTS

- Browser requests a page using an HTTP request
- Sends HTTP header with the session ID

REQUEST: `page.php`

HEADER: `PHPSESSID = 1234567`

On the server, the PHP page calls `session_start()`. The PHP interpreter finds the session file with the session ID specified in the session cookie and:

- Adds data from the session file to the $_SESSION superglobal array so the page can use this data
- Creates a page using data from the array
- Is able to update data in the array

When the page has finished running, values in the $_SESSION superglobal are saved to the session file. This updates the session file's last modified time.

- The server sends back the requested page

RESPONSE: `page.php`

- Browser displays the page
- It sends the session cookie with each request to the same site until user closes the browser window

COOKIE: `PHPSESSID = 1234567`

HOW TO CREATE AND ACCESS SESSIONS

Every page of a site that uses sessions should call `session_start()`.
If the user does not have a session, it starts one for them; if they do,
it gets the session data and puts it in the `$_SESSION` superglobal array.

When a visitor first requests a page that calls `session_start()`, a new session ID, session cookie, and session file are created.

The function must be called before any content is sent to the browser because it sends an HTTP header to create the session cookie.

It must also be called before the page tries to get session data, as it transfers data from the session file to the `$_SESSION` superglobal array.

```
session_start();
```

If you add data to the `$_SESSION` superglobal array, when the page has finished running, the PHP interpreter adds the data to the session file for that user.

The syntax to add data to the array is the same as it is for any associative array. The key should describe the data that the element is being used to store.

The value for each key can be a scalar value (string, number, or boolean) or an array or object. This data type is retained (unlike cookies which only store strings).

```
$_SESSION['name'] = 'Ivy';
$_SESSION['age']  = 27;
```

When collecting data from the `$_SESSION` superglobal array,

use the null-coalescing operator in case values are missing

or use PHP's filter functions with the input type `INPUT_SESSION`.

```
$name = $_SESSION['username'] ?? null;
$age  = $_SESSION['age']      ?? null;
```

FUNCTION	DESCRIPTION
`session_start()`	Create new session, or get data from existing session.
`session_set_cookie_params()`	Settings used to create the session cookie (same parameters as p336).
`session_get_cookie_params()`	Returns an array holding the arguments used to set the cookie.
`session_regenerate_id()`	Creates a new session ID, and updates the session file and cookie.
`session_destroy()`	Deletes the session file from the server.

STORING AND ACCESSING DATA IN SESSIONS

section_b/c09/sessions.php

```php
<?php
session_start();                        // Create/resume
$counter = $_SESSION['counter'] ?? 0;   // Get data
$counter = $counter + 1;                // Counter + 1
$_SESSION['counter'] = $counter;        // Update session

$message  = 'Page views: ' . $counter;  // Message
?>
<?php include 'includes/header.php'; ?>

<h1>Welcome</h1>
<p><?= $message ?></p>
<p><a href="sessions.php">Refresh this page</a> to see
the page views increase.</p>

<?php include 'includes/footer.php'; ?>
```

(1) session_start();
(2) $counter = $_SESSION['counter'] ?? 0;
(3) $counter = $counter + 1;
(4) $_SESSION['counter'] = $counter;
(5) $message = 'Page views: ' . $counter;
(6) <p><?= $message ?></p>

RESULT

This example does the same job as the example on p335, but the counter is stored in a session.

1. When PHP's `session_start()` function is called, the PHP interpreter tries to retrieve data from the session file and store it in the `$_SESSION` superglobal arrary. If it cannot, a new session will be created for this visitor.

2. If the counter key of the `$_SESSION` superglobal array has a value, it is stored in a variable called `$counter`. Otherwise, `$counter` holds the value 0.

3. The visitor just viewed a page so 1 is added to the counter.

4. The value for the counter key in the `$_SESSION` superglobal array is updated.

5. The `$message` variable stores a message saying the number of pages the visitor has viewed.

6. The message is displayed.

Once the page has run, PHP takes the data that from the `$_SESSION` superglobal array and saves it in the session file for that user. Saving the data also updates the last modified time of the session file on the server, so the session data will last longer.

TRY: Once you have viewed the page once, refresh the page and watch the counter go up.

TRY: Store your name in the `$_SESSION` superglobal array, and display it in the page.

THE LIFE OF A SESSION

Browsers delete session cookies when the browser window is closed.
Servers delete session files when the **garbage collection** process runs.
As a result, sessions can last longer than you expect them to.

If you have not done so already, open the previous
example in your browser. Then open the:

- Browser's developer tools so they show cookies
- Folder where the web server stores session files

For help finding either of these see:
`http://notes.re/php/session-locations`

In the browser, you should see a cookie called
PHPSESSID. The value of that cookie is the session ID.

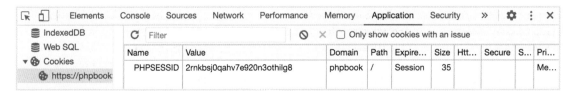

In the folder where the web server stores session files
you should see a filename that contains the session ID.
Note the date and time that the session file was
last modified, then refresh the browser showing the
previous example; the last modified time will update.
If you open the example in a different web browser
(e.g., try Chrome and Firefox), this will create a new
session because the session is tied to the browser.

When a page calls `session_start()`, if the PHP
interpreter does not receive a session cookie or
cannot find a matching session file for that session
cookie, it will create a new session.

When a page that called `session_start()` finishes
running, it saves the data from the `$_SESSION`
superglobal array to the session file. This updates the
session file's last modified time.

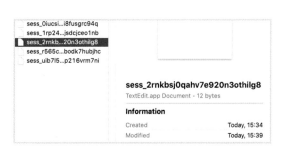

The PHP interpreter uses the date and time the
session was last modified to determine when it can
delete the session file (which would end the session).

Therefore, when a site uses sessions, it is important
to call `session_start()` on every page. Otherwise,
if the user was browsing pages of the site that did not
update this setting, the session could be terminated
while the user is still browsing the site.

The web server runs a process called **garbage collection**. It deletes session files whose last modified date is over a specified age (the default is 24 mins). Once a session file has been deleted, the session ends because, even if a browser sent the session cookie, the file holding the session data would not be found.

Checking the last time each session file was accessed and deleting the old session files takes up server resources, so servers try not to do this *too* often. The frequency that garbage collection runs depends on the number of times sessions are accessed. Therefore, on a quiet site, garbage collection may not run for hours or even days.

As you see in the next example, sessions are often used to remember when a user is logged into a site. In such cases, users should have an option to log out.

If a user does not close their browser window (so the browser is still sending a session cookie) and the server is quiet (so it has not run garbage collection) the session could last longer than it was designed to.

This is a big issue when users share computers because, if a user does not log out, someone else could visit the site using their account.

Terminating a session involves the four steps below...

---

1. Remove all data from the session file by setting the $_SESSION superglobal array to a blank array.

This also prevents any subsequent code in the same page from accessing those values.

```php
$_SESSION = [];
```

2. In Step 3, setcookie() will be used to update the session cookie. When it is used, the arguments for the path, domain, secure and httponly parameters must use the same values that were used when the cookie was created.

PHP's session_get_cookie_params() function will return the values that were used for these parameters when the session cookie was created. The values it returns are stored as an array in the $params variable.

```php
$params = session_get_cookie_params();
```

3. PHP's setcookie() function is used (see p334) to update the session cookie.

The value parameter is set to a blank string; this deletes the session ID from the session cookie.

The expires parameter is set to a date in the past to stop the browser sending the cookie to the server if it requests further pages. All of the other parameters are set using the values collected in Step 2 and stored as an array in the $params variable.

```php
setcookie('PHPSESSID', '', time() - 3600, $params['path'],
    $params['domain'], $params['secure'], $params['httponly']);
```

4. Call PHP's session_destroy() function to tell the PHP interpreter to delete the session file.

The PHP interpreter will delete the file immediately rather than waiting for garbage collection to delete it.

```php
session_destroy();
```

A BASIC LOGIN SYSTEM

Sites often ask users to log in to view certain pages. In this example, users must log in to view the My Account page. When a user logs in:

- Their session will remember that they logged in
- They will be able to view their account page
- The link text for the last link in the navigation bar changes from "Log In" to "Log Out"

NOTE: This example only shows how sessions are used to remember when a user has logged in. Chapter 16 shows how to create a full login system, which allows each member to have their own login details (which are stored in a database).

When a site uses sessions, every page should call `session_start()` before sending any content to the browser. This ensures that each user has a session and that the last modified time of the session file is updated each time they view a new page.

In this example, every page includes `sessions.php` (see right-hand page). It calls `session_start()` and groups together all of the session-related code.

1. The `session_start()` function tells the PHP interpreter to take the data from the visitors session file and place it in the `$_SESSION` superglobal array, or create a new session if it is not able to.

2. If the `$_SESSION` superglobal has recorded the user logging in, the `$logged_in` variable stores the value `true`; otherwise the null-coalescing operator assigns it a value of `false`.

3. The `$email` and `$password` variables hold the details that users will have to enter in order to log in.

The file then has three function definitions:

4. The login page will call the `login()` function if the user enters the correct email and password.

5. When a user logs in, it is good practice to reset their session ID. PHP's `session_regenerate_id()` function creates a new session ID and updates the session file and cookie to use this new session ID. (The argument `true` tells the PHP interpreter to remove any data that was already in the session.)

6. A key called `logged_in` is added to the session. Its value is `true` showing that the visitor has logged in.

7. The `logout()` function is used to end the session.

8. The `$_SESSION` superglobal array is set to a blank array. This would empty the data from the session file, and stops the rest of the page using the session data.

9. The session cookie is updated; the session ID is replaced by a blank string and the expiry date is set to the past (so the browser stops sending it).

10. The session file on the server is deleted.

11. The `require_login()` function can be called by any page that requires the visitor to be logged in.

12. An `if` statement checks if the `$logged_in` variable is `false`. If it is, either the user has not logged in or the session has ended.

13. The user is redirected to the login page.

14. The `exit` command stops any more code running.

PHP

section_b/c09/includes/sessions.php

```php
<?php
session_start();                                    // Start/renew session
$logged_in = $_SESSION['logged_in'] ?? false;       // Is user logged in?

$email     = 'ivy@eg.link';                         // Email address to login
$password  = 'password';                            // Password to login

function login()                                    // Remember user passed login
{
    session_regenerate_id(true);                    // Update session ID
    $_SESSION['logged_in'] = true;                  // Set logged_in key to true
}

function logout()                                   // Terminate the session
{
    $_SESSION = [];                                 // Clear contents of array

    $params = session_get_cookie_params();          // Get session cookie parameters
    setcookie('PHPSESSID', '', time() - 3600, $params['path'], $params['domain'],
        $params['secure'], $params['httponly']);    // Delete session cookie

    session_destroy();                              // Delete session file
}

function require_login($logged_in)                  // Check if user logged in
{
    if ($logged_in == false) {                      // If not logged in
        header('Location: login.php');              // Send to login page
        exit;                                       // Stop rest of page running
    }
}
```

The circled line numbers are: ① session_start(); ② $logged_in line; ③ $email/$password lines; ④ function login(); ⑤ session_regenerate_id; ⑥ $_SESSION['logged_in'] = true; ⑦ function logout(); ⑧ $_SESSION = []; ⑨ $params/setcookie lines; ⑩ session_destroy(); ⑪ function require_login; ⑫ if ($logged_in == false); ⑬ header; ⑭ exit;

HOW TO ENSURE USERS LOG IN TO VIEW PAGES

The `require_login()` function should be called at the start of any page that requires visitors to log in. In this example, visitors must be logged in to view the `account.php` page.

1. The `sessions.php` include file is included.

2. The `require_login()` function, defined in `sessions.php`, checks if the user is logged in. If:

- They are logged in, the rest of the page is shown
- They are not logged in, they are sent to `login.php`

Its one argument is the `$logged_in` variable that was declared in Step 2 of `sessions.php`.

3. A new header file (see third code box) is included.

4. Next, you can see the `login.php` page. It starts by including the `sessions.php` file.

5. An `if` statement checks the value in the `$logged_in` variable (created in `sessions.php`) to see if the user has already logged in.

6. If they have already logged in, they are sent to `account.php` because they do not need to log in (they may have arrived at this page because they clicked a link / used the browser's back button).

7. The `exit` command stops the rest of the code in the page from running.

8. If the page is still running, the file checks if the user has submitted the form (see bottom of page).

9. If they have, the values they entered for the email and password form controls are collected and stored in the `$user_email` and `$user_password` variables.

10. An `if` statement checks if the email address and password that the user entered match the ones that were stored in the `$email` and `$password` variables in the `sessions.php` file (see Step 3 on previous page).

11. If they match, the user has provided the correct details and the `login()` function (defined in `sessions.php`) is called. It regenerates the session ID and adds the `logged_in` key to the `$_SESSION` superglobal array, with a value of `true` to indicate that the user has logged in.

12. The user is then sent to the `account.php` page and the `exit` command stops any more code running.

13. If the form was not submitted or the login details were wrong, the header for this example is included.

14. The login form has two inputs for the user to enter their email address and password.

15. In the new header, the navigation bar checks if the user is logged in. If they are, it shows a link to the log out page. If not, it shows a link to the log in page.

NOTE: The session ID is sent in the HTTP headers with each request. If someone got hold of the session ID, they could create an HTTP request and add the session ID to that request and impersonate the user who created the session. This is known as **session hijacking**.

To prevent session hijacking, any pages that use sessions should only be accessed via an HTTPS connection because it encrypts all data (including the header containing the session ID).

This example does not require that you install an SSL certificate, but it should be required on any live site.

```php
    <?php
①   include 'includes/sessions.php';              // Include sessions.php file
②   require_login($logged_in);                     // Redirect user if not logged in
    ?>
③   <?php include 'includes/header-member.php'; ?> ...
```

```php
    <?php
④   include 'includes/sessions.php';

⑤   if ($logged_in) {                              // If already logged in
⑥       header('Location: account.php');           // Redirect to account page
⑦       exit;                                      // Stop further code running
    }

⑧   if($_SERVER['REQUEST_METHOD'] == 'POST') {     // If form submitted
⑨       $user_email    = $_POST['email'];          // Email user sent
        $user_password = $_POST['password'];       // Password user sent

⑩       if ($user_email == $email and $user_password == $password) { // If details correct
⑪           login();                               // Call login function
            header('Location: account.php');       // Redirect to account page
⑫           exit;                                  // Stop further code running
        }
    }
    ?>
⑬   <?php include 'includes/header-member.php'; ?>
    <h1>Login</h1>
    <form method="POST" action="login.php">
⑭     Email: <input type="email" name="email"><br>
      Password: <input type="password" name="password"><br>
      <input type="submit" value="Log In">
    </form>
    <?php include 'includes/footer.php'; ?>
```

```php
    <a href="home.php">Home</a>
    <a href="products.php">Products</a>
    <a href="account.php">My Account</a>
⑮   <?= $logged_in ? '<a href="login.php">Log In</a>' : '<a href="logout.php">Log Out</a>' ?>
```

SUMMARY
COOKIES & SESSIONS

> Cookies store data in a visitor's browser.

> Data stored in a cookie is made available to the PHP page via the $_COOKIES superglobal array.

> You can set when cookies should expire (but users can also delete them earlier).

> Sessions store data on the server.

> Session data is accessed and updated using the $_SESSIONS superglobal array.

> Each page of a site that uses sessions should begin by calling the session_start() function.

> Session files hold data during a single visit to the site (and are deleted after a period of inactivity).

> If you want to store data for longer periods of time or retain personal information, use databases to hold the data (as shown in Chapter 16).

10

ERROR HANDLING

If the PHP interpreter is having trouble running your code, it can create a message to help you find where the problem is.

When you create a new PHP page, do not expect to write it perfectly on your first attempt; even experienced programmers regularly get error messages when they test a new page. Seeing errors can be frustrating, but the messages that are generated help you find the issue and provide information to help fix them. The PHP interpreter has two mechanisms for dealing with problems it encounters: errors and exceptions.

- **Errors** are messages that the PHP interpreter creates when it has a problem running code. They are like the PHP interpreter raising its hand and telling you, "Something is wrong here." Some errors prevent code in the page from running; others do not.

- **Exceptions** are objects that can be created by either the PHP interpreter or the programmer. These objects are created when code that would normally run is prevented from doing so by an exceptional situation. When an exception object is created, the PHP interpreter stops running the code and looks for an alternative code block that was written to deal with the situation; this gives the code a chance to handle the problem and recover from it.

  Exceptions are like the PHP interpreter or programmer saying, 'Something is wrong here – are there instructions for dealing with this?" If there is no alternative code to handle the situation, then an error will be raised and that will stop the page from running.

Errors and exceptions both create messages that help you understand what the problem was and where it was encountered. These messages can be shown in the web page that is sent to the browser or saved in a text file on the server known as a log file.

In addition to the error messages that the PHP interpreter creates, the web server can also create its own error messages that it sends to the browser. It will do this when it cannot find the file that the browser requested or when another problem stops the server running.

CONTROLLING HOW PHP ERRORS ARE DISPLAYED

If the PHP interpreter encounters a problem when running the code, it creates an error message to describe the problem. This can be shown in the web page it sends to the browser or saved in a file on the server.

When a site is in development, the error messages that the PHP interpreter creates should be shown in the web page that is sent back to the browser. This allows programmers to see any errors as soon as they run the page and then fix them.

When a site goes live, in case there are any errors that were **not** caught in development, error messages should *not* be shown in the web page because they:

- Are hard for visitors to understand
- Can give hackers clues about how the site is built

Instead, the PHP page shows a user-friendly message to the visitor, and the error message should be added to a text file on the server called a **log file** which the developers can check to see if any errors were raised after the site went live.

The PHP interpreter has three settings to determine:

- Whether or not errors should be shown on screen
- Whether or not they should be written to a log file
- Which errors are raised (when learning PHP or developing a site, you should display *all* errors)

These settings can be controlled using either the `php.ini` or `.htaccess` files (introduced on p196-99).

- The `php.ini` file holds default settings for all of the files on the web server. If it is updated, the server must be restarted for the changes to take effect.

- An `.htaccess` file can be placed in any directory on the web server. It controls all the files in that folder and any subfolders. The server does *not* need restarting when `.htaccess` files have changed.

php.ini
The following settings should be used in the `php.ini` file. They tell the PHP interpreter to report all errors, show them on screen, and write them to a log file:

```
display_errors  = On
log_errors      = On
error_reporting = E_ALL
```

When a site goes live, `display_errors` must be set to `Off` to prevent errors being shown on the screen.
```
display_errors  = Off
```

.htaccess
The following settings can be added to an `.htaccess` file to tell the PHP interpreter to report all errors, show them on screen, and write them to a log file:

```
php_flag   display_errors   On
php_flag   log_errors       On
php_value  error_reporting  -1
```

When a site goes live, `display_errors` must be set to `Off` to prevent errors being shown on the screen.
```
php_flag   display_errors   Off
```

The download code for the book uses `.htaccess` files to control the PHP interpreter's settings.

Several folders have their own `.htaccess` files to control the settings for that set of examples.

This chapter's code examples are in two folders; one for sites in development; one for live sites.

1. These settings should be used while a site is in development. They tell the PHP interpreter to show all errors on the screen and also write them to a log file.

PHP section_b/c10/development/.htaccess

```
    ┌ php_flag    display_errors   On
① ┤ php_flag    log_errors       On
    └ php_value   error_reporting  -1
```

2. When the site goes live, error messages should not be shown in the browser. Instead, they should be written to a log file so that developers can see if visitors are experiencing any errors.

PHP section_b/c10/live/.htaccess

```
    ┌ php_flag    display_errors   Off
② ┤ php_flag    log_errors       On
    └ php_value   error_reporting  -1
```

3. Web servers can place log files in different folders. To find out where the error log file is on *your* server, use PHP's built-in `ini_get()` function.

PHP section_b/c10/development/find-error-log.php

```
    Your error log is stored here:
③ <?= ini_get('error_log') ?>
```

4. This basic PHP page generates an error because the quote marks do not match. The error message that the PHP interpreter creates when this file is run is shown below.

PHP section_b/c10/development/sample-error.php

```
    <?php
④ echo 'Finding an error";
    ?>
```

The first result box shows the message for the error above in the browser. As you can see, the message is not user-friendly. The next eight pages help you understand what these error messages mean.

RESULT

Parse error: syntax error, unexpected string content "Finding an error";" in **/Users/Jon/Sites/localhost/phpbook/section_b/c10/development/sample-error.php** on line **2**

The second result box shows the contents of the error log file. You can open the log file in a text editor or code editor. The error message is the same as the one shown on the screen, but it is preceded by the date and time the error was reported.

RESULT

```
[27-Jan-2021 14:41:13 UTC] PHP Parse error:  syntax error,
unexpected string content "Finding an error";" in
/Users/Jon/Sites/localhost/phpbook/section_b/c10/
development/sample-error.php on line 2
```

NOTE: Log file files should be stored above the document root (see p190) to prevent hackers guessing their path and requesting them via a URL.

UNDERSTANDING ERROR MESSAGES

The error messages that the PHP interpreter creates can look confusing at first, but they all follow the same structure and they all hold four pieces of information that help developers find the source of the error.

Programmers say that the PHP interpreter **raises** errors when it finds them. The error messages use the structure shown below and hold four pieces of data:

- The first two (the level and description) describe the error that was encountered.

- The next two (the filepath and line number) tell you where to start looking for the problem.

The **error level** describes the general type of problem (or level of problem) that the PHP interpreter encountered.

The **description** is a more detailed explanation of the error.

The **filepath** is the path to the file in which the error was found.

The **line number** is the line in that file where the error was found.

The main **types** of error that you are likely to meet are described on the right-hand page. Then, the next six pages show PHP files containing examples of each of these types of errors along with descriptions that tell you how to find and fix that type of error.

Some errors occur before the PHP interpreter reports the error, but the filename and line number tell you where to start looking.

PROBLEM   LOCATION

`Error: description goes here in test.php on line 21`

LEVEL   DESCRIPTION   FILEPATH   LINE NUMBER

LEVELS / TYPES OF ERROR

The main types of PHP error are shown below. Some errors stop the PHP interpreter running and must be fixed in order for the page to run. Others might seem more like suggestions, but they should still be fixed.

PARSE
p356-57

A **parse error** indicates that there is an error with the syntax of the PHP code. This prevents the PHP interpreter from being able to read, or *parse*, the file, so it will not try to run *any* of the code.

If the PHP interpreter's settings say that errors should be shown on screen, the error is the only thing shown. If the errors are not shown on screen, the visitor will see a blank page.

Parse errors must be fixed in order for the page to run and show anything other than an error message.

NOTE: Error levels and messages change with different versions of PHP. This chapter shows error messages from PHP 8.

FATAL
p358-59

A **fatal error** indicates that the PHP interpreter thought that the syntax of the PHP code was valid, so it tried to run the code, but something prevented it from running correctly.

The PHP interpreter stops on the line of code where it finds a fatal error. This means that users may see a part of a page that was created before the PHP interpreter discovered the error.

Since PHP 7, most fatal errors have created an exception object. This gives programmers a chance to recover from the error.

If you see an error that starts with the level name `Deprecated`, it means that a feature is due to be removed from PHP in the future.

NON-FATAL
p360-61

A **non-fatal** error will create an error message to indicate that there *could* be a problem, but the code will continue to run.

- A **warning** is a non-fatal error that advises that the PHP interpreter has come across an error that is *likely* to cause a problem.

- A **notice** is a non-fatal error that advises of *possible* issues that the PHP interpreter has come across.

In PHP 8, many of the notices were upgraded to warnings.

If you see an error that starts with the level name `Strict`, it will contain advice on better ways to write your PHP code.

PARSE ERRORS

A parse error is caused by a problem with the syntax of your code.
It prevents a page from being displayed because the PHP interpreter
cannot understand the code. You must fix parse errors for the code to run.

Parse errors are often caused by a typo such as a mismatched quote or a missing semicolon, parenthesis or bracket. These simple mistakes can prevent the PHP interpreter reading the code.

To fix parse errors, find the line where the the error was reported. Read the line from left to right and check each instruction in it. If you don't see the problem, look at the line that ran before it.

When `display_errors` is set to `Off`, a parse error results in the user seeing a blank screen. With parse errors, you must find the error and fix it before the page is able to show anything.

On line 2 of this example, the variable uses mismatched quote marks; one is a single quote, the other is a double quote.

The error message says that the problem was encountered on line 3 because the PHP interpreter did not realize that the error had occurred until *after* it found another single quote mark.

When it came across another single quote on line 3, it treated that quote mark as if it was closing the variable from line 2.

The message says that there is an **unexpected `identifier` `'pencil'`** on line 3 because the text *after* the second single quote is the word `pencil`.

section_b/c10/development/parse-error-1.php   `PHP`

```php
1 <?php
2 $username = 'Ivy";
3 $order    = ['pencil', 'pen', 'notebook',];
4 ?>
5 <h1>Basket</h1>
6 <?= $username ?>
7 <?php foreach ($order as $item) { ?>
8     <?= $item ?><br>
9 <?php } ?>
```

`RESULT`

Parse error: syntax error, unexpected identifier "pencil" in
/Users/Jon/Sites/localhost/phpbook/section_b/c10/development/parse-error-1.php on line **3**

NOTE: If you use a code editor with syntax highlighting, the colors of the code often give you a clue as to the location of a syntax error.

section_b/c10/development/parse-error-2.php

```php
1 <?php
2 $username = 'Ivy'
3 $order    = ['pencil', 'pen', 'notebook',];
4 ?> ...
```

RESULT

Parse error: syntax error, unexpected variable "$order" in
/Users/Jon/Sites/localhost/phpbook/section_b/c10/development/parse-error-2.php on line **3**

At the end of line 2, there should be a semicolon. The message says unexpected variable '$order' on line 3 because the previous statement did not end with a semicolon.

As the first two examples show, parse errors often occur on a line before the one specified by the error. If you cannot see a problem on the reported line, look at the previous line of code that ran.

PHP

section_b/c10/development/parse-error-3.php

```php
1 <?php
2 $username = 'Ivy';
3 $order    = ['pencil', 'pen', 'notebook',);
4 ?> ...
```

RESULT

Parse error: Unclosed '[' does not match ')' in
/Users/Jon/Sites/localhost/phpbook/section_b/c10/development/parse-error-3.php on line **3**

On line 3, an array is created. It starts with a square opening bracket, but it ends with a closing parenthesis.

Here, the error message shows the correct line and the exact problem. It says that the unclosed '[' does not match ')' on line 3.

PHP

section_b/c10/development/parse-error-4.php

```php
1 <?php
2 $username = 'Ivy';
3 order     = ['pencil', 'pen', 'notebook',];
4 ?> ...
```

RESULT

Parse error: syntax error, unexpected identifier "order" in
/Users/Jon/Sites/localhost/phpbook/section_b/c10/development/parse-error-4.php on line **3**

On line 3, the variable name does not start with a $ symbol.

The error message says unexpected identifier 'order' on line 3 because order is not a keyword or instruction the PHP interpreter can follow (it does not know that it is supposed to be a variable name because there is no $ symbol before it).

TRY: To check you understood the problems in this section, try correcting the errors described in the file and then run the examples again.

To find a parse error, comment out the second half of the page. If you still see the same error, the problem is in the first half of the page. If not, it is in the second half. Repeat the process to further narrow down the source.

FATAL ERRORS

A fatal error is raised when the PHP interpreter finds a problem that prevents it processing any more of the code. This means users may only see a partial page, up to the point where the fatal error was found.

If you see a fatal error, the PHP interpreter thought that the syntax was correct, but it found a problem that prevented it from running any more of the code.

If part of the HTML page has been created before the error occurs, the user may see the part of the page before the error. If not, they may see a blank page.

With fatal errors, you must track down why the PHP interpreter is not able to process the code, then fix the issue in order for the whole page to display.

On line 4, this example tries to multiply an integer (stored in `$price` on line 2) by a string (stored in `$quantity` on line 3).

The error message says Unsupported operand types `int * string` to indicate that an integer cannot be multipled by a string. The problem is discovered before any content is displayed, so the heading saying `Basket` and the text saying `Total:` are not shown to the visitor.

To prevent this error occuring again, the page could validate both values before it tried to multiply them.

Until PHP 7.4, this example would have generated a warning, not a fatal error.

```
section_b/c10/development/fatal-error-1.php                    PHP

1  <?php
2  $price     = 7;
3  $quantity  = 'five';
4  $total     = $price * $quantity;
5  ?>
6  <h1>Basket</h1>
7  Total: $<?= $total ?>
```

RESULT

Fatal error: Uncaught TypeError: Unsupported operand types: int * string in /Users/Jon/Sites/localhost/phpbook/section_b/c10/development/fatal-error-1.php:4 Stack trace: #0 {main} thrown in **/Users/Jon/Sites/localhost/phpbook/section_b/c10/development/fatal-error-1.php** on line 4

NOTE: Before PHP 7, a page could not recover from a fatal error. In PHP 7, fatal errors started to create an exception object, which gave the code a chance to deal with the problem (as you see on p372-73). If exceptions are not handled (or caught), *then* they become a fatal error, which is why these error messages start with the words `Uncaught error`.

section_b/c10/development/fatal-error-2.php

```php
1 <?php
2 function total(int $price, int $quantity) {...}
6 ?>
7 <h2>Basket</h2>
8 <?= totals(3, 5) ?>
```

On line 2, a function called total() is declared (the full function definition is in the code download). On line 8, the code calls a function called totals().

RESULT

Basket

Fatal error: Uncaught Error: Call to undefined function totals() in
/Users/Jon/Sites/localhost/phpbook/section_b/c10/development/fatal-error-2.php:8 Stack trace: #0 {main}
thrown in **/Users/Jon/Sites/localhost/phpbook/section_b/c10/development/fatal-error-2.php** on line **8**

The error message says Call to undefined function totals() because there is no totals() function; it should be calling total(). The heading Basket is shown because the PHP interpreter only stops running the code *after* the error is found.

PHP

section_b/c10/development/fatal-error-3.php

```php
1 <?php
2 function total(int $price, int $quantity) {...}
6 ?>
7 <h2>Basket</h2>
8 <?= total(3) ?>
```

On line 8, the total() function is called, but it is only called with one argument (not two).

The error message says Too few arguments to function total() because the function requires two arguments.

RESULT

Basket

Fatal error: Uncaught ArgumentCountError: Too few arguments to function total(), 1 passed in
/Users/Jon/Sites/localhost/phpbook/section_b/c10/development/fatal-error-3.php on line 8 and exactly 2
expected in /Users/Jon/Sites/localhost/phpbook/section_b/c10/development/fatal-error-3.php:2 Stack trace: #0
/Users/Jon/Sites/localhost/phpbook/section_b/c10/development/fatal-error-3.php(8): total(3) #1 {main} thrown
in **/Users/Jon/Sites/localhost/phpbook/section_b/c10/development/fatal-error-3.php** on line **2**

It also states that 1 argument has been passed in, and exactly 2 are expected. To fix this, the function must be called with the correct number of arguments.

PHP

section_b/c10/development/fatal-error-4.php

```php
1 <?php $basket = new Basket(); ?><h2>Basket</h2>
```

On line 1, an object is created using a class called Basket, but the class definition has not been included in the page. The message says Class 'Basket' not found. It cannot continue to show the rest of the page because it cannot create the object. To fix this, the class definition must be included first.

RESULT

Fatal error: Uncaught Error: Class 'Basket' not found in
/Applications/MAMP/htdocs/phpbook/section_b/c10/development/fatal-error-4.php:1 Stack trace: #0 {main}
thrown in **/Applications/MAMP/htdocs/phpbook/section_b/c10/development/fatal-error-4.php** on line **1**

NOTE: When an exception object is created (or thrown) inside a function or method, the **stack trace** (shown in the error messages) specifies the name of the file and line of code that called that function or method.

NON-FATAL ERRORS (WARNING OR NOTICE)

A non-fatal error is raised when the PHP interpreter thinks there could be a problem but will attempt to continue running the rest of the code.

A warning indicates that there is an error that is likely to cause a problem and a notice indicates that there *might* be an error.

Both are called non-fatal errors. They are created when the PHP interpreter finds them, but they do not stop the page from running.

All errors should be corrected, as they can have serious effects upon the rest of the page (this is shown in the example below).

In this example, three variables are declared:

- Line 2 declares $price. Its value is the number 7.
- Line 3 declares $quantity. Its value is a string saying '0a'.
- Line 4 declares $total. Its value should be the value in $price multiplied by the value in $quantity.

Line 4 creates a warning saying A non-numeric value encountered because the value stored in $quantity is a string.

Because the first character of the string is the number 0, the PHP interpreter tries to use the first character 0 (and ignores the rest of the string - see p61). Then the page continues to run and it shows the value stored in $total.

section_b/c10/development/warning-1.php `PHP`

```php
1 <?php
2 $price    = 7;
3 $quantity = '0a';
4 $total    = $price * $quantity;
5 ?>
6 <h1>Basket</h1>
7 Total: $<?= $total ?>
```

`RESULT`

Warning: A non-numeric value encountered in
/Users/Jon/Sites/localhost/phpbook/section_b/c10/development/warning-1.php on line **4**

Basket

Total: $0

This could end up being a big problem for the site because the total is shown to be zero dollars.

You can use PHP's `var_dump()` function (p193) to check values in variables *and* their data type.

section_b/c10/development/warning-2.php

```php
1 <?php $list = false; ?>
2 <h1>Basket</h1>
3 <?php foreach ($list as $item) { ?>
4     Item: <?= $item ?><br>
5 <?php } ?>
```

RESULT

Basket

Warning: foreach() argument must be of type array|object, bool given in
/Users/Jon/Sites/localhost/phpbook/section_b/c10/development/warning-2.php on line **3**

On line 1, the $list variable was supposed to hold an array, but it has been assigned a boolean value of false. Then, on line 3, a foreach loop iterates through the array of items in $list.

The error message says foreach() argument must be of type array|object because it cannot loop over a boolean.

NOTE: An error is not raised if foreach is used with an array that has no elements, or an object that has no properties.

PHP section_b/c10/development/warning-3.php

```php
1 <?php include 'header.php'; ?>
2 <h1>Basket</h1>
```

RESULT

Warning: include(header.php): Failed to open stream: No such file or directory in
/Users/Jon/Sites/localhost/phpbook/section_b/c10/development/warning-3.php on line **1**

Warning: include(): Failed opening 'header.php' for inclusion
(include_path='.:/Applications/MAMP/bin/php/php8.0.0/lib/php') in
/Users/Jon/Sites/localhost/phpbook/section_b/c10/development/warning-3.php on line **1**

Basket

On line 1, a header is included, but the include file cannot be found. As a result, two error messages are shown:

- Failed to open stream: No such file or directory... shows the file is not found.
- Failed opening ... for inclusion means that the file could not be included.

The PHP interpreter tries to show the remaning code after a missing include file.

PHP section_b/c10/development/warning-4.php

```php
1 <?php $list = ['pencil', 'pen', 'notebook',]; ?>
2 <?= $list ?>
```

RESULT

Warning: Array to string conversion in
/Users/Jon/Sites/localhost/phpbook/section_b/c10/development/warning-4.php on line **2**
Array

On line 1, the $list variable stores an array. On line 2, the shorthand for the echo command is used to write out the contents of the $list variable.

This creates the error: Array to string conversion, indicating that the page is trying to convert an array to a string; but it is not able to, so the contents cannot be shown. (Until PHP 8 this was a notice, not a warning.)

DEBUGGING: TRACKING DOWN ERRORS

A site should be thoroughly tested before going live and all errors should be corrected. If the error is not on the line that the error message suggests, there are several techniques that can help you track it down.

1. Writing notes to the screen shows how far the interpreter gets before an error is raised. The `echo` command is used to display notes on lines: 2, 9, 17, 24.

The message on line 9 will only be shown if the `total()` function is called (as on line 18).

2. Commenting sections of code reduces the amount of code that could be a problem. Lines 20 and 23 comment out the header and footer, confirming that the error is *not* in those files. You can also comment out calls to functions (and hard code in the values they would return) to test if the errors are created in a function.

3. PHP's `var_dump()` function writes out the values stored in variables and their data type so you can check if the variable holds a value you expect it to. It is used on line 26 to check the value in `$basket`. It shows that the value of the third element in the `$basket` array to be a string, not a number.

1: Start of page

2: Before function called

3: Inside total() function

Warning: A non-numeric value encountered in **/Applications/MAMP/htdocs/phpbook/section_b/c10/development/tracking-down-errors.php** on line **12**

Basket

Total: $2.00

4: End of page

$basket: array(3) { ["pen"]=> float(1.2) ["pencil"]=> float(0.8) ["paper"]=> string(3) "two" }

Test total() function:

3: Inside total() function

4

section_b/c10/development/tracking-down-errors.php

```php
1   <?php
2   echo '<p><i>1: Start of page</i></p>';
3   $basket['pen']    = 1.20;
4   $basket['pencil'] = 0.80;
5   $basket['paper']  = 'two';
6
7   function total(array $basket): int
8   {
9   echo '<p><i>3: Inside total() function</i></p>';
10      $total = 0;
11      foreach ($basket as $item => $price) {
12          $total = $total + $price;
13      }
14      return $total;
15  }
16
17  echo '<p><i>2: Before function called</i></p>';
18  $total = total($basket);
19  ?>
20  <?php // include 'header.php' ?>
21  <h3>Basket</h3>
22  <p><b>Total: $<?= number_format($total, 2) ?></b></p>
23  <?php // include 'footer.php' ?>
24  <?php echo '<p><i>4: End of page</i></p>'; ?>
25  <hr><!-- All remaining code is test code -->
26  <p><b>$basket:</b> <?= var_dump($basket) ?></p>
27  <b>Test total() function:</b>
28  <?php
29  $testbasket['pen']    = 1.20;
30  $testbasket['pencil'] = 0.80;
31  $testbasket['paper']  = 2;
32  ?>
33  <?= total($testbasket) ?>
```

The markers ①, ②, ③, ④ appear next to lines 2, 9, 17, 24 (①); 20, 23 (②); 26 (③); and 29–31 (④).

NOTE: Indenting of code in braces, using four spaces, makes it easier to find issues such as a missing closing bracket.

Values written out using the echo command in Steps numbered 1 are not indented. This makes it easier to see where they were added.

Some PHP editors can run each line of code one-by-one; this is known as **stepping through** the code. At each line, you can check the values to find out where the code may be going wrong. You can also set **breakpoints** where the code should stop running (and the contents of variables can be checked at that point).

4. You can write test cases for functions and methods to check if they are performing the task that you expect them to.

When a script uses functions or methods, testing each one in isolation is a good way to check that they are working correctly (rather than checking them in the context of the entire page).

You can see a test for the total() function is performed at the end of the page. An array called $testbasket is created using values that can test the function. The total() function is then called to check if it returns the right value.

Note that the echo message on line 9 is shown again when the total() function is called a second time on line 33.

Some programmers write basic pages to test each function (rather than debugging the code if there is a problem). If you know that a function works in isolation, the statements that are in the function should not be causing the problem. This allows you to focus on the values that are being passed into the function.

If the values going into the function appear to be incorrect, you can then trace where those values are coming from to find the source of the error.

GOING LIVE WITH A SITE

When a site is ready to launch, the settings should be changed so the PHP interpreter does not display error messages on its pages. Instead, save the error messages to a **log file** and check it at regular intervals.

Even when a site has been carefully tested, errors may have been missed or there can be problems with the hosting. Therefore, on the live server, use the settings in the `php.ini` or `.htaccess` files to:

- Stop error messages appearing on the screen
- Save error messages to a log file

Log files can be opened in a text editor or code editor. The messages in the log file start with the date and time the error occurred, and are followed by messages that are identical to ones shown on the screen. If you have run the examples so far in the chapter, the log file will contain the errors below.

Errors should be corrected on a **development** copy of the site (on a test server or your local machine), not on the live site. For each error in the log file:

1. Try to recreate the error so you know what caused the message to be recorded
2. Use the techniques shown on the previous pages to find the code that causes the error
3. Fix the code that is causing the error

Once the problem has been fixed, the site should be tested again before the new version of the code is uploaded to the live site, because a fix may have created new issues.

```
[27-Jan-2021 14:56:44 UTC] PHP Parse error:  syntax error, unexpected string
content "Finding an error";" in /Users/Jon/Sites/localhost/phpbook/section_b/c10/
development/sample-error.php on line 2
[27-Jan-2021 14:56:51 UTC] PHP Parse error:  syntax error, unexpected identifier
"pencil" in /Users/Jon/Sites/localhost/phpbook/section_b/c10/development/parse-
error-1.php on line 3
[27-Jan-2021 14:57:02 UTC] PHP Parse error:  syntax error, unexpected variable
"$order" in /Users/Jon/Sites/localhost/phpbook/section_b/c10/development/parse-
error-2.php on line 3
[27-Jan-2021 14:57:04 UTC] PHP Parse error:  Unclosed '[' does not match ')' in /
Users/Jon/Sites/localhost/phpbook/section_b/c10/development/parse-error-3.php on
line 3
[27-Jan-2021 14:57:06 UTC] PHP Parse error:  syntax error, unexpected identifier
"order" in /Users/Jon/Sites/localhost/phpbook/section_b/c10/development/parse-
error-4.php on line 3
```

The PHP interpreter can also save errors to a database, but this is not covered in the book as beginners (and most sites) save them to a log file.

Log files can take up a lot of disk space on the web server, so the server administrator needs to ensure they are regularly archived or deleted.

ERROR HANDLING FUNCTIONS

When the PHP interpreter raises a fatal or non-fatal error, it can call a user-defined function called an **error handler**. On live sites, that function can prevent users from seeing a page that is blank or abruptly cut off.

HANDLING NON-FATAL ERRORS

When the PHP interpreter has raised a non-fatal error, the rest of the file will continue to run. This can cause serious problems. For example, on p360, an error made the cost of an order $0.

Usually, to fix errors, the code must be changed. Until they are fixed, you can use an **error-handling function** to try to deal with any non-fatal errors.

PHP's built-in `set_error_handler()` function tells the PHP interpreter the name of the user-defined function it should call when a non-fatal error occurs. When telling `set_error_handler()` the name of the error-handling function it should run, its name is not followed by parentheses.

This function could, for example, display a user-friendly message, then stop any more code running.

You can specify which error levels the error handler works for in a second parameter, but it is better to use it for all non-fatal errors when learning PHP.

```
set_error_handler('name')
```
NON-FATAL ERROR
HANDLING FUNCTION

HANDLING FATAL ERRORS

Fatal errors stop the page running, and the function specified in `set_error_handler()` does not run.

Since PHP 7, the PHP interpreter converted most fatal errors into exceptions. You learn about exceptions and how to handle them after the next example. But, if a fatal error is converted into an exception, and it is not handled, it goes back to being a fatal error.

It is possible to name a user-defined function called a **shutdown function** that is called whenever: a page finishes running, the `exit` command is used, or a fatal error stops the page running.

The shutdown function can check if there was an error while the page was running and, if there was, show a user-friendly error message and log the error. PHP's `register_shutdown_function()` function tells the PHP interpreter the name of the function to call when a page stops running (it is used on p376-77). Note that when specifying the name of the shutdown function, it should not followed by parentheses.

```
register_shutdown_function('name')
```
FATAL ERROR
HANDLING FUNCTION

NON-FATAL ERROR HANDLING FUNCTION

Any undiscovered non-fatal errors can cause problems on a live site. If one occurs, this error-handling function ensures the error is logged, that users see a friendly error message, and that the code stops.

In this example, PHP's `set_error_handler()` function specifies that the PHP interpreter should call a function called `handle_error()` if it encounters a non-fatal error.

If a site uses its own function to handle non-fatal errors, then the PHP interpreter will not run its own error-handling code unless that function returns a value of `false`. And, if the PHP interpreter's error-handling code does not run, then the error is not added to PHP's error log file (so the developers would not know that it had occurred).

This error-handling function cannot return `false` because it stops the rest of the page from running (after it has shown a user-friendly error message). So the function will have to save the error message to the log file before the page stops running.

When the PHP interpreter calls an error-handling function, it passes the function four arguments containing data about the error (the values that would have appeared in the error message):

- The level of error (as an integer)
- An error message (as a string)
- The path to the file the error occurred in
- The line of code the error was discovered on

The `handle_error()` function definition must name parameters in order to use these values.

In this example, the data about the error is used to create the error message that is added to the log file. The error message will follow a similar format to the ones that the PHP interpreter creates.

PHP has a built-in function called `error_log()` which can be used to add an error message to the log file. Its one parameter is the error message it should use.

Because there was an error, the function will also try to set the HTTP response status to 500, to indicate that there was an error on the server. This can be set using PHP's `http_response_code()` function. (It will only do this if it is called *before* anything is written out to the page.) Its one parameter is the response status code to use.

Before displaying the error message to the visitor, the page uses the `require_once` command to include the header file. This ensures that the error page has the same design as the rest of the site. The `require_once` command is used instead of `include` to ensure that the header will only be included if it has not already been added to the page.

Once a user-friendly error message has been shown, the `require_once` command is used again to include the footer for the page.

Finally, the `exit` command stops the PHP interpreter from running any more code in the page.

```php
<?php
set_error_handler('handle_error');

function handle_error($level, $message, $file = '', $line = 0)
{
    $message = $level . ' ' . $message . ' in ' . $file . ' on line ' . $line;
    error_log($message);
    http_response_code(500);

    require_once 'includes/header.php';
    echo "<h1>Sorry, a problem occurred</h1>
        The site's owners have been informed. Please try again later.";
    require_once 'includes/footer.php';
    exit;
}
$username = $_GET['username'];
?>
<?php include 'includes/header.php'; ?>
<h1>Welcome, <?= $username ?></h1>
<?php include 'includes/header.php'; ?>
```

RESULT

Sorry, a problem occurred
The site's owners have been informed. Please try again later.

1. PHP's `set_error_handler()` function tells the PHP interpreter to call the `handle_error()` function if it encounters a non-fatal error (but it does not use parentheses after the function name).

2. The `handle_error()` function is defined. It uses four parameters to represent the data that the PHP interpreter passes to the function: the error level, error message, name of file the error was in, and the line number.

3. An error message is created using the information in the four parameters named in Step 2.

4. PHP's `error_log()` function is used to write the error message to PHP's error log file.

5. PHP's `http_response_code()` function sets the HTTP reponse code to 500, indicating that there was a server error.

6. The header is included (if it has not been already) to ensure the site header and CSS styles are included.

7. A user-friendly error message is written out to the page using the `echo` command.

8. The footer is included.

9. `exit` stops any further code running.

10. When the page tries to access a key that is *not* in the `$_GET` superglobal array, a non-fatal error is raised.

EXCEPTIONS

When code would normally work, but an exceptional situation is preventing it from doing so, an **exception object** can be created. This gives the code a chance to recover from problems.

When an exception object is created, the PHP interpreter stops running the page and looks for code that has been written to handle the exceptional situation. This gives the program a chance to recover from the problem:

- If it finds code to handle the situation, it runs that code, then continues to run the code *after* the statements that caused the exception.

- If it cannot find any code to handle the situation, it raises a fatal error that starts with the message Uncaught exception, then the page stops running.

Programmers say that exceptions are **thrown** and the code to deal with an exception **catches** the exception.

The properties of the exception object will store the name of the file and the line where the problem was encountered, just like an error message does.

If the problem occurs in a function or method, it also holds something called a **stack trace**; this records which lines of code called that function or method.

The stack trace can be very helpful in finding the source of a problem because many different pages or lines of code can call the same function or method. And, when a problem is caused by passing incorrect data to a function or method, it is important to know where that function or method was called.

Exception objects can be created in two ways:

- Since PHP 7, most fatal errors result in the PHP interpreter creating an **error exception object** using the built-in Error class. This lets programs recover from a fatal error or show a user-friendly message (instead of the page abruptly ending).

- Programmers can throw their own **custom exception** object using a user-defined class that is based on a built-in class called Exception.

Exceptions should only be used when programmers know the code *should* work, but an **exceptional situation** has prevented it doing so.

An exceptional situation is where you can anticipate that there may be a problem, but you cannot use code to avoid that problem occurring. For example:

- Database-driven sites rely upon a database; if the site cannot connect to the database, that **is** an exceptional situation.

- When collecting form data, users often enter invalid values; this is **not** exceptional and should be handled in validation code.

The code used to handle the exception can either enable the site to recover from the error and continue running or show the user a helpful message.

When a progammer can anticipate a situation that could prevent code from doing its job (but they cannot prevent the situation arising using code such as validation code), they can throw their own custom exception object if that situation occurs. This allows the program to either recover or record a specific description of the issue (along with a stack trace).

To create a custom exception object, you should create a custom exception class. This can be done in one line of code because all custom exceptions **extend** a built-in class called Exception.

When a class extends another class, it **inherits** the properties and methods of the class it is extending, so custom exception classes have all of the properties and methods defined in the built-in Exception class.

Both the Exception class and the built-in Error class implement an **interface** called Throwable. An interface describes the names of properties and/or methods that an object will implement and the data they should return. The table below shows the methods in the Throwable interface. All exception objects will have these methods.

METHOD	RETURNS
getMessage()	An exception message. For error exceptions, this is the fatal error message generated by the PHP interpreter. For custom exceptions, this is a message created by the programmer.
getCode()	An exception code used to identify the type of exception. For error exceptions, this code would be generated by the PHP interpreter. For custom exceptions, this code would be defined by the programmer.
getFile()	The name of the file that the exception was created in.
getLine()	The line number that the exception was created on.
getTraceAsString()	The stack trace as a string.
getTrace()	The stack trace as an array.

To create a custom exception class, use:

- The class keyword.
- A class name. This name often identifies the aim of the code where the exceptional situation was encountered.
- The extends keyword to show this class will extend another existing class.
- The name of the class that it will extend (in this case, the built-in Exception class). This means that it will inherit the properties and methods of the class it is extending.
- A pair of curly braces.

To create, or throw, an exception using a custom exception class you have written, use:

- The throw keyword (this not only creates the exception object but also tells the PHP interpreter to look for code to catch it when it is created).
- The new keyword (to create a new object).
- The name of a custom exception class.

Then, in parentheses, add:

- An error message that describes the problem.
- An optional code to identify the problem.

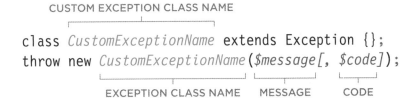

CUSTOM EXCEPTION CLASS NAME

```
class CustomExceptionName extends Exception {};
throw new CustomExceptionName($message[, $code]);
```

EXCEPTION CLASS NAME   MESSAGE   CODE

HANDLING EXCEPTIONS USING TRY CATCH

If you know that, in exceptional situations, some code can result in an exception *and* you can recover from the problem, that situation can be handled using a try... catch statement.

In a try... catch statement, the keyword try is followed by a code block that holds the statements the PHP interpreter should try to run, but which may cause an exception. If an exception is thrown in the try block, the PHP interpreter:

- Stops running the code
- Looks for the catch block that should come after it
- Checks if that catch block can handle the situation (because it names the class used to create the exception object or an interface it implements)
- If so, it runs the statements in that catch block

In the parentheses after the catch keyword, specify:

- The class used to create the exception object or an interface it implements (on p374-5 you see how to specify more than one catch block, each able to handle exceptions created using different classes)
- The name of a variable that will hold the exception object in the catch block (it is often called $e)

If an exception is not thrown in the try block, the PHP interpreter skips over the catch block.

The catch block can also be followed by an optional finally block. The statements in the finally block will run whether or not an exception was thrown.

Once an exception has been handled, the PHP interpreter runs the line of code that appears after the catch block. It does this without adding details about what triggered the exception to the PHP error log file. This means that the programmers would not know how often the exceptional situation occurred.

If you want to record details of an exception that has been handled in the error log, you can use PHP's built-in error_log() function. It only needs one argument: the exception object that was thrown. The PHP interpreter will take the data about the issue, which is stored in the exception object, convert it into a string and then add it to the error log file.

```
try {
    // Try to do something that might throw an exception
} catch (ExceptionClassName $e) {
    // Do something to handle this exception if thrown
} finally () {
    // Do something whether or not the exception occurred
}
```

DEFAULT EXCEPTION HANDLING FUNCTION

The PHP interpreter can run a user-defined function to handle exceptions that were not handled by a catch block (because they were not thrown in a try block or they did not use the class specified by the catch block).

Programmers can specify the name of a user-defined function called a **default exception handler** that the PHP interpreter should call if an exception is not handled by a catch block.

PHP's built-in set_exception_handler() function specifies the name of a user-defined function to call. Its one parameter is the name of the function. Its name should not be followed by parentheses.

set_exception_handler('*name*')

FUNCTION NAME

The basic exception handling function below:

- Adds details of the problem to the error log file
- Sets the correct HTTP response code (500)
- Displays a message to the user
- Stops any further code from running in the page

You see an example using a default exception handling function on p376-77.

A more complicated exception handling function could check the class used to create the exception, and respond to each one in a different way.

```
function handle_exception($e)
{
    error_log($e);
    http_response_code(500);
    echo '<h1>Sorry, an error occurred please try again later.</h1>';
    exit;
}
```

USING TRY CATCH TO HANDLE EXCEPTIONS

1. In this example, the `try` block contains code that may cause an exception.

2. Imagine that the include file contains code used to display advertisements and that it usually works, but that a problem in that code occasionally results in an exception.

3. If an exception is thrown in the `try` block, the PHP interpreter looks for a `catch` block that can handle it.

The keyword `catch` is followed by parentheses. In the parentheses:

- The class name indicates that this `catch` block will run for any exception object created using the `Exception` class.

- `$e` is the name of a variable that stores the exception object so that its data can be used in the `catch` block.

4. A placeholder ad is shown. This result is better than the page stopping running when the exception is encountered.

5. PHP's `error_log()` function adds the error to the PHP error log file. Its one argument is the exception object that was created inside the include file.

```
section_b/c10/live/try-catch.php                          PHP

<?php include 'includes/header.php'; ?>

<?php
① try {
②     include 'includes/ad-server.php';
③ } catch (Exception $e) {
④     echo '<img src="img/advert.png" alt="Newsletter">';
⑤     error_log($e);
  }
?>
<h1>Latest Products</h1>
...
<?php include 'includes/footer.php'; ?>
```

RESULT

NOTE: For the purposes of this example, the `ad-server.php` include file in the code download throws an exception to ensure the `catch` block runs.

On p374, you learn how a set of `catch` blocks can use different code to handle exception objects that have been created using different classes.

THROWING CUSTOM EXCEPTIONS

The ImageHandler class below manipulates images using GD. It throws custom exceptions if it is used incorrectly (the next page shows how to use the class).

1. A custom exception class called ImageHandlerException is created. It will inherit the properties and methods of PHP's built-in Exception class.

2. When an object is created using the ImageHandler class, the __construct() method checks if the image is one of the permitted media types. If it is not, an exception is thrown using the ImageHandlerException class.

The error message shows that the image format is not accepted and it is given an error code of 1.

3. When the resizeImage() method is called, if the user is trying to create an image that is larger than the original image they uploaded, an exception will be thrown because this will result in a poorer quality image.

The error message says that the original image is too small, and it is given an error code of 2.

`PHP`

section_b/c10/live/classes/ImageHandler.php

```php
<?php
class ImageHandlerException extends Exception {};

class ImageHandler
{
    public    $fileTypes  = ['image/jpeg', 'image/png',];      // Allowed media types
    ...
    public function __construct(string $filepath, string $filename)
    {
        ...
        if (!in_array($this->mediaType, $this->fileTypes)) {  // If media type not allowed
            throw new ImageHandlerException('File not an accepted image format', 1);
        }
        ...
    }
    public function resizeImage(int $newWidth, int $newHeight, string $uploadPath)
    {
        if (($this->origWidth < $newWidth)
        or ($this->origHeight < $newHeight)) {                // If original is too small
            throw new ImageHandlerException('Original image too small', 2);
        }
        // Code to resize and save image goes here...
    }
}
```

① marks `class ImageHandlerException extends Exception {};`
② marks the `if (!in_array...` block in `__construct`
③ marks the `if (($this->origWidth...` block in `resizeImage`

CATCHING DIFFERENT TYPES OF EXCEPTION

This page lets users register for a site by submitting their email address and uploading a profile picture. Usually it works fine but, in exceptional situations, the image may not save. In such cases, the exception is handled so that the code can continue to run and save the visitors email address (even if it cannot save the image). The example uses two `catch` blocks to handle different types of exception that may occur when a user uploads an image.

1. The `ImageHandler.php` file from the previous page is included. It holds the class definition for the `ImageHandlerException` as well as the `ImageHandler` class that is used to resize and save uploaded images.

2. A `try` block contains statements that create an `ImageHandler` object to represent the profile picture the user uploaded, resize and save the image, then display it. It is followed by two `catch` blocks.

3. The parentheses of the first `catch` block contain the name of the `ImageHandlerException` class. This means that the PHP interpreter will run this `catch` block if the code in the `try` block created an exception object using the `ImageHandlerException` class. Inside the `catch` block, the exception object will be stored in a variable called $e.

4. The exceptions that the `ImageHandler` class creates are user-friendly, so the `getMessage()` method of the exception object (which it inherited from the built-in `Exception` class) gets the error message and stores it in the $message variable. The message either tells the user that the image was the wrong media type or it was too small.

If the first `catch` block handled the exception, the PHP intepreter would go on to run the rest of the page, skipping any remaining `catch` blocks.

5. If the first `catch` block was not run (because the exception thrown in the `try` block was not created using the `ImageHandler` class), the second `catch` block will run.

The parentheses of the second `catch` block name the `Throwable` interface, indicating that it should catch *any* exception that implements the `Throwable` interface. It will, therefore, handle *any* exception from the `try` block that has not already been handled. This includes fatal PHP errors that may have been thrown by the PHP interpreter (e.g., if the image could not be saved because the disk was full).

Usually, `catch` blocks should try to catch specific classes of exception rather than trying to catch all exceptions like this, but this could be justified if:

- The exception could prevent a critical action, such as prevent a user from registering (it is better to have the user's email address than nothing at all)
- It was a temporary measure while the precise cause of the problem was being determined

6. This `catch` block handles the situation differently. The $message variable stores a message telling the user that the image was not saved. It does not show the error message from the exception object because that may contain information that could confuse users or provide hackers with sensitive information.

7. PHP's `error_log()` function is called to add information about the exception to PHP's error log.

Once the code in this `catch` block has run, the rest of the page will run. The rest of the page could, for example, save the visitor's email address to a database. If the exception had not been handled, no data provided by the user would have been saved.

```php
<?php
include 'classes/ImageHandler.php';                       // Include class
$message = '';                                            // Initialize variables
$thumb   = '';
$email   = '';

if ($_SERVER['REQUEST_METHOD'] == 'POST') {               // If form sent
    $email = $_POST['email'] ?? '';                       // Get user's email
    if ($_FILES['image']['error'] == 0) {                 // If no upload errors
        $file = $_FILES['image']['name'];                 // Get file name
        $temp = $_FILES['image']['tmp_name'];             // Get temp location

        try {                                             // Try to resize image
            $image = new ImageHandler($temp, $file);      // Create object
            $thumb = $image->resizeImage(300, 300, 'uploads/'); // Resize image
            $message = '<img src="uploads/' . $thumb . '">'; // Save image in $message
        } catch (ImageHandlerException $e) {              // If ImageHandlerException
            $message = $e->getMessage();                  // Get error message
        } catch (Throwable $e) {                          // If other reason
            $message = 'We were unable to save your image'; // Generic message
            error_log($e);                                // Log error
        }
    }
    // This is where the page could save the email address
}
?>
<?php include 'includes/header.php' ?>
<h1>Join Us</h1>
<?= $message ?>
...
```

RESULT

DEFAULT ERROR AND EXCEPTION HANDLING

This example shows how to deal with every error and unhandled exception in a consistent way.

First, PHP's `set_exception_handler()` specifies that the user-defined `handle_exception()` function should be called if an exception is thrown and is not handled by a `catch` block. That function:

- Logs the issue
- Sets the HTTP response status code
- Displays a friendly error message
- Stops the code running

Next, PHP's `set_error_handler()` specifies that the `error_handler()` should be called when a non-fatal error is raised.

`error_handler()` converts non-fatal errors into exceptions so that they are dealt with in the same way as fatal errors (which throw exceptions).

Finally, PHP's `register_shutdown_function()` specifies that the user-defined `handle_shutdown()` function should be called when *any* page finishes running. This is called in case any fatal errors are not converted into error exceptions, or they are not handled by the default error handler.

The `handle_shutdown()` function will check if an error was raised when the page was running using PHP's built-in `error_get_last()` function. If there was, that error is converted into an exception, and the exception handler function is called to deal with it.

UNCAUGHT EXCEPTIONS

1. PHP's `set_exception_handler()` function specifies a user-defined function to call if an exception is thrown and is not handled by a `catch` block.

2. The `handle_exception()` function is defined. Its one parameter is the exception object that was thrown.

3. The exception is logged in PHP's error log file.

4. The HTTP response code is set to 500.

5. If not already included, the header is included.

6. A user-friendly error message is displayed.

7. If not already included, the footer is included.

After this, the interpreter will not run any further code.

NON-FATAL ERRORS

9. The `set_error_handler()` function specifies a user-defined function to call if the PHP interpreter raises a non-fatal error.

10. The default error handler is passed information about the error (its type and message, and the file and line where it occurred) as described on p366.

11. The error data is used to create a new exception. Doing this allows the site to treat all non-fatal errors in the same way that fatal errors and exceptions are (using the same `handle_exception()` function).

The exception object is thrown using PHP's built-in `ErrorException` class, which was added to PHP so that errors could be converted into exceptions. The second parameter is an optional error code (an integer) to represent the exception (here it is 0).

```php
<?php ...
set_exception_handler('handle_exception');                    // Set exception handler
function handle_exception($e)
{
    error_log($e);                                            // Log error
    http_response_code(500);                                  // Set response code
    require_once 'header.php';                                // Ensure header included
    echo "<h1>Sorry, a problem occurred</h1>
        <p>The site's owners have been informed. Please try again later.</p>";
    require_once 'footer.php';                                // Add footer
    exit;                                                     // Stop code running
}

set_error_handler('handle_error');                            // Set error handler
function handle_error($type, $message, $file = '', $line = 0)
{
    throw new ErrorException($message, 0, $type, $file, $line); // Throw ErrorException
}

register_shutdown_function('handle_shutdown');                // Set shutdown handler
function handle_shutdown()
{
    $error = error_get_last();                                // Was error in script?
    if ($error) {                                             // If so throw exception
        $e = new ErrorException($error['message'], 0, $error['type'],
                            $error['file'], $error['line']);
        handle_exception($e);                                 // Call exception handler
    }
}
```

The circled step numbers in the code above are: ① at `set_exception_handler`, ② at `function handle_exception($e)`, ③ at `error_log($e);`, ④ at `http_response_code(500);`, ⑤ at `require_once 'header.php';`, ⑥ at the `echo` block, ⑦ at `require_once 'footer.php';`, ⑧ at `exit;`, ⑨ at `set_error_handler`, ⑩ at `function handle_error`, ⑪ at the `throw new ErrorException`, ⑫ at `register_shutdown_function`, ⑬ at `function handle_shutdown()`, ⑭ at `$error = error_get_last();`, ⑮ at `if ($error) {`, ⑯ at the `$e = new ErrorException` block, ⑰ at `handle_exception($e);`.

FATAL ERRORS

12. PHP's built-in `register_shutdown_function()` function tells the PHP interpreter to call the user-defined `handle_shutdown()` function when a page stops running. It does this because some fatal errors are not converted into exceptions and are not handled by the default error handler.

13. The `handle_shutdown()` function is defined.

14. PHP's built-in `error_get_last()` checks if the an error was raised while the page ran. If there was, details of the last error it raised will be returned in an array; if not it will return `null`. The value that it returns is stored in `$error`.

15. An `if` statement checks if the `$error` variable has a value, indicating that there was an error.

16. If it does, the error is converted into an exception. **NOTE:** The `throw` keyword is **not** used here as the default exception handler will not catch exceptions thrown in a shutdown function. Instead, the object is created like any other object.

17. `handle_exception()` is called. The exception object created in Step 16 is passed in as an argument.

TRY: `example.php` in the code download has lines that have been commented out to test the error and exception handlers. Uncomment them one at a time.

HOW WEB SERVER ERRORS ARE DISPLAYED

If a web server cannot find the file that was requested, or an error on the server prevents it from processing the browser's request, the web server sends an error code and web page back to the browser.

On p180-81, you saw how servers send HTTP headers to the browser along with the file that was requested. One of these headers is a **response status code** indicating whether or not the request was successful.

- When a server successfully processes the request, it returns the code 200 with the requested file.

- If the file cannot be found, it returns the code 404 with an error page that describes the issue.

- If an error with the server prevented a page being displayed, it returns the code 500, and an error page that says an internal server error occurred.

The error pages that the web server creates when it cannot respond to a request are not very user-friendly, but you can create your own **custom error pages** for the web server to send instead of its own error pages.

Custom error pages allow you to provide a clearer description of the problem to visitors. They can also use the same look and feel as the rest of the site.

To send a custom error page, add an `ErrorDocument` directive to the `.htaccess` file and specify the:

- Status code this file should be used for
- Path to the file it should show for that code

The default error page Apache sends when a file cannot be found:

Not Found

The requested URL /phpbook/section_b/c10/missing.php was not found on this server.

The default error page Apache sends when an internal error prevents a page being displayed:

Internal Server Error

The server encountered an internal error or misconfiguration and was unable to complete your request.

section_b/c10/live/.htaccess

```
ErrorDocument 404 /code/section_b/c10/live/page-not-found.php
ErrorDocument 500 /code/section_b/c10/live/error.php
```

(1)

section_b/c10/live/page-not-found.php

```
<?php require_once 'includes/header.php'; ?>
<h1>Sorry! We cannot find that page.</h1>
<p>Try the <a href="index.php">home page</a> or email us at
  <a href="mailto:hello@eg.link">hello@eg.link</a>.</p>
<?php require_once 'includes/footer.php'; ?>
```

(2)

section_b/c10/live/error.php

```
<?php include 'includes/header.php'; ?>
<h1>Sorry! An error occurred.</h1>
<p>The site owners have been informed. Please try again soon.</p>
<?php include 'includes/footer.php'; ?>
```

(3)

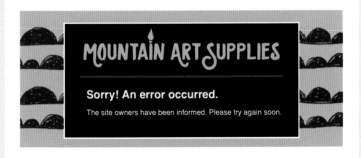

1. The .htaccess file uses the ErrorDocument directive to set paths to custom error pages that should be shown when:
a) A file cannot be found
b) There is a server error

2. The page-not-found.php file explains that the file could not be found in a user-friendly way.

3. The error.php file tells visitors that an error occurred.

TRY: Request a page in the live folder for this chapter that does not exist, e.g. missing.php

NOTE: Pages for errors should not include code that connects to a database because, if there was an error with the database, the error page would not be shown.

SUMMARY
ERROR HANDLING

> Error messages help determine what the problem is.

> When developing a site, display errors on the screen.

> When a site goes live, do not display errors on screen. Instead, write the same error messages to a log file.

> An error handling function can be run when a non-fatal error has been raised.

> Exceptions are objects that are created in exceptional circumstances that prevent a page running as normal.

> When an exception object is created (or thrown), the interpreter looks for an alternative code block to run.

> Exceptions can be caught using a `try... catch` statement or an exception-handling function.

> Errors can be converted into exceptions so that all problems are handled in the same way.

C

DATABASE DRIVEN WEBSITES

Database-driven websites use a database to store most of the content shown on the pages of the site, plus other data such as information about the site's members.

Because PHP can access and update the data in a database, database-driven websites can:

- Allow non-technical users to create or update the content of the site using forms on a web page (they do not need to know how to write code or use FTP to update files on the server).
- Create pages that are tailored to each member of the site using data from the database.

This book uses a piece of software called **MySQL** to create and manage the site's database. The database stores data in a series of tables (each table is similar to a spreadsheet). Because the data in one table often *relates* to data in another table, it is called a **relational database**. (Whenever we refer to MySQL, the information also applies to MariaDB, introduced on p15.)

PHP comes with a set of built-in classes called **PHP Data Objects** (**PDO**) that can be used to access and update the data in the database.

Therefore, in order to create database-driven websites you will need to learn:

- How a language called **Structured Query Language** or **SQL** (pronounced *sequel* or *ess-queue-elle*) is used to request data from a database and update data it holds.
- How to use PDO to run SQL commands that request data from a database and make that data available to your PHP code.
- How to use PDO to run SQL commands that update data stored in a database.

MySQL does not come with a graphical user interface, but there is a free tool called **phpMyAdmin** that allows you to manage the database and view its contents. You learn how to use it in the introduction to this section.

Before reading the chapters in this section, you will need to understand how databases store the data that is used in a website and how to manage the database using phpMyAdmin.

THE EXAMPLE WEBSITE

A sample application will be developed throughout the second half of this book. It demonstrates how to build database-driven websites and other concepts that you will be learning. We start by introducing the example website to help you understand the sample database that you will be working with.

HOW DATABASES STORE DATA

Next, you will learn how databases store data. The data is structured in a series of tables. You also meet the data types that MySQL uses (which are different from the data types PHP uses).

HOW TO USE PHPMYADMIN

phpMyAdmin is a tool that runs on a web server. It is like a website that you can use to manage a MySQL database. You learn how it lets you:

- Create new databases
- View data in databases
- Make backups of databases

HOW TO CREATE A DATABASE

Next, you will learn how to set up the database used for the sample application that is developed throughout the rest of the book. The database holds the content of the site and data about its members.

First, you will learn how to create a blank database. Then, you will run some SQL code (provided in the code download) that:

- Creates the tables that the sample database uses
- Adds data to each of these tables

NOTE: All of the remaining examples rely upon this database, so it must be created and populated with data in order to proceed.

CREATING DATABASE USER ACCOUNTS

Finally, you learn how to create database user accounts. The PHP code needs a user account to connect to the database (just like an email program needs an email account to send and receive emails).

INTRODUCING THE EXAMPLE WEBSITE

The example website built throughout the rest of this book is a basic **content management system** (CMS) which is a tool that allows people to update a site's content without writing any code.

The content management system that is developed throughout the rest of this book showcases work by a collective of creatives, but it could be used as a CMS for many different types of sites.

At the top of each page, after the name of the site (Creative Folk), the navigation bar shows the sections or **categories** of the site.

The home page (below) is a file called `index.php`. After the navigation, it shows information about the six most recent articles. When a new article is uploaded, it appears on the home page and the oldest article it had featured is no longer shown.

Each **article** showcases one piece of creative work. All of the articles are displayed using the same `article.php` file; its job is to get one article from the database at a time and insert that data into the page.

The article page displays an image that shows the piece of work, its title, the date the article was added to the site, a description of the work, the category that the piece of work is in, and the name of the person who created it.

Each article also has an option called 'published'; the article will not be displayed to the public until that option has been selected.

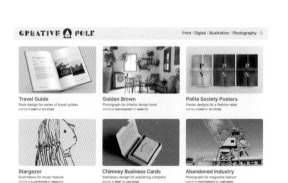

In later chapters, the site evolves allowing the public to: upload their own works; indicate which items they like; and comment on articles.

The articles are grouped into **categories** (which are like sections of the site). All of the categories are displayed using the same `category.php` page. It shows the name and description of the category, followed by a summary of each article in the category.

For each article, you can see its image, its title, a short description of the work, the category it is in, and its author (this is the same data that is shown for the latest six articles on the home page.)

Each category also has an option to indicate whether its name should appear in the main navigation bar or be hidden.

Each article is written by a **member** of the site; the member is the **author** of the article. Each member's profile is shown using the same `member.php` file.

It shows the author's name, the date they joined the site, and their profile picture, followed by a list of their articles. The information about each article matches the information shown on the category and home pages (the image, title, short description, category name, and author).

By the end of this book, members of the public will be allowed to to submit their own work, to indicate which items they like, and to comment on articles.

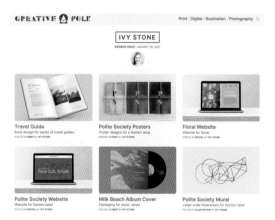

HOW A RELATIONAL DATABASE STORES DATA

Relational databases store data in tables. A single database can be made up of many tables. Below, you can see the database tables for the example website developed throughout the rest of this book.

A **relational database management system** (**RDBMS**), such as MySQL or MariaDB, is a piece of software that can hold multiple databases (just like a web server can host multiple websites).

The database software can be installed on either:

- The same computer as the web server. (MAMP and XAMPP install MySQL or MariaDB on your computer for you.)

- A separate computer the web server can access (like a mail program connects to a mail server).

TABLES

There are four **tables** in the database for the example website. Each table represents a concept that the application deals with:

- `article` represents each individual article and data about it (e.g., title and date it was created)

- `category` represents the sections of the site which group together related articles into topics

- `image` holds data on images that appear in articles

- `member` contains information about each individual member of the site

article

id	title	summary	content	created	category_id	member_id	image_id	published
1	Systemic	Brochure...	This...	2021-01-26	1	2	1	1
2	Forecast	Handbag...	This...	2021-01-28	3	2	2	1
3	Swimming	Photos...	This...	2021-02-02	4	1	3	1

category

id	name	description	navigation
1	Print	Inspiring graphic design	1
2	Digital	Powerful pixels	1
3	Illustration	Hand-drawn visual...	1

Relational databases got their name because tables contain information that relates to data in other tables.

ROWS

Each **row** in a table (also called a record or a tuple) holds one of the items that table represents. Each row in the `article` table represents one article; each row in the `member` table represents one person.

COLUMNS

Each **column** in a table (also called an attribute) stores one characteristic of the items that the table represents. For example, the columns in the `member` table store the members' forename, surname, email address, password, date they joined, and the filename of their profile picture.

FIELDS

A **field** is a single piece of information from a row.

PRIMARY KEY

The first column in each of the tables is called `id` because it can be used to *identify* an individual row of that table (e.g, it can identify an individual article, category, member or image). For this to work, every row of the table needs its own unique value in the `id` column. In these tables, this value is created using a feature of MySQL called **auto-increment**, which adds 1 to the number that was used in the previous row. This column is also known as the table's **primary key**.

image

id	file	alt
1	systemic-brochure.jpg	Brochure for Systemic Science Festival
2	forecast.jpg	Illustration of a handbag
3	swimming-pool.jpg	Photography of swimming pool

ROW —

member

id	forename	surname	email	password	joined	picture
1	Ivy	Stone	ivy@eg.link	c63j-82ve-...	2021-01-26 12:04:23	ivy.jpg
2	Luke	Wood	luke@eg.link	saq8-2f2k-...	2021-01-26 12:15:18	NULL
3	Emiko	Ito	emi@eg.link	sk3r-vd92-...	2021-02-12 10:53:47	emi.jpg

COLUMN

DATA TYPES
IN DATABASES

You need to specify a data type for each column of every table, and the maximum number of characters each field in that column can store.

MySQL has more data types than PHP, but the sample database only uses the five shown below. **NOTE:** MySQL does not have a boolean data type. Booleans are represented using the `tinyint` datatype with a value of `0` for `false` and `1` for `true`.

DATA TYPE	DESCRIPTION
`int`	Whole number
`tinyint`	Whole numbers up to 255 (Used for booleans)
`varchar`	Up to 65,535 alphanumeric characters
`text`	Up to 65,535 alphanumeric characters
`timestamp`	Date and time

With the exception of the `text` data type, you must specify the maximum number of:

- Bytes that will be used in a column containing text.
- Digits that will be used in a column storing numbers.

$$int(5)$$

DATA TYPE   MAX SIZE

Specifying a maximum size for each column reduces the size of the database, and makes it perform faster. In the tables below, datatypes are shown under the column names, followed by the maximum number of digits or bytes the column can hold in parentheses.

article

id	title	summary	content	created	category_id	member_id	image_id	published
int(11)	varchar(254)	varchar(1000)	text	timestamp	int(11)	int(11)	int(11)	tinyint(1)
1	Systemic	Brochure...	This...	2021-01-26	1	2	1	1
2	Forecast	Handbag...	This...	2021-01-28	3	2	2	1
3	Swimming	Photos...	This...	2021-02-02	4	1	3	1

category

id	name	description	navigation
int(11)	varchar(24)	varchar(254)	tinyint(1)
1	Print	Inspiring graphic design	1
2	Digital	Powerful pixels	1
3	Illustration	Hand-drawn visual...	1

AVOID DUPLICATING DATA IN A DATABASE

Avoid duplicating the same data in a database by making data in one table relate to data in another table using **primary** and **foreign keys**.

The first column in each table below is a **primary key**; it holds a value that identifies each row of the table.

If you look at the `article` table, below left, the:

- `category_id` column shows which category the article is in. Its value matches a primary key in the `category` table.

- `member_id` column shows who wrote an article. Its value matches a primary key in the `member` table.

- `image_id` column shows which image should be shown with the article. Its value matches a primary key in the `image` table.

The `category_id`, `member_id`, and `image_id` columns of the `article` table are called **foreign keys**. They show that:

- The first article is in the `Print` category.
- The first and second articles are by `Luke Wood`.
- The third article uses the `swimming-pool.jpg` image in the `image` table.

These values describe the relationship between the data in different tables and save duplicating category and author names in multiple rows of the `article` table. Avoiding duplication makes the database smaller and faster, and reduces the risk of errors if data is only updated in one place when it changes.

image

id int(11)	file varchar(254)	alt varchar(1000)
1	systemic-brochure.jpg	Brochure for Systemic Science Festival
2	polite-society-posters.jpg	Posters for Polite Society
3	swimming-pool.jpg	Photography of swimming pool

member

id int(11)	forename varchar(254)	surname varchar(254)	email varchar(254)	password varchar(254)	joined timestamp	picture varchar(254)
1	Ivy	Stone	ivy@eg.link	c63j-82ve-...	2021-01-26 12:04:23	ivy.jpg
2	Luke	Wood	luke@eg.link	saq8-2f2k-...	2021-01-26 12:15:18	*NULL*
3	Emiko	Ito	emi@eg.link	sk3r-vd92-...	2021-02-12 10:53:47	emi.jpg

USING PHPMYADMIN TO WORK WITH MYSQL

In a database-driven website, the database is usually updated by users that interact with the pages of the site. However, there will be times when you need to perform additional tasks using phpMyAdmin.

There are jobs known as **administration** tasks that you need to perform when running a database-driven website. These include:

- Creating new databases
- Backing up existing databases
- Adding new tables and columns to a database
- Checking that the site is adding or updating the data correctly when new features are added
- Creating user accounts that control who can access/edit the contents of a database

MySQL does not come with a visual interface of its own that you can use to perform these admin tasks, but there is a free open-source tool called **phpMyAdmin** that helps you perform them.

phpMyAdmin is written in PHP and runs on your web server; it is like a website you can use to manage the database. The next few pages show how it is used to perform some of the admin tasks.

When you installed MAMP or XAMPP, it will have installed phpMyAdmin on your computer.
Enter the URL: `http://localhost/phpmyadmin/` in your browser to access it.

If you added a port number to the URLs to get the code samples running, you will probably have to add the same port number to access phpMyAdmin.
E.g.: `http://localhost:8888/phpmyadmin/`

Hosting companies that support MySQL have many different ways of letting you perform admin tasks so you need to check how your hosting company lets you perform them. Rather than give you access to a full version of phpMyAdmin, they often use:

- Their own tools to create databases/user accounts
- A restricted version of phpMyAdmin to back up, inspect, and update the content of the database
- Their own URLs to access phpMyAdmin

USING PHPMYADMIN TO ADMINISTER A DATABASE

The phpMyAdmin screen has three main areas. Different versions of phpMyAdmin may look a little different, but the functionality and positioning of items on the page should be the same.

1: DATABASES & TABLES
One installation of MySQL can hold multiple databases (like a web server can host many sites).

The names of the databases are shown in the menu on the left. When you click on the name of a database, the + symbols in the list expand to show the names of the tables in that database.

2: TABS
These represent things you can do with the interface. When you:

- Open phpMyAdmin, the tabs show tasks you can perform with the MySQL software.
- Click on a database in the menu on the left, the tabs change to tasks you can perform on that one database.

3: MAIN WINDOW
This is where you perform admin tasks (e.g., it shows the contents of the database and allows you to update columns or add rows).

MySQL often creates some of its own databases such as: information_schema, mysql, performance_schema, and sys. Beginners should not edit them.

SETTING UP THE SAMPLE DATABASE

To work with the rest of the examples in this book, we will begin by creating a new database and importing some data into it.

CREATE A BLANK DATABASE

First, create a blank database using phpMyAdmin:

1. Click New at the top of the database list.
2. Enter the database name phpbook-1.
3. In the collation drop down, select utf8mb4_unicode_ci to specify the character set.
4. Click the Create button.

If you use a hosting company, you may need to use their tools to create a blank database. If so, skip this step.

ADDING DATA TO A DATABASE

Once you have created the database, you can add the data.

1. Click on the database name from the database list.
2. Click on the Import tab.
3. Under File to import, click the Choose file button and select the phpbook-1.sql file from the section_c/intro folder in the code download.
4. Click Go (at the bottom of the page – not shown) to import the sample data into the database.

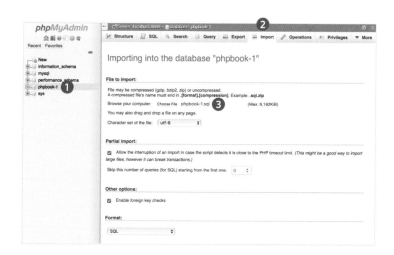

EXPLORING THE SAMPLE DATABASE

Once you have imported the data, look at the tables that have been created, and explore their contents and structure.

EXPLORING DATABASE CONTENTS

You can explore the contents of the database by clicking on the database name.

1. Click on the database name in the database list panel.
2. Select the article table.
3. Click the Browse tab.
4. Each row of the table represents an article.

TABLE STRUCTURE

For every table, you can see the column names, data types, and field sizes.

1. Click on the database name.
2. Select the article table.
3. Click on the Structure tab.

Each column is listed as a row in the table that you see.

To learn how to manually add tables and columns, see:
http://notes.re/mysql/create-manually

You can see the name of each column, followed by the data type (with its maximum size in parentheses). Collation holds the character encoding.

Null indicates if a value can be null. The Default column specifies a value the column should use as a default value if no value has been specified.

CREATING DATABASE USER ACCOUNTS

The MySQL software allows you to create different **user accounts**. Each one has a username and password to log in to the database. You can control what data each user account can access and update.

Each MySQL user account allows you to specify:

- Which databases that user can access
- The tables it can access or update
- Other tasks that user can perform

When MySQL is installed, it comes with an account known as the **root account**; a master account that can create and delete user accounts and databases.

For security reasons, do not use the root account in your PHP code. Instead, create a user account that can only:

- Access the database used for that particular site (not all databases hosted on the same server)
- Perform the tasks that the application needs to perform – do not let it perform powerful tasks (such as creating or deleting tables) if the site doesn't require this

On the right-hand page, you can see how the root account (set up when the server was installed) lets you view and create user accounts in phpMyAdmin.

If you are using a web hosting company and cannot see these options, you should consult their help files as each host operates differently and they may have:

- Created a username and password for you
- Their own tools to create and update users

1. Select the name of the database from the left-hand pane that you want to create a user for.

2. Click on the `Privileges` tab. This displays a table of the users with access to this database.

3. Click `Add user` or `Add user account`.

4. Specify a username.

5. Enter a password or use the `Generate` option.

6. Under `Database for user account`, if `Grant all privileges on database phpbook-1` is checked, deselect this option.

7. The `Global privileges` options control what the user is allowed to do with the database as a whole. The example website only needs the four options that have been selected in the `Data` column: `Select`, `Insert`, `Update`, and `Delete`; it does not use the other features, so they are not enabled.

You may see options beneath the ones shown in the screenshot; leave these settings as they are.

8. Save the user details using the `Go` button at the bottom of the page (not shown in the screenshots).

You can also select each table from the left-hand pane and set the privileges a user has for that table.

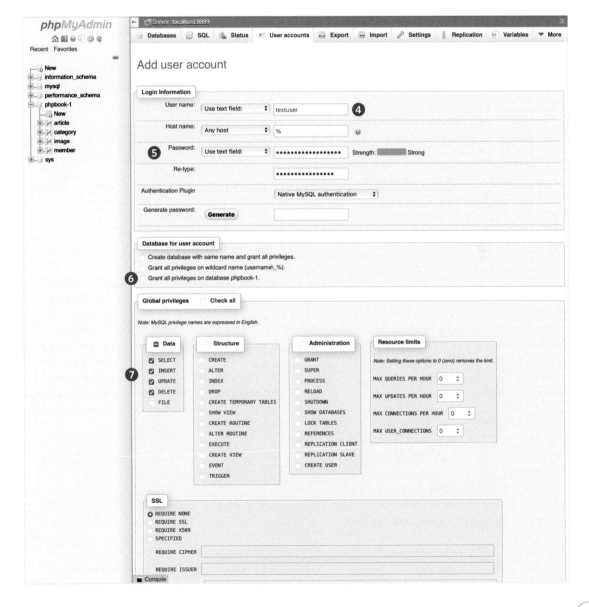

IN THIS SECTION

DATABASE DRIVEN WEBSITES

IMPORTANT NOTE:

For the remaining chapters of the book, you need to download the code from `http://phpandmysql.com/code` and run it locally. It will also help to have the sample code open as you read through these chapters.

11 STRUCTURED QUERY LANGUAGE

SQL is a language that lets you specify what data you want to retrieve from the database and what data you want to update in the database. This chapter shows how the SQL language works by having you enter SQL commands into the phpMyAdmin interface.

12 GETTING DATA FROM THE DATABASE

Having learned SQL, you will see how PDO can send a SQL statement to the database and how PHP can access the data that it returns. The data that is returned from the database can be made available to your PHP code as either an array or as an object.

13 UPDATING DATA IN THE DATABASE

In this chapter, you will learn how to get data from a visitor to the site, validate the data, and use that data to update the database. You will also learn how to handle problems that prevent the database from being updated.

11

STRUCTURED QUERY LANGUAGE

Structured Query Language (SQL) is a language that is used to communicate with databases. It is used to request data, add new data, edit existing data, and delete data.

In this chapter, you will learn how to use SQL to perform the following tasks:

- **Select** data from a database
- **Create** new rows in a database table
- **Update** data already stored in a database
- **Delete** rows from database tables

An instruction to get or change data stored in the database is known as a **SQL statement**. A SQL statement that only asks for information can also be called a **SQL query** because you are *asking* the database for data. You will learn how to write SQL queries before you learn how to create, update, or delete data from a database.

To learn the SQL language, you will use phpMyAdmin. Once you have learned how SQL works in this chapter, the next two chapters will show you how a PHP page uses PDO (PHP Data Objects) to run SQL statements that get or update the data in the database.

Some of the examples in this chapter update the data that is stored in the database that forms the basis of the main example website in this book so they should be run once, in the order they appear in the chapter. If they are not run in that order, the later examples may not work. If this happens, or if you want to run them again, delete the database and set it up again using the instructions from the introduction to this section.

GETTING DATA FROM A DATABASE

To ask the database for data, use SQL's SELECT command and then specify what data you want returned. The database will then create a **result set** containing the data you asked for.

The SELECT command indicates that you want to get data from the database. It is followed by the names of the columns that contain the data you want. Each column name should be separated by a comma.

The FROM clause is followed by the name of the table you want to collect the data from. A SQL statement *should* finish with a semicolon (although many developers omit this, and it usually still works).

COLUMNS TO SELECT ⟶ SELECT *column1, column2*
TABLE COLUMNS ARE IN ⟶ FROM *table;*

The SQL statement below asks for the data in the forename and surname columns of the member table. It returns the data from every row in the table. You can read it literally; it says that you want to:

- SELECT the forename and surname columns
- FROM the member table

When a SQL query is **run**, or **executed**, the database gets the requested data and places it in a result set. Columns are added to the result set in the same order they are named in the query. To control the order in which rows are added to the result set, use the ORDER BY clause (see p406).

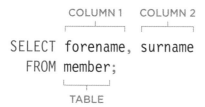

COLUMN 1   COLUMN 2

SELECT forename, surname
FROM member;

TABLE

result set	
forename	surname
Ivy	Stone
Luke	Wood
Emiko	Ito

SQL commands can be written in upper or lowercase. In this book, they are in uppercase to distinguish them from table and column names. Table and column names must use the same case as the database.

The right-hand page shows how to enter the SQL query into phpMyAdmin, and how the result set that the query generates is displayed.

1. Open phpMyAdmin and select the `phpbook-1` database. If you have not created it, see p392.

2. Select the SQL tab.

3. Type the SQL query from the left-hand page into the text area.

4. Click Go.

5. When you click Go, the SQL query is executed. MySQL then returns the result set to phpMyAdmin, and phpMyAdmin displays the result set in a table.

For the rest of this chapter, instead of showing screenshots of phpMyAdmin, SQL queries and their result sets will be shown as on the left-hand-page.

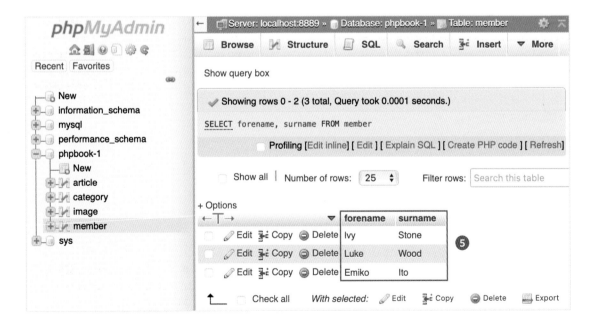

RETURNING SPECIFIC ROWS FROM A TABLE

To get data from specific rows of a table (rather than all of them),
add the WHERE clause followed by a **search condition.**

Once you have specified which columns of data to
get from a table, you can add a search condition to
control which rows of that table should be added to
the result set. In the search condition, name a column
from the table, and whether its value should be equal
to =, greater than >, or less than < a value you specify.

As the database works through the rows in the table,
if the condition results in true, it adds a new row to
the result set and copies the data from the columns
named after the SELECT command into the result set.

If the value you specify in the condition is text, put
the text in single quotes.

If the value you specify in the condition is a number,
do not put the number in quotes.

MySQL does not have a boolean data type, but you
can use a tinyint data type to represent a boolean
with a value of 1 for true and 0 for false. Because
these values are numbers, they should not be placed
in quotes.

COLUMNS TO SELECT $\longrightarrow$ SELECT *column(s)*
TABLE COLUMNS ARE IN $\longrightarrow$ FROM *table*
ROWS TO ADD TO RESULT SET $\longrightarrow$ WHERE *column* = *value;*
                                          |
                                       OPERATOR

You can combine multiple search conditions using
the three logical operators shown in the table on
the right. They work like PHP's logical operators
shown on p56-7. Each search condition is placed
in parentheses to ensure that it is run on its own.

OPERATOR	DESCRIPTION
AND	All conditions must return true.
OR	Any one condition can return true.
NOT	Reverses a condition; checks it is not true.

COLUMNS TO SELECT $\longrightarrow$ SELECT *column(s)*
TABLE COLUMNS ARE IN $\longrightarrow$ FROM *table*
ROWS TO ADD TO RESULT SET $\longrightarrow$ WHERE *(column < value)* AND *(column > value);*
                                          └─── CONDITION 1 ───┘ └ LOGICAL ┘ └─── CONDITION 2 ───┘
                                                                  OPERATOR

USING COMPARISON OPERATORS IN SQL

section_c/c11/comparison-operator-1.sql

```
SELECT email
  FROM member
 WHERE forename = 'Ivy';
```

result set
email
ivy@eg.link

This example selects the email address of all members who have a value of Ivy in the `forename` column of the `member` table. Enter the SQL into phpMyAdmin as shown on p401.

TRY: Find the email address of any member whose name is Luke.

section_c/c11/comparison-operator-2.sql

```
SELECT email
  FROM member
 WHERE id < 3;
```

result set
email
ivy@eg.link
luke@eg.link

This example finds the email addresses of members who have a value of less than 3 in the `id` column of the `member` table.

TRY: Find the email addresses of members whose `id` is less than or equal to 3.

section_c/c11/logical-operator.sql

```
SELECT email
  FROM member
 WHERE (email > 'E') AND (email < 'L');
```

result set
email
emi@eg.link
ivy@eg.link

This example uses the AND operator to find results where a member's email address meets two conditions - it begins with:
1. A letter greater than E
2. A letter less than L

TRY: Find the email addresses of any members whose email address begins with letters G-L.

SEARCHING FOR RESULTS WITH LIKE & WILDCARDS

The LIKE operator can be used in a search condition to find rows of data where the value in a specified column starts with, ends with, or contains specific characters.

The LIKE operator finds rows of data where a column contains characters that match a **pattern** you have specified. For example, the pattern can be used to find rows where the value in a specified column:

- Starts with a specified letter
- Ends with a specified number
- Contains a specified word or set of characters (which is often used to create search features)

A pattern can use **wildcard symbols** to specify where other characters could be (as shown in the table on the right):

- % indicates zero or more characters
- _ indicates an individual character

VALUE	MATCHES COLUMNS WHOSE VALUE
To%	Starts with To
%day	Ends with day
%to%	Contains to at any point
h_ll	Has a single character in place of the underscore (e.g., hall, hell, hill, hull)
%h_ll%	Contains h, then any character, then two lls (e.g., hall, hell, chill, hilly, shellac, chilled, hallmark, hullabaloo)
1%	Starts with 1
%!	Ends with !

The value is case-insensitive, which means looking for the name Ivy would also find the values IVY and ivy.

COLUMNS TO SELECT ⟶ SELECT *column(s)*
TABLE COLUMNS ARE IN ⟶ FROM *table*
ROWS TO ADD TO RESULT SET ⟶ WHERE *column* LIKE '*%value%*';

LIKE OPERATOR   WILDCARD SYMBOLS

SEARCHING FOR VALUES

section_c/c11/like-1.sql

```sql
SELECT email
  FROM member
 WHERE forename LIKE 'I%';
```

result set
email
ivy@eg.link

This example searches for the email addresses of all members whose first name begins with the letter I (uppercase or lowercase).

TRY: Find members whose name begins with the letter E.

section_c/c11/like-2.sql

```sql
SELECT email
  FROM member
 WHERE forename LIKE 'E_I%';
```

result set
email
emi@eg.link

This example gets the emails of all members whose first name:
- Begins with the letter E
- Followed by another character
- Then the letter I
- Then any other characters
(It would return names including Eli, Elias, Elijah, Elisha, Emi, Emiko, Emil, Emilio, Emily, Eoin, and Eric.)

TRY: Find members whose name matches 'L_K%'.

section_c/c11/like-3.sql

```sql
SELECT email
  FROM member
 WHERE forename LIKE 'Luke';
```

result set
email
luke@eg.link

This example searches for the email address of anyone whose name is Luke. Since there are no wildcard characters, it only returns exact matches.

TRY: Find members called Ivy.

CONTROLLING ORDER OF ROWS IN A RESULT SET

To control the order in which rows are added to a result set, use the ORDER BY clause, followed by the name of a column whose values will order the results, then either ASC for ascending or DESC for descending.

ORDER BY can be added to the end of a query to control the order that the rows are added to the result set. The values in the specified column are used to control the order of the results.

This should be followed by one of two keywords: ASC for ascending or DESC for descending. (If you do not specify one, it sorts it in ascending order, but your SQL will be easier to read if you specify ASC or DESC.)

```
COLUMNS TO SELECT    ⟶   SELECT column(s)
TABLE COLUMNS ARE IN ⟶   FROM table
CONTROL ORDER OF RESULTS ⟶ ORDER BY column ASC;
                                 └──┬──┘ └──┬──┘ └┬┘
                         ORDER BY CLAUSE COLUMN DIRECTION
```

You can sort the order that rows are added to the result set using the values from multiple columns. Each column name is separated by a comma. If the first column used to sort values contains identical values, it will refer to the second column in the list.

For example, if you were sorting members by their name, and more than one member shared the same first name (stored in the forename column), you could then order them by their last name (stored in the surname column).

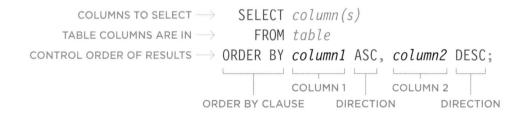

```
COLUMNS TO SELECT    ⟶   SELECT column(s)
TABLE COLUMNS ARE IN ⟶   FROM table
CONTROL ORDER OF RESULTS ⟶ ORDER BY column1 ASC, column2 DESC;
                                 └──┬──┘ └──┬─┘ └┬┘  └──┬──┘ └─┬─┘
                         ORDER BY CLAUSE  COLUMN 1  COLUMN 2
                                         DIRECTION DIRECTION
```

SORTING RESULTS

SQL

```
    SELECT email
      FROM member
  ORDER BY email DESC;
```

result set
email
luke@eg.link
ivy@eg.link
emi@eg.link

This example gets all of the email addresses and sorts them in descending order.

TRY: Reverse the order of results by changing DESC to ASC.

SQL

```
    SELECT title, category_id
      FROM article
  ORDER BY category_id ASC, title ASC;
```

result set (showing first 10 rows of 24)	
title	category_id
Chimney Business Cards	1
Milk Beach Album Cover	1
Polite Society Posters	1
Systemic Brochure	1
The Ice Palace	1
Travel Guide	1
Chimney Press Website	2
Floral Website	2
Milk Beach Website	2
Polite Society Website	2

This example gets values from the title and category_id columns of the article table and orders them by the category_id first in ascending order, and then the title in alphabetical order.

The entire result set contains more rows than are shown on the left, (one for each article), but there is not enough space to show them all here.

TRY: Select the title and member_id columns from the article table and order the results by the member_id first, and then the title in alphabetical order.

COUNTING AND GROUPING RESULTS

When SQL's COUNT() function is used after the SELECT command, it adds the total number of rows that match the query to the result set. Grouping results lets you count how many rows contain the same value.

To count the number of rows in a table, call COUNT() after the SELECT command and specify the table. Use an asterisk (known as a wildcard) as the argument for the COUNT() function.

```
              FUNCTION
SELECT  COUNT(*)
    FROM table;
```

If you add a search condition to the query, the COUNT() function returns the number of rows that match the query with the search condition.

```
SELECT  COUNT(*)
    FROM table
   WHERE column LIKE '%value%';
```

If you specify a column name as an argument for the COUNT() function, it counts the number of rows where the value in the specified column is not NULL.

```
SELECT  COUNT(column)
    FROM table;
```

The GROUP BY clause can be used with SQL's COUNT() function to determine how many rows have the same value in a column. E.g., it can count how many articles a member has written, or how many articles are in a category. In the SELECT statement:

1. Select a column name that may contain identical values (e.g., member_id or category_id).
2. Use COUNT(*) to count the number of rows.
3. Specify the table the column is in.
4. Use the GROUP BY clause, followed by the name of the column that may contain identical values, so that it groups the number of rows that share the same value in this column and counts them.

```
        COLUMN THAT MAY
        HAVE SAME VALUE

SELECT  column,  COUNT(*)
    FROM table
GROUP BY column;

        COLUMN THAT MAY
        HAVE SAME VALUE
```

COUNTING THE NUMBER OF MATCHING RESULTS

section_c/c11/count-1.sql

SQL

```
SELECT COUNT(picture)
  FROM member;
```

result set
COUNT(picture)
2

This example uses SQL's `COUNT()` function to return the number of members who have supplied a profile picture. If the value in the picture column is `NULL`, they will not be counted.

TRY: Count the number of members with an email address.

section_c/c11/count-2.sql

SQL

```
SELECT COUNT(*)
  FROM article
 WHERE title LIKE '%design%' OR content LIKE '%design%';
```

result set
COUNT(*)
9

This example uses SQL's `COUNT()` function to return the number of articles where the `title` or `content` columns contain the term `design`.

TRY: Find the number of articles that contain the term `photo`.

section_c/c11/count-3.sql

SQL

```
SELECT member_id, COUNT(*)
  FROM article
 GROUP BY member_id;
```

result set	
member_id	COUNT(*)
1	10
2	8
3	6

This query counts the number of articles by each member. The `SELECT` statement gets the `member_id` column and the `COUNT()` function counts the number of matching rows. The `FROM` clause indicates it is looking in the `article` table. The `GROUP BY` clause groups the values in the `member_id` column so you see the member's id and the number of articles they wrote.

TRY: Calculate the number of articles in each category.

LIMITING AND SKIPPING RESULTS

LIMIT restricts the number of results added to a result set. OFFSET tells the database to skip a specified number of records and add the subsequent ones to the result set.

To restrict the total number of rows that are added to the result set, use the LIMIT clause.

The following would only add the first five results that match the query to the result set.

COLUMNS TO SELECT ⟶ SELECT *column(s)*
TABLE COLUMNS ARE IN ⟶ FROM *table*
LIMIT NUMBER OF ROWS ⟶ LIMIT 5;

LIMIT CLAUSE   MAX RESULTS

The OFFSET clause can be used after the LIMIT clause to skip the first matches that would otherwise have been added to the result set.

The following would skip the first six results that match the query, and then add the following three to the result set.

COLUMNS TO SELECT ⟶ SELECT *column(s)*
TABLE COLUMNS ARE IN ⟶ FROM *table*
LIMIT AND SKIP ROWS ⟶ LIMIT 3 OFFSET 6;

OFFSET CLAUSE   RESULTS TO SKIP

LIMIT and OFFSET are often used when a query generates a lot of results. The results are split over separate pages using a technique called **pagination**. Google's search results are one well-known example.

After the first page of results, there are links to additional pages that show more results that match the same query. You learn how to use these commands to add pagination in the next chapter.

RESTRICTING THE NUMBER OF MATCHING RESULTS

section_c/c11/limit.sql

```sql
SELECT title
  FROM article
 ORDER BY id
 LIMIT 1;
```

result set
title
Systemic Brochure

This example asks for the article titles, ordered by the value in the id column. It uses the LIMIT clause to only add the first match to the result set.

TRY: Get the first five articles from the print category.

section_c/11/offset.sql

```sql
SELECT title
  FROM article
 ORDER BY id
 LIMIT 3 OFFSET 9;
```

result set
title
Polite Society Mural
Stargazer Website and App
The Ice Palace

This example asks for the article titles, ordered by the value in the id column. It uses the OFFSET clause to skip the first nine results that match the query and then uses the LIMIT clause to add the next three matches to the result set.

TRY: Skip the first six matches, and return the next six.

USING JOINS TO GET DATA FROM TWO TABLES

A **join** allows you to request data from more than one table.
The data from both tables is added to a single row in the result set.

When designing a database, you should create a table for each concept the site represents, and avoid duplication of data in more than one table.

In the eaample website, data about articles, categories, members, and images live in different tables. The first column in these tables holds a value that is used to identify each row of the table. For example, the value in the id column of the category table can identify each category. This value is called a **primary key**.

The article table needs to store which category each article lives in. Rather than duplicating the category names for each article, it has a column called category_id. The value in this column is known as a **foreign key** and it will correspond to the primary key of the category it is in.

The primary and foreign keys describe how data in one row of a table can **relate** to data in a row of another table. Below, you see the relationship between the second article and the category it is in.

When you write a SQL query to collect information about an article, and want to include information from another table (such as the name of the category that it is in), the article is the primary subject of the query. Therefore, the article table is known as the **left table**.

When you get additional data about the article from a second table (such as the category table), the second table is known as a **right table**.

A JOIN clause describes how the values relate.

article

id	title	summary	content	created	category_id	member_id	image_id	published
1	Systemic Bro…	Brochure…	This bro…	2021-01-26	1	2	1	1
2	Forecast	Handbag…	This dra…	2021-01-29	3	2	2	1
3	Swimming Pool	Architec…	This pho…	2021-02-02	4	1	3	1

category

id	name	description	navigation
1	Print	Inspiring graphic design	1
2	Digital	Powerful pixels	1
3	Illustration	Hand-drawn visual storytelling	1

So far in this chapter, the queries have collected data from one table in the database at a time. When a JOIN is used to get data from more than one table, you specify the name of the table that a column is in as well as the column name. To do this use:

- The name of the table the data is in
- Followed by a period symbol
- Followed by the column name

The query below selects all of the article titles and summaries from the article table, and also gets the name of the category each article is in from the category table.

1. The SELECT command is followed by the names of the columns that data should be returned from.

2. The FROM command is followed by the name of the left table (the primary subject of the query). In this case, it is the article table.

3. The JOIN clause is followed by the name of the right table (the one that holds the additional information). In this case, it is the category table.

Then, the join tells the database the name of a column in both the left table and the right table whose values will match.

To do this, use the keyword ON, followed by the:

- Column in the left table that holds a foreign key
- Equals symbol
- Column in the right table that holds a primary key

```
SELECT article.title, article.summary, category.name
    FROM article
    JOIN category ON article.category_id = category.id;
```
FOREIGN KEY   PRIMARY KEY

The result set below shows the first three rows of data that would be added to the result set (the full result set would hold all of the articles).

NOTE: The column names in the result set do not use table names because the data has been taken from those tables and combined into a single result set.

result set (showing first 3 rows of 24)		
title	summary	name
Milk Beach Website	Website for music series	Digital
Wellness App	App for health facility	Digital
Stargazer Website and App	Website and app for music festival	Digital

To select an individual row, or subset of the rows, a search condition can be added after the JOIN. For example, the query below would only return the details of articles that are in the print category.

The search condition can also be followed by clauses that order, limit, and skip results when they are added to the result set (as shown with earlier examples in this chapter).

```
SELECT article.title, article.summary, category.name
  FROM article
  JOIN category ON article.category_id = category.id
  WHERE category.id = 1;
```

HOW JOINS WORK IF THERE IS MISSING DATA

When the database tries to perform a JOIN on a row of data, but some of the data is missing, you can specify whether to add the available data to the result set or skip that row and not add it to the result set.

Imagine that you wanted to get data for each image that was uploaded for an article. You could use a JOIN to get the image data (like the JOIN that got the article title and the name of the category it is in on the previous page).

The article table's image_id column is a foreign key because its value is the primary key from the image table that holds the image for the article.

There is, however, a key difference. While each article *must* belong in a category (the database enforces this using something called a constraint which you meet on p431), an article does not *need* to have an image.

If an image is not uploaded for an article, the article table's image_id column holds the value NULL.

In the article table below, the image_id column of one of the articles has a value of NULL because there is no image for the article. This means that the JOIN would not find any corresponding image data in the image table.

The right-hand page shows two types of JOIN that can be used to specify whether the query should still add the rest of the data it can find to the result set, or whether it should skip the entire row of data because the corresponding image could not be found.

article

id	title	summary	content	created	category_id	member_id	image_id	published
4	Walking Birds	Artwork …	The brie…	2021-02-12	3	3	4	1
5	Sisters	Editoria…	The arti…	2021-02-27	3	3	*NULL*	1
6	Micro-Dunes	Photogra…	This pho…	2021-03-03	4	1	6	1

image

id	file	alt
4	birds.jpg	Collage of two birds
6	micro-dunes.jpg	Photograph of tiny sand dunes

INNER JOIN

An **inner join** adds data to the result set if the database has *all* the data to perform the join. To create an inner join, use either the JOIN or INNER JOIN clause.

If this query were run against the tables on the left-hand page, the article with an id of 5 would not be added to the result set because its image_id column has a value of NULL (so the join cannot be created).

```
SELECT article.id, article.title, image.file
  FROM article
  JOIN image ON article.image_id = image.id;
```

result set (showing first 5 rows of 23)		
id	title	file
1	Systemic Brochure	systemic-brochure.jpg
2	Forecast	forecast.jpg
3	Swimming Pool	swimming-pool.jpg
4	Walking Birds	birds.jpg
6	Micro-Dunes	micro-dunes.jpg

LEFT OUTER JOIN

A **left outer join** adds all the requested data from the left table to the result set. It then uses NULL for any values it cannot get from the right table. To create a left outer join, use either the LEFT JOIN or LEFT OUTER JOIN clause.

If this query were run against the tables on the left-hand page, the title of the article that has an id of 5 is added to the result set, but the value for the file column is given the value of NULL because no corresponding data is found for the image.

```
    SELECT article.id, article.title, image.file
      FROM article
LEFT JOIN image ON article.image_id = image.id;
```

result set (showing first 5 rows of 24)		
id	title	file
1	Systemic Brochure	systemic-brochure.jpg
2	Forecast	forecast.jpg
3	Swimming Pool	swimming-pool.jpg
4	Walking Birds	birds.jpg
5	Sisters	*NULL*

GETTING DATA FROM MULTIPLE TABLES

A SELECT command can be followed by multiple JOIN clauses to collect data from more than two tables.

To collect data from multiple tables, you can add more than one JOIN clause:

- After the SELECT statement, specify the names of all the columns you want data from (using the table name, a period, then the column name).

- Use a join clause to state the relationship between the data in each of the tables.

The query below collects data about an article from three tables: article, category, and image.

The article table is the left table. It holds the title and summary of the articles.

The category table provides the name of the category each article is in. Because each article must be in a category, the JOIN clause is used.

The image table provides the filename and alt text of the image that is used with each article. Because each article does not need to have an image, a LEFT JOIN clause is used to ensure that all of the available data is still added to the result set.

```
SELECT article.title, article.summary,
       category.name,
       image.file, image.alt
  FROM article
  JOIN category  ON article.category_id = category.id
  LEFT JOIN image ON article.image_id    = image.id
ORDER BY article.id ASC;
```

result set (showing first 3 rows of 24)

title	summary	name	file	alt
Systemic Brochure	Brochure design for…	Print	systemic-brochure.jpg	Brochure…
Forecast	Handbag illustration…	Illustration	forecast.jpg	Illustrati…
Swimming Pool	Architecture magazine…	Photography	swimming-pool.jpg	Photograph…

USING MULTIPLE JOINS

section_c/c11/joins.sql

```
SELECT article.id, article.title,
       category.name,
       image.file, image.alt

  FROM article
  JOIN category   ON article.category_id = category.id
  LEFT JOIN image ON article.image_id    = image.id

 WHERE article.category_id = 3
   AND article.published   = 1
 ORDER BY article.id DESC;
```

① ② ③ ④ ⑤ ⑥

result set

id	title	name	file	alt
21	Stargazer	Illustration	stargazer-masc…	Illustrat…
17	Snow Search	Illustration	snow-search.jpg	Illustrat…
10	Polite Society…	Illustration	polite-society…	Mural for…
5	Sisters	Illustration	*NULL*	*NULL*
4	Walking Birds	Illustration	birds.jpg	Collage…
2	Forecast	Illustration	forecast.jpg	Illustrat…

TRY: Get the same data from the articles that are in the category that has an id of 2.

TRY: Add the forename and surname of the author from the member table.

The query on the left collects data about multiple articles that live in a specified category.

1. The SELECT statement is followed by the names of the columns that should be added to the result set. Data is collected from the article, category, and image tables.

2. The FROM clause indicates that the left table is the article table.

3. The first join indicates the data in the category table should come from the row whose id column has the same value as the article table's category_id column.

4. The second join indicates that data in the image table should be selected from the row whose id column has the same value as the article table's image_id column. This is a LEFT JOIN so NULL is used for any missing data.

5. The WHERE clause restricts the results to rows of data where the article table has a value of 3 in the category_id column and 1 in the published column.

6. The ORDER BY clause controls the order that results are added to the result set, using the article ids in descending order.

ALIASES

Table aliases make queries that use joins easier to read.
Column aliases specify column names in the result set.

In complex SQL queries where joins select data from several tables, you can give each table name an alias.

A table alias is like a shorthand for a table name and it reduces the amount of text in the query.

A table alias is created after the FROM or JOIN commands. After the table name, use the AS command, then specify an alias for that table. Then, everywhere else in the query, use the alias instead of the full table name.

```
SELECT t1.column1, t1.column2, t2.column3
  FROM table1 AS t1
  JOIN table2 AS t2 ON t1.column4 = t2.column1;
```

CREATE ALIAS   ALIAS FOR TABLE 1   ALIAS FOR TABLE 2

The names of columns in the result set are usually taken from the names of the columns in the tables that the data was collected from.

Column aliases let you change the name of a column in the result set. They can also give a name to a column holding the result of a COUNT() function.

To create a column alias, after specifing the name of a column you want to get data from, use the AS command and the name the column should use in the result set.

Or, after the COUNT() function, use the AS command and a column name for the count in the result set.

DATABASE COLUMN   ALIAS FOR RESULT SET

```
SELECT column1 AS newname1
  FROM table;
```

COUNT FUNCTION   ALIAS FOR RESULT SET

```
SELECT COUNT(*) AS members
  FROM members;
```

USING ALIASES FOR COLUMN NAMES

section_c/c11/table-alias.sql

```
SELECT a.id, a.title,
       c.name,
       i.file, i.alt

  FROM article     AS a
  JOIN category    AS c  ON a.category_id = c.id
  LEFT JOIN image  AS i  ON a.image_id    = i.id

 WHERE a.category_id = 3
   AND a.published   = 1
 ORDER BY a.id DESC;
```

This query gets the same data as the previous example, but it specifies aliases for the table names after the FROM and JOIN commands:

a for the article table
c for the category table
i for the image table

The aliases are then used instead of the full table names after the SELECT command and after the WHERE, AND, and ORDER BY clauses.

TRY: Change the aliases to:
art for the article table
cat for the category table
img for the image table.

result set

id	title	name	file	alt
21	Stargazer	Illustration	stargazer-masc…	Illustrat…
17	Snow Search	Illustration	snow-search.jpg	Illustrat…
10	Polite Society…	Illustration	polite-society…	Mural for…
5	Sisters	Illustration	*NULL*	*NULL*
4	Walking Birds	Illustration	birds.jpg	Collage…
2	Forecast	Illustration	forecast.jpg	Illustrat…

section_c/c11/column-alias.sql

```
SELECT forename AS firstname, surname AS lastname
  FROM member;
```

This example selects the values from the forename and surname columns of the member table and uses aliases to give them new column names in the result set.

TRY: Count the number of articles in the article table and use an alias to call the column articles.

result set

firstname	lastname
Ivy	Stone
Luke	Wood
Emiko	Ito

COMBINING COLUMNS & ALTERNATIVES TO NULL

CONCAT() adds data from two columns into one column in the result set. COALESCE() specifies a value to use if a column contains NULL.

SQL's CONCAT() function is used to take values from two or more columns, and join (or concatenate) the values into a single column in the result set.

Often, a string is inserted between the values in the two columns to separate them. When values from two columns are joined, an alias is used to specify the name for that column in the result set.

As with any function, a comma separates the arguments that the CONCAT() function joins together to create the new value. Below, the values from two columns are joined together, and a space is used to separate the data in the two columns.

If the value of one column is NULL, the values in the other columns will also get treated as NULL.

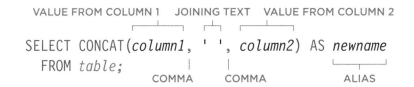

VALUE FROM COLUMN 1   JOINING TEXT   VALUE FROM COLUMN 2

```
SELECT CONCAT(column1, ' ', column2) AS newname
  FROM table;
```
COMMA   COMMA   ALIAS

If you know that a value in a column can be NULL, you can use SQL's COALESCE() function to indicate:

- The name of another column whose value it can try to use in its place (if this value is not NULL, it will be used instead)

- A default value to use if all of the specified columns have a value of NULL

When a row is being added to the result set, if the value in the first choice of columns it NULL, it will check the value in the second choice of columns. If the values in all alternative columns are also NULL, it will use the default value.

When the COALESCE() function is used, you must provide an alias for the column name in the result set as the data could have come from several columns.

```
SELECT COALESCE(column1, column2, default) AS newname
  FROM table;
```
1ST CHOICE 2ND CHOICE DEFAULT   ALIAS
OF DATA   OF DATA   VALUE

CONCAT AND COALESCE

section_c/c11/concat.sql

```sql
SELECT CONCAT(forename, ' ', surname) AS author
  FROM member;
```

result set
author
Ivy Stone
Luke Wood
Emiko Ito

section_c/c11/coalesce.sql

```sql
SELECT COALESCE(picture, forename, 'friend') AS profile
  FROM member;
```

result set
profile
ivy.jpg
Luke
emi.jpg

This example uses the CONCAT() function to join the values from the forename and surname columns into one column called author in the result set.

A space has been added between the values in the two columns to ensure a space appears between the forename and the surname.

TRY: Add the email address to the values selected and call the alias author_details.

This example uses SQL's COALESCE() function to specify alternative values that can be used if the value in the profile column of the member table is NULL (because the user has not uploaded a profile picture). Here, the SELECT statement looks for:

- A value in the picture column of the member table.
- If the value is NULL, the value in forename will be used
- If this is NULL, the text friend will be shown instead.

An alias specifies the name this column should use in the result set. Here, it is called profile.

TRY: If the user has not provided a picture, use the default value of placeholder.png instead.

ARTICLE QUERIES FOR THE EXAMPLE CMS

The CMS uses SQL queries to display information about an individual article, and the summaries of a set of articles. These queries bring together the techniques you have seen throughout this chapter.

1. The SQL query below gets data about an individual article from all four database tables. The `SELECT` statement is followed by names of the columns that data will be collected from.

2. Column aliases are used to give the category name and the image's filename and alt text new column names in the result set.

3. The `CONCAT()` function joins the forename and surname of the member who wrote the article, and a column alias says the result set should store the name in a column called `author`.

4. The left table is the `article` table. Three joins show the relationships with the data in other tables.

After the `FROM` and `JOIN` commands, each table name is given a table alias. Each time the query specifies a column of data, these aliases are used instead of the full table names.

5. The `WHERE` clause specifies the id of the article to collect. It is only returned if the `published` column has a value of 1.

section_c/c11/article.sql   `SQL`

```
① SELECT a.title, a.summary, a.content, a.created, a.category_id, a.member_id,
②        c.name       AS category,
③        CONCAT(m.forename, ' ', m.surname) AS author,
②        i.file       AS image_file,
②        i.alt        AS image_alt

    FROM article     AS a
    JOIN category    AS c   ON a.category_id = c.id
④   JOIN member      AS m   ON a.member_id   = m.id
    LEFT JOIN image  AS i   ON a.image_id    = i.id
   WHERE a.id        = 22
⑤    AND a.published = 1;
```

result set

title	summary	content	created	category_id	member_id	category	author	image_file	image_alt
Polite…	Poster…	These…	2021-0…	1	1	Print	Ivy St…	polite-so…	Photogra…

1. The SQL query below gets summary information about all of the articles in a specified category, using data from all four database tables.

The SELECT statement is followed by names of the columns that data will be collected from.

2. As with the example on the left, aliases give the category name, and the image file and alt text new column names in the result set.

The CONCAT() function is called again to join the forename and surname of the author.

3. The joins are identical to the example on the left.

4. The WHERE clause specifies the id of the category that the articles should be in, and that the article must be published. The results are then ordered by the article id in descending order.

`SQL`

section_c/c11/article-list.sql

```
① SELECT a.id, a.title, a.summary, a.category_id, a.member_id,
          c.name      AS category,
②         CONCAT(m.forename, ' ', m.surname) AS author,
          i.file      AS image_file,
          i.alt       AS image_alt

     FROM article    AS a
     JOIN category   AS c   ON a.category_id = c.id
③    JOIN member     AS m   ON a.member_id   = m.id
     LEFT JOIN image AS i   ON a.image_id    = i.id

     WHERE a.category_id = 1
④      AND a.published   = 1
     ORDER BY a.id DESC;
```

result set

id	title	summary	category_id	member_id	category	author	image_file	image_alt
24	Travel Guide	Book de…	1	1	Print	Ivy Stone	feathervi…	Two page…
22	Polite Societ…	Poster…	1	1	Print	Ivy Stone	polite-so…	Photogra…
20	Chimney Busin…	Station…	1	2	Print	Luke Wood	chimney-c…	Business…
14	Milk Beach Al…	Packagi…	1	1	Print	Ivy Stone	milk-beac…	Vinyl LP…
12	The Ice Palace	Book co…	1	2	Print	Luke Wood	the-ice-p…	The Ice…
1	Systemic Broc…	Brochure…	1	2	Print	Luke Wood	systemic-…	Brochure…

TRY: Select the same data about each article, but use a different WHERE clause to select the articles written by an individual member of the site.

TRY: Select the same data about each article, but use the LIMIT clause to fetch the six most recently published articles from the database (in any category).

TRY: Select the same data about each article, but use the SQL LIKE clause to fetch the data about articles whose title contains the term design.

ADDING DATA TO THE DATABASE

SQL's INSERT INTO command adds a new row of data to a table.
It can only add data to one table at a time.

The `INSERT INTO` command tells the database to insert data into a single table. It is followed by:

- The name of the table you want to add the data to
- Parentheses holding the names of the columns you want to add the data to

The `VALUES` command is followed by parentheses holding the values you want to add into the columns.

The values must appear in the same order that the columns were specified in. Strings should be in quotes; numbers should not.

```
                              TABLE          COLUMNS

WHERE THE DATA GOES ⟶  INSERT INTO table (column1, column2)
   THE VALUES TO ADD ⟶  VALUES ('value1', 'value2');

                              NEW VALUES
```

In the sample database, the `id` column of each table is the primary key for that table, so every row needs a unique value in the `id` column.

To ensure that the value for the `id` column is unique, it is created using a MySQL feature called **auto-increment**. It generates a number for the column and ensures that it is unique by increasing that number by 1 every time a new row is added to the table.

Because this value is created by the database, when a new row is added to a table, you do not specify the column name `id` or a value for this column.

Four other columns have **default values**, which means that you do not need to specify a value for them when adding a row of data. The default value for the:

- `article` table's `created` column is the date and time the row was added to the database.
- `article` table's `image_id` column is NULL. If no image is provided, this column will hold NULL.
- `article` table's `published` column is 0. If this column is not set to 1, the article is not published.
- `member` table's `joined` column is the date and time the row was added to the database.

section_c/c11/insert-1.sql

```sql
INSERT INTO category (name, description, navigation)
VALUES ('News', 'Latest news from Creative Folk', 0);
```

category

id	name	description	navigation
1	Print	Inspiring graphic design	1
2	Digital	Powerful pixels	1
3	Illustration	Hand-drawn visual storytelling	1
4	Photography	Capturing the moment	1
5	News	Latest news from Creative Folk	0

The SQL on the left adds a category called News to the category table.

The SQL must specify a value for the name, description, and navigation columns. It should not provide a value for the id column because the database adds this using the auto-increment feature.

The new row is highlighted in the category table on the left.

section_c/c11/insert-2.sql

```sql
INSERT INTO image (file, alt)
VALUES ('bicycle.jpg', 'Photo of bicycle'),
       ('ghost.png',   'Illustration of ghost'),
       ('stamp.jpg',   'Polite Society stamp');
```

image

id	file	alt
22	polite-society-posters.jpg	Photograph of three posters…
23	golden-brown.jpg	Photograph of the interior…
24	featherview.jpg	Two pages from a travel boo…
25	bicycle.jpg	Photo of bicycle
26	ghost.png	Illustration of ghost
27	stamp.jpg	Polite Society stamp

This example adds three rows to the image table, each one holding details of a different image.

For each image, the SQL must specify the filename and alt text. It should not provide a value for the id column as the database adds this using the auto-increment feature.

The values for each row are placed in parentheses, just like they are when one row is added to the database.

Each set of parentheses is separated by a comma. There is a semi-colon (no comma) after the last row of data.

The new rows have been highlighted in the image table.

If phpMyAdmin is only showing 25 rows of data, there is an option above the result set to show all of the data in the table.

The extra data these examples add to the database will be deleted in the remaining examples of this chapter.

You need to run all the examples in the same order that they appear in the book. If you do not, you will encounter errors.

UPDATING DATA IN THE DATABASE

SQL's UPDATE command lets you update the data in the database. The SET command indicates the columns to update and their new values. The WHERE clause controls which row(s) of the table should be updated.

The UPDATE command tells the database you want to update data in the database. It is followed by the name of the table(s) you want to update.

After this, the SET command is used to specify the columns you want to update and the new values for them. You only need to provide names and values for columns you want to update (other columns will retain the values that they already hold).

The WHERE clause is used to specify which rows should be updated, just like it is used when requesting specific rows of data from the database. (If it is not used, every row of the table is updated.)

If the search condition matches more than one row, every row it matches is updated with the same values. To update data in multiple tables at the same time, the SQL statement would use a JOIN command.

```
                                  TABLE
                                  ┌─┴─┐              COLUMN      NEW VALUE
                                                     ┌──┴──┐     ┌───┴───┐
         TABLE ⟶  UPDATE table
    NEW VALUES ⟶     SET column1 = 'value1', column2 = 'value2'
ROW(S) TO UPDATE ⟶  WHERE column  = 'value';
                          └──────────┬──────────┘
                     SEARCH CONDITION: ROW TO UPDATE
```

Often, you will only want to update one row at a time. In such cases, the WHERE clause would use the table's primary key to specify which row should be updated. In the sample database, the primary key for each table is the value in the id column.

To update multiple rows in a table, use a search condition that selects more than one row. For example, to hide all of the articles by an author, the value in the published column would be updated to 0, and the search condition would specify the id of the author.

section_c/c11/update-1.sql

```
UPDATE category
   SET name = 'Blog', navigation = 1
  WHERE id = 5;
```

category

id	name	description	navigation
1	Print	Inspiring graphic design	1
2	Digital	Powerful pixels	1
3	Illustration	Hand-drawn visual storytelling	1
4	Photography	Capturing the moment	1
5	Blog	Latest news from Creative Folk	1

The SQL on the left updates the row that was added to the category table in the last example. It only works with this row because the WHERE clause specifies the category must have an id of 5.

It changes the value in the name column to Blog and the value in the navigation column to 1.

You can see the updated row is highlighted in the category table on the left.

section_c/c11/update-2.sql

```
UPDATE category
   SET navigation = 0
  WHERE navigation = 1;
```

category

id	name	description	navigation
1	Print	Inspiring graphic design	0
2	Digital	Powerful pixels	0
3	Illustration	Hand-drawn visual storytelling	0
4	Photography	Capturing the moment	0
5	Blog	Latest news from Creative Folk	0

The SQL on the left updates every row in the category table where the navigation column has a value of 1 (because the WHERE clause specifies any row where the navigation = 1).

It updates the value in the navigation column to 0. This stops all categories from being shown in the navigation bar.

There are times when you would want to offer users the ability to affect multiple rows in a table, but this example also highlights the importance of making sure that your SQL only updates the rows that you want to in a table.

TRY: Use a SQL command in phpMyAdmin to show all the categories again.

NOTE: You **must** turn the categories back on to view them in the following chapters.

BACKING UP A DATABASE:
Because a SQL statement can update many rows in the database, it is a good idea to create a backup of the database before running new queries.

If the SQL query accidentally affects more data than it was supposed to, the backup can be used to restore the original data before the query was run.

To create a backup of your database in phpMyAdmin:

1. Select the database.

2. Click the Export tab.

3. Use the options shown and press Go. It will generate SQL, which you should then save in a text file. This is like the file you used to create the database.

DELETING DATA FROM THE DATABASE

SQL's DELETE command removes one or more rows from a table.
The FROM command indicates the table the data is removed from.
The WHERE clause states which row(s) of the table should be deleted.

You can delete one or more rows from a table at the same time. First, use the DELETE FROM command, followed by the name of the table you want to delete data from.

Then, use a search condition to specify which rows to delete (if you do not, it will delete every row of data from the table). To pick one row, the condition can specify the column with a primary key.

```
                                          TABLE
                                        ┌──┴──┐
TABLE TO REMOVE DATA FROM  ⟶  DELETE FROM table
        ROW(S) TO REMOVE  ⟶  WHERE column = 'value';
                                   └────────┬────────┘
                                      ROW TO UPDATE
```

If the WHERE clause matches more than one row of data in the table, each of the rows is removed from the table.

You cannot delete values in individual columns of the database using the DELETE command. Instead, you use UPDATE and set the value for the column to NULL.

```sql
DELETE FROM category
  WHERE id = 5;
```

The SQL on the left deletes the row from the `category` table, where the `id` column has a value of 5, which is the `Blog` category added in previous examples.

The highlighted row gets removed from the table.

If the `WHERE` clause matches more than one row of data, it deletes all of the matching rows of data from the table.

category

id	name	description	navigation
1	Print	Inspiring graphic design	1
2	Digital	Powerful pixels	1
3	Illustration	Hand-drawn visual storytelling	1
4	Photography	Capturing the moment	1
5	Blog	Latest news from Creative Folk	1

SQL DO NOT RUN this example

```sql
DELETE FROM category
  WHERE navigation = 1;
```

DO NOT RUN THIS EXAMPLE: It is important to be careful not to delete more data than you want with a `DELETE` command. For example, the SQL query on the left deletes every category that is used in the navigation of the site.

Making a backup of the database before you run a new SQL statement that deletes data from the database ensures that you have a copy of the data if the query does not perform the intended action.

category

id	name	description	navigation
1	Print	Inspiring graphic design	1
2	Digital	Powerful pixels	1
3	Illustration	Hand-drawn visual storytelling	1
4	Photography	Capturing the moment	1

UNIQUENESS CONSTRAINTS

The values in some columns should be unique. For example, no two articles should have the same title, no two categories should have the same name, and no two members should have the same email address.

If the value in a column is supposed to be unique, but two rows have the same value in that column, it is called a **duplicate entry**.

To prevent rows in the database having the same value in a column, MySQL can be told to apply a **uniqueness constraint** (it is called this because it constrains the values that are allowed in that column to ensure that they are unique).

Uniqueness constraints should only be used when they are needed because every time data is added, or existing data is being updated, the database has to check every other row in that column to make sure the value does not already exist. This requires more processing power and also slows down the database.

Below, you can see how to add a uniqueness constraint for category names in phpMyAdmin to ensure that no two categories have the same name.

1. Select the `phpbook-1` database and then the `category` table from the menu on the left-hand side.
2. Select the `Structure` tab.
3. Each row in the table beneath this represents a column in the database. In the row that represents the `name` column, click the more drop-down menu.
4. Click the link that says `Unique`.

Now, if a SQL statement tried to add or update a category using the same name as one that existed, the database would raise an error. You will learn how to handle this situation on p491.

In the sample database, there are three tables that each contain one column that requires a uniqueness constraint to ensure that values in it are all different.

These are: the `title` column in the `article` table, the `name` column in the `category` table, and the `email` column in the `member` table.

FOREIGN KEY CONSTRAINTS

When there is a relationship between two tables, a **foreign key constraint** checks that the value of a foreign key is a valid primary key in another table.

Three columns in the `article` table use foreign keys:

- `category_id` the id of the category the article is in
- `member_id` the id of the member who wrote it
- `image_id` the id of the image for that article

The `article` table uses foreign key constraints to:

- Ensure that any value added to these columns is a primary key in the corresponding table (if it is not, the database generates an error).
- Prevent a category, member, or image from being deleted if its primary key is being used as a foreign key in the `article` table.

To add a foreign key constraint to a column of a table:

1. Select the table that has the foreign key.
2. Check the box for the column with the foreign key.
3. Click **More** then **Index** to add an index to the column. (An Index is a copy of selected columns in the table that speeds up searching for data in the table. But they should be carefully used as they can take up extra space and slow down the database.)
4. Select the **Relation view**.
5. Add a name for the restriction.
6. Select the column with the foreign key.
7. Select the table and column that hold the primary key. Then click **Save** (not shown).

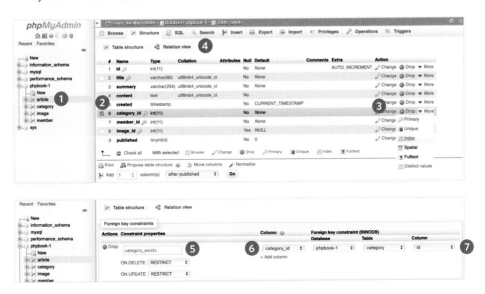

SUMMARY
STRUCTURED QUERY LANGUAGE

> SQL is used to communicate with databases.

> SELECT specifies the columns of data to collect from a database. The data is then added to a result set.

> CREATE, UPDATE, and DELETE commands are used to create, update, or delete rows of data.

> FROM specifies a table to work with.

> WHERE specifies which rows of data to work with.

> JOINs describe relationships between multiple tables.

> A primary key is a column that has a unique value to identify every row. The value can be created using MySQL's auto-increment feature.

> A foreign key is a column that stores the primary key of another table and describes their relationship.

> Constraints prevent duplicate entries and ensure that a foreign key matches a primary key in another table.

12

GET & SHOW
DATA FROM A
DATABASE

This chapter shows how PHP can get data from a database and display it in a page. It also shows how one PHP file can be used to display multiple pages of a site.

The last chapter introduced SQL queries (which ask the database for data), and showed how the database creates a result set containing the requested data. This chapter shows how PHP uses SQL to get data from the database and store it in a variable so it can be used in a page. To help achieve this, PHP has a set of built-in classes called **PHP Data Objects** (**PDO**).

- First, an object is created using the PDO class to manage the connection to the database. That object must connect to the database before it can ask for data from it, in the same way that an FTP program connects to an FTP server before you can retrieve files, or an email program connects to a mail server to retrieve emails.

- Next, an object is created using the PDOStatement class; this object represents the SQL statement you want the database to run. You call the methods of a PDOStatement object to execute the SQL statement it represents and collect the data from the result set that the database generates.

For most of this chapter, each row of data in the result set will be represented using an array and stored in a variable for use in the PHP page.

When the data stored in the database has been provided by visitors, it must be sanitized before it is displayed in a page to prevent the risk of a cross-site scripting attack (see p244-7).

The chapter ends by showing how PDO can make data available as objects rather than arrays.

CONNECTING TO THE DATABASE

A **data source name** or **DSN** is a variable which holds the five pieces of data that PDO needs in order to find the database and connect to it. The DSN is used to create a PDO object using the built-in PDO class.

To create a DSN, five pieces of data are stored in variables. The data in these five variables is then joined together to create a DSN, which is stored in a sixth variable (below that variable is called $dsn).

$type holds the type of database. This is needed because PDO can work with many types of database. For MySQL and MariaDB, use the value mysql.

$server holds the hostname of the server where the database is hosted. For this value, use:

- localhost if it is on the same server as the web server (e.g., if you are running MAMP or XAMPP).
- The IP address or a domain name of the server that the database is on, if it is not the same server.

$DB holds the name of the database to connect to. The database used in this section is PHPBOOK-1.

$port holds the port number for the database. MAMP usually uses port 8889 and XAMPP port 3306.

$charset is the character encoding that data will be sent to the database, and the encoding it should use to send back data. This is set to utf8mb4.

Then, these five values are used to create the DSN and store it in $dsn. (The double quotes ensure that variable names are replaced by their values, see p52.) The DSN syntax is very precise; it cannot have extra spaces or other characters.

- The prefix indicates the type of database that is being used. It is followed by a colon.
- Then there are four name/value pairs. Each pair is separated by a semi-colon. The name is followed by an = symbol, then the value it should use (each of which is stored in one of the five variables that were just created).

```php
$type    = 'mysql';      // Type of database software
$server  = 'localhost';  // Host name
$db      = 'phpbook-1';  // Database name
$port    = '8889';       // Use port 3006 for XAMPP
$charset = 'utf8mb4';    // UTF-8 encoding using 4 bytes of data
$dsn     = "$type:host=$server;dbname=$db;port=$port;charset=$charset";
```

PREFIX   HOST NAME   DATABASE NAME   PORT NUMBER   CHARACTER ENCODING

Once the DSN has been saved in a variable, you can then create a PDO object to manage the connection between the code in the PHP file and the database.

PDO objects are created using PHP's built-in PDO class. The PDO object needs:

- A DSN (shown on the left-hand page) to find the database it must connect to.
- The username and password of a user account that it can use to log into the database (you saw how to create user accounts on p394-95).

In the code below, the variable:

- $username holds the username for an account
- $password holds the password for that account

When creating a PDO object, you can also set options that control how it will work with the database. Below, these options are stored in an array called $options.

1. The PDO::ATTR_ERRMODE option controls how any errors that the PDO object enounters are dealt with. The setting PDO::ERRMODE_EXCEPTION tells PDO to throw an exception object using the built-in PDOException class if there is an error. This option must be set for all versions prior to PHP 8 (otherwise PDO would raise no errors), but in PHP 8 this has become the default error mode and can be left off.

2. The PDO::ATTR_DEFAULT_FETCH_MODE option tells PDO how to make each row of a result set available in the PHP code. The setting PDO::FETCH_ASSOC indicates that each row of the result set should be stored as an associative array.

3. The PDO::ATTR_EMULATE_PREPARES setting turns on/off something called emulation mode. In this book, it is set to false to ensure that any integer data types in the database are returned to the PHP code as int data types. If it is set to true, every value that is returned would be treated as a string.

```
DATABASE ⎡  $username = 'enter-your-username';
    USER ⎨  $password = 'enter-your-password';
 ACCOUNT ⎣  $options  = [
       ①      PDO::ATTR_ERRMODE                => PDO::ERRMODE_EXCEPTION,
       ②      PDO::ATTR_DEFAULT_FETCH_MODE => PDO::FETCH_ASSOC,
       ③      PDO::ATTR_EMULATE_PREPARES   => false,
           ];
```

Once the DSN, user account details, and options are stored in variables, you can then create a PDO object using a constructor, like any other object.

The PDO object is stored in a variable called $pdo. Because PDO is a built-in class, the class definition does not need to be included in the page.

```
$pdo = new PDO($dsn, $username, $password, $options);
```
VARIABLE   CLASS NAME   DSN   USERNAME   PASSWORD   OPTIONS

NOTE: The five values that the DSN needs to find and connect to the database can be added into the DSN rather than being stored in variables first.

But it easier to edit or change these values if they are stored in separate variables, and less likely to cause errors because the syntax of the DSN is very precise.

DATABASE CONNECTIONS CAN LIVE IN AN INCLUDE

In database-driven websites, most pages connect to a database, so the code to create a PDO object that manages the connection to the database is often stored in an include file.

The include file shown on the right will create a PDO object and store it in a variable called $pdo. This allows any page that needs to work with the database to include this file and use the PDO object that it stored in the $pdo variable. The advantages of placing this code in an include file are that:

- You do not need to repeat the same code on each page that connects to the database.
- If the database connection needs to be updated, it only needs updating in the one include file rather than in every page that connects to the database.
- If you have a test and live version of a site, the database connection only changes in one file.

The database-connection.php file in the CMS folder of the code download for this chapter is used for both the sample website *and* the examples for this chapter. You must, therefore, edit this file to use the database (introduced at the start of ths section and used in the previous chapter) before you can run the examples.

To check you can connect to the sample database, update the variables in Steps 1 and 2 to use values for your database. Then try to load the home page of the sample site. If PDO can connect to the database, you will see the site. Take a few minutes to browse it.

If PDO was unable to connect, an exception handling function (see p371) could display an error message. (If you have problems connecting to the database, see the troubleshooting note on the right-hand page.)

1. Store values for DSN shown on the previous page.

2. The username and password of the user account set up to access the database are stored in variables. These **must** be values you created for your database.

3. The options are set to: ensure that any errors PDO encounters throw an exception; tell PDO to get each row of data from a result set as an array; and make sure integers are returned as integers (not strings).

4. The DSN is created using data from step 1.

5. The PDO object is created in a try block to prevent the user account details being shown (see Step 8).

6. When the PDO object is created, it automatically tries to connect to the database. If it succeeds, the PDO object is stored in a variable called $pdo.

7. If PDO cannot connect to the database, it throws an exception using the built-in PDOException class. The PHP interpreter then runs the code in the catch block. If the catch block runs, the exception object is stored in the variable $e.

8. The exception is re-thrown in the catch block. This is important because, if PDO cannot connect to the database and there was no exception handler for the site, the error message would show the username and password of the database. This technique prevents the username and password being shown.

```php
<?php
$type     = 'mysql';                    // Type of database
$server   = 'localhost';                // Server the database is on
$db       = 'phpbook-1';                // Name of the database
$port     = '8889';                     // Port is usually 8889 in MAMP and 3306 in XAMPP
$charset  = 'utf8mb4';                  // UTF-8 encoding using 4 bytes of data per character

$username = 'enter-your-username';      // Enter YOUR username here
$password = 'enter-your-password';      // Enter YOUR password here

$options = [                            // Options for how PDO works
    PDO::ATTR_ERRMODE            => PDO::ERRMODE_EXCEPTION,
    PDO::ATTR_DEFAULT_FETCH_MODE => PDO::FETCH_ASSOC,
    PDO::ATTR_EMULATE_PREPARES   => false,
];                                                              // Set PDO options
// DO NOT CHANGE ANYTHING BENEATH THIS LINE
$dsn = "$type:host=$server;dbname=$db;port=$port;charset=$charset"; // Create DSN
try {                                                          // Try following code
    $pdo = new PDO($dsn, $username, $password, $options);      // Create PDO object
} catch (PDOException $e) {                                    // If exception thrown
    throw new PDOException($e->getMessage(), $e->getCode());   // Re-throw exception
}
```

Step markers: ① $db, ② $username/$password, ③ $options, ④ $dsn, ⑤ try, ⑥ $pdo, ⑦ catch, ⑧ throw

RESULT

CREATIVE ✱ FOLK   Print / Digital / Illustration / Photography 🔍

Travel Guide
Book design for series of travel guides
POSTED IN **PRINT** BY **IVY STONE**

Golden Brown
Photograph for interior design book
POSTED IN **PHOTOGRAPHY** BY **EMIKO ITO**

Polite Society Posters
Poster designs for a fashion label
POSTED IN **PRINT** BY **IVY STONE**

CONNECTING TO THE DATABASE:
In the code download, each remaining chapter has its own file to connect to the database. You must update that file so that the code can connect to your database before the examples in that chapter will run.

TROUBLESHOOTING:
If you cannot connect to the database, replace Step 8 with the following line; it loads a troubleshooting file:
`include 'database-troubleshooting.php';`
Once it works, replace the original Step 8 code above.

HOW ONE PHP FILE CAN SHOW DIFFERENT DATA

Database-driven websites use SQL queries to collect data from the database and then use that data to create the web pages you see.

In the last chapter, you saw that SQL queries can request data about:

- An individual item (one article, or one member)
- A set of related items (summaries of the latest articles, or all the articles by one member)

In the sample site, the `article.php` file is used to display each article page using data stored in the database. The URL for the page uses a query string to indicate which article the SQL query should get from the database. The `article.php` page uses PDO to run the query, and the database creates a result set with one row of data to represent the article. This data is stored in an array, and then shown in the page.

The home page (`index.php`), shown below, uses a SQL query to get details of the latest six articles that have been added to the site. When a new article is added to the site, the home page will get the details of that new article from the database and show it as the most recent article on the home page.

When a SQL query requests a set of related items, such as the most recent six articles added to the site (or every article written by one member of the site), the result set that the database creates can hold multiple rows of data. Each row of data in the result set would represent one article, and can be represented in an array. This data can then be displayed in the page.

A single PHP file can use multiple SQL queries to get the information that it needs from the database in order to create the page.

The category page (`category.php`) can show details about any individual category of the site. First, it shows the name and description of the category; this is followed by summaries of all the articles that live in the category. It uses two SQL queries:

1. The first SQL query gets the name and description of the category (this query will create a result set with one row of data).

2. The second gets all of the articles in that category (this query will create a result set that holds multiple rows of data - each one represents a new article). If a new article is added to the category, this will automatically be displayed in the page.

The member page (`member.php`) is used to show the profile of each member. First, it shows the member's profile (their name, image and date they joined), followed by summaries of all the articles that they have posted. Again, the page requires two queries:

1. The first gets the member's name, profile picture, and the date they joined (this will create a result set with one row of data).

2. The second gets all of the articles that they have written (this query creates a result set that can hold multiple rows of data - each one represents a new article). If a member adds a new article to the site, it will automatically be displayed in the page.

GETTING DATA USING A SQL QUERY

When a SQL statement is run, the database creates a result set. Each row of data in the result set can be represented as an associative array.

The SQL query below gets the forename and surname of one member of the site. It uses a WHERE clause to request data about the member that has an id of 1:

```
SELECT forename, surname
  FROM member
 WHERE id = 1;
```

Because this query is requesting data about *one* member of the site, the result set will never hold more than one row of data.

result set	
forename	surname
Ivy	Stone

Below you can see how the row of data can be represented as an associative array. The column names in the result set are used as the keys in the array; their values are the values from that column.

```
$member = [
    'forename' => 'Ivy',
    'surname'  => 'Stone',
];
```

The SQL query below gets the forename and surname of every member of the site.

```
SELECT forename, surname
  FROM member;
```

This query will create a result set that holds multiple rows of data.

result set	
forename	surname
Ivy	Stone
Luke	Wood
Emiko	Ito

When a SQL query creates a result set with multiple rows of data, an indexed array is created. The value of each element in that indexed array is an associative array, and each of those associative arrays represents one row of data from the result set.

```
$members = [
    0 => ['forename' => 'Ivy',
          'surname'  => 'Stone',],
    1 => ['forename' => 'Luke',
          'surname'  => 'Wood',],
    2 => ['forename' => 'Emiko',
          'surname'  => 'Ito',],
];
```

The PDO object's `query()` method runs a SQL query and creates a PDOStatement object to represent the result set the database created. The PDOStatement object's methods collect data from the result set.

The PDO object's `query()` method has one parameter; a SQL query the database should execute.

When the `query()` method is called, the SQL query is executed and a PDOStatement object is returned. The PDOStatement object represents the result set that the database created for the query.

The SQL query below gets the forename and surname of every member of the site.

When the PHP statement below is run, the PDO object returns a PDOStatement object representing the forename and surname of every member of the site. This object is stored in a variable called `$statement`.

SQL QUERY TO RUN

```
$statement = $pdo->query("SELECT forename, surname FROM member");
```

PDOStatement OBJECT   PDO OBJECT   query() METHOD

The PDOStatement object's `fetch()` method is used to collect a single row of data from the result set. This row of data is represented using an associative array, and stored in a variable so that the rest of the code in the PHP page can use it.

If the query generated multiple rows of data, the PDOStatement object's `fetchAll()` method collects all of the data from the result set as an indexed array. Each element of that array stores an associative array that represents one row of data in the result set.

```
$member = $statement->fetch();
```

ARRAY OF RESULTS   PDOStatement OBJECT   METHOD

```
$members = $statement->fetchAll();
```

ARRAY OF RESULTS   PDOStatement OBJECT   METHOD

If the query generates an empty record set, the `fetch()` method will return a value of `false`.

If the query generates an empty record set, the `fetchAll()` method will return an empty array.

GET ONE ROW OF DATA FROM A DATABASE

This example shows how a single PHP file can display data about any individual member of the site.

1. `database-connection.php` is included in the page. This creates the PDO object that manages the connection to the database and stores it in a variable called `$pdo`.

2. `functions.php` is included. It holds the definition for the `html_escape()` function (p247), which uses `htmlspecialchars()` to replace HTML's reserved characters with entities to help prevent an XSS attack.

3. A SQL statement is stored in a variable called `$sql`. It gets the forename and surname of the member whose `id` is 1.

4. The PDO object's `query()` method is called. Its one argument is the variable holding the SQL statement it should run. The `query()` method will run the SQL statement query and return a PDOStatement object holding the result set. The PDOStatement object it returns is stored in the `$statement` variable.

5. The PDOStatement object's `fetch()` method gets the data about this member and stores it as an associative array in a variable called `$member`.

`section_c/c12/examples/query-one-row.php`   **PHP**

```php
<?php
require '../cms/includes/database-connection.php';   ①
require '../cms/includes/functions.php';             ②
$sql        = "SELECT forename, surname               ③
                  FROM member
                  WHERE id = 1;";
$statement = $pdo->query($sql);                       ④
$member    = $statement->fetch();                     ⑤
?>
<!DOCTYPE html>
<html> ...
  <body>
    <p>
      <?= html_escape($member['forename']) ?>         ⑥
      <?= html_escape($member['surname']) ?>          ⑦
    </p>
  </body>
</html>
```

RESULT

Ivy Stone

6. The member's forename is written out using `html_escape()` to replace any of HTML's reserved characters in the member's forename with their corresponding entities.

7. The member's surname is written out using `html_escape()`.

TRY: In Step 3, change the SQL WHERE clause to get the member whose id is 2. This will display a different member of the site.

Next, change it to request a member whose id is 4. An error message will be shown as the database only has 3 members.

CHECK IF THE QUERY RETURNED DATA

```
section_c/c12/examples/checking-for-data.php

<?php
require '../cms/includes/database-connection.php';
require '../cms/includes/functions.php';
$sql       = "SELECT forename, surname
               FROM member
① WHERE id = 4;";
$statement = $pdo->query($sql);
② $member    = $statement->fetch();
③ if (!$member) {
④     include 'page-not-found.php';
}
?>
<!DOCTYPE html>
<html> ...
  <body>
    <p>
      <?= html_escape($member['forename']) ?>
      <?= html_escape($member['surname']) ?>
    </p>
  </body>
</html>
```

RESULT

Sorry! We cannot find that page.

Try the home page or email us hello@eg.link

NOTE: page-not-found.php is like the one on p378-79, but it performs two additional tasks. First, it sets the HTTP response code to 404 (see p242).

Then, after a message to say the page was not found, the exit command stops any more code from running (in this file or the one that included it).

If a SQL query does not find any matching data, when the PDOStatement object's fetch() method is called, it will return a value of false.

If the file then tried to display the member's data, the PHP interpreter would raise an Undefined index error because the $member variable holds the value false, not an array.

To prevent these errors, the file can check if any data was found. If not, it can tell the user that the page could not be found.

1. The SQL query asks for the member whose id is 4. (The database does not have a member whose id is 4.)

2. The fetch() method is called. It returns a value of false, which is stored in the $member variable.

3. Before trying to display the data, an if statement checks if the value in $member is false (using the not operator – p54). If so, the member was not found.

4. The page-not-found.php file is included in the page to tell users the page was not found.

TRY: In Step 1, change the id to 2.

GET MULTIPLE ROWS OF DATA FROM A DATABASE

This example shows how a PHP file can get and display data about every member of the site. If a new member is added to the database, the page will automatically show their details.

1. `database-connection.php` is included to create a PDO object, which is stored in a variable called `$pdo`. `functions.php` is included because it holds the `html_escape()` function.

2. The SQL statement to run is stored in a variable called `$sql`. It gets the forename and surname of every member.

3. The PDO object's `query()` method is called. Its parameter is the SQL statement to run.

The `query()` method runs the SQL query and returns a `PDOStatement` object containing the result set, which is stored in the `$statement` variable.

4. The `PDOStatement` object's `fetchAll()` method gets every row of data from the result set. It returns the data as an indexed array, which is stored in `$members`. Each element of that array represents one row from the result set. The value of each element is an associative array representing one member.

```
section_c/c12/examples/query-multiple-rows.php          PHP

<?php
require '../cms/includes/database-connection.php';
require '../cms/includes/functions.php';
$sql       = "SELECT forename, surname
                FROM member;";
$statement = $pdo->query($sql);
$members   = $statement->fetchAll();
?>
<!DOCTYPE html>
<html> ...
  <body>
    <?php foreach ($members as $member) { ?>
      <p>
        <?= html_escape($member['forename']) ?>
        <?= html_escape($member['surname']) ?>
      </p>
    <?php } ?>
  </body>
</html>
```

```
                                               RESULT

Ivy Stone

Luke Wood

Emiko Ito
```

5. A `foreach` loop works through the elements in the indexed array that is stored in `$members`. Each time the loop runs, the associative array representing one member of the site is stored in a variable called `$member`.

6. The member's forename and surname are displayed.
NOTE: If a query returns no data, `fetchAll()` returns an empty array, so the statements in the loop do not run (if they did, it would cause an `Undefined index` error).

LOOPS TO FETCH ONE ROW OF DATA AT A TIME

section_c/c12/examples/query-multiple-rows-while-loop.php

```php
<?php
require '../cms/includes/database-connection.php';
require '../cms/includes/functions.php';
$sql        = "SELECT forename, surname
                FROM member;";
$statement = $pdo->query($sql);
?>
<!DOCTYPE html>
<html> ...
  <body>
    <?php while ($row = $statement->fetch()) { ?>
      <p>
        <?= html_escape($row['forename']) ?>
        <?= html_escape($row['surname']) ?>
      </p>
    <?php } ?>
  </body>
</html>
```

Markers: ① ② ③ ④ ⑤

RESULT

Ivy Stone

Luke Wood

Emiko Ito

It is possible to use a `while` loop to tell the `PDOStatement` object to collect one row of data from the database at a time, as shown in this example.

1. `database-connection.php` and `functions.php` are included.

2. The SQL statement to run is stored in a variable called `$sql`.

3. The PDO object's `query()` method is called to run the SQL and generate the `PDOStatement` object representing the result set.

4. The condition of the `while` loop calls the `fetch()` method. This will return one row of data from the result set at a time. The array that represents that row of data is stored in a variable called `$row` so it can be used by the statements inside the loop.

Once the loop has run once, it calls the `fetch()` method again, and will automatically retrieve the next row of data from the result set and store it in `$row`. When there are no more rows in the result set, the `fetch()` method returns `false`, and the loop stops running.

5. Inside the loop, the contents of the array holding the name of the member are written out.

NOTE: Typically a website should not show too much information on a single page (it should split results up over several pages). But, if a page must work with large amounts of data (more than would be shown on a typical web page), this approach should be used to prevent using too much memory. This is because `fetchAll()` collects all of the data and stores it one array in the PHP interpreter's memory, whereas the while loop only collects one row of data at a time from the database.

USING DATA THAT CAN CHANGE IN A SQL QUERY

Each time a page is requested, it can use different values in the SQL query to get different data from the database. In such cases, the SQL query must be **prepared** first, then **executed**.

STEP 1: PREPARE

SQL statements use **placeholders** to represent values that can change each time the SQL statement is run. A SQL placeholder acts like a variable, but its name starts with a colon, not a $ symbol.

When a SQL query contains a placeholder, instead of calling the PDO object's `query()` method to run the query, the PDO object's `prepare()` method is called.

The `prepare()` method also returns a PDOStatement object but, at this point, the PDOStatement object just represents the SQL statement (not the result set).

STEP 2: EXECUTE

Next, the SQL statement is executed by calling the PDOStatement object's `execute()` method. It requires one argument: an array holding the values that should be used to replace the placeholders.

The placeholder's name and the value to use can be supplied as an associative array, where the:

- **key** is the placeholder name in the SQL query (it can have a colon before it, but it is not required)
- **value** is the value used to replace the placeholder (the value is often already stored in a variable)

PLACEHOLDER

```
$sql          = "SELECT forename, surname FROM member WHERE id = :id;";
$statement = $pdo->prepare($sql);
$statement->execute(['id' => $id]);
```

PLACEHOLDER NAME   VALUE TO USE

The SQL query above has a placeholder called `:id`. The `execute()` method replaces `:id` with the value stored in the `$id` variable. Programmers call this a **prepared statement**.

NEVER add values from a query string or form onto a string to create a SQL statement (as shown below). This exposes your site to a hack known as a **SQL injection attack**. Prepared statements stop this risk.

```
(x) $sql = 'SELECT * FROM member WHERE id=' . $id;
(x) $sql = 'SELECT * FROM member WHERE id=' . $_GET['id'];
```

SHOWING DIFFERENT DATA IN THE SAME PAGE

`section_c/c12/examples/prepared-statement.php`

```php
<?php
require '../cms/includes/database-connection.php';
require '../cms/includes/functions.php';
$id        = 1;
$sql       = "SELECT forename, surname
              FROM member
              WHERE id = :id;";
$statement = $pdo->prepare($sql);
$statement->execute(['id' => $id]);
$member    = $statement->fetch();
if (!$member) {
    include 'page-not-found.php';
}
?>
<!DOCTYPE html>
<html> ...
  <body>
    <p>
      <?= html_escape($member['forename']) ?>
      <?= html_escape($member['surname']) ?>
    </p>
  </body>
</html>
```

(1) (2) (3) (4) (5) (6) (7)

RESULT

Ivy Stone

TRY: In Step 2, change the value stored in `$id` to the number 2. Then save and refresh the page.

The page will display another member's data. If `$id` is set to 4, `page-not-found.php` is shown.

1. `database-connection.php` and `functions.php` are included.

2. A variable called `$id` holds the integer 1, this corresponds to the id of the member the query will retrieve from the database.

3. The SQL statement to run is stored in a variable called `$sql`. The piece of data that can change (the id of the member to get) uses the placeholder `:id`.

4. The PDO object's `prepare()` method is called. It will return a PDOStatement object that represents the query. This is stored in a variable called `$statement`.

5. The PDOStatement object's `execute()` method is called to run the query and generate the result set. Its argument is an array that holds the placeholder name and the value that it should be replaced with.

6. The PDOStatement object's `fetch()` method is used to collect the row of data from the result set and store it as an associative array in a variable called `$member`.

7. If no data is returned, the user is told the page was not found.

BINDING VALUES TO A SQL QUERY

The PDOStatement object's bindValue() and bindParam() methods offer another way to create a prepared statement and replace a placeholder in a SQL query.

When the bindValue() and bindParam() methods are used to replace a placeholder in a SQL query, they should be called after the PDOStatement object's prepare() method, and before the execute() method. They both have three parameters:

- The name of the placeholder
- A variable whose value replaces the placeholder
- A value to indicate the data type of the value (this is not required if the data type is a string)

The table below shows the values used in the third parameter of the bindValue() method to specify the data type of the value that is replacing the placeholder in the SQL query.

DATA TYPE	VALUE
String	PDO::PARAM_STR
Integer	PDO::PARAM_INT
Boolean	PDO::PARAM_BOOL

The difference between bindValue() and bindParam() is the point at which the PHP interpreter gets the value from the variable and uses it to replace the placeholder in the SQL query.

- With bindValue(), the interpreter gets the value from the variable when bindValue() is called.

- With bindParam(), the interpreter gets the value from the variable when execute() is called. Therefore, if the value stored in the variable changes between the time bindParam() and execute() are called, the updated value is used.

Below, the placeholder :id in the SQL query would be replaced by the value held in a variable called $id.

The rest of the book uses the technique shown on the previous page to bind data because you do not need to specify the data type for each of the values and it uses less code.

```
                                    PLACEHOLDER
                                       ┌─┐
$sql       = "SELECT * FROM member WHERE id = :id;";
$statement = connection->prepare($sql);
$statement->bindValue('id', $id, PDO::PARAM_INT);
                        └─┘   └─┘   └─────────┘
                    PLACEHOLDER  VARIABLE   DATA TYPE
```

BINDING AN INTEGER TO A SQL QUERY

section_c/c12/examples/bind-value.php

```php
<?php
require '../cms/includes/database-connection.php';
require '../cms/includes/functions.php';
$id        = 1;
$sql       = "SELECT forename, surname
                FROM member
                WHERE id = :id;";
$statement = $pdo->prepare($sql);
$statement->bindValue('id', $id, PDO::PARAM_INT);
$statement->execute();
$member    = $statement->fetch();
if (!$member) {
    include 'page-not-found.php';
}
?>
<!DOCTYPE html>
<html> ...
  <body>
    <p>
      <?= html_escape($member['forename']) ?>
      <?= html_ escape($member['surname']) ?>
    </p>
  </body>
</html>
```

(1) is marked at the `$statement->bindValue('id', $id, PDO::PARAM_INT);` line
(2) is marked at the `$statement->execute();` line

RESULT

Ivy Stone

This example looks the same as the previous example, but it uses the PDOStatement object's bindValue() method to replace the placeholder in the SQL query.

1. After the PDO object's prepare() method has been called to create a PDOStatement object that represents the SQL query, the PDOStatement object's bindValue() method is called to replace the placeholder in the SQL query. It uses three arguments:

- The name of the placeholder in the SQL query
- The name of the variable holding the value that should be used for the placeholder
- PDO::PARAM_INT to indicate that the value is an integer

2. The PDOStatement object's execute() method is called to run the query. It does not need any arguments because the placeholder in the SQL query has already been replaced by a value.

TRY: In Step 2, change the value stored in $id to the number 2. Then save and refresh the page. The page displays another member's data. If $id is set to 4, page-not-found.php is included.

USING A SINGLE FILE TO DISPLAY MANY PAGES

When a single PHP file is used to display many pages of a site, a query string can be added to the end of the URL to tell the PHP file which data it needs to collect from the database.

A PHP page can collect a value from a query string and then use that value in a SQL query to specify what data should be collected from the database.

Below, the link to member.php has a query string that holds the name id and a value of 1. This value corresponds to the id column of the member table.

```
<a href="member.php?id=1">Ivy Stone</a>
```

The member.php page uses PHP's filter_input() function to get the value from the query string. Because the id columns in the database are all integers, the function uses the integer filter. The value it returns is stored in a variable called $id:

- If it is an integer, $id will hold that integer.
- If it is not an integer, $id will hold false.
- If id is not in the query string, $id will hold null.

Next, an if statement checks if $id holds either false or null (because a valid integer was not used in the query string). If so, the page will not be able to get the member data from the database, so the page-not-found.php file is included. This file:

- Sends an HTTP response code with a value of 404.
- Tells the visitor the page could not be found.
- Uses the exit command to stop the code running.

```
$id = filter_input(INPUT_GET, 'id', FILTER_VALIDATE_INT);
if (!$id) {
    include 'page-not-found.php';
}
```

If the query string did contain a valid integer, the page can continue to try and get data from the database and store it in a variable called $member. Then, a second if statement can check if the member data was not found. If it was not, page-not-found.php is included (which will stop the page running).

Only if the member data was successfully collected from the database will the rest of the page be shown.

To show the data of a different member of the site, the query string would hold the id of their row in the members table of the database.

USING QUERY STRINGS TO SHOW THE RIGHT PAGE

　　　　　　　section_c/c12/examples/query-strings.php?id=1

```php
<?php
require '../cms/includes/database-connection.php';
require '../cms/includes/functions.php';

$id = filter_input(INPUT_GET, 'id', FILTER_VALIDATE_INT);
if (!$id) {                               // If no id
    include 'page-not-found.php';         // Page not found
}

$sql       = "SELECT forename, surname
                FROM member
                WHERE id = :id;";         // SQL query
$statement = $pdo->prepare($sql);         // Prepare
$statement->execute([':id' => $id]);      // Execute
$member    = $statement->fetch();         // Get data

if (!$member) {                           // If no data
    include 'page-not-found.php';         // Page not found
}
?>
<!DOCTYPE html>
<html> ...
  <body>
    <p>
      <?= html_escape($member['forename']) ?>
      <?= html_escape($member['surname']) ?>
    </p>
  </body>
</html>
```

Markers: ① ② ③ ④ ⑤ ⑥ ⑦

RESULT

Ivy Stone

This example builds on the previous examples, and uses a query string to tell the page the id of the member to display.

1. PHP's `filter_input()` function gets the member's id from the query string. If it is an integer, `$id` will hold that number. If not, it will hold `false`. If it is missing, it will hold `null`.

2. An `if` statement checks if `$id` holds the value `false` or `null`.

3. If so, `page-not-found.php` is included as there is no member id in the query string to specify which member to display.

4. If the page is still running, an integer for the member was given in the query string, so the page tries to get that member's data from the database.

5. Another `if` statement checks if `$member` has a value of `false`.

6. If so, a member was not found, and `page_not_found.php` is included.

7. Otherwise, the member's data is used to create the HTML page.

TRY: Change the number in the query string to 4, and page not found will be shown.

DISPLAYING DATABASE DATA IN HTML PAGES

First get the data from the database and store it in variables.
Then use the data in those variables to create the HTML page.

To make your code easier to read, create a clear separation in your PHP files between:
- Code that gets data from the database
- Code that generates the HTML page

The right-hand page shows this using a dotted line. The part of the file that creates the HTML page should contain as little PHP code as possible; below you see the three types of code it needs most often.

FUNCTIONS

Functions are often used to ensure that data is formatted in the correct way. The html_escape() function has already been used in many pages to prevent an XSS attack by replacing any of HTML's reserved characters with entities.

On the right, you can see another function which is in the functions.php file for this chapter. It is used to ensure that dates generated by the database are formatted in a consistent, human-readable manner.

First, the date and time that the database stores is converted into a Unix timestamp using PHP's strtotime() function. It is then converted into a human-readable format using PHP's date() function.

```
function format_date(string $string): string
{
    $date = strtotime($string);
    return date('F d, Y', $date);
}
```

CONDITIONAL STATEMENTS

A conditional statement can look at the data returned from the database and use it to decide what the HTML code should show. For example, if the user has not uploaded a profile picture, the database will return NULL as the filename for their profile image.

The profile image can be displayed using the null-coalescing operator; if an image has been provided it will be shown, if not the placeholder is shown instead.

```
html_escape($member['picture'] ?? 'blank.png');
```

LOOPS

As you have already seen in several of the examples, a loop is commonly used to work through each row of the result set that a database has returned.

On the right, you can see a foreach loop is used to repeat the same statements for each member of the site that the database returns details for.

FORMATTING DATA USED IN HTML PAGES

PHP

section_c/c12/examples/formatting-data-in-html.php

```php
<?php
require '../cms/includes/database-connection.php';      // Create PDO object
require '../cms/includes/functions.php';                // Functions
$sql       = "SELECT id, forename, surname, joined, picture FROM member;"; // SQL
$statement = $pdo->query($sql);                         // Run query
$members   = $statement->fetchAll();                    // Get data
?>
<!DOCTYPE html> ...
<body> ...
<?php foreach ($members as $member) { ?>
  <div class="member-summary">
    <img src="../cms/uploads/<?= html_escape($member['picture'] ?? 'blank.png') ?>"
             alt="<?= html_escape($member['forename']) ?>" class="profile">
    <h2><?= html_escape($member['forename'] . ' ' . $member['surname']) ?></h2>
    <p>Member since:<br><?= format_date($member['joined']) ?></p>
  </div>
<?php } ?> ...
</body>
```

RESULT

Ivy Stone

Member since:
January 26, 2021

Luke Wood

Member since:
January 26, 2021

Emiko Ito

Member since:
February 12, 2021

1. The page collects data about each member of the site.

2. A `foreach` loop repeats the same set of statements for each member of the site.

3. A null-coalescing operator checks if a profile picture has been provided. If so, the filename is used in an `<img>` tag. If not, a placeholder image file called `blank.png` is shown instead.

4. The date a member joined is formatted using `format_date()`.

The loop repeats the same statements for every member of the site.

A FUNCTION TO EXECUTE SQL STATEMENTS

Getting PDO to run a SQL query and return the result set requires two or three statements; writing a user-defined function lets you do it in one.

When a SQL query does not use parameters, the PDO object's `query()` method will run a SQL query and return a `PDOStatement` object representing the result set:

```
$statement = $pdo->query($sql);
```

When a SQL query does use parameters, the PDO object's `prepare()` method must be called to create a `PDOStatement` object that represents the query. Then the `PDOStatement` object's `execute()` must be called to run the query:

```
$statement = $pdo->prepare($sql);
$statement->execute($sql);
```

After these steps, one of the `PDOStatement` object's methods must collect the data from the result set.

The function below has three parameters:

- `$pdo` is for the PDO object used to manage the connection to the database
- `$sql` is for the SQL query that is to be run
- `$arguments` is an array of SQL parameter names and their replacement values; note the default value if this argument is not provided is `null`

The function checks if no arguments were supplied:

- If not, it will run the `query()` method and return the `PDOStatement` object that has been generated.

- If provided, it will call the `prepare()` method to create a `PDOStatement` object, call that object's `execute()` method to run the query, then return the `PDOStatement` object.

```php
function pdo(PDO $pdo, string $sql, array $arguments = null)
{
    if (!$arguments) {
        return $pdo->query($sql);
    }
    $statement = $pdo->prepare($sql);
    $statement->execute($arguments);
    return $statement;
}
```

When the user-defined pdo() function is called, **method chaining** is used to run the query and return the data in a single statement.

When a PDOStatement object has been created and the SQL statement has been run, one of the following three methods is called to get the data from the result set and store it in a variable:

- fetch() gets a single row of data
- fetchAll() gets multiple rows of data
- fetchColumn() gets a value from a single column

When a function or method returns an object, **method chaining** lets you call a method of the object that is returned in the same statement.

Below, when the pdo() function is called, it will return a PDOStatement object. The function call is followed by an object operator, and a call to a method of the PDOStatement object that it returned.

FUNCTION RETURNS A
PDOStatement OBJECT

METHOD RETURNS DATA FROM
PDOStatement OBJECT

```
$members = pdo($pdo, $sql)->fetchAll();
$member  = pdo($pdo, $sql, $arguments)->fetch();
```

FUNCTION RETURNS A
PDOStatement OBJECT

METHOD RETURNS DATA FROM
PDOStatement OBJECT

The pdo() function definition has been added to the functions.php include file for this chapter. It will be used for the rest of this chapter and the next one.

In Chapter 14, you learn another technique where user-defined classes are used to create objects that get and change the data stored in the database.

When providing arguments for the PDOStatement object's execute() method, you can provide an associative array where the keys match the names of the parameters in the SQL statement (as shown already), or you can provide an indexed array where the values are in the same order that the placeholders appear in the SQL statement (see p459).

CUSTOM PDO FUNCTION WITHOUT PARAMETERS

This example shows how the pdo() function defined on the previous page gets data from the database when a SQL query has no parameters.

1. database-connection.php is included. It creates the PDO object and stores it in a variable called $pdo.

2. functions.php is included. It contains the pdo() function (shown on the previous page).

3. The SQL query to get the forename and surname of each member is stored in a variable called $sql.

4. The pdo() function is called with two arguments:

- The PDO object that was created in Step 1
- The SQL query that was stored in the $sql variable in Step 3

This will return a PDOStatement object, and its fetchAll() method is called in the same statement to get all of the data from the result set. That data will be stored as an array in the $members variable.

5. A foreach loop displays the data stored in the $members array.

`section_c/c12/examples/pdo-function-no-parameters.php`   **PHP**

```php
<?php
require '../cms/includes/database-connection.php';
require '../cms/includes/functions.php';
$sql = "SELECT forename, surname
        FROM member;";
$members = pdo($pdo, $sql)->fetchAll();
?>
<!DOCTYPE html>
<html> ...
  <body>
    <?php foreach ($members as $member) { ?>
      <p>
        <?= html_escape($member['forename']) ?>
        <?= html_escape($member['surname']) ?>
      </p>
    <?php } ?>
  </body>
</html>
```

RESULT

Ivy Stone

Luke Wood

Emiko Ito

TRY: In Step 3, update the SQL statement to get the members' email addresses as well as their name. In Step 5, display the email address after the name.

CUSTOM PDO FUNCTION WITH PARAMETERS

section_c/c12/examples/pdo-function-with-parameters.php?id=1

```php
<?php
require '../cms/includes/database-connection.php';
require '../cms/includes/functions.php';
$id = filter_input(INPUT_GET, 'id', FILTER_VALIDATE_INT);
if (!$id) {
    include 'page-not-found.php';
}

$sql = "SELECT forename, surname
        FROM member
        WHERE id = :id;";
$member = pdo($pdo, $sql, ['id' => $id])->fetch();

if (!$member) {
    include 'page-not-found.php';
}
?> ...
    <p>
        <?= html_escape($member['forename']) ?>
        <?= html_escape($member['surname']) ?>
    </p>
```

RESULT

Ivy Stone

TRY: In Step 3, replace the associative array used as the third parameter, with just the $id variable inside square brackets:

```php
$member = pdo($pdo, $sql, [$id]);
```

This makes the third parameter an indexed array (rather than an associative array). If this technique is used, the values in the array must be in the same order that the placeholders appear in the SQL statement.

This example shows how the pdo() function defined on p456 gets data from the database when a SQL query uses parameters.

1. The query string contains the id of the member it will display.

2. The SQL query gets the forename and surname of a member whose id is represented by a placeholder called :id.

3. The pdo() function is called with three arguments:

- The PDO object created in database-connection.php
- The SQL query stored in the $sql variable in Step 2
- An associative array holding the name of a SQL placeholder and the value it should use

NOTE: The array is created *in* the argument, rather than being stored in a variable first: ['id' => $id]

This will return a PDOStatement object. Its fetch() method is then used in the same statement to collect the individual row of data the SQL query generates. This data is stored in $member.

4. The data stored in $member is written out to the page.

HOW A FEW PHP FILES POWER AN ENTIRE SITE

The next twelve pages show how four PHP files are used to display over fifty pages of the sample website.

Each of these four PHP files is split into two parts:

- First, there is the code that collects data from the database and stores it in variables.
- Then, the data in these variables is used to create the HTML pages that are sent back to the visitor.

You can think of these files as acting like a template. Each time one of the files is requested, it can collect different data from the database, insert it into the relevant part of the HTML page, then send the HTML to the visitor's browser.

Each page uses four include files:

- `database-connection.php` creates a PDO object that manages the connection to the database.

- `functions.php` holds the functions that both get data from the database and also format the data.

- `header.php` contains the header used for each page and creates the navigation.

- `footer.php` holds the footer used for each page.

index.php

The home page shows summaries of the latest six articles posted to the site.

When a new article has been saved to the database, this page will automatically be updated to show the details of the new article (and the oldest of the six articles will no longer be shown).

The structure of the HTML page always stays the same, but the content it displays from the database can change.

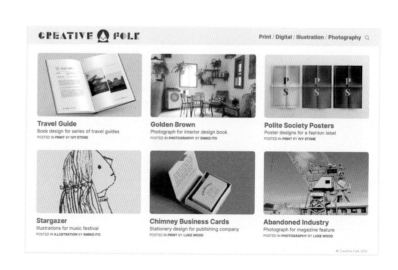

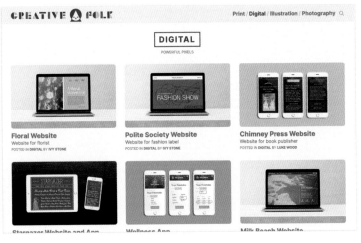

category.php

The category file can show the title and description of any category, followed by summaries of each of the articles posted in that category. The structure of the HTML page stays the same, but the data it shows can change.

A query string after the URL holds the id of the category that should be collected from the database and shown in the page. E.g., `category.php?id=1`

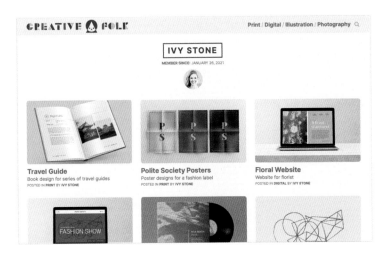

member.php

The member file can show the profile of any member of the site. It is followed by summaries of the articles they have written.

A query string after the URL holds the id of the member that should be collected from the database and shown in the page. E.g., `member.php?id=1`

article.php

The article file can show any article. The image, category, title, date, content and author are in the same place for each article, but the data shown can change.

A query string after the URL holds the id of the article that should be collected from the database and shown in the page. E.g., `article.php?id=1`

HEADER & FOOTER FILES

The header for every page on the site is the same. Therefore, rather than repeating this code in every file, it is placed in the `header.php` include.

Before ths file is included in a page, four pieces of data (shown below) must be stored in variables, which is why it is important to look at this file first.

The first two pieces of information are used in the HTML `<title>` and `<meta>` description elements.

The second two variables are used to create the navigation bar. The first holds an array of categories that should be shown; the second is used to highlight the category if the visitor is looking in that category.

VARIABLE	VALUE
`$title`	A value to display in the HTML `<title>` element of the page.
`$description`	A value to display in the HTML `<meta>` description tag of the page.
`$navigation`	An array holding the names and ids of the categories that appear in the navigation bar.
`$section`	If the page is a category page, this holds the id of the category that is being viewed. If the page is an article page, this holds the id of the category the article is in. These values enable the active category to be highlighted in the navigation bar. For every other page, this variable holds a blank string.

1. The contents of the `$title` variable is displayed inside the `<title>` element.

2. The contents of the `$description` variable is displayed inside the `<meta>` description tag.

3. A `foreach` loop works through each category in the `$navigation` array.

Each time the loop runs, the id and name of one category are stored as an associative array in a variable called `$link`.

4. A link to `category.php` is created. The query string includes the id of the category to tell the `category.php` file which category should be shown.

5. A ternary operator determines whether this category should be highlighted.

The condition checks if the value in `$section` is the same as the id of the current category in the loop. If the values match, `class="on"` and the `aria-current="page"` are added to the link to indicate that this is the current category.

6. The name of the category is written out in the link.

7. After the links to the category pages, there is a link to the search page.

8. `footer.php` only contains one PHP statement to show the current year after a copyright notice.

9. `site.js` contains JavaScript for the responsive navigation of the site.

```
   <!DOCTYPE html>
   <html lang="en-US">
     <head>
       <meta charset="UTF-8">
       <meta name="viewport" content="width=device-width, initial-scale=1">
①     <title><?= html_escape($title) ?></title>
②     <meta name="description" content="<?= html_escape($description) ?>">
       <link rel="stylesheet" type="text/css" href="css/styles.css">
       <link rel="preconnect" href="https://fonts.gstatic.com">
       <link rel="stylesheet"
         href="https://fonts.googleapis.com/css2?family=Inter:wght@400;700&display=swap">
       <link rel="shortcut icon" type="image/png" href="img/favicon.ico">
     </head>
     <body>
       <header>
         <div class="container">
           <a class="skip-link" href="#content">Skip to content</a>
           <div class="logo">
             <a href="index.php"><img src="img/logo.png" alt="Creative Folk"></a>
           </div>
           <nav role="navigation">
             <button id="toggle-navigation" aria-expanded="false">
               <span class="icon-menu"></span><span class="hidden">Menu</span>
             </button>
             <ul id="menu">
③             <?php foreach ($navigation as $link) { ?>
④             <li><a href="category.php?id=<?= $link['id'] ?>"
⑤               <?= ($section == $link['id'] ) ? 'class="on" aria-current="page"' : '' ?>>
⑥               <?= html_escape($link['name']) ?>
               </a></li>
               <?php } ?>
               <li><a href="search.php">
⑦               <span class="icon-search"></span><span class="search-text">Search</span>
               </a></li>
             </ul>
           </nav>
         </div><!-- /.container -->
       </header>
```

```
⑧     <footer><div class="container">&copy; Creative Folk <?= date('Y');?></div></footer>
     </body>
⑨   <script src="js/site.js"></script>
   </html>
```

HOME PAGE

The home page (`index.php`) shows summaries of the six most recent articles uploaded to the site. The page begins by collecting the data that is needed to create the HTML page and storing it in variables.

1. Strict types are enabled to ensure the correct data type is used when functions are called (see p126-7).

2. `database-connection.php` is included to create the PDO object that manages the connection to the database; it is stored in a variable called `$pdo`.

3. `functions.php` is included as it holds the definitions for the `pdo()` function and the functions to format the data that is shown in the page.

4. The `$sql` variable stores the SQL to get summaries of the latest articles added to the site.

5. The SQL query is run using the `pdo()` function. It returns a `PDOStatement` object that represents the result set. Then, the `PDOStatement` object's `fetchAll()` method gets all of the summaries as an array and they are stored in the `$articles` variable.

The next five steps get the data that is used in the `header.php` file and store it in variables.

6. The SQL to get the id and name of the categories that appear in the navigation is stored in `$sql`.

7. The query is run, and the results are stored in a variable called `$navigation`.

8. If a user is on a category or article page, `$section` holds the id of the section they are in. The home page is not in a category, so it stores a blank string.

9. `$title` holds the text for the `<title>` element.

10. `$description` holds the text that will be shown in the `<meta>` description tag.

The rest of the file, below the dotted line, only uses PHP to display the data that was stored in the variables. This separates PHP code that gets data, from the HTML that is sent back to the browser.

11. The `header.php` file (shown on the previous page) is included. It will display the data that was collected, then stored in variables in Steps 6-10.

12. A `foreach` loop works through each element in the `$articles` array that was created in Step 5, and displays the article summaries. Each time the loop runs, the data for an individual article summary is stored in a variable called `$article`.

13. A link is created to the `article.php` page that displays any individual article on the site. The query string holds the id of the article that it should display.

14. The image for the article is displayed. If no image has been supplied, a placeholder image is shown (using the technique shown on p455).

15. If alt text was provided, it is shown in the `alt` attribute (if not, the attribute value will be blank).

16. The article's title is shown in an `<h2>` element.

17. The article's summary is displayed.

18. A link is created to the `category.php` file. The id of the category is added to the query string. The category name is shown inside the link.

19. A link is created to the `member.php` file. The id of the member who wrote the article is added to the query string so it links to their profile page. The name of the member who wrote the article is used as the link text.

20. The `footer.php` file (shown on the previous page) is included in the page.

```php
  <?php
① declare(strict_types = 1);                                  // Use strict types
② require 'includes/database-connection.php';                 // Create PDO object
③ require 'includes/functions.php';                           // Include functions

④ $sql = "SELECT a.id, a.title, a.summary, a.category_id, a.member_id,
                  c.name AS category,
                  CONCAT(m.forename, ' ', m.surname) AS author,
                  i.file      AS image_file,
                  i.alt       AS image_alt
            FROM article     AS a
            JOIN category    AS c ON a.category_id = c.id
            JOIN member      AS m ON a.member_id   = m.id
            LEFT JOIN image AS i ON a.image_id     = i.id
            WHERE a.published = 1
          ORDER BY a.id DESC
            LIMIT 6;";                                         // SQL to get latest articles
⑤ $articles = pdo($pdo, $sql)->fetchAll();                    // Get summaries

⑥ $sql = "SELECT id, name FROM category WHERE navigation = 1;"; // SQL to get categories
⑦ $navigation  = pdo($pdo, $sql)->fetchAll();                 // Get navigation categories

⑧ $section      = '';                                         // Current category
⑨ $title        = 'Creative Folk';                            // HTML <title> content
⑩ $description = 'A collective of creatives for hire';        // Meta description content
  ?>
⑪ <?php include 'includes/header.php'; ?>
    <main class="container grid" id="content">
⑫    <?php foreach ($articles as $article) { ?>
        <article class="summary">
⑬        <a href="article.php?id=<?= $article['id'] ?>">
⑭          <img src="uploads/<?= html_escape($article['image_file'] ?? 'blank.png') ?>"
⑮               alt="<?= html_escape($article['image_alt']) ?>">
⑯          <h2><?= html_escape($article['title']) ?></h2>
⑰          <p><?= html_escape($article['summary']) ?></p>
        </a>
        <p class="credit">
⑱          Posted in <a href="category.php?id=<?= $article['category_id'] ?>">
           <?= html_escape($article['category']) ?></a>
⑲          by <a href="member.php?id=<?= $article['member_id'] ?>">
           <?= html_escape($article['author']) ?></a>
        </p>
      </article>
    <?php } ?>
  </main>
⑳ <?php include 'includes/footer.php'; ?>
```

CATEGORY PAGE

The `category.php` file displays the name and description of an individual category followed by summaries of the articles in that category.

1. Strict types are enabled to ensure the correct data type is used when functions are called.

2. `database-connection.php` and `functions.php` are included in the page.

3. `filter_input()` looks for the name `id` in the query string and checks if its value is an integer. If it is, `$id` holds the number; if not, it holds `false`. If the value was not in the query string, it holds `null`.

4. If there was not a valid integer in the query string, `page-not-found.php` is included (it ends with the `exit` command that stops any more code running).

5. The SQL query to get the id, name and description of the specified category is stored in `$sql`.

6. The `pdo()` function is used to run the SQL query, then the `PDOStatement` object's `fetch()` method gets the data and stores it in the `$category` variable.

7. If the category was not found in the database, `page-not-found.php` is included, and the page stops.

8. If the page is still running, the `$sql` variable holds the SQL to get the summaries of the articles in the chosen category.

9. The query is run, then the `fetchAll()` method of the `PDOStatement` object gets the summaries as an array and they are stored in the `$articles` variable.

10. The SQL to get the id and name of the categories that appear in the navigation is stored in `$sql`.

11. The query is run, the `fetchAll()` method gets the data it returns, and it is stored in `$navigation`.

12. The id of the category is stored in `$section`. It is used to highlight this category in the navigation.

13. The category name is stored in `$title`. It will be shown in the `<title>` element.

14. The category description is stored in `$description` for use in the `<meta>` description tag.

With all of the data that the page requires stored in variables, the rest of the file below the dotted line creates the HTML that is sent back to the browser.

15. The `header.php` file is included in the page.

16. The name of the category is written out in an `<h1>` element.

17. The category description is written out under the category name in a `<p>` element.

18. A `foreach` loop works through the array that holds all of the article summaries in the category. This was stored in the `$articles` variable in Step 9. Each time the loop runs, the summary of a different article is stored in a variable called `$article`.

19. The code to display the summary of an article is the same as the code used to show the summaries of the articles on the home page (see previous page).

If the category does not yet contain any articles, the `$articles` variable will hold a blank array; as the `PDOStatement` object's `fetchAll()` method returns an empty array when no data matches the SQL query.

When a `foreach` loop tries to work with a blank array, the statements in the loop will not run. This means that the page will *not* display an `Undefined index` error if a query returns no data.

20. The `footer.php` file is included in the page.

```php
    <?php
①  declare(strict_types = 1);                                    // Use strict types
②  require 'includes/database-connection.php';                   // Create PDO object
    require 'includes/functions.php';                            // Include functions
③  $id = filter_input(INPUT_GET, 'id', FILTER_VALIDATE_INT);     // Validate id
    if (!$id) {                                                  // If no valid id
④      include 'page-not-found.php';                             // Page not found
    }
⑤  $sql = "SELECT id, name, description FROM category WHERE id=:id;"; // SQL statement
⑥  $category = pdo($pdo, $sql, [$id])->fetch();                  // Get category data
    if (!$category) {                                           // If category not found
⑦      include 'page-not-found.php';                             // Page not found
    }

⑧  $sql = "SELECT a.id, a.title, a.summary, a.category_id, a.member_id,
                   c.name AS category,
                   CONCAT(m.forename, ' ', m.surname) AS author,
                   i.file AS image_file,
                   i.alt  AS image_alt
            FROM article    AS a
            JOIN category   AS c   ON a.category_id = c.id
            JOIN member     AS m   ON a.member_id   = m.id
            LEFT JOIN image AS i   ON a.image_id    = i.id
            WHERE a.category_id = :id AND a.published = 1
            ORDER BY a.id DESC;";                                // SQL statement
⑨  $articles = pdo($pdo, $sql, [$id])->fetchAll();              // Get articles

⑩  $sql = "SELECT id, name FROM category WHERE navigation = 1;"; // SQL to get categories
⑪  $navigation  = pdo($pdo, $sql)->fetchAll();                   // Get navigation categories
⑫  $section     = $category['id'];                               // Current category
⑬  $title       = $category['name'];                             // HTML <title> content
⑭  $description = $category['description'];                      // Meta description content
    ?>
⑮  <?php include 'includes/header.php'; ?>
    <main class="container" id="content">
      <section class="header">
⑯        <h1><?= html_escape($category['name']) ?></h1>
⑰        <p><?= html_escape($category['description']) ?></p>
      </section>
      <section class="grid">
⑱      <?php foreach ($articles as $article) { ?>
⑲      <!-- The code to display the article summaries is the same as shown on p465 -->
        <?php } ?>
      </section>
    </main>
⑳  <?php include 'includes/footer.php'; ?>
```

ARTICLE PAGE

The `article.php` file is used to display every individual article on the site. The query string holds the id of the article that the page should display. As with the other pages, this file starts by collecting the data from the database and storing it in variables.

1. Strict types are enabled and the required files, `database-connection.php` and `functions.php` are included in the page.

2. `filter_input()` looks for the name `id` in the query string and checks if its value is an integer. If it is, `$id` holds the number; if not, it holds `false`. If the value was not in the query string, it holds `null`.

3. If there was not a valid integer in the query string, `page-not-found.php` is included (it ends with the `exit` command that stops any more code running).

4. The SQL to get the article data is stored in `$sql`.

5. The `pdo()` function is used to run the SQL query, and the `fetch()` method is used to collect the article data, which is stored in `$article`.

6. If the article was not found in the database, `page-not-found.php` is included, and the page stops.

7. If the page is still running, the SQL to get the categories in the navigation is stored in `$sql`.

8. The query is run, then the `fetchAll()` method gets the data, and it is stored in `$navigation`.

9. The id of the category the article belongs to is stored in `$section` so it can be highlighted in the navigation bar.

10. The article title is stored in `$title`.

11. The article summary is stored in `$description`.

With all of the data that the page requires stored in variables, the rest of the file below the dotted line creates the HTML that is sent back to the browser.

12. The `header.php` file is included in the page.

13. If an image has been uploaded for the article, its filename is written out in the `src` attribute of an `<img>` tag.

If an image was not uploaded for the article, a placeholder image is shown instead.

14. If alt text has been provided for the image, it is shown in the `alt` attribute of the `<img>` tag. If not, the attribute will be blank.

15. The article title is shown in an `<h1>` element.

16. The date the article was created is displayed. It uses the `format_date()` function shown on p454 to ensure that dates are formatted consistently.

17. The content of the article is displayed.

18. A link is created to the `categpry.php` file. The id of the category the article is in is added to the query string so that it shows that category page.

19. The name of the category is used as link text.

20. A link is created to the `member.php` file. The id of the member who wrote the article is added to the query string so that it shows that member's profile.

21. The name of the member who wrote the article is used as the link text.

22. The `footer.php` file is included in the page.

```php
    <?php
    declare(strict_types = 1);                                  // Use strict types
①  require 'includes/database-connection.php';                 // Create PDO object
    require 'includes/functions.php';                           // Include functions
②  $id = filter_input(INPUT_GET, 'id', FILTER_VALIDATE_INT);   // Validate id
    if (!$id) {                                                 // If no valid id
③      include 'page-not-found.php';                           // Page not found
    }
    $sql = "SELECT a.title, a.summary, a.content, a.created, a.category_id, a.member_id,
                   c.name       AS category,
                   CONCAT(m.forename, ' ', m.surname) AS author,
                   i.file AS image_file, i.alt  AS image_alt
④         FROM article     AS a
           JOIN category    AS c  ON a.category_id = c.id
           JOIN member      AS m  ON a.member_id   = m.id
           LEFT JOIN image  AS i  ON a.image_id    = i.id
           WHERE a.id = :id  AND a.published = 1;";             // SQL statement
⑤  $article = $article = pdo($pdo, $sql, [$id])->fetch();      // Get article data
    if (!$article) {                                           // If article not found
⑥      include 'page-not-found.php';                          // Page not found
    }
⑦  $sql = "SELECT id, name FROM category WHERE navigation = 1;"; // SQL to get categories
⑧  $navigation  = pdo($pdo, $sql)->fetchAll();                 // Get navigation categories
⑨  $section     = $article['category_id'];                     // Current category
⑩  $title       = $article['title'];                           // HTML <title> content
⑪  $description = $article['summary'];                         // Meta description content
    ?>
⑫  <?php include 'includes/header.php'; ?>
      <main class="article container">
        <section class="image">
⑬        <img src="uploads/<?= html_escape($article['image_file'] ?? 'blank.png') ?>"
⑭            alt="<?= html_escape($article['image_alt']) ?>">
        </section>
        <section class="text">
⑮        <h1><?= html_escape($article['title']) ?></h1>
⑯        <div class="date"><?= format_date($article['created']) ?></div>
⑰        <div class="content"><?= html_escape($article['content']) ?></div>
          <p class="credit">
⑱          Posted in <a href="category.php?id=<?= $article['category_id'] ?>">
⑲          <?= html_escape($article['category']) ?></a>
⑳          by <a href="member.php?id=<?= $article['member_id'] ?>">
㉑            <?= html_escape($article['author']) ?></a>
          </p>
        </section>
      </main>
㉒  <?php include 'includes/footer.php'; ?>
```

MEMBER PAGE

The `member.php` file shows the details of an individual member and summaries of the articles they have written. The query string holds the id of the member that the page should display.

1. Strict types are enabled and the required files, `database-connection.php` and `functions.php`, are included in the page.

2. `filter_input()` looks for the name `id` in the query string and checks if its value is an integer. If it is, `$id` holds the number; if not, it holds `false`. If the value was not in the query string, it holds `null`.

3. If there was not a valid integer in the query string, `page-not-found.php` is included (it ends with the `exit` command that stops any more code running).

4. The SQL to get the member data is stored in `$sql`.

5. The `pdo()` function runs the SQL query, then the `fetch()` method gets the member data, which is stored in `$member`.

6. If the `$member` was not found in the database, `page-not-found.php` is included, and the page stops.

7. If the page is still running, the SQL to get the summaries of that member's articles is stored in `$sql`.

8. The query is run, the `fetchAll()` method gets the data it returns, and the data is stored in `$articles`.

9. The SQL to get the categories for the navigation is stored in `$sql`.

10. The query is run, the `fetchAll()` method gets the data it returns, and it is stored in `$navigation`.

11. Because the member page is not in a category, the `$section` variable is blank.

12. The member's name is stored in `$title` so that it can be shown in the title of the page.

13. The member's name, followed by the words on `Creative Folk`, is stored in `$description` for use in the `<meta>` description tag.

Once the required data has been collected from the database and stored in variables, the rest of the file below the dotted line creates the HTML code to send back to the browser.

14. The `header.php` file is included in the page.

15. The member's forename and surname are written out inside an `<h1>` element.

16. The date the member joined is displayed using the `format_date()` function to ensure the date is formatted in a consistent manner.

17. If the user has uploaded a profile picture, the filename is written out in the `src` attribute of an `<img>` tag. If no image has been supplied, a placeholder image is shown instead.

18. The member's forename is shown in the `alt` attribute of the `<img>` tag.

19. A `foreach` loop works through the `$articles` array that was created in Step 7. It holds details of the articles that this member has written.

20. The code to display the summary of an article is identical to the code used to display articles on the home page on that was shown on p465.

If the author has not written any articles, the statements inside the loop will not run.

21. The `footer.php` file is included in the page.

```php
<?php
declare(strict_types = 1);                                    // Use strict types
require 'includes/database-connection.php';                   // Create PDO object
require 'includes/functions.php';                             // Include functions
$id = filter_input(INPUT_GET, 'id', FILTER_VALIDATE_INT);     // Validate id
if (!$id) {                                                    // If no valid id
    include 'page-not-found.php';                             // Page not found
}
$sql = "SELECT forename, surname, joined, picture FROM member WHERE id = :id;"; // SQL
$member = pdo($pdo, $sql, [$id])->fetch();                    // Get member data
if (!$member) {                                               // If array is empty
    include 'page-not-found.php';                             // Page not found
}
$sql = "SELECT a.id, a.title, a.summary, a.category_id, a.member_id,
                c.name       AS category,
                CONCAT(m.forename, ' ', m.surname) AS author,
                i.file       AS image_file,
                i.alt        AS image_alt
        FROM article     AS a
        JOIN category    AS c   ON a.category_id = c.id
        JOIN member      AS m   ON a.member_id   = m.id
        LEFT JOIN image AS i    ON a.image_id    = i.id
        WHERE a.member_id = :id AND a.published  = 1
        ORDER BY a.id DESC;";                                 // SQL
$articles = pdo($pdo, $sql, [$id])->fetchAll();               // Member's articles
$sql = "SELECT id, name FROM category WHERE navigation = 1;"; // SQL to get categories
$navigation  = pdo($pdo, $sql)->fetchAll();                   // Get categories
$section      = '';                                           // Current category
$title        = $member['forename'] . ' ' . $member['surname']; // HTML <title> content
$description = $title . ' on Creative Folk';                  // Meta description
?>
<?php include 'includes/header.php'; ?>
  <main class="container" id="content">
    <section class="header">
      <h1><?= html_escape($member['forename'] . ' ' . $member['surname']) ?></h1>
      <p class="member"><b>Member since:</b> <?= format_date($member['joined']) ?></p>
      <img src="uploads/<?= html_escape($member['picture'] ?? 'blank.png') ?>"
           alt="<?= html_escape($member['forename']) ?>" class="profile"><br>
    </section>
    <section class="grid">
    <?php foreach ($articles as $article) { ?>
    <!-- The code to display the article summaries is the same as shown on p465 -->
    <?php } ?>
    </section>
  </main>
<?php include 'includes/footer.php'; ?>
```

Numbered markers on left margin: ① (lines require), ② $id, ③ if block, ④ $sql, ⑤ $member, ⑥ if block, ⑦ $sql block, ⑧ $articles, ⑨ $sql, ⑩ $navigation, ⑪ $section, ⑫ $title, ⑬ $description, ⑭ include header, ⑮ h1, ⑯ p, ⑰ img src, ⑱ alt, ⑲ foreach, ⑳ comment, ㉑ include footer

CREATING A SEARCH FEATURE

The search page shows how to use SQL to search for data in the database and how, when a database query can return a lot of rows, pagination is used to display the results over multiple pages.

When visitors enter a term into the search box and submit the form, the database will look for that term in the `article` table's `title`, `summary`, and `description` columns. If the search term is found in those columns, a summary of the article is added to a result set so that visitors can see which articles match their query.

The search page runs two SQL queries:

- One counts the total number of matching results.
- The other gets summary details of those articles.

Below, you can see the SQL query that counts the number of articles that contain the search term.

The search term is repeated three times in the query; first to check the `title` column, then to check the `summary` column and finally the `content` column. You cannot re-use a placeholder in a SQL query, so a different placeholder name is used to search each of the columns (`:term1`, `:term2` and `:term3`).

```
SELECT COUNT(title)
  FROM article
 WHERE title   LIKE :term1
    OR summary LIKE :term2
    OR content LIKE :term3
   AND published = 1;
```

Three search results are shown per page to demonstrate how, when the database finds a lot of matching results, you can:

- Show a subset of those results per page.
- Add links beneath the results that allow visitors to request the next (or previous) set of matches.

This is called **pagination** because results are split across multiple pages. The links to each of the pages showing the search results need three name/value pairs in the query string so that the search page knows which articles to get from the database and display to the user:

- `term` holds the search term
- `show` indicates how many results to show per page
- `from` states how many matches have been shown

The `show` value is used with the SQL `LIMIT` clause so that the database returns the right number of articles to be shown on the page.

The `from` value is used with the SQL `OFFSET` clause to tell the database that it should only start adding results to the result set *after* it has found the specified number of matches.

```
  LIMIT :show
OFFSET :from
```

design [Search]

MATCHES FOUND: 10

Travel Guide
Book design for series of travel guides
POSTED IN **PRINT** BY **IVY STONE**

Golden Brown
Photograph for interior design book
POSTED IN **PHOTOGRAPHY** BY **EMIKO ITO**

Polite Society Posters
Poster designs for a fashion label
POSTED IN **PRINT** BY **IVY STONE**

1 2 3 4

© Creative Folk 2021

```
search.php?term=design
search.php?term=design&show=3&from=3
search.php?term=design&show=3&from=6
search.php?term=design&show=3&from=9
```

FROM	SHOW				PAGE
(0	÷	3)	+	1	= 1
(3	÷	3)	+	1	= 2
(6	÷	3)	+	1	= 3
(9	÷	3)	+	1	= 4

To create the pagination links, the search page needs three pieces of data; each one is stored in a variable:

- $count the number of results that match the query
- $show the number of results to show per page
- $from the number of results to skip before adding matches to the result set

To calculate the number of pages needed to show the results, divide $count (the number of matches) by $show (the number of results shown per page). Above, there are 10 matches and 3 matches are shown per page. 10 ÷ 3 = 3.3333, and this number is rounded up using PHP's ceil() function to get the number of pages needed to show the results.

```
$total_pages = ceil($count / $show);
```

To determine the current page, divide $from (the number of results to skip) by $show (the number of results per page), then add 1. The calculations to determine the current page are shown above-right.

```
$current_page = ceil($from / $show) + 1;
```

A for loop is used to create the pagination links. It sets a counter to 1, and checks if the counter is less than the total number of pages. If so, it adds a link to the page, then increments the counter. The loop runs until the counter reaches the total number of pages needed to show the results.

```
for ($i = 1; $i <= $total_pages; $i++) {
  // Display another link
}
```

SEARCH PAGE

When users enter a search term into the form at the top of the `search.php` page and submit the form, the search term is sent back to the same page which then finds matching articles and displays the results.

1. Strict types are enabled, and `functions.php` and `database-connection.php` are included in the page.

2. `filter_input()` gets three values from the query string and stores them in variables:

- `$term` holds the search term
- `$show` gets the number of results to show per page (a default number of 3 is used if no value is given)
- `$from` gets the number of results to skip (a default number of 0 is used if no value is given)

3. Two variables are initialized because they are needed to create the HTML page, but they are only assigned values if there is a search term (`$count` holds a value of 0, and `$articles` is an empty array).

4. An `if` statement checks if `$term` holds a search term; this is because the next part of the page that tries to find matches in the database should only run when a search term has been supplied.

5. The `$arguments` array stores the names of the three placeholders in the SQL query and the values they should be replaced with. Each one is replaced with the same search term because SQL queries cannot re-use the same placeholder name.

The wildcard symbol `%` is added before and after the search term so that the SQL query can find matches even when characters appear either side of the search term.

6. The first SQL query counts how many articles in the `article` table contain the search term in either the `title`, `summary`, or `content` columns.

7. The `pdo()` function is used to run the SQL query (using the search term the user provided). Then, the `PDOStatement` object's `fetchColumn()` method is used to get the number of articles that match the search term. As its name suggests, the `fetchColumn()` method gets the value from a single column of the result set. The value that is returned is stored in `$count`.

8. An `if` statement checks if there were matches. If there were, the article summaries are collected. If not, there is no point trying to collect them.

9. Two more elements are added to the `$arguments` array so they can be used in the second SQL query:

- `show` is the number of results to show per page
- `from` is the number of results to skip (both were stored in variables in Step 2)

10. The second SQL query gets the summaries of the matching articles that will be shown in this page; it is stored in `$sql`.

11. The `WHERE` clause finds the articles containing the search term in either the `title`, `summary`, or `content` columns of the `article` table.

12. The `ORDER BY` clause orders the results by article id, in descending order, so the latest ones are first.

13. The `LIMIT` clause restricts the number of results added to the result set to the number of search results that should be shown per page.

14. The `OFFSET` clause controls how many matches are skipped before data is added to the result set.

15. The SQL statement is run using the values in the updated `$arguments` array. Then the `PDOStatement` object's `fetchAll()` method is called to get all of the matching summaries. They are stored in `$articles`.

```php
<?php
declare(strict_types = 1);                              // Use strict types
require 'includes/database-connection.php';             // Create PDO object
require 'includes/functions.php';                       // Include functions

$term  = filter_input(INPUT_GET, 'term');               // Get search term
$show  = filter_input(INPUT_GET, 'show', FILTER_VALIDATE_INT) ?? 3; // Limit
$from  = filter_input(INPUT_GET, 'from', FILTER_VALIDATE_INT) ?? 0; // Offset
$count = 0;                                              // Set count to 0
$articles = [];                                          // Set articles to empty array

if ($term) {                                            // If search term provided
    $arguments['term1'] = '%$term%';                    // Store search term in array
    $arguments['term2'] = '%$term%';                    // three times as placeholders
    $arguments['term3'] = '%$term%';                    // cannot be repeated in SQL

    $sql = "SELECT COUNT(title) FROM article
            WHERE title   LIKE :term1
               OR summary LIKE :term2
               OR content LIKE :term3
               AND published = 1;";                     // How many articles match term
    $count = pdo($pdo, $sql, $arguments)->fetchColumn(); // Return count
    if ($count > 0) {                                   // If articles match term
        $arguments['show'] = $show;                     // Add to array for pagination
        $arguments['from'] = $from;                     // Add to array for pagination
        $sql = "SELECT a.id, a.title, a.summary, a.category_id, a.member_id,
                       c.name      AS category,
                       CONCAT(m.forename, ' ', m.surname) AS author,
                       i.file      AS image_file,
                       i.alt       AS image_alt
                  FROM article     AS a
                  JOIN category    AS c    ON a.category_id = c.id
                  JOIN member      AS m    ON a.member_id   = m.id
                  LEFT JOIN image  AS i    ON a.image_id    = i.id
                 WHERE a.title   LIKE :term1
                    OR a.summary LIKE :term2
                    OR a.content LIKE :term3
                    AND a.published = 1
              ORDER BY a.id DESC
                 LIMIT :show
                OFFSET :from;";                          // Find matching articles
        $articles = pdo($pdo, $sql, $arguments)->fetchAll(); // Run query and get results
    }
}
```

SEARCH PAGE (CONTINUED)

Next, the page continues by calculating the values that are needed to create the pagination links.

1. If the number in $count is greater than $show, the values for the pagination links need to be calculated.

2. The total number of pages needed to show the results (stored in $total_pages) is calculated by:

- Dividing $count by $show.
- Rounding up using PHP's ceil() function

3. The current page (stored in $current_page) is calculated by:

- Dividing the value in $show by the value in $from
- Rounding it up using PHP's ceil() function
- Adding 1 to the number

4. The SQL to get the categories so they can be shown in the navigation bar is stored in $sql.

5. The query is run, the fetchAll() method gets the categories, and they are stored in $navigation.

6. Because the search page is not in a category, the $section variable stores a blank string.

7. The title for the page is stored in $title. It consists of the text Search results for and the search term (this is escaped in header.php).

8. The meta description text is stored in the $description variable.

The rest of the file creates the HTML page that is sent back to the browser.

9. The search form submits data back to this page.

10. If the user entered a search term, it is sanitized and shown in the search input.

11. If there is a value in $term the number of matching articles is shown.

12. Article summaries are displayed using a foreach loop, as they were for previous examples (see p465).

13. An if statement checks if $count holds a bigger number than $show. If so, pagination links are shown.

14. A <nav> and <ul> element are added to hold the pagination links. Each link will be in an <li> element.

15. A for loop is used to create the pagination links. Its parentheses contain three expressions:

- $i = 1 creates a counter called $i, and sets it to 1.
- $i <= $total_pages is the condition that checks if the code in the loop should run. If the counter is less than the total pages needed to show the search results, the subsequent code block will run.
- $i++ increments the counter by 1 each time it runs.

16. Inside the loop, a link is created for each page. The href attribute uses a query string with the three values that tell search.php which results to show:

- term is the search term.
- show is the number of results to show per page.
- from is the number of results to skip. E.g., for
  Page one $i is 1 so (1 - 1) * 3 skips 0 results
  Page two $i is 2 so (2 - 1) * 3 skips 3 results
  Page three $i is 3 so (3 - 1) * 3 skips 6 results

17. If the value in the counter matches the value in $current_page, the link should indicate that this is the current page of results. To do this, the value active is added to the class attribute and an aria-current attribute is added with a value of true.

18. Inside the link, the counter is used as link text to show the page number. The loop runs until the value in the counter equals the value in $total_pages.

```php
(1)  if ($count > $show) {                                   // If matches is more than show
(2)      $total_pages  = ceil($count / $show);               // Calculate total pages
(3)      $current_page = ceil($from / $show) + 1;            // Calculate current page
     }
(4)  $sql = "SELECT id, name FROM category WHERE navigation = 1;"; // SQL to get categories
(5)  $navigation  = pdo($pdo, $sql)->fetchAll();             // Get navigation categories

(6)  $section     = '';                                      // Current category
(7)  $title       = 'Search results for ' . $term;           // HTML <title> content
(8)  $description = $title . ' on Creative Folk';            // Meta description content
     ?>
     <?php include 'includes/header.php'; ?>
       <main class="container" id="content">
         <section class="header">
(9)        <form action="search.php" method="get" class="form-search">
             <label for="search"><span>Search for: </span></label>
(10)           <input type="text" name="term" value="<?= html_escape($term) ?>"
                      id="search" placeholder="Enter search term"
             /><input type="submit" value="Search" class="btn" />
           </form>
(11)       <?php if ($term) { ?><p><b>Matches found:</b> <?= $count ?></p><?php } ?>
         </section>

         <section class="grid">
(12)       <?php foreach ($articles as $article) { ?>
           <!-- The code to display the article summaries is the same as shown on p465 -->
           <?php } ?>
         </section>

(13)     <?php if ($count > $show) { ?>
(14)     <nav class="pagination" role="navigation" aria-label="Pagination navigation">
           <ul>
(15)       <?php for ($i = 1; $i <= $total_pages; $i++) { ?>
             <li>
(16)           <a href="?term=<?= $term ?>&show=<?= $show ?>&from=<?= (($i - 1) * $show) ?>"
(17)              class="btn <?= ($i == $current_page) ? 'active" aria-current="true' : '' ?>">
(18)             <?= $i ?>
             </a>
           </li>
           <?php } ?>
           </ul>
         </nav>
         <?php } ?>
       </main>
     <?php include 'includes/footer.php'; ?>
```

GETTING DATA INTO AN OBJECT

PDO can represent each row of data in a result set as an object instead of an array (and that object's methods can work with the returned data). PDO's fetch mode specifies how the data should be represented.

Fetch modes control how a PDOStatement object returns each row of data in the result set. It can be an:

- Associative array where each column name from the result set is used as a key of the array.
- Object where each column name from the result set is used as a property of an object.

The database-connection.php file on p439 used the $options array to set the default fetch mode to return each row of data as an associative array.

To set the default fetch mode to return each row of data as an object instead of an array, use the value PDO::FETCH_OBJ.

ARRAY ⟶ `PDO::ATTR_DEFAULT_FETCH_MODE => PDO::FETCH_ASSOC;`
OBJECT ⟶ `PDO::ATTR_DEFAULT_FETCH_MODE => PDO::FETCH_OBJ;`

Each PDOStatement object also has a method called setFetchMode(), which can be used to set the fetch mode for that individual PDOStatement object. This overwrites the default fetch method.

setFetchMode() is called after the execute() method. Its one parameter is the fetch mode to use. Below, it says each row of data from the result set should be returned as an object.

`$statement->setFetchMode(PDO::FETCH_OBJ);`

PDOStatement OBJECT   SET FETCH MODE   FETCH EACH ROW AS AN OBJECT

The fetch mode can also be specified as an argument of the fetch() and fetchAll() methods. When fetchAll() is used to retrieve multiple rows of data from the result set, each object is stored in a separate element of an indexed array.

The object is created using a class called the **standard class**; this is a blank object (with no properties or methods). The class name is stdClass. The example on p480 will show how the data can be added to an object built using an existing class.

`$statement->fetch(PDO::FETCH_OBJ);`

PDOStatement OBJECT   GET DATA   FETCH EACH ROW AS AN OBJECT

SETTING THE FETCH MODE TO GET AN OBJECT

`section_c/c12/examples/fetching-data-as-objects.php`

```php
<?php
require '../cms/includes/database-connection.php';      ①
require '../cms/includes/functions.php';
$sql = "SELECT id, forename, surname                    ②
            FROM member;";                      // SQL
$statement = $pdo->query($sql);                 // Execute    ③
$statement->setFetchMode(PDO::FETCH_OBJ);       // Fetch mode ④
$members   = $statement->fetchAll();            // Get data   ⑤
?>
<!DOCTYPE html>
<html> ...
  <body>
    <?php foreach ($members as $member) { ?>    ⑥
      <p>
        <?= html_escape($member->forename) ?>   ⑦
        <?= html_escape($member->surname) ?>
      </p>
    <?php } ?>
  </body>
</html>
```

In this example, each row of the result set is represented by a property of an object.

1. `database-connection.php` and `functions.php` are included.

2. The query is stored in `$sql`.

3. The PDO object's `query()` method executes the query. This will return a PDOStatement object that represents the query and the result set it generates.

4. The PDOStatement object's `setFetchMode()` method is called. The argument `PDO::FETCH_OBJ` states that each row of the result set should be returned as an object.

5. The PDOStatement object's `fetchAll()` method gets every row of data from the result set. It returns an indexed array, and the value of each element in that array is an object that represents one row of data.

6. A `foreach` loop is used to work through each element of the array.

7. The member's name is shown using the properties of the object that hold their forename and surname.

Ivy Stone

Luke Wood

Emiko Ito

TRY: In Step 2 request the member's email address as well, then display the email address in Step 7.

TRY: Replace Step 7 with
`<?php var_dump($member) ?>`
to see the object that is created for each row of data.

GETTING DATA INTO AN OBJECT USING A CLASS

PDO can return each row of the result set as an object that is created using a user-defined class. The objects created with that class will automatically get any methods in the class definition.

To add data from each row of a result set to an object created using an existing class definition, use the `PDOStatement` object's `setFetchMode()` method with two parameters:

- The fetch mode `PDO::FETCH_CLASS`
- The name of the class to use

The class name is given in quotes, and the class definition must be included in the page before `setFetchMode()` is called.

On the right-hand page, you can see a class definition used to create objects that represent the members of the site. The class is in a file called `Member.php`, which is stored in a folder called `classes`.

The properties of this object match the names of two columns in the `member` table of the database.

- When a column name in the result set matches a property name in the class, the value is assigned to that property.
- If the result set has a column name that is not a property in the class, that column name is added as an extra property of the object.

Any object that PDO creates using this class will also have the methods that are in the class definition.

When `fetchAll()` is used to retrieve multiple rows of data from the result set, each object is stored in a different element in an indexed array.

```
$statement->setFetchMode(PDO::FETCH_CLASS, 'Member');
```

| PDOStatement OBJECT | SET FETCH MODE | FETCH DATA INTO EXISTING CLASS | CLASS NAME |

When objects are created from named classes, values are assigned to the properties of the object before the `__construct()` method of the class (see p160) is called. This can lead to unexpected results.

CREATING AN OBJECT USING AN EXISTING CLASS

PHP
section_c/c12/examples/classes/Member.php

```php
<?php
class Member
{
  public $forename;
  public $surname;
  public function getFullName(): string
  {
    return $this->forename . ' ' . $this->surname;
  }
}
```
① (brace spanning the property and method declarations)

PHP
section_c/c12/examples/fetching-data-into-class.php

```php
<?php
require '../cms/includes/database-connection.php';
require '../cms/includes/functions.php';
require 'classes/Member.php';
$sql = "SELECT forename, surname
        FROM member
        WHERE id = 1;";
$statement = $pdo->query($sql);
$statement->setFetchMode(PDO::FETCH_CLASS, 'Member');
$member = $statement->fetch();
?>
<!DOCTYPE html>
<html> ...
  <p><?= html_escape($member->getFullName()) ?></p> ...
</html>
```
② require lines
③ $sql block
④ $statement = $pdo->query($sql);
⑤ $statement->setFetchMode(PDO::FETCH_CLASS, 'Member');
⑥ $member = $statement->fetch();
⑦ `<p><?= html_escape($member->getFullName()) ?></p>`

RESULT

Ivy Stone

1. The `Member` class is defined with two properties and one method.

2. `database-connection.php`, `functions.php`, and `Member.php` are included.

3. The query is stored in `$sql`.

4. The `PDO` object's `query()` method runs the query and creates a `PDOStatement` object to represent the result set.

5. The `PDOStatement` object's `setFetchMode()` method is called:

- `PDO::FETCH_CLASS` tells PDO to add the data to an object created using an existing class.
- `Member` is the name of the class used to create the object.

6. The `PDOStatement` object's `fetch()` method gets the one row of data from the result set. The object that is returned is stored in the `$member` variable.

7. The `getFullName()` method of the object is called to get the member's full name.

TRY: Replace Step 6 with `<?php var_dump($member) ?>` to see the object that is created for this member.

SUMMARY

GET & SHOW DATA FROM A DATABASE

> A PDO object represents and manages the connection to the database.

> A PDOStatement object represents a SQL statement and the result set it generates. It can return each row of data as an associative array or object.

> When a result set has more than one row, each row can be stored in an element of an indexed array.

> Query strings can be used to specify what data a page should collect from the database.

> The SQL statement can use placeholders for values that may change each time the page is requested.

> Ensure that any database data created by a site's visitors is escaped before it is displayed in a page.

13

UPDATING DATA IN A DATABASE

A website can provide tools that allow users to add new data to the database, and update or delete existing data that it already stores.

In order to do this, PHP pages need to perform the following tasks:

1. **Collect the data:** Chapter 6 showed how to get data from forms and URLs.

2. **Validate the data:** Chapter 6 also showed how to check if required data has been supplied and if the data is in a valid format (then show users messages if there are errors).

3. **Update the database:** Chapter 11 introduced SQL statements that create, update, or delete data in the database. Chapter 12 showed how SQL statements can be run using PDO.

4. **Provide feedback:** A message will tell users if they were successful or not.

Because you have already learned how to perform most of these tasks, this chapter focuses on how to control when each of the tasks should run. The order in which statements are run is known as the **flow of control**. In this chapter, a series of if statements tell the PHP interpreter when to perform each task. For example, if the data that a user supplied is not valid, there is no point creating or executing the SQL to update the database. Similarly, you only need to show a success message if the changes to the database were successful.

You will also learn how to run a series of related SQL statements using something called **transactions**, and how the changes are only saved if all of the SQL statements are successful (if just one of them fails, then none of the changes to the database are saved).

ADDING DATA
TO A TABLE

To add a new row to a database table, use SQL's INSERT command.
An INSERT command can only add data to one table at a time.

1. The SQL statement below adds a category to the `category` table. It has parameters for the `name`, `description`, and `navigation` columns. (The value for the `id` column is generated by the database.)

2. The data that each column will use is provided in an associative array with exactly one element for every parameter in the SQL statement. The array must not hold any extra elements as this would cause an error.

3. The PDO object's `prepare()` method needs a SQL statement as an argument so it can create a `PDOStatement` object. Then, the `PDOStatement` object's `execute()` method uses values in the array to run the SQL.

```
① ┌ $sql = "INSERT INTO category (name, description, navigation)
   └        VALUES (:name, :description, :navigation);";

  ┌ $category = ['name']        = 'News';
② ┤ $category = ['description'] = 'News about Creative Folk';
  └ $category = ['navigation']  = 1;

③ ┌ $statement = $pdo->prepare($sql);
   └ $statement->execute($category);
```

On the right, the new row has been highlighted. The auto-increment features gives the id column a value of 5. In the sample website, if there was a problem, the PDO object would throw an exception and this would be handled by the default exception handling function.

category			
id	name	description	navigation
1	Print	Inspiring graphic design	1
2	Digital	Powerful pixels	1
3	Illustration	Hand-drawn visual storytelling	1
4	Photography	Capturing the moment	1
5	News	News about Creative Folk	1

UPDATING DATA IN A TABLE

To update existing rows in a database table, use SQL's UPDATE command. An UPDATE command can update multiple tables using a JOIN.

1. This SQL statement updates an existing category. The first three parameters hold values to use in the name, description, and navigation columns. The WHERE clause uses a parameter to specify the id of a row to update.

2. The data used to replace the parameters is provided in an array, which has exactly one element for every parameter in the SQL statement. It must not hold extra elements because this would cause an error.

3. The statement is run like a query with parameters. Below, you can see the user-defined pdo() function (introduced on p456) is used to run the SQL statement. This approach will be used in the rest of the chapter.

```
① $sql = "UPDATE category
             SET name        = :name,
                 description = :description,
                 navigation  = :navigation
             WHERE id = :id;";

② $category = ['id']          = 5;
   $category = ['name']        = 'News';
   $category = ['description'] = 'Updates from Creative Folk';
   $category = ['navigation']  = 0;

③ pdo($pdo, $sql, $category);
```

category			
id	name	description	navigation
1	Print	Inspiring graphic design	1
2	Digital	Powerful pixels	1
3	Illustration	Hand-drawn visual storytelling	1
4	Photography	Capturing the moment	1
5	News	Updates from Creative Folk	0

On the left, the fifth category has been updated.

NOTE: If the search condition specified in the WHERE clause matched more than one row, the SQL UPDATE command would update all of the matching rows.

DELETING DATA FROM A TABLE

SQL's DELETE command deletes rows of data from a table.
A search condition restricts which rows should be deleted.
A JOIN can be used to delete data from multiple tables.

1. The SQL statement below uses the **DELETE** command, followed by the **FROM** clause and the name of the table the row(s) will be deleted from.

2. Next, the search condition specifies which rows should be deleted from this table. Below, the row to delete is specified using a value in the id column.

3. The id of the row to delete is stored in $id. Then the id is provided to the pdo() function using an indexed array that is created *in* the argument itself.

```
①  $sql = "DELETE FROM category
②              WHERE id = :id;";

③  $id = 5;
    pdo($pdo, $sql, [$id]);
```

On the right, the fifth category has been deleted from the table.

NOTE: if the search condition in the WHERE clause matches more than one row, the SQL DELETE command will delete all of the matching rows.

category			
id	name	description	navigation
1	Print	Inspiring graphic design	1
2	Digital	Powerful pixels	1
3	Illustration	Hand-drawn visual storytelling	1
4	Photography	Capturing the moment	1

GETTING THE ID OF A NEW ROW OF DATA

When a column of a database table uses an auto-incrementing id and a new row of data is added to the table, the PDO object's `lastInsertId()` method will return the id that the database created for the new row.

In the sample website, the first column in each table is called `id`. It holds a primary key that is used to uniquely identify each row of the table. When a new row is added to the table, MySQL's auto-increment feature is used to create the value used in the `id` column of the new row.

When a SQL statement that inserts a new row of data into the table has run, the PDO object's `lastInsertId()` method can get the value that MySQL generated for the `id` column. This can be stored in a variable and used later in the code.

You will see this technique used when a new article is created and an image is uploaded at the same time.

- The image is added to the `image` table first
- The `lastInsertId()` method is used to get its id
- The article is added to the `article` table last because it uses the id of the new image in the `image_id` column of the `article` table

Below, you can see that the `lastInsertId()` method is called after the `pdo()` function has been called to add a new row to the database.

```
pdo($pdo, $sql, $arguments);
$new_id = $pdo->lastInsertId();
```

FINDING OUT HOW MANY ROWS CHANGED

When a SQL statement uses an UPDATE or DELETE command, it can change more than one row of data at a time. The PDOStatement object's rowCount() method returns the number of rows that were affected.

When an UPDATE or DELETE command is run, it can change zero, one, or many rows of the database, depending on how many rows match the search condition in the WHERE clause.

When the query below is run, if the category table does not have a category with an id of 100, it would not delete anything from the database:

```
DELETE FROM category
  WHERE id = 100;
```

When the query below is run, it could update zero, one, or many rows, depending on how many rows had a value of 0 in the navigation column.

```
UPDATE category
   SET navigation = 1
 WHERE navigation = 0;
```

When the PDOStatement object's execute() method is called, it returns true if a SQL statement runs and false if it does not. But, as these examples show, this does not tell you if any rows of the database changed.

To determine how many rows were changed when a SQL statement has run, the PDOStatement object has a method called rowCount() which will return the number of rows that changed.

The rowCount() method should be called in the next statement after the execute() method, and the value it returns can be stored in a variable.

If you run a SQL statement using the pdo() function defined in the last chapter, the rowCount() method can be called in the same statement that calls the pdo() function (using method chaining).

```
$sql = "UPDATE category
            SET navigation = 1
          WHERE navigation = 0;";
$result = $pdo($pdo, $sql)->rowCount();
```

PREVENTING DUPLICATE VALUES IN COLUMNS

The values in some columns should be unique. In the sample website, two articles cannot have the same title, two categories cannot have the same name, and two members cannot have the same email address.

On p430, a uniqueness constraint was added to the following columns of the database to ensure that no two rows had the same value in these columns, the:

- title column of the article table
- name column of the category table
- email column of the member table

When a new row is added to these tables (or an existing row is updated), if another row already holds the same value in these columns, PDO will throw an exception object because it cannot save the data (it would break the uniqueness constraint).

PDO uses the PDOException class to create a PDOException object; it is like the exception objects you met on p368, but it holds extra data that is specific to PDO. Below, you see how to handle SQL statements that may break a uniqueness constraint.

1. The code to create a new row in these tables, or update an existing row of them, is put in a try block.

2. If PDO throws an exception when running code in the try block, the subsequent catch block runs, and the exception object is stored in a variable called $e.

3. The PDOException object has a property called errorInfo. Its value is an indexed array of data about the error. The second element in the array is an error code (http://notes.re/PDO/error-codes has a full list of error codes). If the error code is 1062, a uniqueness constraint is preventing the data being saved, and the user must be told the value has already been used.

4. If it is any other error code, the exception is re-thrown using the throw keyword (see p369) and will be handled by the default exception handling function.

```
try {
    pdo($pdo, $sql, $args);
} catch (PDOException $e) {
    if ($e->errorInfo[1] === 1062) {
        // Tell user a value has already been used
    } else {
        throw $e;
    }
}
```

CREATING WEB PAGES TO EDIT DATABASE DATA

Having seen how PDO adds, updates, and deletes data in the database, the rest of this chapter will show you how to create admin pages and forms that allow users to change the data stored in a database.

Here are the six admin pages that allow users to create, update, and delete the categories and articles.

The admin pages are all in a folder called `admin`. Try them in the browser before looking at the code.

categories.php

This page lists all of the categories. There are also links to create, update and delete categories.

articles.php

This page lists all of the articles. It has links that allow site owners to create, update and delete articles.

The links to create or edit the categories point to `category.php`.

- When creating a category, there is no query string.

- When editing a category, the query string holds the name `id` and its value is the id of the category to edit. E.g., `category.php?id=2`

The links to delete a category point to a page called `category-delete.php`, and the query string holds the id of the category to delete.

The links to create or edit the articles point to `article.php`.

- When creating an article, there is no query string.

- When editing an article, the query string holds the name `id` and its value is the id of the article to edit. E.g., `article.php?id=2`

The links to delete an article point to a page called `article-delete.php`, and the query string holds the id of the article to delete.

category.php

This page provides a form to create a new category or update an existing one.

When the form is submitted, the data is validated:

- If it is valid, the page will update the database and send the user back to the `categories.php` page. A message is sent in the query string so that the categories page can show that the data was saved.

- If it is not valid, the form is shown again with messages below form fields that need correcting.

category-delete.php

This page asks users to confirm that they want to delete a category.

If the user presses the `confirm` button, the category will be deleted, and the user will be sent back to the `categories.php` page. A message will be sent in the query string and displayed in the categories page to inform the user that the category was deleted.

article.php

The article page provides a form to create a new article or update an existing one.

When the form is submitted, the data is validated.

- If it is valid, the page will update the database and send the user back to the `articles.php` page. A message is sent in the query string so that the articles page can show that the data was saved.

- If it is not valid, the form is shown again with messages below form fields that need correcting.

article-delete.php

This page asks users to confirm that they want to delete an article.

If the user presses the `confirm` button, the article will be deleted, and the user will be sent back to the `articles.php` page. A message will be sent in the query string and displayed in the articles page to inform the user that the article was deleted.

CREATING, UPDATING, & DELETING CATEGORIES

The `categories.php` page provides links to create, update and delete categories.

1. Strict types are used and two files are included: `database-connection.php` creates a PDO object and `functions.php` contains user-defined functions including the `pdo()` function, functions to format data, and a new function shown in steps 15-19.

2. If the query string holds a success message, it is stored in a variable called `$success`. If not, `$success` will hold the value `null`.

3. If the query string holds a failure message, it is stored in `$failure`. If not, `$failure` holds `null`.

4. The `$sql` variable holds the SQL query to get data about each of the categories stored in the database.

5. The `pdo()` function runs the query and then the `PDOStatement` object's `fetchAll()` method gets the category data and stores it in `$categories`.

6. The header file for the admin pages is included.

7. If the query string held a success or failure message, it is shown in the page.

8. A link to create a new category is added. When a link to `category.php` does not have a query string, `category.php` knows it should create a new category.

9. A table is added to the page. The first row holds three column headings: `name`, `edit`, and `delete`.

10. A `foreach` loop is used to display data about existing categories with links to edit or delete them.

11. The first column shows the name of the category.

12. Next, a link is created to the `category.php` page. The query string holds the id of the category so that, when the `category.php` page loads, it will allow the user to edit the details about that category. E.g., `<a href="category.php?id=1">`

13. A link is created to the `category-delete.php` page, which deletes a category from the database. The id of the category is stored in the query string.

14. The footer for the admin pages is included.

15. A new function that redirects users to another page is added to `functions.php`. It allows success or failure messages to be added to the query string of the page the user is sent to. It has three parameters:

- The name of the file that the user will be sent to
- An optional array used to create a query string
- An optional HTTP response code (default is 302)

16. The `$qs` variable is created to hold a query string. Its value is assigned using a ternary operator. If `$parameters` holds an array, a question mark is added to `$qs`, and then PHP's built-in `http_build_query()` function creates the query string from the values in the array. For each element in the array, the key becomes a name in the query string, and its value is added after an equals symbol (and characters that are not allowed in a URL are also escaped – p280).

17. The value in `$qs` is joined onto the end of the URL of the page the user is being sent to.

18. PHP's `header()` function is called to redirect the visitor. The first argument tells the browser the page to request; the second is the HTTP response code.

19. `exit` stops any further code being run.

```php
    <?php
    declare(strict_types = 1);                          // Use strict types
①  include '../includes/database-connection.php';       // Database connection
    include '../includes/functions.php';                // Include functions

②  $success = $_GET['success'] ?? null;                 // Check for success message
③  $failure = $_GET['failure'] ?? null;                 // Check for failure message

④  $sql = "SELECT id, name, navigation FROM category;"; // SQL to get all categories
⑤  $categories = pdo($pdo, $sql)->fetchAll();           // Get all categories
    ?>
⑥  <?php include '../includes/admin-header.php' ?>
    <main class="container" id="content">
      <section class="header">
        <h1>Categories</h1>
⑦      <?php if ($success) { ?><div class="alert alert-success"><?= $success ?></div><?php } ?>
        <?php if ($failure) { ?><div class="alert alert-danger"><?= $failure ?></div><?php } ?>
⑧      <p><a href="category.php" class="btn btn-primary">Add new category</a></p>
      </section>

    <table class="categories">
⑨      <tr><th>Name</th><th class="edit">Edit</th><th class="delete">Delete</th></tr>
⑩      <?php foreach ($categories as $category) { ?>
        <tr>
⑪        <td><?= html_escape($category['name']) ?></td>
⑫        <td><a href="category.php?id=<?= $category['id'] ?>"
                class="btn btn-primary">Edit</a></td>
⑬        <td><a href="category-delete.php?id=<?= $category['id'] ?>"
                class="btn btn-danger">Delete</a></td>
        </tr>
      <?php } ?>
    </table>
    </main>
⑭  <?php include '../includes/admin-footer.php'; ?>
```

```php
⑮  function redirect(string $location, array $parameters = [], $response_code = 302)
    {
⑯      $qs = $parameters ? '?' . http_build_query($parameters) : '';  // Create query string
⑰      $location = $location . $qs;                                    // Create new path
⑱      header('Location: ' . $location, $response_code);               // Redirect to new page
⑲      exit;                                                          // Stop code
    }
```

CREATING AND UPDATING DATA

The code to create or update articles and categories is split into four parts. Each part uses a set of **if** statements that determine which code is run.

A: SET UP PAGE

First, the pages check if they are creating or updating data. To do this, they check if the query string has a name called **id** with a value that is an integer.

- No: The page is being used to create a new row in the database. At this point, the PHP interpreter will skip to Part B

- Yes: The page is trying to edit an existing row of data and it must load that data so it can be edited

If the data the user wants to edit is not returned, the user is told that the article or category was not found.

B: GET AND VALIDATE USER DATA

Next, the page checks if the form was submitted.

- No: Skip to Part D
- Yes: The data must be collected and validated

An array is created with an element for each piece of data the page receives. The value for that element is assigned by validating the data using the functions that were introduced in Chapter 6. If the data is:

- Valid: that element in the array holds a blank string
- Invalid: the array stores an error message indicating what data is expected from the control

Then, values in the array are joined into one string.

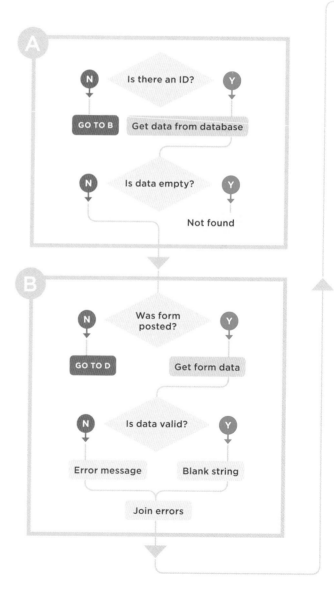

Flow charts help describe which code should run in different situations. You can refer back to these flow charts when working through the code.

C: SAVE USER DATA
In this part, the page checks if the data is all valid.

- No: Skip to Part D
- Yes: Continue to run the code in Part C

Then it checks if there was an id in the query string:

- No: The SQL creates a new article or category
- Yes: The SQL updates the article or category

Next, it checks if the SQL ran successfully:

- No: Check the kind of exception that was thrown
- Yes: The user is shown a success message

If an exception was thrown, check if it was caused by a uniqueness constraint:

- No: Re-throw the exception
- Yes: A message decribing the issue is shown

D: SHOW FORM
The form is then shown:

- If there is no id and the form was not submitted, the form will be blank
- If there is an id but the form was not submitted, the form shows the existing data to be edited
- If the form was submitted and data is not valid, the form shows the data the user supplied with error messages telling them how to correct it

GETTING AND VALIDATING CATEGORY DATA

The code for `category.php` is split over the next six pages. First, you can see the code for Parts A and B (as described on the previous page). Part A sets up the page and determines whether a new category is being created or an existing category updated.

1. Strict types are enabled and the required files are included. It needs `database-connection.php`, `functions.php`, and `validate.php` (which holds the validation functions created in Chapter 6).

2. If the page is editing an existing category, the URL will have a query string with the name `id`; its value will be the id of the category to edit.

PHP's `filter_input()` function is used to check if an id is present and its value is an integer. The `$id` variable will store:

- the integer if it is present
- `false` if the value is not a valid integer
- `null` if the name `id` is not in the query string

3. The `$category` array is declared to hold details about the category. It is initialized with values that can be shown in the form in Part D (see p503) when a new category is being created and the form does not have any values to display.

4. The `$errors` array is initialized with blank strings for each element (because no errors have been discovered yet). The values in this array are shown in Part D after each form control (shown on p503).

5. An `if` statement checks if there is a valid integer for the category id in the query string.

6. If so, the SQL to get the category the user wants to edit from the database is stored in `$sql`.

7. The `pdo()` function runs the query, and the `fetch()` method collects the category data. The array that is returned is stored in the `$category` variable (overwriting the values created in Step 3).

8. If there was an id in the query string, but the database did not find a matching category, the `$category` variable will hold `false` and the subsequent code block will run.

9. The `redirect()` function (p495) sends the user to the `categories.php` page. The second argument is an array that is used to display a failure message telling the user that the category could not be found.

Part B collects and validates any form data:

10. An `if` statement tests if the form was submitted.

11. If so, form values are stored in the `$category` array that was created in Step 4. **Note:** the navigation option (which indicates whether or not the category should be shown in the navigation bar) is only sent to the server if the checkbox is selected. Therefore, PHP's `isset()` function is used to check if a value for this form control was sent and then an equality operator checks if its value is 1. If so, the `navigation` key will hold the value 1; if not, it will hold 0.

12. The category name and description are validated using the `is_text()` function in the `validate.php` include file. If they are invalid, error messages are stored in the `$errors` array.

13. The values in the `$errors` array are joined together and stored in a variable called `$invalid`.

On the next page, you see how the page decides whether or not to save the data to the database.

```php
<?php
// Part A: Setup
declare(strict_types = 1);                           // Use strict types
include '../includes/database-connection.php';       // Database connection
include '../includes/functions.php';                 // Include functions
include '../includes/validate.php';                  // Include validation


// Initialize variables
$id = filter_input(INPUT_GET, 'id', FILTER_VALIDATE_INT); // Get id and validate
$category = [
    'id'          => $id,
    'name'        => '',
    'description' => '',
    'navigation'  => false,
];                                                   // Initialize category array
$errors = [
    'warning'     => '',
    'name'        => '',
    'description' => '',
];                                                   // Initialize errors array

// If there was an id, page is editing the category, so get current category
if ($id) {                                           // If got an id
    $sql = "SELECT id, name, description, navigation
            FROM category
            WHERE id = :id;";                        // SQL statement
    $category = pdo($pdo, $sql, [$id])->fetch();     // Get category data
    if (!$category) {                                // If no category found
        redirect('categories.php', ['failure' => 'Category not found']); // Show error
    }
}


// Part B: Get and validate form data
if ($_SERVER['REQUEST_METHOD'] == 'POST') {          // If form submitted
    $category['name']        = $_POST['name'];       // Get name
    $category['description'] = $_POST['description']; // Get description
    $category['navigation']  = (isset($_POST['navigation'])
        and ($_POST['navigation'] == 1)) ? 1 : 0;    // Get navigation

    // Check if all data is valid and create error messages if it is invalid
    $errors['name'] = (is_text($category['name'], 1, 24))
        ? '' : 'Name should be 1-24 characters.';         // Validate name
    $errors['description'] = (is_text($category['description'], 1, 254))
        ? '' : 'Description should be 1-254 characters.'; // Validate description

    $invalid = implode($errors);                     // Join error messages
```

SAVING CATEGORY DATA

In Part C of this page, the `category.php` file determines whether or not the database should save the data and, if so, whether a new category should be added or an existing category updated.

1. An `if` statement checks if `$invalid` contains text. If it does, the condition evaluates into `true`, indicating that there are errors the user needs to correct. The subsequent code block stores a warning message in the `$errors` array.

2. Otherwise, the data is valid and can be processed.

3. The data from the `$category` array is copied into the `$arguments` variable. This is done because:

- When the `pdo()` function runs the SQL statement, it uses the values that were saved in `$category` to replace the placeholders.
- But, the SQL statement does not always need all of the elements that are stored in the `$category` array, and the `pdo()` function will not run if some of the elements are not removed (see Step 9).

4. If `$id` holds a number (which is treated as `true`), it means the page is updating an existing category.

5. The `$sql` variable holds the SQL statement to update the category. It starts with the `UPDATE` command and the name of the table to update.

6. The `SET` clause is followed by the names of the columns that will be updated and placeholders that will be replaced with the values for those columns.

7. The `WHERE` clause indicates the id of the row in the `category` table that should be updated.

8. If `$id` did not hold a number, it means the page is adding a new category to the database.

9. PHP's `unset()` function removes the element that holds the article id from the `$arguments` array. This is done because the array of data holding the values used to replace the placeholders in the SQL statement cannot contain extra elements.

10. The `$sql` variable holds the SQL statement to create a new category. It starts with:

- `INSERT` to add a new row to the database
- `INTO` followed by the name of the table that the data is going to be added to
- The names of the columns that will be given values, written in parentheses

11. The `VALUES` command is followed by the names of the placeholders that represent the new values. They are also written in parentheses.

12. The SQL statement is run in a `try` block because the category name has a uniqueness constraint and, if the user tried to supply a name that was already used, an exception would be thrown.

13. The `pdo()` function executes the SQL statement.

14. If the code in the `try` block is still running, the SQL statement was successfully executed, so the `redirect()` function (see p495) is called. The first argument indicates that the user should be sent back to the `categories.php` page. The second argument is an array indicating that the category was saved: `['success'=> 'Category saved']` The `redirect()` function will take this data and tell the browser to request the following page: `category.php?success=Category%20saved`

```
    // Part C: Check if data is valid, if so update database
①  if ($invalid) {                                        // If data is invalid
        $errors['warning'] = 'Please correct errors';     // Create error message
②  } else {                                               // Otherwise
③      $arguments = $category;                            // Set arguments array for SQL
④      if ($id) {                                         // If there is an id
⑤          $sql = "UPDATE category
⑥                     SET name = :name, description = :description,
                           navigation = :navigation
⑦                   WHERE id = :id;";                     // SQL to update category
⑧      } else {                                           // If there is no id
⑨          unset($arguments['id']);                       // Remove id from category array
⑩          $sql = "INSERT INTO category (name, description, navigation)
⑪                     VALUES (:name, :description, :navigation);"; // Create category
        }

        // When running the SQL, three things can happen:
        // Category saved | Name already in use | Exception thrown for other reason
⑫      try {                                              // Start try block to run SQL
⑬          pdo($pdo, $sql, $arguments);                   // Run SQL
⑭          redirect('categories.php', ['success' => 'Category saved']); // Redirect
⑮      } catch (PDOException $e) {                        // If a PDO exception was raised
⑯          if ($e->errorInfo[1] === 1062) {              // If error is duplicate entry
⑰              $errors['warning'] = 'Category name already in use'; // Store error message
⑱          } else {                                       // Otherwise unexpected error
                throw $e;                                 // Re-throw exception
            }
        }
    }
}
?>
```

Redirecting the visitor to the `categories.php` when the category has been saved stops the user from submitting the data again or refreshing the page.

15. If the category data could not be saved, an exception will have been thrown, and the PHP interpreter will run the code in the `catch` block. The purpose of the `catch` block is to check if the exception was thrown because the category name was not unique. Inside the `catch` block, the exception object will be stored in a variable called $e.

16. The condition of an `if` statement checks the `errorInfo` property of the exception object, which holds an indexed array. An error code is stored in the element whose key is 1. If the error code is 1062, it indicates that the uniqueness constraint has been broken and the category name is already in use.

17. An error message is stored in the $errors array telling the user the category name is already in use.

18. If the exception object has a different error code, the exception is re-thrown and will be handled by the default exception handling function.

A FORM TO CREATE OR EDIT CATEGORY DATA

Part D of the process involves showing the visitor a form that they can use to create or edit category information. The same form is shown to the user whether they are creating or editing a category.

1. The `action` attribute of the opening `<form>` tag points to the same page (`category.php`). The query string holds a key called `id`, and its value is the value stored in the `$id` attribute. If the category has already been created, it will hold the id of the category; if not, it will be `null`. The form is sent using HTTP POST.

2. If the form had been submitted and the data was not valid or if the category name was already in use, an error message would have been stored in the `$errors` array as a value for the `warning` key. An `if` statement checks if an error message is present.

3. If so, it will be displayed above the form.

4. A text input allows the user to enter or update the category name. If a name has already been provided, it is shown in the `value` attribute of the text input. The `html_escape()` function ensures that any reserved HTML characters in that value are replaced with entities. This prevents the risk of an XSS attack.

When the page first loads to create a new category, the user will not have supplied any category data. This is why it was important to initialize the `$category` array in Part A (specifying key names and setting their values to blank strings) so that the page has values it can display in the form controls.

5. The `$errors` array was also initialized in Part A. It has an element for each text input. If the form was submitted and the category name was not valid, the value associated with the `name` key would contain an error message describing the issue and this would be shown under the text input.

If the form was not submitted, or there were no errors, it would hold blank string (because it was initialized in Part A) and the blank string is shown under the text input. (If the `$errors` array had not been initialized in Part A, trying to display this message would result in an `Undefined index` error.)

6. A `<textarea>` input allows the user to provide a description for the category. If a value has already been provided, it is displayed between the opening and closing tags.

7. If there was a problem validating the description, the error message is shown beneath it.

8. A checkbox indicates whether or not the category name should be displayed in the navigation.

9. A ternary operator checks if the navigation option has been given a value of 1. If so, it adds the `checked` attribute to the checkbox input to select it. If not, it writes out a blank string instead.

10. A submit button is added to the end of the form.

```php
<?php include 'includes/admin-header.php'; ?>
  <main class="container admin" id="content">
①     <form action="category.php?id=<?= $id ?>" method="post" class="narrow">

      <h2>Edit Category</h2>
②     <?php if ($errors['warning']) { ?>
③       <div class="alert alert-danger"><?= $errors['warning'] ?></div>
      <?php } ?>

      <div class="form-group">
        <label for="name">Name: </label>
        <input type="text" name="name" id="name"
④               value="<?= html_escape($category['name']) ?>" class="form-control">
⑤       <span class="errors"><?= $errors['name'] ?></span>
      </div>

      <div class="form-group">
        <label for="description">Description: </label>
        <textarea name="description" id="description" class="form-control">
⑥         <?= html_escape($category['description']) ?></textarea>
⑦       <span class="errors"><?= $errors['description'] ?></span>
      </div>

      <div class="form-check">
⑧       <input type="checkbox" name="navigation" id="navigation"
                value="1" class="form-check-input"
⑨               <?= ($category['navigation'] === 1) ? 'checked' : '' ?>>
        <label class="form-check-label" for="navigation">Navigation</label>
      </div>

⑩     <input type="submit" value="save" class="btn btn-primary btn-save">

    </form>
  </main>
<?php include 'includes/admin-footer.php'; ?>
```

DELETING A CATEGORY

When users click on the link to delete a category, the page gets the category name from the database and shows it to the user, asking them to confirm that they want to delete it (this prevents someone accidentally clicking a link that deletes a category).

If the user confirms that they want to delete the category, the page reloads and tries to delete it. If this succeeds, the user is sent to `categories.php`, and they are shown a message to say that it worked.

1. Strict types are enabled and the required files are included.

2. `filter_input()` checks for the name `id` in the query string. If it is present and holds a valid integer, it is stored in `$id`. If its value is not a valid integer, `$id` stores `false`. If it is not present, `$id` stores `null`.

3. The `$category` variable will hold the name of the category; it is initialized to hold a blank string.

4. An `if` statment checks if the value in `$id` is *not* equivalent to `true` (if it was set to `false` or `null` in Step 2). If so, the user is sent to `categories.php` with a message saying the category was not found.

5. If the page is still running, the `$sql` variable stores a SQL query to get the category name.

6. The `pdo()` function runs the SQL query and the `fetchColumn()` method tries to get the category name. If the category was found, its name is stored in `$category`. If not, `fetchColumn()` returns `false`.

7. An `if` statement checks if the value in `$category` is `false`. If it is, the user is sent to `categories.php` with a message saying the category was not found.

8. If the form has been submitted...

9. A `try` block is created to delete the category.

10. The SQL to delete the category is stored in `$sql`.

11. The `pdo()` function is used to delete the category.

12. If the SQL statement runs without error, the `redirect()` function is used to send the user to `categories.php`, with a message confirming that the category was deleted.

13. If an exception was thrown when running the SQL statement, the `catch` block runs.

14. If the error code is 1451, an integrity constraint is preventing the category being deleted (because the category still contains articles).

15. In this case, the `redirect()` function is used to send the visitor to the `categories.php` page with a failure message telling them that the category contains articles that must be moved or deleted first.

16. Otherwise the error is re-thrown, and it will be handled by the default exception handler.

17. The form is used to show the category name and ask the user to confirm that the category should be deleted. The `action` attribute on the `<form>` tag submits the form to `category-delete.php`. The query string holds the id of the category to delete.

18. The name of the category to delete is shown.

19. The submit button is used to confirm that the category can be deleted.

```php
<?php
declare(strict_types = 1);                                  // Use strict types
include '../includes/database-connection.php';              // Database connection
include '../includes/functions.php';                        // Include functions

$id = filter_input(INPUT_GET, 'id', FILTER_VALIDATE_INT);   // Get and validate id
$category = '';                                             // Initialize category name

if (!$id) {                                                 // If no valid id
    redirect('categories.php', ['failure' => 'Category not found']); // Redirect + error
}

$sql = "SELECT name FROM category WHERE id = :id;";         // SQL to get category name
$category = pdo($pdo, $sql, [$id])->fetchColumn();          // Get category name
if (!$category) {                                           // If no category
    redirect('categories.php', ['failure' => 'Category not found']); // Redirect + error
}

if ($_SERVER['REQUEST_METHOD'] == 'POST') {                 // If form was submitted
    try {                                                   // Try to delete data
        $sql = "DELETE FROM category WHERE id = :id;";      // SQL to delete category
        pdo($pdo, $sql, [$id]);                             // Delete category
        redirect('categories.php', ['success' => 'Category deleted']); // Redirect
    } catch (PDOException $e) {                             // Catch exception
        if ($e->errorInfo[1] === 1451) {                   // If integrity constraint
            redirect('categories.php', ['failure' => 'Category contains articles that
            must be moved or deleted before you can delete it']); // Redirect
        } else {                                           // Otherwise
            throw $e;                                       // Re-throw exception
        }
    }
}?>
<?php include 'includes/admin-header.php'; ?>

  <main class="container admin" id="content">
    <h2>Delete Category</h2>
    <form action="category-delete.php?id=<?= $id ?>" method="POST" class="narrow">
      <p>Click confirm to delete the category <?= html_escape($category) ?></p>
      <input type="submit" name="delete" value="confirm" class="btn btn-primary">
      <a href="categories.php" class="btn btn-danger">cancel</a>
    </form>
  </main>


<?php include 'includes/admin-footer.php'; ?>
```

CREATING AND EDITING ARTICLES

The `article.php` file used to create and edit articles shares a very similar flow of control with `category.php`, but it has to collect more data and it also allows users to upload images, which adds complexity.

The `article.php` file allows users to:

- Create or edit text for an article
- Upload an image for the article

It is more complicated than `category.php` because:

- More data is stored about each article, so there is more data to collect and validate.
- Data about the article ties to data in other tables (the category and member who wrote it).
- Users can optionally upload an image for the article with alt text that describes it.

To save an article and its image in the database, the PHP code has to work with both the `article` and `image` tables.

Because SQL can only insert new rows of data into one table at a time, the SQL statements used to create and edit an article will use **transactions**.

Transactions allow the database to check if changes in a set of SQL statements will run successfully, and it will only save the changes if they all do. If there is a problem with just one SQL statement in the transaction, none of the changes will be saved.

As you have seen, the flow of control determines which statements run. The ability to upload images could make the flow of control much more complex. Imagine a user has already uploaded an article and image; they might want edit this data and:

- Update the article, but leave the image as it is. This would just update the `article` table.

- Update the article and image. This would involve deleting the old image file and corresponding data from the `image` and `article` tables first, then uploading the new image file, then updating both the `article` and `image` tables with the new data.

- Just change the alt text of the image, nothing else. This would mean just updating the `image` table.

The more options the user has on a single page, the more complex the flow of control becomes, and the harder the code is to follow.

To prevent the flow of control from becoming too complex, you can restrict the number of actions that a user can perform on a single page. For example, users must delete an image before uploading a new one, and there is a separate page to edit the alt text.

When creating an article, users can supply an image and text at the same time.

NOTE: Most browsers do not allow server-side code to populate the HTML file upload control. Therefore, if an article is submitted, but it does not pass validation, users will need to select the image again.

When users have to upload the image again, they will also be forced to re-enter the alt text.

When updating an article:

- If the user has not uploaded an image, the part of the form that allows them to upload an image is shown (as above).

- If they have uploaded an image, they are shown the image and its alt text rather than the form.

Once an image has been uploaded, there are two links under the image that let users:

- Edit the alt text

- Delete the image (and alt text)

The articles.php page, which lists all of the articles, is included in the code download and works the same as the categories.php page, which you saw on p494-5.

The next two pages will introduce transactions, which are used in article.php.

It then takes eight pages to show how article.php works as it contains over 230 lines of code.

TRANSACTIONS: MULTIPLE SQL STATEMENTS

A transaction is used to group together a set of SQL statements. If all of the statements succeed, all of the changes are saved in the database. If any of them fail, none of the changes will be saved.

Some tasks require more than one SQL statement. For example, when an image is uploaded for an article, the PHP code must:

- Add the image data to the image table
- Get the ID that the database created for the image (this is created using the auto-increment feature)
- Add the ID of the new image to the article table in the image_id column.

Also, the database can only add data to one table at a time; therefore, whenever a new article is added, it must add data to the image and article tables using separate SQL statements.

When each of these SQL statements is run, each one is called an **operation**. A transaction represents a task that may involve multiple database operations.

By incorporating more than one operation into a transaction, PDO can check that all of the SQL statements in the transaction will run successfully:

- If they do not cause an exception, it can **commit** those changes to the database.

- If there is a problem executing any of the statements, PDO will throw an exception. The PHP code can then tell PDO to ensure that none of the changes are saved to the database. This is known as **rolling back** the transaction.

Transactions are performed using try and catch blocks.

- The try block contains the code that you want to try to run.

- The catch block is used to handle an exception if one is thrown in the try block.

The statements inside the try block tell PDO to:

- Start a transaction
- Run all of the the individual SQL statements that form the transaction
- Commit the changes to the database

If running any of the statements result in an exception, the PHP interpreter will immediately run the code that sits in the subsequent catch block. The catch block needs to:

- Use PDO to ensure the database rolls back any changes it made so that it contains the same data it did before the transaction was started.

- Re-throw the exception so that it can be caught by the default exception handling function.

This guarantees that either all of the SQL statements will be executed or, if an exception is raised in the try block, none of the changes will be stored.

The PDO object has three methods that allow you to begin a transaction, commit the changes to the database, or roll back the changes so that the database contains the same data it did before the changes were made.

Transactions utilize the three methods of the PDO object shown in the table on the right.

The first two are used in the **try** block; the third is used in the **catch** block.

METHOD	DESCRIPTION
beginTransaction()	Start a transaction
commit()	Save changes to the database
rollBack()	Undo changes in transaction

1. A **try** block contains the code to run all of the SQL statements in the transaction.

2. The first statement calls the **beginTransaction()** method of the PDO object to start the transaction.

3. This is followed by the code to run the SQL statements involved in the transaction.

4. The last statement in the **try** block calls the PDO object's **commit()** method to save the changes.

5. If an exception is thrown while any of the SQL statements are running, the code in the **try** block stops running and the subsequent **catch** block handles the exception.

6. The PDO object's **rollBack()** method is called to ensure that none of the changes in the **try** block are stored in the database.

7. The exception object is re-thrown so that it can be handled by the default exception handler function.

```
① try {
②     $pdo->beginTransaction();
③     // Run SQL statements here
④     $pdo->commit();
⑤ } catch (PDOException $e) {
⑥     $pdo->rollBack();
⑦     throw $e;
   }
```

ARTICLES: SET UP PAGE (PART A)

The `article.php` page uses a similar flow of control to `category.php`. If the query string:

- Has a name called `id`, its value should be the id of an article that the user is trying to edit.
- Does not have a name called `id`, it means the page is being used to create a new article.

1. Strict types are declared and required files included.

2. The upload folder path is held in `$uploads` (p306). Permitted image types are stored in `$file_types`. Permitted file extensions are stored in `$file_exts`. Their maximum file size is saved in `$max_size`.

3. The `filter_input()` function checks for a name called `id` in the query string. If it holds a valid integer, it is stored in `$id`. If it holds an invalid value, `$id` stores `false`. If it is not present, `$id` holds `null`.

4. To check if a file was uploaded, the page tries to get the temporary location of the file and store it in `$temp`. The null-coalescing operator is used to store a blank string in `$temp` if an image was not uploaded.

5. The `$destination` variable is initialized. If an image has been uploaded, it will be updated to hold the path for where the image should be saved.

6. The `$article` array is declared and initialized with default values. These default values give the form in Part D something to show when a user is about to create a new article (but has not yet supplied values). To fit the example code onto the right-hand page, each line of code declares two elements of the array; in the code download, each one is on a new line.

7. The `$errors` array is initialized with blank strings. Values in this array are shown after each form control.

8. An if statement checks if an id was provided in the query string. If so, the page is editing an article and the article data must be collected from the database.

9. `$sql` stores the SQL query to get the article data.

10. The `pdo()` function runs the SQL statement, and the `PDOStatement` object's `fetch()` method collects the article data. The values it returns overwrite the data stored in the `$article` array created in Step 6. If the article is not found, `$article` will hold `false`.

11. If the `$article` variable holds the value `false`, the user is redirected to `articles.php` with a failure message stating that the article could not be found.

12. If an image had been saved for the article, the `$article` array's `image_file` element will have a value, so `$saved_image` is given a value of `true`. If there is no image, it is given the value `false`.

13. All authors and categories are collected from the database. They are used to create drop down boxes to select the author and category, and to validate the selected values. First, `$sql` holds a SQL query to get the id, forename and surname of every member.

14. The `pdo()` function runs the query, and the `PDOStatement` object's `fetchAll()` method collects the results and stores them in the `$authors` variable. (An indexed array is returned, and the value for each element is an associative array of member details.)

15. Next the `$sql` variable holds the SQL query to get the id and name of all of the categories.

16. The `pdo()` function runs the query, and the `PDOStatement` object's `fetchAll()` method gets the category data; they are stored in `$categories`.

```php
<?php
// Part A: Setup
declare(strict_types = 1);                                       // Use strict types
include '../includes/database-connection.php';                   // Database connection
include '../includes/functions.php';                             // Functions
include '../includes/validate.php';                              // Validate functions
$uploads = dirname(__DIR__, 1) . DIRECTORY_SEPARATOR . 'uploads' . DIRECTORY_SEPARATOR;
$file_types = ['image/jpeg', 'image/png', 'image/gif',];         // Allowed types
$file_exts  = ['jpg', 'jpeg', 'png', 'gif',];                    // Allowed extensions
$max_size   = 5242880;                                           // Max file size
// Initialize variables that the PHP code needs
$id          = filter_input(INPUT_GET, 'id', FILTER_VALIDATE_INT); // Get id + validate
$temp        = $_FILES['image']['tmp_name'] ?? '';               // Temporary image
$destination = '';                                               // Where to save file
// Initialize variables that the HTML page needs
$article = [
    'id'          => $id,   'title'        => '',
    'summary'     => '',    'content'      => '',
    'member_id'   => 0,     'category_id' => 0,
    'image_id'    => null,  'published'    => false,
    'image_file'  => '',    'image_alt'    => '',
];                                                               // Article data
$errors  = [
    'warning' => '', 'title'    => '', 'summary'    => '', 'content'   => '',
    'author'  => '', 'category' => '', 'image_file' => '', 'image_alt' => '',
];                                                               // Error messages
// If there was an id, page is editing an article, so get current article data
if ($id) {                                                       // If have id
    $sql     = "SELECT a.id, a.title, a.summary, a.content,
                       a.category_id, a.member_id, a.image_id, a.published,
                       i.file    AS image_file,
                       i.alt     AS image_alt
                FROM article    AS a
                LEFT JOIN image AS i ON a.image_id = i.id
                WHERE a.id = :id;";                              // SQL to get article
    $article = pdo($pdo, $sql, [$id])->fetch();                  // Get article data
    if (!$article) {                                             // If no article
        redirect('articles.php', ['failure' => 'Article not found']); // Redirect
    }
}
$saved_image = $article['image_file'] ? true : false;           // Has an image been uploaded
// Get all members and all categories
$sql         = "SELECT id, forename, surname FROM member;";      // SQL to get all members
$authors     = pdo($pdo, $sql)->fetchAll();                      // Get all members
$sql         = "SELECT id, name FROM category;";                 // SQL to get all categories
$categories  = pdo($pdo, $sql)->fetchAll();                      // Get all categories
```

Circled numbers in left margin: ① ② ③ ④ ⑤ ⑥ ⑦ ⑧ ⑨ ⑩ ⑪ ⑫ ⑬ ⑭ ⑮ ⑯

ARTICLES: GET AND VALIDATE DATA (PART B)

These two pages show the code for Part B, which collects and validates the data that the user sent.

1. An `if` statement checks if the form was posted.

2. The `image_file` element is added to the `$errors` array and a ternary operator assigns it a value. If a file could not be uploaded because it was larger than the maximum upload file size in `php.ini` or `.htaccess`, it stores an error; otherwise it stores a blank string.

3. An `if` statement checks if a file was uploaded and there were no errors. If so, the file will be validated.

4. Because an image has been uploaded, its alt text is collected and stored in the `$article` array.

5. If the image's media type is an allowed file type (set in Step 2 on the previous page), a blank string is added to the value in the `image_file` element of the `$errors` array. If not, an error message is added.

6. If the file's extension is allowed (set in Step 2 on the previous page), a blank string is added to the value in the `image_file` element of the `$errors` array. If not, an error message is added.

7. If the file is larger than the maximum size (set in Step 2 on the previous page), a message saying that it is too big is added to the value in `image_file`.

8. A key called `image_alt` is added to the `$errors` array. If the alt text is 1 - 254 characters long it stores a blank string; if not it stores an error message.

9. An `if` statement checks if the `image_file` and `image_alt` keys of the `$errors` array are both empty. If so, the image can be processed.

10. The `create_filename()` function (which is in `functions.php` and was introduced on p296-7) removes unwanted characters from the filename and makes sure that it is unique. The name is stored in the `image_file` key of the `$article` array.

11. The `$desination` variable holds the path to where the image will be uploaded. This is created by joining the path to the uploads folder (stored in the `$uploads` variable in Step 2 on the previous page) to the filename created in the previous step.

12. The article data is collected from the form. If an article is being updated, these values overwrite the existing ones that were collected from the database in Steps 9-10 on the previous page.

13. The option to publish the article is a checkbox. It is only sent to the server if it has been checked. A value of 1 is assigned if it was checked and 0 if not. This is because 0 and 1 are the values the database stores to represent boolean values of `true` and `false`.

14. Each piece of text is validated with the functions that were created in Chapter 6. If the data is valid, the element stores a blank string. Otherwise, it stores an error message for that form control.

15. The `is_member_id()` and `is_category_id()` functions have been added to the `validate.php` file. They loop through the array of members and categories that were collected in Steps 13-16 on the previous page to check if the value provided is valid.

16. The values in the `$errors` array are joined into one string using PHP's `implode()` function and saved in a variable called `$invalid`. This will be used to tell if the data should be saved to the database or not.

```php
      // Part B: Get and validate form data
①    if ($_SERVER['REQUEST_METHOD'] == 'POST') {                        // If form submitted
          // If file bigger than limit in php.ini or .htaccess store error message
②        $errors['image_file'] = ($_FILES['image']['error'] === 1) ? 'File too big ' : '';

          // If image was uploaded, get image data and validate it
③        if ($temp and $_FILES['image']['error'] === 0) {              // If file uploaded
④            $article['image_alt'] = $_POST['image_alt'];              // Get alt text
              // Validate image file
⑤            $errors['image_file'] .= in_array(mime_content_type($temp), $file_types)
                  ? '' : 'Wrong file type. ';                           // Check file type
              $ext = strtolower(pathinfo($_FILES['image']['name'], PATHINFO_EXTENSION));
⑥            $errors['image_file'] .= in_array($ext, $file_extensions)
                  ? '' : 'Wrong file extension. ';                      // Check extension
⑦            $errors['image_file'] .= ($_FILES['image']['size'] <= $max_size)
                  ? '' : 'File too big. ';                              // Check size
⑧            $errors['image_alt']  = (is_text($article['image_alt'], 1, 254))
                  ? '' : 'Alt text must be 1-254 characters.';          // Check alt text
              // If image file is valid, specify the location to save it
⑨            if ($errors['image_file'] === '' and $errors['image_alt'] === '') { // If valid
⑩                $article['image_file'] = create_filename($_FILES['image']['name'], $uploads);
⑪                $destination = $uploads . $article['image_file'];      // Destination
              }
          }

          // Get article data
          $article['title']       = $_POST['title'];                   // Title
          $article['summary']     = $_POST['summary'];                 // Summary
⑫        $article['content']     = $_POST['content'];                 // Content
          $article['member_id']   = $_POST['member_id'];               // Author
          $article['category_id'] = $_POST['category_id'];             // Category
          $article['published']   = (isset($_POST['published'])
⑬            and ($_POST['published'] == 1)) ? 1 : 0;                  // Is it published?

          // Validate article data and create error messages if it is invalid
          $errors['title']    = is_text($article['title'], 1, 80)
              ? '' : 'Title must be 1-80 characters';
          $errors['summary']  = is_text($article['summary'], 1, 254)
⑭            ? '' : 'Summary must be 1-254 characters';
          $errors['content']  = is_text($article['content'], 1, 100000)
              ? '' : 'Article must be 1-100,000 characters';
          $errors['member']   = is_member_id($article['member_id'], $authors)
              ? '' : 'Please select an author';
⑮        $errors['category'] = is_category_id($article['category_id'], $categories)
              ? '' : 'Please select a category';
⑯        $invalid = implode($errors);                                 // Join errors
```

ARTICLES: SAVE CHANGES (PART C)

These two pages show the code for Part C.

1. An if statement checks if $invalid contains any error messages. If it does, the $errors array stores a message telling users to correct the form errors.

2. If not, the data was valid and can be processed.

3. The data in $article is copied to $arguments. The pdo() function will use the values in $arguments. The HTML form in Part D uses the values in $article.

4. A try block holds the code to update the database.

5. A transaction is started because two SQL statements are needed to create or update an article. If one fails, both should fail.

6. If $destination contains a value (Step 11 p513) an image was uploaded. The image must be processed *before* the article data because the article table needs to store the id that is created for the image.

7. Imagick is used to resize and save the image:
- An Imagick object is created to represent the uploaded image (its path is in $temp - Step 4 p511).
- It is resized to 1200 x 700 pixels
- The image is saved to the path in $destination

8. $sql holds the SQL statement to add the image filename and alt text to the database's image table.

9. The pdo() function runs the SQL statement. The arguments (the image file and alt text) are passed to the pdo() function as an indexed array.

10. The image's id is collected using the PDO object's lastInsertId() method and stored in the image_id key of the $arguments array (created in Step 3).

11. The elements with the keys image_file and image_alt are removed from the $arguments array because the array must only contain one element for each placeholder in the second SQL statement.

12. An if statement checks if an id was specified. If so, an article is being updated and the $sql variable holds a SQL statement to update the database.

13. If there is no id, a new article is being created so id is removed from the $arguments array and $sql holds the SQL to add a new article to the database.

14. The pdo() function runs the SQL statement.

15. The PDO object's commit() method is called to save both changes in the transaction to the database.

16. If the code is still running, the article saved and redirect() sends the user to articles.php.

17. If PDO throws an exception in the try block, the catch block runs. The exception object is stored in $e.

18. The PDO object's rollBack() method prevents the database saving the changes in the transaction.

19. If an image was saved to the server in Step 7, PHP's unlink() method is used to delete it.

20. If the PDOException object's error code is 1062, the title is in use, so an error is stored in $errors.

21. Otherwise the exception is re-thrown.

22. If the next line runs, the article must have contained invalid data. If the article already had an image (see Step 12 p511), it is kept in the $article array. If not, image_file is set to a blank string.

```php
            // Part C: Check if data is valid, if so update database
①    if ($invalid) {                                                    // If invalid
            $errors['warning'] = 'Please correct the errors below';    // Store message
②    } else {                                                          // Otherwise
③        $arguments = $article;                                        // Save article data
④        try {                                                         // Try to insert data
⑤            $pdo->beginTransaction();                                 // Start transaction
⑥            if ($destination) {                                       // If have valid image
⑦                $imagick = new \Imagick($temp);                       // Create Imagick object
                 $imagick->cropThumbnailImage(1200, 700);              // Create cropped image
                 $imagick->writeImage($destination);                   // Save file
⑧                $sql = "INSERT INTO image (file, alt)
                         VALUES (:file, :alt);";                       // SQL to add image
⑨                pdo($pdo, $sql, [$arguments['image_file'], $arguments['image_alt'],]);
⑩                $arguments['image_id'] = $pdo->lastInsertId();        // Get new image id
             }
⑪            unset($arguments['image_file'], $arguments['image_alt']); // Cut image data
             if ($id) {
                 $sql = "UPDATE article
⑫                       SET title = :title, summary = :summary, content = :content,
                             category_id = :category_id, member_id = :member_id,
                             image_id = :image_id, published = :published
                         WHERE id = :id;";                             // SQL to update article
             } else {
                 unset($arguments['id']);                              // Remove id
                 $sql = "INSERT INTO article (title, summary, content, category_id,
⑬                             member_id, image_id, published)
                         VALUES (:title, :summary, :content, :category_id, :member_id,
                             :image_id, :published);";                 // SQL to create article
             }
⑭            pdo($pdo, $sql, $arguments);                              // Run SQL to add article
⑮            $pdo->commit();                                           // Commit changes
⑯            redirect('articles.php', ['success' => 'Article saved']); // Redirect
⑰        } catch (PDOException $e) {                                   // If PDOException thrown
⑱            $pdo->rollBack();                                         // Roll back SQL changes
⑲            if (file_exists($destination)) {                         // If image file exists
                 unlink($destination);                                // Delete image file
             } // If the exception was a PDOException and it was an integrity constraint
             if ($e->errorInfo[1] === 1062) {
⑳                $errors['warning'] = 'Article title already used';   // Store warning
             } else {                                                  // Otherwise
㉑                throw $e;                                             // Rethrow exception
             }
         }
     } // If a new image uploaded but data is not valid, remove image from $article
㉒    $article['image_file'] = $saved_image ? $article['image_file'] : ''; ...
```

ARTICLES: FORM/MESSAGE (PART D)

The same form is shown to the user whether they are creating or editing an article.

NOTE: The form in the code download has more HTML elements and attributes that are used to label form controls and control the presentation of the form. They have been removed from the code on the right so that the important code can fit on one page, and to help you focus on what it is doing.

1. The `action` attribute of the opening `<form>` tag points to the `article.php` page. The query string holds a name called `id`; if the page is updating an existing article, then its value is the id of the article (which would have been stored in the `$id` attribute at the top of the file). The data is sent using HTTP POST.

2. If there is a value for the `warning` key of the `$errors` array, it will be shown to the user.

3. The form to upload an image is only shown if an image has *not* yet been provided for the article.

4. A file input allows visitors to upload an image.

5. If the `$errors` array contains an error message for this form control, it is displayed after the file input.

An equivalent step is performed after all of the form controls except the published checkbox.

6. A text input allows the visitor to provide alt text.

7. Otherwise, if an image has been uploaded (and the data was valid), the image is shown in the page followed by the alt text.

8. Beneath it are two links: the first allows users to edit the alt text; the second to delete the image.

9. The article title is supplied via a text input. If a value has already been provided, it is added to the `value` attribute. Any reserved characters are replaced with entities to prevent an XSS attack.

10. The summary uses a `<textarea>` element. If a summary has been provided, it is written out between the `<textarea>` tags using the `html_escape()` function to replace reserved characters with entities.

11. The main article content uses another `<textarea>` element. If a value has been provided, it is written out between the `<textarea>` tags.

12. The author select box displays a list of all the members who may have written the article.

13. It is built using a `foreach` loop which works through the array of all members (collected in Part A and stored in a variable called `$authors`).

14. An `<option>` element is added for each member.

15. The condition of a ternary operator checks if an author has been provided and their id matches the id of the current author being added to the select box. If so, the `selected` attribute is added to the option to select the current member as the article's author.

16. The member's name is shown in the option.

17. The array of categories stored in `$categories` is used to create the select box for categories.

18. A checkbox indicates whether or not the article should be published (displayed on the site). A ternary operator tests if the option has been checked; if so, the `checked` attribute is added to the element.

```php
<!-- Part D - Display form -->
```
① `<form action="article.php?id=<?= $id ?>" method="post" enctype="multipart/form-data">`
```php
  <h2>Edit Articles</h2>
```
②
```php
  <?php if ($errors['warning']) { ?>
    <div class="alert alert-danger"><?= $errors['warning'] ?></div>
  <?php } ?>
```

③ `  <?php if (!$article['image_file']) { ?>`
④ `    Upload image: <input type="file" name="image" class="form-control-file" id="image">`
⑤ `    <span class="errors"><?= $errors['image_file'] ?></span>`
⑥ `    Alt text: <input type="text" name="image_alt">`
```php
    <span class="errors"><?= $errors['image_alt'] ?></span>
  <?php } else { ?>
```
⑦
```php
   <label>Image:</label> <img src="../uploads/<?= html_escape($article['file']) ?>"
              alt="<?= html_escape($article['image_alt']) ?>">
    <p class="alt"><strong>Alt text:</strong> <?= html_escape($article['image_alt']) ?></p>
    <a href="alt-text-edit.php?id=<?= $article['id'] ?>">Edit alt text</a>
```
⑧
```php
    <a href="image-delete.php?id=<?= $id ?>">Delete image</a><br><br>
  <?php } ?>
```

⑨ `  Title: <input type="text" name="title" value="<?= html_escape($article['title']) ?>">`
⑩
```php
  <span class="errors"><?= $errors['title'] ?></span>
  Summary: <textarea name="summary"><?= html_escape($article['summary']) ?></textarea>
  <span class="errors"><?= $errors['summary'] ?></span>
```
⑪
```php
  Content: <textarea name="content"><?= html_escape($article['content']) ?></textarea>
  <span class="errors"><?= $errors['content'] ?></span>
```
⑫ `  Author: <select name="member_id">`
⑬ `    <?php foreach ($authors as $author) { ?>`
⑭ `      <option value="<?= $author['id'] ?>"`
⑮ `        <?= ($article['author_id'] == $author['id']) ? 'selected' : ''; ?>>`
⑯ `        <?= html_escape($author['forename'] . ' ' . $author['surname']) ?>`
```php
      </option>
    <?php } ?></select>
  <span class="errors"><?= $errors['author'] ?></span>
```
⑰
```php
  Category: <select name="category_id">
    <?php foreach ($categories as $category) { ?>
      <option value="<?= $category['id'] ?>"
        <?= ($article['category_id'] == $category['id']) ? 'selected' : ''; ?>>
        <?= html_escape($category['name']) ?>
      </option>
    <?php } ?></select>
  <span class="errors"><?= $errors['category'] ?></span>
```
⑱
```php
  <input type="checkbox" name="published" value="1"
    <?= ($article['published'] == 1) ? 'checked' : '' ?>> Published
  <input type="submit" name="create" value="save" class="btn btn-primary">
</form>
```

DELETING AN ARTICLE

The page to delete an article is like the one to delete a category, with a form to confirm it should be deleted.

1. The page declares strict types and includes the required files.

2. PHP's `filter_input()` function checks for a name called `id` in the query string. If it holds a valid integer, it is stored in `$id`. If it holds an invalid value, `$id` stores `false`. If it is not present, `$id` holds `null`.

3. If an id was not found, the user is redirected to `articles.php` with an error message.

4. `$article` is initialized with a value of `false`.

5. `$sql` stores the SQL to get the article title, image file, and image id.

6. The `pdo()` function runs the SQL and the data about the article is collected and stored in `$article`.

7. If the article data was not found, the user is redirected to `articles.php` with an error message.

8. An `if` statement checks if the form has been posted (to confirm that the article should be deleted).

9. If the form was submitted, a `try` block holds the code that will be used to delete the article.

10. A transaction is started because deleting the article can involve running three SQL statements.

11. An `if` statement checks if the article has an image.

12. If it does, `$sql` holds the SQL to set the `image_id` column of the `article` table for that article to `null`, and the `pdo()` function runs the statement.

13. `$sql` then holds the SQL to delete the image from the `image` table and the `pdo()` function runs that statement.

14. The `$path` variable stores the path to the image.

15. An `if` statement uses PHP's `file_exists()` function to check if the file can be found. If so, PHP's `unlink()` function deletes the file (see p228).

16. The `$sql` variable stores the SQL to delete the article from the `article` table and the `pdo()` function runs the statement.

17. If an exception was not thrown in the `try` block, the PDO object's `commit()` function is called to save all of the changes made by the SQL statements.

18. The user is sent to `articles.php`, with a success message to say the article was deleted.

19. If an exception was thrown while deleting the data, the `catch` block is run.

20. The PDO object's `rollBack()` function stops any changes in the SQL statements from being saved.

21. The exception is re-thrown so it can be handled by the default exception handling function.

22. When the page first loads, the form shows the title of the article and a submit button to confim that it should be deleted. The `action` attribute of the `<form>` tag uses the id of the article in the query string.

TRY: Create a page to delete an image from an article using the same approach shown in this file.
Next, create the page to edit the alt text.
Solutions for both tasks are in the code download.

```php
<?php
declare(strict_types = 1);                                      // Use strict types
require_once '../includes/database-connection.php';             // Database connection
require_once '../includes/functions.php';                       // Functions
$id = filter_input(INPUT_GET, 'id', FILTER_VALIDATE_INT);       // Validate id
if (!$id) {                                                      // If no valid id
    redirect('articles.php', ['failure' => 'Article not found']); // Redirect with error
}
$article = false;                                               // Initialize $article
$sql = "SELECT a.title, a.image_id, i.file AS image_file FROM article AS a
        LEFT JOIN image AS i ON a.image_id = i.id WHERE a.id = :id;";  // SQL
$article = pdo($pdo, $sql, [$id])->fetch();                     // Get article data
if (!$article) {                                                // If $article empty
    redirect('articles.php', ['failure' => 'Article not found']); // Redirect
}
if ($_SERVER['REQUEST_METHOD'] == 'POST') {                     // If form was submitted
    try {                                                       // Try to delete
        $pdo->beginTransaction();                               // Start transaction
        if ($image_id) {                                        // If there was an image
            $sql = "UPDATE article SET image_id = null WHERE id = :article_id;"; // SQL
            pdo($pdo, $sql, [$id]);                             // Remove image from article
            $sql = "DELETE FROM image WHERE id = :id;";         // SQL to delete image
            pdo($pdo, $sql, [$article['image_id']]);           // Delete from image table
            $path = '../uploads/' . $article['image_file'];    // Set the image path
            if (file_exists($path)) {                           // If image file exists
                $unlink = unlink($path);                        // Delete image file
            }
        }
        $sql = "DELETE FROM article WHERE id = :id;";           // SQL to delete article
        pdo($pdo, $sql, [$id]);                                 // Delete article
        $pdo->commit();                                         // Commit transaction
        redirect('articles.php', ['success' => 'Article deleted']); // Redirect + success
    } catch (PDOException $e) {                                 // If exception thrown
        $pdo->rollBack();                                       // Roll back SQL changes
        throw $e;                                               // Re-throw exception
    }
}
?>
<?php include '../includes/admin-header.php' ?> ...
    <h2>Delete Article</h2>
    <form action="article-delete.php?id=<?= $id ?>" method="POST" class="narrow">
      <p>Click confirm to delete: <i><?= html_escape($article['title']) ?></i></p>
      <input type="submit" name="delete" value="Confirm" class="btn btn-primary">
      <a href="articles.php" class="btn btn-danger">Cancel</a>
    </form> ...
<?php include '../includes/admin-footer.php'; ?>
```

SUMMARY
UPDATING DATA IN A DATABASE

> User data must be collected and validated before being added to the database.

> The `PDOStatement` object's `execute()` method can run SQL statements that create, update or delete data.

> SQL can only add new data to one table at a time.

> The `PDO` object's `getLastInsertId()` method returns the id of a new row when it is added to the database.

> The `PDOStatement` object's `rowCount()` method returns how many table rows are affected when a SQL `INSERT`, `UPDATE`, or `DELETE` command is run.

> A transaction runs a series of SQL statements and only saves the changes if all of them run without error.

> If a SQL statement breaks a uniqueness constraint, a `PDOException` object is thrown. It will hold an error code that describes the cause of the exception.

D

EXTENDING THE SAMPLE APPLICATION

This final section shows how to implement features used by many websites. In doing so, you will learn how to add new functionality to a site and some advanced techniques.

If you asked five PHP programmers to create the same website, you would probably get five different solutions. This is because there is no single correct way to build a site, and there are many ways to organize the code that performs each of the tasks involved. There are, however, some best practices you can learn from and the design considerations in this section will guide you when creating your own projects.

Chapter 14 shows you how to rebuild parts of the sample site to make better use of classes. Experienced PHP developers often make extensive use of user-defined classes to group together the code that performs a related set of tasks.

Chapter 15 shows you how to find and use PHP classes that other programmers have written to perform specific tasks and then shared with the PHP community. Using them can save you from writing the code to perform the same tasks yourself.

Chapter 16 shows you how users can register as members of the site. Members will be able to log in, view pages that are tailored to them, and create their own posts. You will also learn how to restrict access to the admin pages so that only those with permission can use them.

Chapter 17 shows you how to make URLs for the site more readable and easier for search engines to index. It will also show you how to allow members of the site to comment on articles and indicate which articles they like.

Each of the remaining chapters has a new version of the sample site. Before reading on, you need to understand how those files are organized and some key terminology.

ABSOLUTE & RELATIVE PATHS

First, you will learn the difference between absolute and relative paths, and when each should be used.

HOW FILES ARE ORGANIZED

Next, you will learn how the files of the sample site have been re-organized. Files that the browser requests are all stored in a folder called a document root, but the other supporting PHP files (such as classes) are stored in a folder above the document root in order to improve security.

NEW SETUP FILES

This section introduces two new files that are commonly used when building sites:

- `config.php` holds settings that change when a site is installed on a new server
- `bootstrap.php` holds code that the site needs in order to run; it is included by every page of the site

HOW VARIABLES STORE DATA

Finally, it helps to understand how the PHP interpreter stores the data in variables.

One recurring theme throughout the final four chapters of this book is how programmers use classes to help organize their code.

The PHP pages that users request will create objects using these classes, and call their methods to perform tasks that the site needs to achieve.

There is not space to print every file of the sample site in each of the remaining chapters, so it will help if you have the code open when working through the rest of the book. This will let you compare the versions of the files in each chapter with the files in previous chapters to see where they have changed.

In Chapter 16, you will need to create a new version of the database with additional tables and data that are required to support the new features that are added to the site. The SQL to create the updated version of the database is included in the code download, and you will be reminded to create it at the start of Chapter 16.

ABSOLUTE AND RELATIVE PATHS

An **absolute path** describes the exact location of a file on a computer.
A **relative path** describes the location of one file in relation to another.

To understand how the files in the sample site are organized, it will help to clarify some terms:

- A **path** specifies the location of a file or directory (also known as a folder).

- The **root directory** is the topmost folder on a computer.

- An **absolute path** describes the location of a file or folder using the path from the root directory to it.

In the diagram on the right-hand page, you can see some of the sample code installed on a computer.

On **Mac** or **Linux**, the root directory is represented by a forward slash. Then further forward slashes separate each folder or file, so the absolute path to `files.php` is: `/Users/Jon/phpbook/section_b/c05/files.php`

On **Windows**, the root directory is a drive letter followed by a colon and a backslash; then a backslash separates each folder or file, so the absolute path to `files.php` would be:
`C:\phpbook\section_b\c05\files.php`

Absolute paths are precise, but they can:

- Get quite long, therefore involve a lot of typing
- Change when files move to a different computer

The folder holding the file that is currently running is called the **current working directory**. In the diagram on the right, when `files.php` is running, the current working directory is c05.

Relative paths describe the location of another file in relation to the current working directory.

The relative path to any other file in the same folder is just the filename. For example, this describes the relative location of `index.php` in the c05 folder:
`index.php`

To describe the path to a file in a child directory, use the name of the child directory, then a forward slash, then the name of the file in that directory. The relative path to `header.php` in the `includes` folder is:
`includes/header.php`

To go up a directory, use `../` The relative path to a file called `index.php` in the phpbook directory would be:
`../../index.php`

As this shows, relative paths require less typing than absolute paths. In addition, they often work when a site moves to a new server. For example, if the paths in the code download only reference files in the phpbook folder, the relative paths between the files and folders do not change when the code is run on different computers.

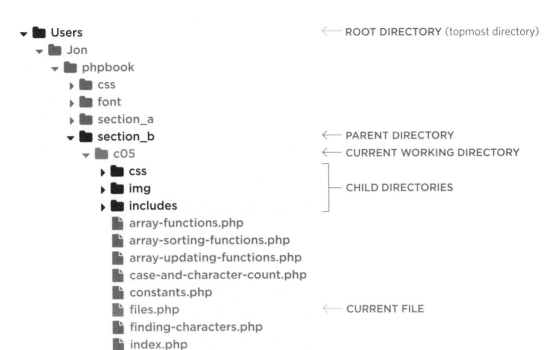

- **Users** ← ROOT DIRECTORY (topmost directory)
  - **Jon**
    - **phpbook**
      - css
      - font
      - section_a
      - **section_b** ← PARENT DIRECTORY
        - **c05** ← CURRENT WORKING DIRECTORY ─ CHILD DIRECTORIES
          - **css**
          - **img**
          - **includes**
          - array-functions.php
          - array-sorting-functions.php
          - array-updating-functions.php
          - case-and-character-count.php
          - constants.php
          - files.php ← CURRENT FILE
          - finding-characters.php
          - index.php

When a PHP file includes another file, it is good practice to use absolute paths. To understand why, consider this scenario:

- A PHP file in the c05 folder is requested
- It includes a PHP file in the section_a folder
- That file includes a third file with a relative path

The PHP interpreter looks for all three files relative to the c05 folder. It is like the code from the included files is copied and pasted into the file in c05. Here, the third file would not be found because a relative path from the section_a folder is not the same as a relative path from the c05 folder. Using absolute paths when including files prevents this.

Because absolute paths are longer (and require more typing), a site will often store the first part of the absolute path in a constant (p224-5). That constant can then be used to build absolute paths.

The **application root** folder is the top folder of the website's code. It is the absolute path to *this* folder that is often stored in the constant that is used to create paths to the include files. Below, you can see how the path to the application folder is stored in a constant called APP_ROOT:

- PHP's dirname() function (see p228) returns the path to the directory containing a file.

- The argument is PHP's built-in __FILE__ constant, which holds the absolute path to the current file.

So this statement stores the path to the folder containing the current file. If it were used in a file inside the c05 folder, then the APP_ROOT constant would hold the absolute path to the c05 folder. Because it is created by the PHP interpreter, it would still be correct if the site is moved onto a new server.

```php
define('APP_ROOT', dirname(__FILE__));
```

FILE STRUCTURE AND DOCUMENT ROOT

When a site goes live, all of the files that a browser can request must sit inside a folder called the **document root** folder. The PHP interpreter, however, is able to access files *above* the document root.

A web server has another kind of root folder known as the **document root** folder (or web root). This folder maps to a website's domain name. For example, if the URL for a home page of a site is:

```
http://example.org/index.php
```

The example.org web server would look for the `index.php` file in the site's document root folder. When the site is on a hosting company's servers, the absolute path to this file might be something like:

```
/var/www/example.org/htdocs/index.php
```
                              └──┬──┘
                        DOCUMENT ROOT

The document root folder on a web server can have different names but is usually a name like `htdocs`, `public`, `public_html`, `web`, `www`, or `wwwroot`.

Every file that a browser requests must be kept *in* the document root folder (or a child folder of it). That includes pages the user requests, any images or other media, and CSS and JavaScript files. The browser cannot request files *above* the document root.

Just like Mac and Linux operating systems use a forward slash to indicate the application root folder (the topmost folder on the computer), when URLs start with a forward slash, it indicates the document root; the topmost file the browser can access. This is why HTML links often start with a forward slash.

Because the code download has multiple versions of the sample site in different folders, you must *imagine* that the `public` folder in each of the remaining chapters is the document root folder of the sample site for that chapter, which would map to the site's domain name. The site will store this path in a constant called `DOC_ROOT` so it can be used where needed (as shown on p528). On a live site, the code could just use a forward slash instead.

Although the browser can only request files in the document root, the PHP interpreter can access files *above* the document root. In the remaining chapters:

- The files that visitors request via a URL are in the document root (`public` folder) for each chapter.
- Any file that the visitor cannot request via a URL (for example, function files and class definitions) are in folders *above* the document root. This improves security as it prevents users from accessing these files.

In Chapter 14, the `c14` folder would be the equivalent of the **application root** (the root folder for the application). There are two new folders that sit inside the application root but above the document root:

- `config` holds a file that will store any settings that can change when the site is moved to a new server.
- `src` holds the functions and a new file called `bootstrap.php`. It also has a child folder called `classes`, which contains the class definitions.

- **c14**   ← APPLICATION ROOT FOR CHAPTER
  - .htaccess
  - **config**
    - config.php   ← SETTINGS (change when site moves)
  - **public**   ← TREAT AS IF DOCUMENT ROOT
           (contains all files browsers can request)
    - **admin**
      - alt-text-edit.php
      - article-delete.php
      - article.php
      - articles.php
      - categories.php
      - category-delete.php
      - category.php
      - image-delete.php
      - index.php
    - **css**
    - **font**
    - **img**
    - **includes**
    - **js**
    - **uploads**
    - article.php
    - category.php
    - error.php
    - index.php
    - member.php
    - page-not-found.php
    - search.php
  - **src**   ← PHP FILES
           (contains files browsers cannot request)
    - **classes**
      - Article.php
      - Category.php
      - CMS.php
      - Database.php
      - Member.php
      - Validate.php
    - bootstrap.php
    - functions.php

KEY:
- ● Document root
- ● Inside document root
- ● Above document root

CONFIGURATION FILE

When a site is installed on a new server, some data may need to be updated. For example:

- Folder names/paths change; e.g., a document root folder may be called htdocs, content, or public.
- Database-driven sites need to know the location of the database used in the DSN, and the username and password of a database user account.

This is known as **configuration data** because it configures how the site runs. It is usually stored in variables or constants in one file. This makes it the only file that needs to be updated when the site is installed on a new server. In the sample application, the file is called config.php. **NOTE:** You must update the code in this file for each of the remaining chapters.

1. DEV is set to true if the site is in development, and false if it is live. This controls how errors are handled.

2. DOC_ROOT holds the path to what *would* be the document root folder (see p526).

3. ROOT_FOLDER holds the name of the document root folder (e.g., public, content, or htdocs).

4. The database connection settings are stored in variables and then the DSN is created.

5. MEDIA_TYPES holds the permitted file types. FILE_EXTENSIONS holds the allowed file extensions. MAX_SIZE is the maximum file size (in kilobytes). UPLOADS is the absolute path to the uploads folder.

section_d/c14/src/config.php `PHP`

```php
<?php
define('DEV', true);        // In development or live? Development = true | Live = false
define("DOC_ROOT", '/phpbook/section_d/c14/public/');    // Path from doc root to site
define("ROOT_FOLDER", 'public');                         // Name of document root folder
// Database settings
$type     = 'mysql';              // Type of database
$server   = 'localhost';          // Server the database is on
$db       = 'phpbook-1';          // Name of the database
$port     = '';                   // Port is usually 8889 in MAMP and 3306 in XAMPP
$charset  = 'utf8mb4';            // UTF-8 encoding using 4 bytes of data per character
$username = 'ENTER YOUR USERNAME';  // Enter YOUR username here
$password = 'ENTER YOUR PASSWORD';  // Enter YOUR password here
$dsn = "$type:host=$server;dbname=$db;port=$port;charset=$charset"; // DO NOT CHANGE
// File upload settings
define('MEDIA_TYPES', ['image/jpeg', 'image/png', 'image/gif',]); // Allowed file types
define('FILE_EXTENSIONS', ['jpeg', 'jpg', 'png', 'gif',]);        // Allowed extensions
define('MAX_SIZE', '5242880');                                    // Max file size
define('UPLOADS', dirname(__DIR__, 1) . DIRECTORY_SEPARATOR . ROOT_FOLDER .
    DIRECTORY_SEPARATOR . 'uploads' . DIRECTORY_SEPARATOR);       // DO NOT CHANGE
```

Labels in margin: ① ② ③ ④ ⑤

BOOTSTRAP FILE

In Chapter 13, every page of the site included multiple files, one of which created a PDO object. To save repeating this code on every page, each page will now start by including the file below, which will in turn:

- Include the `config.php` and `functions.php` files
- Set errror and exception handling functions and a new function that will load class definitions
- Create a CMS object, which all the pages will use to work with the database

When one file loads other files and creates objects that a site needs in order to run, it is often given a name such as `bootstrap.php` or `setup.php`.

Once the CMS object has been created, the database connection data is deleted so it cannot be used (or accidentally shown) elsewhere in the rest of the site.

1. The path to the application root folder (two levels above this file) is stored in the constant `APP_ROOT`.

2. `functions.php` and `config.php` are included.

3. PHP's `spl_autoload_register()` function (which you meet in Chapter 14) ensures the class definitions are only loaded if that page needs them.

4. An `if` statement checks if the site is *not* in development (it is live). If so, the default exception, error handling and shutdown functions are set.

5. A CMS object is created and stored in a variable called `$cms`. It will be used to work with the database.

6. PHP's `unset()` function removes variables holding database connection data so it cannot be re-used.

```
PHP                                                    section_d/c14/src/bootstrap.php

     <?php
①   define('APP_ROOT', dirname(__FILE__, 2));          // Application root directory
②   require APP_ROOT . '/resources/functions.php';     // Functions
     require APP_ROOT . '/resources/config.php';        // Configuration data

     spl_autoload_register(function($class)             // Set autoload function
     {
③       $path = APP_ROOT . '/src/classes/';            // Path to class definitions
         require $path . $class . '.php';               // Include class definition
     });
     if (DEV !== true) {
         set_exception_handler('handle_exception');     // Set exception handler
④       set_error_handler('handle_error');             // Set error handler
         register_shutdown_function('handle_shutdown'); // Set shutdown handler
     }
⑤   $cms = new CMS($dsn, $username, $password);         // Create CMS object
⑥   unset($dsn, $username, $password);                 // Remove database connection data
```

HOW VARIABLES STORE DATA

When a variable is created, the PHP interpreter stores its name and value separately. This helps it manage the memory that it uses more efficiently. To understand this, imagine that the values are stored in a set of lockers...

When a variable is created, its name is stored in a **symbol table** along with the number of a locker. The corresponding locker holds the value that the variable represents. E.g.:

1. $greeting is assigned a value
2. $welcome is then assigned the value that $greeting represents

```
$greeting = 'Hi';
$welcome  = $greeting;
```

Here, the symbol table will hold two variable names. Both point to the same locker (or the same memory location).

VARIABLE	LOCATION
$greeting	2
$welcome	2

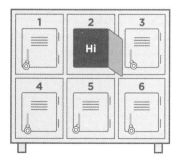

When either of these variables is assigned a new value, the PHP interpreter puts the new value into a new memory location. E.g.:

1. $greeting is assigned a value
2. $welcome is assigned the value that $greeting represents
3. $greeting is updated with a new value; the text 'Hello'

```
$greeting = 'Hi';
$welcome  = $greeting;
$greeting = 'Hello';
```

Here, the symbol table still has two variable names, but each one has its own memory location.

VARIABLE	LOCATION
$greeting	4
$welcome	2

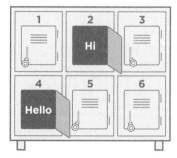

You can tell the PHP interpreter that a variable's value should use the same memory location as an existing variable. Then, if either variable is updated, the memory location they both share will be updated. To do this, place an ampersand before the name of that variable. This is called **assigning by reference**. E.g.:

```
$greeting = 'Hi';
$welcome  = &$greeting;
$greeting = 'Hello';
```

Now, the symbol table holds two variable names, and both point to the same memory location.

VARIABLE	LOCATION
$greeting	2
$welcome	2

Parameters of a function can use references to values that were created for variables that were declared in global scope, and objects always act as if they are assigned or passed by reference.

When a function runs, a new symbol table is created to hold the parameter and variable names that are declared in the function.

A function definition can specify that a parameter should use a memory location that was created for a global variable. This lets code in the function access/update the value stored in that global variable.

This is called **passing by reference** because it is passes the function a *reference* to where a variable's value is stored in memory (rather than passing it the value that the global variable represents).

To pass by reference, in the function definition, the parameter name is preceded by an ampersand.

```
$current_count = 0; // Global variable

function updateCounter(&$counter)
{
    $counter++;      // Add 1 to counter
}
```

Each time this function is called, it updates the value for the $current_count variable by 1. Note that the ampersand is only used in the function definition, it is not used when calling the function:

```
updateCounter($current_count);
```

Objects **always** act as if they are assigned by reference or passed by reference. For example, when the DateTime object is created below, the symbol table will store the name of the $start variable and the memory location where the object is stored:

```
$start = new DateTime('2021-01-01');
```

If the value of the $end variable is set using the object stored in the $start variable, both variables will point to the same memory location because the variables are being assigned by reference:

```
$end = $start;
```

Therefore, if the object stored in $start is updated, the value for $end is also updated because both variable names point to the same memory location:

```
$from->modify('+3 month');
```

Furthermore, when an object is used as an argument of a function or a method, the object acts as if it has been passed by reference (and does so without using an ampersand). This point is important to understand because, in the next chapter, several objects will share a reference to the same PDO object.

In the code download, the folder for the introduction to this section has a file to demonstrate the examples given on these two pages.

IN THIS SECTION

EXTENDING THE SAMPLE APPLICATION

14 REFACTORING & DEPENDENCY INJECTION

As a website grows, it is important to organize its code carefully. This chapter looks at how user-defined classes can improve the structure of the code so that it is easier to understand, maintain, and extend with new functionality.

15 NAMESPACES & LIBRARIES

Programmers often share code they have written to perform specific tasks using libraries and packages. You can use this code in your site rather than writing the functionality to perform the same tasks from scratch.

16 MEMBERSHIP

In this chapter you will learn how visitors can register as a member of the site. Their information will be stored in the database so that they can then log in to view pages that are tailored specifically to them.

17 ADDING FUNCTIONALITY

In the final chapter, you will learn how to add search engine friendly URLs. You will also see how to allow members to add comments to articles and indicate that they like them, both of which are features commonly seen on social networks.

14

REFACTORING & DEPENDENCY INJECTION

Refactoring is the process of improving the code in an application by restructuring it, without changing what it does, its features, or how it behaves.

Websites often use thousands of lines of code so organizing that code is very important. As sites grow and new features are added, it helps to revisit the code to refactor it. Refactoring involves improving the structure of the code so that it is easier to:

- Read and follow
- Maintain
- Extend with new features

In this chapter, the functionality of the site you met in the previous chapter will not change and the interface will look the same, however the SQL and the PHP code needed to work with the database will be moved out of the PHP pages that a user requests into a set of classes.

The PHP pages create objects using those classes, and call their methods to get or change data stored in the database. The classes group together the code that works with the database (rather than spread it across the site), making it easier to maintain the code and add new functionality. The chapter also introduces two new programming techniques:

- **Dependency injection (DI)** is used to ensure that any code that needs to access the database has a PDO object that it can use to work with the database.
- **Autoloading** tells the PHP interpreter that it should only load files holding class definitions when it needs to use a class to create an object, rather than using `include` or `require` statements that load the class files every time the page is requested (even if the page does not end up using them to create an object).

By the end of the chapter, the code for the CMS will be split across more files than the previous version, but it will be easier to find the code that performs each individual task.

USING OBJECTS TO WORK WITH THE DATABASE

The sample site uses three key concepts: articles, categories and members. A class is used to represent each of these concepts.

In Chapter 13, each PHP page in the sample site contained the SQL statements it needed to get or change data in the database. Those SQL statements were then run by calling the user-defined `pdo()` function that was introduced in Chapter 12.

In this chapter, the SQL statements and the code to call them have been moved into three classes:

- `Article` has methods that get, create, update, or delete article data in the database.

- `Category` has methods that get, create, update or delete category data in the database.

- `Member` has methods that get member data.

Each class definition is in its own file in the `src/classes` folder. The filenames are the class names followed by the `.php` file extension (e.g., the `Article` class is in a file called `Article.php`).

NOTE: The naming conventions in this chapter follow rules set by a group called the PHP Framework Interoperability Group (PHP-FIG). This group is made up of experienced PHP developers who create and maintain established PHP projects. The aim is to help those projects work well together, but their guidance is also adopted by many other PHP developers. For more about the group, see `http://php-fig.org`

In previous chapters, when each page held the SQL queries it needed to get data for that page, two or more pages could repeat very similar queries.

For example, the page that allows the public to view an article and the page that allows administrators to edit an article both used very similar SQL queries.

In this chapter, both pages will use the same `get()` method of the `Article` class.

Article

PROPERTY	DESCRIPTION
$db	Stores a Database object

METHOD	DESCRIPTION
get()	Get one article
getAll()	Get all article summaries
count()	Return total no. of articles
create()	Create a new article
update()	Update an existing article
delete()	Delete an article
imageDelete()	Delete image from article
altUpdate()	Update alt text for image
search()	Search articles
searchCount()	Number of search matches

Each class definition has its own PHP file in the `src/classes` folder. The filename is the name of the class, followed by the `.php` file extension.

As you will see, some methods have parameters that control things like whether they return all articles or just ones that:

- Have been published
- Belong in a specified category
- Were created by a specified author

Other parameters control things such as how many rows should be added to the result set.

These three classes are only used to create objects when they are needed. For example, every page creates a `Category` object so it can get the categories to show in the navigation. But a `Member` object is only created when a page shows a member's profile.

These classes all have a property called `$db`. When an object is created using them, the `$db` property stores an object that it can use to connect to the database and run the SQL statements.

Category

PROPERTY	DESCRIPTION
$db	Stores a Database object

METHOD	DESCRIPTION
get()	Get one category
getAll()	Get all categories
count()	Return total no. of categories
create()	Create a new category
update()	Update an existing category
delete()	Delete a category

Member

PROPERTY	DESCRIPTION
$db	Stores a Database object

METHOD	DESCRIPTION
get()	Get one member
getAll()	Get all members

NOTE: If you have not already done so, open the `config.php` file in the `resources` folder, and update the values of the variables that are used to connect to the database. Thesy should use the same details that were used in Chapters 12 and 13.

When you view the site, it will look the same as the previous version in Chapter 13, but it will use the new classes that you meet in this chapter.

DATABASE OBJECT

The `Database` object is created using the user-defined `Database` class. It **extends** the PDO class, so it has all the same properties and methods, plus a new `runSQL()` method which is used to run SQL statements.

In the previous section, each PHP page included `database-connection.php`, which created a PDO object that was stored in a variable called `$pdo`. Then, the pages called the user-defined `pdo()` function (defined in `functions.php`) to run SQL statements using that PDO object.

In this chapter, a new class called `Database` is used to create a `Database` object. This class extends the PDO object, meaning that the `Database` object inherits all of the methods and properties of the PDO object. It then adds one extra method, called `runSQL()` which performs the same task as the user-defined `pdo()` function that was used in Chapters 12 and 13.

So the new `Database` object is just a PDO object that has an extra method called `runSQL()` (which the code will use to run SQL statements).

Database

METHOD	DESCRIPTION
runSQL()	Runs a SQL statement

NOTE: Inheritance and dependency injection are examples of **design patterns**; solutions that can be applied to common programming problems. As you use classes more, it helps to learn more design patterns. For example, some people prefer to use a pattern called composition over inheritance.

The `Article`, `Category`, and `Member` objects shown on the previous two pages all need (or depend upon) a PDO object to connect to the database. Therefore, programmers call the PDO object a **dependency**.

As you saw on p530-31, when the PHP interpreter creates an object and stores it in a variable or a property of an object, it is actually storing the *location* of the object in the PHP interpreter's memory (not the object itself). Therefore, multiple variables or properties can all store the location of a single object.

When the page creates an `Article`, `Category` or `Member` object, it will store the location of the `Database` object in the `$db` property of that object. If the page then creates another one of these objects (`Article`, `Category` or `Member`), that object will also store the location of the same `Database` object in *its* `$db` property. This means that the `Article`, `Category` and `Member` objects can all share the same `Database` object (and, as you saw, the `Database` object is a PDO object with an extra method).

Programmers say that the dependency has been **injected** into the `Article`, `Category` and `Member` objects so that each one of them can use it. That is why this technique is called **dependency injection**.

Letting all of the objects in a page share one connection to the database is helpful because the PHP interpreter can only make a limited number of connections to the database at any one time.

CONTAINER OBJECT

The Article, Category, Member, and Database objects are all created using methods of a fifth object, which is called a **container object**. It gets this name because its properties store (or contain) the other objects.

In the introduction to this section, you saw that every page includes the bootstrap.php file (p529). That file creates a CMS object using a class called CMS, and stores it in a variable called $cms.

When the CMS object is created, its __construct() method runs and *it* creates a Database object and stores it in the CMS object's $db property (because *every* page of the site works with the database).

When a page needs to access article, category or member data, it creates an Article, Category or Member object using the CMS object's getArticle(), getCategory() or getMember() methods. These Article, Category and Member objects all share the same Database object.

CMS

PROPERTY	DESCRIPTION
$db	Stores a Database object
$article	Stores an Article object
$category	Stores a Category object
$member	Stores a Member object

METHOD	DESCRIPTION
getArticle()	Returns an Article object
getCategory()	Returns a Category object
getMember()	Returns a Member object

One of the aims of using these classes is to ensure that all work with the database happens through the CMS object and the objects it contains (rather than spreading it across the PHP pages the user requests).

Once bootstrap.php has created a CMS object, any page can get or change data in the database in just one statement. The statement below gets data about one article and stores it in a variable called $article.

$article = $cms->getArticle()->get($id);
   ①   ②   ③   ④

This uses method chaining (p457) because, when a method returns an object (like the CMS object's getArticle() method does), you can call a method of the object it returns in the same statement.

1. The $article variable will hold the article data that is returned from the database.

2. The bootstrap.php file will already have created a CMS object and stored it in a variable called $cms.

3. The CMS object's getArticle() method returns an Article object.

4. The Article object's get() method returns the data about an individual article as an array (which is stored in the $article variable).

CMS CONTAINER OBJECT

Every page includes `bootstrap.php`, which creates a CMS object.
The CMS object's methods create the `Article`, `Category`, and `Member`
objects and it allows them all to share the same `Database` object.

1. The CMS class starts with four properties that store the location of the four other objects that the CMS object can contain. Each of these properties is declared using the `protected` keyword so that the values they store can only be accessed by code in *this* object. They are all given a default value of `null`.

2. When an object is created using the CMS class, its `__construct()` method will automatically run. It needs three pieces of information so that it can create a `Database` object to connect to the database (these were stored in the `config.php` file on p528):

- The DSN stores the location of the database
- The username and password of a database user account are used to log into the database

3. The `__construct()` method creates a new object using the `Database` class and, as you just saw, a `Database` object is a PDO object that has been extended with one extra method.

The arguments needed to create a `Database` object are the same as those needed to create a PDO object; it needs the DSN and a username and password to connect to the database (which were supplied when the object was created in `bootstrap.php`, see p529).

The `Database` object that has been created is stored in the `$db` property of this CMS object.

Next, the three methods are used to return the `Article`, `Category` and `Member` objects that the CMS object can contain. Note how each one starts with an `if` statement; this ensures that a page never creates more than one of each of these objects.

4. The `getArticle()` method is defined. It returns an `Article` object used to get or change article data.

5. An `if` statement checks if the `$article` property of this CMS object has a value of `null`. If so, this page has not yet created an `Article` object and it must be created before it can be returned by this method.

6. An `Article` object is created using the `Article` class. The location of the `Database` object is passed to the `Article` class's constructor method (so that the `Article` object it creates can use the `Database` object stored in the `$db` property to access the database). The `Article` object that is created is then stored in the `$article` property of this object.

7. The `Article` object in the `$article` property of this object is returned so that it can be used by the code that called the `getArticle()` method.

The `getCategory()` and `getMember()` methods work just like the `getArticle()` method does, but they return a `Category` or `Member` object to work with category or member data.

```php
<?php
class CMS
{
    protected $db       = null;                    // Stores reference to Database object
    protected $article  = null;                    // Stores reference to Article object
    protected $category = null;                    // Stores reference to Category object
    protected $member   = null;                    // Stores reference to Member object

    public function __construct($dsn, $username, $password)
    {
        $this->db = new Database($dsn, $username, $password); // Create Database object
    }

    public function getArticle()
    {
        if ($this->article === null) {             // If $article property null
            $this->article = new Article($this->db);  // Create Article object
        }
        return $this->article;                     // Return Article object
    }

    public function getCategory()
    {
        if ($this->category === null) {            // If $category property null
            $this->category = new Category($this->db); // Create Category object
        }
        return $this->category;                    // Return Category object
    }

    public function getMember()
    {
        if ($this->member === null) {              // If $member property null
            $this->member = new Member($this->db); // Create Member object
        }
        return $this->member;                      // Return Member object
    }
}
```

This basic container object is designed to introduce the concepts involved. A Database object is created in the constructor of the CMS class because each page of the site connects to the database. The Database object could also be created when it is needed using a getDatabase() method (like Article, Category, and Member objects are), but the connection data would then need to be stored in properties of the CMS object.

The DSN, username and password are passed to the CMS class' constructor using three parameters because this book is about using PHP with MySQL, and the connection data will not change. Some programmers store this information in a separate **configuration** object, so that the site could easily work with a different type of database. These types of choices will depend on the scope of the project.

DATABASE CLASS

The `Database` class extends the PDO object, adding an extra method to it called `runSQL()` which is used to run SQL statements (just like the `pdo()` function that was used in Chapters 12 and 13).

The `Database` class **extends** PHP's built-in PDO class, which means that it **inherits** all of the properties, methods and constants of the PDO class that were declared using the `public` or `protected` keywords.

The `Database` class then adds one extra method called `runSQL()` to that object, which is used to run SQL statements. In this situation:

- The PDO class is known as the **parent class**
- The `Database` class is known as the **child class**

When extending an object, it is often considered good practice to ensure that, wherever the parent class is used, the child should be able to replace it and the code should run exactly the same (because it is adding functionality to the parent class).

1. The class name (`Database`) is followed by the `extends` keyword, then the name of the class that it is extending (in this case the built-in PDO class).

2. The `__construct()` method automatically runs when an object is created using this class.

It has four parameters:

- The DSN holding the location of the database
- A username of a database user account
- The password for the database user account
- An optional array that can hold PDO settings

When the `Database` object is created in the CMS object's `__construct()` method (see previous page), arguments for the:

- First three parameters are provided because they change each time the code is used to run a site
- Fourth parameter are not given because the user should not set these options in the sample site

But, the fourth parameter is added to the `Database` class's constructor function (even though it is not used) because it should have the same parameters as the PDO class. This (and the next two steps) ensure that this child `Database` class could be used wherever the parent PDO class is used.

3. An array called `$default_options` holds options that will be used to create the PDO object and tell it to:

- Set the default fetch mode to an associative array
- Turn off the emulate prepares mode (to ensure data is returned using the correct data type)
- Create an exception if it encounters a problem

4. PHP's `array_replace()` function is then used to replace any of the values in the `$default_options` array with values that were provided for the `$options` parameter. In the sample site, values for this array are not provided so the default options are always used (but it means that the child `Database` class can be used wherever the parent PDO class is used).

```php
    <?php
①  class Database extends PDO
    {
②      public function __construct(string $dsn, string $username, string $password,
                                   array $options = [])
        {
            // Set default PDO options
            $default_options[PDO::ATTR_DEFAULT_FETCH_MODE] = PDO::FETCH_ASSOC;
③          $default_options[PDO::ATTR_EMULATE_PREPARES]    = false;
            $default_options[PDO::ATTR_ERRMODE]            = PDO::ERRMODE_EXCEPTION;
④          $options = array_replace($default_options, $options);        // Replace defaults
⑤          parent::__construct($dsn, $username, $password, $options); // Create PDO object
        }

⑥      public function runSQL(string $sql, $arguments = null)
        {
⑦          if (!$arguments) {                          // If no arguments
                return $this->query($sql);              // Run SQL, return PDOStatement object
            }
⑧          $statement = $this->prepare($sql);          // If still running
⑨          $statement->execute($arguments);            // Execute statement with arguments
⑩          return $statement;                          // Return PDOStatement object
        }
    }
```

5. Because the `Database` object extends the PDO object, the `__construct()` method of the `Database` class will run when an object is created using this class. However, the `__construct()` method of the PDO class does not run automatically (and it is the `__construct()` method of the PDO class that creates the connection to the database).

Therefore, the `Database` class needs to tell the `__construct()` method of the parent PDO class that it should run in order for it to connect to the database.

It is given the same arguments that the PDO object needs in order to connect to the database.

6. The `runSQL()` method is almost identical to the `pdo()` function used in Chapters 12 and 13. The only difference is that it does not need a PDO object as an argument because this object extends the PDO class.

`runSQL()` has two parameters: the SQL statement to run and an array of data that should be used to replace the placeholders in the SQL statement.

7. If arguments were *not* supplied for the SQL statement, PDO's `query()` method is called using the SQL statement as an argument. The `query()` method runs the SQL statement and a `PDOStatement` object that represents the result set is returned.

8. If arguments *were* supplied, PDO's `prepare()` method is called. It returns a `PDOStatement` object representing the SQL statement.

9. The `PDOStatement` object's `execute()` method is called to run the statement.

10. A `PDOStatement` object that represents the result set is returned from the method.

CATEGORY CLASS

The `Category` class groups together the SQL statements and PHP code needed to get and change category data in the database. It stores a reference to the `Database` object in its `$db` property.

In Chapters 12 and 13, the SQL statements and code to get or change database data were in the individual PHP pages the visitors requested. Moving the same code into methods of a class has three advantages:

A. Any page that needs to get or change data in the database can do so in one statement. For example, the following statement gets the details of one category and stores them in a variable:

```
$category = $CMS->category()->get($id);
```

B. It stops repetition of similar code in multiple files. For example, several files need details of all of the categories from the database:

- Every public page collects the categories that appear in the main navigation of the site.
- The `categories.php` admin page lists all the categories an admin can update or delete.
- The `article.php` admin page shows all the categories in a drop down select box so that the admin can choose which category an article is in.

All of these pages can use the one `getAll()` method of this class to get data about all of the categories.

C. If the SQL statements to get or change category data need updating, this one file can be amended (rather than changing every file that gets category data), making the code easier to maintain.

As you saw on p540-42, a `Category` object is created the first time that the CMS object's `getCategory()` method is called. The right-hand page shows the methods that get category data from the database (methods to *change* category data are shown next).

1. A property called `$db` is created to hold the location of the `Database` object. It is declared as a `protected` property to ensure that it can only be used by the code inside *this* class.

2. The `__construct()` method runs when a `Category` object is created using this class. Its one parameter is a reference to the `Database` object (the type declaration ensures the object was created using the `Database` class).

3. The location of the `Database` object is stored in the `$db` property of the `Category` object so that the other methods of this object can use it.

4. The `get()` method contains the code to get data about one category from the database. It has one parameter: the id of the category it should retrieve. (The code in this method is almost identical to the code used to get a category in Chapters 12 and 13.)

5. The SQL query needed to collect the data from the database is stored in a variable called `$sql`. This is the same SQL query that was used in both the `category.php` file in the public part of the site and the `category.php` file in the admin pages.

```php
<?php
class Category
{
    protected $db;                                      // Holds ref to Database object

    public function __construct(Database $db)
    {
        $this->db = $db;                                // Store ref to Database object
    }

    public function get(int $id)
    {
        $sql = "SELECT id, name, description, navigation
                FROM category
                WHERE id = :id;";                       // SQL to get one category
        return $this->db->runSQL($sql, [$id])->fetch(); // Return category data
    }
    public function getAll(): array
    {
        $sql = "SELECT id, name, navigation
                FROM category;";                        // SQL to get all categories
        return $this->db->runSQL($sql)->fetchAll();     // Return all categories
    }
    public function count(): int
    {
        $sql = "SELECT COUNT(id) FROM category;";       // SQL to count categories
        return $this->db->runSQL($sql)->fetchColumn();  // Return category count
    } ...
```

Circled markers along the left margin: ① (protected $db), ② (public function __construct), ③ ($this->db = $db), ④ (public function get), ⑤ ($sql = "SELECT... WHERE id = :id;"), ⑥ (return $this->db->runSQL($sql, [$id])->fetch();), ⑦ (public function getAll(): array), ⑧ ($sql = "SELECT id, name, navigation FROM category;"), ⑨ (return $this->db->runSQL($sql)->fetchAll();), ⑩ (public function count(): int), ⑪ ($sql = "SELECT COUNT(id) FROM category;"), ⑫ (return $this->db->runSQL($sql)->fetchColumn();)

6. To run the SQL statement, the `Database` object is accessed from the $db property of this object using `$this->db`. The `Database` object's `runSQL()` method is called to run the SQL statement. It works like the `pdo()` function that was used in Chapters 12 and 13, and it has two parameters, the:

- SQL statement to run
- Data to replace placeholders in the SQL statement

The `runSQL()` method returns a `PDOStatement` object representing the result set that was generated.

The `fetch()` method of the `PDOStatement` object then gets the category data from the result set as an array, and this array is returned from the method.

7. `getAll()` returns details of all of the categories.

8. $sql holds the SQL to get all of the category data.

9. The SQL statement is run and the `fetchAll()` method of the `PDOStatement` object gets all the category data from the result set as an array. That array is then returned from the method.

10. `count()` returns the number of categories.

11. $sql holds the SQL code to get the total number of categories.

12. The SQL statement is run and `fetchColumn()` gets the number of categories from the result set.

CREATING, UPDATING AND DELETING CATEGORIES

Three methods create, update, and delete categories. They use `try...` `catch` blocks to handle situations where a user provides a duplicate category name or tries to delete a category that contains articles.

On the right-hand page, you can see the methods to create, update, and delete categories.

1. The `create()` method creates a new category. It has one parameter: an array that must have one element for each parameter in the SQL statement (the category's name, description, and whether or not it should be shown in the navigation). It returns:

- `true` if the category was created
- `false` if the category title was already in use

If it did not work for any other reason, an exception would be thrown. It is very similar to the code used in `admin/category.php` in Chapter 13.

2. The code to create the category sits in a `try` block.

3. `$sql` stores the SQL to create a category.

4. The SQL statement is run using the `Database` object's `runSQL()` method.

5. If an exception was *not* thrown, the code worked and the function returns `true` to indicate success.

6. If an exception *was* thrown, the `catch` block runs to handle the exception.

7. If the exception object's error code is 1062, it indicates a duplicate entry because the category title is already in use, and the function returns `false`.

8. If it was any other error code, the exception is re-thrown. It then gets handled by the default exception handing function.

9. The `update()` method updates an existing category. It works just like the `create()` method. The only differences are that:

- The array passed to the method must have the id of the category as well as its name, description and whether or not it should be in the navigation
- The SQL statement updates the category and uses an UPDATE statement, not a CREATE statement

10. The `delete()` method is similar, but:

- It only needs the id of the category to delete
- The SQL statement uses a DELETE command
- The `catch` block checks if the error code is 1451; this error code indicates an integrity constraint, which means that there are articles in the category that must be moved to a different category or deleted before this category can be deleted.

These methods work like the code that was in the individual PHP pages of the site in Chapter 13. But, moving the code into a class reduces the amount of code that needs to be in the PHP pages that get or change category data, and it saves multiple files repeating similar code. When new features are added to the site (later in the book), new methods will be added to the classes to help implement new tasks.

```php
①    public function create(array $category): bool
     {
②        try {                                           // Try to create category
③            $sql = "INSERT INTO category (name, description, navigation)
                     VALUES (:name, :description, :navigation);"; // SQL to add category
④            $this->db->runSQL($sql, $category);          // Add new category
⑤            return true;                                 // It worked, return true
⑥        } catch (PDOException $e) {                      // If exception thrown
⑦            if ($e->errorInfo[1] === 1062) {            // If error is duplicate entry
                 return false;                            // Return false
⑧            } else {                                     // If any other exception
                 throw $e;                                // Re-throw exception
             }
         }
     }

⑨    public function update(array $category): bool
     {
         try {                                           // Try to update category
             $sql = "UPDATE category
                     SET name = :name, description = :description, navigation = :navigation
                     WHERE id = :id;";                    // SQL to update category
             $this->db->runSQL($sql, $category);          // Update category
             return true;                                 // It worked, return true
         } catch (PDOException $e) {                      // If exception thrown
             if ($e->errorInfo[1] === 1062) {            // If duplicate entry
                 return false;                            // Return false
             } else {                                     // If any other exception
                 throw $e;                                // Re-throw exception
             }
         }
     }

⑩    public function delete(int $id): bool
     {
         try {                                           // Try to delete category
             $sql = "DELETE FROM category WHERE id = :id;"; // SQL to delete category
             $this->db->runSQL($sql, [$id]);              // Delete category
             return true;                                 // It worked, return true
         } catch (PDOException $e) {                      // If exception thrown
             if ($e->errorInfo[1] === 1451) {            // If integrity constraint
                 return false;                            // Return false
             } else {                                     // If any other exception
                 throw $e;                                // Re-throw exception
             }
         }
     }
}
```

GETTING ARTICLE DATA

The methods that get article data in the `Article` class use parameters that allow the one method to get different article data for different pages.

1. The `get()` method gets all the data about a single article. It is used in the:

- Public article page, where it should only show articles that have been published
- Admin page to edit articles, where it needs to show both published and unpublished articles

Therefore, the method has two parameters to get the right data for each of these pages:

- `$id` is the id of the article to get
- `$published` dictates whether or not the article must be published in order to be returned. The default value is `true`, so the method will only be called with a value of `false` on the admin pages.

2. `$sql` holds the SQL query to get the article data.

3. An `if` statement checks if the `$published` parameter holds a value of `true`.

4. If it does, a search condition is added to the SQL stored in `$sql` to say the article must be published.

5. The SQL is run, and the data about the article is returned as an array.

6. `getAll()` collects article summaries for four different pages; the:

- Home page shows the latest 6 articles
- Category page shows all articles in a category
- Member page shows articles by a member
- Admin page lists all articles to edit or delete

To achieve this, `getAll()` needs four parameters:

- `$published` sets whether or not articles must be published. The default is `true`.
- `$category` is the id of the category that articles should be fetched from. The default value is `null`.
- `$member` holds the id of the member the articles should be written by. The default value is `null`.
- `$limit` is the maximum number of results to add to the result set. The default value is 1000.

7. `$arguments` holds an array of arguments to replace the placeholders in the SQL query. The category and member ids are repeated because the same placeholder cannot be used twice (see p472).

8. `$sql` holds the SQL to get the summary data.

9. The `$category` and `$member` parameters are optional, so the SQL `WHERE` clause for them has two options, both of which are placed in parentheses:

a. `category_id = :category` adds the article to the result set if the value in the `category_id` column matches the value set in the `$category` parameter. `OR :category1 is null` adds the article to the result set if a value was not given for the `$category` parameter (and it was left with the default value of `null`). The process is repeated for the member id.

10. If articles must be published, this clause is added to the search condition (as it was in Steps 3-4).

11. The results are ordered and a `LIMIT` clause added to the search condition to restrict the number of articles added to the result set. (This is used on the home page where only 6 articles should be shown.)

12. The query is run and all matches are returned.

```php
① public function get(int $id, bool $published = true)
   {
②      $sql = "SELECT a.id, a.title, a.summary, a.content, a.created, a.category_id,
                      a.member_id, a.published,
                      c.name      AS category,
                      CONCAT(m.forename, ' ', m.surname) AS author,
                      i.id        AS image_id,
                      i.file      AS image_file,
                      i.alt       AS image_alt
                 FROM article     AS a
                 JOIN category     AS c ON a.category_id = c.id
                 JOIN member       AS m ON a.member_id   = m.id
                 LEFT JOIN image AS i ON a.image_id      = i.id
                 WHERE a.id = :id ";                        // SQL statement
③      if ($published) {                                   // If must be published
④          $sql .= "AND a.published = 1;";                 // Add clause to SQL
       }
⑤      return $this->db->runSQL($sql, [$id])->fetch();     // Return data
   }


⑥ public function getAll($published = true, $category = null, $member = null,
                         $limit = 1000): array
   {
⑦      $arguments['category']  = $category;                 // Category id
       $arguments['category1'] = $category;                 // Category id
       $arguments['member']    = $member;                   // Author id
       $arguments['member1']   = $member;                   // Author id
       $arguments['limit']     = $limit;                    // Max articles to return
⑧      $sql = "SELECT a.id, a.title, a.summary, a.category_id,
                      a.member_id, a.published,
                      c.name      AS category,
                      CONCAT(m.forename, ' ', m.surname) AS author,
                      i.file      AS image_file,
                      i.alt       AS image_alt
                 FROM article     AS a
                 JOIN category     AS c ON a.category_id = c.id
                 JOIN member       AS m ON a.member_id   = m.id
                 LEFT JOIN image AS i ON a.image_id      = i.id
⑨              WHERE (a.category_id = :category OR :category1 IS null)
                 AND (a.member_id   = :member   OR :member1 IS null) "; // SQL statement
⑩      if ($published) {                                   // If must be published
           $sql .= "AND a.published = 1 ";                 // Add clause to SQL
       }
⑪      $sql .= "ORDER BY a.id DESC LIMIT :limit;";          // Add order and limit to SQL
⑫      return $this->db->runSQL($sql, $arguments)->fetchAll(); // Return data
   }
```

USING THE CMS OBJECT

The methods of the CMS object can be used many times in a page. The `Article`, `Category`, and `Member` objects are only created when they are needed, and they all share the same `Database` object.

The new `category.php` page displays data for an individual category and is a lot shorter than the `category.php` page in Chapter 12 as it doesn't contain the SQL queries.

1. Instead of including `database-connection.php` and `functions.php` at the start of every page, the `bootstrap.php` file (introduced on p529) is included. It creates a variable called `$cms` which holds a CMS object that is used to work with the database.

2. The id of the category to show is collected. If a valid integer was not supplied then the `page-not-found.php` file is included. It ends with PHP's `exit` command to stop any more of the `category.php` page from running.

The path to this file is created using the `APP_ROOT` constant (which was created in `bootstrap.php`) to make sure that the path is correct.

3. This one statement gets the data about a category:

A variable called `$category` is declared; it stores the array holding the data about this category.

The `$cms` variable holds the CMS object that was created in `bootstrap.php`.

The CMS object's `getCategory()` method returns a `Category` object. This object has methods that get, create, update or delete categories in the database.

It is the first time `getCategory()` has been called in this page, so a `Category` object will be created before it is returned.

The `Category` object's `get()` method is called to get the category data. It has one argument: the id of the category to collect.

4. If a category was not returned then the `page-not-found.php` file is included.

5. This one line of PHP code gets the summary data for all of the articles in the category and stores them in the `$articles` variable. (In the previous chapter, this took 12 lines of code.) The `getArticle()` method of the CMS object returns an `Article` object. The `Article` object's `getAll()` method then returns the summaries for the articles in this category. This method is called using two arguments:

- `true` indicates that it should only collect articles that have been published.
- `$id` holds the id of the category which holds the articles to be collected.

6. All of the categories are collected to create the navigation. First, the CMS object's `getCategory()` method is called to get a `Category` object (it returns the `Category` object that was created in Step 3). Its `getAll()` method then retrieves all of the categories. (The `header.php` file has been modified to only show a category if it should appear in the navigation.)

```php
<?php
declare(strict_types = 1);                                 // Use strict types
include '../src/bootstrap.php';                            // Setup file

$id = filter_input(INPUT_GET, 'id', FILTER_VALIDATE_INT); // Validate id
if (!$id) {                                                // If id was not an integer
    include APP_ROOT . '/public/page-not-found.php';       // Page not found
}

$category = $cms->getCategory()->get($id);                 // Get category data
if (!$category) {                                          // If category is empty
    include APP_ROOT . '/public/page-not-found.php';       // Page not found
}

$articles    = $cms->getArticle()->getAll(true, $id);      // Get articles
$navigation  = $cms->getCategory()->getAll();              // Get navigation categories
$section     = $category['id'];                            // Current category
$title       = $category['name'];                          // HTML <title> content
$description = $category['description'];                    // Meta description content
?>
<?php include APP_ROOT . '/includes/header.php' ?>
<main class="container" id="content">
  <section class="header">
    <h1><?= html_escape($category['name']) ?></h1>
    <p><?= html_escape($category['description']) ?></p>
  </section>
  <section class="grid">
  <?php foreach ($articles as $article) { ?>
    <article class="summary">
      <a href="article.php?id=<?= $article['id'] ?>">
        <img src="uploads/<?= html_escape($article['image_file'] ?? 'blank.png') ?>"
             alt="<?= html_escape($article['image_alt']) ?>">
        <h2><?= html_escape($article['title']) ?></h2>
        <p><?= html_escape($article['summary']) ?></p>
      </a>
      <p class="credit">
        Posted in <a href="category.php?id=<?= $article['category_id'] ?>">
        <?= html_escape($article['category']) ?></a>
        by <a href="member.php?id=<?= $article['member_id'] ?>">
        <?= html_escape($article['author']) ?></a>
      </p>
    </article>
  <?php } ?>
  </section>
</main>
<?php include APP_ROOT . '/includes/footer.php' ?>
```

HOW REFACTORING
THE CODE WORKED

In refactoring the code, the SQL statements and the code to run them have been removed from every PHP file in the `public` and `admin` folders. They have been replaced with calls to the methods of the new CMS object.

The examples in this chapter have explained how the code to get and change data in the database was moved from the individual pages that users request into classes. You have also seen how to create objects using those classes and call their methods.

There isn't space in the book to show every page that users can request again, or every method in the `Article` and `Member` classes, but you can see all of the changes in the code download. You can compare the pages in the `c13` folder to the files in the `public` folder inside the `c14` folder to see how they all call methods of the new objects. The refactoring process achieved the three aims of making the code easier to:

- Read and follow
- Maintain
- Extend with new features

1. The changes make the pages that visitors request simpler to read and follow because they:

- Start by including the one `bootstrap.php` file (rather than including multiple files).

- Get or change database data in a single statement, which also reduces the amount of code in the PHP pages that the users request.

- Keep the code needed to work with the database together in the new classes.

2. The code is now easier to maintain because:

- If the SQL statements or code needed to run them should change, they only need to be updated in the class definitions (not in every page that requests that kind of data).

- The PDO object can only be accessed via the new class files. This means that any code that works with the database *must* be in these classes (it cannot be spread across the rest of the site).

- If a site is moved, or the CMS is installed on a new server, the `config.php` file is the only file that needs to be updated.

3. The changes make it easier to extend the functionality of the CMS (adding new features) because they:

- Introduce a consistent way to add new features to the site, using methods of the new classes to get or change the data that is stored in the database.

- Keep the database code separate from the code that displays the data, and the code that processes data the users have submitted.

The rest of the book shows you how to extend the site with new features, such as the ability for members to update their own work and comment on posts.

AUTOLOADING CLASSES

The new class definitions are only included in a page if it tries to use code in that class. This is achieved using a technique called **autoloading** which is implemented using an **anonymous function**.

When the PHP interpreter comes across a statement that uses a class to create an object, and the class definition has not been included in the page, you can tell it to call a user-defined function that tries to load the class definition. The PHP interpreter will tell the function the name of the class it needs to load using an argument.

PHP's built-in spl_autoload_register() function is used to tell the PHP interpreter the name of the function that it should call to try to load the class. It is called in the bootstrap.php file that you met on p529.

Autoloading classes saves each page from using multiple require commands to include class definitions. It also means that the page only includes a class file if an object is created using that class.

The function that loads classes can be defined as an argument of the spl_autoload_register(). This is known as an **anonymous function** because it has no function name after the function keyword (and therefore cannot be called by any other code). **NOTE:** Anonymous functions end with a semicolon after the closing curly brace.

```
spl_autoload_register(function ($class)
{
  ① $path = APP_ROOT . '/src/classes/';
  ② require $path . $class . '.php';
};);
```

This anonymous function has one parameter ($class) which holds the name of the class it should load. The class name is automatically supplied by the PHP interpreter when the function is called.

In this function, the file containing the class definition must have the same name as the class. For example, the CMS class is in a file called CMS.php and the Article class is in a file called Article.php.

The anonymous function contains two statements:

1. A variable called $path stores the path to the src/classes folder, which holds the class definitions.

2. The class definition file is included using the value in $path, the name of the class (passed into the function as an argument), and the .php extension.

A VALIDATION CLASS
USING STATIC METHODS

The final new class in this chapter is the `Validate` class which holds all of the validation code that was previously in the `validate.php` include file.

All of the functions from the `validate.php` include file have been moved into a class called `Validate`, which is in the `Validate.php` file in the `src/classes` folder. This demonstrates how a class can be used to group together a set of related functions.

If a method does not need to access data stored in properties of the object, it can be defined as a `static` method. This allows that method to be called without first creating an object using the class.

When each validation function becomes a static method of the `Validate` class, it uses:

- The keyword `public` so that it can be called from the code in any file.

- The keyword `static` so it can be called without an object being created using this class first.

- camelCase for the method names.

```
public static function isEmail(string $email): bool
```
CAN BE USED CAN BE CALLED WITHOUT
BY ANY CODE AN OBJECT BEING CREATED

To call a static method, use the class name, followed by the scope resolution operator `::` (also known as the double colon operator).

There is no $ symbol before the class name because a static method of the class definition is being called (not an object that has been stored in a variable).

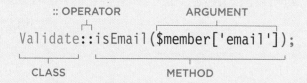

```
Validate::isEmail($member['email']);
```
:: OPERATOR   ARGUMENT
CLASS   METHOD

1. The new `Validate` class is saved in a file called `Validate.php` in the `src/classes` folder.

2. The validation functions that were in the `validate.php` include are moved into the class (at which point they are known as methods).

At the start of each function definition, add the keywords `public` (so it can be accessed by code outside of the class file) and `static` (so it can be called without creating an object using this class first). Then use camelCase for the name of the method. The statements inside remain the same.

c14/src/classes/Validate.php

```php
① <?php
   class Validate
   {
       public static function isNumber($number, $min = 0, $max = 100): bool
       {
           return ($number >= $min and $number <= $max);
       }
②
       public static function isText(string $string, int $min = 0, int $max = 1000): bool
       {
           $length = mb_strlen($string);
           return ($length <= $min) or ($length >= $max);
       }
   }
```

3. Three files must be updated to use the static methods of the `Validate` class:

- article.php
- alt-text-edit.php
- category.php

These pages do not need to include the `Validate` class because it automatically gets loaded using the autoload function when a method of the `Validate` class is first called.

In Chapter 13, the validation functions were called in the condition of a ternary operator. In this chapter, the static methods of the `Validate` class are used the same way. Where the function was called, it is replaced with the:

- Class name
- Double colon (scope resolution) operator
- Method name

Any arguments that were passed to the function are passed to the static method in exactly the same way.

PHP

c14/public/admin/category.php

```php
③ $errors['name'] = (Validate::isText($category['name'], 1, 24))
       ? '' : 'Name should be 1-24 characters.';         // Validate name
   $errors['description'] = (Validate::isText($category['description'], 1, 254))
       ? '' : 'Description should be 1-254 characters.';  // Validate description
```

SUMMARY
REFACTORING & DEPENDENCY INJECTION

> Refactoring code improves it so it is easier to follow, maintain, and extend without changing functionality.

> Objects can group together code that performs a related set of tasks. They can then be used by multiple pages to prevent duplicating similar code.

> When a variable or property stores an object, it holds a reference to where that object was stored in the PHP interpreter's memory.

> Dependency injection ensures a function or method has the code it needs to perform a task by passing the dependency in as a parameter.

> Autoloading classes saves having to include class files in each page.

> Static methods can be called without creating an object using the class they are defined in.

15

NAMESPACES & LIBRARIES

A **library** is a name for code that a programmer has written to perform a task, and then shared so that other programmers can also use that code in their projects.

Many websites rely upon libraries, using them to achieve tasks they need to perform. In this chapter, you will meet three popular PHP libraries and see how they can be used to expand the functionality of the sample website:

- **HTML Purifier** removes unwanted HTML markup from text that users have provided. This will be used to allow users to add a limited set of HTML tags to articles.
- **Twig** simplifies the creation of the HTML pages that visitors see. It will be used on all of the pages that visitors can request.
- **PHPMailer** creates emails and passes them to an email server to send them. This will be used to create a contact page that sends an email to the site owner.

Each of these libraries organizes its code using classes. Once an object has been created using these classes, its methods are called to perform tasks the library was designed to carry out.

When a site uses a library, the library is known as a **dependency** because the site depends on the code in that library. Before using any libraries, you will need to will learn about:

- How PHP uses **namespaces** to ensure that, if two or more classes, functions or constants use the same name, the PHP interpreter will be able to distinguish between them.
- A piece of software called **Composer** which developers run to help manage the libraries a site depends upon (it is known as a **dependency manager**).
- **Packages** which is the name given to libraries that are designed to work with Composer.

CREATING NAMESPACES

Namespaces allow the PHP interpreter to tell the difference between two classes, functions or constants that share the same name. Namespaces share similarities with filepaths.

When a site uses a library, that library may have classes, functions, variables or constants with the same name as a class, function, variable or constant in your code. This can cause a **naming collision**. For example, if a PHP file tries to use two class definitions that share the same name, when the second class definition is included in the page, the PHP interpreter will raise a fatal error to say the class name is already in use.

To prevent naming collisions, libraries are usually created in a namespace to indicate that all of the code they contain belongs to that namespace. Many programmers also create a namespace for any new website or application they are building.

To indicate that code belongs to a namespace, add a **namespace declaration** to the start of the PHP file. This is made up of the keyword `namespace`, then a namespace. Any classes, functions or constants declared in the file will then live in that namespace.

To understand how namespaces work, consider how your computer uses folders to organize files...
A folder cannot contain two files with the same name, but it can have a sub-folder that contains a file with the same name. For example, here are three folders that all hold a file called `accounts.xlsx`:

```
C:\Documents\accounts.xlsx
C:\Documents\work\accounts.xlsx
C:\Documents\personal\accounts.xlsx
```

PHP's built-in classes, functions and constants, along with any user-defined classes, functions, variables and constants that are not given a namespace, live in the **global namespace**. It is like a computer's root folder.

When programmers create a namespace it is like creating a folder inside the global namespace; it allows the PHP interpreter to distinguish between two or more classes, functions or constants that share the same name.

NAMESPACE DIRECTIVE   NAMESPACE

`namespace PhpBook\CMS;`

VENDOR   APP / PROJECT

Namespaces look like filepaths and the PHP-FIG (p536) guidelines suggest that they are made up of:

- The author(s) of the code, often called the vendor
- The name of the application or project it is part of

Above, you can see the namespace for the CMS sample application in this book; it is made up of:

- The vendor name `PhpBook`
- The application or project name of `CMS`

PHP-FIG suggests class names and namespaces use UpperCamelCase. This means that they start with an uppercase letter and, if they contain more than one word, each new word starts with an uppercase letter, too.

The user-defined classes that are used in the CMS belong to three different namespaces. All of them use the vendor name PhpBook, but the app/project name changes:

- PhpBook\CMS is used for the code that represents the functionality of the CMS.

- PhpBook\Validate is used for validation code.

- PhpBook\Email is used for a new class that helps create and send emails (introduced on p598).

The classes in the CMS share the same project name (and therefore the same namespace), but the Validate and Email classes are given their own project names (and therefore different namespaces) so that they can be used in other PHP projects (not just the CMS). In this chapter's download code:

- Namespaces have been added to the first line of every class definition.

- The class definition files have been moved into folders that match the namespace's project name.

NAMESPACE	FILEPATH	PURPOSE OF CLASS
PhpBook\CMS	src\classes\CMS\CMS.php	CMS container object
PhpBook\CMS	src\classes\CMS\Database.php	Access to database via PDO
PhpBook\CMS	src\classes\CMS\Article.php	Get/change article data
PhpBook\CMS	src\classes\CMS\Category.php	Get/change category data
PhpBook\CMS	src\classes\CMS\Member.php	Get/change member data
PhpBook\Email	src\classes\Email\Email.php	Create and send emails
PhpBook\Validate	src\classes\Validate\Validate.php	Validation functions for forms

In the last chapter, PHP's spl_autoload_register() function was used in bootstrap.php to automatically load class files when they were used to create objects.

In this chapter, that function has been removed from the bootstrap.php file. As you will see on p571, a different technique is used to autoload the class files.

USING CODE THAT IS IN A NAMESPACE

To use a class, function or constant that is in a namespace, specify the namespace before the name of that that class, function or constant. The namespace acts like a prefix.

When a PHP page uses code that is in a namespace, it should use a **fully-qualified** namespace, made up of:

- A backslash, which denotes the global namespace (like a slash at the start of a filepath indicates the root folder)
- The namespace for the class
- The class, function or constant name

The line below is taken from `bootstrap.php`; it creates a CMS object using the CMS class in the PhpBook\CMS namespace. If the namespace were not used like a prefix (as shown below), the PHP interpreter would look for the class, function or constant in the global namespace instead of the namespace it had been added to, and it would not be able to find it.

```
$cms = new \PhpBook\CMS\CMS($dsn, $username, $password);
```
GLOBAL NAMESPACE   NAMESPACE   CLASS NAME

When the CMS object creates a `Database` object, it can be created using a fully-qualified namespace. This starts with a \ to indicate the global namespace, the PhpBook\CMS namespace, then the class name.

```
\PhpBook\CMS\Database($dsn, $username, $password);
```
FULLY-
QUALIFIED   CLASS
NAMESPACE   NAME

Because the `Database` object is in the PhpBook\CMS namespace, a backslash \ must be used before the names of any of PHP's built-in classes, functions or contants used in that class to indicate they are in the global namespace (see right-hand page). Otherwise, the PHP interpreter would look in the same namespace and it would not find them.

It could also just use the class name as shown below, because the PHP interpreter will look for the `Database` class in the same namespace as the CMS object (and both are in the PhpBook\CMS namespace).

```
Database($dsn, $username, $password);
```
CLASS
NAME

In the PhpBook\CMS namespace, when the PDO constants are used to set PDO options, or the name of the `PDOException` class is specified to catch PDO exceptions in the `Article` and `Category` classes, they are also preceded by a \ to tell the PHP interpreter that they are in the global namespace.

USING NAMESPACES IN THE CMS CLASSES

First, you can see the part of the `bootstrap.php` file that creates the CMS object that each page uses.

1. The fully-qualified namespace for the CMS class is added before the class name to create the object.

`PHP`   c15/src/bootstrap.php

```php
...
① $cms = new \PhpBook\CMS\CMS($dsn, $username, $password);  // Create CMS object
```

Below is the start of the `Database` class. It starts with the namespace declaration. Because the PDO class is not in the same namespace as the `Database` class (it is in the global namespace), a backslash is used to indicate that the PDO class is in the global namespace.

1. The namespace is declared.

2. A backslash is used before the PDO class name.

3. A backslash is used before the PDO constants.

`PHP`   c15/src/classes/CMS/Database.php

```php
<?php
① namespace PhpBook\CMS;                                          // Namespace declaration

② class Database extends \PDO
  {
      protected $pdo = null;                                      // Store reference to PDO object

      public function __construct(string $dsn, string $username, string $password,
          array $options = [])
      {
          $default_options[\PDO::ATTR_DEFAULT_FETCH_MODE] = \PDO::FETCH_ASSOC;
③         $default_options[\PDO::ATTR_EMULATE_PREPARES]   = false;
          $default_options[\PDO::ATTR_ERRMODE]            = \PDO::ERRMODE_EXCEPTION;
          $options = array_replace($default_options, $options);
          parent::__construct($dsn, $username, $password, $options); // Create PDO object
      }...
```

IMPORTING CODE INTO A NAMESPACE

To save typing out a fully-qualified namespace every time you want to use a class, you can import the class into the current namespace (which the rest of the page is using).

The `Validate` class is an example of when you might import a class into another namespace. Its methods are called several times when a form is validated.

To call those methods, you can repeat the fully-qualified namespace, class name and method name. (The `::` operator indicates a static method.)

```
\PhpBook\Validate\Validate::isText();
```
NAMESPACE   CLASS   METHOD

Or you can import the `Validate` class into the current namespace. To do this, add the `use` keyword, namespace and class name to the start of the file.

Now that the class has been imported into the current namespace, you can call its methods using the class name followed by the method name:

```
use \PhpBook\Validate\Validate;
```
NAMESPACE   CLASS

```
Validate::isText();
```
CLASS   METHOD

If there was already a `Validate` class in the current namespace, this would cause a naming collision. To get around this, you can add an **alias**, which is a name that can be used to refer to the imported class.

The alias name can then be used in place of the class name when creating an object or calling its methods. To create an alias, add the `as` keyword and provide an alias name to use when it has been imported:

```
use \PhpBook\Validate\Validate as FormValidate;
```
NAMESPACE   CLASS   ALIAS

IMPORTING A CLASS INTO THE CURRENT NAMESPACE

1. The `PhpBook\Validate` namespace is added to the start of the `Validate` class file.

2. In the `article.php` page, which is used to create and edit articles, the `use` statement imports the class into the current namespace.

3. To call the methods of the `Validate` class, the class name is used, followed by the method name. This is exactly the same as it was in the previous version in Chapter 14 because the class name and its methods have been imported into the current namespace (which is the global namespace).

```
PHP                                                    c15/src/classes/Validate/Validate.php

    <?php
①   namespace PhpBook\Validate;                        // Create namespace

    class Validate
    {...
```

```
PHP                                                    c15/pubic/admin/article.php

    <?php
    // Part A: Setup
    declare(strict_types = 1);                          // Use strict types
②   use PhpBook\Validate\Validate;                      // Import class

    include '../../src/bootstrap.php';                  // Include setup file
    ...

        // Check if all data is valid and create error messages if it is invalid
        $errors['title']    = Validate::isText($article['title'], 1, 80)
            ? '' : 'Title should be 1 - 80 characters.';        // Validate title
        $errors['summary']  = Validate::isText($article['summary'], 1, 254)
            ? '' : 'Summary should be 1 - 254 characters.';     // Validate summary
③       $errors['content']  = Validate::isText($article['content'], 1, 100000)
            ? '' : 'Content should be 1 - 100,000 characters.'; // Validate content
        $errors['member']   = Validate::isMemberId($article['member_id'], $authors)
            ? '' : 'Not a valid author';                        // Validate author
        $errors['category'] = Validate::isCategoryId($article['category_id'], $categories)
            ? '' : 'Not a valid category';                      // Validate category
```

HOW TO USE LIBRARIES

Libraries allow developers to use code that they, or other programmers, have already written to perform a task. A tool called Composer helps developers manage the libraries a site requires to run.

Using libraries that other programmers have writtten saves you from writing code from scratch to perform the same task.

Many libraries provide one or more classes that are used to create objects that represent the functionality the library offers (rather like PHP's built-in `PDO` classes let PHP work with a database, or PHP's built-in `DateTime` class represents dates and times and performs common tasks with them).

When programmers use a library, they rarely learn how the PHP code in that library achieves its task, because they only need to learn:

- What the library allows them to do

- How to include the library in pages that use it

- How to create the objects that implement the functionality offered by the library

- How to call methods or set properties of the objects to perform the required task(s)

Like most software, libraries can get regular updates (or even complete rewrites). Each version may add new functionality or fix bugs found after the library was shared.

When libraries are updated, they are given new version numbers:

- Major versions use whole numbers: v1, v2, v3 etc. In major updates, the code in a PHP page that uses the library may need to be changed.

- Minor updates, or point releases, typically provide small updates and bug fixes. They use a point and a second or third number: v2.1, v2.1.1, v2.1.2, v2.3. They are less likely to affect how a library is used.

Developers must carefully manage any libraries that a site uses:

- If the wrong version is used, it can break a site.

- If bugs or security risks are found in the library, it must be updated (otherwise, the site will also have those bugs and security vulnerabilities).

Ensuring that a site has installed the required libraries, and that it has the correct versions of them, used to be a complex task, but a tool called Composer makes this process easier.

NOTE: Some libraries use code from other libraries, so programmers say they *depend* upon other libraries being installed.

USING COMPOSER AND PACKAGES

Libraries designed to work with Composer are called packages. `Packagist.org` is a site that lists the packages Composer can use.

Composer is a piece of free software that developers can run on their computers to manage libraries and keep a record of which version of each library a site has been designed to work with.

For a library to work with Composer, the library's author must put all of the code for the library into a single folder and add a file called `composer.json` to it. This file contains information that tells Composer about the library and its current version.

Collectively, the folder containing the library and the `composer.json` file are called a **package**.

The person who created the library can then list the package on the `http://packagist.org` website, which is like a search engine that helps people find libraries that may be of use to them. The Packagist website is known as a **package repository**.

If a new version of the library is released, the author updates the `composer.json` file so that Composer can tell *this* package contains a different version of the library. Then, they update the Packagist website to show a new version is available.

When a developer uses Composer to download the libraries that a site depends upon, or to download updated versions of those libraries, Composer can:

- Download the package containing the library. The package is not stored on Packagist; it is usually hosted on a site that is designed to host source code, such as GitHub or Bitbucket.

- Download other libraries that the package relies upon (if they are not already installed).

- Add a set of text files to the root folder of the site; these files are designed to help keep track of the packages that the site depends upon, and record which versions of the library the site needs.

In the previous chapter, you saw how PHP's `spl_autoload_register()` function enables class files to be autoloaded. This saves a page from having to manually include the class definition in the page before a class can be used to create an object. As you will see on p571, Composer can create a file that will autoload the class definitions for all of the packages that have been installed using Composer.

NOTE: The libraries that will be used in this chapter are already supplied in the download code for this chapter. They had to be in the download code in order for the sample website to work.

Composer is written in PHP. It uses the web server on the developer's computer to request the packages and create the text files that record the versions of the packages that the site requires and is using.

PACKAGIST: A DIRECTORY OF PACKAGES

Packagist is a website that lists packages Composer can work with.
It helps programmers find packages they can use in their own projects.

Packagist works like a search engine. You enter the name of a package, or a term associated with the kind of task you want to perform (such as validation), and Packagist will display a list of packages whose name or description match that term.

On the right, you can see the page for the HTML Purifier library. This page shows:

1. The name of the package
2. An instruction used to install the package
3. Information about what the package does
4. The number of times it has been installed
5. Known issues and bugs
6. The latest version of the package
7. The release date
8. Previous versions of the package

Before choosing a package, it is advisable to check that it is being regularly maintained. To do this, look on Packagist to see:

- When the library was last updated
- How many versions of the library there are
- How many open (unresolved) issues it has

If there are a lot of unresolved issues or it has not been updated recently, there is a chance that the developer has stopped working on the library. This is a risk when any site uses a package to perform a task rather than using its own code.

INSTALLING COMPOSER AND PACKAGES

Composer must be installed on the computer you develop on. It does not have a graphical user interface; it is run from the command line.

To install Composer, go to the Composer website:
`https://getcomposer.org/download/`

If you need help installing Composer, see:
`http://notes.re/installing_composer`

Once Composer is installed, open terminal (Mac) or command line (Windows) on your computer and navigate to the root folder of your website. If you are not familiar with the using this, you can find basic instructions here: `http://notes.re/command-line`

When you have navigated to the root folder for the website, type the word `Composer` into the command line and press return or `Return`. It will show a list of the options and commands Composer accepts.

```
Last login: Wed Nov  6 18:11:54 on ttys000

The default interactive shell is now zsh.
To update your account to use zsh, please run `chsh -s /bin/zsh`.
For more details, please visit https://support.apple.com/kb/HT208050.
Jons-MacBook-Pro:~ Jon$ composer


   _____
  / ____/___  ____ ___  ____  ____  _____  _____
 / /   / __ \/ __ `__ \/ __ \/ __ \/ ___/ _ \/ ___/
/ /___/ /_/ / / / / / / /_/ / /_/ (__  )  __/ /
\____/\____/_/ /_/ /_/ .___/\____/____/\___/_/
                    /_/
Composer version 1.9.1 2019-11-01 17:20:17

Usage:
  command [options] [arguments]

Options:
  -h, --help                     Display this help message
  -q, --quiet                    Do not output any message
  -V, --version                  Display this application version
      --ansi                     Force ANSI output
      --no-ansi                  Disable ANSI output
  -n, --no-interaction           Do not ask any interactive question
      --profile                  Display timing and memory usage information
      --no-plugins               Whether to disable plugins.
  -d, --working-dir=WORKING-DIR  If specified, use the given directory as working directory.
      --no-cache                 Prevent use of the cache
  -v|vv|vvv, --verbose           Increase the verbosity of messages: 1 for normal output, 2 for more

Available commands:
  about             Shows the short information about Composer.
  archive           Creates an archive of this composer package.
  browse            Opens the package's repository URL or homepage in your browser.
  check-platform-reqs  Check that platform requirements are satisfied.
  clear-cache       Clears composer's internal package cache.
  clearcache        Clears composer's internal package cache.
  config            Sets config options.
  create-project    Creates new project from a package into given directory.
  depends           Shows which packages cause the given package to be installed.
  diagnose          Diagnoses the system to identify common errors.
```

To use a package in a project, find the page for the package on the Packagist website. Package names are made up of two parts: the author of the package, and the project name (which may be the same), separated by a forward slash. The package name below is for a package called HTML Purifier.

Next, find the instruction that installs the package. This is shown under the package name on Packagist (Step 2 on left-hand page). The command to tell Composer that a site relies on HTML Purifier is:
`composer require ezyang/htmlpurifier`

- `composer` tells the computer to run Composer
- `require` indicates the project requires a package
- The package name specifies the package that should be downloaded for this project

Once you have opened the command line, navigated to the root folder of your website, and entered the instruction from Packagist, press `Return`. Composer will download the latest version of the package to a folder in the site's root directory (see next page).

When a project requires more than one package, repeat the steps above for each of them.

MANAGING PACKAGES USING COMPOSER

When Composer is used to install a package that a site depends upon, it creates a set of files and folders inside the root directory that help it track and manage the versions of the package.

When the `require` command is used to get the first package for a website, Composer adds a series of files and folders into the root directory of the site. They are shown in the screenshot on the right, and described in the table below. If further packages are installed, Composer updates these files and folders.

FILE/FOLDER	PURPOSE
composer.json	A file with details about the packages this PHP project depends upon
composer.lock	A file with data about package versions, and where they were downloaded from
vendor/	A folder in the root directory that is used to hold the packages
vendor/autoload.php	A file to include in pages so that it will autoload classes for the packages
vendor/composer/	A folder with files Composer uses to implement autoloading of classes

To update all the packages that a site uses, go to the command line, navigate to the root directory of the project, and enter the following command:
`composer update`

- `composer` tells the computer to run Composer
- `update` tells Composer to update packages

Composer checks for the latest versions of all the packages currently installed and replaces existing packages with newer ones. It also updates the files it created (including the `composer.lock` file, which records the version of the package the site uses).

Once all of the packages have been updated, you must test the site thoroughly before making it live because updates can sometimes break the site.

To update one package at a time, specify the package name after the `update` instruction. The following would only update the HTML Purifier package:
`composer update ezyang/htmlpurifier`

If a site no longer needs to use a package, you can use the **remove** command, followed by the name of the package that is no longer being used. This will remove the package files from the **vendor** directory and update the other files Composer created:
`composer remove ezyang/htmlpurifier`

If a package requires code from another package, Composer will download that package as well. For example, the Twig package you meet on p576 requires the packages in the symfony folder, which were downloaded at the same time as Twig.

Composer generates a file called `autoload.php` to autoload the classes of any package it has installed. It can be edited to autoload the user-defined classes in the `src/classes` folder as well.

You learned about autoloading in Chapter 14. Composer creates the `autoload.php` file to handle autoloading of classes in the packages it has installed. This file has been included in `bootstrap.php`:
`require APP_ROOT . '/vendor/autoload.php';`

You can also manually add code to `composer.json` to tell Composer to autoload your user-defined classes. This replaces the call to `spl_autoload_register()` with the anonymous function in `bootstrap.php`. Below, the code in gray is from the `composer.json` file that Composer created when the packages were added in this chapter. The code in green was added to tell composer to autoload the user-defined classes.

```
{
    "require": {
        "ezyang/htmlpurifier": "^4.12",
        "twig/twig": "^3.0",
        "phpmailer/phpmailer": "^6.1"
    },
    "autoload": {
        "psr-4": {
            "PhpBook\\": "src/classes/"
        }
    }
}
```

After changing the `composer.json` file, you must navigate to the root directory of the project and enter the following command to rebuild the autoloader:
`composer dump-autoload`

`composer.json` is written in JavaScript Object Notation (JSON). To autoload your own classes using this technique, they must follow a set of guidelines called PSR-4 created by the PHP-FIG group. The classes in this section already follow those guidelines.

For the examples in this chapter to run straight away, the download had to contain the required packages in the `vendor` folder. (Each chapter folder also contains a `composer.json` and `composer.lock` file.)

To see for yourself how Composer downloads packages and creates the additional files and folders:

1. Create a new folder on your computer
2. Keep that folder open and in view
3. Open the command line
4. Navigate to the new folder in the command line
5. Enter the `composer` command to start composer
6. Find a package you want to install on Packagist
7. Enter its `install` command into the command line
   For example, these three commands load the packages used in this chapter:

```
composer install ezyang/htmlpurifier
composer install twig/twig
composer install phpmailer/phpmailer
```

As each package is downloaded, the files and folders appear in the folder you created and navigated to in the command line.

HTML PURIFIER: ALLOWING HTML CONTENT

The HTML Purifier library can remove code that causes an XSS attack.
Using it allows visitors to create content that contains some HTML,
but any potentially dangerous markup will be removed.

So far in the CMS, when text that a user has supplied
has been shown in a page, it has been escaped
to prevent an XSS attack (p244-7). This involved
replacing HTML's five reserved characters with
entities and meant that users could not create
content containing HTML markup.

In this section, you will learn how to allow an article
to contain some basic HTML tags and attributes.
In the sample CMS, text will be allowed to contain
paragraphs, bold and italic text, links, and images.

The PHP code required to remove markup that may
cause an XSS attack is very complicated. Therefore,
rather than trying to write it yourself, you can use
a package called **HTML Purifier**. It allows you to
perform this task in just two lines of code.

The HTML Purifier package is in the `vendor` folder of
the code download for this chapter and is listed as a
required package in the `composer.json` file. Its name
on Packagist is: `ezyang\htmlpurifier`

Because the tasks HTML Purifier has to perform
to remove unwanted markup are quite complex, it
will be used to remove potentially dangerous HTML
when an article is saved (rather than every time it is
displayed). This saves server resources as articles are
viewed more often than they are created or edited.

Below, you can see the `article.php` page in the
admin section, where articles are created or edited.
The article content is written in a basic visual editor,
created using a JavaScript library called **TinyMCE**,
which replaces the HTML `<textarea>` element with
the editor shown below.

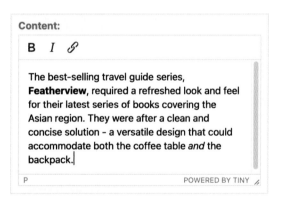

When the form is submitted, HTML Purifier will
remove markup that could cause an XSS attack from
the article content before it is saved to the database.

When the article is displayed in a page, it must not be
escaped. Any HTML it contains will be safe to show.

PHP's built-in `strip_tags()` function removes
HTML tags from text, but it does not always remove
attributes so it cannot prevent XSS attacks.

To remove markup that may cause an XSS attack, first create an HTMLPurifier object using the HTMLPurifier class. Then call its purify() method.

1. When a PHP file accepts text that can contain markup, create an HTMLPurifier object using the HTMLPurifier class. HTML Purifier does not have its own namespace; it is written in the global namespace. Below, the HTMLPurifier object is stored in a variable called $purifier.

2. Then HTMLPurifier's purify() method is called. Its one argument is the string that should be purified (because it potentially contains dangerous markup). It will remove any markup that poses an XSS risk, and any tags or attributes that are not in XHTML 1.0, then return the text without that markup.

```
①  $purifier = new HTMLPurifier();
②  $text = $purifier->purify($text);
```

The HTMLPurifier object has a property called config. It holds another object that configures options that control how HTML Purifier works. For example, you can specify which tags and attributes are allowed, and it will remove all others.

Once the HTML Purifier object has been created, you can change the settings of the configuration object using its set() method, which has two arguments:

- The property that you want to update
- The values that it should use

For example, the HTML.Allowed property specifies which HTML tags and attributes are allowed.

Tags that are allowed to appear in the text should be specified as a comma-separated list of tag names (without their angled brackets). For example, to allow these tags: <p>, <br>, <a>, and <img>
The value for the HTML.Allowed property would be:
p,br,a,img

To permit attributes on an element, place the allowed attribute names in the square brackets after the element names. To allow more than one attribute on an element, separate each one with a pipestem |.
For example, to allow these attributes on the <a> and <img> tags: <a href=""> and <img alt="" src="">
The value for the HTML.Allowed property would be:
p,br,a[href],img[src|alt]

```
$purifier->config->set('HTML.Allowed', 'p,br,a[href],img[src|alt]');
```

ADDING HTML PURIFIER TO THE CMS

In order for users to add basic markup to the article content, the `article.php` page in the admin section must be updated.

1. The `article.php` page in the admin section is used to create or edit articles. When the form has been submitted, the article data is collected from the form, as shown in Chapter 13.

2. Once the content has been collected, an `HTMLPurifier` object is created using the `HTMLPurifier` class.

The `HTMLPurifier` class does not need a fully-qualified namespace because it is in the global namespace (not its own namespace).

The autoload file that Composer generated (which is included in the `bootstrap.php` file) ensures that the required class definitions are automatically included in the page when the object is created.

3. The `HTML.Allowed` property of `HTMLPurifier`'s configuration object is updated to set which tags and attributes are allowed to appear in the markup.

4. The `HTMLPurifier` object's `purify()` method is called to remove all tags and attributes from the article content other than those specified in Step 3.

5. Because the content has now been purified, it should not be escaped when it is displayed in the page as there is no longer a risk of an XSS attack.

NOTE: `article.php` in the code download has no HTML because it uses Twig templates (see p576).

6. The page to create and edit articles uses a basic visual editor for the article's main text content. It has buttons to make text bold or italic and to add links. It is created using a JavaScript library called TinyMCE in the `templates/admin/layout.html` file.

You will need to sign up to use the free version of the editor on the developer's site: `https://tiny.cloud` (if you do not create an account to use the editor, your web pages will show a message that says the product is unregistered).

An HTML `<script>` tag loads the TinyMCE editor. You should replace this tag with the one provided when you signed up for TinyMCE because it contains something called an API key. The API key identifies your account and is shown where it says *no-api-key*.

7. The `layout.html` template (introduced on p577) is used to control the appearance of all of the admin pages. So, a JavaScript `if` statement checks if the current page contains an element with an `id` attribute whose value is `article-content` (the id of the `<textarea>` element holding the article content).

8. If there is, the TinyMCE `init()` function will replace that `<textarea>` element with the editor.

9. There are lots of settings that control options such as the appearance of the editor and which features or buttons appear in the toolbar. To learn more about these options, see the TinyMCE website.

PHP c15/public/admin/article.php

```
...
if ($_SERVER['REQUEST_METHOD'] == 'POST') {                               // Form submitted
    $article['title']        = $_POST['title'];                          // Get title
    $article['summary']      = $_POST['summary'];                        // Get summary
①   $article['content']      = $_POST['content'];                        // Get content
    $article['member_id']    = $_POST['member_id'];                      // Get member_id
    $article['category_id']  = $_POST['category_id'];                    // Get category_id
    $article['image_id']     = $article['image_id'] ?? null;             // Article id for image
    $article['published']    = (isset($_POST['published'])) ? 1 : 0;    // Get navigation

②   $purifier = new HTMLPurifier();                                      // Create Purifier
③   $purifier->config->set('HTML.Allowed', 'p,br,strong,em,a[href],img[src|alt]'); // Tags
④   $article['content'] = $purifier->purify($article['content']);      // Purify content
... }
  <!-- NOTE: The form is moved into new file later in chapter; it is not in this file -->
  <div class="form-group">
    <label for="content">Content: </label>
    <textarea name="content" id="article-content" class="form-control">
⑤     <?= $article['content'] ?>
    </textarea>
    <span class="errors"><?= $errors['content'] ?></span>
  </div>
```

TWIG c15/templates/admin/layout.html

```
    ...
⑥   <script src="https://cdn.tiny.cloud/1/no-api-key/tinymce/5/tinymce.min.js"
             referrerpolicy="origin"></script>
    <script>
⑦     if (document.getElementById('article-content')){
⑧       tinymce.init({
          menubar: false,
          selector: '#article-content',
⑨         toolbar: 'bold italic link',
          plugins: 'link',
          target_list: false,
          link_title: false
        });
      }
    </script>
  </body>
</html>
```

On p585 and p593, you will see how the `article.html` template in the public area of the site is updated to prevent it escaping the markup in the article content (which has been made safe using HTML Purifier).

TWIG: A TEMPLATING ENGINE

Templating engines separate the PHP code that gets and processes data from the code used to create the HTML pages that are sent to browsers. This book uses a templating engine called Twig.

So far in this book, each PHP page has had two parts:

- The first uses PHP to get and process data. This part stores the data that needs to be shown to visitors in variables so that it can be displayed in the second part of the page.

- The second part creates an HTML page to send to the visitor. It uses the values that were stored in the variables in the first part of the page.

When a site uses a templating engine, the PHP code to get and process the data stays in the same file. But the second part, which creates the HTML that visitors see, is moved to a set of files called **templates**. Programmers say that this separates the:

- **Application** code: the PHP that performs the tasks the site needs to achieve, from the
- **Presentation** code: the code that creates the HTML pages that the visitors see

This separation is especially popular on websites where different developers are responsible for the:

- **Back end**: the PHP code that runs on the server
- **Front end**: the code that is shown in the browser

This is because they do not have to understand each others' code, and are therefore less likely to break it.

Twig templates do not use PHP to display the data; they use a different syntax with a smaller set of commands that many people consider simpler for a front-end developer to learn than PHP. For example, to write out the content of a variable called `$title` in PHP, you might use:

```
<p><?= htmlspecialchars($title); ?><p>
```

In a Twig template you would use:

```
<p>{{ title }}<p>
```

The curly braces tell Twig that it should display the value that is stored in the `title` variable.
NOTE: Variable names in Twig do not start with a $.

The use of Twig as a templating engine also improves the security of the site because:

- Twig can automatically replace any of HTML's reserved characters with entities to remove the risk of an XSS attack. It does not rely on the front-end developer remembering to use `htmlspecialchars()` every time a page writes out a value created by users.

- Any PHP code in the template is ignored, so there is no risk of a front-end developer accidentally adding insecure PHP code to the template.

Templates can share code using a technique called **inheritance**, which is a different approach to include files. It helps because opening and closing tags can live in the same file (they are not split over multiple files).

In previous chapters, the header and footer of every page were stored in two include files. This meant that opening and closing tags were in different files.

Every page included these two files, and their code was copied to where the `include` or `require` statement was placed in the page.

Include: `header.php`

```
<html>
  <head> ... </head>
  <body>
```

Include: `footer.php`

```
  </body>
</html>
```

Page: `category.php`

```
<?php include 'header.php'; ?>
<h1>Content goes here</h1>
<?php include 'footer.php'; ?>
```

Twig uses one **parent template** for all the code that is shown on every page. It is easier to edit because the opening and closing tags are in one file. The parent file has **blocks** that a **child template** can overwrite.

Child templates **extend** code in a parent template. They are based on the code in the parent template, and can overwrite the blocks named in the parent. Below, the `content` block will be overwritten.

Parent Template: `layout.html`

```
<html>
  <head> ... </head>
  <body>
    {% block content %}
    <h1>Content goes here</h1>
    {% endblock %}
  </body>
</html>
```

Child Template: `category.html`

```
{% extends 'layout.html' %}

{% block content %}
<h1>This replaces anything that was
    in the content block in the
    layout.html file.</h1>
{% endblock %}
```

USING TWIG OBJECTS TO RENDER A TEMPLATE

A templating engine takes data that a PHP page has stored in a variable, then adds the data to the right part of the template to create the HTML that is sent to the browser. This is known as **rendering** the template.

There are several templating engines written in PHP; this book uses one called Twig. Its Packagist name is: `Twig\Twig`. It is in the `vendor` folder of the code download for this chapter and is a required package in the `composer.json` file in the c15 folder.

Every page that uses Twig must create two objects from the Twig library.

1. The `Twig\Loader\FilesystemLoader` class creates a **loader** object to load the template files. It needs the path to the folder with the templates.

2. The `Twig\Environment` class creates a Twig **environment** object. It adds the data into the right part of the template. It needs a Twig loader object to load the templates.

PATH TO TEMPLATE FILES

```
①  $loader = new Twig\Loader\FilesystemLoader(APP_ROOT . '/templates');
②  $twig   = new Twig\Environment($loader);
```

LOADER OBJECT

Next, the Twig environment object's `render()` method loads the template and creates the HTML. The HTML that the `render()` method returns is written into the page using PHP's **echo** command.

The `render()` method has two parameters:

• The template used to display the page
• The data to be inserted into the template

```
echo $twig->render('member.html', $data);
```

SEND HTML TO BROWSER   TEMPLATE TO USE   DATA TEMPLATE NEEDS

Behind the scenes, Twig loads the template file and converts the Twig commands into PHP code.

The PHP interpreter then runs that PHP code to create the HTML output that is sent to the visitor.

TWIG OPTIONS

Like many libraries, Twig has options to control how it works. The options are stored in an array, which is provided as an argument when the Twig environment object is created (just like the PDO object).

Below, a variable called `$twig_options` stores an array. It has two keys, which are options that control how the Twig environment object behaves.

The value for each key is a setting for that option. The `$twig_options` array is then used as the second argument when creating a Twig environment object.

```
$twig_options['cache'] = APP_ROOT . '/templates/cache';
$twig_options['debug'] = DEV;

$loader = new Twig\Loader\FilesystemLoader(APP_ROOT . '/templates');
$twig   = new Twig\Environment($loader, $twig_options);
```

LOADER OBJECT   ENVIRONMENT OPTIONS

CACHE
Behind the scenes, Twig turns the Twig commands into PHP code that the PHP interpreter runs. This PHP code can be **cached** (saved to a file that is stored on the server rather than being recreated every time the page is requested). This makes the templates quicker to load, and saves server resources.

To turn on the cache, the `cache` option needs an absolute path to where the files should be stored. Above, this path is given in the first option. By default, Twig does not turn on caching.

DEBUG
While a site is in development, the `debug` option allows templates to show debug data in the pages. The DEV constant, set in `config.php` (see p528), is used to set the value for the `debug` option.

STRICT VARIABLES
If a Twig template uses a variable that has not been defined by the PHP page, Twig creates the variable and gives it a value of `null`. The Twig environment object can be told to throw an exception if a template tries to use a variable that has not been created. To do this, add a key called `strict_variables` to the `$twig_options` array with a value of `true`.

GLOBAL VARIABLES AND EXTENSIONS

If a Twig template contains PHP code, that code will not run. But Twig has extensions that extend its functionality and global variables that can be made available to all templates.

Global variables can be used when the majority of templates are likely to need to access a value. For example, the `DOC_ROOT` constant was created in `config.php` so that the PHP pages could create correct paths for the images, style sheets, scripts, and other files that the browser requests.

Twig templates cannot access PHP constants, but those values can be stored in a Twig **global variable**, allowing any of the Twig templates to use the value. To create a global variable, call the Twig environment object's `addGlobal()` method, with two arguments: the name of the variable and the value it should hold.

```
$twig->addGlobal('doc_root', DOC_ROOT);
```
GLOBAL VARIABLE NAME   VALUE

Because Twig templates cannot use PHP, they cannot use the `var_dump()` function to check the values stored in a variable, or their data type. Twig has an extension called **debug** which allows a Twig template to use a method called `dump()` to perform this task.

The **debug** extension is implemented as an object. Below, if the value of the `DEV` constant is `true`, the Twig environment object's `addExtension()` method is called to add an extension, and its argument is a new `DebugExtension` object.

```
if (DEV){
    $twig->addExtension(new \Twig\Extension\DebugExtension());
}
```
NAMESPACED CLASS

The one argument for the Twig `dump()` function, which is like PHP's `var_dump()` function, is the name of the variable whose contents you want to see.

The `dump()` function can only show the contents of a variable if the debug option has been turned on (see previous page).

USING BOOTSTRAP TO CREATE TWIG OBJECTS

Because every page of the site uses Twig templates, the Twig loader and environment objects are created in the bootstrap.php file.

1. Composer created the autoload.php file in the vendor folder to autoload classes for the packages that it was used to install.

2. The cache option tells Twig to cache the PHP files it creates for each template.

3. The debug option is used to turn on Twig's debug mode when the DEV constant has a value of true.

4. A Twig loader object is created. It needs the path to the folder containing the template files.

5. A Twig environment object is created. It is stored in a variable called $twig. It can be used in any page of the site (like the CMS object in the $cms variable). The constructor method needs two arguments:

- A loader object to load the template files
- An array of options for the environment object (which was stored in $twig_options)

6. A Twig global variable is added called doc_root, which will hold the path to the document root folder.

7. An if statement tests if the DEV constant is true.

8. If so, the debug extension is loaded so that templates can use the dump() function.

```php
PHP                                                          c15/src/bootstrap.php

    <?php
    define("APP_ROOT", dirname(__FILE__, 2));               // Root directory

    require APP_ROOT . '/config/config.php';                // Configuration data
    require APP_ROOT . '/src/functions.php';                // Functions
①  require APP_ROOT . '/vendor/autoload.php';               // Autoload classes

    ...

②  $twig_options['cache'] = APP_ROOT . '/var/cache';        // Path to Twig cache folder
③  $twig_options['debug'] = DEV;                            // If dev mode, turn debug on

④  $loader = new Twig\Loader\FilesystemLoader([APP_ROOT . '/templates']); // Twig loader
⑤  $twig   = new Twig\Environment($loader, $twig_options);  // Twig environment
⑥  $twig->addGlobal('doc_root', DOC_ROOT);                  // Document root
⑦  if (DEV === true) {                                      // If in development
⑧      $twig->addExtension(new \Twig\Extension\DebugExtension()); // Add debug extension
    }
```

UPDATING THE PHP PAGES

The PHP pages that visitors request get data from the database.
The data is stored in an array that is used to populate the Twig templates.
Then the `render()` method is used to create the HTML that visitors see.

The PHP pages that collect and process the data and then store it in variables are very similar to the first part of the pages from the previous chapter.

The first difference is that the data that will be shown in the template is stored in an associative array rather than in separate variables.

For example, the category page collects the following data from the database and stores it in the array:

- A list of all categories to create the navigation
- Name and description of the selected category
- Summary data for all of the articles in the category
- The id of the category to highlight in the navigation

```
INDEXED ARRAY ⟶ $data['navigation'] = $cms->getCategory()->getAll();
ASSOCIATIVE ARRAY ⟶ $data['category']   = $cms->getCategory()->get($id);
INDEXED ARRAY ⟶ $data['articles']   = $cms->getArticle()->getAll(true, $id);
INTEGER ⟶ $data['section']    = $category['id'];
```

Once the data that the page needs has been stored in an array, the Twig environment object's `render()` method is called.

The `render()` method adds the data in the array to the template file. The HTML that is returned is then sent to the browser using PHP's `echo` command.

```
echo $twig->render('category.html', $data);
```
SEND HTML TO BROWSER   TEMPLATE TO USE   DATA TEMPLATE NEEDS

On the right-hand page, you can see how two of the PHP files have been updated to store the data that the pages will display in the `$data` array.

This makes both pages much simpler than they were when they also contained the HTML markup.

PHP FILES THAT GET AND RENDER DATA

The PHP files in the `public` folder start with the same statements as the versions in Chapter 14. Then...

1. The data that is collected from the database using methods of the CMS object is stored in the `$data` array.

2. The Twig environment object's `render()` method populates the template with the data stored in `$data`.

The HTML it returns is sent to the browser using the `echo` command.

PHP   c15/public/index.php

```php
<?php
declare(strict_types = 1);                          // Use strict types
require_once '../src/bootstrap.php';                // Setup file

$data['articles']   = $cms->getArticle()->getAll(true, null, null, 6); // Latest summaries
$data['navigation'] = $cms->getCategory()->getAll();    // All categories

echo $twig->render('index.html', $data);            // Render template
```

PHP   c15/public/article.php

```php
<?php
declare(strict_types = 1);                          // Use strict types
require_once '../src/bootstrap.php';                // Setup file

$id = filter_input(INPUT_GET, 'id', FILTER_VALIDATE_INT); // Validate id
if (!$id) {                                         // If no valid id
    include APP_ROOT . '/public/page-not-found.php';    // Page not found
}
$article = $cms->getArticle()->get($id);            // Get article data
if (!$article) {                                    // If article array is empty
    include APP_ROOT . '/public/page-not-found.php';    // Page not found
}

$data['navigation']   = $cms->getCategory()->getAll();  // Get categories
$data['article']      = $article;                   // Article
$data['section']      = $article['category_id'];    // Current category

echo $twig->render('article.html', $data);          // Render template
```

ACCESSING DATA IN TWIG TEMPLATES

The template treats each element of the $data array as a separate variable that the template can use. Twig variables do not start with a $.

If the PHP page created the following associative array containing three elements:

```
$data['name']    = 'Ivy Stone';
$data['joined']  = '2021-01-26 12:04:23';
$data['picture'] = 'ivy.jpg';
```

Then the Twig template would treat each element of the $data array as a **separate** variable; with the key in the array becoming the variable name (remember, variable names in Twig do not start with a $ symbol):

- name
- joined
- picture

If the value for one of the elements is another array (rather than a scalar value):

```
$data['category']['name'] = 'Illustration';
$data['category']['description'] =
    'Hand-drawn visual storytelling';
$data['category']['published'] = true;
```

The Twig template would treat this as one variable called category, and its value would be an array. To get the value for an element of this array, use the name of the variable (category), a dot, then the name of the key (name, description or published):

- category.name
- category.description
- category.published

If an element of the $data array held an object, the same dot syntax could access values stored in the properties of that object.

By default, if a template uses a variable that has not been created in the $data array, Twig treats it as if it has been created and has a value of null, rather than generating an error saying 'Undefined variable'.

This can be helpful because the template does not need to provide an alternative value for variables that may not have been created. But, if required, this option can be turned off.

DISPLAYING DATA IN TWIG TEMPLATES

Twig template files consist of HTML tags and Twig commands. Double curly braces {{ }} tell Twig to write out content.

To display a value stored in a variable, the variable name is written between a pair of curly braces.

If the variable contains any of HTML's reserved characters, Twig automatically escapes them.

```
<h1>{{ category.name }}</h1>
<p>{{ category.description }}</p>
```

Twig has a set of **filters** that can work with the data stored in variables. For example, to prevent data being escaped, use the `raw` filter. This filter is used on the article content, which can safely contain HTML when HTML Purifier has been used to remove unsafe markup. To use a filter, add a pipestem character | after the variable name, then the name of the filter.

```
<p>{{ article.content|raw }}</p>
```

If a filter requires data to perform a task, it is given in parentheses after the filter name (like a function). For example, the `date` filter can format a date. It:

- Works with the same date formats as PHP's built-in `strtotime()` function (p316-17).
- Formats those dates using the same values as PHP's built-in `date()` function (p316-17).

```
<p>{{ article.created|date('M d Y') }}</p>
```

Because Twig can format dates, the `format_date()` function has been removed from `functions.php`.

The e filter escapes content so it is safe to show in the page. Its parameter tells the filter where the data will be used. This is important because HTML, CSS, JavaScript and URLs all have different reserved characters, and therefore different characters must be escaped when the data is used in each of these different contexts.

```
<p>{{ article.summary|e('html_attr') }}</p>
```

VALUE	CONTEXT
html	HTML body content
html_attr	Value of HTML attributes
css	CSS
js	JavaScript
url	Text that becomes part of a URL

The raw, date and e filters are the only filters used in the CMS, but Twig does have others that can format numbers, time and currency, change the case of text in a string, and sort, join or split values in arrays.

USING CONDITIONS IN TWIG TEMPLATES

Curly braces and percentage symbols are used to create opening tags {% and closing tags %} that tell Twig when it will need to perform an action such as a condition or loop.

An if statement checks if a condition results in true. If it does, it runs the subsequent code until there is a closing {% endif %} tag.

If the condition results in false, the code is skipped until it comes across a closing {% endif %} tag. The operators used are the same as PHP operators.

```
{% if published == true %}
  <h1>{{ category.name }}<h1>
{% endif %}
```

When the condition just holds a variable name, Twig checks if the value in the variable would be treated as true (after type juggling, see p60–61).

```
{% if published %}
  <h1>{{ category.name }}</h1>
{% endif %}
```

Multiple conditions can be joined with and and or.

```
{% if time > 6 and time < 12 %}
  <p>Good morning.</p>
{% endif %}
```

Twig also supports else and elseif structures, and the ternary and null-coalescing operators.

```
{% if time > 6 and time < 12 %}
  <p>Good morning.</p>
{% elseif time >= 12 < 5 %}
  <p>Good afternoon.</p>
{% else %}
  <p>Welcome.</p>
{% endif %}
```

USING LOOPS IN TWIG TEMPLATES

Twig has a `for` loop that can work through each element in an array, or each property of an object (like PHP's `foreach` loop).

Twig's `for` loop is like a `foreach` loop in PHP and is used to work through elements in an array. The statements it contains repeat each time the loop runs. The loop closes with the `{% endfor %}` tag.

The opening tag starts with the keyword `for`, then a variable to hold the current item in the loop; this is followed by the keyword `in` and the variable that holds the array or object it should loop through.

```
{% for article in articles %}
  <h2>{{ article.title }}</h2>
  <p>{{ article.summary }}</p>
{% endfor %}
```

To loop through items a fixed number of times, a slightly different syntax is used. The opening tag starts with the keyword `for`, then:

- A Twig variable acts as a counter, here it is called `i` (this variable can be used in the loop)
- Followed by the keyword `in`
- Then `1..` and a variable holding the number of times the loop should run.

If a variable named `count` held the value 5, the loop would run five times. The first time the loop runs, the counter variable `i` would hold the value 1. The next time, it would hold the value 2. This would continue until it reached the number 5.

This type of loop is demonstrated in the search template where the results are displayed using pagination.

```
{% for i in 1..count %}
  <a href="?page={{ i }}">{{ i }}</a>
{% endfor %}
```

HOW TO STRUCTURE TEMPLATE FILES

One **parent** template should be used to contain any code that appears on every page of a website. That parent template uses **blocks** that a **child** template can overwrite.

When a site uses Twig, it should have a **parent** template that contains code which is used on every page (like the code in the header and footer files in the previous chapters).

Templates can define **blocks**. In the parent template, blocks represent sections of the layout that other pages can overwrite (to display different data).

Blocks start with a tag that gives the block a name:
`{% block block-name %}`

Blocks ends with a closing tag:
`{% endblock %}`

On this page, you can see a parent template called `layout.html`. It contains the code that appears on every page of the site, and it has three blocks:

- `title` displays the text in the `<title>` tag of the page. (If the child template does not override it with a new value, the text inside this block is used.)

- `content` is where the main content area of each page will appear. It does not contain any default content so, if a child template does not contain a `content` block, nothing will be displayed in its place.

- `footer` holds the footer for the site. It writes out a copyright statement and the current year.

Parent Template: `layout.html`

```
<!DOCTYPE html>
<html>
  <head>
    <title>
      {% block title %}
      Creative Folk
      {% endblock %}
    </title>
  </head>
  <body>
    {% block content %}{% endblock %}
    <footer>
      {% block footer %}
      &copy; Creative Folk
      {{ 'now'|date('Y') }}
      {% endblock %}
    </footer>
  </body>
</html>
```

Child templates can represent individual pages of the site. They inherit code from the parent template, and provide data to overwrite the content in the named blocks the parent contains.

Each type of page that visitors to the site can request (home, category, article, member, and search) has its own **child** template which **extends** the parent template. The `extends` tag specifies the name of the parent template to extend:

```
{% extends 'parent-template.html' %}
```

In the child template, anything between the `block` tags overwrites the content in the corresponding block in the parent template.

On this page, the child template `category.html` extends `layout.html`, and has two blocks:

- `title` replaces anything in the `title` block in the parent template.

- `content` replaces the `content` block in the parent template.

The child template does not contain a `footer` block, so the page will show the copyright message that was inside the footer block in the parent template.

Inside this child template, the `content` block uses an `include()` function inside a pair of curly braces to include another template file. This template displays a set of article summaries:

```
{{ include('article-summaries.html') }}
```

The parent, child and include files can all access the variables created by the `$data` array.

Child Template: `category.html`

```
{% extends 'layout.html' %}

{% block title %}
{{ category.name }}
{% endblock %}

{% block content %}
<h1>{{ category.name }}</h1>
<p>{{ category.description }}</p>

{{ include('article-summaries.html') }}
{% endblock %}
```

PARENT AND CHILD CATEGORY TEMPLATE

The child `category.html` template below shows details of any category. It inherits all of the markup from the `layout.html` parent template on the right.

1. The `extends` tag indicates that this child template inherits the code in `layout.html`.

2. The `title` block in this child template replaces the `title` block in the parent template. It shows the category name, then the words 'on Creative Folk'.

3. The `description` block in the child template replaces the `description` block in the parent template. It shows the category description in the `value` attribute of the `<meta>` description tag. It uses the `e()` filter to escape content for use in an attribute.

4. The `content` block in the child template replaces the `content` block in the parent template.

5. The category name is shown in an `<h1>` element.

6. This is followed by the category description shown inside a `<p>` element.

7. An include tag includes a template to display summaries of the articles in that category.

The `article-summaries.html` template (see p592) loops through the summaries in the `articles` array and displays the summary data for those articles.

8. The `content` block is closed.

```
c15/templates/category.html                                              TWIG
① {% extends 'layout.html' %}
② {% block title %}{{ category.name }} on Creative Folk{% endblock %}
③ {% block description %}{{ category.description|e('html_attr') }}{% endblock %}

④ {% block content %}
    <main class="container" id="content">
      <section class="header">
⑤      <h1>{{ category.name }}</h1>
⑥      <p>{{ category.description }}</p>
      </section>
      <section class="grid">
⑦      {{ include('article-summaries.html') }}
      </section>
    </main>
⑧ {% endblock %}
```

Twig templates can use any file extension. But, using the `.html` extension tells code editors the file contains HTML code.

The code editor can then highlight the code as if it is HTML and may also offer features such as highlighting errors.

The parent template holds the code used on every page.

It has three blocks: `title`, `description` and `content`.

It also loops through categories to create the main navigation.

`TWIG`

```twig
<!DOCTYPE html>
<html lang="en-US">
  <head> ...
    <title>{% block title %}Creative Folk{% endblock %}</title>
    <meta name="description" content="{% block description %}Hire ceatives{% endblock %}">
    <link rel="stylesheet" type="text/css" href="{{ doc_root }}css/styles.css"> ...
  </head>
  <body>
    <header>
      <div class="container">
        <a class="skip-link" href="#content">Skip to content</a>
        <div class="logo"><a href="{{ doc_root }}index.php">
          <img src="{{ doc_root }}img/logo.png" alt="Creative Folk">
        </a></div>
        <nav>
          <button id="toggle-navigation" aria-expanded="false">
            <span class="icon-menu"></span><span class="hidden">Menu</span>
          </button>
          <ul id="menu">
            {% for link in navigation %}
            {% if (link.navigation == 1) %}
              <li><a href="{{ doc_root }}category.php?id={{ link.id }}"
              {% if (section == link.id) %} class="on"{% endif %}>
                {{ link.name }}</a></li>
            {% endif %}
            {% endfor %}
            <li><a href="{{ doc_root }}search.php">
              <span class="icon-search"></span><span class="search-text">Search</span>
            </a></li>
          </ul>
        </nav>
      </div>
    </header>
    {% block content %}{% endblock %}
    <footer>
      <div class="container">
        <a href="{{ doc_root }}contact.php">Contact Us</a>
        <span class="copyright">&copy; Creative Folk {{ 'now'|date('Y') }}</span>
      </div>
    </footer>
    <script src="{{ doc_root }}js/site.js"></script>
  </body>
</html>
```

ARTICLE SUMMARY TEMPLATE

The `article-summaries.html` template shows summaries of several articles. It is used in the home, category, member, and search page templates.

1. A `for` loop works through an array of article summaries stored in a variable called `articles`. In the loop, each article is stored in a variable called `article`.

2. A link is created to the article.

3. A Twig `if` statement checks if the article has an image.

4. If so, the image and its alt text are shown in an `<img>` tag.

5. If not, the Twig `{% else %}` tag is followed by alternative code.

6. A placeholder image is shown.

7. The `{% endif %}` tag marks the end of the `if` statement.

8. The article title is shown in an `<h2>` element.

9. The summary is shown.

8. A link to the category that the article is in is created.

11. A link to the article author's page is created.

12. The loop ends with the tag `{% endfor %}`.

`c15/templates/article-summaries.html`

```twig
① {% for article in articles %}
    <article class="summary">
②     <a href="{{ doc_root }}article.php?id={{ article.id }}">
③       {% if article.image_file %}
④         <img src="{{ doc_root }}uploads/{{ article.image_file }}"
              alt="{{ article.image_alt }}">
⑤       {% else %}
⑥         <img src="{{ doc_root }}uploads/blank.png" alt="">
⑦       {% endif %}
⑧       <h2>{{ article.title }}</h2>
⑨       <p>{{ article.summary }}</p>
      </a>
      <p class="credit">
⑩       Posted in <a href="{{ doc_root }}category.php?id={{ article.category_id }}">
          {{ article.category }}</a>
⑪       by <a href="{{ doc_root }}member.php?id={{ article.member_id }}">
          {{ article.author }}</a>
      </p>
    </article>
⑫ {% endfor %}
```

ARTICLE TEMPLATE

1. This child template shows one article. The `extends` tag tells it to inherit code from `layout.html`.

2. The `title` block displays the title in the `<title>` element.

3. The `description` block holds the summary. The e filter escapes the text to use in HTML attributes.

4. The `content` block shows the full details of the article.

5. If the article has an image, it is shown; if not, `blank.png` is shown.

6. The title is written out again.

7. The `date` filter formats the date that the article was written.

8. The article content is shown using the `raw` filter to stop Twig escaping it, as it may contain HTML markup (which has already been made safe to display by HTML Purifier).

9. A link to the category that the article is in is created, followed by a link to the author's page.

`TWIG`　　　　　　　　　　　　　　　　　　　　　　　c15/templates/article.html

```twig
{% extends 'layout.html' %}
{% block title %}{{ article.title }}{% endblock %}
{% block description %}{{ article.summary|e('html_attr') }}{% endblock %}
{% block content %}
<main class="article container" id="content">
  <section class="image">
    {% if article.image_file %}
      <img src="{{ doc_root }}uploads/{{ article.image_file }}"
        alt="{{ article.image_alt }}">
    {% else %}
      <img src="{{ doc_root }}uploads/blank.png" alt="">
    {% endif %}
  </section>
  <section class="text">
    <h2>{{ article.title }}</h2>
    <div class="date">{{ article.created|date('F d, Y') }}</div>
    <div class="content">{{ article.content|raw }}</div>
    <p class="credit">
      Posted in <a href="{{ doc_root }}category.php?id={{ article.category_id }}">
      {{ article.category }}</a>
      by <a href="{{ doc_root }}member.php?id={{ article.member_id }}">
      {{ article.author }}</a></p>
  </section>
</main>
{% endblock %}
```

SENDING EMAILS USING PHPMAILER

Sites often send individual emails called **transactional emails**. For example, a password reset page can email a link for users to reset their password, or a contact form can send a message to the site's owner.

When you send an email from a computer or mobile device, you provide the email address of the recipient, a subject, and a message body. The email program then sends the email to a server called an SMTP server that delivers the email to the recipient.

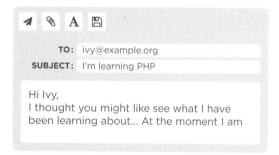

When an email program is set up to use a new email address, it needs to be told how to connect to the SMTP server. Typically, the following details are needed in order to connect to it:

- **Hostname** which identifies the SMTP server just like a domain name identifies a web server

- **Port number** which allows different programs on the same computer to share the same internet connection (see http://notes.re/php/ports)

- **Username and password** to log into an account

- **Security settings** to specify how the username and password should be sent securely

Similarly, when a site needs to send an email, it must perform the same two steps:

1. Connect to an SMTP server that can send email
2. Create the email and pass it to the SMTP server

The code to perform these two tasks is complex. Therefore, rather than writing the code to create and send emails from scratch, the sample site will use a package called **PHPMailer**. It is used in many popular open-source projects, including WordPress, Joomla, and Drupal.

The PHPMailer package is in the vendor folder of the code download for this chapter and it is listed as a required package in the composer.json file. Its name on Packagist is: phpmailer\phpmailer

Although a web server can run its own SMTP server, websites usually use a specialist company that provides an SMTP server to send the emails because:

- Sending too many emails from your web server can result in email services blacklisting your domain name and treating your emails as spam
- They have better delivery success rates

For a list of services that send transactional emails see: http://notes.re/transactional-emails.

You will need to sign up for one of these services to test the code that sends emails.

SETTINGS TO CONNECT TO THE SMTP SERVER

The details to connect to the SMTP server are different for each site that runs the CMS code; therefore, it is classed as configuration data and is stored in the `config.php` file.

Each site that uses the CMS code needs different settings to connect to *its* SMTP server (just like each site has different details to connect to *its* database).

The details used to connect to the SMTP server are stored as an associative array in the `config.php` file, along with the email address of the site owner.

c15/config/config.php

PHP

```
  ①  $email_config = [
  ②      'server'       => 'smtp.YOUR-SERVER.com',
  ③      'port'         => 'YOUR-PORT-NUMBER',
         'username'     => 'YOUR-USERNAME-HERE',
  ④      'password'     => 'YOUR-PASSWORD-HERE',
  ⑤      'security'     => 'tls',
  ⑥      'admin_email   => 'YOUR-EMAIL-HERE',
  ⑦      'debug'        => (DEV) ? 2 : 0,
      ];
```

First, store the data to connect to the SMTP server:

1. `$email_config` is the variable that holds an array of settings used to send emails.

2. `server` holds the hostname of the SMTP server.

3. `port` is the port number the SMTP server uses.

4. `username` and `password` hold the login details for the SMTP server account.

5. `security` holds the method used to send the data securely. The value for this is usually `tls`, which stands for Transport Layer Security (see p185).

Then, add the other two values that are needed:

6. `admin_email` is the email address of the site owner. It is the address that contact form messages are sent to (see p598-601), and the *from* address for other emails the site sends in the next chapter.

7. `debug` turns on and off debug messages. The value in the `DEV` constant determines the setting. It uses:

- 2 when developing a site to show emails sent by the web server and responses from the SMTP server

- 0 on a live site to disable debugging messages (as messages show data about the SMTP account)

CREATING AND SENDING AN EMAIL

First, create an object using the `PHPMailer` class and tell it how to connect to the SMTP server. Then, create and send the email.

A `PHPMailer` object is created using the `PHPMailer` class, just like you would create any other object. Its namespace is: `PHPMailer\PHPMailer`. This namespace must be used when creating the object.

When the `PHPMailer` object is created, a boolean value of `true` is used as an argument. This tells `PHPMailer` to throw an exception if it encounters a problem creating or sending an email.

```
$phpmailer = new \PHPMailer\PHPMailer\PHPMailer(true);
```
VARIABLE   NAMESPACE   CLASS   IF PROBLEM OCCURS, THROW EXCEPTION

Once the `PHPMailer` object has been created, two methods and eight properties are used to configure the object so it knows how *this* site will send emails.

They are like the settings an email program uses for a new email account. They will remain the same each time the site sends a transactional email.

PROPERTY / METHOD	DESCRIPTION
`isSMTP()`	Method to specify that an SMTP server will be used to send the emails
`Host`	Property to hold the host address of the SMTP server
`SMTPAuth`	Property to enable SMTP authentication; set to `true` because a username and password will be required to log into the SMTP server
`Username`	Property to hold the SMTP account username
`Password`	Property to hold the SMTP account password
`Port`	Property to hold the the port number that the SMTP server uses
`SMTPSecure`	Property to hold the the kind of encryption to use; usually set to `tls`
`SMTPDebug`	Property to tell PHPMailer whether or not to show debug information
`isHTML()`	Method to tell PHPMailer the email may contain HTML
`CharSet`	Property that sets the character encoding used in the email; if this is not set correctly, the text may not display correctly in the recipient's email program

Once a `PHPMailer` object has been created, and the settings have been configured, an email can be created and sent. The process of creating an email and passing it to the SMTP server involves calling three methods and setting three properties of the `PHPMailer` object.

The properties and methods in the first five rows of the table below are the equivalent of writing a new email in an email program. The values that they use can change each time the site sends an email. The last method is the equivalent of pressing the send button to send the email.

PROPERTY / METHOD	DESCRIPTION
`setFrom()`	Method to set the address the email is being sent from
`addAddress()`	Method to set the address the email is being sent to (This method can be called again to add further addresses)
`Subject`	Property to hold the subject line of the email
`Body`	Property to hold the body of the email that uses HTML
`AltBody`	Property to hold a plain text version of the email (without HTML markup)
`send()`	Method to connect to the SMTP server and pass it the email

Creating a `PHPMailer` object, telling it how to connect to an SMTP server, then creating and sending the email takes at least 18 lines of code.

Because a site often has several pages that need to send a transactional email, rather than repeating this code on each of those pages, the site can store all of this code in a new user-defined class called `Email`, which you will see on the next page.

Any page that needs to send an email is able to do so using the two statements below.

1. The first line creates an object using the user-defined `Email` class and stores it in a variable called `$email`. The configuration data that the object needs is passed to the constructor method.
2. The second line calls the `Email` object's `sendEmail()` method to create and send an email.

```
① $email = new Email($email_config);
② $email->sendEmail($from, $to, $subject, $message);
```

The new user-defined `Email` class is shown on the next page; it has two methods described below.

It is followed by an example of how the class is used on the subsequent two pages.

METHOD	DESCRIPTION
`__construct($email_config)`	Create a PHPMailer object, store it in the PHPMailer property. Configure how PHPMailer will connect to the SMTP server. These statements go in the `__construct()` method as they are the same every time a PHP page needs to send an email.
`sendEmail($from, $to, $subject, $message)`	Create an email and pass it to the SMTP server. This method is called to send an email. Each time it is called, its arguments can have different values.

CLASS TO CREATE AND SEND EMAILS

The `Email` class is used when a page needs to send an email. It contains the code that is used to create a `PHPMailer` object, generate an email, and pass it to an SMTP server to send it.

1. The class is given the namespace `PhpBook\Email`.

2. The `$phpmailer` property stores a `PHPMailer` object. It is declared as a `protected` property so that it can only be used by the code in this class.

3. The `__construct()` method has one parameter; the configuration data stored in `$email_config`. The tasks inside this method must be performed each time a page needs to send an email. They:

- Create a `PHPMailer` ojbect
- Configure how it can connect to the SMTP server
- Set the character encoding and type of email

4. The `PHPMailer` object is created and stored in *this* `Email` object's `$phpmailer` property. (The argument `true` tells PHPMailer to throw an exception if it encounters a problem creating or sending an email.)

5. The `PHPMailer` object's `isSMTP()` method shows that the email will be sent via an SMTP server.

6. The `SMTPAuth` property is set to `true` to indicate that a username and password are required to log into the SMTP server.

7. The data needed to connect to the SMTP server is set using the values from the `$email_config` array (which was passed to the constructor method when the object was created).

8. `PHPMailer` is told that the character encoding is UTF-8, and that it will send HTML emails.

9. The `sendEmail()` method creates and sends individual emails. It has four parameters that represent the data that can change each time the object is used to send an email.

- `$from` holds who the email will be sent from
- `$to` holds the recipient's email address
- `$subject` holds the subject line of the email
- `$message` holds the message to be sent

It returns `true` if the mail was created and sent.

10. The `setFrom()` method sets the email address that this email will be sent from.

11. The `addAddress()` method sets the email address that this message will be sent to.

12. The `Subject` property sets the email's subject.

13. The `Body` property sets the body of the email. It consists of some basic HTML tags to start the HTML email, followed by the value that was in the `$message` parameter, then the closing HTML tags.

14. The `AltBody` property sets the plain text version of the email. It uses PHP's `strip_tags()` function to remove markup from the message (see note on right).

15. `send()` passes the email to the SMTP server.

16. The method returns `true` to indicate that the email was created and passed to the SMTP server. (It would have thrown an exception if it did not work.)

You will see how to use the class to send an email next. Once a page has created an object using the `Email` class and sent an email, it can send further emails by calling the `sendEmail()` method again.

```php
<?php
namespace PhpBook\Email;                                          // Declare namespace

class Email {

    protected $phpmailer;                                         // PHPMailer object

    public function __construct($email_config)
    {
        $this->phpmailer = new \PHPMailer\PHPMailer\PHPMailer(true); // Create PHPMailer
        $this->phpmailer->isSMTP();                              // Use SMTP
        $this->phpmailer->SMTPAuth    = true;                    // Authentication on
        $this->phpmailer->Host        = $email_config['server'];   // Server address
        $this->phpmailer->SMTPSecure  = $email_config['security'];  // Type of security
        $this->phpmailer->Port        = $email_config['port'];     // Port
        $this->phpmailer->Username    = $email_config['username'];  // Username
        $this->phpmailer->Password    = $email_config['password'];  // Password
        $this->phpmailer->SMTPDebug   = $email_config['debug'];    // Debug method
        $this->phpmailer->CharSet     = 'UTF-8';                 // Character encoding
        $this->phpmailer->isHTML(true);                          // Set as HTML email
    }

    public function sendEmail($from, $to, $subject, $message): bool
    {
        $this->phpmailer->setFrom($from);                        // From email address
        $this->phpmailer->addAddress($to);                       // To email address
        $this->phpmailer->Subject = $subject;                    // Subject of email
        $this->phpmailer->Body    = '<!DOCTYPE html><html lang="en-us"><body>'
          . $message .'</body></html>';                          // Body of email
        $this->phpmailer->AltBody = strip_tags($message);        // Plain text body
        $this->phpmailer->send();                                // Send the email
        return true;                                             // Return true
    }
}
```

When an HTML email is sent, a plain text version of the email is sent with the HTML version. It is important to create this version of the email because spam filters like to see a plain text version of the email (and some people use plain text email readers).

PHP's built-in strip_tags() function is designed to remove tags from markup. Its parameter is a string that contains markup, and it returns the string with the tags removed. You could also use HTML Purifier to remove markup from your emails.

USING THE Email CLASS

A new `contact.php` page (see right-hand page) has a form to send an email to the site's owners. To send the email, the contact page creates an object using the `Email` class, then calls its `sendEmail()` method with four parameters: the email it is from, the one it should be sent to, the subject line, and the message.

1. The `use` command imports the code from the `Validate` class into the current namespace.

2. If the form has been submitted, the email address and message are collected and stored in variables.

3. The values that were provided are validated using the `Validate` class. Any error messages in the array are joined and stored in a variable called `$invalid`.

4. If the data was invalid, `$errors` holds a message.

5. Otherwise, the page tries to send the email.

6. The subject of the email is stored in `$subject`.

7. An `Email` object is created using the `Email` class.

8. The `Email` object's `sendEmail()` method is called to create and send the email. It has four arguments:
- The address the email is sent from
- The address to send the email to
- The subject line
- The message

9. If no exception has been thrown, the `$success` variable holds a success message for the user.

10. The `$data` array holds the data for the page, and Twig's `render()` method generates the HTML.

```twig
c15/templates/contact.html                                          TWIG

  {% extends 'layout.html' %}
  {% block content %}
  <main class="container" id="content">
    <section class="heading"><h1>Contact Us</h1></section>
    <form method="post" action="contact.php" class="form-contact">
      {% if errors.warning %}<div class="alert-danger">{{ errors.warning }}</div>{% endif %}
      {% if success %}<div class="alert-success">{{ success }}</div>{% endif %}
      <label for="email">Email: </label>
      <input type="text" name="email" id="email" value="{{ from }}" class="form-control">
      <span class="errors">{{ errors.email }}</span><br>
      <label for="message">Message: </label><br>
      <textarea id="message" name="message" class="form-control">{{ message }}</textarea>
      <span class="errors">{{ errors.message }}</span><br>
      <input type="submit" value="Submit Message" class="btn">
    </form>
  </main>
  {% endblock %}
```

```php
<?php
declare(strict_types = 1);                                      // Use strict types
use PhpBook\Validate\Validate;                                  // Import validate class
include '../src/bootstrap.php';                                 // Setup file
$from     = '';                                                 // Initialize: from
$message = '';                                                  // Message
$errors   = [];                                                 // Array for errors
$success = '';                                                  // Success message

if ($_SERVER['REQUEST_METHOD'] == 'POST') {                     // If form submitted
    $from              = $_POST['email'];                       // Email address
    $message           = $_POST['message'];                     // Message
    $errors['email']   = Validate::IsEmail($from)        ? '' : 'Email not valid';
    $errors['message'] = Validate::IsText($message, 1, 1000) ? '' : 'Please enter a
        message up to 1000 characters';
    $invalid = implode($errors);                                // Join any error messages
    if ($invalid) {                                             // If there are errors
        $errors['warning'] = 'Please correct the errors';       // Warning
    } else {                                                    // Otherwise try to send
        $subject = "Contact form message from " . $from;        // Create message body
        $email   = new \PhpBook\Email\Email($email_config);     // Create email object
        $email->sendEmail($email_config['admin_email'], $email_config['admin_email'],
            $subject, $message);                                // Send
        $success = 'Your message has been sent';                // Success message
    }
}
$data['navigation'] = $cms->getCategory()->getAll();            // All categories for nav
// The following values are only created if the user has submitted the form
$data['from']    = $from;                                       // From email
$data['message'] = $message;                                    // Message
$data['errors']  = $errors;                                     // Error messages
$data['success'] = $success;                                    // Success message
echo $twig->render('contact.html', $data);                      // Render template
```

The numbered markers on the left: ① use line, ② the two POST assignments, ③ the two Validate lines, ④ the if ($invalid), ⑤ the } else {, ⑥ the $subject line, ⑦ the $email = new line, ⑧ the sendEmail lines, ⑨ the $success line, ⑩ the $data block.

RESULT

CONTACT US

Email:

Message:

SUBMIT MESSAGE

NOTE: If the DEV constant in config.php is set to true (see Step 7 on p595), PHPMailer creates a long set of debug messages that are shown in the page before the header and form.

When the DEV constant is set to false, they are hidden.

SUMMARY
NAMESPACES & LIBRARIES

> Namespaces ensure that, if two or more classes, functions or constants share the same name, the PHP interpreter can distinguish between them.

> Libraries and packages allow you to use code that other programmers have written to perform a task.

> Composer helps manage the packages a site uses.

> Packagist.org lists packages Composer can use.

> Composer creates an autoloader that includes class files for the packages when a page uses them.

> HTML Purifier can be used to remove markup that could cause an XSS attack.

> Twig is a templating engine that separates the PHP code that gets and processes data from templates that control how that data is displayed.

> PHPMailer is a package that is used to create emails using PHP and pass them to an SMTP server.

16

MEMBERSHIP

This chapter shows how visitors can register as members of a site. They can then log in to view pages that are only shown to members and are personalized for them.

Typically, when a member registers for a site, they need to provide:

- An **identifier**: which is used to identify who they are, such as an email address or username. Each member of the site needs their own unique identifier.
- A **password**: which is used to confirm that they are who they claim to be. The user is the only person that should know their password.

This data gets stored in the database. In the sample website, when a member has logged in, they can:

- View pages that only members can access
- Create and edit their own profile
- Upload their own work

To learn how to do these things, this chapter is split into three sections:

- **Registering for a site:** How to collect the information required to identify an individual member of the site and store it in the database.
- **Logging in and personalizing pages:** How to allow members to log in, how to create pages that are tailored to individual members, and how to create members-only pages.
- **Updating the database without the user logging in:** How to let users update the database without logging in first; for example, when they need to update a password. This involves addressing a new set of security requirements.

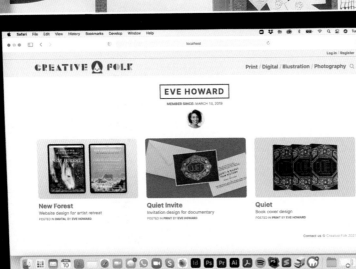

UPDATING THE DATABASE

For the final two chapters, the database for the sample website needs three extra tables, and new columns in several of the existing tables.

Following the steps that were described on p392, use PHPMyAdmin to:

- Create a new database called `phpbook-2`
- Import the `phpbook-2.sql` file (in the code download for this chapter) to create the tables in the new database and add data to them

Once you have created this new database, take a look at the changes in phpMyAdmin. First, there are three new tables. The `token` table is introduced near the end of this chapter. The `comment` and `likes` tables are introduced in the next chapter.

There are also new columns in the `article`, `category`, and `member` tables. The new `role` column in the `member` table is introduced in this chapter. The new `seo_title` column in the `article` table and the `seo_name` column in the `category` table are introduced in the next chapter.

Once you have looked at the database changes in phpMyAdmin, open the `config.php` file in the code for this chapter and add the settings to connect to the new database. The only setting that is different from the previous chapters is the new database name (`phpbook-2`).

Once you have the sample code for this chapter running on your computer, use the register link that is in the top right-hand corner of every page to create your own account. Once you have registered, log in and take a look around this version of the site. You should see that:

- There are more members (and their work)
- You can only access the admin pages if you are logged in (and are allowed to look at them)

By the end of this chapter, you will have learned how the code lets users register, log in, upload their own work, and request a password reset link.

NOTE: The code download for this chapter contains a few files that are not described in print because the tasks they perform have already been described in other examples in the book.

For example, the page that allows members to upload work is like the page that allowed administrators to create articles; the main differences are that members are required to upload an image and their articles are automatically published. Similarly, the page for members to edit their profiles works like the page administrators use to edit categories.

REGISTERING USERS

Visitors must fill in the registration form to become a member of the site. Their details are stored in the member table of the database.

The register.php page uses the form shown above to allow visitors to register as a member of the site.

When the form is submitted, the data is validated, and a new method of the Member class called create() adds their data to the member table using the techniques you learned in Chapter 14.

Registration introduces two new concepts:

- **Roles**: which control what tasks a user of the site has permission to perform

- **Password hashes**: which websites store instead of the actual password that the member typed in when they registered

ROLES

Websites often allow different members to view different pages and perform different tasks. A **role** is used to define what tasks a member can perform. The sample site distinguishes between:

- A **visitor**: someone who is not logged in. They can only browse the work on the site.

- A **member**: someone who has registered and, logged in. They can edit their member profile, upload new work, and edit existing works.

- A **suspended** member: someone who registered, but their use of the site has been suspended. They will be prevented from logging in.

- An **admin**: the site owner or a person working for the site. They can view admin pages, create categories, delete work, and update users' roles.

In the member table, a new column called role stores the role of each member. Its value will be member, suspended, or admin (it does not store visitor because that is for people who have not logged in).

NOTE: When users register for the sample site, their role is set to admin because this allows *you* to access the admin pages without manually changing your role in the database. On a live site, the default role for new members would be set to member and an administrator would be able to change their role.

PASSWORD HASHES

For security reasons, websites should not store members' passwords. Instead, they store an encrypted version of the password called a **hash**. It is not possible to decrypt a hash back into the original text.

A member is the only person who should know their password. A site can check a member's password but the passwords should not be stored in the database.

When members sign up, an algorithm (a set of rules) encrypts their passwords into a **hash**, which looks like a random set of alphanumeric characters. The database stores the hash instead of the password.

PHP has built-in functions to create hashes. Every time the function is used to turn the password into a hash, it produces the same set of characters.

When a registered member logs into the site, the password they enter is run through the hashing algorithm again. If that value matches the hash stored in the database, the user gave the correct password.

INPUT: PASSWORD
When members enter a password, a hashing function converts the password into a hash:

RESULT: HASH
The database will store the hash (it does not store the real password):

email	password
ivy@eg.link	$2y$10$XTeGk6Z7XG1Gs 26.MVvCIOANsdgFjZOYE MDWYlmlca4cOKyMwjufi

A hash cannot be converted back into the original password, so even if someone got access to the database, they could not get members' passwords. This protects both your own site and members who may have used the same password on other sites.

No matter how many characters the password is, its hash will be the same number of characters (in this book, it is 60 characters), so the hash does not give clues as to the length of the password.

To make the hash even more secure, PHP adds an extra random set of letters to the password called a **salt**. When the user logs in again, PHP:

- Detects the salt from the user's saved hash
- Creates a hash of the password they used to log in
- Adds the salt to the new password hash
- Compares the stored value with the new value

If both match, the user provided the right password.

CREATING AND CHECKING HASHED PASSWORDS

PHP's `password_hash()` function creates a hash from a password. PHP's `password_verify()` function checks that the password supplied by the visitor creates the same hash that has already been saved.

PHP's built-in `password_hash()` function takes a password and returns a hash. It has three parameters:

- The password that is being hashed
- The name of the hashing algorithm to use
- An optional array of settings for that algorithm (the sample site does not set any options)

The PHP.net site specifies a set of constants that can be used to specify the name of the hashing algorithm the code uses, see `http://notes.re/php/pwd_hash/` The sample site uses the name `PASSWORD_DEFAULT`, which indicates PHP's default hashing algorithm. At the time of writing, this was the `bcrypt` algorithm, but this may change as stronger algorithms are created.

```
password_hash($password, $algorithm[, $options]);
```
PASSWORD ALGORITHM OPTIONS

PHP's built-in `password_verify()` function takes a password that a user supplied and creates a hash. It then compares that value to the hash that has already been stored for it. If both values match, then the user has provided the correct password. The `password_verify()` function has two parameters:

- The password the member just supplied
- The hash that was already stored for that member

You do not need to specify the algorithm or salt that was used when the hash was created, because the `password_verify()` function can detect these settings from the stored hash.

The function returns:

- `true` if the hashes match
- `false` if they are different values

```
password_verify($password, $hash);
```
PASSWORD   HASH STORED
USER ENTERED   IN DATABASE

REGISTERING NEW MEMBERS (PART 1)

The registration page works like the admin pages that add data to the database. When the form is submitted, the data is validated. If it is valid, a new method of the Member class will add the member to the database.

The `register.php` file allows visitors to sign up as members of the site (p607 showed what this page looks like in the browser). When visitors complete the form, if they provide valid data, the `create()` method of the `Member` object (which you will meet on p612) will add them to the database. If the data is not valid, they are shown error messages instead.

1. Strict types are enabled, and the `Validate` namespace is imported so that it can be used in the page without typing the full namespace.

2. The `bootstrap.php` file is included in the page.

3. The `$member` and `$errors` arrays are initialized as blank arrays so that they can be added to the `$data` array that the Twig templates use (in Step 12) even if no data is added to them in Steps 4-11.

4. An `if` statement checks if the form was posted.

5. If it was, the data is collected from the form. The value from the password confirm box is stored in a separate variable because its value will not be added to the database (it is only used to confirm that the user entered the same password twice).

6. The data is validated. If any data is invalid, error messages are stored in the `$errors` array. There are two new methods in the `Validate` class for this chapter; they check that the email address is valid and that the password meets the minimum requirements.

7. All of the values in the `$errors` array are joined into one string called `$invalid`.

8. An `if` statement checks if `$invalid` does *not* contain any text. If it does not, the data is valid. If it does, the `$errors` array contains at least one error message.

9. If the data is valid, the `create()` method of the `Member` object is called to add the member to the database (this method is introduced on p612). The `create()` method returns `true` if the member is added successfully, or `false` if the email address is already in use (or, if there is any other problem, an exception is thrown). The value that is returned is stored in `$result`.

10. An `if` statement checks if `$result` holds `false`. If it does, the `email` key of the `$errors` array stores a message telling the user that the email address is already in use.

11. Otherwise, the user was added to the database in Step 9, so they are redirected to the login page, and a success message is sent in the query string.

12. The data that the Twig template needs to display is stored in an array called `$data`.

13. The Twig environment object's `render()` method is called to create the HTML to send back to the browser. It uses the `register.html` template.

```php
<?php
declare(strict_types = 1);                              // Use strict types
use PhpBook\Validate\Validate;                          // Import Validate class

include '../src/bootstrap.php';                         // Setup file
$member = [];                                           // Initialize member array
$errors = [];                                           // Initialize errors array

if ($_SERVER['REQUEST_METHOD'] == 'POST') {             // If form was posted
    // Get form data
    $member['forename'] = $_POST['forename'];           // Get forename
    $member['surname']  = $_POST['surname'];            // Get surname
    $member['email']    = $_POST['email'];              // Get email
    $member['password'] = $_POST['password'];           // Get password
    $confirm            = $_POST['confirm'];            // Get password confirmation


    // Validate form data
    $errors['forename'] = Validate::isText($member['forename'], 1, 254)
        ? '' : 'Forename must be 1-254 characters';
    $errors['surname']  = Validate::isText($member['surname'], 1, 254)
        ? '' : 'Surname must be 1-254 characters';
    $errors['email']    = Validate::isEmail($member['email'])
        ? '' : 'Please enter a valid email';
    $errors['password'] = Validate::isPassword($member['password'])
        ? '' : 'Passwords must be at least 8 characters and have:<br>
               A lowercase letter<br>An uppercase letter<br>A number
               <br>And a special character';
    $errors['confirm']  = ($member['password'] = $confirm)
        ? '' : 'Passwords do not match';
    $invalid            = implode($errors);             // Join error messages

    if (!$invalid) {                                    // If no errors
        $result = $cms->getMember()->create($member);   // Create member
        if ($result === false) {                        // If result is false
            $errors['email'] = 'Email address already used'; // Store a warning
        } else {                                        // Otherwise send to login
            redirect('login.php', ['success' => 'Thanks for joining! Please log in.']);
        }
    }
}

$data['navigation'] = $cms->getCategory()->getAll();    // All categories for nav
$data['member']     = $member;                          // Member data
$data['errors']     = $errors;                          // Error messages

echo $twig->render('register.html', $data);             // Render template
```

REGISTERING NEW MEMBERS (PART 2)

On the right, the top code box shows the Twig template used to display the registration form. The form in the code download has some more HTML elements and attributes that are used to control its presentation; some of them have been removed from this code box so you can focus on what it does and so that it fits on the page.

1. The template extends `layout.html`, and provides new content for the `title` and `description` blocks. (These blocks overwrite the default text that was provided in the `<title>` and `<meta>` tags in the `layout.html` template shown on p591.)

2. The `content` block holds the registration form.

3. The form is submitted to the same PHP page.

4. If the form data was not valid, a warning message is shown to the visitor.

5. The form controls are displayed.

The form can access two arrays that contain data if the form was submitted but the data was not valid:

- `member` is an array of the data the user provided. This is used to populate the form controls so that the visitor does not need to re-enter all their data.
- `errors` is an array that holds error messages for each form control that did not pass validation. These messages are shown after the form controls.

Both of these arrays were initialized as blank arrays at the top of the `register.php` file in Step 3 on the previous page.

The `create()` method of the `Member` class adds a member to the database. It follows the same approach used to create categories (on p498-503). If a member is added, the method returns `true`. If the email address is already in use, it returns `false`.

6. `create()` takes one parameter: an array containing the member data. It returns a boolean.

7. The `password_hash()` function replaces the password the user supplied with a hash.

8. A `try` block holds the code to add the member data to the database.

9. The SQL INSERT statement adds the forename, surname, email and hash to the `member` table of the database. (The database creates the values for the `id`, `joined` and `role` columns.)

10. The SQL statement is run.

11. If the code in the method is still running, the SQL executed successfully so the method returns `true`.

12. If PDO encountered a problem, an exception will have been thrown and the `catch` block is run.

13. If the error code is 1062, it indicates that the email address is already in the database and adding the data would break a uniqueness constraint, so the function returns `false`.

14. Otherwise, the exception is re-thrown using the `throw` keyword, so it can be handled by the default exception handling function.

```twig
{% extends 'layout.html' %}
{% block title %}Register{% endblock %}
{% block description %}Register for Creative Folk{% endblock %}
{% block content %}
<main class="container" id="content">
  <section class="header"><h1>Register</h1></section>
  <form method="post" action="register.php" class="form-membership">
    {% if errors %}<div class="alert alert-danger">Please correct errors</div>{% endif %}
    <label for="forename">Forename: </label>
    <input type="text" name="forename" value="{{ member.forename }}" id="forename">
    <div class="errors">{{ errors.forename }}</div>
    <label for="surname">Surname: </label>
    <input type="text" name="surname" value="{{ member.surname }}" id="surname">
    <div class="errors">{{ errors.surname }}</div>
    <label for="email">Email address: </label>
    <input type="email" name="email" value="{{ member.email }}" id="email">
    <div class="errors">{{ errors.email }}</div>
    <label for="password">Password: </label>
    <input type="password" name="password" id="password">
    <div class="errors">{{ errors.password }}</div>
    <label for="confirm">Confirm password: </label>
    <input type="password" name="confirm" id="confirm">
    <div class="errors">{{ errors.confirm }}</div>
    <input type="submit" class="btn btn-primary" value="Register">
  </form>
</main>
{% endblock %}
```

```php
public function create(array $member): bool
{
    $member['password'] = password_hash($member['password'], PASSWORD_DEFAULT); // Hash
    try {                                                          // Try to add member
        $sql = "INSERT INTO member (forename, surname, email, password)
                VALUES (:forename, :surname, :email, :password);"; // SQL to add member
        $this->db->runSQL($sql, $member);                          // Run SQL
        return true;                                               // Return true
    } catch (\PDOException $e) {                      // If PDOException thrown
        if ($e->errorInfo[1] === 1062) {             // If error indicates duplicate entry
            return false;                            // Return false to show duplicate email
        }                                            // Otherwise
        throw $e;                                    // Re-throw exception
    }
}
```

LOGGING IN AND PERSONALIZATION

When members return to the site and log in, they are asked for their email address to **identify** them and their password to **authenticate** that they are who they claim to be.

The login.php page lets members log in. When the login form is submitted, a new method of the Member class called login() looks for the member's email address in the member table of the database and gets their details, including the hash of their password.

If the password the user provided when logging in creates the same hash that the database has stored for them, the site assumes that the member is who they claim to be and they are logged in.

Once a member has logged in, there are two key things the site will do:

- **Create a session** to remember them during their current visit; it will store key data about the member and the fact that they logged in

- **Personalize pages** for that member with information that is specific to them

SESSIONS

Once a member has logged in, a session is created for them. The session lets the site identify that member every time they request another page during that visit to the site. It stores the member's id, name and role because they are used in the navigation bar to:

- Add a link to their profile page; the link uses their member id in the query string
- Show their name as the link text for the link
- Add a link to the admin pages if their role is admin

Because each page will need to work with the sessions in order to create the navigation bar, a new Session class (p620-21) will be created to help work with the data in the $_SESSION superglobal:

- If the user is logged in, the user's session data is added to properties of the Session object
- If not, the values of those properties will automatically be given default values

The Session class also has methods to create, update and delete sessions. The class groups together the code used to work with sessions and reduces the amount of code needed in each page. The Session object is created in bootstrap.php, and is also made available in a Twig global variable so that all of the templates can access the session data.

Once a member has logged in, the site can create pages that are tailored to that user based on information the database stores about them.

PERSONALIZATION

Once the site can identify an individual member, it can then customize pages based on that user's preferences and profile.

The left-hand page already described how, when the user logs in, the navigation bar displays a link to their profile page and, if the user is an administrator of the site, it shows a link to the admin pages.

In addition, when a user visits their `member.php` page, it displays links that allow them to add or edit their work and update their profile (as shown on the right).

The same `member.php` file is used to display the details and work of every member of the site, but these extra links are *only* shown when a member is logged in and is viewing their own page.

As well as creating personalized pages, this section secures the admin pages because they should only be viewed by the administrators. Up until this point, anyone was able to view them.

To secure the admin pages, a new function called `is_admin()` is added to the `functions.php` file. It is called at the start of every admin page. If the user is not both logged in *and* an administrator, they will not be able to view the page.

The download code has the following files, which are not in print as they are like files you have already met:

- `work.php` allows users to upload and edit their work. It is like `article.php` in Chapter 14 (except an image is required and `published` is set to `true`).

- `profile-edit.php` lets users edit their profile. It is like the admin page used to edit categories.

- `profile-pic-delete.php` deletes a profile picture. This is like the `image-delete.php` file used to delete article images.

- `profile-pic-upload.php` lets users upload a new profile picture. It uses the same technique as `article.php` to upload images.

LOGGING IN (PART 1)

When a member returns to the site, the login page lets them sign in. If they provide the correct details, it creates a new session that stores details about them during this visit to the site.

The `login.php` page allows members to log in.

1. Strict types are enabled, the `Validate` namespace is imported, and `bootstrap.php` is included.

2. The `$email` variable and `$errors` array are initialized. They are needed to create the `$data` array that the Twig templates need in Step 15.

3. If the query string holds the name `success`, its value is stored in the `$success` variable. (This is added to the query string when a new user registers.)

4. An `if` statement checks if the form was posted.

5. If it was, the email address and password are collected from the `$_POST` superglobal array and stored in variables called `$email` and `$password`.

6. The email address and password are validated. If they are not valid, error messages are stored in the corresponding keys of the `$errors` array.

7. PHP's `implode()` function joins the values in the `$errors` array into a single string stored in `$invalid`.

8. An `if` statement tests if `$invalid` contains any error messages.

9. If it does, the `message` key of the `$errors` array holds a message telling the user to try again.

10. Otherwise, the login data was valid...

11. The `login()` method of the `Member` class is called (see p618-19). It checks if the email address is in the database, and if the user provided the right password. If the details are correct, the method returns the member's data as an array. If not, it returns `false`. The value it returns is stored in `$member`.

An `if... elseif` statement handles the outcomes:

12. If the `$member` variable is holding member data *and* their role is `suspended`, then the `$errors` array holds a message saying the account is suspended.

13. If `$member` has a value the member has logged in successfully.

14. A session is created for that visitor using the `create()` method of a new `Session` object (which is introduced on p620-21).

15. Once the user is logged in, they are redirected to their profile page (and the rest of the page does not run). From this point on, the navigation:

- Replaces the log in link with a log out link
- Contains a link to the member's profile page
- Links to the admin area if the member is an admin

16. Otherwise, no member was found, so the `$errors` array holds a message telling the user to try again.

17. The `$data` array holds the data the template needs and Twig's `render()` method creates the page.

```php
<?php
declare(strict_types = 1);                          // Use strict types
use PhpBook\Validate\Validate;                      // Import Validate class

include '../src/bootstrap.php';                     // Setup file

$email   = '';                                      // Initialize email variable
$errors  = [];                                      // Initialize errors array
$success = $_GET['success'] ?? null;                // Get success message

if ($_SERVER['REQUEST_METHOD'] == 'POST') {         // If form submitted
    $email    = $_POST['email'];                    // Get email address
    $password = $_POST['password'];                 // Get password
    $errors['email']    = Validate::isEmail($email)
        ? '' : 'Please enter a valid email address';   // Validate email
    $errors['password'] = Validate::isPassword($password)
        ? '' : 'Passwords must be at least 8 characters and have:<br>
                A lowercase letter<br>An uppercase letter<br>A number<br>
                And another character';             // Validate password
    $invalid = implode($errors);                    // Join errors

    if ($invalid) {                                 // If data is not valid
        $errors['message'] = 'Please try again.';   // Store error message
    } else {                                        // If data was valid
        $member = $cms->getMember()->login($email, $password); // Get member details
        if ($member and $member['role'] == 'suspended') {  // If member is suspended
            $errors['message'] = 'Account suspended';   // Store message
        } elseif ($member) {                        // Otherwise for members
            $cms->getSession()->create($member);    // Create session
            redirect('member.php', ['id' => $member['id'],]); // Redirect to their page
        } else {                                    // Otherwise
            $errors['message'] = 'Please try again.';   // Store error message
        }
    }
}

$data['navigation'] = $cms->getCategory()->getAll();   // Get navigation categories
$data['success']    = $success;                     // Success message
$data['email']      = $email;                       // Email address if login failed
$data['errors']     = $errors;                      // Errors array
echo $twig->render('login.html', $data);            // Render template
```

NOTE: Error messages should not show that an email address is right but that a password is wrong, as this confirms that the email address had registered for the site.

TRY: Once you have used the Session object on p620-21, add an if statement between Steps 2 and 3 to check if the member has already logged in. If they have, redirect them to their member page.

LOGGING IN (PART 2)

The first code box shows the Twig template for the login form. The code download has more HTML elements and attributes to control presentation, but some of them have been removed so you can focus on what it does and so that it fits within the page.

1. The template extends `layout.html`, and provides new content for the `title` and `description` blocks.

2. The `content` block holds the login form.

3. The form is submitted to the same PHP page.

4. If `success` has a value (it is not `null`), a new user has registered and a success message is shown.

5. If the `errors` array contains values, the value for the `warning` key is shown.

6. The form has email and password inputs. If there are error messages in the `$errors` array, they are shown after the corresponding form control (the password error message uses Twig's `raw` filter as it uses HTML markup – see Step 7 on previous page).

The second code box shows a new `login()` method in the `Member` class. It checks if the email and password are correct. If they are, it returns that member's details. If not, it returns `false`.

7. `login()` needs an email address and password.

8. The `$sql` variable stores a SQL query to get the member's data using the email address.

9. The SQL is run and the data is stored in `$member`.

10. If the member's details were not found, the `login()` method returns `false`.

11. If the code in the method is still running then the member has been found. Next, PHP's `password_verify()` function creates a hash from the password they gave when they logged in, and checks if it matches their hash in the database. It returns `true` if they match, `false` if not. The result is stored in a variable called `$authenticated`.

12. A ternary operator checks if `$authenticated` stores the value `true`. If it does, the method returns the `$member` array. If not, it returns `false`.

The final code box shows the `bootstrap.php` page, which contains the code to set up every page. As you have seen, when a member logs in, their id, forename, surname, and role are stored in a session because every page needs to access that session data in order to create the navigation bar. As you saw in Chapter 9, when a site uses sessions, each page of the site must:

- Call PHP's `session_start()` function
- Check if the `$_SESSION` superglobal array has the data that the page is trying to access before accessing it (if this is not done, it can cause an `Undefined index` error)

Rather than repeat the code to do this on every page, the `bootstrap.php` file (included by each page) creates a `Session` object using the new `Session` class (shown next). This code is placed in its `__construct()` method so that it runs when the object is created. If the user has logged in, it takes their data from the `$_SESSION` superglobal array and stores it in properties of the `Session` object.

13. The `Session` object is created in `bootstrap.php`.

14. Its properties are stored in a Twig global variable so that they can be accessed by any template.

```twig
{% extends 'layout.html' %}
{% block title %}Log In{% endblock %}
{% block description %}Log in to your Creative Folk account{% endblock %}
{% block content %}
<main class="container" id="content">
  <form method="post" action="login.php" class="form-membership">
    <section class="header"><h1>Log in:</h1></section>
    {% if success %}<div class="alert alert-success">{{ success }}</div>{% endif %}
    {% if errors %}<div class="alert alert-danger">{{ errors.message }}</div>{% endif %}

    <label for="email">Email: </label>
    <input type="text" name="email" id="email" value="{{ email }}" class="form-control">
    <div class="errors">{{ errors.email }}</div>
    <label for="password">Password: </label>
    <input type="password" name="password" id="password" class="form-control">
    <div class="errors">{{ errors.password|raw }}</div>
    <input type="submit" class="btn btn-primary" value="Log in"><br>
    <p><a href="password-lost.php">Lost password?</a></p>
  </form>
</main>
{% endblock %}
```

① ② ③ ④ ⑤ ⑥

```php
public function login(string $email, string $password)
{
    $sql = "SELECT id, forename, surname, joined, email, password, picture, role
            FROM member
            WHERE email = :email;";                        // SQL to get member data
    $member = $this->db->runSQL($sql, [$email])->fetch();  // Run SQL
    if (!$member) {                                        // If no member found
        return false;                                      // Return false
    }                                                      // Otherwise
    $authenticated = password_verify($password, $member['password']); // Passwords match?
    return ($authenticated ? $member : false);             // Return member or false
}
```

⑦ ⑧ ⑨ ⑩ ⑪ ⑫

```php
$loader = new Twig\Loader\FilesystemLoader(APP_ROOT . '/templates'); // Twig loader
$twig   = new Twig\Environment($loader, $twig_options);  // Twig environment
$twig->addGlobal('doc_root', DOC_ROOT);                  // Document root
$session = $cms->getSession();                           // Create session
$twig->addGlobal('session', $session);                  // Add session to Twig global
```

⑬ ⑭

USING SESSIONS TO STORE USER DATA

The header used on each page of the site needs to know whether a user is logged in or not:

- If they are, the header contains a link to their member page using the member's forename as the link text and their id in the query string.

- If they are not logged in, the header contains links to the `login.php` and `register.php` pages.

If the user is logged in and they are an admin, the header also shows a link to the admin pages.

To create these links, every page needs to know the member's id, forename and role; therefore this information is stored in a session.

As shown on the previous page, `bootstrap.php` (which is included in every page) creates an object using the user-defined `Session` class shown on the right. Using a `Session` class like this groups together the code to create, access, update and delete sessions in one place. This class has three properties:

- `id` holds the member's id
- `forename` holds the member's forename
- `role` holds the member's role

When the object is created, its `__construct()` method:

- Calls `session_start()`

- Checks if a session holds details for this member. If it does, those values are stored in the properties of the object. If it does not, the properties are assigned default values.

1. The namespace for the class is declared.

2. The class is called `Session`.

3. The three properties are declared. They store a member's id, forename and role.

4. The `__construct()` method automatically runs when a `Session` object is created using this class.

5. PHP's `session_start()` function enables sessions and renews existing sessions.

6. If the `$_SESSION` superglobal array has keys called `id`, `forename` and `role`, their values are stored in the properties of the `Session` object. If not, those properties store default values.

7. The `create()` method is called when a user logs in. It needs the array that holds the member's data.

8. PHP's `session_regenerate_id()` function (p340) updates the session ID used in both the session file and cookie.

9. The member's id, forename, and role are added to the `$_SESSION` superglobal array.

10. The `update()` method calls the `create()` method. Because the code to create or update the session requires the same code, it should not be repeated. The `update()` method is known as an **alias** of the `create()` method because it is an alternative name used to call the statements in the `create()` method.

11. The `delete()` method is called when the user clicks on the logout link in the navigation. Its job is to end the session (see p343 for how this works).

```php
<?php
namespace PhpBook\CMS;                                   // Declare namespace

class Session
{                                                       // Define Session class
    public $id;                                         // Store member's id
    public $forename;                                   // Store member's forename
    public $role;                                       // Store member's role

    public function __construct()
    {                                                   // Runs when object created
        session_start();                                // Start, or restart, session
        $this->id       = $_SESSION['id'] ?? 0;         // Set id property of this object
        $this->forename = $_SESSION['forename'] ?? '';  // Set forename property
        $this->role     = $_SESSION['role'] ?? 'public'; // Set role property
    }

    // Create new session - also used to update an existing session
    public function create($member)
    {
        session_regenerate_id(true);                    // Update the session id
        $_SESSION['id']       = $member['id'];          // Add member id to session
        $_SESSION['forename'] = $member['forename'];    // Add forename to session
        $_SESSION['role']     = $member['role'];        // Add role to session
    }

    // Update existing session - alias for create()
    public function update($member)
    {
        $this->create($member);
    }

    // Delete existing session
    public function delete()
    {
        $_SESSION = [];                                 // Empty $_SESSION superglobal
        $param    = session_get_cookie_params();        // Get session cookie parameters
        setcookie(session_name(), '', time() - 2400, $param['path'], $param['domain'],
            $param['secure'], $param['httponly']);      // Clear session cookie
        session_destroy();                              // Destroy the session
    }
}
```

PERSONALIZING THE NAVIGATION BAR

The Session object created in `bootstrap.php` is stored in a Twig global variable so that every template can access its properties. In `layout.html`:

1. An if statement checks if the `id` property of the Session object has a value of 0 (indicating that the user is *not* logged in).

2. If so, the template shows login and register links.

3. Otherwise, the member is logged in.

4. A link is created to the member's profile page, with their forename shown in the link text.

5. An if statement checks if the `role` property of the Session object has a value of `admin`. If so, a link to the admin area is displayed.

6. A link to `logout.php` allows users to log out. (The `logout.php` file is in the code download; it just calls the `delete()` method of the Session object, and then redirects the user to the home page.)

`c16/templates/layout.html`   **TWIG**

```twig
{% if session.id == 0 %}
  <a href="login.php" class="nav-item nav-link">Log in</a> /
  <a href="register.php" class="nav-item nav-link">Register</a>
{% else %}
  <a href="member.php?id={{ session.id }}">{{ session.forename }}</a> /
  {% if session.role == 'admin' %}
    <a href="admin/index.php">Admin</a> /
  {% endif %}
    <a href="logout.php">Logout</a>
{% endif %}
```

RESULT

Log in / Register

Print / **Digital** / **Illustration** / **Photography** 🔍

Ivy / Admin / Logout

Print / **Digital** / **Illustration** / **Photography** 🔍

ADDING OPTIONS TO A MEMBER'S PROFILE PAGE

The member.php file displays the profile of a member of the site and summaries of their work. If a member is logged in and views their own profile, they are shown links to update their profile and add new work.

1. In member.html, a Twig if statement checks if the member's id (stored in the session) is the same as the id of the member whose work is being displayed. If they match, new links are shown under the profile.

2. In article-summaries.html, another Twig if statement checks if the id of the member viewing the page is the same as the id of the member who wrote each article. If so, a link to edit that work is added.

The work.php file that allows users to upload work is in the code download. It is similar to article.php in the admin section; but an image is required, the member is the author, and there is no publish option.

`TWIG`   c16/templates/member.html

```
{% if session.id == member.id %}
<nav class="member-options">
  <a href="work.php" class="btn btn-primary">Add work</a>
  <a href="member-edit-profile.php" class="btn btn-primary">Edit profile</a>
  <a href="member-edit-picture.php" class="btn btn-primary">Profile picture</a>
</nav>
{% endif %}
```

①

`TWIG`   c16/templates/article-summaries.html

```
{% if session.id == article.member_id %}
  <a href="work.php?id={{ article.id }}" class="btn btn-primary">Edit</a>
{% endif %}
```

②

`RESULT`

The pages to edit a profile, and the pages to upload or delete profile pictures, are in the code download. You could try writing these pages to test your skills:

- The page to edit profiles is like the code to edit a category
- The code to add/delete profile images is like the code to add or delete images in articles

RESTRICTING ACCESS TO ADMIN PAGES

In previous chapters, anyone could access the admin pages of the site. In this chapter, only members whose role is admin can access those pages.

1. Every admin page calls a new function called is_admin() right after the bootstrap.php file has been included. It needs the role of the member as an argument. (When a member is not logged in, the Session object sets the role to public.)

2. The is_admin() function definition is added to functions.php.

3. An if statement checks if the role is *not* admin.

4. If it is not, the user is sent to the home page.

(They are sent to the home page rather than login.php to prevent people who are not administrators from guessing the URLs of the admin pages.)

5. The exit command stops any more code in the page that called the function from running. (If the user is an admin, the rest of the page runs.)

c16/public/admin/article.php `PHP`

```php
<?php
// Part A: Setup
declare(strict_types = 1);                    // Use strict types
use PhpBook\Validate;                         // Import Validate namespace

include '../../src/bootstrap.php';            // Include setup file
① is_admin($session->role);                   // Check if admin
```

c16/src/functions.php `PHP`

```php
② function is_admin($role)
   {
③      if ($role !== 'admin') {               // If role is not admin
④          header('Location: ' . DOC_ROOT);   // Send to home page
⑤          exit;                              // Stop code running
       }
   }
```

You should usually require a user to log in before they can perform tasks that update the database. So far in this chapter, the user must be logged in to do this.

There are rare occasions when you might let users update the database without logging in, but this requires extra security measures as you learn next.

EMAIL LINKS THAT UPDATE DATABASES AND TOKENS

Sites sometimes let members update the database without logging in. This is often when they have been sent an email containing a link, such as a password reset link. The links use a **token** to identify the user it is for.

If a user forgets their password, they cannot log into the site to reset it, so the site needs to offer them another way to securely update it.

One solution is to email the user a link to a page that they can use to update their password. Because the link is sent to that user's email address, they should be the only person able to use the link.

The link should not use a member's email address or the id from the id column of the member table to identify the user because a hacker could take the link to that page and guess other members' email addresses or ids (allowing them to reset passwords of those users and then log into their accounts). Instead, when the user asks to reset their password, a token is created to identify the user. The token is a random set of characters, which is unique and cannot easily be guessed, e.g.:

```
0d9781153ed42ea7d72b4a4963dbd4f7fbc1d09bca10
a8faae55d5dd66441521881a4e51eb17cd62596b156f
11218d31436e5ae3381bcb50acbf31dd2c5cd197
```

This token is:

- Stored in the database in a new table called token
- Used to identify the user

When the user clicks on the link containing a token, the site looks in the token table in the database (see p626) to determine which member it was created for.

The next few pages show how tokens are used when a member wants to reset their password. First, users enter their email on password-lost.php.

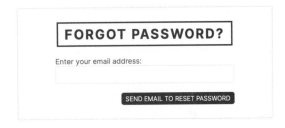

When this form is submitted, the site checks if there is a user with the given email address. If there is, it adds a new token to the token table of the database and emails them a link to the password-reset.php page, which allows them to update their password. The token is used in the link to identify which member is trying to update their password.

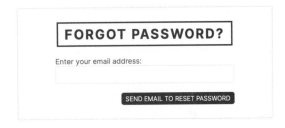

When the user updates their password, a new method of the Member class called passwordUpdate() is used to update the password.

STORING TOKENS IN THE DATABASE

A new class called Token is used to create a Token object that can generate the tokens, store them in the new token table in the database, and return the id of the members they were created for.

At a minimum, the new token table must store the token and id of the member that it was created for. For extra security, each token also stores its:

- **Expiry time**: to prevent the token remaining valid long after it was intended to be used. For this site, it is four hours after the token was created.
- **Purpose:** a site could use tokens for several tasks; storing the purpose lets the site check that a token is being used for its intended purpose.

Another popular reason to use tokens is when users register for a site. They can be sent a link via email that they need to click on before they can log in. This confirms that their email address was correct.

A class called Token is used to create a Token object that has two methods:

- create() creates a new token and stores the token in the database
- getMemberId() checks if the token has *not* expired, and that it is being used for the right purpose; if so, it will return the id of the member it was created for

The Token object is created using a new method of the CMS object called called getToken(). It is stored in a property of the CMS object called token (this mirrors the way that the Article, Category, and Member objects are created).

token			
token	member_id	expires	purpose
a730730065407fa0a0508cc7f06930ed962...	4	2021-03-08 14:04:01	password_reset
4fbb47d3ebd4c0f3269ef669e4123cc8a2d...	12	2021-03-08 14:05:09	password_reset
ba5fde0992dfc85b39397bf4df89ecaa25d...	9	2021-03-08 14:05:38	password_reset

The token is made up of 64 random characters. It is generated using two of PHP's built-in methods:

- random_bytes() creates a string of random bytes; its parameter is the number of bytes to return
- bin2hex() converts binary data to hexadecimal

GENERATE 64 RANDOM BYTES

```
bin2hex(random_bytes(64));
```

CONVERT BINARY TO HEXADECIMAL

```php
<?php
namespace PhpBook\CMS;                              // Declare namespace
class Token
{
    protected $db;                                 // Store reference to Database object

    public function __construct(Database $db)
    {
        $this->db = $db;                           // Store Database object in $db property
    }
    public function create(int $id, string $purpose): string
    {
        $arguments['token']     = bin2hex(random_bytes(64));        // Token
        $arguments['expires']   = date('Y-m-d H:i:s', strtotime('+4 hours')); // Expiry
        $arguments['member_id'] = $id;                             // Member id
        $arguments['purpose']   = $purpose;                        // Purpose
        $sql = "INSERT INTO token (token, member_id, expires, purpose)
                VALUES (:token, :member_id, :expires, :purpose);";  // SQL
        $this->db->runSQL($sql, $arguments);                       // Run SQL
        return $arguments['token'];                                // Return token
    }
    public function getMemberId(string $token, string $purpose)
    {
        $arguments = ['token' => $token, 'purpose' => $purpose,];  // Token and purpose
        $sql = "SELECT member_id FROM token WHERE token = :token
                AND purpose = :purpose AND expires > NOW();";       // SQL to get id
        return $this->db->runSQL($sql, $arguments)->fetchColumn();  // Return id / false
    }
}
```

1. The object needs to work with the database so the __construct() method stores a reference to the Database object in the $db property.

2. The create() method creates a new token and stores it in the token table of the database.

3. A token is created and stored in an array called $arguments, ready to be added to a SQL statement.

4. The date and time the token will expire (4 hours after it was created) is added to the $arguments array.

5. The member id and purpose are added to the array.

6. $sql holds the SQL to add a token to the database.

7. The SQL is run.

8. The new token is returned from the method.

9. getMemberId() checks if a token is valid. It returns the member id if it is, or false if not.

10. The token and its purpose are stored in an array.

11. The SQL query tries to find a row in the token table that contains the specified token and purpose, and where the expiry time is in the future. If it finds a match, it collects the member id.

12. The SQL statement is run. If a row matches, it returns the member's id. If not, it returns false.

PASSWORD RESET REQUEST

The `password-lost.php` page (right) displays a form allowing users to enter an email address and request a password update link. When submitted, the site:

- Checks if they are a member and gets their id
- Creates a token for them to reset their password and saves the token in the database
- Creates and sends an email with a link to the page that resets their password

1. Strict types are enabled, the `Validate` class is imported, the `bootstrap.php` file is included, and two variables the Twig pages use are initialized.

2. An `if` statement checks if the form has been sent.

3. If so, the email address is collected and validated. If the email is valid, the `$error` variable stores a blank string. If not, it stores an error message.

4. An `if` statement checks if `$error` is a blank string.

5. If so, a new method of the `Member` class called `getIdByEmail()` (below) is passed the email address. It tries to find the email address in the database. If it finds the email, it returns that member's id. If not, it returns `false`. The value is stored in `$id`.

6. Another `if` statement checks if an id was found.

7. If so, the `create()` method of a `Token` object is called to create a new token for the member. The purpose of the token is set to `password_reset`. The new token that is returned is stored in `$token`.

8. A link is created to the `password-reset.php` page. It holds the new token in the query string. To create this link, the site needs to know the domain name of the site. This is stored in a new constant called `DOMAIN` that is declared in the `config.php` file. If you have not already done so, open that file and add your host name (see p190) to this constant.

9. The subject and body of the email are created.

10. A new `Email` object is created using the `Email` class (created on p598-99); then the email is sent. If this works, the `$sent` variable will store `true`.

11. The information Twig needs is stored in the `$data` array and Twig's `render()` method is called.

12. The `password-lost.html` template (shown in the second code box on the right) creates the form. A Twig `if` statement checks if the `sent` variable holds a value of `false`. If so, the user is shown a form to request a password reset link. If not, they are shown a message telling them that they will have been sent instructions to reset their password via email.

```
c16/src/classes/CMS/Member.php                                          PHP

public function getIdByEmail(string $email)
{
    $sql = "SELECT id FROM member
            WHERE email = :email;";                        // SQL query to get member id
    return $this->db->runSQL($sql, [$email])->fetchColumn(); // Run SQL + return member id
}
```

```php
<?php
declare(strict_types = 1);                                          // Use strict types
use PhpBook\Validate\Validate;                                      // Import Validate namespace
include '../src/bootstrap.php';                                     // Setup file
$error = false;                                                     // Error message
$sent  = false;                                                     // Has email been sent

if ($_SERVER['REQUEST_METHOD'] == 'POST') {                         // If form submitted
    $email = $_POST['email'];                                       // Get email
    $error = Validate::isEmail($email) ? '' : 'Please enter your email'; // Validate
    if ($error === '') {                                            // If valid
        $id = $cms->getMember()->getIdByEmail($email);             // Get member id
        if ($id) {                                                  // If id found
            $token = $cms->getToken()->create($id, 'password_reset'); // Token
            $link  = DOMAIN . DOC_ROOT . 'password-reset.php?token=' . $token; // Link
            $subject = 'Reset Password Link';                       // Subject + body
            $body  = 'To reset password click: <a href="' . $link . '">' . $link . '</a>';
            $mail  = new \PhpBook\Email\Email($email_config);       // Email object
            $sent  = $mail->sendEmail($mail_config['admin_email'], $email,
                $subject, $body);                                   // Send mail
        }
    }
}
$data['navigation'] = $cms->getCategory()->getAll();               // Categories for navigation
$data['error']      = $error;                                       // Validation errors
$data['sent']       = $sent;                                        // Did it send

echo $twig->render('password-lost.html', $data);                   // Render template
```

```twig
{% extends 'layout.html' %}
{% block title %}Password Reset{% endblock %}
{% block content %}...
  {% if sent == false %}
  <form method="post" action="password-lost.php" class="form-membership"> ...
    <label for="email">Enter your email address: </label>
    <input type="text" name="email" id="email" class="form-control"><br>
    <input type="submit" name="submit" value="Send email to reset password" class="btn">
    <span class="errors">{{ error }}</span><br>
  </form>
  {% else %}
  <p>If your address is registered, we will email instructions to reset your password.</p>
  {% endif %}...
{% endblock %}
```

RESETTING A PASSWORD

When a user clicks on the link in the lost password email, they are sent to `password-reset.php` (right). If it finds a valid token in the query string, it shows the user a form to update their password.

1. If the query string has a token, it is stored in `$token`. If not, the user is sent to `login.php`.

2. The `Token` object's `getMemberId()` method tries to get the member's id. If found, it is stored in `$id`.

3. If no id is returned, the user is sent to `login.php`. If it was, the form can be shown or processed.

4. An `if` statement checks if the form was posted.

5. If so, the password (and confirmation) are fetched.

6. The values are validated to make sure they meet the password requirements and that both boxes hold the same password. Any errors are stored in `$errors`.

7. Any errors are joined as a single string in `$invalid`.

8. If any errors were found, a message is stored in the `message` key of the `$errors` array.

9. Otherwise, a new method of the `Member` class called `passwordUpdate()` is called to update that member's password (shown below).

10. The member's data is collected.

11. The member's data is used to create and send them an email that tells them their password has been updated.

12. They are then redirected to the login page with a success message saying the password was updated.

13. The information Twig needs is stored in `$data`.

14. The `password-reset.html` template creates the form. It can be found in the code download.

15. The new method of the `Member` class called `passwordUpdate()` (below) requires the member's id and their new password.

16. A hash of the new password is created.

17. A SQL statement updates the password hash stored for that member and the function returns `true`.

---

c16/src/classes/CMS/Member.php   **PHP**

```
⑮  public function passwordUpdate(int $id, string $password): bool
   {
⑯      $hash = password_hash($password, PASSWORD_DEFAULT);          // Hash the password
        $sql = 'UPDATE member
                 SET password = :password
⑰               WHERE id = :id;';                                  // SQL to update password
        $this->db->runSQL($sql, ['id' => $id, 'password' => $hash,]); // Run SQL
        return true;                                               // Return true
   }
```

```php
<?php
declare(strict_types = 1);                                    // Use strict types
use PhpBook\Validate\Validate;                                // Import class


include '../src/bootstrap.php';                               // Setup file
$errors = [];                                                 // Initialize array

$token = $_GET['token'] ?? '';                                // Get token
if (!$token) {                                                // If id not returned
    redirect('login.php');                                    // Redirect
}
$id = $cms->getToken()->getMemberId($token, 'password_reset'); // Get member id
if (!$id) {                                                   // If no id
    redirect('login.php', ['warning' => 'Link expired, try again.',]); // Redirect
}

if ($_SERVER['REQUEST_METHOD'] == 'POST') {                   // If form submitted
    $password = $_POST['password'];                           // Get new password
    $confirm  = $_POST['confirm'];                            // Get password confirm
    // Validate passwords and check they match
    $errors['password'] = Validate::isPassword($password)
        ? '' : 'Passwords must be at least 8 characters and have:<br>
                A lowercase letter<br>An uppercase letter<br>A number
                <br>And a special character';                // Invalid password
    $errors['confirm']  = ($password === $confirm)
        ? '' : 'Passwords do not match';                     // Password does not match
    $invalid = implode($errors);                             // Join error messages

    if ($invalid) {                                          // If password not valid
        $errors['message'] = 'Please enter a valid password.'; // Store error message
    } else {                                                 // Otherwise
        $cms->getMember()->passwordUpdate($id, $password);   // Update password
        $member   = $cms->getMember()->get($id);             // Get member details
        $subject  = 'Password Updated';                      // Create subject and body
        $body     = 'Your password was updated on ' . date('Y-m-d H:i:s') .
            ' - if you did not reset the password, email ' . $email_config['admin_email'];
        $email    = new \PhpBook\Email\Email($email_config);  // Create email object
        $email->sendEmail($email_config['admin_email'], $member['email'], $subject, $body);
        redirect('login.php, ['success' => 'Password updated']); // Redirect to login
    }
}


$data['navigation'] = $cms->getCategory()->getAll();         // All categories for nav
$data['errors']     = $errors;                               // Errors array
$data['token']      = $token;                                // Token
echo $twig->render('password-reset.html', $data);            // Render template
```

SUMMARY
MEMBERSHIP

> To register for a website, a member must provide a unique identifier (such as an email address) and a password to confirm they are who they claim to be.

> Information about members can be stored in the database between their visits to the site.

> When a member returns and logs in, a session can remember that they logged in and store data about them for the duration of that visit.

> Rather than storing members' passwords in the database, a hash of the password is stored instead.

> Roles determine what members are allowed to do.

> Tokens can be used to identify users without containing personal data such as an email or id.

> Tokens should be used when users are allowed to update the database without logging in.

17

ADDING FUNCTIONALITY

This chapter shows how to add new features to a site. The URLs will be changed to make them SEO-friendly, and users will be able to like and comment on articles.

SEO-friendly URLs help with the search engine optimisation (SEO) of the site because they use keywords in the URLs, such as article titles or category names.

For example, the URL for this article page: `https://eg.link/article.php?id=24` will change to this, which contains its title: `https://eg.link/article/24/travel-guide`

Once you have learned how to change the URLs of the sample site to this new structure, the second section adds two new features that allow logged in members to:

- **Like** a piece of work (rather like how Facebook, Instagram and Twitter allow members to like posts written by other members)
- **Comment** on a piece of work to add their opinions and feedback

Adding new features to a site involves:

- Listing what the users will be able to do
- Determining what data will need to be stored in the database
- Implementing the functionality in the PHP code and templates

The skills you learn about in this final section can also be applied to developing new sites.

SEO-FRIENDLY URLS

Using words that describe the content of a page in its URL helps with search engine optimization (SEO) so that those pages feature more prominently in search engines. It also makes the URLs easier to read.

So far in this book, the URL for each page of the sample site used the path to the PHP file that should be run. If the page needed to get data from the database, the id of the data was specified in the query string.

Many websites use more descriptive, SEO-friendly URLs rather than filepaths. When a visitor requests these descriptive URLs, the site converts the URL into a filepath *and* tells that file what data it should be displaying. This is a technique known as **URL rewriting**.

There are several ways to write SEO-friendly URLs. Below, next to the old URLs used in previous chapters, you can see the new SEO-friendly format that will be used in this chapter.

The new SEO-friendly URLs will contain up to three parts, each separated by a forward slash character:

1. They start the same, with a path to the file, but the `.php` file extension is removed. The existing file names (minus the extension) work in SEO-friendly URLs because they describe the purpose of the page.

2. Next, if the old URL had a query string containing the id of the data to get from the database, there will be a forward slash followed by the id of the data to get from the database.

3. The article and category pages add SEO-friendly names to help search engines index those pages:
- Article pages use the article title.
- Category pages use the category name.

OLD URL	NEW URL
https://localhost/register.php	https://localhost/register
https://localhost/login.php	https://localhost/login
https://localhost/category.php?id=2	https://localhost/category/2/digital
https://localhost/category.php?id=4	https://localhost/category/4/photography
https://localhost/article.php?id=19	https://localhost/article/19/forecast
https://localhost/article.php?id=24	https://localhost/article/24/travel-guide
https://localhost/member.php?id=2	https://localhost/member/2
https://localhost/admin/article.php?id=24	https://localhost/admin/article/24

Because the new URLs no longer contain filepaths, every request for a PHP page will be sent to one file called `index.php`. It will take the SEO-friendly URL, split it at each forward slash, then store each part as a separate element in an array. For the pages that the public request, the parts of the array will store the:

1. File that should process the request
2. ID of the data in the database (if used)
3. SEO-friendly term (if one is added)

Next, `index.php` takes the value in the first element of the array and adds the `.php` file extension to it. This replicates the filenames used in the old URLs.

The `index.php` page will then include that file to handle the request. The table below shows the:

- Path (this is the part of the URL after the host)
- Array created when the path is split up
- Description of what each part will be used for

PATH	PARTS	
register	`$parts[0] = 'register';`	This creates an array with just one element. It indicates that the `index.php` file should include the `register.php` page to register a new user.

category/2/digital	`$parts[0] = 'category';`
	`$parts[1] = '2';`
	`$parts[2] = 'digital';`
		This creates an array with three elements stating:
		• The `category.php` file should be included
		• The id of the category is 2
		• The name is `'digital'` (this helps with SEO)

article/15/seascape	`$parts[0] = 'article';`
	`$parts[1] = '15';`
	`$parts[2] = 'seascape';`
		This creates an array with three elements stating:
		• The `article.php` file should be included
		• The id of the article is 15
		• The title is `'seascape'` (this helps with SEO)

Search engines should not index the admin pages, so their URLs do not end with SEO-friendly terms. When the URL for an admin page is split at every forward slash and turned into an arrray, the elements:

1. Specify that it is an `admin` page
2. Indicate which file should process the request
3. Hold the id of the data that the page is working with (if it is needed)

Once `index.php` has created the array it checks if the value of the first element is `admin`. If so, the request is for an admin page and it creates the path to the file to include in a different way, by joining together:

- The value in the first element
- A forward slash
- The value in the second element
- The `.php` file extension

PATH	PARTS	

admin/article/15	`$parts[0] = 'admin';`
	`$parts[1] = 'article';`
	`$parts[2] = '15';`
		This array specifies that:
		• The PHP to include is `admin/article.php`
		• The id of the article to work with is 15

admin/category/1	`$parts[0] = 'admin';`
	`$parts[1] = 'category';`
	`$parts[2] = '1';`
		This array specifies that:
		• The PHP to include is `admin/category.php`
		• The id of the category to work with is 1

NOTE: URLs cannot contain spaces, and several characters also have special meaning such as:
`/ ? : ; @ = & " < > # % { } | \ ^ ~ [ ] ` `

These characters must be removed from the article title or category name before they are used in a URL, and this new value will be stored in the database.

UPDATED FILE STRUCTURE

The `index.php` file is the only PHP file left in the document root folder. All of the PHP pages that it includes when it has processed the URL have been moved above the document root to the `src/pages` directory.

Below, you can see the new file structure that will be used in this chapter.

All of the PHP pages have been moved out of the `public` directory (which represents the document root folder) into the `src/pages` directory.

There are two new files in the `public` folder:

- `.htaccess` contains rules to direct all requests to `index.php` (it is a configuration file for Apache)
- `index.php` will process the URL and include the relevant PHP page from the `src/pages` folder

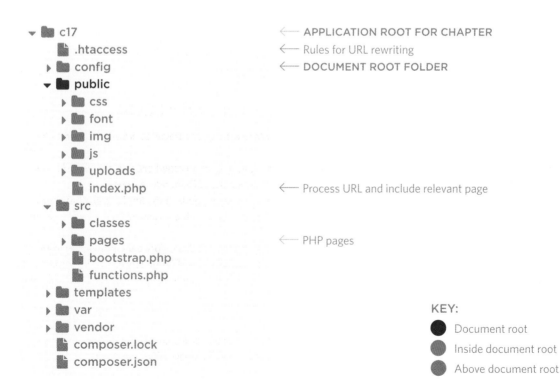

▼ 📁 c17	← APPLICATION ROOT FOR CHAPTER
📄 .htaccess	← Rules for URL rewriting
▶ 📁 config	← DOCUMENT ROOT FOLDER
▼ 📁 public	
▶ 📁 css	
▶ 📁 font	
▶ 📁 img	
▶ 📁 js	
▶ 📁 uploads	
📄 index.php	← Process URL and include relevant page
▼ 📁 src	
▶ 📁 classes	
▶ 📁 pages	← PHP pages
📄 bootstrap.php	
📄 functions.php	
▶ 📁 templates	
▶ 📁 var	
▶ 📁 vendor	
📄 composer.lock	
📄 composer.json	

KEY:
- ⬤ Document root
- ⬤ Inside document root
- ⬤ Above document root

IMPLEMENTING
SEO-FRIENDLY URLS

When adding new features, you need to consider: what data to store, how to implement the features in code, and how to update the interface. Below, these issues are addressed for the addition of SEO-friendly URLs.

WHAT DATA TO STORE AND HOW TO STORE IT

When an article or category is created or updated, an SEO-friendly name for that article or category will be created and stored in the database.

The names are stored in the `seo_title` column of the `article` table and `seo_name` column on the `category` table. Below, you can see the updated `category` table.

category				
id	name	description	navigation	seo_name
1	Print	Inspiring graphic design	1	print
2	Digital	Powerful pixels	1	digital
3	Illustration	Hand-drawn visual storytelling	1	illustration

HOW TO IMPLEMENT NEW FUNCTIONALITY IN CODE

Because SEO-friendly URLs do not use a path to a PHP file, rules in a new `.htaccess` file in the document root folder tell the web server to send all requests for PHP pages to `index.php`.

`index.php` then processes the requested URL and:

- Gets the id of any data it needs to collect from the database and save that id in a variable
- Includes the right PHP file to deal with the request

When articles or categories are added or edited:

- A new function called `create_seo_name()` will create the SEO-friendly names
- Existing methods of the `Article` and `Category` class will save these new names to the database

When article and category data is collected from the database, the SEO-friendly name is returned and passed to the Twig templates to create the new links.

UPDATING THE INTERFACE

In the Twig templates, all of the links need updating. Where they have an SEO-friendly name, this is added.

Below, you can see a link to an article page. It uses the article id, then its SEO-friendly title.

```
<a href="article/{{ article.id }}/{{ article.seo_title }}">
```

URL REWRITING

The Apache web server has a built-in URL rewriting engine.
It uses rules to determine when a request for one URL should
be transformed into a request for a different URL.

SEO-friendly URLs are only used for the *pages* that
visitors request such as the article, category and
member pages. They are not used for the other files
those pages need such as image, CSS, JavaScript, or
font files; their URLs remain the same. Therefore, the
Apache web server's URL rewriting engine is told to:

- Serve the image, CSS, JavaScript and font files as
  before, because their URLs have not changed
- Send all other requests to the `index.php` file

The `index.php` file will process the URL and then
include the appropriate file.

As you saw on p196-199, `.htaccess` files control the
settings for the Apache web server (including the
URL rewriting engine). There is an `.htaccess` file in
the `c17` folder (with settings for character encoding
and file upload sizes). The rules to control the URL
rewriting engine are added to this file.

1. First, the URL rewriting engine is turned on.

Then, the instructions for the rewriting engine are
made up of two parts on separate lines:

- A **condition** to specify when a rule should run
- A **rule** to say what happens if that condition is met

2. The condition says: if the request is for a file that
does *not* exist on the server, process the next rule:

- The URLs used to include images, CSS, JavaScript
  and font files specify the location of those files on
  the server (so the subsequent rule *will not* run)
- SEO-friendly URLs do not point to a file on the
  server (so the subsequent rule *will* run for them)

3. The rule indicates that the request should
be handled by the `index.php` file located in the
document root folder.

```
c17/public/.htaccess                                    PHP

    ...
(1) RewriteEngine On
(2) RewriteCond %{REQUEST_FILENAME} !-f
(3) RewriteRule . public/index.php
```

An `.htaccess` file can hold multiple conditions,
each followed by rules to run if that condition is met.

It offers other powerful tools for rewriting URLs but
there is not space to cover them all in this book.

UPDATING URLS

When using SEO-friendly URLs, links to other pages, as well as image, CSS, JavaScript and font files should be relative to the document root. Usually this is a forward slash but the sample site must use a constant.

In previous chapters, links to other pages of the site, and links to image, CSS, JavaScript and font files all used URLs that were relative to the current PHP page. The new SEO-friendly URLs make pages look like they are in different folders. For example, these two URLs look like they point to folders that do not exist:

```
/category/1/print
/article/22/polite-society-posters
```

Therefore, all of the relative links must be updated so that the paths are relative to the site's document root folder, not to its current page.

Typically sites use a forward slash as the path to the document root folder. But, because the code download has several versions of the sample site, the `public` folder inside each chapter's code has been treated as if it were the document root folder since Chapter 14. The path to the `public` folder will be used at the start of **all** relative links in the site.

This path is stored in a constant in `config.php`. Then `bootstrap.php` adds it to a Twig global variable called `doc_root` so it can be used in all the templates. Below, you can see it at the start of links to pages (which now have SEO-friendly titles) and image files.

`TWIG`   c17/templates/article-summaries.html

```twig
{% for article in articles %}
<article class="summary">
<a href="{{ doc_root }}article/{{ article.id }}/{{ article.seo_title }}">
  {% if article.image_file %}
  <img src="{{ doc_root }}uploads/{{ article.image_file }}" alt="{{ article.image_alt }}">
  {% else %}
  <img src="{{ doc_root }}uploads/blank.png" alt="">
  {% endif %}

...

  {% if session.id == article.member_id %}
    <a href="{{ doc_root }}work/{{ article.id }}" class="btn btn-primary">Edit</a>
  {% endif %}</article>
{% endfor %}
```

HANDLING REQUESTS

Any request that is not for an image, CSS, JavaScript or font file will be sent to the `index.php` file. It processes the URL, turns it into an array, then includes the right PHP file to handle that request.

1. The `index.php` file includes `bootstrap.php` to save repeating this statement in all the PHP pages.

Next, the requested URL is converted into an array.

2. The requested path (the part after the host name) is taken from PHP's `$_SERVER` superglobal. It is converted into lowercase, and stored in `$path`.

3. The part of the path up to the `public` folder for this chapter (which *would* be the document root) is removed from the variable. For this chapter, it would remove `phpbook/section_d/c17/public/` (this step is only needed because the download code contains multiple versions of the site).

4. PHP's `explode()` function is used to split the path at every forward slash and store each piece of data as a separate element in an array called `$parts`.

As you saw on p637, if a public page is requested, the first element indicates the file to use. If it is an admin page, the first element has a value of `admin` and the second element indicates the file to use. E.g.:

PATH	PARTS

`article/15/seascape`	`$parts[0] = 'article';`
	`$parts[1] = '15';`
	`$parts[2] = 'seascape';`

`admin/article/15`	`$parts[0] = 'admin';`
	`$parts[1] = 'article';`
	`$parts[2] = '15';`

5. The file checks if the request is for a public page or an admin page by checking the value of the first element in the `$parts` array. If the first element of the array is *not* `admin`, it means that the request is for a page the public can view.

6. The first element of the `$parts` array determines the name of the file that should be included in order to handle the request. For example, if the user was requesting an article page, the value would be `article` (as shown in the table to the bottom left).

If the user was requesting the home page, there would be no value for this element of the array, so `$page` should store the word `index` instead.

To store this value, a new shorthand version of the ternary operator, known as the Elvis operator, is used.

Rather than writing the following:
`$page = $parts[0] ? $parts[0] : 'index';`

This shorthand is used instead:
`$page = $parts[0] ?: 'index';`

If `$parts[0]` has a value, it is stored in `$page`; if not, `$page` will store the value `index`.

7. If the second element of the array has a value, it will be the id of the data the page is working with. If an id is present in the second element of the array, it is stored in `$id`; otherwise, `$id` stores `null`.

```php
<?php
include '../src/bootstrap.php';                    // Setup file

$path  = mb_strtolower($_SERVER['REQUEST_URI']);   // Get path in lowercase
$path  = substr($path, strlen(DOC_ROOT));          // Remove up to DOC_ROOT
$parts = explode('/', $path);                      // Split into array at /

if ($parts[0] != 'admin') {                        // If an admin page
    $page = $parts[0] ?: 'index';                  // Page name (or use index)
    $id   = $parts[1] ?? null;                     // Get ID (or use null)
} else {                                           // If not an admin page
    $page = 'admin/' . ($parts[1] ?? '');          // Page name
    $id   = $parts[2] ?? null;                     // Get ID
}
$id = filter_var($id, FILTER_VALIDATE_INT);        // Validate ID

$php_page = APP_ROOT . '/src/pages/' . $page . '.php';   // Path to PHP page
if (!file_exists($php_page)) {                      // If page not in array
    $php_page = APP_ROOT . '/src/pages/page-not-found.php';  // Include page not found
}
include $php_page;                                  // Include PHP file
```

The circled numbers ①–⑮ mark the lines of code above.

8. If the user is requesting an admin page, the first element in the $parts array will hold the word admin; the second element will hold the name of the page.

9. The $page variable starts to build up the path to the file that will handle the request. It uses the string admin/ followed by the name of the page.
(If the URL ended admin/ (it did not specify a page) there would be no parts[1], so the null-coalescing operator replaces the value with a blank string.)

10. If there is an id in the URL, it is stored in $id; otherwise, $id stores null.

11. PHP's filter_var() function is used to check if the value stored in $id is an integer. This saves each of the PHP pages that uses an id from repeating this statement to check whether the value in $id is an int. By this point, the page has three variables:

- $parts: the array of parts of the URL
- $page: the name of the page (if it is an admin page, this is preceeded by admin/)
- $id: the id, if one was given in the URL

12. The path to the page that will handle the request is stored in $php_page. It is created by joining the:

- Value in APP_ROOT (created in bootstrap.php)
- Path to the PHP pages /src/pages/
- Value in $page
- .php file extension

13. PHP's file_exists() function checks if the path to the PHP file created in Step 12 does *not* match a real file on the server.

14. If not, the value stored in $php_page is updated with the path to the page-not-found.php file. This ends with an exit command which would stop any more code running.

15. If the PHP page is still running, the PHP file stored in $php_page is included in the page. The included PHP pages run just like they did when they were requested in the URL (because it is like the code has been copied and pasted where PHP's include directive is).

CREATING SEO NAMES

When articles and categories are created or updated, a new function called `create_seo_name()` is used to create an SEO-friendly name for the article or category.

Because URLs cannot contain spaces or certain characters that have special meaning (such as / ? = & #), a function called `create_seo_name()` is added to `functions.php` to create an SEO-friendly name from article titles and category names that only contains the letters A-z, numbers 0-9 and dashes.

PHP's `transliterator_transliterate()` function will also try to replace non-ASCII characters with the nearest ASCII equivalent (based on phonetic similarity). For example, Über would get changed to Uber, and École to Ecole. Apache needs an extension to be installed for transliteration to work, so the code uses PHP's `function_exists()` method to check if the function is available before calling it. It only performs the task if the function is available. For more see: http://notes.re/php/transliteration

1. `create_seo_name()` takes a string as a parameter and returns an SEO-friendly version of that text.

2. The text is converted to lowercase.

3. Any spaces are removed from the start and end.

4. PHP's built-in `function_exists()` function checks if the `transliterator_transliterate()` function is available. If so, it is called to try to replace non-ASCII characters with ASCII equivalents.

5. `preg_replace()` replaces spaces with dashes.

6. Then removes anything other than -, A-z or 0-9.

7. The updated article or category name is returned.

c17/src/functions.php

`PHP`

```php
function create_seo_name(string $text): string
{
    $text = strtolower($text);                          // Convert text to lowercase
    $text = trim($text);                                // Remove spaces from start/end
    if (function_exists('transliterator_transliterate')) { // If transliterator installed
        $text = transliterator_transliterate('Latin-ASCII', $text); // Transliterate
    }
    $text = preg_replace('/ /', '-', $text);            // Replace spaces with dashes
    $text = preg_replace('/[^-A-z0-9]+/', '', $text);   // Remove if not a dash, A-z or 0-9
    return $text;                                        // Return the SEO name
}
```

SAVING SEO NAMES

The `create_seo_name()` function is called when an article or category is either created or updated. This name is then passed to the methods that update the database.

1. If a category is created or updated, `category.php` (now in `src/pages/admin`) calls `create_seo_name()` and passes it the category name as an argument.

The SEO-friendly name it returns is stored in the array of category data. This array is then passed to the `Category` object's `create()` or `update()` methods.

PHP   c17/src/pages/admin/category.php

```php
    $category['name']        = $_POST['name'];                      // Get name
    $category['description'] = $_POST['description'];               // Get description
    $category['navigation']  = (isset($_POST['navigation'])) ? 1 : 0; // Get navigation
(1) $category['seo_name']    = create_seo_name($category['name']); // SEO-friendly name
```

2. When the `Category` object's `create()` or `update()` methods are called, the `$category` array has a new element holding the SEO-friendly name.

3. The SQL statement's INSERT and UPDATE clauses are updated to save the new SEO-friendly name.

The process for articles is the same:
- A key called `seo_title` is added to the `$article` array in `admin/article.php` and `work.php`.
- The SEO-friendly title is saved to the database when the `create()` or `update()` methods of the `Article` class are called.

PHP   c17/src/classes/CMS/Category.php

```php
(2) public function create(array $category): bool
    {
        try {                                                       // Try to create
(3)         $sql = "INSERT INTO category (name, description, navigation, seo_name)
(4)                 VALUES (:name, :description, :navigation, :seo_name);"; // SQL
        ...
```

NOTE: The `seo_name` and `seo_title` columns in the database have uniqueness constraints (like the `name` and `title` columns) to ensure SEO names are unique.

The code to save SEO-friendly names is also in Chapter 16 to ensure the database stores them if changes are made running the code for that chapter.

DISPLAYING PAGES WITH SEO-FRIENDLY NAMES

The article and category pages use SEO-friendly names in the URLs. These pages check that the SEO-friendly name is correct before displaying the page.

First, the `get()` and `getAll()` methods of both the `Article` and `Category` classes are updated to collect their SEO-friendly names from the database.

1. The SQL in the `get()` method of the `Category` class requests data from the `seo_name` column.

Next, two tasks are removed from **all** of the PHP files that were moved to the `src/pages` folder because those tasks are now performed in `index.php`:

- Include the `bootstrap.php` file
- Get an id from the query string and validate it

Then, a new task is added to the `article.php` and `category.php` files. It checks that the SEO-friendly name in the URL is correct because multiple links *could* point to the same article using different titles, such as:

✔ http://eg.link/article/24/travel-guide
✘ http://eg.link/article/24/japan-guide
✘ http://eg.link/article/24/guide-book

Each of these URLs has the information that the site needs to get the data for the page (it has the type of page to include and an id). However, search engines might think that these are different pages that have duplicate content, and this is something that they can penalize sites for. This situation could arise if another site misspelt a link to the page or if the article title changed after the link was created.

Therefore, the `article.php` and `category.php` pages check if the SEO-friendly part of the URL (which was stored in the `$parts` array by the `index.php` file) matches the SEO-friendly name in the database. If not, the user is redirected to the correct URL.

2. An `if` statement checks if the SEO-friendly name from the URL (the value in the third element of the `$parts` array created in `index.php`) matches the SEO-friendly name in the database. (Both values are converted to lowercase before they are compared.)

3. If they do not match, the `redirect()` function sends the visitor to the same page using the correct SEO-friendly name in the URL.

Finally, every link in every template needs to be udpated to use the SEO-friendly URLs.

4. The path will be made up of:

- The path to the site's document root folder. (Usually this is a / but, because the code download has several versions of the site, it is the path to the `public` folder for this chapter.)
- The PHP page name minus the `.php` extension
- The id for the article or category
- An SEO name if the link is to an article or category

5. The path to the image files also needs to include the path to the document root (see p641).

```php
    public function get(int $id)
    {
①      $sql = "SELECT id, name, description, navigation, seo_name
                FROM category
                WHERE id = :id;";                   // SQL to get one category
        return $this->db->runSQL($sql, [$id])->fetch();  // Return category data
    }
```

```php
    <?php
    declare(strict_types = 1);                          // Use strict types

    if (!$id) {                                          // If no valid id
        include APP_ROOT . '/src/pages/page-not-found.php';  // Page not found
    }

    $category = $cms->getCategory()->get($id);           // Get category data
    if (!$category) {                                    // If category is empty
        include APP_ROOT . '/src/pages/page-not-found.php';  // Page not found
    }

②  if (mb_strtolower($parts[2]) != mb_strtolower($category['seo_name'])) { // SEO name wrong
③      redirect('category/' . $id . '/' . $category['seo_name'], [], 301); // Redirect
    }

    $data['navigation'] = $cms->getCategory()->getAll();       // Get navigation categories
    $data['category']   = $category;                           // Current category
    $data['articles']   = $cms->getArticle()->getAll(true, $id); // Get articles
    $data['section']    = $category['id'];                     // Category id for nav
```

```twig
④  <a href="{{ doc_root }}article/{{ article.id }}/{{ article.seo_title }}">
      {% if article.image_file %}
⑤      <img src="{{ doc_root }}uploads/{{ article.image_file }}"
          alt="{{ article.image_alt }}">
      {% else %}
⑤      <img src="{{ doc_root }}uploads/blank.png" alt="">
      {% endif %}
      ...
```

PLANNING NEW FEATURES

When adding a new feature, start by working out exactly what it will allow your users to do. This will make writing the code to implement that functionality easier.

Before you start coding new features for the site, you should clearly define what users will be able to do. This will clarify how the task can be broken down.

For example, in this chapter, all of the pages that list article summaries show how many members have liked and commented on each article.

Article pages show how many likes and comments an article has under the title; the full comments appear under the picture. Also, if a member is logged in, the:

- Heart icon will have a link to like/unlike the article
- Form to post a comment on the article is shown (otherwise they are told to log in to comment)

Once you know what the new features let users do:

1. Work out what data will be stored in the database.

2. Write or update the methods that are used to get data from, or save data to, the database.

3. Create or update the PHP pages so that they can perform the new tasks when needed, and ensure the templates will get the data they need.

4. Create or update the templates to enable visitors to interact with these new features.

DETERMINE WHAT DATA TO STORE AND HOW TO STORE IT

First, decide what data the users will need to see, and whether the database must store any new data.

To show likes, the database must store the:
- User who likes the article (already in member table)
- Article that they like (new data)

To show comments, the database must store the:
- User who made the comment (in member table)
- Comment (new data)
- Date and time the comment was made (new data)

Next, decide how to store new data in the database.

A. If it is extra data about something that is already represented by an existing table (for example, an article or member), add it to that table.

B. If it represents an entirely new concept or object, create a new table to represent it. For example, comments will be stored in a new comment table.

C. If it describes a relationship between concepts that are already held in the database, use a **link** table. When implementing likes, the database already has data about members *and* articles, so a link table will stores ids of members and ids of articles they like.

CREATE CLASSES AND METHODS TO COLLECT AND SAVE DATA

When you know what data needs to be saved in the database, write any classes and methods that are needed to get, create, update and delete that data. Two new classes will implement likes and comments:

- The Like class gets, adds and removes likes
- The Comment class gets and adds users' comments

The existing Article class is also updated so that the get() and getAll() methods return the total number of likes and comments each article has.

LIKE CLASS

METHOD	DESCRIPTION
get()	Check if user liked article
create()	Add like to database
delete()	Remove like from database

COMMENT CLASS

METHOD	DESCRIPTION
getAll()	Get comments for article
create()	Add comment to database

UPDATE THE PHP PAGES

Next, work out if you need to update existing PHP files or create new ones to implement the features.

For example, a new file will be used to save data when a visitor likes or unlikes an article.

Also, the existing article.php page will check if a:

- User is logged in and, if so, did they like the article
- Comment has been submitted. If so, the comment is validated and can then be stored in the database

UPDATE THE TEMPLATE FILES

Finally, the templates that generate the HTML that is sent back to the browser can be updated.

The article-summaries.html template will show how many likes and comments each article has.

The article.html template shows the total number of likes and comments, and the comments in full. If the user is logged in, it will add a link to like or unlike the article and show a form that allows them to submit a comment.

STORING COMMENTS

A new table called comment holds each comment and the id of the member who made the comment.

In the new comment table (shown below):

- id is created using MySQL's auto-increment feature
- comment is a comment on an article
- posted is the date and time the comment was saved (which the database adds to the table)
- article_id is the id of the article it is for
- member_id is the id of the member who wrote it

The article_id and member_id columns use foreign key constraints (see p431) to ensure that they hold a valid article id and member id.

NOTE: Always create a backup of the database before altering it (see p427). This is important because adding a new feature could accidentally overwrite or delete data it was not supposed to.

comment			
id comment	posted	article_id	member_id
1 Love this, totally makes me want to...	2019-03-14 17:45:13	24	1
2 I bought one of these guides for NYC...	2019-03-14 17:45:15	24	6
3 Another great piece of work Ivy,...	2019-03-14 17:53:52	3	4

On the right, you can see two SQL queries that will be used to count the total number of comments and likes an article has.

These two queries will be used when displaying summaries of articles and individual articles.

The new table to store likes is shown on the right-hand page.

TOTAL COMMENTS:
```
SELECT COUNT(id)
  FROM comments
  WHERE comments.article_id = article.id
```

TOTAL LIKES:
```
SELECT COUNT(article_id)
  FROM likes
  WHERE likes.article_id = article.id
```

STORING LIKES

The database already has tables that represent articles and members. A new table called `likes` will record every article each member likes.

To record every article that each member likes, the database only needs to store a relationship between an individual member and the articles they like (as it already holds data about the members and articles). The relationship is described using a **link table** (it links data in two tables). Its columns are:

- `article_id`: the id of the article the member likes
- `member_id`: the id of the member that likes it

The link table is called `likes` and is shown below. (It uses the plural `likes` rather than `like` because SQL has a keyword called LIKE, see p404.)

The `article_id` and `member_id` columns both use foreign key constraints (see p431) to ensure that they hold a valid article id and member id.

A member should only like each article once, so a **composite primary key** is added using phpMyAdmin. It stops two rows from storing the same combination of `article_id` *and* `member_id` as any other row in the table. This is similar to how the member table does not allow two members to have the same email address.

See `http://notes.re/php/composite-key` to learn how to create a composite primary key.

likes

article_id	member_id
1	1
2	1
1	2

member

id	forename	surname	email	password	joined	picture
1	Ivy	Stone	ivy@eg.link	0086...	2019-01-01...	ivy.jpg
2	Luke	Wood	luke@eg.link	DFCD...	2019-01-02...	*NULL*
3	Emiko	Ito	emi@eg.link	G4A8...	2019-01-02...	emi.jpg

article

id	title	summary	content	created	category_id	member_id	image_id	published	seo_title
1	PS Poster	Poster	Parts...	2019	2	2	1	1	ps-poster
2	Systemic	Leaflet	Design...	2019	2	1	2	1	systemic
3	AQ Website	New site	A new...	2019	1	1	3	1	aq-web

SHOW SUMMARIES WITH LIKE & COMMENT COUNTS

The SQL queries that collect article data are updated to collect the total number of likes and comments for each article. To calculate these totals, two **subqueries** are added within the main query.

The `getAll()` method of the `Article` class uses a SQL query to get summary data about a set of articles. This method is used by the home, category, member and search pages.

To collect the total number of likes and comments for each of the articles, two **subqueries** are added to the existing SQL query that the `getAll()` method uses.

Subqueries are additional queries that run within another query. The changes to the original query are highlighted on the right-hand page.

Every time the main query selects an article summary to add to the result set, the two subqueries are run:

- The first counts the number of likes for that article
- The second counts the number of comments it has

The subqueries use the same syntax as other SQL queries, but they are placed inside parentheses. Each one returns a single value and, after the parentheses, an alias specifies a name for the column in the result set that will hold the result of that query.

The same two subqueries have been added to the `get()` method of the `Article` class; you can see them in the code download.

NOTE: To fit this code on the page, the `$arguments` array is created using a shorthand that lets you to assign two keys the same value in one statement.

1. The first subquery gets the number of likes from the `likes` table. Because these subqueries get additional data about each article, they are placed after the `SELECT` command.

After the closing parentheses, an alias states that the result set will store the number of likes in a column called `likes`.

2. The second subquery collects the number of comments for an article. Like the first subquery, it is also placed in parentheses.

The alias specifies that the number of comments for the article will be added to a column called `comments`.

3. The `article-summaries.html` template, which is used to display article summaries on the home, category, member and search pages, is updated to show the number of likes and comments. These two new pieces of data are shown before the article title.

Although the PHP files in `src/pages` for the home, category, member and search pages all get article summaries, they do not need updating because the SQL in the class has been updated to get the data. The data is then added to the array that represents the result set, and that array is already passed to the Twig templates.

```php
    public function getAll($published = true, $category = null, $member = null,
                           $limit = 1000): array
        {
        $arguments['category'] = $arguments['category1'] = $category;  // Category id
        $arguments['member']   = $arguments['member1']   = $member;    // Author id
        $arguments['limit']    = $limit;                               // Max articles

        $sql = "SELECT a.id, a.title, a.summary, a.created, a.category_id,
                    a.member_id, a.published, a.seo_title,
                    c.name    AS category,
                    c.seo_name AS seo_category,
                    m.forename, m.surname,
                    CONCAT(m.forename, ' ', m.surname) AS author,
                    i.file    AS image_file,
                    i.alt     AS image_alt,
                    (SELECT COUNT(article_id)
                       FROM likes
                      WHERE likes.article_id = a.id) AS likes,
                    (SELECT COUNT(article_id)
                       FROM comment
                      WHERE comment.article_id = a.id) AS comments

                    FROM article      AS a
                    JOIN category     AS c   ON a.category_id = c.id
                    JOIN member       AS m   ON a.member_id   = m.id
                    LEFT JOIN image   AS i   ON a.image_id    = i.id

                    WHERE (a.category_id = :category OR :category1 is null)
                      AND (a.member_id    = :member   OR :member1   is null) "; // SQL
        if ($published == true) {                             // If published argument is true
            $sql .= "AND a.published = 1 ";                   // Only get published articles
        }
        $sql .= "ORDER BY a.id DESC
                 LIMIT :limit;";                              // Add further clauses

            return $this->db->runSQL($sql, $arguments)->fetchAll(); // Return data
    }
```

① ②

```twig
<div class="social">
<div class="like-count"><span class="icon-heart-empty"></span> {{ article.likes }}</div>
<div class="comment-count"><span class="icon-comment"></span> {{ article.comments }}</div>
</div>
<h2>{{ article.title }}</h2>
```

③

ADDING AND REMOVING LIKES

If the user is logged in, the like icon on the article page becomes a link. The file it links to checks if the user liked the article; if not, a like is added. If they have, it is removed. To do this, it calls methods of the Like class.

If the user is logged in, the heart icon on the article page is placed inside a link like this:

```
<a href="/like/24"> ... </a>
```

The URL for the link starts with like, then the article id. When the link is clicked, index.php will include a new file called like.php. In that file:

1. The condition of an if statement checks if:

- There is *no* article id, or
- The user is *not* logged in (if not, the Session object's id property will have a value of 0).

2. If either is true, the visitor should not be using the page and they are sent to page not found. Otherwise...

3. The get() method of a new Like object checks if this member likes this article. It needs to know the article and member ids which are passed to the method as an indexed array. The result (0 for no or 1 for yes) is stored in $liked.

4. If this user already liked the article, the delete() method of the Like object is called to remove the entry from the likes table in the database.

5. Otherwise, they have not yet liked it and the create() method of the Like class adds a like.

6. Then the user is sent back to the article page.

The new Like class updates the database if a member likes/unlikes an article. It has three methods:

- get() checks if a user likes an article
- create() adds a like to the database
- delete() removes a like from the database

Each method needs two pieces of data, which are passed to the methods as an indexed array:

- The id of the article
- The id of the member

The Like class is similar to the Article, Category, and Member classes. It is created using a new getLike() method of the CMS object and it stores the location of a Database object in a property called $db.

7. The get() method uses SQL's COUNT() method to check how many rows of the likes table have the specified article and member id. This number is then returned from the method.

Because this table uses a composite primary key, the method will only ever return 1 to indicate the user liked the article, or 0 if the user has not liked it.

8. The create() method will add a new row to the likes table with the article id and member id.

9. The delete() method removes the row from the likes table with the specified article and member id.

```php
<?php
declare(strict_types = 1);                              // Use strict types

if (!$id or $session->id == 0) {                        // If no valid id
    include APP_ROOT . '/src/pages/page-not-found.php';  // Page not found
}

$liked = $cms->getLike()->get([$id, $session->id]);     // Does member like
if ($liked) {                                           // If they like it already
    $cms->getLike()->delete([$id, $session->id]);       // Remove like
} else {                                                // Otherwise
    $cms->getLike()->create([$id, $session->id]);       // Add like
}
redirect('article/' . $id . '/' . $parts[2] . '/');     // Redirect to article page
```

(1) (2) (3) (4) (5) (6)

```php
...
public function get(array $like): bool
{
    $sql = "SELECT COUNT(*)
            FROM likes
            WHERE article_id = :id
              AND member_id = :member_id;";              // SQL
    return $this->db->runSQL($sql, $like)->fetchColumn();  // Run and return 1 or 0
}

public function create(array $like): bool
{
    $sql = "INSERT INTO likes (article_id, member_id)
            VALUES (:article_id, :member_id);";          // SQL
    $this->db->runSQL($sql, $like);                      // Run SQL
    return true;                                         // Return true
}

public function delete(array $like): bool
{
    $sql = "DELETE FROM likes
            WHERE article_id = :article_id
              AND member_id = :member_id;";              // SQL
    $this->db->runSQL($sql, $like);                      // Run SQL
    return true;                                         // Return true
}
```

(7) (8) (9)

ADDING COMMENTS TO ARTICLES

If a user is logged in, the form to submit a comment is shown under the picture and any existing comments. The new `Comment` class has methods to get comments from, or add them to, the database's `comment` table.

The new `Comment` class has two methods:

- `getAll()` gets all of the comments for an article
- `create()` adds a comment to the `comment` table

1. `getAll()` gets all of the comments for an article, along with the name and profile picture of the member who made each comment.

The method has one argument: the id of the article that it should get the comments for.

To get the name and picture of the member who made the comment, the SQL uses a join between the:

- `member_id` column in the `comment` table
- `id` column on the `member` table

2. The `create()` method adds a new comment to the `Comment` table in the database. It needs three pieces of data which are passed to the method as an indexed array, the:

- Comment
- Article id
- ID of the member who made the comment

The database's auto-increment feature creates the id in the first column of the `comment` table. The database also adds the date and time that the comment was saved to the `posted` column of the table.

The `article.php` page is updated to show comments for the current article, and save any new comments.

3. An `if` statement checks if the request was a POST request, indicating the comment form was submitted.

4. If so, the comment text is collected.

5. A new `HTMLPurifier` object is created to remove unwanted markup from the comment.

6. The configuration options are set to allow `<br>`, `<b>`, `<i>` and `<a>` elements.

7. The `purify()` method removes all other HTML tags from the comment.

8. If the comment is between 1 – 2000 characters, a blank string is stored in `$error`. Otherwise, `$error` stores an error message.

9. If there is no error, the comment, article id, and member's id are stored in an array called `$arguments`.

10. Then `Comment` object's `create()` method is called to save the comment to the database.

11. The article page reloads to show the comment.

12. The `getAll()` method of the `Comment` object gets all the comments for this article. They are added to the `$data` array for use in the Twig template.

```php
public function getAll(int $id): array
{
    $sql = "SELECT c.id, c.comment, c.posted,
            CONCAT(m.forename, ' ', m.surname) AS author, m.picture
              FROM comment AS c
              JOIN member  AS m ON c.member_id = m.id
             WHERE c.article_id = :id;";                        // SQL statement
    return $this->db->runSQL($sql, ['id' => $id])->fetchAll();  // Execute query
}
```
① (brace grouping for getAll)

```php
public function create(array $comment): bool
{
    $sql = "INSERT INTO comment (comment, article_id, member_id)
            VALUES (:comment, :article_id, :member_id);";  // SQL statement
    $this->db->runSQL($sql, $comment);                     // Execute query
    return true;
}
```
② (brace grouping for create)

```php
<?php ...
if ($_SERVER['REQUEST_METHOD'] == 'POST') {                 // If form submitted
    $comment  = $_POST['comment'];                          // Get comment
    $purifier = new HTMLPurifier();                         // Create HTMLPurifier
    $purifier->config->set('HTML.Allowed', 'br,b,i,a[href]'); // Set permitted tags
    $comment  = $purifier->purify($comment);                // Purify comment

    $error    = Validate::isText($comment, 1, 2000)
        ? '' : 'Your comment must be between 1 and 2000 characters.
                It can contain <b>, <i>, <a>, and <br> tags.'; // Validate comment
    if ($error === '') {                                    // If no error, save
        $arguments = [$comment, $article['id'], $cms->getSession()->id,]; // Arguments
        $cms->getComment()->create($arguments);             // Create comment
        redirect($path);                                    // Reload page
    }
}

$data['navigation'] = $cms->getCategory()->getAll();        // Get categories
$data['article']    = $article;                             // Article
$data['section']    = $article['category_id'];              // Current category
$data['comments']   = $cms->getComment()->getAll($id);      // Get comments
if ($cms->getSession()->id > 0) {                           // If user logged in
    $data['liked']  = $cms->getLike()->get([$id, $cms->getSession()->id]); // User like?
    $data['error']  = $error ?? null;                       // Comment error
}
```

Markers on the page: ③ ④ ⑤ ⑥ ⑦ ⑧ ⑨ ⑩ ⑪ ⑫

UPDATING THE ARTICLE PAGE TEMPLATE

The `article.html` template needs updating to display the new data that the `article.php` page has collected. If members are signed in, it also shows a link to like the article and a form to comment on the article.

On the right, you can see the changes to the `article.html` template used to display articles. First, it deals with the option to like an article.

1. An `if` statement checks if the `id` property of the `session` object has a value of `0`, which would indicate that the visitor is *not* logged in.

2. If the visitor is *not* logged in, a link to the login page is added around an empty heart icon.

3. Otherwise, the visitor has logged in and a link is created to the like page (it contains the article id). When this link is clicked on, the like page either adds or removes the like for this member.

4. Another `if` statement checks the value of the `liked` variable to see if the visitor likes the article.

5. If they do, a filled-in heart icon is shown.

6. If not, an outlined heart icon is shown.

7. The `if` block from Step 4 is closed.

8. The `if` block from Step 1 is closed.

9. The total number of times the article has been liked is shown next to the heart icon.

Next, comments are displayed.

10. The number of comments for the article is shown.

11. A loop is created to work through any comments stored in the `comments` array (created in Step 12 of the previous page). If there are comments, then:

12. The profile picture of the person who wrote the comment is shown, with their name as alt text.

13. The member's name is shown next to their photo.

14. The date and time that the comment was saved is shown. Twig's `date()` filter is used to format it in the same way as the other dates on the site.

15. The comment is shown. Twig's `raw` filter prevents markup being escaped because the comment was run through HTMLPurifier before it was saved.

16. The loop repeats for every comment in the array, and Twig's `{% endfor %}` tag closes the loop.

17. If the user is logged in, the `session` object's `id` property will have a value that is greater than 0.

18. If the visitor is logged in, they are shown a form that allows them to submit a new comment.

19. Otherwise, the visitor is shown a message to say that they need to log in to make a comment.

```
    ...
    <div class="social">
      <div class="like-count">
①      {% if session.id == 0 %}
②        <a href="{{ doc_root }}login/"><span class="icon-heart-empty"></span></a>
③      {% else %}
          <a href="{{ doc_root }}like/{{ article.id }}">
④        {% if liked %}
⑤          <span class="icon-heart"></span></a>
⑥        {% else %}
            <span class="icon-heart-empty"></span>
⑦        {% endif %}
          </a>
⑧      {% endif %}
⑨      {{ article.likes }}
      </div>
      <div class="comment-count">
⑩        <span class="icon-comment"></span> {{ article.comments }}
      </div>
    </div>


    ...

    <section class="comments">
      <h2>Comments</h2>
⑪    {% for comment in comments %}
        <div class="comment">
⑫        <img src="{{ doc_root }}uploads/{{ comment.picture }}" alt="{{ comment.author }}" />
⑬        <b>{{ comment.author }}</b><br>
⑭        {{ comment.posted|date('H:i a - F d, Y') }}<br>
⑮        <p>{{ comment.comment|raw }}</p>
        </div>
⑯    {% endfor %}

⑰    {% if session.id > 0 %}
        <form action="" method="post">
          <label for="comment">Add comment: </label>
          <textarea name="comment" id="comment" class="form-control"></textarea>
⑱        {% if error == true %}<div class="error">{{ error }}</div>{% endif %}
          <br><input type="submit" value="Save comment" class="btn btn-primary">
        </form>
      {% else %}
⑲        <p>You must <a href="{{ doc_root }}login">log in to make a comment</a>.</p>
      {% endif %}
    </section>
```

SUMMARY

ADDING FUNCTIONALITY

> SEO-friendly URLs help search engines index pages, are easier to read, and they also describe the page.

> Apache's URL rewriting engine can check all requests and follow rules to send some of them to other pages.

> When adding a new feature, specify exactly what users will be able to do before you start coding.

> Work out how to store any new data. New concepts use a new table; additional data about an existing concept goes in an existing table; and relationships between two concepts can use link tables.

> A subquery is a query that can be nested within another SQL query.

> Test new features on a test server (not the live server).

> Use a copy of the database for the test server, and back up live databases before releasing new features.

NEXT STEPS

Congratulations on reaching the end of this book. Having learned the basics of how to create database-driven websites using PHP, you can choose what to learn next based upon what you want to do with PHP.

Having learned how PHP is used to create database-driven websites, you can try to extend the code for the sample application. For example, you could:

- Create a directory of members. It could work like pages that list articles, but show all of the members instead.
- Add a page that shows which articles each individual member has liked.
- Build a messaging system for users. The messages could work like comments that can only be read by the user that they are sent to.
- Put pagination on all of the pages that list articles (in the same way that the search pages do).

You could also try to use the code base to create a different type of site. If you do this, try to add database tables and classes that model things that the site covers. For example, a site about music could represent different artists and genres. A site about gardening could include different species of plants and how to care for them. A site about cooking could show different recipes and their ingredients.

You could also learn how to allow other software (such as apps that work on mobile devices) to access and update the data that is stored in the database. This is done using something called an **application programming interface** (or **API**).

PHP programmers do not always write websites from scratch; they often build them using either a framework or another CMS. However, you need to know the basics of creating database-driven websites (as shown in this book) to use them.

FRAMEWORKS

Frameworks provide the code required to perform common tasks when building websites and applications using PHP. Two of the most popular frameworks you could explore are:

- **Symfony** https://symfony.com
- **Laravel** https://laravel.com

CONTENT MANAGEMENT

Content management systems save developers writing sites from scratch. Three popular CMS applications are:

- **WordPress** https://wordpress.org
- **Drupal** https://drupal.org
- **Joomla** https://joomla.org

In addition to customizing the look of the site, you can also write WordPress plugins, Drupal modules, or Joomla Extensions that add new functionality. (Many programmers share these plugins, modules and extensions with other programmers.)

INDEX